Communications in Computer and Information Science 2578

Series Editors

Gang Li ®, *School of Information Technology, Deakin University, Burwood, VIC, Australia*
Joaquim Filipe ®, *Polytechnic Institute of Setúbal, Setúbal, Portugal*
Zhiwei Xu, *Chinese Academy of Sciences, Beijing, China*

Rationale

The CCIS series is devoted to the publication of proceedings of computer science conferences. Its aim is to efficiently disseminate original research results in informatics in printed and electronic form. While the focus is on publication of peer-reviewed full papers presenting mature work, inclusion of reviewed short papers reporting on work in progress is welcome, too. Besides globally relevant meetings with internationally representative program committees guaranteeing a strict peer-reviewing and paper selection process, conferences run by societies or of high regional or national relevance are also considered for publication.

Topics

The topical scope of CCIS spans the entire spectrum of informatics ranging from foundational topics in the theory of computing to information and communications science and technology and a broad variety of interdisciplinary application fields.

Information for Volume Editors and Authors

Publication in CCIS is free of charge. No royalties are paid, however, we offer registered conference participants temporary free access to the online version of the conference proceedings on SpringerLink (http://link.springer.com) by means of an http referrer from the conference website and/or a number of complimentary printed copies, as specified in the official acceptance email of the event.

CCIS proceedings can be published in time for distribution at conferences or as post-proceedings, and delivered in the form of printed books and/or electronically as USBs and/or e-content licenses for accessing proceedings at SpringerLink. Furthermore, CCIS proceedings are included in the CCIS electronic book series hosted in the SpringerLink digital library at http://link.springer.com/bookseries/7899. Conferences publishing in CCIS are allowed to use Online Conference Service (OCS) for managing the whole proceedings lifecycle (from submission and reviewing to preparing for publication) free of charge.

Publication process

The language of publication is exclusively English. Authors publishing in CCIS have to sign the Springer CCIS copyright transfer form, however, they are free to use their material published in CCIS for substantially changed, more elaborate subsequent publications elsewhere. For the preparation of the camera-ready papers/files, authors have to strictly adhere to the Springer CCIS Authors' Instructions and are strongly encouraged to use the CCIS LaTeX style files or templates.

Abstracting/Indexing

CCIS is abstracted/indexed in DBLP, Google Scholar, EI-Compendex, Mathematical Reviews, SCImago, Scopus. CCIS volumes are also submitted for the inclusion in ISI Proceedings.

How to start

To start the evaluation of your proposal for inclusion in the CCIS series, please send an e-mail to ccis@springer.com.

Riccardo Guidotti · Ute Schmid · Luca Longo
Editors

Explainable Artificial Intelligence

Third World Conference, xAI 2025
Istanbul, Turkey, July 9–11, 2025
Proceedings, Part III

Springer

Editors
Riccardo Guidotti
University of Pisa
Pisa, Italy

Ute Schmid
University of Bamberg
Bamberg, Germany

Luca Longo
Technological University Dublin
Dublin, Ireland

ISSN 1865-0929   ISSN 1865-0937 (electronic)
Communications in Computer and Information Science
ISBN 978-3-032-08326-5   ISBN 978-3-032-08327-2 (eBook)
https://doi.org/10.1007/978-3-032-08327-2

© The Editor(s) (if applicable) and The Author(s), under exclusive license
to Springer Nature Switzerland AG 2026. This book is an open access publication.

Open Access This book is licensed under the terms of the Creative Commons Attribution 4.0 International License (http://creativecommons.org/licenses/by/4.0/), which permits use, sharing, adaptation, distribution and reproduction in any medium or format, as long as you give appropriate credit to the original author(s) and the source, provide a link to the Creative Commons license and indicate if changes were made.
The images or other third party material in this book are included in the book's Creative Commons license, unless indicated otherwise in a credit line to the material. If material is not included in the book's Creative Commons license and your intended use is not permitted by statutory regulation or exceeds the permitted use, you will need to obtain permission directly from the copyright holder.
The use of general descriptive names, registered names, trademarks, service marks, etc. in this publication does not imply, even in the absence of a specific statement, that such names are exempt from the relevant protective laws and regulations and therefore free for general use.
The publisher, the authors and the editors are safe to assume that the advice and information in this book are believed to be true and accurate at the date of publication. Neither the publisher nor the authors or the editors give a warranty, expressed or implied, with respect to the material contained herein or for any errors or omissions that may have been made. The publisher remains neutral with regard to jurisdictional claims in published maps and institutional affiliations.

This Springer imprint is published by the registered company Springer Nature Switzerland AG
The registered company address is: Gewerbestrasse 11, 6330 Cham, Switzerland

If disposing of this product, please recycle the paper.

Preface

Over the last decade, Explainable Artificial Intelligence (XAI) has developed into an ever-growing research field dedicated to approaches that make AI systems—especially those based on machine-learned black box models—more transparent, interpretable, and comprehensible to humans. The demand for XAI methods rises with the growing number of application areas for AI methods, from image-based medical diagnostics to personalised recommenders to scientific discovery. In the context of the European AI Act, requirements for trustworthy AI systems have been defined, including human agency and oversight, robustness, fairness, and transparency. Trustworthiness is crucial for critical application domains, such as healthcare, industrial production, and finance. XAI methods can help meet these requirements.

A growing variety of XAI methods has emerged over the last decade. Initially, a strong focus has been placed on feature relevance methods for classification models applied to images and tabular data. These methods are beneficial for model developers to assess the quality of learned models, particularly in addressing issues such as overfitting to training data or unwanted biases. Soon, the importance of non-expert users of AI systems was recognised, especially professionals in the respective application domain of an AI system and end-users who interact with AI systems in a private context. Consequently, the need for XAI methods that consider the specific information needs of these user groups has been recognised. This has resulted in a rich set of XAI methods, including counterfactual or contrastive explanations, prototype-based explanations, and concept-based explanations. Furthermore, it has been recognised that XAI must be an interdisciplinary endeavour to consider the cognitive demands of the explainees and design helpful human-AI interfaces.

While most XAI research has focused on local, post-hoc explanations for classifiers, XAI methods have expanded to unsupervised learning and generative AI approaches. Additionally, methods for explaining inherently interpretable AI models and providing global explanations are investigated. Methods of explanatory interactive learning broaden the scope of XAI research, shifting from explanation to understanding and revision. Over recent years, the need to systematically evaluate XAI methods has been recognised. To support understanding the output of a model, an explanation needs to be faithful concerning its inferential mechanisms.

To bring together the growing number of researchers dedicated to developing and evaluating XAI methods, the World Conference of Explainable Artificial Intelligence (xAI) was established in 2023. This conference aims to connect researchers from AI, computer science, cognitive science, human-computer interaction, social sciences, law, philosophy, and practitioners from all continents to share and discuss knowledge, new perspectives, experiences, and innovations in XAI. The Third World Conference on Explainable Artificial Intelligence (xAI 2025) took place in Istanbul, Turkey, from July 9 to 11, 2025. It attracted 224 submissions worldwide for the main track, as well as over

60 submissions for the late-breaking work and demo tracks. The conference also had a doctoral consortium, and 14 doctoral proposals were accepted.

Split over five volumes, the proceedings aggregate the best contributions received and presented at xAI 2025, describing recent approaches, methods, and techniques for explainability. The acceptance rate has been roughly 40 per cent, with 96 accepted papers for the main track. The accepted contributions were selected through a rigorous, single-blind peer-review process. Each article received at least three reviews, with an average of four reviews per paper, from more than 300 scholars in academia and industry. All accepted research contributions are included in these proceedings and their authors were invited to give oral presentations.

Several thematic sessions were organised, each proposed and chaired by various researchers. A parallel track was organised for work in progress, specifically preliminary novel research studies relevant to xAI, which were presented as posters during the event. A demo track was held, where researchers from academia and industry presented their software prototypes, focusing on explainability or real-world applications of explainable AI-based systems. A doctoral consortium was organised, with lecturers for PhD scholars who submitted their doctoral proposals on future research in XAI. Finally, two panel discussions were organised with renowned scholars in XAI, offering multidisciplinary views while inspiring the attendees with tangible recommendations to tackle challenges toward designing responsible, trustworthy AI-based technologies through explainable AI.

We would like to thank the volunteers who helped in the xAI 2025 organising committee, our local chair, Berrin Yanikoglu, and Pınar Karadayı Ataş. Thank you to the doctoral consortium chairs, Przemysław Biecek and Slawomir Nowarczyk, and the late-breaking work and demo chair Gitta Kutyniok. Also, a special thank you goes to Wojciech Samek, the keynote speaker for xAI 2025. A word of appreciation goes to the proposers of the special tracks and those who chaired them during the conference, and to all the senior chairs, including Charlie Abela, Christopher Anders, Omran Ayoub, Pietro Barbiero, Przemysław Biecek, Enrico Ferrari, Pascal Friederich, Francesco Giannini, Paolo Giudici, Julia Herbinger, Verena Klös, Tuwe Löfström, Gianmarco Mengaldo, Maurizio Mongelli, Anna Monreale, Grégoire Montavon, Francesca Naretto, Ann Nowe, Ruairi O'Reilly, Roberto Pellungrini, Alan Perotti, Salvatore Rinzivillo, Christin Seifert, Francesco Sovrano, Lenka Tětková, Giulia Vilone, Philipp Wintersberger, and Bartosz Zieliński. A word of appreciation goes to all the moderators and panellists of the two engaging sessions "Integrating XAI in industry processes challenges for responsible AI" and "From Explanations to Impact". Special thanks go to the researchers and practitioners who submitted their work, the various program committee members who provided valuable feedback during the peer-review process, and all who attended the event, making it a fantastic networking opportunity to share findings and learn from one another as a community.

July 2025

Riccardo Guidotti
Ute Schmid
Luca Longo

Organization

Programme Committee Chairs

Riccardo Guidotti   University of Pisa, Italy
Ute Schmid   University of Bamberg, Germany

Doctoral Consortium Chairs

Przemysław Biecek   Warsaw University of Technology, Poland
Slawomir Nowarczyk   Halmstad University, Sweden

Late-Breaking Work and Demo Chair

Gitta Kutyniok   LMU Munich, Germany

Local Chairs

Berrin Yanikoglu   Sabancı University, Turkey
Pınar Karadayı Ataş   Istanbul Arel University, Turkey

General Chair

Luca Longo   Technological University Dublin, Ireland

Steering Committee

Sebastian Lapuschkin   Fraunhofer Heinrich Hertz Institute, Germany
Paolo Giudici   University of Pavia, Italy
Luca Longo   Technological University Dublin, Ireland
Christin Seifert   University of Marburg, Germany
Grégoire Montavon   Freie Universität Berlin, Germany

Programme Committee

Ad Feelders	Utrecht University, Netherlands
Adrian Byrne	CeADAR UCD/Idiro Analytics, Ireland
Alan Perotti	CENTAI Institute, Italy
Alberto Fernández	University of Granada, Spain
Alberto Freitas	University of Porto, Portugal
Alberto Tonda	INRAE, France
Alessandro Antonucci	IDSIA, Switzerland
Alessandro Renda	Università degli Studi di Firenze, Italy
Alex Freitas	University of Kent, UK
Alexander Schulz	Bielefeld University, Germany
Alexandros Doumanoglou	Information Technologies Institute, Greece
Amparo Alonso-Betanzos	University of A Coruña, Spain
André Artelt	Bielefeld University, Germany
André Panisson	CENTAI Institute, Italy
Andrea Apicella	University of Naples Federico II, Italy
Andrea Campagner	Università degli Studi di Milano-Bicocca, Italy
Andrea Passerini	University of Trento, Italy
Andrea Pazienza	NTT DATA Italia SpA & A3K Srl, Italy
Andrea Pugnana	University of Pisa, Italy
Andreas Holzinger	University of Natural Resources and Life Sciences, Vienna, Austria
Andreas Theissler	Aalen University of Applied Sciences, Germany
Andres Paez	Universidad de los Andes, Colombia
Andrew Lensen	Victoria University of Wellington, New Zealand
Angela Lombardi	Politecnico di Bari, Italy
Angelica Liguori	ICAR-CNR, Italy
Ann Nowe	Vrije Universiteit Brussel, Belgium
Anna Monreale	University of Pisa, Italy
Annalisa Appice	Università degli Studi di Bari Aldo Moro, Italy
Antonio Mastropietro	Università di Pisa, Italy
Antonio Moreno	Universitat Rovira i Virgili, Spain
Antonio Jesús Banegas-Luna	Universidad Católica de Murcia, Spain
Anurag Koul	Microsoft Research, USA
Arianna Agosto	University of Pavia, Italy
Aris Anagnostopoulos	Sapienza University of Rome, Italy
Astrid Rakow	German Aerospace Center (DLR) e.V., Germany
Athanasios Voulodimos	University of West Attica, Greece
Autilia Vitiello	University of Naples Federico II, Italy
Axel-Cyrille Ngonga Ngomo	Paderborn University, Germany
Barbara Hammer	Bielefeld University, Germany

Bartosz Zieliński	Jagiellonian University, Poland
Benoît Frénay	Université de Namur, Belgium
Bernard Zenko	Jožef Stefan Institute, Slovenia
Bettina Finzel	Otto-Friedrich-Universität Bamberg, Germany
Björn-Hergen Laabs	Universität zu Lübeck, Germany
Bruno Martins	INESC-ID - Instituto Superior Técnico, University of Lisbon, Portugal
Bruno Veloso	University of Porto & LIAAD - INESC TEC, Portugal
Carlo Metta	University of Florence, Italy
Carlos Soares	University of Porto, Portugal
Caroline Petitjean	Université de Rouen - LITIS EA 4108, France
Carsten Schulte	University of Paderborn, Germany
Caterina Senette	IIT-CNR, Italy
Cèsar Ferri	Universitat Politècnica de València, Spain
Charlie Abela	University of Malta, Malta
Chiara Renso	ISTI-CNR Pisa, Italy
Chirag Agarwal	University of Illinois Chicago, USA
Christian Lovis	University Hospitals of Geneva, Switzerland
Christin Seifert	University of Marburg, Germany
Christoph Schommer	University of Luxembourg, Luxembourg
Christophe Labreuche	Thales R&T, France
Christopher Anders	Technische Universität Berlin, Germany
Christos Dimitrakakis	University of Neuchâtel, Switzerland
Ciara Heavin	University College Cork, Ireland
Clemens Dubslaff	Eindhoven University of Technology, Netherlands
Corrado Mencar	Università degli Studi di Bari Aldo Moro, Italy
Damiano Verda	Rulex Innovation Labs Srl, Italy
Dariusz Brzezinski	Poznań University of Technology, Poland
Dave Braines	IBM United Kingdom Ltd., UK
David Leake	Indiana University, USA
David H. Glass	University of Ulster, UK
Diego Borro	CEIT and University of Navarra, Spain
Dino Ienco	IRSTEA, France
Domenico Talia	University of Calabria, Italy
Donato Malerba	Università degli Studi di Bari Aldo Moro, Italy
Duarte Folgado	Associação Fraunhofer Portugal Research, Portugal
Edel Garcia	CCG, Portugal
Eliana Pastor	Politecnico di Torino, Italy
Elio Masciari	University of Naples Federico II, Italy
Elvio Gilberto Amparore	Università di Torino, Italy

Emmanuel Müller	TU Dortmund University, Germany
Enea Parimbelli	University of Pavia, Italy
Enrico Ferrari	Rulex Innovation Labs Srl, Italy
Erasmo Purificato	Joint Research Centre, European Commission, Italy
Fabian Fumagalli	Bielefeld University, Germany
Fabio Fassetti	University of Calabria, Italy
Fabrizio Angiulli	University of Calabria, Italy
Fabrizio Marozzo	University of Calabria, Italy
Federico Cabitza	Università degli Studi di Milano-Bicocca, Italy
Florije Ismaili	South East European University, North Macedonia
Floris Bex	Utrecht University, Netherlands
Francesca Naretto	Scuola Normale Superiore, Italy
Francesco Flammini	University of Florence, Italy
Francesco Giannini	Scuola Normale Superiore, Italy
Francesco Guerra	Università di Modena e Reggio Emilia, Italy
Francesco Marcelloni	Università di Pisa, Italy
Francesco Sovrano	University of Zurich, Switzerland
Francesco Spinnato	University of Pisa, Italy
Françoise Fessant	Orange Labs, France
Frederic Jurie	University of Caen Normandie, France
Gabriella Casalino	Università degli Studi di Bari Aldo Moro, Italy
Ganna Grynova	University of Birmingham, UK
Georgiana Ifrim	University College Dublin, Ireland
Gesina Schwalbe	University of Lübeck, Germany
Gianmarco Mengaldo	National University of Singapore, Singapore
Giovanna Dimitri	University of Siena, Italy
Giovanni Ciatto	University of Bologna, Italy
Giulia Vilone	Technological University Dublin, Ireland
Giulio Rossetti	KDD Lab ISTI-CNR, Italy
Giuseppe Casalicchio	Ludwig-Maximilians-Universität München, Germany
Giuseppe Manco	ICAR-CNR, Italy
Giuseppe Marra	KU Leuven, Belgium
Gizem Gezici	Scuola Normale Superiore, Italy
Gjergji Kasneci	Technical University of Munich, Germany
Grégoire Montavon	Freie Universität Berlin, Germany
Grzegorz J. Nalepa	Jagiellonian University, Poland
Guido Bologna	University of Applied Sciences and Arts of Western Switzerland, Switzerland
Hamed Ayoobi	Imperial College London, UK

Heike Buhl	Paderborn University, Germany
Hendrik Baier	Eindhoven University of Technology, Netherlands
Henning Müller	HES-SO and University of Geneva, Switzerland
Henrik Boström	KTH Royal Institute of Technology, Sweden
Henrique Lopes Cardoso	University of Porto, Portugal
Heta Gandhi	Nurix Therapeutics, USA
Howard Hamilton	University of Regina, Canada
Ilir Jusufi	Blekinge Institute of Technology, Sweden
Iordanis Koutsopoulos	Athens University of Economics and Business, Greece
Isacco Beretta	Università di Pisa, Italy
Isel Grau	Eindhoven University of Technology, Netherlands
Jaesik Choi	Korea Advanced Institute of Science and Technology, South Korea
Jan Arne Telle	University of Bergen, Norway
Jane Courtney	Technological University Dublin, Ireland
Jaromir Savelka	Carnegie Mellon University, USA
Jasper S. van der Waa	TNO, Netherlands
Jaumin Ajdari	South East European University, North Macedonia
Jenny Benois-Pineau	LaBRI Université de Bordeaux, CNRS, France
Jérôme Guzzi	IDSIA, Switzerland
Jerzy Stefanowski	Poznań University of Technology, Poland
Jesús Alcalá-Fdez	University of Granada, Spain
João Gama	Porto University, Portugal
Jörg Hoffmann	Saarland University, Germany
Johannes Fürnkranz	Johannes Kepler University Linz, Austria
Johannes Langer	University of Bamberg, Germany
John Gilligan	Technological University Dublin, Ireland
John Lawrence	University of Dundee, UK
Jonathan Ben-Naim	Institut de Recherche en Informatique de Toulouse (IRIT-CNRS), France
Jonathan Dunne	IBM, Ireland
Jose Juarez	Universidad de Murcia, Spain
Jose M. Molina	Universidad Carlos III de Madrid, Spain
Jose Paulo Marques dos Santos	University of Maia, Portugal
Josep Domingo-Ferrer	Universitat Rovira i Virgili, Spain
Juan Corchado	University of Salamanca, Spain
Juan A. Recio-Garcia	Universidad Complutense de Madrid, Spain
Julia Herbinger	Ludwig-Maximilians-Universität München, Germany
Julien Delaunay	Université Rennes, France

Juri Belikov	Tallinn University of Technology, Estonia
Kary Främling	Umeå University, Sweden
Katharina Rohlfing	University of Paderborn, Germany
Katharina Weitz	Fraunhofer Heinrich Hertz Institute, Germany
Kirsten Thommes	Padeborn University, Germany
Konstantinos Makantasis	University of Malta, Malta
Kristoffer Wickstrøm	UiT The Arctic University of Norway, Norway
Larisa Soldatova	Goldsmiths, University of London, UK
Lars Kai Hansen	Technical University of Denmark, Denmark
Lenka Tětková	Technical University of Denmark, Denmark
Luca Ferragina	University of Calabria, Italy
Luca Oneto	University of Genoa, Italy
Lucas Rizzo	Technological University Dublin, Ireland
Lucie Charlotte Magister	University of Cambridge, UK
Luis Galárraga	Inria, France
Luis Macedo	University of Coimbra, Portugal
Luís Rosado	Fraunhofer Portugal AICOS, Portugal
Maguelonne Teisseire	Irstea - UMR Tetis, France
Malika Bendechache	University of Galway, Ireland
Manuel Mazzara	Innopolis University, Russia
Marcelo G. Manzato	University of São Paulo, Brazil
Marcilio De Souto	LIFO/University of Orléans, France
Marcin Luckner	Warsaw University of Technology, Poland
Marco Baioletti	Università degli Studi di Perugia, Italy
Marco Podda	University of Pisa, Italy
Marco Polignano	Università degli Studi di Bari Aldo Moro, Italy
Maria Kaselimi	National Technical University of Athens, Greece
Maria Riveiro	Jönköping University, Sweden
Marija Bezbradica	Dublin City University, Ireland
Mario Brcic	University of Zagreb, Croatia
Mario Giovanni C. A. Cimino	University of Pisa, Italy
Mark Hall	Airbus, UK
Markus Löcher	Berlin School of Economics and Law, Germany
Marta Marchiori Manerba	Università di Pisa, Italy
Martin Atzmueller	Osnabrück University, Germany
Martin Gjoreski	Università della Svizzera italiana, Switzerland
Martin Holeňa	Czech Academy of Sciences, Czechia
Martin Jullum	Norwegian Computing Center, Norway
Marvin Wright	Leibniz Institute for Prevention Research and Epidemiology - BIPS & University of Bremen, Germany
Massimo Guarascio	ICAR-CNR, Italy

Mathieu Roche	Cirad, TETIS, France
Mattia Cerrato	Johannes Gutenberg University Mainz, Germany
Mattia Setzu	University of Pisa, Italy
Maurizio Mongelli	CNR-IEIIT, Italy
Mauro Dragoni	Fondazione Bruno Kessler, Italy
Md Shajalal	University of Siegen, Germany
Megha Khosla	Delft University of Technology, Netherlands
Meiyi Ma	Vanderbilt University, USA
Melinda Gervasio	SRI International, USA
Mexhid Ferati	Linnaeus University, Sweden
Michail Mamalakis	University of Cambridge, UK
Michelangelo Ceci	Università degli Studi di Bari Aldo Moro, Italy
Miguel Couceiro	Inria, France
Miguel A. Gutiérrez-Naranjo	University of Seville, Spain
Miguel Angel Patricio	Universidad Carlos III de Madrid, Spain
Mirna Saad	Scuola Universitaria Professionale della Svizzera Italiana, Switzerland
Myra Spiliopoulou	Otto von Guericke University Magdeburg, Germany
Nick Bassiliades	Aristotle University of Thessaloniki, Greece
Nicolas Boutry	EPITA Research Laboratory (LRE), Le Kremlin-Bicêtre, France
Niki van Stein	Leiden University, Netherlands
Nikolay Tcholtchev	Fraunhofer FOKUS, Germany
Nikos Deligiannis	Vrije Universiteit Brussel, Netherlands
Nikos Karacapilidis	University of Patras, Greece
Nirmalie Wiratunga	Robert Gordon University, UK
Nuno Silva	INESC TEC & ISEP - IPP, Portugal
Oliver Eberle	Technische Universität Berlin, Germany
Oliver Ray	University of Bristol, UK
Omran Ayoub	Scuola Universitaria Professionale della Svizzera Italiana, Switzerland
Özgür Lütfü Özcep	University of Hamburg, Germany
Pance Panov	Jožef Stefan Institute, Slovenia
Paola Cerchiello	University of Pavia, Italy
Paolo Giudici	University of Pavia, Italy
Paolo Pagnottoni	University of Insubria, Italy
Paolo Soda	Umeå University, Sweden
Pascal Friederich	Karlsruhe Institute of Technology, Germany
Pascal Germain	Inria, France
Paulo Cortez	University of Minho, Portugal
Paulo Lisboa	Liverpool John Moores University, UK

Paulo Novais	University of Minho, Portugal
Pedro Sequeira	SRI International, USA
Peter Kieseberg	St. Pölten University of Applied Sciences, Austria
Peter Vamplew	Federation University Australia, Australia
Philipp Cimiano	Bielefeld University, Germany
Prasanna Balaprakash	Oak Ridge National Laboratory, USA
Przemysław Biecek	Polish Academy of Sciences, University of Wrocław, Poland
Renato De Leone	Università di Camerino, Italy
Ricardo Prudêncio	Universidade Federal de Pernambuco, Brazil
Riccardo Cantini	University of Calabria, Italy
Richard Jiang	Lancaster University, UK
Rita P. Ribeiro	University of Porto, Portugal
Rob Brennan	University College Dublin, Ireland
Roberta Calegari	Alma Mater Studiorum–Università di Bologna, Italy
Roberto Capobianco	Sapienza University of Rome, Italy
Roberto Interdonato	CIRAD - UMR TETIS, France
Roberto Pellungrini	University of Pisa, Italy
Roberto Prevete	University of Naples Federico II, Italy
Rocio Gonzalez-Diaz	University of Seville, Spain
Romain Bourqui	Université Bordeaux 1, Inria Bordeaux-Sud Ouest, France
Romain Giot	LaBRI Université de Bordeaux, CNRS, France
Rosa Lillo	Universidad Carlos III de Madrid, Spain
Rosa Meo	University of Turin, Italy
Rosina Weber	Drexel University, USA
Ruairi O'Reilly	Munster Technological University, Ireland
Ruben Laplaza	École Polytechnique Fédérale de Lausanne, Switzerland
Ruggero G. Pensa	University of Turin, Italy
Rui Mao	Nanyang Technological University, Singapore
Sabatina Criscuolo	University of Naples Federico II, Italy
Salvatore Greco	Politecnico di Torino, Italy
Salvatore Rinzivillo	ISTI-CNR Pisa, Italy
Salvatore Ruggieri	Università di Pisa, Italy
Sandra Mitrović	IDSIA, Switzerland
Sang Won Baae	Stevens Institute of Technology, USA
Santiago Quintana Amate	Airbus, UK
Sebastian Lapuschkin	Fraunhofer Heinrich Hertz Institute, Germany
Severin Kacianka	Technical University of Munich, Germany
Shahina Begum	Mälardalen University, Sweden

Shai Ben-David	University of Waterloo, Canada
Shujun Li	University of Kent, UK
Silvia Giordano	Scuola Universitaria Professionale della Svizzera Italiana, Switzerland
Simon See	Nvidia, Singapore
Simona Nisticò	University of Calabria, Italy
Simone Piaggesi	University of Bologna, Italy
Simone Stumpf	University of Glasgow, UK
Slawomir Nowaczyk	Halmstad University, Sweden
Sriraam Natarajan	University of Texas at Dallas, USA
Stefano Bistarelli	Università di Perugia, Italy
Stefano Mariani	Università di Modena e Reggio Emilia, Italy
Stefano Melacci	University of Siena, Italy
Stéphane Galland	Université de Technologie de Belfort-Montbéliard, France
Sylvio Barbon Junior	University of Trieste, Italy
Szymon Bobek	AGH University of Science and Technology, Poland
Takafumi Nakanishi	Musashino University, Japan
Tania Cerquitelli	Politecnico di Torino, Italy
Telmo Silva Filho	University of Bristol, UK
Teodor Chiaburu	Berliner Hochschule für Technik, Germany
Thach Le Nguyen	University College Dublin, Ireland
Thomas Guyet	Inria, France
Thomas Lukasiewicz	University of Oxford, UK
Tiago Pinto	Universidade de Trás-os-Montes e Alto Douro/INESC-TEC, Portugal
Tjitze Rienstra	Maastricht University, Netherlands
Tomáš Kliegr	Prague University of Economics and Business, Czechia
Tommaso Turchi	University of Pisa, Italy
Tran Cao Son	New Mexico State University, USA
Tuan Pham	Queen Mary University of London, UK
Tuwe Löfström	Jönköping University, Sweden
Udo Schlegel	University of Konstanz, Germany
Ulf Johansson	Jönköping University, Sweden
Vân Anh Huynh-Thu	University of Liège, Belgium
Vedran Sabol	Know-Center GmbH, Austria
Verena Klös	Carl von Ossietzky Universität Oldenburg, Germany
Vincent Andrearczyk	HES-SO, Switzerland
Vincenzo Moscato	University of Naples, Italy

Vincenzo Pasquadibisceglie	Università degli Studi di Bari Aldo Moro, Italy
Weiru Liu	University of Bristol, UK
Werner Bailer	JOANNEUM Research, Austria
Wojciech Samek	Technical University of Berlin, Germany
Yazan Mualla	Université de Technologie de Belfort-Montbéliard, France
Zahraa S. Abdallah	University of Bristol, UK

Contents – Part III

Generative AI Meets Explainable AI

Reasoning-Grounded Natural Language Explanations for Language Models 3
   Vojtech Cahlik, Rodrigo Alves, and Pavel Kordik

What's Wrong with Your Synthetic Tabular Data? Using Explainable AI to Evaluate Generative Models 19
   Jan Kapar, Niklas Koenen, and Martin Jullum

Explainable Optimization: Leveraging Large Language Models for User-Friendly Explanations 44
   Bram Biemans, Pavel Troubil, Isel Grau, and Wim P. M. Nuijten

Large Language Models as Attribution Regularizers for Efficient Model Training 68
   Davor Vukadin, Marin Šilić, and Goran Delač

GraphXAIN: Narratives to Explain Graph Neural Networks 91
   Mateusz Cedro and David Martens

Intrinsically Interpretable Explainable AI

MSL: Multi-class Scoring Lists for Interpretable Incremental Decision-Making 117
   Stefan Heid, Jaroslaw Kornowicz, Jonas Hanselle, Kirsten Thommes, and Eyke Hüllermeier

Interpretable World Model Imaginations as Deep Reinforcement Learning Explanation 140
   Nils Wenninghoff and Maike Schwammberger

Unsupervised and Interpretable Detection of User Personalities in Online Social Networks 162
   Alessio Cascione, Laura Pollacci, and Riccardo Guidotti

An Interpretable Data-Driven Approach for Modeling Toxic Users via Feature Extraction 180
   Laura Pollacci, Jacopo Gneri, and Riccardo Guidotti

Assessing and Quantifying Perceived Trust in Interpretable Clinical
Decision Support 202
    Mohsen Abbaspour Onari, Isel Grau, Chao Zhang, Marco S. Nobile,
    and Yingqian Zhang

Benchmarking and XAI Evaluation Measures

When Can You Trust Your Explanations? A Robustness Analysis
on Feature Importances 225
    Ilaria Vascotto, Alex Rodriguez, Alessandro Bonaita, and Luca Bortolussi

XAIEV – A Framework for the Evaluation of XAI-Algorithms for Image
Classification 250
    Carsten Knoll, Julian Ullrich, Thomas Manjooran, Kilian Göller,
    Haadia Amjad, Ronald Tetzlaff, and Steffen Seitz

From Input to Insight: Probing the Reasoning of Attention-Based MIL
Models 264
    Paulina Tomaszewska, Michał Gozdera, Elżbieta Sienkiewicz,
    and Przemysław Biecek

Uncovering the Structure of Explanation Quality with Spectral Analysis 289
    Johannes Maeß, Grégoire Montavon, Shinichi Nakajima,
    Klaus-Robert Müller, and Thomas Schnake

Consolidating Explanation Stability Metrics 310
    Jeremie Bogaert, Antonin Descampe, and François-Xavier Standaert

XAI for Representational Alignment

Latent Space Interpretation and Mechanistic Clipping of Subject-Specific
Variational Autoencoders of EEG Topographic Maps for Artefacts
Reduction 327
    Taufique Ahmed, Przemyslaw Biecek, and Luca Longo

Metric-Guided Synthesis for Class Activation Mapping 351
    Alejandro Luque-Cerpa, Elizabeth Polgreen, Ajitha Rajan,
    and Hazem Torfah

Which Direction to Choose? An Analysis on the Representation Power
of Self-Supervised ViTs in Downstream Tasks 376
    Yannis Kaltampanidis, Alexandros Doumanoglou, and Dimitrios Zarpalas

XpertAI: Uncovering Regression Model Strategies for Sub-manifolds 400
Simon Letzgus, Klaus-Robert Müller, and Grégoire Montavon

An XAI-Based Analysis of Shortcut Learning in Neural Networks 424
Phuong Quynh Le, Jörg Schlötterer, and Christin Seifert

Author Index 447

Generative AI Meets Explainable AI

Reasoning-Grounded Natural Language Explanations for Language Models

Vojtech Cahlik[✉], Rodrigo Alves, and Pavel Kordik

Faculty of Information Technology, CTU in Prague, Prague, Czech Republic
{vojtech.cahlik,rodrigo.alves,pavel.kordik}@fit.cvut.cz

Abstract. We propose a large language model explainability technique for obtaining faithful natural language explanations by grounding the explanations in a reasoning process. When converted to a sequence of tokens, the outputs of the reasoning process can become part of the model context and later be decoded to natural language as the model produces either the final answer or the explanation. To improve the faithfulness of the explanations, we propose to use a joint predict-explain approach, in which the answers and explanations are inferred directly from the reasoning sequence, without the explanations being dependent on the answers and vice versa. We demonstrate the plausibility of the proposed technique by achieving a high alignment between answers and explanations in several problem domains, observing that language models often simply copy the partial decisions from the reasoning sequence into the final answers or explanations. Furthermore, we show that the proposed use of reasoning can also improve the quality of the answers.

Keywords: Explainable AI · Large Language Models · Natural Language Explanations · Reasoning

1 Introduction

Today's prevalent large language model (LLM) explainability techniques lack the expressivity of natural language, as the explanations are limited in detail and hard to interpret for an untrained user [1]. On the other hand, natural language explanations [2] can potentially be easy to follow and unlimited in expressivity, but their faithfulness is typically questionable, such as with the simple *answer-then-explain* setting which tends to lead models into fabulating their explanations. Moreover, it is even questionable whether LLMs produce their outputs in a thought process that is anyhow related to human reasoning, as they are in essence mere enhancements of traditional n-gram models [3,4]. Chain-of-thought reasoning is one notable improvement of the decision process as the answers tend to follow from the preceding natural language reasoning sequences, but it is too computationally intensive for ubiquitous use.

We propose to ground natural language explanations, as well as the answers, in a suitable resource-efficient LLM reasoning process. When converted to a sequence of tokens, the result of the reasoning process can then become part of the context observed by the model when producing its final answer or explanation. The reasoning sequence does not have to be directly human-readable, as it merely has to encode the explanation together with the answer. This information can then be simply decoded from the reasoning sequence to natural language when the model generates the final answer or explanation. In order for the explanations to be credible, a joint predict-explain setting can be used, in which the answer and explanation are inferred independently of each other. To demonstrate the plausibility of this approach, we experiment with compact reasoning sequences that we refer to as *compressed chain-of-thought reasoning*. We present the high-level overview of our methodology in Fig. 1.

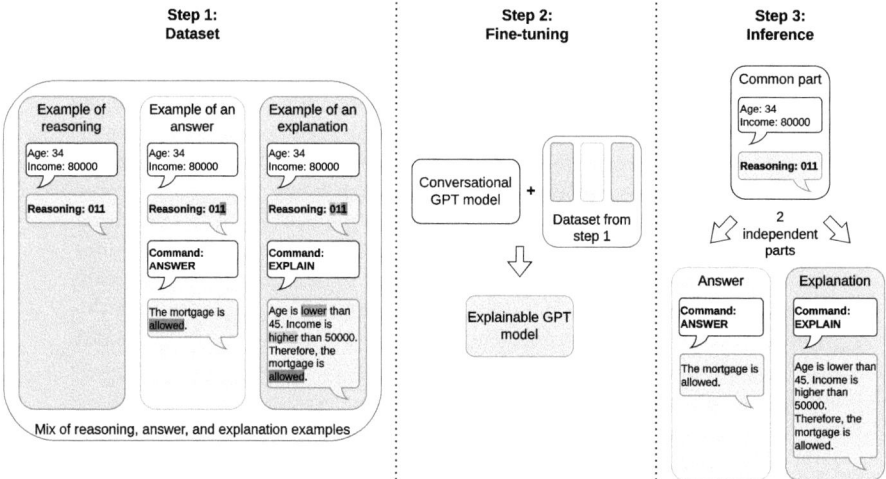

Fig. 1. Overview of our methodology. As a first step, we gather a conversational dataset in which for each user input, the triplet of reasoning-answer-explanation ground truths is present. In the second step, we fine-tune a conversational GPT model on the dataset from step 1. As a last step, we perform inference using the fine-tuned model by first computing a reasoning sequence and then including it in the conversation to produce the final answer or explanation, which are obtained independently of each other.

We evaluate our explainability framework in an "LLM-as-a-classifier" setting, in which we train LLMs to mimic the behavior of simple machine learning classifiers such as decision trees. This setting is convenient for our approach as it can be framed so that the final model outputs are affected by multiple intermediate decisions, and also allows for simple and deterministic evaluation of results. Our paper makes the following contributions to the field of LLM explainability:

1. We propose an LLM explainability technique for producing faithful natural language explanations grounded in reasoning.

2. We observe that when a suitable reasoning process is included in LLM training, and the outputs of the reasoning process are placed in the LLM input contexts, LLMs will often copy the partial decisions from the reasoning sequence into their answers or explanations.
3. We demonstrate the plausibility of our proposed explainability technique by achieving a high alignment between answers and explanations in several problem domains.
4. We show that besides enabling faithful natural language explanations, the inclusion of the reasoning process can also improve the quality of answers.

2 Related Work

2.1 LLM Explanations

LLMs are by default complex black boxes, and without proper explainability, it is difficult to understand their capabilities, limitations, and potential failures [1,5]. Explainability techniques in general are commonly categorized based on whether explainability is incorporated into the model's architecture and thus the explanation is part of the model's prediction (*ante-hoc* or *intrinsic explanations*), or if explanations are calculated after the model has been trained and a prediction has been obtained (*post-hoc explanations*). Explainability techniques can be further classified based on whether they are related to a single prediction (*local explanations*) or to the general behavior of the model across all predictions (*global explanations*).

Zhao et al. [1] categorize local LLM explainability techniques into 4 main approaches: feature attribution-based explanations, attention-based explanations, example-based explanations, and natural language explanations.

Feature Attribution-Based Explanations. These explanations measure the importance of each input feature (such as an input token) in relation to outputs. *Perturbation-based techniques* perturb the inputs using removal or masking [6,7], which may however generate out-of-distribution data. *Gradient-based* techniques measure partial derivatives of outputs with respect to the input features, using well-established explainability techniques such as *gradient × input* or *integrated gradients* [8–11] which address some of the difficulties that occur when using gradients naively [12]. *Surrogate model methods* employ simpler white-box models to explain individual predictions, notably using the SHAP technique, which utilizes Shapley values and has also been adapted to Transformer models [13].

Attention-Based Explanations. Attention-based explanations analyze the parameters or behavior of attention heads. Numerous studies have focused on explaining attention heads using visualizations, such as with token-level bipartite graphs and heatmaps or neuron-level heatmaps [14,15]. Other works have adopted gradient-based methods using various definitions of gradient in attention heads [11,16]. However, there is ongoing debate on the reliability of attention-based explainability techniques [1].

Example-Based Explanations. These explanations analyze how changes in model inputs affect the outputs. A popular approach is to generate *counterfactual examples* that cause important changes in the outputs by adding, altering, masking, removing, or shuffling words in the input text [17]. On the other hand, *adversarial examples* aim to substantially alter the model outputs with barely noticeable changes to the input text [18,19]. These examples can be added to the training data to improve the robustness of the final model. Another family of methods aims to analyze the impact of the individual training examples on the behavior of the trained model, remarkably without the need for multiple rounds of training [20,21].

Natural Language Explanations. Natural language explanations refer to explanations that take the form of text in natural language, thus making them suitable even for a lay audience [1,2]. The quality of natural language explanations is commonly assessed according to plausibility, which checks if the explanations are logically sound, faithfulness, which assesses whether the explanations describe the true decision process of the model, and readability [22]. Although being a relatively large field, most natural language explanation studies focus on other types of models than LLMs. The approaches for LLMs include using simple explain-then-predict and predict-then-answer methods [23], training the models using datasets of synthetic [24] or human-written explanations [25,26], and translation of natural language to symbolic solver domains [27].

2.2 LLM Reasoning

The field of LLM reasoning covers a wide range of methods aimed at improving the model outputs or answers. Chain-of-Thought [28] is perhaps the most well-known technique, in which the LLM is simply tasked to reason first before stating the final answer. Extensions of this approach include self-consistency [29], in which multiple reasoning paths are sampled, and Tree of Thoughts [30], where the reasoning trajectories form a tree which is explored using search strategies such as BFS and DFS. Other notable reasoning methods include multi-agent collaboration [31], knowledge distillation [32], process-based reward models [33], Monte Carlo Tree Search [34], and reinforcement learning [35].

3 Methods

3.1 Reasoning-Grounded Natural Language Explanations

To achieve faithful natural language explainability, we propose to ground LLM explanations as well as answers in a reasoning process. In order to decrease computational complexity, we suggest that the output of the reasoning process does not have to be inherently human-readable, but that it should merely contain the information necessary to be later decoded by the LLM into the final answer or natural language explanation. Such reasoning can be used in a two-step conversational framework, where as the first step, the reasoning sequence is generated, and as the second step, the user (or the chat interface) sends a *command* message indicating whether the model should answer the question or explain the answer, and the model responds accordingly. In case the user chooses to obtain both the answer as well as the explanation, it is crucial that both are obtained independently by the chat interface to prevent the model from fabulating the explanation or the answer being affected by the explanation.

For a clearer definition of the conversational inference process, we can define the conversation history H_n as a sequence of user question messages U_i and model answer messages A_i:

$$H_n = U_1 \cdot A_1 \cdot U_2 \cdot A_2 \cdot \ldots \cdot U_{n-1} \cdot A_{n-1} \cdot U_n \qquad (1)$$

With this notation, the message with reasoning output R_n can be defined by the formula

$$R_n = \text{ReasoningModel}(H_n), \qquad (2)$$

and the model's answer message A_n and explanation message E_n can be defined by the formulas

$$A_n = \text{LLM}(H_n \cdot R_n \cdot C_\text{answer}) \qquad (3)$$

and

$$E_n = \text{LLM}(H_n \cdot R_n \cdot C_\text{explain}), \qquad (4)$$

where C_answer and C_explain are the "ANSWER" and "EXPLAIN" command messages.

As a proof of concept, we experiment with using the LLM to generate compact reasoning sequences in an approach that we refer to as *compressed chain-of-thought reasoning*. With the use of the previous notation, we therefore set ReasoningModel = LLM. We suggest to put three requirements on such reasoning sequences:

1. The reasoning sequences should encode all the partial decisions necessary for the model to produce the right answers.
2. The reasoning sequences should encode all the partial decisions necessary for the model to produce the natural language explanations in the desired level of detail.
3. The encoding of the partial decisions in the reasoning sequences should follow a chain-of-thought ordering to allow accurate token-by-token generation by the LLM.

Similarly to regular chain-of-thought reasoning, compressed chain-of-thought reasoning can also potentially improve the quality of LLM answers, as more circuit layer operations can be performed by the LLM before the final answer is produced.

3.2 LLM as a Classifier

In our experiments, we adopt an "LLM-as-a-classifier" approach in which the LLM is tasked with mimicking the behavior of a machine learning classifier. This approach is convenient for our study as reasoning and explanation sequences can be formulated so that they involve chains of various decisions, and we can calculate evaluation metrics deterministically without using methods such as LLM-as-a-judge. We experiment with three problem domains: Logistic regression, decision tree classification, and a natural language dataset generated using decision tree logic. For each problem domain, we design the ground-truth answers to simply state the classification result. For explanations, we use detailed chain-of-thought sequences that describe the intermediate decisions necessary to reach correct classification, and for reasoning, we extract or encode the most important values from the explanation sequence to form minimal, "compressed" chain-of-thought sequences. For each of the datasets, an example of an input, reasoning, answer, and explanation text for a single instance is shown in Table 1.

Table 1. Examples of instances from our experimental datasets. For each instance, the sections corresponding to values included in the reasoning sequence are highlighted with bold text, and the occurrences of the ground truth class are underlined.

	Dataset		
	Logistic regressor	Decision tree	Natural language decision tree
Input	X: [−0.4408, 0.7812, −0.3482, 0.9094, 0.869, −0.0214, −0.0555, −0.8395]	X: [0.923, 0.252]	Loan amount: $115000.0 Loan-to-value ratio: 92.266 Debt-to-income ratio: <20% Applicant's age: 25–34 Loan term: 120.0 Income: $83000.0 Property value: $475000.0 Total loan costs: $0.0
Reasoning	**−1.2465** −1.2465; **−2.9536** −4.2001; **−2.3885** −6.5886; **7.2595 0.6709;** −4.5762 −3.9053; **0.2138** −3.6915; −0.5065 −4.198; **6.8913 2.6933;** <u>1</u>	0, 0, 0, 1, 1, 1, 0, <u>0</u>	1, 0, 0, 0, <u>1</u>
Answer	<u>1</u>	<u>0</u>	The mortgage is <u>issued</u>.
Explanation	[[0, "w[0] * x[0] = **−1.2465**", "y − 1.2465 = **−1.2465**"], [1, "w[1] * x[1] = **−2.9536**", "y − 2.9536 = **−4.2001**"], [2, "w[2] * x[2] = **−2.3885**", "y − 2.3885 = **−6.5886**"], [3, "w[3] * x[3] = **7.2595**", "y + 7.2595 = **0.6709**"], [4, "w[4] * x[4] = **−4.5762**", "y − 4.5762 = **−3.9053**"], [5, "w[5] * x[5] = **0.2138**", "y + 0.2138 = **−3.6915**"], [6, "w[6] * x[6] = **−0.5065**", "y − 0.5065 = **−4.198**"], [7, "w[7] * x[7] = **6.8913**", "y + 6.8913 = **2.6933**"], ["OUTPUT", <u>**1**</u>]]	[["0.923 < 0.3562", **false**], ["0.252 > 0.6825", **false**], ["0.923 < 0.5613", **false**], ["0.252 < 0.2597", **true**], ["0.923 > 0.8087", **true**], ["0.252 > 0.0709", **true**], ["0.923 < 0.8676", **false**], ["OUTPUT", <u>**0**</u>]]	The loan-to-value ratio is **higher than 79%**. The income is **lower than $110000**. The applicant's age is **lower or equal to 34** years. The debt-to-income ratio is **lower or equal to 40%**. Therefore, the mortgage is <u>issued</u>.

Logistic Regression. In this setting, we randomly generate a parameter vector $\mathbf{w}$ of a logistic regression model without a bias parameter and train the LLM to classify random 8-dimensional input vectors $\mathbf{x}$ according to the following formula:

$$y(\mathbf{x}) = \begin{cases} 1 & \text{if } \mathbf{w}^T\mathbf{x} > 0 \\ 0 & \text{otherwise.} \end{cases} \quad (5)$$

Decision Tree. In this setting, we randomly generate a binary decision tree of depth 7 with the following node selection logic at each non-leaf node:

$$next(N) = \begin{cases} left(N) & \text{if } s_N \times x_{index(N)} > s_N \times t_N \\ right(N) & \text{otherwise,} \end{cases} \quad (6)$$

where $next(N)$ is the next node to be evaluated after the current node N, $left(N)$ and $right(N)$ are the left and right child nodes of node N, t_N is a random threshold, $index(N)$ is a function that selects the index of $\mathbf{x}$ (defined so that two consecutive nodes can not use the same index), and s_N is a random sign of -1 or 1 that can effectively flip the comparison operator.

Leaf nodes are assigned a class of 0 or 1.

Decision Tree Encoded in Natural Language. In the last setting, we experiment with a decision tree that represents a mortgage application review process encoded in natural language. We take a subset of randomly selected mortgage applications from the 2022 version of the *HMDA National Loan Level Dataset* [36] as input data and using a manually designed decision tree that represents a fictional mortgage application review process, we generate paragraphs in which each sentence describes a decision branch comparison for one of the input features. Decisions are evaluated for each dataset instance from the top of the decision tree to the leaf with the final class of issued or not issued.

4 Experiments

4.1 Categorization of Experiments

Separate Fine-Tuning for Answers and Explanations. In this setting, the training dataset is split into two separate datasets, each composed of either input-command-answer or input-command-explanation instances. The LLM is then fine-tuned on each of the two datasets independently, resulting in two fine-tuned models. The inference for answers and explanations is then performed separately using the corresponding model.

Joint Fine-Tuning. This setting is similar to the previous one, but the answer and explanation instances are not separated into two training datasets. Instead, fine-tuning is performed jointly on the mix of input-command-answer and input-command-explanation examples. Inference is performed in the joint predict-explain approach, with the answers generated independently of the explanations and vice versa, according to the command "ANSWER" or "EXPLAIN".

Joint Fine-Tuning with Reasoning. In this setting, the training dataset is composed of a mix of input-reasoning, input-reasoning-command-answer, and input-reasoning-command-explanation instances. Inference is performed in two steps, where in the first step, the model generates a reasoning sequence, and in the second step, the answer and explanation are generated independently according to the "ANSWER" or "EXPLAIN" command.

In-Context Learning. To understand how strongly the performance of LLMs is affected by fine-tuning to the specific problem domain, we include results for in-context learning [37] as an informative baseline. In this setting, the LLMs are not fine-tuned to the specific classification model, but instead obtain their problem domain knowledge only from classification input-output example pairs included in their input prompt. For each few-shot example, both the answer and explanation target is included. In order to prevent the influence of human prompt engineering, we pre-train the LLMs on a training dataset where each training instance belongs to a different problem domain, corresponding to a randomly generated classifier from the same model family but with different values of model parameters than those used in the test dataset. The input of each few-shot example is randomly generated to achieve greater diversity. We omit the in-context learning setting in the experiments with natural language decision trees due to the complexity of random generation of meaningful decision processes in this problem domain.

4.2 Experimental Setup

All experiments were performed using a similar methodology.[1] For each of the five LLMs tested, the model's instruction-tuned variant was used. LLMs were trained using low-rank adaptation [39] and Adam optimizer [40] for a single epoch on a train dataset created using 2000 classification inputs. During training, the test loss was periodically measured on a test dataset created using 200 inputs, and at the end of training, the best model checkpoint was kept. In the in-context learning experiments, the number of few-shot examples was 5 for logistic regression and 20 for decision trees. The same training hyperparameters were used in all experiments, namely a batch size of 4 and a learning rate of 5×10^{-5} with a linear schedule and 100 warmup steps.

4.3 Evaluation Metrics

In our experiments, we separately measure the classification accuracy of answers and explanations on test datasets created using 200 classification inputs. For explanations, determining the resulting classification is possible as we have designed the explanations as chain-of-thought sequences in which the output

---

[1] The source code, together with our datasets, is available under the CC0 license at https://github.com/vcahlik/reasoning-grounded-explanations and at Zenodo [38].

class is always stated at the end. Furthermore, we measure the rate of alignment between the answer and explanation classifications. The predicted classes are determined using automated rules such as regular expressions; outputs that could not be reliably parsed are counted as errors.

5 Results

5.1 Logistic Regression Results

The results for the logistic regression dataset are shown in Table 2. In-context learning has near-perfect classification accuracy for explanations, as the parameters of the logistic regressor are stated in the few-shot examples and therefore it is simple for the model to generate correct chain-of-thought explanations. However, for answers, classification accuracy is equivalent to random guessing due to the difficulty of the task when a chain-of-thought process is not used. The gap between the classification accuracy for answers and explanations is also wide for most of the fine-tuning experiments without reasoning. However, when reasoning is used, the classification accuracies of answers increase to the level of classification accuracies for explanations, indicating that the reasoning process helps the LLMs achieve correct answers.

Table 2. Results on the logistic regression dataset. The experimental setup differs in whether training was performed separately or jointly for answers and explanations, whether in-context learning (ICL) was used, and whether reasoning was used. Outputs that could not be parsed into a valid class are counted towards errors and their rate is additionally shown in parentheses.

Ans./exp.training	ICL	Reas.	Metric	Llama 3 8B	Mistral NeMo	Mistral 7B	Zephyr SFT	Phi-4
Separately	Yes	No	Answer acc.	0.455	0.515	0.470	0.495	0.470
			Expl. acc.	0.990	1.000	0.995	1.000	0.990
			Align. rate	0.455	0.515	0.475	0.495	0.460
Separately	No	No	Answer acc.	0.610	0.890	0.830	0.555	0.620
			Expl. acc.	0.615(0.140)	0.990(0.005)	0.995	0.995	0.990
			Align. rate	0.455(0.140)	0.880(0.005)	0.835	0.560	0.620
Jointly	No	No	Answer acc.	0.640	0.530	0.555	0.470	0.470
			Expl. acc.	0.990	1.000	1.000	0.995	1.000
			Align. rate	0.630	0.530	0.555	0.475	0.470
Jointly	No	Yes	Answer acc.	0.890(0.020)	0.995	1.000	1.000	0.945
			Expl. acc.	0.875(0.030)	0.995	1.000	1.000	0.940(0.005)
			Align. rate	0.965(0.035)	1.000	1.000	1.000	0.995(0.005)

5.2 Decision Tree Results

The results for the decision tree dataset, belonging to a tree of depth 7, are shown in Table 3. Even though 4 times as many few-shot examples were used than in the logistic regression experiments, the classification accuracy of in-context learning is low even for explanations, as the number of few-shot examples is still lower than the number of decision tree leaves. The results for fine-tuning without reasoning are similar to those with the logistic regression dataset. Results for reasoning show higher error rates than in the logistic regression experiments, presumably due to the less detailed reasoning process. However, answers and explanations now remarkably contain the same classification errors in almost all cases, as can be seen from the near-perfect alignment rates. We visualize this phenomenon by plotting the classifications for one of the experiments in Fig. 2.

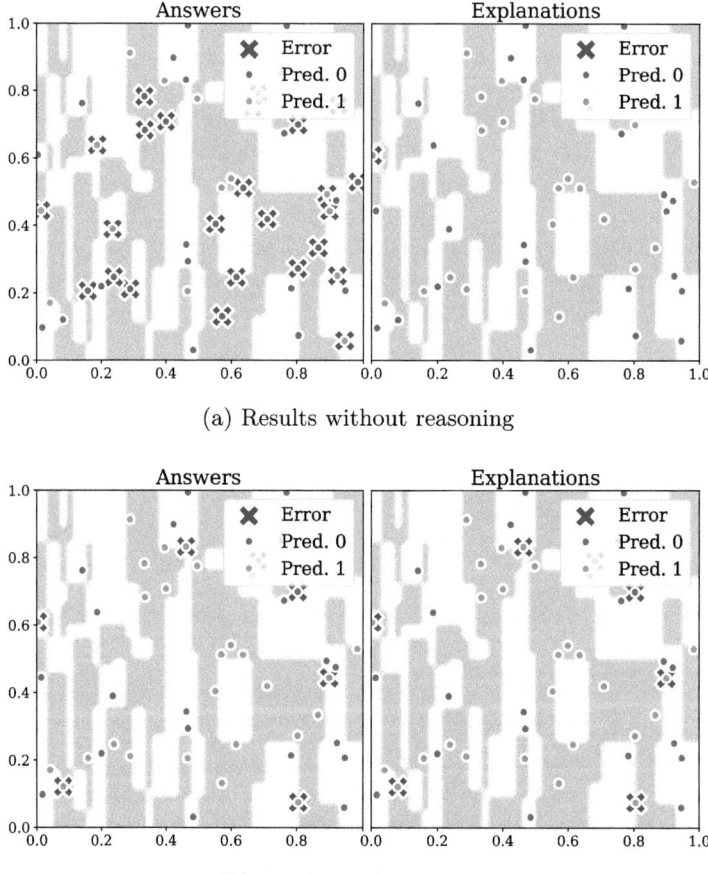

Fig. 2. Experiments with joint training of answers and explanations on a decision tree dataset. The colored regions correspond to ground-truth classes. When reasoning is used, answer and explanation classification errors are typically near-perfectly aligned.

Figure 3 shows the results for the Mistral 7B model on datasets of varying decision tree depths, indicating that classification accuracy tends to decrease as the complexity of the trees increases. With reasoning, answer and explanation classifications are near-perfectly aligned for all of the depths, in contrast to the alignment rates for experiments without reasoning. However, explanations without reasoning tend to have the highest classification accuracy in these experiments, supposedly due to the chain-of-thought explanation sequences being more thorough than the compressed chain-of-thought reasoning sequences.

Table 3. Results on the decision tree dataset, with the same semantics as in Table 2

Ans./exp.training	ICL	Reas.	Metric	Llama 3 8B	Mistral NeMo	Mistral 7B	Zephyr SFT	Phi-4
Separately	Yes	No	Answer acc.	0.535	0.510	0.490	0.490	0.535
			Expl. acc.	0.670	0.685	0.695	0.695	0.700
			Align. rate	0.565	0.565	0.495	0.485	0.505
Separately	No	No	Answer acc.	0.475	0.525	0.530	0.565	0.565
			Expl. acc.	0.975	0.985	0.985	1.000	0.955
			Align. rate	0.480	0.540	0.515	0.565	0.580
Jointly	No	No	Answer acc.	0.475	0.450	0.500	0.475	0.520
			Expl. acc.	0.985	0.985	0.995	0.975	0.985
			Align. rate	0.480	0.435	0.505	0.460	0.505
Jointly	No	Yes	Answer acc.	0.745	0.835	0.845	0.875	0.715
			Expl. acc.	0.745	0.835	0.840(0.005)	0.875	0.715
			Align. rate	1.000	1.000	0.995(0.005)	1.000	1.000

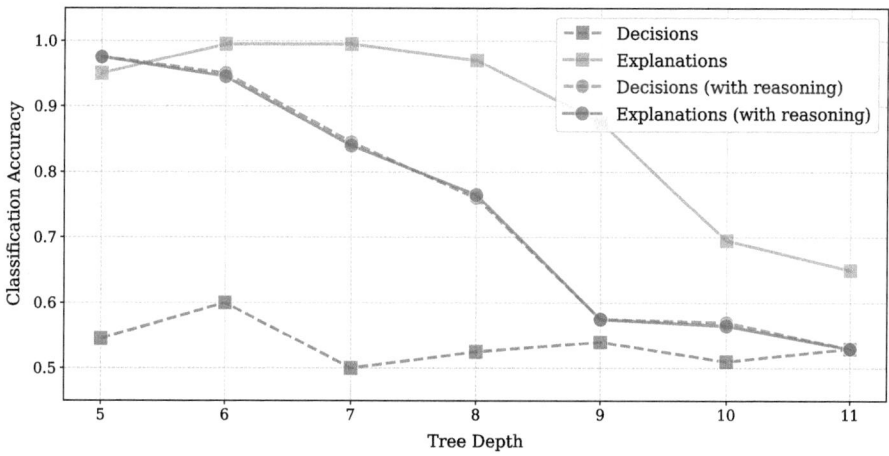

Fig. 3. Classification accuracies for experiments with decision trees of various depths

5.3 Natural Language Decision Tree Results

The results for the natural language decision tree dataset, shown in Table 4, are similar to those for the decision tree dataset. However, in this case, the use of reasoning is associated with near-perfect classification accuracies for both answers and explanations and with perfect alignment of classification errors.

Table 4. Results on the natural language decision tree dataset, with the same semantics as in Table 2

Ans./exp.training	ICL	Reas.	Metric	Llama 3 8B	Mistral NeMo	Mistral 7B	Zephyr SFT	Phi-4
Separately	No	No	Answer acc.	0.810	0.825	0.850	0.850	0.815
			Expl. acc.	0.950	0.975	0.950	0.995	0.970
			Align. rate	0.860	0.840	0.850	0.855	0.835
Jointly	No	No	Answer acc.	0.840	0.840	0.810	0.865	0.845
			Expl acc.	0.935	0.975	0.980	0.990	0.975
			Align. rate	0.825	0.855	0.820	0.875	0.830
Jointly	No	Yes	Answer acc.	0.985	0.970	0.985	1.000	1.000
			Expl acc.	0.985	0.970	0.985	1.000	1.000
			Align. rate	1.000	1.000	1.000	1.000	1.000

5.4 Analysis of Errors

As a further analysis, we study the partial decisions present in the reasoning and explanation sequences generated on the decision tree dataset by the Llama 3 8B model. As shown in Table 5, the final classification errors in both the reasoning and explanation sequences are caused by the accumulation of mistakes in partial decisions. It is noteworthy that all of the decisions are perfectly aligned between the reasoning and explanation sequences. Although not shown in the table, we also observed perfect alignment between the answer classifications and reasoning classifications, meaning that all partial decisions as well as the final classifications are aligned between the generated answers, explanations, and reasoning in this case.

Table 5. Analysis of the correctness of the reasoning and explanation chain-of-thought sequences generated by Llama 3 8B on the decision tree dataset

	Partial decision							Final classification
	1	2	3	4	5	6	7	
Reasoning accuracy	0.995	1.000	0.990	0.960	0.895	0.830	0.745	0.745
Explanation accuracy	0.995	1.000	0.990	0.960	0.895	0.830	0.745	0.745
Alignment rate	1.000	1.000	1.000	1.000	1.000	1.000	1.000	1.000

6 Discussion

It may not be immediately clear why the inclusion of reasoning sequences in LLM input contexts leads to alignment between answers and explanations. It seems that during training, the LLM must learn the relatively simple task of reproducing the compressed chain-of-thought reasoning sequence to succeed at the more difficult task of producing the one-step answer classifications. We hypothesize that once the model learns to produce accurate reasoning sequences, the internal mechanism by which the LLM produces its explanations also degrades to the copying of the partial decisions from the reasoning sequence. To gain supporting evidence for this hypothesis, we further experimented with randomly flipping the partial decisions as well as the final classification decisions present in the reasoning sequences produced by fine-tuned Llama 3 8B. As was suspected, we observed that almost all of the changes were propagated into the produced explanations as well as to the answers.

Our approach presented in this paper can be extended in numerous possible ways, which we leave for future work. Primarily, the reasoning process that we chose for our proof-of-concept experiments could be extended to wider problem domains or even to general-purpose assistant datasets, for example by straightforwardly using chain-of-thought reasoning or similar approaches, such as the reasoning process used by DeepSeek-r1 [35]. It would also seem beneficial to introduce a training loss that directly penalizes the mismatch between answers, explanations, and reasoning. Furthermore, we believe that LLM applications could benefit from other output modes besides answering and explaining. We envision a multitask setting with additional implemented commands, such as those for obtaining explanations of varying detail, classification of user intent, content filtering analysis, metadata generation, and so on.

7 Conclusion

In this paper, we have proposed an LLM explainability technique for obtaining faithful natural language explanations by grounding the LLM answers and explanations in a reasoning process. We have shown that LLMs often simply copy the partial decisions from the reasoning sequence into their answers or explanations, and we utilized this phenomenon to achieve high alignment between answers and explanations in several problem domains. Furthermore, we have shown that besides enabling faithful explanations, the use of a reasoning process can also lead to improvements in the quality of answers. We hope that our study inspires further research or real-world use-cases that advance the current state of explainability in LLMs.

Acknowledgments. This work was supported by the project "PoliRuralPlus: Fostering Sustainable, Balanced, Equitable, Place-based and Inclusive Development of Rural-Urban Communities' Using Specific Spatial Enhanced Attractivenes Mapping ToolBox" funded by the European Union (REA), grant No. 101136910.

Disclosure of Interests. The authors have no competing interests to declare that are relevant to the content of this article.

References

1. Zhao, H.: Explainability for large language models: a survey. ACM Trans. Intell. Syst. Technol. **15**(2), 1–38 (2024)
2. Cambria, E., Malandri, L., Mercorio, F., Mezzanzanica, M., Nobani, N.: A survey on XAI and natural language explanations. Inf. Process. Manag. **60**(1), 103111 (2023)
3. Russell, S.: Human Compatible: AI and the Problem of Control. Penguin UK (2019)
4. Hrytsyna, A., Alves, R.: From representation to response: assessing the alignment of large language models with human judgment patterns. ACM Trans. Intell. Syst. Technol. (2024)
5. Weidinger, L., et al.: Ethical and social risks of harm from language models. arXiv preprint arXiv:2112.04359 (2021)
6. DeYoung, J., et al.: ERASER: a benchmark to evaluate rationalized NLP models. arXiv preprint arXiv:1911.03429 (2019)
7. Wu, Z., Chen, Y., Kao, B., Liu, Q.: Perturbed masking: parameter-free probing for analyzing and interpreting BERT. arXiv preprint arXiv:2004.14786 (2020)
8. Sikdar, S., Bhattacharya, P., Heese, K.: Integrated directional gradients: feature interaction attribution for neural NLP models. In: Proceedings of the 59th Annual Meeting of the Association for Computational Linguistics and the 11th International Joint Conference on Natural Language Processing (Volume 1: Long Papers), pp. 865–878 (2021)
9. Sanyal, S., Ren, X.: Discretized integrated gradients for explaining language models. arXiv preprint arXiv:2108.13654 (2021)
10. Enguehard, J.: Sequential integrated gradients: a simple but effective method for explaining language models. arXiv preprint arXiv:2305.15853 (2023)
11. Hao, Y., Dong, L., Wei, F., Ke, X.: Self-attention attribution: Interpreting information interactions inside transformer. In: Proceedings of the AAAI Conference on Artificial Intelligence, vol. 35, pp. 12963–12971 (2021)
12. Lyu, Q., Apidianaki, M., Callison-Burch, C.: Towards faithful model explanation in NLP: survey. Comput. Linguist., 1–67 (2024)
13. Kokalj, E., Škrlj, B., Lavrač, N., Pollak, S., Robnik-Šikonja, M.: BERT meets shapley: extending SHAP explanations to transformer-based classifiers. In: Proceedings of the EACL Hackashop on News Media Content Analysis and Automated Report Generation, pp. 16–21 (2021)
14. Vig, J.: A multiscale visualization of attention in the transformer model. arXiv preprint arXiv:1906.05714 (2019)
15. Hoover, B., Strobelt, H., Gehrmann, S.: exBERT: a visual analysis tool to explore learned representations in transformers models. arXiv preprint arXiv:1910.05276 (2019)
16. Barkan, O., et al.: Grad-SAM: explaining transformers via gradient self-attention maps. In: Proceedings of the 30th ACM International Conference on Information & Knowledge Management, pp. 2882–2887 (2021)
17. Wu, T., Ribeiro, M.T., Heer, J., Weld, D.S.: Polyjuice: generating counterfactuals for explaining, evaluating, and improving models. arXiv preprint arXiv:2101.00288, 2021

18. Jin, D., Jin, Z., Zhou, J.T., Szolovits, P.: Is BERT really robust? A strong baseline for natural language attack on text classification and entailment. In: Proceedings of the AAAI Conference on Artificial Intelligence, vol. 34, pp. 8018–8025 (2020)
19. Garg, S., Ramakrishnan, G.: BAE: BERT-based adversarial examples for text classification. arXiv preprint arXiv:2004.01970 (2020)
20. Koh, P.W., Liang, P.: Understanding black-box predictions via influence functions. In: International Conference on Machine Learning, pp. 1885–1894. PMLR (2017)
21. Yeh, C.-K., Kim, J., Yen, I.E.-H., Ravikumar, P.K.: Representer point selection for explaining deep neural networks. Adv. Neural Inf. Process. Syst. **31** (2018)
22. Jacovi, A., Goldberg, Y.: Towards faithfully interpretable NLP systems: How should we define and evaluate faithfulness? arXiv preprint arXiv:2004.03685 (2020)
23. Huang, S., Mamidanna, S., Jangam, S., Zhou, Y., Gilpin, L.H.: Can large language models explain themselves? A study of LLM-generated self-explanations. arXiv preprint arXiv:2310.11207 (2023)
24. Chen, Y., et al.: Towards consistent natural-language explanations via explanation-consistency finetuning. arXiv preprint arXiv:2401.13986 (2024)
25. Camburu, O.-M., Rocktäschel, T., Lukasiewicz, T., Blunsom, P.: e-SNLI: natural language inference with natural language explanations. Adv. Neural Inf. Process. Syst. **31** (2018)
26. Rajani, N.F., Mccann, B., Xiong, C., Socher, R.: Explain yourself! Leveraging language models for commonsense reasoning. arXiv preprint arXiv:1906.02361 (2019)
27. Lyu, Q., et al.: Faithful chain-of-thought reasoning. In: The 13th International Joint Conference on Natural Language Processing and the 3rd Conference of the Asia-Pacific Chapter of the Association for Computational Linguistics (IJCNLP-AACL 2023) (2023)
28. Kojima, T., Gu, S.S., Reid, M., Matsuo, Y., Iwasawa, Y.: Large language models are zero-shot reasoners. Adv. Neural. Inf. Process. Syst. **35**, 22199–22213 (2022)
29. Wang, X., et al.: Self-consistency improves chain of thought reasoning in language models. arXiv preprint arXiv:2203.11171 (2022)
30. Yao, S.: Tree of thoughts: deliberate problem solving with large language models. Adv. Neural. Inf. Process. Syst. **36**, 11809–11822 (2023)
31. Li, X., Wang, S., Siqi Zeng, Y.W., Yang, Y.: A survey on LLM-based multi-agent systems: workflow, infrastructure, and challenges. Vicinagearth **1**(1), 9 (2024)
32. West, P., et al.: Symbolic knowledge distillation: from general language models to commonsense models. arXiv preprint arXiv:2110.07178 (2021)
33. Lightman, H., et al.: Let's verify step by step. In: The Twelfth International Conference on Learning Representations (2023)
34. Feng, X., et al.: Alphazero-like tree-search can guide large language model decoding and training. arXiv preprint arXiv:2309.17179 (2023)
35. Guo, D., et al.: DeepSeek-R1: incentivizing reasoning capability in LLMs via reinforcement learning. arXiv preprint arXiv:2501.12948 (2025)
36. Consumer Financial Protection Bureau: HMDA National Loan Level Dataset 2022 (2022)
37. Dong, Q., et al.: A survey on in-context learning. arXiv preprint arXiv:2301.00234 (2022)
38. Cahlik, V.: Research data of the scientific paper "reasoning-grounded natural language explanations for language model" (2025). https://zenodo.org/records/15149693. https://doi.org/10.5281/zenodo.15149693.

39. Hu, E.J., et al.: LoRA: low-rank adaptation of large language models. ICLR **1**(2), 3 (2022)
40. Kingma, D.P., Ba, J.: Adam: a method for stochastic optimization. arXiv preprint arXiv:1412.6980 (2014)

Open Access This chapter is licensed under the terms of the Creative Commons Attribution 4.0 International License (http://creativecommons.org/licenses/by/4.0/), which permits use, sharing, adaptation, distribution and reproduction in any medium or format, as long as you give appropriate credit to the original author(s) and the source, provide a link to the Creative Commons license and indicate if changes were made.

The images or other third party material in this chapter are included in the chapter's Creative Commons license, unless indicated otherwise in a credit line to the material. If material is not included in the chapter's Creative Commons license and your intended use is not permitted by statutory regulation or exceeds the permitted use, you will need to obtain permission directly from the copyright holder.

What's Wrong with Your Synthetic Tabular Data? Using Explainable AI to Evaluate Generative Models

Jan Kapar[1,2], Niklas Koenen[1,2], and Martin Jullum[3(✉)]

[1] Leibniz Institute for Prevention Research and Epidemiology – BIPS, Bremen, Germany
[2] Faculty of Mathematics and Computer Science, University of Bremen, Bremen, Germany
[3] Norwegian Computing Center, Oslo, Norway
jullum@nr.no

Abstract. Evaluating synthetic tabular data is challenging, since they can differ from the real data in so many ways. There exist numerous metrics of synthetic data quality, ranging from statistical distances to predictive performance, often providing conflicting results. Moreover, they fail to explain or pinpoint the specific weaknesses in the synthetic data. To address this, we apply explainable AI (XAI) techniques to a binary detection classifier trained to distinguish real from synthetic data. While the classifier identifies distributional differences, XAI concepts such as feature importance and feature effects, analyzed through methods like permutation feature importance, partial dependence plots, Shapley values and counterfactual explanations, reveal *why* synthetic data are distinguishable, highlighting inconsistencies, unrealistic dependencies, or missing patterns. This interpretability increases transparency in synthetic data evaluation and provides deeper insights beyond conventional metrics, helping diagnose and improve synthetic data quality. We apply our approach to two tabular datasets and generative models, showing that it uncovers issues overlooked by standard evaluation techniques.

Keywords: Synthetic data quality · Generative artificial intelligence · Explainable artificial intelligence · Interpretable machine learning · Interpretable evaluation · Synthetic data detection · Tabular data

1 Introduction

The rapid development of generative modeling, also known as generative artificial intelligence (GenAI), is driving profound changes in business, science, education, creative processes, and our everyday lives. While the maturation of transformer-based architectures [62] and diffusion models [33,59] has led to previously unimaginable possibilities and quality leaps in text, image, audio, and video generation, the advances in tabular data synthesis lag behind. However, generative modeling has great potential for tabular data: A large amount of data in organizations, research and medicine is organized in a tabular format, and there is a wide range of useful applications, such as privacy-preserving data sharing, data augmentation and balancing, missing data imputation and what-if analyses [35].

What is it that makes tabular data synthesis so difficult for methods which excel in image and text domains? How can we examine which exact parts of a synthetic dataset contain implausible values or patterns? Answering these questions is not trivial, as already measuring the quality of synthetic data is not straightforward: As opposed to supervised learning, there are no direct performance measures for generative modeling as a mainly unsupervised discipline through the absence of labels. Moreover, even in relatively low dimensions, dependencies between features – of numerical or categorical nature – are hard to comprehend for humans. This makes the evaluation of tabular data synthesis quality even more challenging compared to image or text data where human experts can assess the results more easily. There are many different concepts for evaluating the performance of generative models, and not all of them are available for every model and data type. New measures are also frequently proposed to address the shortcomings of the previous ones. However, transparency regarding the underlying *reasons* for poorer synthesis quality, reflected in lower performance scores, is rarely available. Furthermore, while some of the measures allow for evaluation at individual observation level [5,39], it often remains unclear which specific feature values or combinations are responsible for the poor quality of a specific synthetic observation. (See Sect. 3.1 for more background about generative models and their evaluation.)

Explainable artificial intelligence (XAI), also referred to as interpretable machine learning (IML), tries to explain the outputs and decision-making of machine learning models. This is an emerging machine learning discipline, as high performing machine learning models are often black boxes due to their complexity, and there is an urgent demand for methods to make them more transparent and easier to trust. Some XAI methods are able to attribute to each feature - or even feature interaction - its contribution to a model's output. However, the majority of these XAI methods is designed for supervised learning and not directly applicable to generative modeling. (See Sect. 3.2 for more background about XAI.)

Contributions. We propose to leverage a synthetic data detection model to evaluate the performance of a generative model and to use it as a supervised proxy model in order to obtain more detailed insights about the strengths and weaknesses of the synthetic data via common XAI methods. While the detection model itself can give an indication of the overall and individual discernibility of real and synthetic data and about the fidelity and diversity of the synthetic data (Sect. 4.1), we go one step further: As our main contribution, we provide a set of suitable global and local XAI tools which can be used to unlock more detailed insights by answering the following questions (Sect. 4.2):

Q1. Which features and feature dependencies were most challenging for the generative model?
Q2. How do the generative models behave in low and high density areas of feature distributions? Which areas are under- or overrepresented in the synthetic data?
Q3. Which features and feature dependencies/interactions contributed most to the detection of an individual real or synthetic observation?
Q4. Which minimal changes to a correctly classified synthetic observation could be performed to make it look realistic?

We demonstrate the utility of this approach by answering these questions for real data examples (Sect. 5). This work is primarily aimed at practitioners and researchers in the field of generative modeling, who want to gain deeper insights about the quality of their synthetic data or about the strengths and limitations of their generative models. Secondarily, within the XAI community, we want to raise awareness of the specific challenges in explainability for generative models that have not yet been adequately addressed.

2 Related Work

The intersection of XAI and generative modeling has not yet been sufficiently researched. Schneider [55] underscores the demand for interpretability methods for generative models and gives a road map for this research direction but does not refer to explaining synthetic data quality explicitly. Several works have focused on finding meaningful representations of the latent space of generative models [20,22,32] to better understand and control the data generation process or have specifically examined the explainability of the attention mechanism and transformers [3,63]. XAI has successfully been incorporated in the training process of generative models to increase their performance [45,71], but these approaches are specifically aimed at image data generation.

In the opposite direction, generative modeling has supported XAI methods to explain the inner workings of neural networks [47], create more human-understandable interpretations of model decisions [23], calculate conditional feature importances [4,13], and produce more plausible counterfactuals [21,46,52].

The following works are most closely related to our approach, though they emphasize different aspects and do not extend as far in our primary focus area of explaining synthetic data quality: Lopez-Paz et al. [39] suggest to train a detection model to evaluate if two samples derive from the same distribution and analyze the statistical properties of such classifier two-sample tests. Zein et al. [67] follow this strategy to demonstrate that machine learning utility as an evaluation measure may not be a reliable indicator for synthetic data quality. Both underline the interpretability of such classifier models and even perform a limited analysis using XAI, but do not focus on this aspect: Lopez-Paz et al. [39] briefly mention several feature importance methods and show an example on image data, Zein et al. [67] use impurity-based and permutation-based feature importances for synthetic tabular data detection. Neither of these works go beyond feature importance techniques which represent only an initial analysis step in the set of XAI tools presented in this work.

On image data, a wide range of existing studies use binary classifiers and their image-specific interpretation techniques for deep fake detection [2,8,11].

3 Background

Since this work lies at the intersection of generative modeling and XAI and is intended for researchers and practitioners who do not necessarily have expertise in both disciplines, we provide a high-level overview of both fields.

3.1 Generative Modeling of Tabular Data

Generative modeling or generative artificial intelligence is a machine learning sub-discipline concerned with generating realistic synthetic data: Let D_{real} denote a dataset with instances from a feature space $\mathcal{X}$, each of which is a realization of a random variable $\mathbf{X}$. Given D_{real}, generative modeling tries to generate synthetic data D_{syn} which follow the same joint distribution $p_{\mathbf{X}}$. As this original data distribution is unknown in real-world settings, generative modeling *explicitly* or *implicitly* approximates $p_{\mathbf{X}}$ in order to generate realistic instances and is therefore related to the discipline of joint density estimation [35,42]: Explicit generative models $G : \mathcal{X} \to \mathbb{R}_0^+$ directly model the underlying joint distribution ($G = \hat{p}_{\mathbf{X}}$) and provide a sampling routine to generate new instances. On the other hand, implicit generative models $G : \mathcal{L} \to \mathcal{X}$ are trained to generate realistic samples given random noise $\mathbf{z}$ from a latent-space $\mathcal{L}$ without being able to compute density likelihoods ($G(\mathbf{z}) \sim \hat{p}_{\mathbf{X}}$).

Early deep learning approaches such as variational autoencoders (VAEs) [37], generative adversarial networks (GANs) [29], and normalizing flows (NFs) [53] have set the ground for the success of generative AI within the past decade. Modern transformer-based architectures [62], denoising diffusion probabilistic models (DDPMs) [33,59], often combined with autoregressive models (ARs) [10], are responsible for the recent hype about generative AI for realistic text, image, audio, and video synthesis [14].

While numerous adaptions of these methods for tabular data synthesis have been proposed [38,66,69], these often struggle to achieve the same overwhelming results as on image or text data. Tree-based generative methods [48,64] have demonstrated competitive or superior performance while being significantly less computationally demanding than deep learning approaches [26,49], which aligns to well-known findings from discriminative modeling [15,30,57]: This type of models showed the capacity to effectively deal with the challenges specific to tabular data, such as different feature types (e.g., continuous, discrete, categorical), odd-shaped feature distributions (e.g., multimodality, skew, truncation), complex feature dependencies, and lack of a natural positional or syntactical feature order as for image or text data. However, recent advances in deep learning for both discriminative and generative modeling seem to be promising steps towards closing the gap to tree-based methods [34,68].

Another inherent challenge in tabular data synthesis is the assessment of its quality. Generative models in general lack direct evaluation methods, since they are usually trained in an unsupervised manner. An evaluation via test likelihoods as in density estimation is only available for explicit generative models and does not necessarily allow for implications about the synthetic data quality [61]. On top of that, tabular data quality cannot innately be evaluated like data modalities such as images and text, which humans are able to process and judge naturally. Various evaluation concepts exist which try to cover different aspects of the complexity of tabular data: *Fidelity* or *precision* metrics measure the resemblance of a synthetic dataset to the original data, and *coverage* or *recall* its diversity [5,54]. This is often measured by assessing how much of the synthetic data is covered by the original data distribution and vice versa. As a trivial synthesizer returning an exact copy of the original dataset would receive perfect scores in both previous metrics, a third dimension is often added: *Authenticity*, *overfitting* or – closely related – *privacy* metrics measure the generalization or privacy preservation ability of the generative model [5,35]. The so-called *detection score* or *classifier two-sample test* gives a measure of how well binary machine learning classifiers can distinguish between original and synthetic data [39,49]. Alternatively, the distance between original and synthetic data distributions can be assessed using statistical tests and distance measures such as *Kullback-Leibler divergence*, *Wasserstein distance*, and *maximum mean discrepancy* [12,42]. Utility-based evaluations assess how well predictive machine learning tasks or statistical analyses can be repeated on synthetic data, using measures of *machine learning utility* or *statistical utility* [26,35,66]. So far, no gold standard has been established in measuring the quality of synthetic data. Good performance in one of the previous approaches does not imply the same for a different one [35,61,67]. Moreover, none of these possibilities to measure synthetic data quality provides a data-based explanation of their scores or insights into *why* the quality of some synthetic dataset has been evaluated to be good or bad.

3.2 Explainable Artificial Intelligence

Due to their high performance, machine learning models are increasingly implemented in high-stake decision-making. However, the gain in performance often comes at the cost of reduced interpretability. XAI methods aim to enhance transparency and trustworthiness by developing inherently interpretable models or creating post-hoc methods that provide insights into the behavior of complex black box models.

Post-hoc XAI methods can be categorized along several dimensions, which should be taken into account when selecting the most suitable approach in a given context [43,44]: *Model-agnostic* methods can be applied to any model, whereas *model-specific* methods are tailored to particular model classes, making them often more computationally efficient. For instance, Shapley additive explanation values (SHAP) [41] are not limited to any specific model class, DeepSHAP [41] and TreeSHAP [40] can only be used for deep learning architectures and tree-based learners, respectively. Another central axis of differentiation is the scope of interpretability: *Global* methods provide explanations for the overall model behavior across all data points, *local* ones for single instances. Partial dependence plots (PDP) [27], as an example, provide a global assessment of feature influence, while individual conditional expectation (ICE) [6] curves refine this perspective by depicting variation at a local level. A further distinction arises regarding the perspective of explanations: *Prediction-based* methods, such as SHAP, concentrate on how the model's predictions change in response to different inputs, while *loss-based* methods, such as permutation feature importance (PFI) [25], focus on how the model learns and generalizes rather than how it predicts. Explanation methods differ in how they account for relationships between features: *Marginal* explanations evaluate the effect of a feature ignoring dependencies with other features while *conditional* explanations account for feature relationships based on the data distribution [1,13,17]. Marginal methods are said to be "true to the model" because they reflect how the model internally processes features, even if the resulting explanations are unrealistic given the data due to ignored correlations. In contrast, conditional methods are said to be "true to the data", ensuring that explanations align with real-world feature dependencies [18].

The reliability of any interpretability method highly depends on the model's capacity to generalize. If a model underfits, explanations may reflect oversimplified patterns, whereas an overfitting model may yield explanations that are driven by noise rather than meaningful structure.

4 Methods

To not only assess the quality of synthetic data but also gain more granular insights into their limitations, we propose applying XAI methods to a synthetic data detection model. Specifically, we introduce methods capable of addressing questions Q1.–Q4. from Sect. 1, which represent increasing levels of explanatory detail.

In the following, $D := \{D_{\text{real}}, D_{\text{syn}}\}$ denotes a dataset of size n and dimensionality p consisting of original data D_{real} and equally-sized synthetic data D_{syn} from an arbitrary (explicit or implicit) generative model G. Furthermore, let $\mathbf{x}_j$ denote the j-th feature of D, $\mathbf{x}_{-j}$ the subset of features excluding j, and $\mathbf{x}^{(i)}$ the i-th instance.

4.1 Synthetic Data Detection Model

A synthetic data detection model is a binary classifier $C : \mathcal{X} \to [0, 1]$ trained on $X_{\text{train}} \subset D$ with corresponding binary labels $\mathbf{y}_{\text{train}}$ marking if an observation is real or synthetic. It outputs a probability $C(\mathbf{x})$ for a given data point to be real. Its performance on unseen test data X_{test} and $\mathbf{y}_{\text{test}}$ can be evaluated by metrics such as accuracy and the area under the ROC curve (AUC), and serves as a measure for the quality of the synthetic data: Intuitively, high quality synthetic data should almost be indistinguishable from real data for C. False positive rates and false negative rates can be used to assess fidelity and diversity of the synthetic data [58]. If additionally a train-test-split is introduced before generative model training so that C gets trained on different real data than G, the performance of C also reflects the generalization ability of G.

Different types of binary classifiers can be used as a synthetic data detection model. In order to obtain reliable evaluation scores and explanations, it is vital to select a highly capable model and ensure it does not overfit substantially. For tabular data, well-tuned gradient-boosted tree ensembles such as XGBoost [19] are a robust choice [67].

4.2 Explaining Synthetic Data Detection with XAI Methods

Given a synthetic data classifier C and a dataset of original and synthetic instances D, we present suitable XAI methods addressing questions Q1. – Q4. and discuss their properties, advantages and shortcomings. For a more holistic and detailed discussion of XAI methods, we refer to Molnar [43].

Q1.: Feature Importance Measures. To determine which features or feature combinations were not reproduced realistically in synthetic data, feature importance measures can be leveraged. High feature importance values can point to the features or dependencies most responsible for low synthetic data quality.

Permutation feature importance (PFI) is a global loss-based method for assessing feature importance. It quantifies the impact of a feature $\mathbf{x}_j$ by the drop in model performance, measured by the model loss L, averaged over all instances when this feature is replaced by a permuted version $\tilde{\mathbf{x}}_j$ of itself:

$$\text{PFI}_j = \frac{1}{n} \sum_{i=1}^{n} \left(L\left(C(\tilde{\mathbf{x}}_j; \mathbf{x}_{-j}^{(i)}), y^{(i)}\right) - L\left(C(\mathbf{x}^{(i)}), y^{(i)}\right) \right).$$

As an effect of the permutation across the whole dataset, the associations between $\mathbf{x}_j$ and y, as well as all other features, are removed. The more the model's performance declines, the more important the feature is considered. Since the model's performance is involved in the computation of PFI, it is preferable to calculate it on test data [43]. PFI can yield inaccurate results in the presence of highly correlated features as the permutation procedure leads to the generation of off-manifold data. This can be tackled by replacing the marginal permutation routine by conditional sampling techniques [13, 65].

Alternatively, Shapley values [56] can be leveraged to obtain feature importances: The *Shapley feature importance* [40] is calculated as the mean absolute Shapley value

$$\phi_j = \frac{1}{n} \sum_{i=1}^{n} |\phi_j^i|,$$

where ϕ_j^i denotes the Shapley value for instance i and feature j. For an introduction to Shapley values, see Sect. 4.2 Q3.

Q2.: Feature Effect Plots. The marginal effect of a feature on the detection model's prediction can be graphically represented by feature effect plots. This allows for the identification of unrealistic feature value regions in the synthetic data, as well as areas of the original data distribution that are not covered or underrepresented by the synthetic data. To facilitate understanding of feature effect plots in the context of synthetic data detection, Fig. 3 and its interpretation in Section 5.2 Q2. can already be considered alongside their methodological discussion in this section.

At a single-instance level, this can be visualized using *individual conditional expectation* (ICE) curves, represented by the graph of the function

$$\text{ICE}_j^i(x_j) = C(x_j; \mathbf{x}_{-j}^{(i)}),$$

where model predictions are evaluated for different values of the j-th feature while keeping all other features constant. Non-parallel ICE curves of different individuals indicate the presence of an interaction effect with other features on the prediction, suggesting that some feature dependencies present in the original data were not consistently retained in the synthetic data.

By averaging over each feature value, a global *partial dependence plot* (PDP) can be derived from local ICE curves:

$$\text{PDP}_j(x_j) = \frac{1}{n} \sum_{i=1}^{n} \text{ICE}_j^i(x_j).$$

This provides a comprehensive view of the feature's marginal effect on the prediction. Regions where the PDP drops significantly below 0.5 indicate unrealistic feature values in the synthetic data, making them easily identifiable for the classifier. Conversely, regions where the PDP rises well above 0.5 highlight feature value areas that are absent or underrepresented in the synthetic data. Often, PDP and ICE curves are presented together in a joint plot.

Both ICE and PDP assume independent features, which can lead to misleading interpretations when features are correlated. Accumulated local effects (ALE) [7] plots are an alternative to PDP for this case, as they compute localized instead of marginal effects by measuring changes in model predictions within small conditional neighborhoods.

Q3.: Shapley Values. Rooted in cooperative game theory, *Shapley values* [56] were originally designed to fairly distribute a total payoff among players in a game. In the context of machine learning, the most common approach treats features as players, and distributes a single observation's prediction among them based on their contribution. This is done in an inclusion-removal manner considering all possible feature coalitions S:

$$\phi_j^i = \sum_{S \subseteq \{1,\ldots,p\} \setminus \{j\}} \frac{|S|!(p-|S|-1)!}{p!} \left(v^i(S \cup \{j\}) - v^i(S) \right). \tag{1}$$

The function v^i returns the model's expected output when only a given subset of features of an instance i is considered. In the classical marginal approach

[41], the remaining features are marginalized out using their *marginal* expectations, implicitly assuming independence between observed and unobserved features. In the conditional approach [1], the remaining features are integrated out based on their *conditional* expectations given the considered features, preserving dependencies in the data. This results in conditional Shapley values, which are often more realistic when estimated accurately. However, their estimation can be challenging and entails higher computational costs [1,17]. Equation (1) can be slightly modified to compute contributions of feature interactions [60]. For large datasets and high-dimensional feature spaces, computing exact Shapley values can be computationally expensive or even infeasible. Often, only a subset of all possible coalitions is considered to make computations feasible, for instance with the model-agnostic KernelSHAP method [1,41]. Also model-specific adaptions such as DeepSHAP and TreeSHAP can speed up calculations significantly.

In the setting of synthetic data detection, Shapley values decompose the predictions of individual synthetic observations to reveal which features (or feature interactions, in the case of Shapley interaction values) make instances appear unrealistic to the detection model. Conversely, they also help identify which values and feature combinations of a real instance are insufficiently represented in the synthetic data distribution. Thus, Shapley values quantify the relevance of the *presence* of each feature value (or feature combination) in determining how realistic this observation appears to the detection model: For real observations with $C(\mathbf{x}) \gg 0.5$, the features with the largest Shapley values indicate that the feature values they correspond to are the main reasons the detection model is able to separate them from the synthetic data. This suggests that these feature values may be underrepresented in the synthetic data. The same applies to synthetic observations with $C(\mathbf{x}) \ll 0.5$.

Q4.: Counterfactuals. Counterfactual explanations (CE) present examples of minimal feature changes that would alter the model's prediction to a different outcome. For our binary classification setting, a different outcome will correspond to crossing the threshold of 0.5. We will leverage this method to study how we can most easily modify the feature values of a correctly detected synthetic sample so that it looks realistic to the detection model (i.e., has $C(\mathbf{x}) > 0.5$). The best counterfactual examples possess several quality properties [31], where sparsity/proximity (changes are as few and small as possible), plausibility (changes are realistic and align with the feature distribution), validity (actually resulting in a changed outcome) are the most relevant in our case.

As discussed in Sect. 2, many methods for counterfactual generation rely on generative models themselves in order to produce realistic counterfactuals. The *Monte Carlo sampling of realistic counterfactual explanations* (MCCE) method [52], used in Sect. 5.2 Q4., directly aims to achieve the aforementioned quality properties and leverages an autoregressive tree-based synthesizer to generate on-manifold counterfactuals, making it particularly well-suited for tabular data.

5 Real Data Examples

We demonstrate our approach on real world data. First, we examine the performance of different synthetic data detection models (Sect. 5.1) on various datasets and generative models. After that, we answer questions Q1.–Q4. with the XAI methods presented in Sect. 4.2 for synthetic adult data [9] generated with TabSyn [68] (Sect. 5.2). In Appendix A, we do a similar, but simplified exercise for synthetic nursery data [50] generated with CTGAN [66]. Generic scripts for detection model tuning and training, for applying the XAI methods discussed in this paper, as well as for reproducing our presented tables and figures can be found in the repository accompanying this paper.[1] Additionally, it includes an overview and descriptive statistics of all datasets and further context for our experiments with all synthesizers considered.

5.1 Performance of Different Synthetic Data Detection Models

In order to obtain reliable explanations, we need to ensure that we use a high performing classifier as our synthetic data detection model. For this purpose, we performed hyperparameter tuning for XGBoost via Bayesian optimization, e.g., for the tree depth, learning rate and regularization parameters. As already stated in 4.1, a well-tuned XGBoost model is typically a robust choice for classification tasks on tabular data. Figure 1a supports this statement: Across six different state-of-the-art or frequently used generative models [48,64,66,68,70] and eleven standard machine learning datasets from publicly available sources [24,36], tuned XGBoost models consistently show the strongest classification performance against logistic regression and random forest as baseline models.

Figure 1b shows the performance of the tuned XGBoost models for the two datasets (adult and nursery) we use in the following to illustrate our approach.

5.2 Answering Q1.–Q4. for Synthetic Adult Data

Before synthesis, we removed all rows with missing values from the adult dataset as well as the categorical feature `education`, since its information value is identical to `education_num`, resulting in a dataset with 47 876 instances and 14 columns (6 numeric and 8 categorical). We generated ten synthetic datasets using TabSyn, a state-of-the-art DDPM for tabular data. On each of these generated datasets, we trained an XGBoost model for synthetic data detection using Bayesian optimization for hyperparameter tuning and a train-test split of 30%, while keeping the real data points the same across all ten synthetic datasets.

Q1. To address our first research question on identifying the most challenging features and feature dependencies for TabSyn, we analyze feature importances using both loss-based and prediction-based XAI methods. Figure 2a shows results for PFI and global TreeSHAP (mean absolute Shapley values estimated

---

[1] https://github.com/bips-hb/XAI_syn_data_detection.

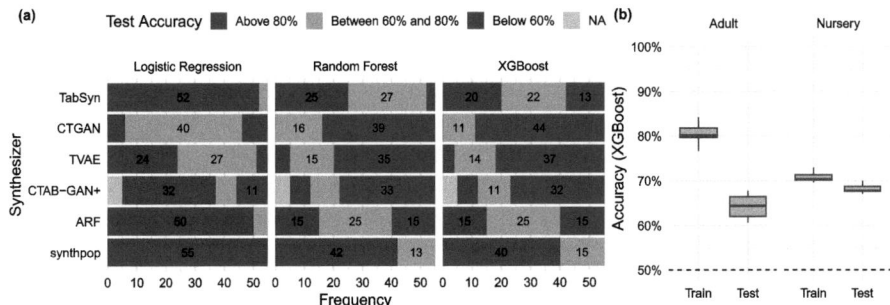

Fig. 1. (a) Synthetic data detection performance of logistic regression, random forest [16] and XGBoost models with six generative models generating five synthetic datasets for eleven original datasets each. CTAB-GAN+ did not converge for all runs. (b) Synthetic data detection performance for XGBoost on train and test data for adult and nursery data with ten replications.

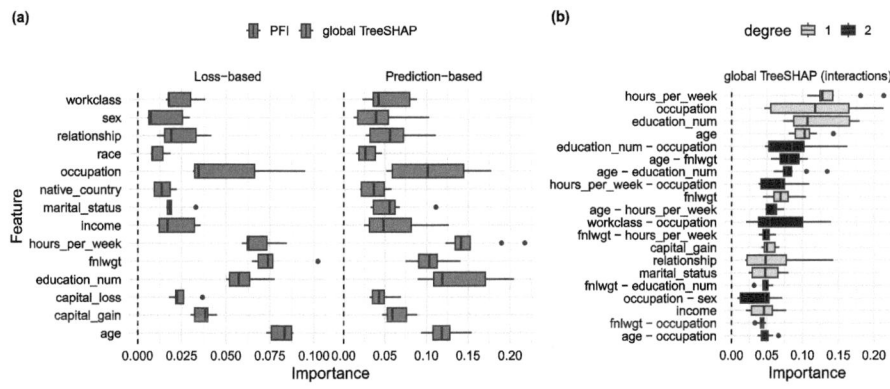

Fig. 2. Feature importance values for synthetic data detection with XGBoost for ten TabSyn-generated synthetic adult datasets. Higher importance values indicate poorer synthesis quality. (a) PFI and global TreeSHAP values. (b) Global TreeSHAP interaction values of degree 1 and 2 (top 20 most important).

by TreeSHAP), while Fig. 2b provides a finer examination of the interaction effects inherently obtained using TreeSHAP. In general, if a feature has a high importance, it indicates patterns in the synthetic data that make a differentiation on a global level easier for the detection model, whereas low importance suggests more realistic feature values.

At a broad level, both methods in Fig. 2a identify similar key features for the XGBoost detection model, such as `age`, `hours_per_week`, `fnlwgt`, and `education_num`, highlighting these features as weak spots in the synthetic data where marginal distributions or dependencies to other features are not replicated accurately. Moreover, the relatively low variance (except for `occupation`) in the boxplots suggests that the detection models rely on the same features across all ten synthesized dataset versions, indicating a consistent decision basis. The high variance for occupation may be due to its strong dependencies with multiple important features (see Fig. 2b), which seem challenging to retain for TabSyn. Comparing PFI and global TreeSHAP, both yield similar feature rankings and relative differences. However, their importance values differ in scale: As mentioned in Sect. 4.2, TreeSHAP sums absolute contributions across instances, leading to larger values, while PFI measures the average performance drop of a feature removal. An exception is the feature fnlwgt, which is ranked considerably higher in PFI than in TreeSHAP. This is likely due to its strong interactions with other important features, such as age and hours_per_week (see Fig. 2b). Since PFI disrupts feature dependencies through permutation, it fully attributes interaction effects to each involved feature once, not multiple times, whereas TreeSHAP distributes them fairly among the interacting features [28].

Figure 2b shows that, alongside strong main effects, many interaction effects contribute substantially to the model's predictions, which are inherently calculated with TreeSHAP for XGBoost models (interaction TreeSHAP). The features hours_per_week, education_num, and age remain the most important individually, but interactions, such as education_num with occupation and age with fnlwgt and education_num, also show a strong influential effect. Their appearance within the most important features (main and interactions) indicates that TabSyn struggles to fully recreate this complex dependence structure. An interesting case is occupation, which, as previously noted, appears in numerous interactions (with education_num, hours_per_week and workclass). The variability in this interaction across all ten dataset versions further confirms that the dependencies involving occupation are difficult for the synthesizer to capture consistently. Another notable observation is that the importance ranking of occupation in Fig. 2b including the interactions is much higher than in both PFI and TreeSHAP in Fig. 2a. One possible explanation is that occupation's interactions partially cancel out or reduce the main effect due to different contribution signs in the standard TreeSHAP decomposition, whereas for interaction TreeSHAP, the separation of interactions prevents this effect. This may happen if the marginal distribution of occupation deviates from the real distribution (i.e., making it easier to distinguish), but the dependencies for influential classes of occupation to other features are realistically generated.

Q2. Using feature effect plots, we now take a closer look at the numerical feature education_num and the categorical feature occupation which were among the top-ranked features and appeared in several interactions in Fig. 2b. From now on, we base our explanations on one synthetic dataset only and do not further examine the variation across different TabSyn-generated datasets. ICE curves and PDP for education_num are shown in Fig. 3a with indicated marginal distributions for real and synthetic data on the x-axis. We observe that especially in the low-density region of the real data for feature values below 4, the PDP is located considerably below 0.5, implying that TabSyn learned unrealistic patterns in this area which make the identification of synthetic data easy for XGBoost. Furthermore, the PDP and the plotted data distributions reveal

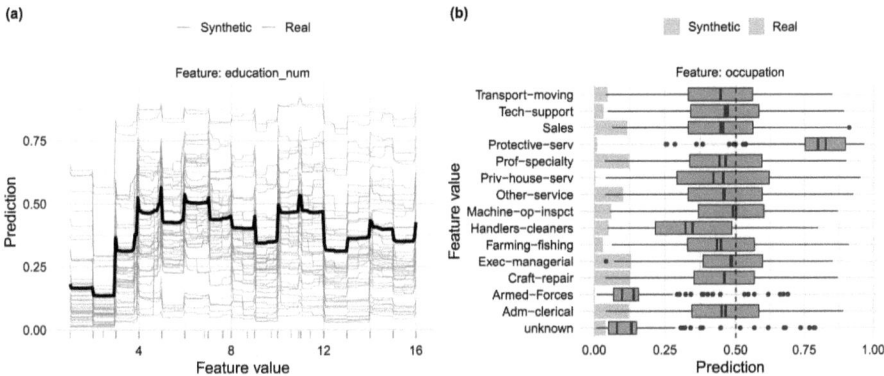

Fig. 3. ICE/PDP for synthetic data detection with XGBoost for TabSyn-generated synthetic adult data. (a) Numeric feature `education_num`, distribution for original and synthetic data on x-axis. (b) Categorical feature `occupation`, PDP in red, frequencies for real and synthetic data on y-axis.

unrealistic synthetic feature values: While in the real data only integer values occur for `education_num`, TabSyn also generates non-integer values, resulting in a periodical PDP drop between integers. Looking at the ICE curves, we see that not all curves run in parallel and that some cross each other. This indicates the presence of interactions with `education_num` which alter the course of the curves individually on top of the marginal effects, which aligns to the findings presented in Fig. 2b. Another observation is that the share of real data ICE curves markedly falling under 0.5 is higher than the share of synthetic data ICE curves over 0.5. This means that it is harder for the model to correctly classify real data than synthetic data based on this feature, indicating low fidelity but high diversity of the synthetic data for this feature.

Figure 3b shows results for the categorical variable `occupation`. For each class, the variation of ICE values across instances is displayed by box plots, the PDP values are represented by red lines. On the y-axis, the class frequencies are shown for real and synthetic data. We observe that the classes `Protective-serv`, `Armed-Forces` and `unknown` with most deviation from 0.5 have a low number of occurrences, while the most frequent classes such as `Prof-specialty` and `Exec-managerial` tend to have values close to 0.5. This implies that data generation quality is low for rare classes and improves for more frequent ones. Looking at `Protective-serv` and the corresponding class frequencies for real and synthetic data, we notice that this class is substantially underrepresented in the synthetic data, which can be an explanation for its PDP value close to 1 (prediction as real). On the contrary, the class `Handlers-cleaners` seems to be moderately overrepresented in the synthetic data, which can be the reason why its PDP and ICE values are consistently smaller than 0.5 (prediction as synthetic). The class `unknown` appears to be equally represented in real and synthetic data. However, its PDP value is close to 0, indicating that synthetic instances with this class are

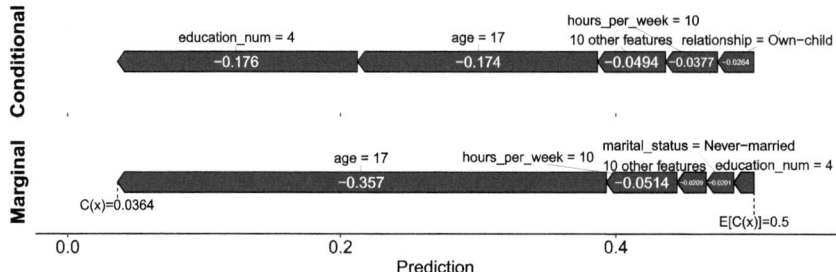

Fig. 4. Force plots for conditional and marginal Shapley values decomposing the XGBoost prediction for an exemplary instance of TabSyn-generated synthetic adult data.

often unrealistic. A reason for this can be that combinations of this class with other feature values are not retained realistically in the synthetic data. This aligns to the presence of important interactions with occupation in 2b.

Q3. While the first two questions focused mainly on the detection model's global behavior, we now examine how features and feature interactions contribute to the classification of specific individual predictions. To explore this, we analyze two correctly classified samples – one synthetic and one real. Note that these two examples illustrate key aspects that should be considered when interpreting predictions of the detection model. However, for a comprehensive assessment of local behavior, a structured analysis across many more observations is required.

We first explore a specific synthetic observation corresponding to a young (age = 17), white female with low education (education_num = 4, indicating education up to the 7th or 8th grade) based in the United States with marginal and conditional Shapley values. Note that potential issues with the region around education_num = 4 were already visible in Fig. 3a. The feature distributions in the conditional approach are estimated with conditional inference trees [51] and both approaches use the KernelSHAP method with 2000 coalitions to approximate the Shapley values. The force plots in Fig. 4 visualize how differently marginal and conditional Shapley values drive the prediction from the baseline value of 0.5 down to a very low predicted probability of $C(\mathbf{x}) = 0.0364$: The marginal approach attributes the majority of the contribution to this prediction to the young age, whereas the conditional approach distributes the contribution almost evenly between education_num and age. As noted already in Sect. 4.2, the marginal and conditional approaches differ in the presence of (local) feature dependence. Upon closer inspection of these two features, we find that the combination present in our synthetic example is highly unlikely in the real data: Only 0.7% of 17-years-old real individuals have a value of 4 for education_num, the average value is 6.69 for this age. Moreover, the mean age for education_num = 4 is the oldest across all education levels with 49.12 years. An explanation for these numbers can be the fact that it was common for older generations to quit school after the 8th grade to start working, as younger generations typically attend school for longer than that. Moreover, their global correlation in the real data is small (0.03), but larger for the younger (0.54 for age≤ 20). The stronger feature dependence among younger individuals is natural, as many are still in education and have yet to attain higher degrees. With this in mind, we consider the conditional approach the more appropriate, and argue that this synthetic sample is weak not only in terms of age, but also in education_num.

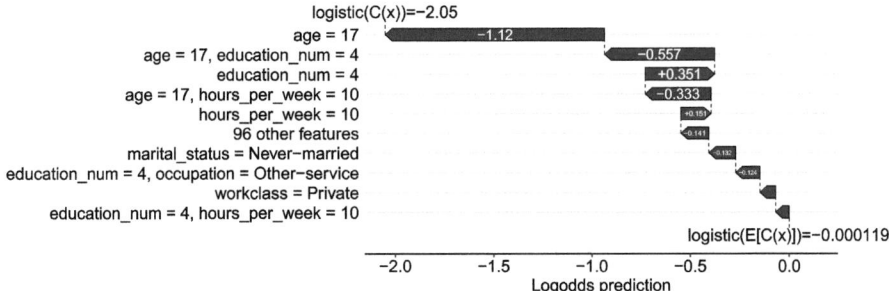

Fig. 5. Waterfall plots for Shapley interaction values decomposing the XGBoost prediction for an exemplary instance of TabSyn-generated synthetic adult data. Note that TreeSHAP decomposes the prediction on the log-odds/logistic scale rather than on the probability scale.

Figure 5 confirms this line of reasoning: It displays a waterfall plot with the largest (in absolute value) Shapley interaction values for the same synthetic female as above, computed with the (path dependent) TreeSHAP algorithm [40], which partially accounts for feature dependencies, placing it between the conditional and marginal approaches: The interaction between age and education_num is identified as a key factor for correctly classifying the sample. Interestingly, when adjusting for interactions, education_num alone actually makes the sample look more similar to the real observations. This suggests that locally around this sample, education_num itself aligns well with real observations, but its combination with the specific age is causing the discrepancy.

For the majority of the features, the overall average dependence in this dataset is relatively small, such that the conditional and marginal Shapley values more or less agree for most of the samples. However, as seen above, the features may be highly dependent locally. Going forward, we therefore stick to the conditional approach. Figure 6 displays both conditional Shapley values and Shapley interaction values for a 47-year-old, self-employed, male in the real dataset, which was easily correctly classified by the detection model $C(\mathbf{x}) = 0.94$. The main contributor to that was the capital_gain feature, while the interactions also reveal that the dependencies between education_num and occupation play a role. As seen from Fig. 2, capital_gain was not very important globally, which exemplifies that there may be local areas in the feature space which are not adequately represented in the synthetic data even if the feature is globally well represented. The education_num–occupation interaction, on the other hand, is already highlighted as a potential issue globally.

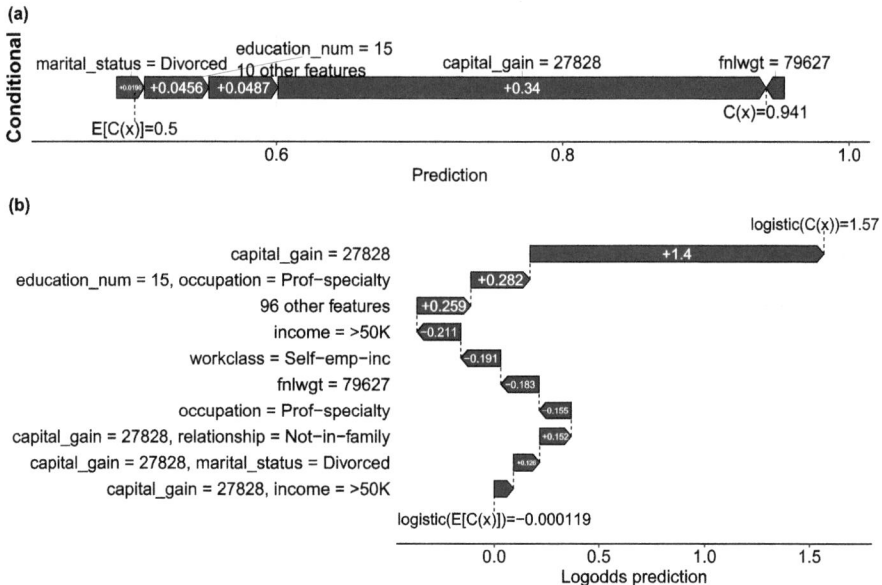

Fig. 6. Force and waterfall plots for, respectively, (a) conditional Shapley values and (b) Shapley interaction values decomposing the XGBoost prediction for an exemplary real instance of the adult data. Note that TreeSHAP decomposes the prediction on the log-odds/logistic scale rather than on the probability scale.

Q4. Finally, we investigate how minimal changes to synthetic observations can be performed to make them look realistic. We proceed to exemplify this with the same synthetic sample as in Sect. 5.2 Q3. , the young female with low education. Figure 7 provides four counterfactual examples which modify a few of the feature values in different ways to change the classification to real. The counterfactual examples are generated with the MCCE method of [52] with all features mutable and 5×10^5 Monte Carlo samples.

First, observe that fnlwgt is changed in all counterfactuals. This feature reflects the number of people each observation represents in the population, making it natural that it must be adjusted when other features change to maintain consistency. Moreover, Fig. 2b indicated issues in the synthetic data for its dependencies with other features on a global level, so that its value might not have aligned to other features. Apart from fnlwgt, the first counterfactual (CF1) changes only education_num, while CF2 and CF3 perform slightly smaller changes in education_num while also increasing respectively age by 1 year and occupation. Finally, CF4 illustrates that education_num does not need to be

	Original	CF1	CF2	CF3	CF4
age	17	17	18 ↑	17	22 ↑
workclass	Private	Private	Private	Private	Private
fnlwgt	261872.28	215990 ↓	191784 ↓	206066 ↓	213700 ↓
education_num	4	8 ↑	7 ↑	7 ↑	4
marital_status	Never-married	Never-married	Never-married	Never-married	Never-married
occupation	Other-service	Other-service	Other-service	Adm-clerical ↔	Other-service
relationship	Own-child	Own-child	Own-child	Own-child	Own-child
race	White	White	White	White	White
sex	Female	Female	Female	Female	Female
capital_gain	0	0	0	0	0
capital_loss	0	0	0	0	0
hours_per_week	10	10	10	10	25 ↑
native_country	United-States	United-States	United-States	United-States	United-States
income	<=50K	<=50K	<=50K	<=50K	<=50K

Fig. 7. Four counterfactual explanations for an exemplary instance of TabSyn-generated synthetic adult data. Highlighted features are changed.

changed for the synthetic observation to appear real – increasing `age` by five years and `hours_per_week` by 15 h also changes the classification to real.

6 Discussion

In this paper, we demonstrate that the application of XAI methods on a synthetic data detection model can generate valuable insights about synthetic data quality. We provide a set of suitable global and local XAI tools, such as feature importance measures, feature effect plots, Shapley values and counterfactuals. These XAI tools can be used to identify the most challenging features and dependencies in the original data for successful data synthesis and to detect unrealistic patterns in the synthetic data on dataset- and single-instance level. The experiments in Sect. 5 illustrate this on real world data and underline the gain in explanatory depth in comparison to traditional synthetic data quality metrics and visual approaches such as histograms and correlation plots. The insights generated from our suggested XAI-driven analysis can be used for synthetic data auditing to explain overall utility, synthesis quality in low density areas of the real data, and to determine low fidelity instances. It could also be leveraged to analyze and compare the strengths and weaknesses of different generative models on different datasets and to debug or further improve generative models.

One limitation of this approach is that it is not directly applicable to a generative model itself but depends on the performance of a binary classifier used for synthetic data detection. Special care has to be taken during the tuning and training process of this classifier as low detection accuracy values can both be caused by insufficient classification performance and by high quality synthetic data. For some purposes, the detection model can even be too sensitive and might detect deviations such as different numeric precision which might not be relevant to assess the practical utility of the synthetic data. Moreover, it is critical to choose an appropriate XAI method considering data dependencies and explanation goal in order to obtain reliable explanations. As is generally true for all applications of XAI methods, there is no one-fits-all solution and it is important to know the strength and limitations of different tools. For instance, it is important to be aware of the differences of loss-based and prediction-based methods as well as marginal and conditional approaches [44]. Some of the XAI methods, especially conditional approaches and counterfactuals generators, are even based on generative modeling themselves. As stated in Sect. 3.1, one should keep in mind that generative models for tabular data synthesis are not yet as mature as for image and text data generation, which could lower the quality of explanations created with these methods.

We restricted this work to the explanation of synthetic data fidelity and diversity and did not consider the generalization and privacy dimension of data quality. Following a different routine for generative model training as described in Sect. 4.1, our approach could be extended to cover these aspects as well. We leave this for future work.

Especially in the light of the current worldwide rise of generative models and the increasing use of synthetic data in all relevant areas of daily life, we strongly believe that the identification and explainability of synthetic data quality as well as the intersection of XAI and generative AI in general is of highest importance.

Acknowledgments. This project was supported by the German Research Foundation (DFG), Grant Numbers 437611051, 459360854, by the U Bremen Research Alliance/AI Center for Health Care, financially supported by the Federal State of Bremen, the Norwegian Research Council through the Integreat Center of Excellence, Project Number 332645, and EU's HORIZON Research and Innovation Programme, project ENFIELD, grant number 101120657. The project was initiated at a workshop supported by a PhD grant of the Minds, Media, Machines Integrated Graduate School Bremen.

We thank Marvin N. Wright for his valuable comments during the revision of the first draft of the manuscript.

Disclosure of Interests. The authors have no competing interests to declare that are relevant to the content of this article.

A Answering Q1.–Q4. for Synthetic Nursery Data

We provide another exemplary application of our approach using the nursery dataset and the generative model CTGAN [66]. The nursery dataset has 12 958 instances and 9 columns (all categorical). CTGAN is a widely used GAN-based generative model for tabular data. Again, on each of these generated datasets, we trained an XGBoost model for synthetic data detection using Bayesian optimization for hyperparameter tuning and a train-test split of 30%, while keeping the real data points the same across all ten synthetic datasets. The mean accuracy and its variation on both train and test data are shown in Fig. 1b: The accuracy is consistently around 70%, with slightly lower values on test data.

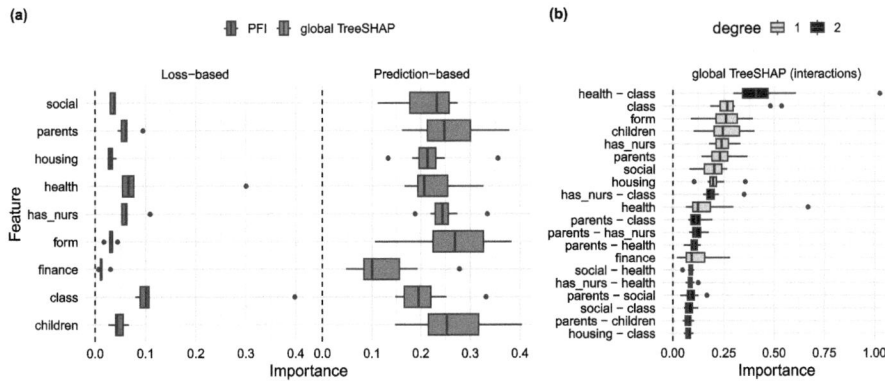

Fig. 8. Feature importance values for synthetic data detection with XGBoost for ten CTGAN-generated synthetic nursery datasets. Higher importance values indicate poorer synthesis quality. (a) PFI and global TreeSHAP values. (b) Global TreeSHAP interaction values of degree 1 and 2 (top 20 most important).

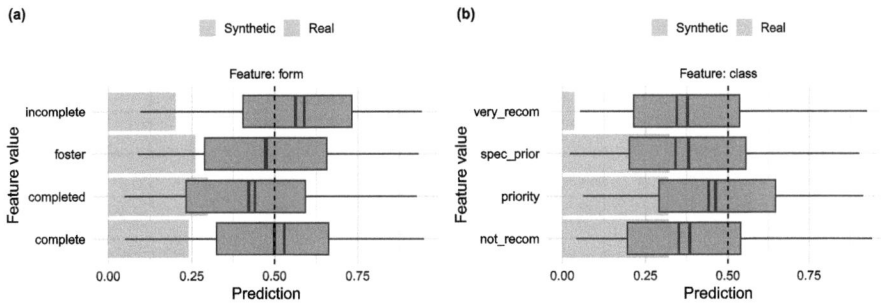

Fig. 9. ICE/PDP for synthetic data detection with XGBoost for CTGAN-generated synthetic nursery data. (a) Feature `form`, (b) feature `class`. PDP in red, frequencies for real and synthetic data on y-axis.

Figure 8 shows that CTGAN struggled to accurately reproduce multiple features. On top of that, especially the dependency between `health` and `class` appears to be insufficiently retained. In alignment with Fig. 8b, the ICE and PDP values for the feature `form` in Fig. 9a indicate a poor reconstruction of the marginal distribution with over- and underrepresented classes. The situation differs for the feature `class`, as shown in Fig. 9: Except for the rare class `very_recom`, the classes appear to be equally represented in real and synthetic data. The low ICE and PDP values for the three frequent classes are therefore likely due to inadequately captured dependencies with other features, consistent with the presence of multiple relevant interactions for `class` in Fig. 8b.

Finally, we consider a specific correctly classified ($C(\mathbf{x}) = 0.07$) synthetic observation with pretentious parents, one child and non-problematic social conditions, to mention some key features. The Shapley interaction values of this

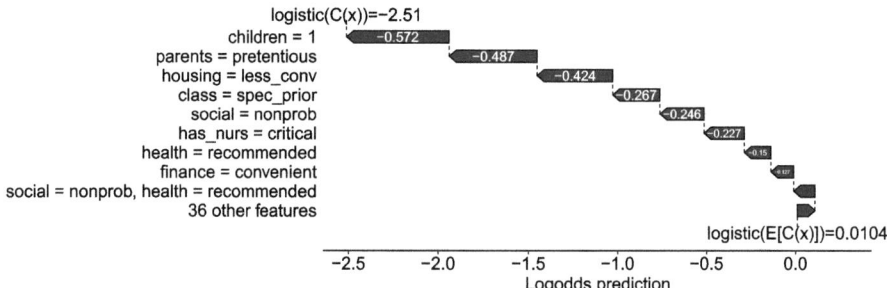

Fig. 10. Waterfall plots for Shapley interaction values decomposing the XGBoost prediction for an exemplary instance of CTGAN-generated synthetic nursery data. Note that TreeSHAP decomposes the prediction on the log-odds/logistic scale rather than on the probability scale.

	Original	CF1	CF2	CF3	CF4
parents	pretentious	great_pret	great_pret	usual	pretentious
has_nurs	critical	critical	critical	critical	critical
form	complete	complete	complete	complete	complete
children	1	3	1	3	3
housing	less_conv	less_conv	less_conv	less_conv	less_conv
finance	convenient	convenient	convenient	convenient	convenient
social	nonprob	nonprob	nonprob	problematic	slightly_prob
health	recommended	recommended	recommended	recommended	priority
class	spec_prior	spec_prior	priority	spec_prior	spec_prior

Fig. 11. Four counterfactual explanations for an exemplary instance of CTGAN-generated synthetic nursery data. Highlighted features are changed.

prediction, displayed in Fig. 10, indicate that correct classification is mainly driven by single features as opposed to feature interactions. The feature values `children = 1` and `parents = pretentious` contribute the most, but nearly all other features also have a substantial impact, implying that the majority of the features values are unrealistic or overrepresented. Figure 11 shows four counterfactual examples for the same individual. Modifying the `parents` feature and changing the `children` feature to 3 are commonalities in three of the examples. However, like in Sect. 5.2, the synthetic observation can be altered in quite different ways to appear realistic to the detection model.

References

1. Aas, K., Jullum, M., Løland, A.: Explaining individual predictions when features are dependent: more accurate approximations to Shapley values. Artif. Intell. **298**, 103502 (2021)
2. Abir, W.H., et al.: Detecting deepFake images using deep learning techniques and explainable AI methods. Intell. Autom. Soft Comput. **35**(2), 2151–2169 (2023)

3. Abnar, S., Zuidema, W.: Quantifying attention flow in transformers. In: Proceedings of the 58th Annual Meeting of the Association for Computational Linguistics, pp. 4190–4197 (2020)
4. Agarwal, C., Nguyen, A.: Explaining image classifiers by removing input features using generative models. In: Computer Vision – ACCV 2020, pp. 101–118 (2020)
5. Alaa, A., Van Breugel, B., Saveliev, E.S., van der Schaar, M.: How faithful is your synthetic data? Sample-level metrics for evaluating and auditing generative models. In: International Conference on Machine Learning. PMLR, vol. 162, pp. 290–306 (2022)
6. Goldstein, A., Kapelner, A., Bleich, J., Pitkin, E.: Peeking inside the black box: visualizing statistical learning with plots of individual conditional expectation. J. Comput. Graph. Stat. **24**(1), 44–65 (2015)
7. Apley, D.W., Zhu, J.: Visualizing the effects of predictor variables in black box supervised learning models. J. R. Stat. Soc. Ser. B Stat Methodol. **82**(4), 1059–1086 (2020)
8. Baraheem, S.S., Nguyen, T.V.: AI vs. AI: Can AI detect AI-generated images? J. Imaging **9**(10), 199 (2023)
9. Becker, B., Kohavi, R.: Adult. UCI Machine Learning Repository (1996). https://doi.org/10.24432/C5XW20
10. Bengio, Y., Ducharme, R., Vincent, P.: A neural probabilistic language model. In: Advances in Neural Information Processing Systems, vol. 13 (2000)
11. Bird, J.J., Lotfi, A.: CIFAKE: image classification and explainable identification of AI-generated synthetic images. IEEE Access **12**, 15642–15650 (2024)
12. Bischoff, S., et al.: A practical guide to sample-based statistical distances for evaluating generative models in science. Trans. Mach. Learn. Res. (2024)
13. Blesch, K., et al.: Conditional feature importance with generative modeling using adversarial random forests. In: Proceedings of the AAAI Conference on Artificial Intelligence, vol. 39, no. 15, pp. 15596–15604 (2025)
14. Bond-Taylor, S., Leach, A., Long, Y., Willcocks, C.G.: Deep generative modelling: a comparative review of VAEs, GANs, normalizing flows, energy-based and autoregressive models. IEEE Trans. Pattern Anal. Mach. Intell. **44**(11), 7327–7347 (2022)
15. Borisov, V., Leemann, T., Seßler, K., Haug, J., Pawelczyk, M., Kasneci, G.: Deep neural networks and tabular data: a survey. IEEE Trans. Neural Netw. Learning Syst. **35**(6), 7499–7519 (2024)
16. Breiman, L.: Random forests. Mach. Learn. **45**, 5–32 (2001)
17. Chen, H., Covert, I.C., Lundberg, S.M., Lee, S.I.: Algorithms to estimate Shapley value feature attributions. Nat. Mach. Intell. **5**(6), 590–601 (2023)
18. Chen, H., Janizek, J.D., Lundberg, S., Lee, S.I.: True to the model or true to the data? arXiv preprint arXiv:2006.16234 (2020)
19. Chen, T., Guestrin, C.: XGBoost: a scalable tree boosting system. In: Proceedings of the 22nd ACM SIGKDD International Conference on Knowledge Discovery and Data Mining, KDD 2016, pp. 785–794 (2016)
20. Chen, X., Duan, Y., Houthooft, R., Schulman, J., Sutskever, I., Abbeel, P.: InfoGAN: interpretable representation learning by information maximizing generative adversarial nets. In: Advances in Neural Information Processing Systems, vol. 29 (2016)
21. Dandl, S., et al.: CountARFactuals – generating plausible model-agnostic counterfactual explanations with adversarial random forests. In: Explainable Artificial Intelligence, pp. 85–107 (2024)

22. Dombrowski, M., Reynaud, H., Müller, J.P., Baugh, M., Kainz, B.: Trade-offs in fine-tuned diffusion models between accuracy and interpretability. In: Proceedings of the AAAI Conference on Artificial Intelligence, vol. 38, no. 19, pp. 21037–21045 (2024)
23. Dravid, A., Schiffers, F., Gong, B., Katsaggelos, A.K.: medXGAN: visual explanations for medical classifiers through a generative latent space. In: 2022 IEEE/CVF Conference on Computer Vision and Pattern Recognition Workshops (CVPRW), pp. 2935–2944 (2022)
24. Dua, D., Graff, C.: UCI machine learning repository (2017). http://archive.ics.uci.edu/ml
25. Fisher, A., Rudin, C., Dominici, F.: All models are wrong, but many are useful: learning a variable's importance by studying an entire class of prediction models simultaneously. J. Mach. Learn. Res. **20**(177), 1–81 (2019)
26. Fössing, E., Drechsler, J.: An evaluation of synthetic data generators implemented in the Python library synthcity. In: Privacy in Statistical Databases, pp. 178–193 (2024)
27. Friedman, J.H.: Greedy function approximation: a gradient boosting machine. Ann. Stat. **29**(5), 1189–1232 (2001)
28. Fumagalli, F., Muschalik, M., Hüllermeier, E., Hammer, B., Herbinger, J.: Unifying feature-based explanations with functional ANOVA and cooperative game theory. In: The 28th International Conference on Artificial Intelligence and Statistics (2025). https://openreview.net/forum?id=tp3Aw6t0QF
29. Goodfellow, I., et al.: Generative adversarial nets. In: Advances in Neural Information Processing Systems, vol. 27 (2014)
30. Grinsztajn, L., Oyallon, E., Varoquaux, G.: Why do tree-based models still outperform deep learning on typical tabular data? In: Advances in Neural Information Processing Systems, vol. 35, pp. 507–520 (2022)
31. Guidotti, R.: Counterfactual explanations and how to find them: literature review and benchmarking. Data Min. Knowl. Disc. **38**(5), 2770–2824 (2024)
32. Higgins, I., et al.: Beta-VAE: learning basic visual concepts with a constrained variational framework. In: International Conference on Learning Representations (2017)
33. Ho, J., Jain, A., Abbeel, P.: Denoising diffusion probabilistic models. In: Advances in Neural Information Processing Systems, vol. 33, pp. 6840–6851 (2020)
34. Hollmann, N., Müller, S., Eggensperger, K., Hutter, F.: TabPFN: a transformer that solves small tabular classification problems in a second. In: NeurIPS 2022 First Table Representation Workshop (2022)
35. Jordon, J., et al.: Synthetic data–what, why and how? arXiv preprint arXiv:2205.03257 (2022)
36. Kaggle: Kaggle datasets repository. https://www.kaggle.com/datasets. Accessed 19 Feb 2025
37. Kingma, D.P., Welling, M.: Auto-encoding variational bayes. In: International Conference on Learning Representations (2014)
38. Kotelnikov, A., Baranchuk, D., Rubachev, I., Babenko, A.: TabDDPM: modelling tabular data with diffusion models. In: Proceedings of the 40th International Conference on Machine Learning. PMLR, vol. 202, pp. 17564–17579 (2023)
39. Lopez-Paz, D., Oquab, M.: Revisiting classifier two-sample tests. In: International Conference on Learning Representations (2017)
40. Lundberg, S.M., Erion, G.G., Lee, S.I.: Consistent individualized feature attribution for tree ensembles. arXiv preprint arXiv:1802.03888 (2018)

41. Lundberg, S.M., Lee, S.I.: A unified approach to interpreting model predictions. In: Advances in Neural Information Processing Systems, vol. 30 (2017)
42. Mohamed, S., Lakshminarayanan, B.: Learning in implicit generative models. arXiv preprint arXiv:1610.03483 (2016)
43. Molnar, C.: Interpretable Machine Learning, 2 edn. (2022). https://christophm.github.io/interpretable-ml-book
44. Molnar, C., et al.: General pitfalls of model-agnostic interpretation methods for machine learning models. In: International Workshop on Extending Explainable AI Beyond Deep Models and Classifiers, pp. 39–68 (2022)
45. Nagisetty, V., Graves, L., Scott, J., Ganesh, V.: xAI-GAN: enhancing generative adversarial networks via explainable AI systems. arXiv preprint arXiv:2002.10438 (2020)
46. Nemirovsky, D., Thiebaut, N., Xu, Y., Gupta, A.: CounteRGAN: generating counterfactuals for real-time recourse and interpretability using residual GANs. In: Proceedings of the Thirty-Eighth Conference on Uncertainty in Artificial Intelligence. PMLR, vol. 180, pp. 1488–1497 (2022)
47. Nguyen, A., Dosovitskiy, A., Yosinski, J., Brox, T., Clune, J.: Synthesizing the preferred inputs for neurons in neural networks via deep generator networks. In: Advances in Neural Information Processing Systems, vol. 29 (2016)
48. Nowok, B., Raab, G.M., Dibben, C.: synthpop: bespoke creation of synthetic data in R. J. Stat. Softw. **74**(11), 1–26 (2016)
49. Qian, Z., Cebere, B.C., van der Schaar, M.: Synthcity: facilitating innovative use cases of synthetic data in different data modalities. arXiv preprint arXiv:2301.07573 (2023)
50. Rajkovic, V.: Nursery. UCI Machine Learning Repository (1989). https://doi.org/10.24432/C5P88W
51. Redelmeier, A., Jullum, M., Aas, K.: Explaining predictive models with mixed features using Shapley values and conditional inference trees. In: ICross-Domain Conference for Machine Learning and Knowledge Extraction, pp. 117–137 (2020)
52. Redelmeier, A., Jullum, M., Aas, K., Løland, A.: MCCE: Monte Carlo sampling of valid and realistic counterfactual explanations for tabular data. Data Min. Knowl. Disc. **38**(4), 1830–1861 (2024)
53. Rezende, D., Mohamed, S.: Variational inference with normalizing flows. In: Proceedings of the 32nd International Conference on Machine Learning. PMLR, vol. 37, pp. 1530–1538 (2015)
54. Sajjadi, M.S., Bachem, O., Lucic, M., Bousquet, O., Gelly, S.: Assessing generative models via precision and recall. In: Advances in Neural Information Processing Systems, vol. 31 (2018)
55. Schneider, J.: Explainable generative AI (GenXAI): a survey, conceptualization, and research agenda. Artif. Intell. Rev. **57**(11), 289 (2024)
56. Shapley, L.S.: A value for n-person games. In: Kuhn, H.W., Tucker, A.W. (eds.) Contributions to the Theory of Games, pp. 307–317. Princeton University Press, Princeton (1953)
57. Shwartz-Ziv, R., Armon, A.: Tabular data: deep learning is not all you need. Inform. Fusion **81**, 84–90 (2022)
58. Simon, L., Webster, R., Rabin, J.: Revisiting precision recall definition for generative modeling. In: Proceedings of the 36th International Conference on Machine Learning. PMLR, vol. 97, pp. 5799–5808 (2019)
59. Song, Y., Sohl-Dickstein, J., Kingma, D.P., Kumar, A., Ermon, S., Poole, B.: Score-based generative modeling through stochastic differential equations. In: International Conference on Learning Representations (2021)

60. Sundararajan, M., Dhamdhere, K., Agarwal, A.: The Shapley Taylor interaction index. In: Proceedings of the 37th International Conference on Machine Learning. PMLR, vol. 119, pp. 9259–9268 (2020)
61. Theis, L., van den Oord, A., Bethge, M.: A note on the evaluation of generative models. In: International Conference on Learning Representations (2016)
62. Vaswani, A., et al.: Attention is all you need. In: Advances in Neural Information Processing Systems, vol. 30 (2017)
63. Vig, J.: A multiscale visualization of attention in the transformer model. In: Proceedings of the 57th Annual Meeting of the Association for Computational Linguistics: System Demonstrations, pp. 37–42 (2019)
64. Watson, D.S., Blesch, K., Kapar, J., Wright, M.N.: Adversarial random forests for density estimation and generative modeling. In: Proceedings of The 26th International Conference on Artificial Intelligence and Statistics. PMLR, vol. 206, pp. 5357–5375 (2023)
65. Watson, D.S., Wright, M.N.: Testing conditional independence in supervised learning algorithms. Mach. Learn. **110**(8), 2107–2129 (2021). https://doi.org/10.1007/s10994-021-06030-6
66. Xu, L., Skoularidou, M., Cuesta-Infante, A., Veeramachaneni, K.: Modeling tabular data using conditional GAN. In: Advances in Neural Information Processing Systems, vol. 32 (2019)
67. Zein, E.H., Urvoy, T.: Tabular data generation: can we fool XGBoost ? In: NeurIPS 2022 First Table Representation Workshop (2022)
68. Zhang, H., et al.: Mixed-type tabular data synthesis with score-based diffusion in latent space. In: International Conference on Learning Representations (2024)
69. Zhao, Z., Birke, R., Chen, L.: TabuLa: harnessing language models for tabular data synthesis. arXiv preprint arXiv:2310.12746 (2023)
70. Zhao, Z., Kunar, A., Birke, R., Scheer, H., Chen, L.Y.: CTAB-GAN+: enhancing tabular data synthesis. Front. Big Data **6**, 1296508 (2024)
71. Zhou, Z., et al.: Activation maximization generative adversarial nets. In: International Conference on Learning Representations (2018)

Open Access This chapter is licensed under the terms of the Creative Commons Attribution 4.0 International License (http://creativecommons.org/licenses/by/4.0/), which permits use, sharing, adaptation, distribution and reproduction in any medium or format, as long as you give appropriate credit to the original author(s) and the source, provide a link to the Creative Commons license and indicate if changes were made.

The images or other third party material in this chapter are included in the chapter's Creative Commons license, unless indicated otherwise in a credit line to the material. If material is not included in the chapter's Creative Commons license and your intended use is not permitted by statutory regulation or exceeds the permitted use, you will need to obtain permission directly from the copyright holder.

Explainable Optimization: Leveraging Large Language Models for User-Friendly Explanations

Bram Biemans[1,2], Pavel Troubil[3(✉)], Isel Grau[2,4], and Wim P. M. Nuijten[1,2]

[1] Department of Mathematics and Computer Science, Eindhoven University of Technology, Eindhoven, The Netherlands
[2] Eindhoven AI Systems Institute, Eindhoven University of Technology, Eindhoven, The Netherlands
[3] Dassault Systèmes, 's-Hertogenbosch, The Netherlands
pavel.troubil@3ds.com
[4] Department of Industrial Engineering and Innovation Sciences, Eindhoven University of Technology, Eindhoven, The Netherlands

Abstract. Progress in operations research allowed for the widespread use of mathematical optimization in supply chain planning. Despite its numerous practical and economic benefits, human planners often doubt the solutions provided by automated optimizers, which limits their potential effectiveness. Although Explainable Artificial Intelligence (XAI) offers innovative methods to improve the transparency of various models, the tools available to explain optimization algorithms remain underdeveloped. Existing solutions tend to present explanations in numerical formats difficult to interpret. This study explores the application of Large Language Models (LLMs) to enhance the interpretability and persuasiveness of these explanations. Specifically, it investigates whether LLMs can convert numerical explanations into clear, context-aware narratives, thereby fostering greater trust among planners in the optimizer outputs.

We worked on top of a supply chain planning optimizer with a LIME-inspired algorithm to generate explanations for typical supply chain scenarios. Explanations generated by LLMs were evaluated using various metrics and compared to the expectations of experienced experts in the field. Our results show that LLMs can substantially improve the clarity and persuasiveness of XAI explanations, increasing human planners' confidence in the optimizer's outputs. We also identify future improvements needed to fully meet the ideal standards set by expert planners.

Keywords: Explainable Optimization · Explainable AI · Large Language Models

1 Introduction

Advances in Operations Research (OR) have led to a broad industrial adoption of mathematical optimization technology to solve supply chain planning problems [24]. Despite that progress, seamless deployment and adoption of the technology remains a challenge in business reality. The common business practice is that solutions to a supply chain planning problem proposed by optimization technology must be reviewed and confirmed by a human planner before they are executed. Human planners often have many years of experience with the planning tasks at hand, during which they acquired a lot of knowledge about what constitutes feasible high-quality solutions and how to obtain them. Solutions generated by optimization technology that do not satisfy the expectations of human planners tend to face distrust, leading to their feasibility and/or quality being challenged [33].

Such distrust towards generated solutions hinders the benefits obtainable from mathematical optimization technology. While the technology is being deployed, gaining trust consumes time and introduces costs [17]. In practice, concerns about the quality of the technology delay its introduction into the daily planning process, thus also postpone realization of the benefits. After the deployment project is over, planners who do not trust the technology tend to manually modify the solutions more often [33]. The manual modifications made for trust reasons take time and potentially reduce the quality of the plan and thus hinder the benefits of the automated optimization.

In recent years, research has increasingly focused on enhancing the interpretability of *black box* models. Explainable Artificial Intelligence (XAI) has become a central area of investigation, with efforts aimed at developing techniques to increase the transparency of complex machine learning and deep learning models. XAI methods strive to deconstruct model predictions, providing insights into how specific input features impact outcomes. This growing emphasis on interpretability is crucial for fostering trust, improving model robustness, and ensuring the ethical and legal deployment of AI systems. However, less attention has been given to explaining OR-based optimization models [6]. While existing XAI techniques can clarify some optimizer decisions, the explanations provided are often too complex for human planners without technical background, preventing them from full understanding.

This study introduces a methodology to utilize Large Language Models (LLMs) to generate human-centered explanations for the outcomes produced by a tactical supply chain planning optimizer. The primary aim is to evaluate the capacity of LLMs to interpret and understand the numerical outputs of XAI techniques, which are currently employed to elucidate the complex decision-making processes of the optimization system. Furthermore, the research seeks to determine whether LLMs can effectively convey these XAI-generated insights in a manner that is context-aware, clear, coherent, and easily interpretable by human users. The ultimate goal is to enhance the quality of information provided to human planners, thereby fostering greater trust in the optimization system. By comparing LLM-generated explanations with authoritative explanations provided by domain experts, we investigate whether LLMs, given specific input contexts, can approach or match the quality of expert-derived explanations. The contribution of our work is to develop and validate a methodology capable of providing human-readable explanations for questions related to a complex and highly interdependent optimization problem, thereby advancing research in the developing field of explainable optimization.

2 Literature Review

2.1 Explainable AI

The challenge of building user trust in machine learning predictions has become a widely explored area of research. As black-box predictive models are increasingly deployed across various domains, the demand for transparency and interpretability in their decision-making processes has intensified [26,30]. Certainly in high-stakes fields such as finance, healthcare, and criminal justice, where model decisions directly affect people's lives, but also in any domain where people collaborate closely with models, it is essential that models not only deliver accurate predictions, but also offer interpretable and understandable explanations. In addressing this need, a research domain, termed eXplainable Artificial Intelligence (XAI), has emerged, with the primary goal of fostering trust and confidence in AI models when applied in real-world settings [10].

In recent years, various XAI methods have been introduced [23], focusing on both *local* explanations for individual predictions and *global* explanations that capture overall model behavior. Local explanation techniques include counterfactual and contrastive explanations, while global explanations are often derived from transparent surrogate models or feature attribution aggregations. Among the widely-used state-of-the-art methods are LIME [25] and SHAP values [19]. However, outcomes of these methods demand a technical background to be understood, presenting challenges for non-expert users to fully comprehend [21].

Within the research field of human-centric XAI, considerable attention is devoted to addressing this challenge. One potential solution involves the graphical representation of explanations, where visualizations are used to enhance the comprehensibility of technical XAI outputs [3]. By leveraging (interactive) visual tools, complex information can be conveyed more intuitively, making it easier for users without a technical background to understand the underlying model behaviors [11]. An additional method for improving the interpretability of XAI outputs involves translation into natural language. A dedicated section will later provide a more in-depth discussion of this aspect.

2.2 Explainability in Optimization

While XAI provides methods for interpreting proposed decisions of machine learning models, explainability in optimization specifically addresses the challenge of clarifying the reasoning behind proposed decisions within complex systems. This subsection explores the techniques and approaches developed to enhance the interpretability of optimization models, bridging the gap between opaque mathematical formulations and user-friendly explanations.

In XAI, counterfactual and contrastive explanations are foundational methods for providing clear and human-friendly interpretations of model predictions. Counterfactual explanations operate by illustrating the smallest change in feature values that would alter the prediction to a desired outcome, a method that resonates with how people naturally describe causal situations—e.g., "If your income had been $10,000 higher, your loan application would have been approved" [23]. These explanations are effective because they are both contrastive, as they highlight differences between the actual prediction and a specified alternative, and selective, as they focus on the most relevant features or changes. To generate counterfactuals in optimization contexts, Korikov & Beck [14] introduced the concept of *Inverse Optimization*. In a standard (or forward) optimization problem $\langle c, f, X \rangle$, the goal is to determine the decision vector $x \in X \subseteq \mathbb{R}^n$ that optimizes an objective function f, given a parameter vector $c \in C \subseteq \mathbb{R}^n$. However, in some cases, a user may wish to understand why the optimal solution x^* does not align with an expected or desired outcome x^d, typically characterized by additional constraints. These constraints define a refined feasible set $X_\psi = X \cap \psi$. Inverse optimization addresses this challenge by identifying the minimal adjustments to the initial parameter vector c, giving c', required to make x^d optimal for the forward problem $\langle c', f, X \rangle$. The proposed solution, however, is currently limited to cases involving a specific structure of partial assignment constraints and imposes restrictions on the explanation parameters. More complex problems remain outside the scope of this approach for now.

Contrastive explanations, another approach within XAI, address the question "Why was A chosen instead of B?"—a common mode of human reasoning [22]. Instead of identifying inputs that would lead to an expected or desired outcome, contrastive explanations highlight differences between the actual and expected outcomes, often by emphasizing distinctions in objective values. This provides insights into why a specific decision was made over alternatives. The Explainable Planning (XAIP) framework [7] is built around contrastive explanations. It recognizes that contrastive questions arise when a planning algorithm suggests an action that diverges from user expectations. Like counterfactual explanations, these expected plans can be conceptualized in various ways, making it crucial to identify the most suitable alternative from the set of possible explanations.

The methods discussed earlier require generating alternative solutions for comparison with the optimal solution, which can be computationally expensive and even prohibitive for optimization models. Additionally, users often prefer immediate explanations and are unwilling to wait for these alternatives to be generated [28]. An alternative approach involves employing surrogate models, which serve as simplified approximations of the original optimization model by learning the underlying relationships between inputs and outputs in the system. By adopting a simpler, ante-hoc (*white-box*) model for this purpose, surrogate models offer transparency in their internal workings, allowing users to understand and interpret the decision-making process while providing a computationally efficient solution [29]. In cases where data is limited due to the high computational cost of generating candidate solutions, gray-box models can provide an effective approach. These models combine the accuracy of black-box models with the interpretability of white-box models by generating additional labeled instances to train a more interpretable model, aiming to closely approximate the original model [8]. Although gray-box models are not typically designed for optimization problems, their effectiveness in addressing the challenge of generating alternatives within machine learning highlights their potential to inform innovative approaches to similar challenges in optimization.

2.3 LLMs and XAI

Recent advancements in LLMs have greatly enhanced their applicability across various tasks. Due to their extensive parameterization and pre-training, LLMs excel in pattern recognition and understanding long-term dependencies, making them effective tools for natural language processing tasks, such as text generation, translation, summarization, and conversational AI. Additionally, LLMs can be further optimized for specific tasks using techniques such as Retrieval-Augmented Generation, Prompt Engineering, and Fine-Tuning.

LLMs typically store factual knowledge within their parameters [12], which are learned during pre-training, without direct access to external information. This architecture can result in limitations such as difficulties in updating knowledge over time, as well as potential inaccuracies or hallucinations if the model lacks access to relevant or up-to-date information. One approach to mitigate this issue is *Retrieval-Augmented Generation (RAG)*, which integrates a pre-trained LLM with an external, non-parametric memory system, such as specialized documents or databases [16]. This allows the model to retrieve relevant information during generation, reducing hallucinations and improving performance in specialized or evolving contexts [9,31].

Additionally, *Prompt Engineering* plays a crucial role in optimizing LLM performance for specific tasks. This technique involves strategically designing prompts to guide LLMs toward generating accurate and contextually relevant responses. It is an iterative process that refines prompts to achieve the desired output [27]. A key strategy within prompt engineering is in-context learning, which uses a limited set of examples and/or instructions within the prompt to teach LLMs new skills, often referred to as one-shot or few-shot learning. By carefully structuring prompts, prompt engineering enhances the effectiveness of in-context learning, enabling LLMs to adapt to specific tasks more efficiently.

Kroeger et al. [15] explore the potential of leveraging LLMs to enhance the interpretability of black-box machine learning models by instructing the LLM to identify the most important features influencing a model's predictions. The effectiveness of this approach depends largely on prompt engineering, with prompts structured to include contextual introductions, dataset examples (features and outcomes), queries, and specific instructions. The LLM's feature rankings are compared to traditional XAI techniques such as SHAP and LIME using four metrics: Feature Agreement (FA), Rank Agreement (RA), Prediction Gap on Important feature perturbation (PGI), and Prediction Gap on Unimportant feature perturbation (PGU). Results showed that the LLM outperformed SHAP and performed comparably to LIME in most cases. However, the experiment was conducted on relatively small datasets with limited features, potentially leading to an optimistic bias in the outcomes. As dataset size increases, challenges in prompt design may become more pronounced, given the token constraints of LLMs, which limit the number of dataset examples that can be processed simultaneously. More fundamentally, LLMs are not inherently designed for feature attribution tasks, raising concerns about their suitability for such applications.

The rapid advancement of LLMs presents significant opportunities for generating clear and readable explanations. Building on this foundation, this research aims to determine whether LLMs can effectively produce human-readable explanations by transforming specialized XAI explanations related to optimization problems into accessible text, thereby establishing a so-called *LLM-XAI tandem*.

The concept of an XAI-LLM tandem, where an LLM interprets and conveys XAI outputs in accessible language, is relatively new and still in early development. However, it holds significant potential for enhancing user understanding of complex model behaviors. Yu et al. [34] presented the first framework that combines XAI techniques with natural language processing to generate human-readable explanations. This integration enables the provision of explanations in accessible, everyday language, a critical aspect for facilitating user engagement and fostering critical evaluation of AI systems, which may contribute to greater trust and understanding. Mavrepis et al. [21] developed a model that generates summaries of various XAI methods, tailoring the explanations to the knowledge and expertise level of the target audience. Use-case studies demonstrated that the model effectively delivers easy-to-understand, audience-specific explanations, regardless of the XAI method employed. The primary limitation identified in this paper is that the LLM tends to create lengthy, long-winded explanations, where users often want quick, direct information without excessive detail that can obscure the main points. In the realm of cybersecurity, Ali & Kostakos [2] introduced HuntGPT, a dashboard designed to clarify the results of a predictive model for identifying cyber attacks. This dashboard presents initial explanations of XAI outcomes, followed by further insights provided by an LLM. Additionally, it offers the opportunity for discussion with a chat assistant.

Martens et al. [20] demonstrate the effectiveness of integrating LLMs with XAI through their introduction of the *XAIstories* technique. This method employs counterfactual explanations for image classification and SHAP explanations for tabular data classification, presenting them as coherent narratives. Their findings underscore the value that data scientists attribute to this approach, particularly in enhancing decision-making across diverse applications. Building on this framework, Cedro & Martens [5] utilize it to improve the comprehensibility of numeric, XAI-generated explanations for individual predictions in graph neural networks. Similarly, Zytek et al. [35] explore the potential of LLMs in transforming XAI explanations into human-readable narratives, a focus that aligns closely with our research objectives. However, our study differentiates itself by specifically examining the capability of LLMs to generate human-readable explanations in the context of optimization problems, with a particular emphasis on supply chain optimization. Our work uniquely considers the importance of incorporating supply chain context within these explanations.

3 Methodology

The methodology proposed in this study works within a framework of three key components for generating narrative explanations: (1) formulation of the optimization problem and its solver, (2) application of an XAI technique, inspired by LIME, to produce numerical explanations of the optimizer, and (3) utilization of language models to craft prompts and generate narrative explanations. The first two components are established techniques, while the third represents the novel contribution of this work. These components are designed to work in tandem to address the challenge of producing human-readable explanations. Figure 1 provides a schematic representation of the methodology, highlighting its structure and flow. The subsequent sections provide a detailed discussion of each component.

3.1 Optimization Problem and Optimizer

The problem addressed in this experiment is the Master Production Scheduling Problem (MPSP) as described in [32]. This problem involves balancing demand

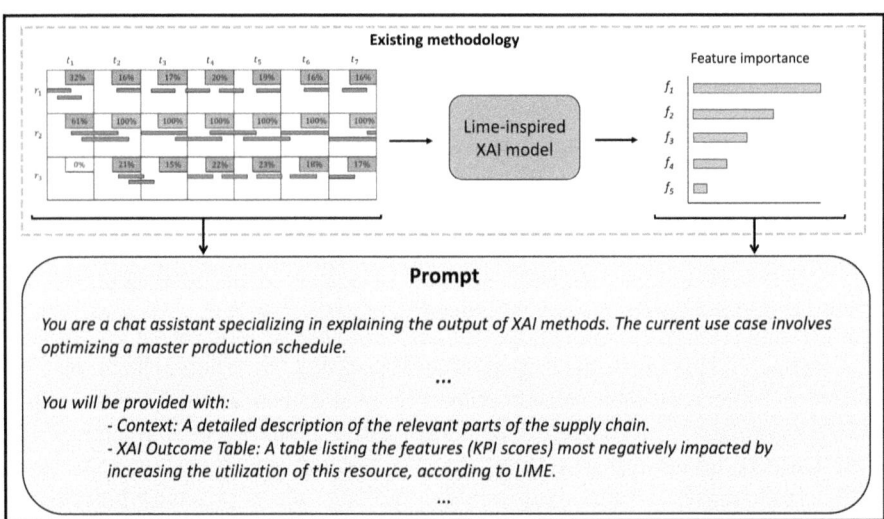

Fig. 1. Schematic overview of the methodology. The current approach utilizes an optimizer to produce an optimized schedule, which is then explained using a LIME-inspired technique to generate feature importances. Our approach integrates both information about the optimized schedule and the feature importances into a prompt provided to the LLM.

and supply across supply chains while simultaneously scheduling supply orders and managing resource capacities. Unlike detailed scheduling, where specific operations are allocated to resources in sequence with exact starting and ending times, the MPSP emphasizes allocation of bucketed capacity in longer horizon. The focus is therefore on coarse-grained resource capacity utilization rather than fine-grained scheduling.

Feasible solutions need to respect constraints on individual multi-level supply chains of various complex structures from diverse industries, aggregate constraints on variable resource capacity in presence of wandering bottlenecks, or stocking limits. The objective is a complex combination of factors measuring, among others, delivery performance, adherence to inventory targets, or minimization of inventory and work-in-progress. To address these complexities throughout a multi-month horizon, a specifically tailored optimizer is used. Relying on large-scale neighborhood search [1] and mathematical programming, it delivers high-quality solutions virtually impossible to improve by humans. While further details of the proprietary optimizer remain undisclosed, they do not influence the further study, since the explanation method is independent of the actual optimization algorithm as long as provided solutions are of high quality.

3.2 LIME-Inspired XAI Model

Local Interpretable Model-agnostic Explanations (LIME) [25] is a widely used model-agnostic framework for interpreting the predictions of complex machine learning models. By generating locally faithful explanations, LIME approximates the behavior of any given model in the vicinity of a specific prediction using interpretable surrogate models, typically linear models. It operates by perturbing the input data to observe how changes affect the model's predictions, allowing for an analysis of feature importance and contribution to the decision-making process.

This paper builds on the work of Tullemans [32], which presents a method for identifying explanations for underutilized resource periods. Such phenomenon occurs even in optimal solutions to the MPSP, and often raises concern among human planners occurring. To address the explanation task, a generic LIME-inspired method was designed and then implemented specifically for the resource utilization use case in the MPSP. The original plan generated by the optimizer is perturbed by systematically increasing utilization of the resource in question. For each perturbed plan, the difference in each partial objective metric (further called KPI score) is compared to that of the original plan. Repeating this process multiple times yields a value that quantifies the impact of the perturbations on each individual KPI score.

3.3 Prompt Engineering

Our experiment follows the prompt design methodology established by Zytek et al. [35], which provides a structured approach to creating and evaluating prompt templates across multiple LLMs. Using this methodology, we constructed a series of prompt templates with recurring components, each adjusted to enhance the prompt's overall effectiveness. Table 1 details all prompt components utilized in our study, along with explanations of their functions and intended effects. The process involves methodical combination, reordering, and rephrasing of these components to achieve an effective design, which is a crucial aspect of prompt engineering [27]. The resulting templates are presented in Table 2. This prompt engineering methodology allows us to systematically explore and refine the interactions between different prompt components, ultimately leading to more effective and nuanced model outputs. The methodology for evaluating and identifying the most effective combination of prompt template and model is detailed in Sect. 4.3.

Table 1. Overview of the key components in the prompt engineering process, along with their explanations.

Component	Description
[A] Role	The role component specifies the assumed perspective that the LLM is expected to adopt during the interaction.
[B] Data Examples	Raw data examples of alternative plans that include KPI scores and Resource Utilization Scores. This data is utilized by LIME to determine which features are most significant. The raw data serves as a component to assess whether the LLM can extract specific information independently.
[C] LIME Examples	The actual LIME outcomes, describing the most important features related to the XAI question.
[D] XAI Context	Context about the XAI itself, including the specific question or challenge we want to address. This ensures the LLM understands the context in which it should provide explanations or insights.
[E] Supply Chain Context	Context related to the specific supply chain dynamics and operations. This information helps the LLM connect LIME outcomes with real-world scenarios, enhancing the relevance and applicability of the insights generated.
[F] Task	Define a step-by-step plan to achieve the primary objective that the LLM is intended to fulfill. This involves breaking down the objective into manageable actions or milestones, ensuring clarity and focus in the model's execution.
[G] Instructions	Guide the model towards the desired output by providing clear and concise directives that outline the expected format, tone, and content of the response. This ensures that the model aligns with user expectations and requirements effectively.

Table 2. Overview of the constructed prompt templates (T1–T5) and their corresponding component composition and order, as defined in Table 1.

Template	Component Sequence
T1	ACF
T2	ABCF
T3	ADCEF
T4	ADECF
T5	ADCEFG

4 Experiments

4.1 Data

The experimental dataset consists of three test instances, each representing a distinct use case: two from a bulk production supply chain (denoted Metals-A and Metals-B) and one from an automotive assembly supply chain (further called Assembly). Each case study focuses on a specific resource within the respective supply chain that is planned as not fully utilized at some period within the horizon of the problem instance. Test instances were based on data of actual real-world supply chain planning challenges.

The dataset incorporates the results of the LIME explanations derived from the method proposed by Tullemans [32]. Furthermore, it is supplemented with raw input data of the optimization problems, like resources and production processes, and solution data like inventory levels of all production stages throughout the planning horizon.

4.2 LLMs

We tested several LLMs to evaluate their performance in transforming XAI explanations into human-readable form. The models tested include OpenAI's ChatGPT-3.5, Meta's Llama-3-8B-Instruct and Llama-3-70B-Instruct, as well as Mistral AI's Mixtral-8x7B-Instruct-v0.1 and Mistral-7B-Instruct-v0.2. These models represent a diverse set of architectures and parameter sizes, allowing for a comprehensive comparison of their capabilities in this context. All LLMs were accessed via APIs on a remote server, ensuring consistent interaction protocols and enabling automated evaluation across different model types. Local simulations were executed on a system with a 2100 Mhz Intel Core i7 processor and 32 GB RAM.

4.3 Evaluation

Three distinct evaluation protocols were considered. The first protocol assesses the quality of LLM-generated responses across different prompt templates and models to identify the best combination. The second protocol evaluates whether

LLM-generated narrative explanations enhance the numerical explanations from the LIME-inspired approach. The third protocol compares LLM-generated explanations to expert explanation, to assess if the use of large language models supports the goal of providing high-quality explanations.

Evaluation of LLM Response Quality. To evaluate the LLMs' responses across the different combinations of prompt templates and models, we used the same four metrics as employed by Zytek et al. in [35], i.e., completeness, soundness, fluency, and context-awareness, and added consistency next to the set. Completeness refers to the extent to which the response covers all relevant aspects of the question or topic. Soundness evaluates validity of the response, ensuring that it is based on accurate information and reasoning. Fluency measures the clarity and readability of the language used in the response. Context-awareness refers to the extent to which contextual information is integrated into the explanation. This aspect serves as a crucial metric for evaluating and achieving impactful outcomes in the transition from LIME to our proposed method. Additionally, we introduced the evaluation of answer consistency, which assesses the stability of the LLM responses across different iterations and contexts, extending the analysis beyond the scope of the study of Zytek et al. [35]. An authoritative expert knowledgeable in the optimization problem and its explanations evaluated all LLM responses.

Comparison of Numerical and Narrative Explanations. To assess whether integrating LLM-generated narrative explanations enhances numerical explanations from the LIME-inspired approach for human planners, a questionnaire was developed to collect qualitative feedback from five domain experts who were not part of the previous evaluation. The questionnaire aims to explore the clarity, utility, and completeness of the generated explanations. Additionally, it seeks to determine whether narrative explanations provide added value to the current numerical explanations. It is conducted in an interview format, allowing for a conversational approach where experts can elaborate on their responses and provide detailed insights. This interactive method facilitates a deeper understanding of their perspectives and experiences. The collected responses are subsequently analyzed using thematic analysis, a systematic approach to identify and interpret recurring patterns and themes, providing a comprehensive evaluation of the proposed methodology's effectiveness [4].

Alignment with Expert Explanations. To establish a benchmark for model response quality, experts were initially asked to provide their explanations in natural language, as they would to a customer. They did this without prior exposure to the model-generated explanations, thereby minimizing potential biases. These explanations are gathered during an interview in which the expert had to think out loud about their approach, providing insights into their reasoning and decision-making process. Besides establishing a benchmark, this also provides an opportunity to understand the aspects experts focus on when creating explanations, which could be valuable for future research.

Since optimization problems can be explained from multiple angles, experts' responses naturally differ depending on the aspects they emphasize or omit. To create a standardized reference, the same authoritative expert, who evaluated the LLMs earlier, later reviewed all explanations provided for the same use case. Gaining insight into different perspectives, they formulated the collective understanding into a single, aggregated explanation. This explanation is considered to be the *Authoritative* explanation, designed to be the most complete, sound, and high-level representation of the given scenario.

Ultimately, the experts' explanations, as well as the Authoritative explanation, were compared with the LLM-generated explanations using the proposed *Human Similarity* metric from Ichmoukhamedov et al. [13]. Specifically, both the expert-generated explanations and LLM-generated explanations were encoded as high-dimensional embeddings, represented by vectors **a** and **b**, with an angular relationship defined by the angle θ_{ab}. Following the methodology in [13], we used voyage-large-2-instruct as the embedding model, which converts a narrative into a 1024-dimensional vector. The similarity between the explanations was quantified using the distance metric $d = 1 - \cos(\theta_{ab})$. This quantitative measure provides an interpretable indication of the degree of alignment between the LLM-generated and the expert-generated explanations.

5 Results and Discussion

This section presents the results and discussion of the experimental evaluations outlined in Sect. 4.3. Additionally, examples of LLM-generated explanations, along with an authoritative explanation, are provided in Sect. 5.4.

5.1 LLM Response Quality

An evaluation of responses generated by different LLMs, combined with various prompt templates, reveals that models with a higher number of parameters, such as OpenAIs GPT-3.5 and Meta's Llama-3-70B-Instruct, consistently perform better across the metrics of completeness, soundness, fluency, consistency, and context-awareness, as shown in Table 3. Larger models demonstrate a stronger ability to capture contextual information and produce fact-based responses, receiving higher evaluations from the authoritative expert in both completeness and soundness. In contrast, smaller models are more likely to generate incomplete or inaccurate responses, often displaying 'hallucinations' that negatively impact their consistency and factual reliability. While fluency remains robust across all models, larger models provide outputs that are more coherent and contextually relevant.

The prompt template, structured as Role → XAI Context → Supply Chain Context → LIME Examples → Tasks, was evaluated as the most effective by the expert based on five key metrics and will be used in further experiments requiring prompt outputs. This approach ensures that the LLM is initially assigned a clear role and provided with a well-defined XAI use case. The absence of this step led to unsound responses, as the LLM lacked guidance on how to approach the task. Following this, the provision of specific contextual details proved critical, with the order of presentation—starting with the supply chain context—significantly influencing the model's ability to accurately interpret the information. This finding aligns with the conclusions of [18]. By enforcing strict task definitions, additional instructions became redundant, thus reducing unnecessary complexity in the prompt. Furthermore, the inclusion of data points as in-context examples was found to have no significant effect on response quality and was therefore excluded.

Table 3. Binary evaluation scores indicating compliance with authoritative expert expectations for LLMs across different prompt templates (see Table 2), assessing Completeness (C), Soundness (S), Fluency (F), Consistency (O), and Context-Awareness (A).

	T1					T2					T3					T4					T5				
	C	S	F	O	A	C	S	F	O	A	C	S	F	O	A	C	S	F	O	A	C	S	F	O	A
ChatGPT-3.5	✓	✗	✓	✗	✗	✓	✗	✓	✗	✗	✓	✗	✓	✓	✓	✓	✓	✓	✓	✓	✓	✓	✓	✓	✓
Llama-3-8B-Instruct	✗	✗	✓	✗	✗	✗	✗	✓	✗	✗	✗	✗	✓	✓	✓	✗	✗	✓	✓	✓	✗	✗	✓	✓	✓
Llama-3-70B-Instruct	✓	✗	✓	✗	✗	✓	✗	✓	✗	✗	✓	✗	✓	✓	✓	✓	✓	✓	✓	✓	✓	✓	✓	✓	✓
Mixtral-8x7B-Instruct-v0.1	✗	✗	✓	✗	✗	✗	✗	✓	✗	✗	✗	✗	✗	✓	✗	✗	✗	✗	✓	✗	✗	✗	✗	✓	✗
Mistral-7B-Instruct-v0.2	✗	✗	✓	✗	✗	✗	✗	✓	✗	✗	✓	✓	✓	✗	✗	✗	✓	✓	✗	✗	✗	✓	✓	✗	✗

5.2 Comparison of Numerical and Narrative Explanations

Thematic analysis revealed five central themes regarding the use of numerical and narrative explanations: added value of narrative explanations, limitations of narrative explanations, user role in interpretation, completeness of explanations, and suggestions for improvement. These themes underscore the relationship between different explanation styles and their effects on expert trust, usability, and decision-making.

Added Value of Narrative Explanations. A prominent theme identified in the analysis was the positive impact of narrative explanations compared to numerical ones. Experts emphasized that narrative explanations provided additional context, which not only helped in understanding the optimization process but also saved time. Moreover, they played a crucial role in fostering trust in the optimizer's decision-making. Notably, four out of five experts explicitly highlighted the importance of the "in-context" placement of explanations. As one expert noted:

"That really is an added value: having the information placed into context. I think that's particularly useful when you're just starting out. And indeed, having examples and that extra level of detail—like which resource is involved—goes beyond what the numerical explanation can show, and I find that to be a real advantage."

This ability to embed the explanation in context was contrasted with the abstract nature of numerical explanations, which were often seen as detached and difficult to interpret. Experts consistently noted that the narrative format made the optimizer's decision-making process more relatable. Another expert mentioned:

"Numbers are fine, but they don't tell a story. Narratives give me the reasoning and examples. That's what builds trust."

Limitations of Narrative Explanations. While narrative explanations were well-received, their limitations were also acknowledged. The length of the explanations emerged as a challenge, particularly for experienced users who may not require a too detailed contextualization. As one expert observed:

"The explanations were sometimes overly verbose. I don't need a full story every time—I just need the key insights."

Additionally, the potential for bias in narrative explanations was highlighted. Experts noted that the framing and wording of these explanations could subtly influence decision-making, raising concerns about objectivity. One expert cautioned:

"Narratives are helpful, but they can steer you in a direction without you realizing it. There's a fine line between explaining and persuading, where you might start believing one option is the only valid choice, even if other possibilities exist."

One final limitation of the narrative explanation noted by some experts was the lack of clarity regarding the magnitude of a feature's importance, which is conveyed in the numerical explanation. Numerical explanations provide insight into the relative importance of features, allowing users to discern whether one feature is significantly more important than others, or if multiple features contribute equally. In contrast, this level of detail is absent in the narrative explanation, which focuses more on providing context and reasoning without emphasizing the relative significance of each feature. At the same time, it should be also taken into account that the relative values of feature importance as delivered by the LIME-inspired algorithm are hard to interpret, especially for users who lack expertise in XAI. And their imprecise interpretation based on insufficiently grounded assumptions could be actually misleading.

User Role in Interpretation. The analysis also revealed that the effectiveness of narrative explanations varied depending on expert experience levels. Experienced experts often required less detailed explanations, relying more on their domain knowledge to interpret outcomes. This aligns with findings discussed in the previous theme, where it was noted that experienced users tend to prioritize efficiency over elaboration. One expert summarized this sentiment:

"As an experienced user, I value narrative explanations but prefer concise ones that highlight key points. Newer users might need longer narratives."

This suggests a need for customization in the presentation of explanations, tailoring the level of detail to the user's expertise. In line with this, another expert emphasized the practicality of narrative explanations, highlighting the differences between experienced and less experienced users when it comes to sharing insights and making decisions with other stakeholders:

"A planner with extensive experience, such as someone who's worked in supply chain for years, can likely interpret the numerical data or might just need a narrative explanation highlighting key points. However, they can't present the numerical explanation directly to their manager. In contrast, the narrative explanation is more suitable for sharing with managers."

Completeness of Explanations. The narratives were frequently endorsed for addressing the inherent limitations of numerical methods. Experts appreciated how narrative explanations filled gaps left by numerical outputs, which often lack nuance.

"The narrative explanation was clarifying; it provides context, such as explaining what the KPI means and highlighting key areas to focus on. It [allows me to skip] a step, because when I look at the numerical data, I have to deduce things myself to figure out what happened based on the numbers. But with the narrative, it's already pointed out for me."

However, this strength also underscored a key limitation: the risk of oversimplification. One expert commented:

"Narratives provide the bigger picture, but sometimes they simplify too much. It's important to balance completeness with clarity."

This ties back to the concern about bias, as oversimplification or selective framing in narratives could lead to incomplete or skewed interpretations of the data.

The overall conclusion from most experts regarding the completeness of both numerical and narrative explanations is that neither tells the full story. This limitation stems from the inherent nature of the numerical method, which relies exclusively on KPI values to explain a specific use case. While this can be effective in many machine learning applications, optimization problems often involve greater complexity. Experts highlighted factors such as constraints and parameter input values, which they routinely consider in their own explanations but are absent from the numerical method's approach. One expert noted:

"The issue with the method, even before converting graphs into text, is that it focuses on KPIs but misses underlying reasons, like hard constraints. For instance, if a [resource is unavailable], it won't recognize that as the root cause— it will point to a KPI [measuring inventory holding] instead. However, the real issue might be the [unavailable resource] or a long lead time. This limitation seems inherent to the method itself, not just the textual explanation."

Since narrative explanations are derived from these numerical methods, they inherit the same shortcomings. This lack of depth becomes particularly apparent in supply chain contexts, where constraints and parameter interactions are integral to understanding the decision-making process.

Additionally, the LIME-inspired numerical approach focuses only on local perturbations, making it difficult to capture the broader system-level dynamics of the supply chain. This local perspective can sometimes obscure the true underlying explanations of complex optimization problems. As one expert summarized:

"The limitation of LIME is that it focuses solely on the immediate impact on the KPI without considering the broader consequences. For example, it might suggest increased utilization of a resource, but this could exacerbate the situation by causing delays elsewhere in the supply chain. Since LIME is designed to analyze local perturbations, it often overlooks cascading effects, such as unnecessary [inventory] holding. Consequently, it may fail to identify the true root cause of an issue."

These limitations underscore the need for complementary approaches that go beyond local KPI-based methods, integrating a more holistic view of the system to enhance explanation completeness.

Suggestions for Improvement. Several experts proposed improvements to enhance the utility of narrative explanations. Key suggestions included:

- Adjusting explanation length: Offering tiered or collapsible explanations to suit diverse user preferences.
- Addressing bias: Ensuring that suggestions provided by the explanations are either entirely accurate or accompanied by a clear warning for users to verify the information.
- Enhancing interactivity: Introducing features like hyperlinks that allow users to quickly access key points within the explanation for immediate clarity.

One expert suggested:
"If I could toggle between a short summary and a detailed explanation, it would make the tool more versatile."

These recommendations align with the broader themes of customization and user-centric design, emphasizing the need for explanations that are both accessible and adaptable.

The analysis highlights the significant advantages of narrative explanations over numerical ones, with experts praising their ability to provide valuable context, foster trust, and enhance interpretability. These benefits represent a major improvement, particularly in addressing the abstract and often detached nature of numerical explanations. While narratives do have some limitations, such as verbosity, potential bias, and oversimplification, their strengths in facilitating understanding and collaboration were widely recognized. The primary shortcoming of narrative explanations—completeness—largely stems from the LIME-inspired numerical approach that underpins them, which focuses on local perturbations and KPI values while overlooking broader contextual factors. Nevertheless, narrative explanations effectively bridge important gaps by embedding numerical insights into a meaningful context. This directly supports the objective of this paper: making explanations for optimization problems more human-friendly.

Looking ahead, experts proposed several improvements, including customizable explanation length, enhanced interactivity, and clearer communication of uncertainties. These suggestions underscore the value of narrative explanations as a critical enhancement to traditional methods, paving the way for even more user-friendly and adaptable explanatory approaches.

5.3 Alignment with Expert Explanations

As outlined in Sect. 4.3, experts were tasked with generating their own explanations for the given use cases. It became apparent that each expert employed a unique approach to both constructing and conveying their explanations. To further analyze these variations, the experts' explanations were compared quantitatively using the cosine distance metric, including comparisons with the Authoritative explanation. The results of these comparisons for the different use cases are presented in Tables 4, 5, and 6. The cosine distance values between each expert' explanation and the Authoritative explanation highlight the variation in how experts interpret and convey the reasoning behind the optimization decisions. Lower cosine distance values indicate greater similarity, while higher values reflect more divergence. These comparisons offer insight into the consistency and variability of expert interpretations, as well as the potential for alignment with the Authoritative explanation.

Table 4. Cosine distance values between expert-generated explanations and the Authoritative explanation for the Metals-A use case.

	Expert 1	Expert 2	Expert 3	Expert 4	Expert 5	Authoritative
Expert 1	X	0.237	0.179	0.215	0.194	0.173
Expert 2	0.237	X	0.114	0.201	0.185	0.089
Expert 3	0.179	0.114	X	0.229	0.22	0.067
Expert 4	0.215	0.201	0.229	X	0.213	0.234
Expert 5	0.194	0.185	0.22	0.213	X	0.195
Authoritative	0.173	0.089	0.067	0.234	0.195	X

The comparison of expert-generated explanations using cosine distance values reveals notable variation in how different experts approach the same use cases, highlighting the subjectivity inherent in expert reasoning. Across all use cases, expert explanations exhibit a wide range of cosine distances, both in relation to one another and to the Authoritative explanation. This variability confirms that

Table 5. Cosine distance values between expert-generated explanations and the Authoritative explanation for the Metals-B use case.

	Expert 1	Expert 2	Expert 3	Expert 4	Expert 5	Authoritative
Expert 1	X	0.307	0.187	0.265	0.191	0.127
Expert 2	0.307	X	0.369	0.197	0.207	0.311
Expert 3	0.187	0.369	X	0.286	0.222	0.038
Expert 4	0.265	0.197	0.286	X	0.157	0.22
Expert 5	0.191	0.207	0.222	0.157	X	0.153
Authoritative	0.127	0.311	0.038	0.22	0.153	X

Table 6. Cosine distance values between expert-generated explanations and the Authoritative explanation for the Assembly use case.

	Expert 1	Expert 2	Expert 3	Expert 4	Expert 5	Authoritative
Expert 1	X	0.236	0.179	0.132	0.164	0.141
Expert 2	0.236	X	0.314	0.283	0.217	0.27
Expert 3	0.179	0.314	X	0.174	0.211	0.106
Expert 4	0.132	0.283	0.174	X	0.171	0.081
Expert 5	0.164	0.217	0.211	0.171	X	0.163
Authoritative	0.141	0.27	0.106	0.081	0.163	X

experts construct explanations in distinct ways, suggesting they rely on different strategies, domain knowledge, and interpretations.

The differences in expert explanations can also be attributed to the multifaceted nature of supply chain optimization problems, which involve interconnected variables such as resource capacities, inventory levels, and constraints. Experts emphasize different aspects based on their experience and knowledge, leading to diverse yet valid interpretations. While each expert may focus on different elements, their explanations remain generally correct and offer meaningful perspectives. Therefore, a high cosine distance does not necessarily indicate an error. Instead, this variability underscores the complexity of optimization problems, where multiple valid viewpoints can coexist without one being inherently more accurate than another.

Similarly, differences between expert explanations and the Authoritative explanation stem from their distinct approaches. Experts tend to focus on specific aspects of a use case based on their expertise, whereas the Authoritative explanation aims to provide a comprehensive, neutral overview by incorporating multiple perspectives and factors. Some experts align more closely with the Authoritative explanation, as indicated by a smaller cosine distance, suggesting that their focus and reasoning reflect its broader, all-encompassing nature.

Table 7 presents the cosine distances between the LLM-generated narrative explanation and the explanations produced by individual experts, as well as the

Authoritative explanation, for all three use cases. These distances offer insights into how closely the LLM-generated explanations align with those produced by human experts and the aggregated Authoritative explanation.

Table 7. Cosine distance values between expert-generated explanations or the Authoritative explanation and the LLM-generated explanation for the Metals-A, Metals-B and Assembly use cases.

	Metals-A	Metals-B	Assembly
Expert 1	0.284	0.197	0.293
Expert 2	0.192	0.322	0.371
Expert 3	**0.161**	0.178	0.245
Expert 4	0.281	0.248	0.258
Expert 5	0.243	0.201	0.271
Authoritative	0.182	**0.151**	**0.239**

A key observation is that for two of the three use cases (Metals-B and Assembly), the Authoritative explanation shows the closest alignment to the LLM-generated explanation, as indicated by the lowest cosine distance values of 0.151 and 0.239 respectively. This suggests that the LLM is capable of producing explanations that are broadly consistent with the Authoritative explanation, which is considered the best and most comprehensive representation for these use cases. However, it is worth noting that even in these cases, a noticeable gap remains between the Authoritative explanation and the LLM-generated output. To provide context, [13] conducted a similar analysis for machine learning purposes and reported significantly lower cosine distances (ranging from 0.01 to 0.08). This contrast might indicate a potential for improvement in the LLM's approach to explainability in optimization, but could also stem from a different nature of optimization problems compared to AI, or even properties of this particular problem.

For the Metals-A use case, however, the Authoritative explanation is not the closest match. Instead, Expert 3's explanation has the smallest cosine distance (0.161) to the LLM-generated explanation. As shown in Table 4, Expert 3's explanation aligns most closely with the Authoritative explanation. Yet, the LLM-generated explanation remains closer to Expert 3's formulation than to the Authoritative. This suggests that the LLM's reliance on predefined features and patterns may, in this case, align more with individual expert styles rather than a consensus-driven authoritative perspective.

Discrepancies between LLM-generated explanations and both Authoritative and individual expert explanations may stem from a fundamental limitation in the LLM's methodology, which focuses primarily on numerical features derived from the LIME-inspired approach and restricts its ability to account for broader contextual factors. As described earlier, experts tend to incorporate additional context, such as operational constraints or domain-specific nuances, into their explanations. These contextual elements, while critical for a holistic understanding, are not always directly reflected in the feature set used by the LLM. This reliance on feature-based reasoning could explain why the LLM struggles to fully replicate the depth and complexity of expert explanations. While it captures key patterns and relationships within the data, it may overlook subtleties that experts intuitively factor into their reasoning, such as interdependencies between features, constraints, or prior knowledge.

To address this gap, future research should explore alternative methods that go beyond local perturbations and incorporate richer data representations from the supply chain. For instance, developing machine learning models that directly learn explanations from raw data of the optimization model could enable a more comprehensive understanding of the system. These models would analyze complete datasets, including historical trends, constraints, and parameter interactions, to produce explanations that better mirror the depth and complexity of expert reasoning. By replacing or augmenting the current LIME-inspired methodology with more holistic approaches, future work can aim to bridge the gap between machine-generated and expert-level explanations. This progression holds promise for creating more human-friendly, accurate, and actionable insights, ultimately advancing the utility of AI in optimization problem-solving.

5.4 Examples of Explanation

This section presents examples of LLM-generated and Authoritative explanations for the Metals-B use case. The LLM-generated explanation interprets the top three features from the numerical explanation, which had importance magnitudes of 0.129, 0.113, and 0.109.

LLM-Generated Explanation. Hello! I'd be happy to help you understand the output of the LIME method, which explains why the [resource] is underutilized during a particular time period. Let's dive into the LIME outcome table, which highlights the features most negatively impacted by increasing the utilization of the [resource]. The top three features are:

1. **KPI [work-in-progress on resource]:** This feature indicates that increasing the utilization of [resource] would lead to a higher KPI [work-in-progress]. In the context of our supply chain, this means that more products would be held in the [resource] operation, waiting to be processed. This could be due to upstream constraints, such as delays in the [upstream operations] or inventory shortages of the [required input materials] in the [stocking area]. As a result, increasing the utilization of [resource] would exacerbate these holding times, leading to a less optimal schedule.
2. **KPI [inventory adherence of upstream product X]:** This feature suggests that increasing the utilization of [resource] would negatively impact the KPI [measuring inventory adherence] of [input material] in [stocking area].

This implies that there might be inventory shortages or constraints in [stocking area], which would be further strained if more products were pushed through the [resource] operation. This could be due to delays in the supply of [upstream materials] from the [supplier] or inefficiencies in the [two upstream] operations. By increasing the utilization of [resource], we would be exacerbating these inventory shortages, leading to a less optimal schedule.

3. **KPI [inventory adherence of upstream product Y]:** Similar to the previous feature, this suggests that increasing the utilization of [resource] would negatively impact the KPI [inventory adherence] of [input material] in [stocking area]. This reinforces the idea that there are inventory constraints in [stocking area], which would be worsened by increasing the utilization of [resource]. This could be due to similar upstream constraints, such as delays in the supply of [upstream materials] or inefficiencies in the [two upstream] operations.

In general, these features suggest that increasing the utilization of [resource] would lead to a less optimal schedule due to upstream constraints and inventory shortages in [stocking area]. This highlights the importance of considering the entire supply chain when optimizing the master production schedule.

Authoritative Explanation. The input materials for the [resource] consist of [input materials], which are stored at [stocking area]. During the specified period, the inventory levels of [input materials] are at or below their minimum target levels. Any increase in the utilization of this resource will further deplete these inventories, resulting in a higher KPI [inventory adherence].

Replenishments of these input materials cannot be planned earlier, as lead times would not allow that so early in the planning horizon. While some [resource] supply orders could be moved earlier, advancing them would increase stock levels, i.e., reduce the [inventory holding costs] before [resource] but increase the [work-in-progress cost] between [resource] and [next resource], leading to a higher [total objective] overall.

Downstream of the [resource], the [next bottleneck resource] is at full capacity, preventing earlier scheduling. Advancing processes would lead to inventory holding costs between operations, negatively affecting the KPI [work-in-progress].

Most of the [resource] tasks are scheduled on time or early, so pushing them earlier offers no tangible benefit. The resource shows minimal lateness, with only minor delays that are not significant enough to warrant rescheduling. Underutilization of specific resources can be influenced by KPI configurations, but the current setup does not prioritize unused periods as a cost.

6 Conclusion

In conclusion, this study presents two key findings. First, qualitative research through expert interviews illustrates the potential of LLMs to bridge the gap between advanced optimization technologies and human planners. By transforming complex, technical explanations from XAI models into more accessible and persuasive narratives, LLMs significantly enhance the interpretability of optimization outputs. The findings suggest that incorporating LLMs into the supply chain planning process can increase trust and acceptance among experts, thereby improving the overall effectiveness of optimization models in practical applications, in line with the objectives of this paper. While promising, there remain limitations in narrative explanations that can be refined to further improve their clarity and applicability.

Second, a quantitative comparison between LLM-generated and expert explanations reveals a gap regarding the contextual richness. In particular, the experts mentioned factors missing in explanations coming from the underlying LIME method. We hypothesize that expanding the underlying explanations would also improve the narrative ones. The comparison further highlights the variability in expert explanations, reflecting the difficulty of generating a comprehensive explanation for supply chain optimization problems due to their multifaceted nature. Future research should focus on integrating LLMs with other models, utilizing more specific and granular data within optimization frameworks. This will refine the applicability of LLM-generated explanations, ensuring better alignment with expert expectations and practical requirements, and ultimately enhancing the overall utility of these technologies in optimization contexts.

Acknowledgments. This research is part of the LEO project which is co-funded by Holland High Tech | TKI HSTM via the PPS allowance scheme for public-private partnerships, and by Dassault Systèmes. I. Grau is supported by the European Union's HORIZON Research and Innovation Programme under grant agreement No 101120657, project ENFIELD (European Lighthouse to Manifest Trustworthy and Green AI).

References

1. Ahuja, R.K., Orlin, J.B., Sharma, D.: Very large-scale neighborhood search. Int. Trans. Oper. Res. **7**(4–5), 301–317 (2000)
2. Ali, T., Kostakos, P.: HuntGPT: integrating machine learning-based anomaly detection and explainable AI with large language models (LLMs) (2023)
3. Alicioglu, G., Sun, B.: A survey of visual analytics for explainable artificial intelligence methods. Compute. Graph. **102**, 502–520 (2022)
4. Braun, V., Clarke, V.: Using thematic analysis in psychology. Qual. Res. Psychol. **3**(2), 77–101 (2006)
5. Cedro, M., Martens, D.: GraphXAIN: narratives to explain graph neural networks (2024)
6. Bock, K.W., Coussement, K., Caigny, A.D., et al.: Explainable AI for operational research: a defining framework, methods, applications, and a research agenda. Eur. J. Oper. Res. **317**(2), 249–272 (2024)
7. Fox, M., Long, D., Magazzeni, D.: Explainable Planning (2017). https://arxiv.org/abs/1709.10256

8. Grau, I., Sengupta, D., Lorenzo, M.M.G., Nowe, A.: An interpretable semi-supervised classifier using rough sets for amended self-labeling. In: 2020 IEEE International Conference on Fuzzy Systems (FUZZ-IEEE). IEEE (2020)
9. Guu, K., Lee, K., Tung, Z., Pasupat, P., Chang, M.: Retrieval augmented language model pre-training. In: ICML 2020, pp. 3929–3938 (2020)
10. Hassija, V., et al.: Interpreting black-box models: a review on explainable artificial intelligence. Cogn. Comput. **16** (2023)
11. Hoque, M.N., Shin, S., Elmqvist, N.: Harder, better, faster, stronger: interactive visualization for human-centered AI tools (2024). https://arxiv.org/abs/2404.02147
12. Hu, X., et al.: Do large language models know about facts? (2023). https://arxiv.org/abs/2310.05177
13. Ichmoukhamedov, T., Hinns, J., Martens, D.: How good is my story? Towards quantitative metrics for evaluating LLM-generated XAI narratives (2024). https://arxiv.org/abs/2412.10220
14. Korikov, A., Beck, J.C.: Counterfactual explanations via inverse constraint programming. In: Leibniz International Proceedings in Informatics. LIPIcs, vol. 210, no. 48, pp. 1–17 (2021)
15. Kroeger, N., Ley, D., Krishna, S., Agarwal, C., Lakkaraju, H.: Are large language models post hoc explainers? In: XAI in Action: Past, Present, and Future Applications (2023). https://openreview.net/forum?id=mAzhEP9jPv
16. Lewis, P., et al.: Retrieval-augmented generation for knowledge-intensive NLP tasks (2021)
17. Liu, J., Marriott, K., Dwyer, T., Tack, G.: Increasing user trust in optimisation through feedback and interaction. ACM Trans. Comput.-Hum. Interact. **29**(5) (2023)
18. Liu, N.F., et al.: Lost in the middle: how language models use long contexts. Trans. Assoc. Comput. Linguist. **12**, 157–173 (02 2024)
19. Lundberg, S., Lee, S.I.: A unified approach to interpreting model predictions (2017). https://arxiv.org/abs/1705.07874
20. Martens, D., Hinns, J., Dams, C., Vergouwen, M., Evgeniou, T.: Tell me a story! Narrative-driven XAI with large language models (2024). https://arxiv.org/abs/2309.17057
21. Mavrepis, P., Makridis, G., Fatouros, G., Koukos, V., Separdani, M.M., Kyriazis, D.: XAI for all: can large language models simplify explainable AI? (2024). https://arxiv.org/abs/2401.13110
22. Miller, T.: Explanation in artificial intelligence: insights from the social sciences. Artif. Intell. **267**, 1–38 (2019)
23. Molnar, C.: Interpretable Machine Learning (2022). https://christophm.github.io/interpretable-ml-book
24. Petropoulos, F., Laporte, G., Aktas, E., et al.: Operational research: methods and applications. J. Oper. Res. Soc. **75**(3), 423–617 (2023)
25. Ribeiro, M.T., Singh, S., Guestrin, C.: Why should i trust you?: Explaining the predictions of any classifier. In: KDD 2016, pp. 1135–1144 (2016)
26. Saeed, W., Omlin, C.: Explainable AI (XAI): a systematic meta-survey of current challenges and future opportunities. Knowl.-Based Syst. **263**, 110273 (2023)
27. Schulhoff, S., Ilie, M., Balepur, N., et al.: The prompt report: a systematic survey of prompting techniques (2024). https://arxiv.org/abs/2406.06608
28. Sokol, K., Flach, P.: Explainability fact sheets: a framework for systematic assessment of explainable approaches. In: 2020 ACM Conference on Fairness, Accountability, and Transparency, pp. 56–67 (2020)

29. Speith, T.: A review of taxonomies of explainable artificial intelligence (XAI) methods. In: 2022 ACM Conference on Fairness, Accountability, and Transparency, pp. 2239–2250 (2022)
30. Susnjak, T.: Beyond predictive learning analytics modelling and onto explainable artificial intelligence with prescriptive analytics and ChatGPT. Int. J. Artif. Intell. Educ. **34** (2023)
31. Tsutsui, S., Karino, M., Kuroki, K., et al.: A case study on enhancing inquiry response in a non-life insurance company using generative AI. In: 5th ACM International Conference on AI in Finance, pp. 108–116 (2024)
32. Tullemans, R.: Explaining underutilized resource periods in a master production scheduling problem. Master's thesis, Eindhoven University of Technology (2022)
33. Vieira, J., Deschamps, F., Valle, P.: Advanced Planning and Scheduling (APS) Systems: A Systematic Literature Review (2021)
34. Yu, J., et al.: INTERACTION: a generative XAI framework for natural language inference explanations. In: 2022 International Joint Conference on Neural Networks (2022)
35. Zytek, A., Pidò, S., Veeramachaneni, K.: LLMs for XAI: future directions for explaining explanations (2024). https://arxiv.org/abs/2405.06064

Open Access This chapter is licensed under the terms of the Creative Commons Attribution 4.0 International License (http://creativecommons.org/licenses/by/4.0/), which permits use, sharing, adaptation, distribution and reproduction in any medium or format, as long as you give appropriate credit to the original author(s) and the source, provide a link to the Creative Commons license and indicate if changes were made.

The images or other third party material in this chapter are included in the chapter's Creative Commons license, unless indicated otherwise in a credit line to the material. If material is not included in the chapter's Creative Commons license and your intended use is not permitted by statutory regulation or exceeds the permitted use, you will need to obtain permission directly from the copyright holder.

Large Language Models as Attribution Regularizers for Efficient Model Training

Davor Vukadin(✉), Marin Šilić, and Goran Delač

Faculty of Electrical Engineering and Computing, University of Zagreb, 3 Unska Street, Zagreb, Croatia
{davor.vukadin,marin.silic,goran.delac}@fer.hr

Abstract. Large Language Models (LLMs) have demonstrated remarkable performance across diverse domains. However, effectively leveraging their vast knowledge for training smaller downstream models remains an open challenge, especially in domains like tabular data learning, where simpler models are often preferred due to interpretability and efficiency.

In this paper, we introduce a novel yet straightforward method for incorporating LLM-generated global task feature attributions into the training process of smaller networks. Specifically, we propose an attribution-matching regularization term that aligns the training dynamics of the smaller model with the insights provided by the LLM. By doing so, our approach yields superior performance in few-shot learning scenarios. Notably, our method requires only black-box API access to the LLM, making it easy to integrate into existing training pipelines with minimal computational overhead.

Furthermore, we demonstrate how this method can be used to address common issues in real-world datasets, such as skewness and bias. By integrating high-level knowledge from LLMs, our approach improves generalization, even when training data is limited or imbalanced. We validate its effectiveness through extensive experiments across multiple tasks, demonstrating improved learning efficiency and model robustness.

Keywords: Large Language Models · Attribution Regularization · Data-Efficient Learning

1 Introduction

The recent expansion in model parameters and training data for large language models (LLMs) has driven a significant breakthrough in natural language processing (NLP) [9,13,25,54]. These models exhibit remarkable performance across various evaluation paradigms, such as zero-shot [33] and few-shot inference, leveraging in-context learning [39,56]. This capability stems from the extensive text corpora used for training, which embed rich prior knowledge into LLMs, allowing them to approximate expert knowledge across diverse domains. Although their strong performance and generalization capabilities have been successfully extended to other modalities, such as images [37] and speech [59], their application in tabular learning settings remains limited.

Several challenges hinder the adoption of LLMs for tabular data tasks. Firstly, their large parameter counts demand substantial computational resources, typically reliant on GPUs, which significantly increases operational costs. Secondly, tabular learning is often employed in domains where transparency and interpretability are critical, such as healthcare and finance. In these fields, simpler and more interpretable models, such as logistic regression or decision trees, are often preferred. Although techniques exist to enhance LLM interpretability [3,34], they currently fall short compared to the inherent explainability of simpler models.

In this paper, we investigate the potential of utilizing LLMs as training regularizers to enhance few-shot learning performance and improve generalization, especially in scenarios with skewed or biased training data. Specifically, we propose a method called **L**arge Language Model **A**ttribution **A**ligned **T**raining (**LAAT**), which introduces an attribution-matching regularization term that aligns the local, feature-wise explanations of smaller models with the global, task-specific explanations generated by LLMs. This approach harnesses the strong generalization capabilities of LLMs while preserving the efficiency and transparency of smaller models. We share our code at: https://github.com/davor10105/laat.

2 Related Work

2.1 Standard Machine Learning Approaches

Inspired by the success of deep learning in other domains, numerous efforts have sought to apply self-supervised learning to tabular data to develop transfer learning-ready models. These approaches include masked feature prediction [4,38], feature corruption correction [6,58], and contrastive pre-training [52]. However, comparative studies indicate that gradient-boosted tree ensembles still outperform these methods [21,49]. More recently, Nam et al. [41] introduced Self-generated Tasks from UNlabeled Tables (STUNT), leveraging self-generated few-shot tasks for tabular learning, though its reliance on large unlabeled datasets may limit practical applicability. Additionally, Hollmann et al. [26] proposed the Tabular Prior-data Fitted Network (TabPFN), a tabular foundation model pre-trained on millions of synthetic datasets.

2.2 Large Language Models in Tabular Learning

Most approaches integrating large language models (LLMs) into tabular learning rely on encoding task and feature descriptions in natural language, serializing the data, and leveraging LLMs for inference—either through in-context learning [50] or additional fine-tuning [14,24,55]. However, these methods face significant drawbacks, including the high cost of LLM inference for individual samples and the computational demands of fine-tuning.

In sensitive domains such as medicine or finance [48], where transparency is critical, the opaque decision-making of LLMs is less desirable than traditional, smaller models. Alternative approaches involve using LLMs to generate synthetic examples to augment existing datasets, employing both in-context learning and fine-tuning [46,51,60]. However, these methods inherit the same scalability issues, particularly when dealing with high-dimensional datasets, where generating sufficiently large datasets becomes computationally expensive.

Recently, Han et al. [22] introduced FeatLLM, a novel approach that utilizes LLMs as feature engineers. Instead of directly performing inference, FeatLLM employs code-generating LLMs to create preprocessing functions that transform the original dataset into a more suitable representation for few-shot classification. This method implements an ensemble classifier to combine insights from multiple feature transformations, improving robustness and classification accuracy. FeatLLM significantly reduces resource requirements by relying solely on pretrained LLMs with API-level access. Moreover, FeatLLM outperforms existing fine-tuned and in-context learning approaches while maintaining lower computational costs. However, even though FeatLLM achieves state-of-the-art performance on few-shot tabular classification problems, its many iterations of rule and preprocessing function generation incur significant costs. Furthermore, during preprocessing, FeatLLM produces only binary features, which may limit expressiveness compared to the original data.

2.3 Explanation Guided Learning

A growing line of research explores enhancing model behavior through additional supervision derived from explainable artificial intelligence (XAI) techniques. This field can be broadly categorized into local explanation-guided learning and global explanation-guided learning [18].

Local explanation guidance applies supervision signals or regularization terms to individual model explanations, steering learning at the sample level. This approach is more prevalent due to the extensive development of local explanation techniques, particularly in the image domain, such as Grad-CAM [47], Layer-wise Relevance Propagation (LRP) [5], and attention-based attributions [2]. Ross et al. [45] propose regularizing differentiable models by penalizing input gradients, aligning them with expert-defined attribution maps. Dharma et al. [30] use object bounding boxes as explanation supervision signals. In text classification, several studies leverage per-sample human-annotated rationales [12,29,61]. Gao et al. [19] demonstrate the effectiveness of local explanation supervision under limited training data. However, a key limitation of this approach is its reliance on per-sample attribution annotations, which are often difficult and costly to obtain, particularly in expert-driven fields like medicine.

Global explanation guidance, in contrast, does not require instance-level attributions, instead offering a broader, more scalable approach to shaping model behavior. Liu et al. [36] reduce undesired biases by penalizing nonzero attributions on sensitive tokens. Erion et al. [17] aggregate local feature attributions via expected gradients to improve interpretability. Weinberger et al. [57] extract prior knowledge from multiple gene expression datasets to construct meta-features, training a deep global attribution model alongside a predictive model with a regularization loss. However, this method assumes the availability of additional datasets related to the problem, which may not always be feasible.

3 Method

In contrast to other methods that utilize LLMs for tabular data prediction, we seek to minimize both the computational and price overhead of their use, while simultaneously still effectively using their generalization abilities and providing small, interpretable models that can be readily used in existing pipelines.

3.1 Formulation

Given a trained binary classification model $m_\theta : \mathbb{R}^N \to [0, 1]$ parametrized by θ, an attribution produced by an attribution method a for an input $\mathbf{x}$ is a vector $a(x) = (s_1, ..., s_n)$, where s_i is the attribution score of the input feature x_i. We are interested in the expected value of the attribution scores over the entire dataset, given by $\mathbf{s}_\mathbb{E} = \mathbb{E}_{\mathbf{x} \sim \mathcal{D}}[a(\mathbf{x})]$, where $\mathcal{D}$ represents the data distribution.

For certain datasets where the expected attribution follows an intuitive pattern that humans can interpret, we hypothesize that this expected value can be approximated using a large language model and thus serve as a valuable local attribution guide during training.

Taking a step back, given an untrained model along with a task description and feature descriptions, we query an LLM to generate importance scores for each feature, producing a vector $\mathbf{s}_{\text{LLM}}$. During model training, we then regularize the local attribution scores of the model to align with these LLM-derived scores. This regularization acts as a guiding signal, helping the model maintain behavior that aligns with intuitive, human-understandable reasoning.

The final model's loss function consists of two components: the standard binary cross-entropy loss and an attribution regularization term. The regularization term is the mean squared error between the normalized attribution scores and the normalized LLM-derived scores, weighted by γ. The overall loss is given as a weighted sum of these terms:

$$\mathcal{L}(\theta) = \frac{1}{n} \sum_{i=1}^{n} (\ell_{\text{BCE}}(m_\theta(\mathbf{x}_i), \mathbf{y}_i) + \gamma \ell_{\text{MSE}}(\frac{a(\mathbf{x}_i)}{\|a(\mathbf{x}_i)\|}, \frac{\mathbf{s}_{\text{LLM}}}{\|\mathbf{s}_{\text{LLM}}\|})) \quad (1)$$

Following Ross et al. [45], we employ the input gradient as our chosen attribution method.

3.2 LLM Prompting and Score Parsing

To enable Large Language Models (LLMs) to generate meaningful feature attribution scores for guiding downstream models, we developed a structured prompting methodology. This approach ensures score accuracy and relevance through three key components.

Task and Dataset Contextualization. We embed task and dataset details within the prompt. Task descriptions succinctly define classification objectives and outcomes, e.g., *"Predict whether this patient's breast cancer will reoccur. Yes or no?"*, following established methodologies [22,24]. Feature descriptions clarify dataset attributes, e.g., *"Age: The age of the patient at diagnosis."*. Categorical features are one-hot encoded with explicit descriptions for each category, enabling the LLM to assign distinct attribution scores per category rather than per feature. Unlike prior approaches that use LLMs for tabular data classification, our method avoids serializing dataset examples into the prompt, thereby reducing prompt length and computational cost.

Score Generation Protocol. We instruct the LLM to assign integer scores between -10 and 10, establishing a standardized feature importance scale. Using chain-of-thought prompting [56], we ensure explicit reasoning before score assignment, enhancing interpretability. The full prompt template is provided in Prompt 1.1 in the Appendix.

Score Extraction and Aggregation. A secondary LLM instance extracts numerical scores from the primary LLM's textual output via function calling, converting semi-structured responses into a standardized list format. To enhance stability, we generate scores multiple times ($N_{estimates}$) and compute their mean, yielding the final LLM-based feature attribution vector (s_{LLM}).

This methodology provides a robust framework for leveraging LLM capabilities to generate reliable feature attribution scores that effectively inform downstream predictive models.

4 Experiments

We conducted a comprehensive evaluation of LAAT across diverse tabular datasets, examining its performance in few-shot learning contexts and scenarios where significant bias was present in the training data. Furthermore, we performed supplementary experiments to investigate the impact of various hyperparameter configurations on the proposed methodology.

4.1 Few-Shot Learning

While large volumes of data are readily available in many domains, expert-labeled data remains scarce in fields requiring specialized knowledge, such as medicine. To address this challenge, recent research has focused on enhancing the generalization capabilities of tabular classification models under minimal labeled data constraints [22,24,41]. In this experiment, we assess the effectiveness of our proposed approach in leveraging LLM-derived knowledge as a guiding signal during extremely low-shot training scenarios.

We evaluate our approach on ten publicly available binary classification datasets:

- **adult** [7] - predicting whether an individual earns over $50,000 annually
- **bank** [40] - predicting whether a client will subscribe to a term deposit
- **bodyfat** [43] - predicting whether an individual's body fat percentage exceeds the mean
- **breast-ljub** [62] - predicting whether a patient's breast cancer will reoccur
- **cdc-diabetes** [1] - predicting whether an individual has diabetes
- **contraceptive** [53] - predicting whether an individual uses contraception
- **diabetes** [28] - predicting whether an individual has diabetes
- **electricity** [23] - predicting the price change of electricity (up or down) in New South Wales
- **indian-liver** [8] - predict whether a patient has liver disease
- **myocardial** [20] - predicting whether the myocardial infarction complications data for an individual shows chronic heart failure

The datasets vary in size and complexity, and their additional basic information is outlined in Table 6 in the Appendix.

Baselines. We compare our proposed method with several baselines: logistic regression (LR), 2-layer MLP with ReLU activation and 100 hidden units (MLP), random forest (RF), XGBoost (XGB) [10], CatBoost [15], TabPFN [26] and FeatLLM [22].

Implementation Details. We employ three distinct foundation models as our importance score estimators: Llama 3.3 70B ($LLa_{3.3}$) [16], Gemini 2.0 Flash ($Gem_{2.0}$) [44] and GPT-4o-mini (G_{4om}) [27]. As simple downstream models, we utilized logistic regression and a two-layer multilayer perceptron (MLP) with ReLU activation and 100 hidden units. Optimization was performed using the Adam optimizer [31] with a learning rate of 1×10^{-2} and no weight decay, leveraging LAAT's internal regularization via the γ factor, which was set to 100. Additionally, the number of importance score estimations for LAAT was set to 5. LAAT was executed without early stopping. Data preprocessing involved one-hot encoding categorical variables and standardizing numerical features using z-score normalization. Feature descriptions were derived from dataset repository metadata or original publications, whereas task descriptions were formulated based on prior research on tabular data classification using LLMs [22,24]. As prompt engineering is not the focus of our work, we leave the exploration of alternative prompting strategies to future research. Exact task descriptions used can be found in Table 7 in the Appendix.

For traditional machine learning models (logistic regression, MLP, random forest, XGBoost, and CatBoost), we performed hyperparameter optimization through grid search with 5-fold cross-validation, with the exception of 1-shot learning scenarios where default scikit-learn [42] hyperparameters were applied. The complete baseline hyperparameter search spaces are detailed in Table 8 in the Appendix. TabPFN and FeatLLM were implemented with their respective default parameter configurations as described in the original publications. Additionally, FeatLLM incorporated early stopping mechanisms in the 5-shot and

10-shot experimental settings. Due to the inherent complexity of generating multiple conditions and preprocessing functions in the FeatLLM method, Llama 3.3 exhibited inconsistencies in producing valid outputs. As a result, we excluded it from the FeatLLM experiments.

All models were trained using k-shot examples as the training set, while the remaining data served as the test set. To ensure statistical robustness, we conducted twenty independent experimental runs for each model. The significance of the difference in the mean values of the total scores was verified using the Wilcoxon signed-rank test with $p = 0.05$.

In the following sections, we present our experimental results and provide additional analyses on LAAT's robustness to noise, as well as an examination of how LAAT influences the training loss landscape through the lens of the bias-variance tradeoff.

Results. The results of our experiments, averaged over twenty repetitions, are presented in Tables 1 (for non-LLM methods) and 2 (for LLM-based methods). As demonstrated, LAAT models consistently rank among the top-performing methods, securing the highest or shared highest scores in 28 out of 30 experiments. Notably, the highest-performing variants of LAAT were LAAT^{MLP}_{G4om} and $\text{LAAT}^{LR}_{Gem2.0}$, securing 12 and 21 top or shared top scores respectively. Furthermore, the LAAT-trained models statistically significantly outperformed their non-LAAT counterparts in 24, 28, and 27 out of 30 experiments using logistic regression with Llama 3.3 70B, Gemini 2.0 Flash, and GPT-4o-mini as scoring models, respectively. For MLP, LAAT models significantly exceeded the performance of vanilla MLP in 23, 28, and 29 experiments, respectively. These results underscore the positive impact of LLM attribution alignment on the generalization capabilities of even simple models, achieving significant improvements without the need for extensive hyperparameter tuning, which is often required for other approaches.

Figure 1 illustrates the average ROC AUC performance across all datasets, highlighting the superior performance of LAAT model variants across all shot settings. While FeatLLM closely matches LAAT in the 1-shot scenario, its performance plateaus beyond this point. We hypothesize that this occurs for two reasons: first, FeatLLM generates binary features, which may lack the expressiveness of the continuous features present in the original dataset. Second, the serialized few-shot examples significantly increase the length of the input prompt, potentially reducing the effectiveness of the rule and preprocessing function generation procedure. This may occur because the expanded prompt causes the initial instruction and relevant data to become less prominent among the large number of tokens. In contrast, LAAT models demonstrate a substantial advantage in both the 5-shot and 10-shot settings, significantly outperforming all other methods. Among the scoring models evaluated, Gemini 2.0 Flash-Lite emerged as the top performer, with GPT-4o-mini following closely behind. Although Llama 3.3 70B lagged behind these two LLMs, it consistently matched or outperformed all baseline methods across all settings. In addition to outperforming FeatLLM,

Table 1. ROC AUC scores of baseline models on the few-shot experiments. Best scores for each dataset, across both LLM and non-LLM approaches, are emphasized in **bold**. Multiple bolded values indicate that their differences were not statistically significant according to the Wilcoxon signed-rank test at $p = 0.05$.

Dataset	Shot	LR	MLP	RF	XGB	CatBoost	TabPFN
adult	1	$58.9_{19.5}$	$57.9_{14.1}$	$67.9_{11.8}$	$50.0_{0.0}$	$64.7_{14.5}$	$64.9_{16.3}$
	5	$76.7_{6.6}$	$72.8_{7.0}$	$73.8_{9.2}$	$63.9_{11.9}$	$78.1_{4.8}$	$78.1_{4.7}$
	10	$81.0_{3.4}$	$78.4_{4.8}$	$76.4_{8.1}$	$77.4_{3.3}$	$82.3_{3.5}$	$82.2_{3.5}$
bank	1	$51.2_{12.5}$	$55.5_{10.7}$	$56.0_{9.1}$	$50.0_{0.0}$	$56.8_{9.2}$	$56.2_{8.7}$
	5	$63.9_{8.7}$	$64.6_{7.8}$	$65.7_{8.4}$	$56.4_{9.3}$	$68.2_{8.1}$	$67.5_{9.1}$
	10	$66.7_{3.9}$	$67.0_{6.3}$	$69.1_{6.8}$	$71.4_{6.9}$	$74.7_{5.1}$	$74.5_{7.6}$
bodyfat	1	$62.7_{22.4}$	$69.0_{14.2}$	$64.4_{19.1}$	$50.0_{0.0}$	$67.1_{15.6}$	$68.6_{13.7}$
	5	$78.3_{9.6}$	$78.7_{10.1}$	$74.8_{8.0}$	$64.3_{14.1}$	$75.2_{11.9}$	$78.0_{10.4}$
	10	$84.4_{3.1}$	$84.3_{3.7}$	$79.4_{6.9}$	$80.2_{5.0}$	$83.6_{2.6}$	$86.2_{3.9}$
breast-ljub	1	$55.1_{9.7}$	$56.7_{12.7}$	$55.8_{7.2}$	$50.0_{0.0}$	$52.8_{9.1}$	$53.1_{9.8}$
	5	$58.4_{10.6}$	$57.9_{6.5}$	$61.6_{8.3}$	$55.0_{7.8}$	$60.2_{10.0}$	$59.9_{9.8}$
	10	$61.6_{5.9}$	$61.2_{5.6}$	$60.9_{8.2}$	$61.6_{8.1}$	$64.6_{6.5}$	$66.4_{5.6}$
cdc-diabetes	1	$58.0_{12.9}$	$62.4_{11.9}$	$59.1_{15.6}$	$50.0_{0.0}$	$59.7_{12.5}$	$64.1_{11.4}$
	5	$69.3_{5.9}$	$63.3_{11.5}$	$66.0_{8.4}$	$60.6_{5.7}$	$73.0_{4.5}$	$72.1_{4.0}$
	10	$71.8_{4.3}$	$67.0_{12.1}$	$66.7_{8.5}$	$69.8_{5.6}$	$75.5_{3.0}$	$73.3_{4.1}$
contraceptive	1	$50.9_{4.9}$	$52.4_{5.0}$	$54.4_{5.7}$	$50.0_{0.0}$	$51.9_{3.7}$	$51.3_{5.6}$
	5	$54.2_{4.9}$	$53.0_{5.2}$	$54.5_{6.7}$	$52.2_{4.9}$	$56.0_{6.8}$	$56.9_{5.9}$
	10	$56.5_{3.9}$	$53.6_{6.1}$	$57.3_{3.9}$	$57.5_{4.9}$	$59.2_{4.6}$	$59.4_{3.8}$
diabetes	1	$53.9_{13.6}$	$58.3_{15.6}$	$63.5_{7.9}$	$50.0_{0.0}$	$59.2_{8.3}$	$58.5_{10.1}$
	5	$70.6_{6.4}$	$64.2_{9.8}$	$66.0_{7.4}$	$61.6_{8.7}$	$72.6_{5.1}$	$72.9_{5.3}$
	10	$73.8_{7.9}$	$72.7_{5.8}$	$68.8_{7.2}$	$70.9_{7.4}$	$75.3_{5.1}$	$75.8_{5.9}$
electricity	1	$51.5_{12.3}$	$54.1_{13.1}$	$58.5_{9.5}$	$50.0_{0.0}$	$60.2_{11.8}$	$58.9_{10.2}$
	5	$65.2_{7.9}$	$69.0_{6.4}$	$63.6_{8.3}$	$58.3_{9.9}$	$65.4_{8.1}$	$66.8_{7.9}$
	10	**$72.6_{4.5}$**	$68.0_{8.8}$	$70.7_{4.4}$	$70.5_{7.2}$	**$74.5_{2.2}$**	**$73.2_{5.1}$**
indian-liver	1	$54.3_{14.7}$	$55.6_{14.8}$	$60.0_{11.6}$	$50.0_{0.0}$	$58.5_{11.3}$	$61.1_{11.8}$
	5	$61.3_{10.5}$	$60.4_{12.3}$	$60.3_{10.3}$	$58.9_{7.1}$	$67.7_{4.5}$	$63.4_{6.3}$
	10	$67.4_{7.3}$	$65.9_{4.7}$	$62.1_{6.8}$	$62.7_{7.0}$	$70.6_{3.2}$	$69.4_{4.2}$
myocardial	1	$50.5_{5.7}$	$52.1_{3.0}$	$51.9_{5.8}$	$50.0_{0.0}$	$50.8_{4.0}$	$50.8_{4.1}$
	5	$55.3_{5.2}$	$53.3_{7.6}$	$52.3_{6.8}$	$50.9_{3.4}$	$53.3_{6.0}$	$54.6_{5.4}$
	10	$59.3_{5.4}$	$58.5_{5.2}$	$53.4_{5.5}$	$52.3_{4.4}$	$58.7_{5.0}$	$61.0_{5.8}$

LAAT utilizes, on average, 79% fewer input tokens and 60% fewer output tokens, as shown in Table 3, demonstrating significant conservation of computational resources.

Table 2. ROC AUC scores of LLM-based models on the few-shot experiments. Best scores for each dataset, across both LLM and non-LLM approaches, are emphasized in **bold**. Multiple bolded values indicate that their differences were not statistically significant according to the Wilcoxon signed-rank test at $p = 0.05$.

Method		FeatLLM		LAAT					
Model		Ensemble		LR			MLP		
Dataset	Shot	$Gem_{2.0}$	G_{4om}	$LLa_{3.3}$	$Gem_{2.0}$	G_{4om}	$LLa_{3.3}$	$Gem_{2.0}$	G_{4om}
adult	1	**81.2**$_{6.1}$	**80.4**$_{4.7}$	68.9$_{11.6}$	67.0$_{13.1}$	70.5$_{10.3}$	70.5$_{8.6}$	71.4$_{9.9}$	72.8$_{7.6}$
	5	**85.3**$_{2.5}$	81.1$_{4.2}$	79.2$_{4.5}$	81.5$_{4.6}$	77.9$_{4.2}$	76.3$_{4.8}$	78.7$_{5.2}$	77.5$_{4.5}$
	10	**84.4**$_{3.0}$	78.5$_{5.1}$	82.4$_{3.4}$	**85.2**$_{3.4}$	81.0$_{3.2}$	79.1$_{4.8}$	82.1$_{4.4}$	78.6$_{3.7}$
bank	1	71.4$_{3.3}$	66.3$_{3.0}$	61.3$_{8.7}$	**76.2**$_{10.3}$	**77.2**$_{7.5}$	58.1$_{9.4}$	72.5$_{10.1}$	74.4$_{7.8}$
	5	71.9$_{5.0}$	66.3$_{4.3}$	65.6$_{2.2}$	**85.6**$_{2.0}$	83.8$_{0.8}$	64.4$_{4.9}$	82.0$_{5.0}$	83.4$_{2.6}$
	10	70.3$_{4.0}$	64.2$_{5.1}$	64.7$_{1.4}$	**86.0**$_{0.9}$	84.7$_{1.0}$	65.6$_{4.5}$	81.9$_{3.9}$	84.4$_{2.1}$
bodyfat	1	67.6$_{11.5}$	76.0$_{7.4}$	88.2$_{1.6}$	**89.6**$_{0.8}$	89.0$_{1.2}$	84.9$_{6.1}$	85.6$_{6.6}$	85.5$_{6.2}$
	5	82.6$_{2.4}$	81.6$_{2.4}$	89.0$_{0.5}$	**90.2**$_{0.4}$	89.7$_{0.4}$	89.0$_{0.5}$	**90.2**$_{0.5}$	89.7$_{0.5}$
	10	82.6$_{2.4}$	78.8$_{7.1}$	89.0$_{0.6}$	**90.2**$_{0.5}$	89.7$_{0.6}$	89.0$_{0.7}$	**90.2**$_{0.6}$	89.8$_{0.7}$
breast-ljub	1	60.9$_{6.9}$	61.5$_{7.9}$	74.0$_{0.9}$	73.9$_{1.1}$	**74.4**$_{0.7}$	72.7$_{3.0}$	72.6$_{2.7}$	72.6$_{3.1}$
	5	65.0$_{7.1}$	61.4$_{5.5}$	74.4$_{0.8}$	**74.7**$_{0.8}$	74.4$_{0.8}$	74.1$_{1.0}$	**74.4**$_{1.0}$	74.0$_{1.1}$
	10	63.9$_{6.8}$	61.0$_{8.5}$	73.8$_{1.1}$	**74.2**$_{1.1}$	73.7$_{1.1}$	73.6$_{1.3}$	73.8$_{1.4}$	73.2$_{1.4}$
cdc-diabetes	1	**73.7**$_{2.8}$	72.6$_{2.9}$	72.5$_{2.8}$	**75.1**$_{2.7}$	72.6$_{2.1}$	70.8$_{4.2}$	74.3$_{2.9}$	72.1$_{3.2}$
	5	71.4$_{11.1}$	75.3$_{1.5}$	74.4$_{1.9}$	**78.1**$_{0.9}$	75.1$_{1.2}$	74.7$_{2.2}$	**78.2**$_{0.9}$	75.6$_{1.5}$
	10	73.2$_{3.3}$	73.4$_{2.6}$	74.8$_{1.3}$	**78.5**$_{0.6}$	75.7$_{0.9}$	75.2$_{1.4}$	**78.6**$_{0.6}$	76.3$_{1.1}$
contraceptive	1	55.7$_{4.5}$	55.6$_{4.3}$	**62.8**$_{0.8}$	61.6$_{2.4}$	61.1$_{1.3}$	**63.1**$_{2.3}$	61.2$_{3.3}$	61.3$_{2.2}$
	5	53.4$_{5.8}$	53.1$_{5.5}$	62.7$_{0.2}$	**64.2**$_{0.7}$	61.7$_{0.1}$	62.9$_{0.4}$	**64.2**$_{1.4}$	61.7$_{0.3}$
	10	54.7$_{4.6}$	53.6$_{4.0}$	62.6$_{0.2}$	64.9$_{0.4}$	61.6$_{0.2}$	62.9$_{0.4}$	**65.2**$_{0.7}$	61.7$_{0.3}$
diabetes	1	75.6$_{4.5}$	73.1$_{3.7}$	72.8$_{8.1}$	**78.9**$_{2.9}$	75.0$_{8.0}$	68.4$_{9.8}$	69.8$_{9.3}$	69.7$_{9.4}$
	5	73.1$_{8.9}$	75.0$_{2.0}$	78.7$_{1.5}$	**79.8**$_{0.4}$	**79.7**$_{0.6}$	78.8$_{1.5}$	**79.8**$_{0.5}$	**79.7**$_{0.7}$
	10	70.9$_{5.7}$	75.4$_{2.3}$	79.1$_{0.7}$	79.6$_{0.3}$	79.7$_{0.4}$	79.2$_{0.7}$	**79.7**$_{0.4}$	**79.8**$_{0.4}$
electricity	1	63.9$_{4.9}$	66.5$_{5.7}$	65.3$_{7.6}$	66.8$_{3.4}$	**73.3**$_{5.3}$	61.4$_{7.1}$	61.8$_{8.2}$	65.4$_{9.8}$
	5	71.8$_{4.1}$	67.6$_{5.3}$	67.6$_{0.6}$	68.3$_{0.2}$	**74.9**$_{1.5}$	67.4$_{0.7}$	68.2$_{0.4}$	**74.9**$_{1.6}$
	10	70.8$_{3.8}$	65.5$_{6.3}$	67.4$_{0.4}$	68.4$_{0.3}$	**74.1**$_{2.0}$	67.4$_{0.5}$	68.3$_{0.4}$	**74.2**$_{2.0}$
indian-liver	1	68.5$_{4.1}$	67.6$_{4.9}$	**73.1**$_{1.6}$	**73.4**$_{1.1}$	72.7$_{1.7}$	72.0$_{2.1}$	72.1$_{1.7}$	71.4$_{2.2}$
	5	72.2$_{1.7}$	72.7$_{0.8}$	**73.8**$_{1.0}$	**73.7**$_{0.9}$	73.2$_{1.0}$	**73.7**$_{0.9}$	73.5$_{1.0}$	73.1$_{0.9}$
	10	70.3$_{3.8}$	70.5$_{2.5}$	**74.0**$_{0.9}$	73.9$_{0.7}$	73.3$_{0.9}$	**73.9**$_{0.9}$	73.9$_{1.0}$	73.4$_{1.1}$
myocardial	1	59.0$_{3.5}$	59.1$_{4.4}$	54.8$_{5.3}$	58.3$_{6.3}$	57.9$_{6.3}$	58.5$_{2.9}$	**63.1**$_{3.9}$	61.7$_{4.4}$
	5	59.7$_{5.0}$	60.6$_{3.0}$	60.7$_{3.7}$	65.9$_{2.5}$	64.9$_{3.0}$	62.0$_{1.8}$	**66.1**$_{1.8}$	64.4$_{2.6}$
	10	58.7$_{2.8}$	60.7$_{3.2}$	63.0$_{2.7}$	67.2$_{2.2}$	66.5$_{3.0}$	62.6$_{2.4}$	**66.7**$_{2.5}$	65.9$_{2.7}$

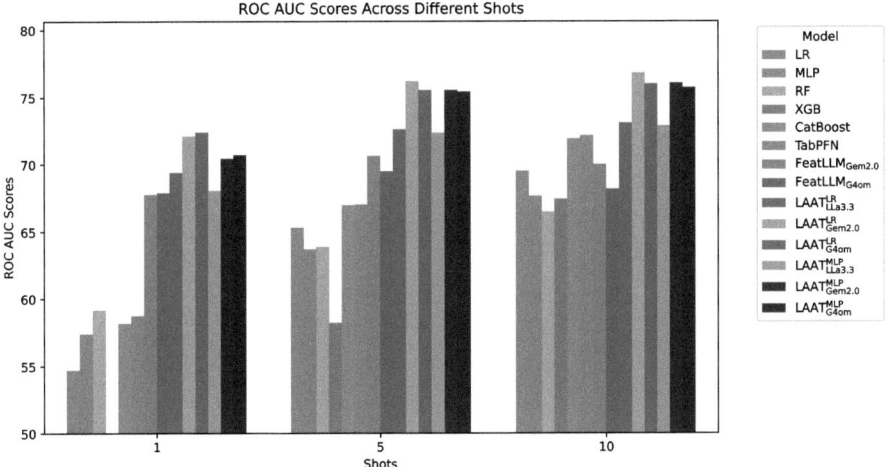

Fig. 1. ROC AUC scores for baseline models and LLM-based methods, averaged across all datasets. In the 1-shot setting, FeatLLM achieves the highest average performance. However, in subsequent shots, LAAT-based approaches, both Logistic Regression and MLP variants, outperform the baselines and FeatLLM.

Table 3. FeatLLM and LAAT average token count comparison. LAAT consumes significantly less input and output tokens, conserving computational resources.

Method	FeatLLM						LAAT	
k-shot	1		5		10		N/A	
Token Type	Input	Output	Input	Output	Input	Output	Input	Output
Count	37866	19730	51704	20067	62310	20282	**10570**	**7990**

Sensitivity to Importance Score Noise. We assess the robustness of the LAAT method by introducing controlled noise into the importance scores provided by the LLM. Specifically, we define a noise ratio $\epsilon \in [0,1]$ and compute the perturbed importance scores, $\mathbf{s}_{\text{LLM}}^{\text{noisy}}$, as a linear interpolation between the original scores and randomly generated scores, $\mathbf{s}_{\text{noise}}$, sampled from a uniform integer distribution in the range $[-10, 10]$:

$$\mathbf{s}_{\text{LLM}}^{\text{noisy}} = (1-\epsilon)\mathbf{s}_{\text{LLM}} + \epsilon \mathbf{s}_{\text{noise}} \qquad (2)$$

Figure 2 presents the average performance across all shot scenarios for both LR and MLP LAAT variants using the GPT-4o mini model under varying noise conditions. As expected, the performance of LAAT declines as the noise ratio increases. However, even with noise ratios as high as 0.6, LAAT variants continue to outperform their non-LAAT counterparts. These results demonstrate LAAT's ability to enhance baseline model performance even when the LLM-derived importance scores are imperfect.

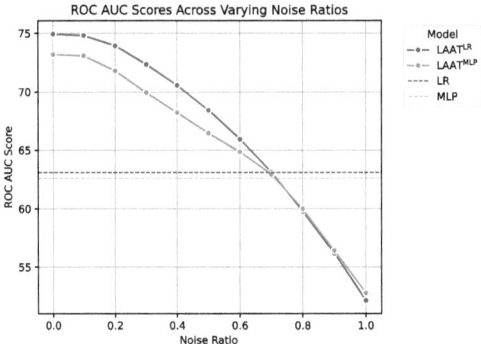

Fig. 2. LAAT robustness to noisy importance scores. Despite performance degradation with increasing noise ϵ, LAAT variants outperform non-LAAT counterparts up to $\epsilon = 0.6$, demonstrating resilience to imperfect LLM scores.

Exploring the Loss Landscape. To understand why LAAT consistently outperforms other methods, we analyze the training and test loss landscapes [35] of two logistic regression models: one trained with standard binary cross-entropy loss and another incorporating the attribution alignment loss with $\gamma = 100$. We also visualize their respective training trajectories. Each model was trained using Adam for 200 epochs without early stopping or weight decay, with only five training samples per class, while the remaining dataset was used as the test set.

Figure 3 illustrates the results for the **adult** and **bank** datasets, while additional results for the **breast-ljub** and **myocardial** datasets are provided in the Appendix in Fig. 6.

A key observation from these visualizations is that the loss landscape of the standard model exhibits a substantial discrepancy between training and test loss surfaces. This suggests high variance, where the model overfits to the limited training data, learning feature importance patterns that do not generalize well. Conversely, introducing the attribution alignment loss alters the training loss landscape, shifting it closer to the test loss landscape. This shift can be interpreted as a form of inductive bias, where the model is nudged toward an attribution structure informed by the LLM's prior knowledge.

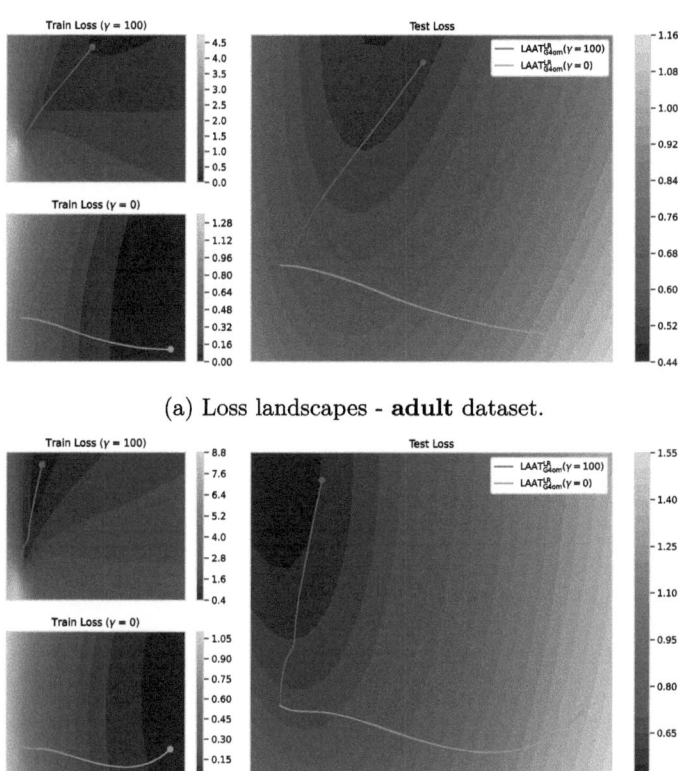

Fig. 3. Train and test loss landscapes for logistic regression on the **adult** and **bank** datasets, comparing models with attribution alignment loss ($\gamma = 100$, top left subfigure) and without it ($\gamma = 0$, bottom left subfigure). The addition of attribution alignment loss results in a closer match between training landscapes (left half) and the test loss landscape (right half), guiding the training process (colored lines ending with a point) towards minima that align well with testing minima, indicating improved generalization. (Color figure online)

From a bias-variance perspective, LAAT's regularization constrains the model's optimization path, discouraging reliance on spurious correlations and guiding it toward more stable, generalizable parameters. Secondly, the model becomes less sensitive to variations in small datasets, lowering the variance, which is preferable in low-data scenarios. This trade-off mitigates overfitting and enhances generalization, ultimately leading to improved predictive performance, as demonstrated in previous experiments.

4.2 Learning on Biased Data

Many real-world datasets exhibit varying degrees of bias, which can negatively impact machine learning models by introducing misleading correlations. For instance, a model trained on historical recruitment data may inherit biases related to gender and job roles [11]. Similarly, systemic biases in criminal justice datasets often lead to strong correlations between demographic attributes and outcomes, potentially reflecting enforcement patterns rather than actual crime rates. In some cases, these confounding factors can be explicitly removed when they are demonstrably unrelated to the target classification. However, the challenge becomes more complex when the relationship is "soft"—i.e., a correlation exists, but its exact influence is difficult to quantify.

To evaluate the performance of baseline methods alongside our proposed LAAT method, we introduce artificial biases into the training portion of the medicine-related datasets used in the previous experiment while keeping the evaluation data distribution unchanged. This approach mimics real-world biases that may arise due to the way data is collected—for example, demographic skews in clinical trials or socioeconomic biases in electronic health records. By training models on biased distributions and assessing them on the original, unbiased test data, we simulate practical scenarios where spurious correlations may mislead models, allowing us to analyze their robustness to such biases. Specifically, we apply the following modifications:

- **bodyfat** - Exclude all individuals under the age of 50 with above-average body fat percentage, introducing a bias that overestimates body fat in elderly individuals.
- **breast-ljub** - Exclude all patients under the age of 50 who experienced breast cancer recurrence, introducing a bias that overestimates recurrence in elderly patients.
- **cdc-diabetes** - Exclude all women with diabetes and all men without diabetes, artificially inflating the apparent prevalence of diabetes among men.
- **contraceptive** - Exclude all working women not using contraceptives and all non-working women using contraceptives, creating a spurious relationship between employment and contraceptive use.
- **diabetes** - Remove all individuals under 50 years old who have diabetes, encouraging models to over-rely on age for diabetes prediction.
- **indian-liver** - Remove all male patients with diagnosed liver disease, biasing models toward associating liver disease more strongly with female patients.
- **myocardial** - Remove all female patients with a history of myocardial infarction, biasing models toward overestimating the risk of myocardial infarction in men.

Results. As in the few-shot experiment, results are presented in Tables 4 for non-LLM methods and 5 for LLM-based methods. LAAT effectively mitigates dataset biases and achieves the highest performance across all datasets, surpassing non-LLM baselines by more than 20 ROC AUC points in some cases.

Although FeatLLM outperforms traditional baselines, it achieves shared top performance with LAAT on only two datasets and lags significantly behind LAAT models on the remaining datasets. The superior performance of LAAT on this challenging benchmark further highlights the benefits of attribution guidance—not only in enhancing performance in data-scarce scenarios but also in addressing subtle, hard-to-detect dataset biases that could otherwise compromise the integrity of the machine learning pipeline.

Table 4. ROC AUC scores of baseline methods on the biased dataset experiments. Best scores for each dataset, across both LLM and non-LLM approaches, are emphasized in **bold**. Multiple bolded values indicate that their differences were not statistically significant according to the Wilcoxon signed-rank test at $p = 0.05$.

Model Dataset	LR	MLP	RF	XGB	CatBoost	TabPFN
bodyfat	$84.5_{4.4}$	$81.1_{4.7}$	$78.1_{6.2}$	$75.0_{7.3}$	$82.3_{4.1}$	$85.0_{3.9}$
breast-ljub	$54.3_{6.6}$	$54.4_{5.4}$	$55.8_{7.4}$	$54.6_{9.5}$	$54.0_{6.6}$	$52.9_{7.6}$
cdc-diabetes	$62.2_{0.4}$	$62.4_{0.3}$	$60.3_{2.3}$	$49.3_{1.3}$	$60.2_{2.1}$	$50.1_{1.3}$
contraceptive	$57.3_{3.0}$	$50.9_{5.8}$	$55.7_{5.3}$	$47.6_{2.2}$	$57.0_{2.8}$	$50.1_{2.9}$
diabetes	$75.8_{3.3}$	$72.9_{4.1}$	$72.9_{4.6}$	$60.7_{8.8}$	$75.0_{3.2}$	$76.4_{3.1}$
indian-liver	$60.4_{6.7}$	$56.8_{5.3}$	$54.9_{8.4}$	$49.3_{6.1}$	$58.9_{5.6}$	$59.8_{5.5}$
myocardial	$55.1_{8.2}$	$55.8_{5.9}$	$58.5_{5.1}$	$54.6_{8.7}$	$55.6_{9.9}$	$50.0_{7.8}$

4.3 Hyperparameter Analysis

We investigate the impact of varying the regularization factor γ and the number of importance score estimations on the final performance of LAAT models. Specifically, we assess the performance of a logistic regression model trained using LAAT alignment with importance scores provided by GPT-4o mini. The experimental results are presented in Figs. 4 and 5, corresponding to the γ variation and the number of importance score estimations, respectively.

Our findings indicate that increasing γ initially enhances model performance, reaching an optimal value around $\gamma = 100$. However, further increases beyond $\gamma = 250$ lead to a substantial decline in performance. In contrast, increasing the number of importance score estimations results in a steady performance improvement, which plateaus at approximately four to five estimations, depending on the k-shot setting. These results suggest that while additional score generation and ensembling can enhance performance, their benefits diminish beyond a certain threshold.

Table 5. ROC AUC scores of LLM-based models on the biased dataset experiments. Best scores for each dataset, across both LLM and non-LLM approaches, are emphasized in **bold**. Multiple bolded values indicate that their differences were not statistically significant according to the Wilcoxon signed-rank test at $p = 0.05$.

Method	FeatLLM		LAAT					
Model	Ensemble		LR			MLP		
Dataset	$Gem_{2.0}$	G_{4om}	$LLa_{3.3}$	$Gem_{2.0}$	G_{4om}	$LLa_{3.3}$	$Gem_{2.0}$	G_{4om}
bodyfat	$80.9_{6.4}$	$79.3_{6.2}$	$84.5_{16.2}$	$83.4_{18.0}$	$84.3_{17.0}$	$89.5_{4.2}$	$\mathbf{91.0_{3.6}}$	$90.4_{4.0}$
breast-ljub	$67.8_{8.7}$	$62.9_{7.2}$	$\mathbf{71.1_{9.6}}$	$71.1_{8.6}$	$70.5_{8.7}$	$\mathbf{73.6_{6.9}}$	$\mathbf{73.5_{6.8}}$	$\mathbf{73.2_{6.9}}$
cdc-diabetes	$75.4_{3.3}$	$76.1_{0.8}$	$72.5_{0.3}$	$\mathbf{79.0_{0.2}}$	$75.6_{0.3}$	$72.4_{0.3}$	$78.9_{0.3}$	$74.1_{0.9}$
contraceptive	$54.8_{8.6}$	$51.8_{3.9}$	$63.9_{3.4}$	$\mathbf{66.6_{2.2}}$	$62.9_{3.4}$	$63.9_{3.4}$	$66.1_{2.2}$	$62.9_{3.5}$
diabetes	$76.8_{3.8}$	$76.3_{2.8}$	$78.8_{6.9}$	$78.4_{7.2}$	$78.6_{7.3}$	$79.9_{4.1}$	$\mathbf{80.0_{3.9}}$	$\mathbf{80.2_{4.0}}$
indian-liver	$67.4_{6.4}$	$\mathbf{69.3_{6.1}}$	$71.1_{5.7}$	$71.4_{5.5}$	$69.3_{5.7}$	$\mathbf{72.1_{4.3}}$	$\mathbf{72.1_{3.9}}$	$71.2_{4.5}$
myocardial	$54.0_{9.2}$	$62.5_{5.1}$	$63.8_{6.2}$	$\mathbf{66.2_{6.4}}$	$64.4_{5.6}$	$59.4_{7.2}$	$\mathbf{64.8_{7.3}}$	$61.6_{7.3}$

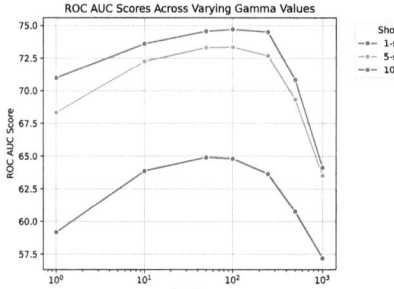

Fig. 4. ROC AUC scores of LAAT aligned logistic regression over varying gamma values.

Fig. 5. ROC AUC scores of LAAT aligned logistic regression over varying number of estimates.

5 Limitations

While LAAT offers significant benefits, it has several limitations. First, the method is restricted to tabular data and supports only binary classification tasks. Additionally, LAAT requires features to be describable in natural language, limiting its applicability to datasets with anonymized or uninterpretable features. Finally, its effectiveness depends on the general knowledge embedded in LLMs, which may vary across different data domains.

6 Conclusion

We introduce **L**arge **L**anguage **M**odel **A**ttribution **A**ligned **T**raining (**LAAT**), a novel approach that leverages importance scores inferred by large language models (LLMs) as local attribution guides. This method effectively harnesses the generalization capabilities of LLMs while employing simple, traditional machine learning models. Although gradient boosting trees have traditionally dominated tabular data learning, LAAT significantly outperforms existing methods in few-shot learning and biased dataset scenarios. Notably, it surpasses FeatLLM, the current state-of-the-art LLM-based few-shot learning approach.

Beyond its standalone effectiveness, LAAT is highly versatile and can be used in conjunction with more complex models, provided they are differentiable—for example, TabPFN. Additionally, it can be combined with feature preprocessing techniques such as FeatLLM. Given the interpretability of LLM-derived importance scores, LAAT could be incorporated into interactive, chat-based interfaces, enabling human experts to refine these scores before finalizing them. This human-in-the-loop refinement could further enhance model performance by leveraging domain expertise.

While we focus on input gradient-based attribution in this work, future research could explore alternative attribution methods to further enhance LAAT's effectiveness. Additionally, future research could explore extending LAAT to multiclass classification problems by generating LLM-based feature attribution vectors for each class. Subsequent training could regularize local attributions based on the class of the current example. Similarly, in regression tasks, the score generation prompt of LAAT could be adapted to accommodate continuous target variables.

Furthermore, LAAT's framework could be expanded beyond tabular data to other modalities, such as images, by integrating it into concept bottleneck models [32]. These architectures produce high-level, human-interpretable features that could serve as input to a LAAT-augmented classifier, facilitating improved feature selection and attribution in vision tasks. Such an extension could enhance both interpretability and generalization in image-based applications. We leave the exploration of these research directions to future work.

Disclosure of Interests. The authors have no competing interests to declare that are relevant to the content of this article.

Appendix

We provide dataset details, task descriptions, score extraction prompt, hyperparameter search spaces, and loss landscapes used in our experiments.

Prompt 1.1. Prompt template for LLM importance score generation.
```
You are an expert at assigning importance scores to features
used for a classification task. For each feature, output an
integer importance score between -10 and 10. Positive scores
suggest that an increase in the feature's value boosts the
class probability, whereas negative scores indicate that an
increase in the feature's value reduces the class probability.
You have to include a score for every feature.
```

Table 6. Basic information about dataset used in our experiments.

Dataset	Samples	Num. features	Cat. features	Pos. label ratio
adult	48842	14	8	23.93%
bank	45211	16	9	11.70%
breast-ljub	277	16	0	29.24%
cdc-diabetes	253680	21	0	13.93%
diabetes	768	8	0	34.90%
electricity	45312	8	0	42.45%
myocardial	686	91	13	22.16%

Table 7. Task descriptions utilized in the experiments.

Dataset	Task Description
adult	Predict whether this person earns more than 50000 dollars per year. Yes or no?
bank	Predict whether this client will subscribe to a term deposit. Yes or no?
breast-ljub	Predict whether this patient's breast cancer will reoccur. Yes or no?
cdc-diabetes	Predict whether the patient has diabetes. Yes or no?
diabetes	Predict whether the patient has diabetes. Yes or no?
electricity	In the electricity market, prices are not fixed and are affected by demand and supply of the market. They are set every five minutes. Electricity transfers in the state A to/from the neighboring state B are done to alleviate fluctuations. Based on the current measurement, predict whether the price of electricity in state A will go up. Yes or no?
myocardial	Predict whether the myocardial infarction complications data of this patient show chronic heart failure. Yes or no?

```
Task: {task_prompt}
Features:
{features_prompt}
Output the importance scores for the class "{label}".

Think step by step and output an integer importance score
between -10 and 10 for each feature. You must specify each
feature individually, in order of its appearance.
```

Table 8. Hyperparameter search spaces for baseline models.

Model	Hyperparameter search space
Logistic Regression	C: [100, 10, 1, 1e−1, 1e−2, 1e−3, 1e−4, 1e−5]
MLP	alpha: [0.001, 0.01, 0.1, 1, 10] learning_rate_init: [0.1, 0.01, 0.001, 0.0001]
XGBoost	max_depth: [2, 4, 6, 8, 10] alpha: [1e−4, 1e−3, 1e−2, 1e−1, 1, 10] lambda: [1e−4, 1e−3, 1e−2, 1e−1, 1, 10] eta: [0.01, 0.03, 0.1, 0.3]
Random Forest	bootstrap: [True, False] max_depth: [2, 4, 6, 8, 10] n_estimators: [2, 4, 8, 16, 32, 64]
CatBoost	colsample_bylevel: [0.01, 0.03, 0.06, 0.1] boosting_type: ["Ordered", "Plain"] depth: [2, 4, 6, 8, 10]

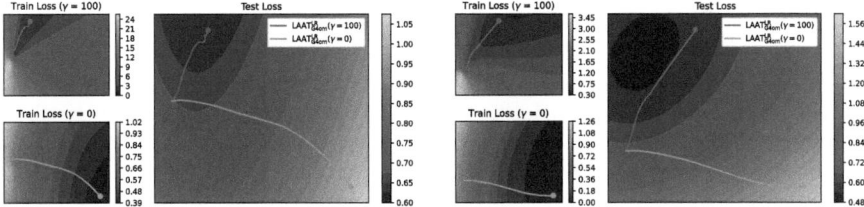

(a) Loss landscapes - **breast-ljub** dataset. (b) Loss landscapes - **myocardial** dataset.

Fig. 6. Loss landscapes for logistic regression on the **breast-ljub** and **myocardial** datasets, comparing models with ($\gamma = 100$, top left) and without ($\gamma = 0$, bottom left) attribution alignment loss. The addition of attribution alignment loss better aligns training (left) and test (right) loss landscapes, guiding the model towards minima that improve generalization.

References

1. U.S. Centers for Disease Control and Prevention, Behavioral Risk Factor Surveillance System, Annual Survey Data. UCI Machine Learning Repository (2015). Accessed 16 Dec 2024
2. Abnar, S., Zuidema, W.H.: Quantifying attention flow in transformers. In: Jurafsky, D., Chai, J., Schluter, N., Tetreault, J.R. (eds.) Proceedings of the 58th Annual Meeting of the Association for Computational Linguistics, ACL 2020, Online, 5–10 July 2020, pp. 4190–4197. Association for Computational Linguistics (2020). https://doi.org/10.18653/V1/2020.ACL-MAIN.385
3. Achtibat, R., et al.: AttnLRP: attention-aware layer-wise relevance propagation for transformers. In: Forty-first International Conference on Machine Learning, ICML 2024, Vienna, Austria, 21–27 July 2024. OpenReview.net (2024)

4. Arik, S.Ö., Pfister, T.: TabNet: attentive interpretable tabular learning. In: Thirty-Fifth AAAI Conference on Artificial Intelligence, AAAI 2021, Thirty-Third Conference on Innovative Applications of Artificial Intelligence, IAAI 2021, The Eleventh Symposium on Educational Advances in Artificial Intelligence, EAAI 2021, Virtual Event, 2–9 February 2021, pp. 6679–6687. AAAI Press (2021). https://doi.org/10.1609/AAAI.V35I8.16826
5. Bach, S., Binder, A., Montavon, G., Klauschen, F., Müller, K.R., Samek, W.: On pixel-wise explanations for non-linear classifier decisions by layer-wise relevance propagation. PLoS ONE **10**(7), e0130140 (2015). https://doi.org/10.1371/journal.pone.0130140
6. Bahri, D., Jiang, H., Tay, Y., Metzler, D.: SCARF: self-supervised contrastive learning using random feature corruption. In: The Tenth International Conference on Learning Representations, ICLR 2022, Virtual Event, 25–29 April 2022. OpenReview.net (2022)
7. Becker, B., Kohavi, R.: Adult. UCI Machine Learning Repository (1996). https://doi.org/10.24432/C5XW20
8. Bendi Ramana, N.V.: ILPD (Indian Liver Patient Dataset) (2022). https://doi.org/10.24432/C5D02C. https://archive.ics.uci.edu/dataset/225
9. Brown, T.B., et al.: Language models are few-shot learners. In: Larochelle, H., Ranzato, M., Hadsell, R., Balcan, M., Lin, H. (eds.) Advances in Neural Information Processing Systems 33: Annual Conference on Neural Information Processing Systems 2020, NeurIPS 2020, 6–12 December 2020, virtual (2020)
10. Chen, T., Guestrin, C.: XGBoost: a scalable tree boosting system. In: Krishnapuram, B., Shah, M., Smola, A.J., Aggarwal, C.C., Shen, D., Rastogi, R. (eds.) Proceedings of the 22nd ACM SIGKDD International Conference on Knowledge Discovery and Data Mining, San Francisco, CA, USA, 13–17 August 2016, pp. 785–794. ACM (2016). https://doi.org/10.1145/2939672.2939785
11. Chen, Z.: Ethics and discrimination in artificial intelligence-enabled recruitment practices. Humanit. Soc. Sci. Commun. **10**(1) (2023). https://doi.org/10.1057/s41599-023-02079-x. http://dx.doi.org/10.1057/s41599-023-02079-x
12. Choi, S., Park, H., Yeo, J., Hwang, S.: Less is more: attention supervision with counterfactuals for text classification. In: Webber, B., Cohn, T., He, Y., Liu, Y. (eds.) Proceedings of the 2020 Conference on Empirical Methods in Natural Language Processing, EMNLP 2020, Online, 16–20 November 2020, pp. 6695–6704. Association for Computational Linguistics (2020). https://doi.org/10.18653/V1/2020.EMNLP-MAIN.543
13. Devlin, J., Chang, M., Lee, K., Toutanova, K.: BERT: pre-training of deep bidirectional transformers for language understanding. In: Burstein, J., Doran, C., Solorio, T. (eds.) Proceedings of the 2019 Conference of the North American Chapter of the Association for Computational Linguistics: Human Language Technologies, NAACL-HLT 2019, Minneapolis, MN, USA, 2–7 June 2019, Volume 1 (Long and Short Papers), pp. 4171–4186. Association for Computational Linguistics (2019). https://doi.org/10.18653/V1/N19-1423
14. Dinh, T., et al.: LIFT: language-interfaced fine-tuning for non-language machine learning tasks. In: Koyejo, S., Mohamed, S., Agarwal, A., Belgrave, D., Cho, K., Oh, A. (eds.) Advances in Neural Information Processing Systems 35: Annual Conference on Neural Information Processing Systems 2022, NeurIPS 2022, New Orleans, LA, USA, November 28–December 9 2022 (2022)
15. Dorogush, A.V., Ershov, V., Gulin, A.: CatBoost: gradient boosting with categorical features support. CoRR **abs/1810.11363** (2018)

16. Dubey, A., et al.: The llama 3 herd of models. CoRR **abs/2407.21783** (2024). https://doi.org/10.48550/ARXIV.2407.21783
17. Erion, G.G., Janizek, J.D., Sturmfels, P., Lundberg, S.M., Lee, S.: Improving performance of deep learning models with axiomatic attribution priors and expected gradients. Nat. Mach. Intell. **3**(7), 620–631 (2021). https://doi.org/10.1038/S42256-021-00343-W
18. Gao, Y., Gu, S., Jiang, J., Hong, S.R., Yu, D., Zhao, L.: Going beyond XAI: a systematic survey for explanation-guided learning. ACM Comput. Surv. **56**(7), 188:1–188:39 (2024). https://doi.org/10.1145/3644073
19. Gao, Y., Sun, T.S., Bai, G., Gu, S., Hong, S.R., Zhao, L.: RES: a robust framework for guiding visual explanation. In: Zhang, A., Rangwala, H. (eds.) KDD 2022: The 28th ACM SIGKDD Conference on Knowledge Discovery and Data Mining, Washington, DC, USA, 14–18 August 2022, pp. 432–442. ACM (2022). https://doi.org/10.1145/3534678.3539419
20. Golovenkin, S., et al.: Myocardial infarction complications. UCI Machine Learning Repository (2020). https://doi.org/10.24432/C53P5M
21. Grinsztajn, L., Oyallon, E., Varoquaux, G.: Why do tree-based models still outperform deep learning on typical tabular data? In: Koyejo, S., Mohamed, S., Agarwal, A., Belgrave, D., Cho, K., Oh, A. (eds.) Advances in Neural Information Processing Systems 35: Annual Conference on Neural Information Processing Systems 2022, NeurIPS 2022, New Orleans, LA, USA, November 28–December 9 2022 (2022)
22. Han, S., Yoon, J., Arik, S.Ö., Pfister, T.: Large language models can automatically engineer features for few-shot tabular learning. In: Forty-First International Conference on Machine Learning, ICML 2024, Vienna, Austria, 21–27 July 2024. OpenReview.net (2024)
23. Harries, M., Wales, N.S., et al.: Splice-2 comparative evaluation: electricity pricing (1999)
24. Hegselmann, S., Buendia, A., Lang, H., Agrawal, M., Jiang, X., Sontag, D.A.: TabLLM: few-shot classification of tabular data with large language models. In: Ruiz, F.J.R., Dy, J.G., van de Meent, J. (eds.) International Conference on Artificial Intelligence and Statistics, Palau de Congressos, Valencia, Spain, 25–27 April 2023. Proceedings of Machine Learning Research, vol. 206, pp. 5549–5581. PMLR (2023)
25. Hoffmann, J., et al.: Training compute-optimal large language models. CoRR **abs/2203.15556** (2022). https://doi.org/10.48550/ARXIV.2203.15556
26. Hollmann, N.: Accurate predictions on small data with a tabular foundation model. Nat. **637**(8044), 319–326 (2025). https://doi.org/10.1038/S41586-024-08328-6
27. Hurst, A., et al.: GPT-4O system card. CoRR **abs/2410.21276** (2024). https://doi.org/10.48550/ARXIV.2410.21276
28. Kahn, M.: Diabetes. UCI Machine Learning Repository. https://doi.org/10.24432/C5T59G
29. Kanchinadam, T., Westpfahl, K., You, Q., Fung, G.: Rationale-based human-in-the-loop via supervised attention. In: Dragut, E.C., Li, Y., Popa, L., Vucetic, S. (eds.) 1st Workshop on Data Science with Human in the Loop, DaSH@KDD 2020, San Diego, California, USA, 24 August 2020 (2020)
30. KC, D., Zhang, C.: Improving the trustworthiness of image classification models by utilizing bounding-box annotations. CoRR **abs/2108.10131** (2021)
31. Kingma, D.P., Ba, J.: Adam: a method for stochastic optimization. In: Bengio, Y., LeCun, Y. (eds.) 3rd International Conference on Learning Representations, ICLR 2015, San Diego, CA, USA, 7–9 May 2015, Conference Track Proceedings (2015)

32. Koh, P.W., et al.: Concept bottleneck models. In: Proceedings of the 37th International Conference on Machine Learning, ICML 2020, 13–18 July 2020, Virtual Event. Proceedings of Machine Learning Research, vol. 119, pp. 5338–5348. PMLR (2020)
33. Kojima, T., Gu, S.S., Reid, M., Matsuo, Y., Iwasawa, Y.: Large language models are zero-shot reasoners. In: Koyejo, S., Mohamed, S., Agarwal, A., Belgrave, D., Cho, K., Oh, A. (eds.) Advances in Neural Information Processing Systems 35: Annual Conference on Neural Information Processing Systems 2022, NeurIPS 2022, New Orleans, LA, USA, November 28–December 9 2022 (2022)
34. Leemann, T., Fastowski, A., Pfeiffer, F., Kasneci, G.: Attention mechanisms don't learn additive models: rethinking feature importance for transformers. Trans. Mach. Learning Res. (2025). https://openreview.net/forum?id=yawWz4qWkF
35. Li, H., Xu, Z., Taylor, G., Studer, C., Goldstein, T.: Visualizing the loss landscape of neural nets. In: Proceedings of the 32nd International Conference on Neural Information Processing Systems, NIPS 2018, pp. 6391–6401. Curran Associates Inc., Red Hook (2018)
36. Liu, F., Avci, B.: Incorporating priors with feature attribution on text classification. In: Korhonen, A., Traum, D.R., Màrquez, L. (eds.) Proceedings of the 57th Conference of the Association for Computational Linguistics, ACL 2019, Florence, Italy, July 28–August 2 2019, Volume 1: Long Papers, pp. 6274–6283. Association for Computational Linguistics (2019). https://doi.org/10.18653/V1/P19-1631
37. Liu, H., Li, C., Wu, Q., Lee, Y.J.: Visual instruction tuning. In: Oh, A., Naumann, T., Globerson, A., Saenko, K., Hardt, M., Levine, S. (eds.) Advances in Neural Information Processing Systems 36: Annual Conference on Neural Information Processing Systems 2023, NeurIPS 2023, New Orleans, LA, USA, 10–16 December 2023 (2023)
38. Majmundar, K., Goyal, S., Netrapalli, P., Jain, P.: MET: masked encoding for tabular data. CoRR **abs/2206.08564** (2022). https://doi.org/10.48550/ARXIV.2206.08564
39. Min, S., et al.: Rethinking the role of demonstrations: what makes in-context learning work? In: Goldberg, Y., Kozareva, Z., Zhang, Y. (eds.) Proceedings of the 2022 Conference on Empirical Methods in Natural Language Processing, EMNLP 2022, Abu Dhabi, United Arab Emirates, 7–11 December 2022, pp. 11048–11064. Association for Computational Linguistics (2022). https://doi.org/10.18653/V1/2022.EMNLP-MAIN.759
40. Moro, S., Rita, P., Cortez, P.: Bank Marketing. UCI Machine Learning Repository (2014). https://doi.org/10.24432/C5K306
41. Nam, J., Tack, J., Lee, K., Lee, H., Shin, J.: STUNT: few-shot tabular learning with self-generated tasks from unlabeled tables. In: The Eleventh International Conference on Learning Representations, ICLR 2023, Kigali, Rwanda, 1–5 May 2023. OpenReview.net (2023)
42. Pedregosa, F., et al.: Scikit-learn: machine learning in Python. J. Mach. Learn. Res. **12**, 2825–2830 (2011)
43. Penrose, K.W., Nelson, A.G., Fisher, A.G.: Generalized body composition prediction equation for men using simple measurement techniques. Med. Sci. Sports Exercise **17**(2), 189 (1985). https://doi.org/10.1249/00005768-198504000-00037. http://dx.doi.org/10.1249/00005768-198504000-00037
44. Reid, M., et al.: Gemini 1.5: unlocking multimodal understanding across millions of tokens of context. CoRR **abs/2403.05530** (2024). https://doi.org/10.48550/ARXIV.2403.05530

45. Ross, A.S., Hughes, M.C., Doshi-Velez, F.: Right for the right reasons: training differentiable models by constraining their explanations. In: Sierra, C. (ed.) Proceedings of the Twenty-Sixth International Joint Conference on Artificial Intelligence, IJCAI 2017, Melbourne, Australia, 19–25 August 2017, pp. 2662–2670. ijcai.org (2017). https://doi.org/10.24963/IJCAI.2017/371
46. Seedat, N., Huynh, N., van Breugel, B., van der Schaar, M.: Curated LLM: synergy of LLMs and data curation for tabular augmentation in low-data regimes. In: Forty-first International Conference on Machine Learning, ICML 2024, Vienna, Austria, 21–27 July 2024. OpenReview.net (2024)
47. Selvaraju, R.R., Cogswell, M., Das, A., Vedantam, R., Parikh, D., Batra, D.: Grad-CAM: visual explanations from deep networks via gradient-based localization. Int. J. Comput. Vis. **128**(2), 336–359 (2020). https://doi.org/10.1007/S11263-019-01228-7
48. Shick, A.A., et al.: Transparency of artificial intelligence/machine learning-enabled medical devices. npj Digit. Med. **7**(1) (2024). https://doi.org/10.1038/S41746-023-00992-8
49. Shwartz-Ziv, R., Armon, A.: Tabular data: deep learning is not all you need. Inf. Fusion **81**, 84–90 (2022). https://doi.org/10.1016/J.INFFUS.2021.11.011
50. Slack, D., Singh, S.: TABLET: learning from instructions for tabular data. CoRR **abs/2304.13188** (2023). https://doi.org/10.48550/ARXIV.2304.13188
51. Solatorio, A.V., Dupriez, O.: REaLTabFormer: generating realistic relational and tabular data using transformers. CoRR **abs/2302.02041** (2023). https://doi.org/10.48550/ARXIV.2302.02041
52. Somepalli, G., Goldblum, M., Schwarzschild, A., Bruss, C.B., Goldstein, T.: SAINT: improved neural networks for tabular data via row attention and contrastive pre-training. CoRR **abs/2106.01342** (2021)
53. Lim, T.-S.: Contraceptive method choice (1999). https://doi.org/10.24432/C59W2D, https://archive.ics.uci.edu/dataset/30
54. Vaswani, A., et al.: Attention is all you need. In: Guyon, I., et al. (eds.) Advances in Neural Information Processing Systems 30: Annual Conference on Neural Information Processing Systems 2017, Long Beach, CA, USA, 4–9 December 2017, pp. 5998–6008 (2017)
55. Wang, Z., Gao, C., Xiao, C., Sun, J.: MediTab: scaling medical tabular data predictors via data consolidation, enrichment, and refinement. In: Proceedings of the Thirty-Third International Joint Conference on Artificial Intelligence, IJCAI 2024, Jeju, South Korea, 3–9 August 2024, pp. 6062–6070. ijcai.org (2024)
56. Wei, J., et al.: Chain-of-thought prompting elicits reasoning in large language models. In: Koyejo, S., Mohamed, S., Agarwal, A., Belgrave, D., Cho, K., Oh, A. (eds.) Advances in Neural Information Processing Systems 35: Annual Conference on Neural Information Processing Systems 2022, NeurIPS 2022, New Orleans, LA, USA, November 28–December 9 2022 (2022)
57. Weinberger, E., Janizek, J.D., Lee, S.: Learning deep attribution priors based on prior knowledge. In: Larochelle, H., Ranzato, M., Hadsell, R., Balcan, M., Lin, H. (eds.) Advances in Neural Information Processing Systems 33: Annual Conference on Neural Information Processing Systems 2020, NeurIPS 2020, 6–12 December 2020, virtual (2020)
58. Yoon, J., Zhang, Y., Jordon, J., van der Schaar, M.: VIME: extending the success of self- and semi-supervised learning to tabular domain. In: Larochelle, H., Ranzato, M., Hadsell, R., Balcan, M., Lin, H. (eds.) Advances in Neural Information Processing Systems 33: Annual Conference on Neural Information Processing Systems 2020, NeurIPS 2020, 6–12 December 2020, virtual (2020)

59. Zhang, P., et al.: InternLM-XComposer2.5-OmniLive: a comprehensive multimodal system for long-term streaming video and audio interactions. CoRR **abs/2412.09596** (2024). https://doi.org/10.48550/ARXIV.2412.09596
60. Zhang, T., Wang, S., Yan, S., Jian, L., Liu, Q.: Generative table pre-training empowers models for tabular prediction. In: Bouamor, H., Pino, J., Bali, K. (eds.) Proceedings of the 2023 Conference on Empirical Methods in Natural Language Processing, EMNLP 2023, Singapore, 6–10 December 2023, pp. 14836–14854. Association for Computational Linguistics (2023). https://doi.org/10.18653/V1/2023.EMNLP-MAIN.917
61. Zhong, R., Shao, S., McKeown, K.R.: Fine-grained sentiment analysis with faithful attention. CoRR **abs/1908.06870** (2019)
62. Zwitter, M., Soklic, M.: Breast Cancer. UCI Machine Learning Repository (1988). https://doi.org/10.24432/C51P4M

Open Access This chapter is licensed under the terms of the Creative Commons Attribution 4.0 International License (http://creativecommons.org/licenses/by/4.0/), which permits use, sharing, adaptation, distribution and reproduction in any medium or format, as long as you give appropriate credit to the original author(s) and the source, provide a link to the Creative Commons license and indicate if changes were made.

The images or other third party material in this chapter are included in the chapter's Creative Commons license, unless indicated otherwise in a credit line to the material. If material is not included in the chapter's Creative Commons license and your intended use is not permitted by statutory regulation or exceeds the permitted use, you will need to obtain permission directly from the copyright holder.

GraphXAIN: Narratives to Explain Graph Neural Networks

Mateusz Cedro[✉] and David Martens

University of Antwerp, 2000 Antwerp, Belgium
{mateusz.cedro,david.martens}@uantwerpen.be

Abstract. Graph Neural Networks (GNNs) are a powerful technique for machine learning on graph-structured data, yet they pose challenges in interpretability. Existing GNN explanation methods usually yield technical outputs, such as subgraphs and feature importance scores, that are difficult to understand, thereby violating the purpose of explanations. Motivated by recent Explainable AI (XAI) research, we propose *GraphXAIN*, a method that generates natural language narratives explaining GNN prediction. GraphXAIN is a model- and explainer-agnostic method that uses Large Language Models (LLMs) to translate explanatory subgraphs and feature importance scores into coherent, story-like explanations of GNN predictions. Evaluation on real-world datasets demonstrates GraphXAIN's ability to improve graph explanations. A survey of machine learning researchers and practitioners reveals that GraphXAIN enhances four explainability dimensions: understandability, satisfaction, convincingness, and suitability for communicating model predictions. When combined with another graph explainer method, GraphXAIN further improves trustworthiness, insightfulness, confidence, and usability. Notably, 95% of participants find GraphXAIN to be a valuable addition to the current GNN explanation methods. By incorporating natural language narratives, our approach serves both graph practitioners and non-expert users by providing clearer and more effective explanations.

Keywords: Explainable AI · Graph Neural Networks · Generative AI · Generative XAI · Natural Language Explanations · XAI Narratives

1 Introduction

The exponential growth in the complexity of machine learning models has led to architectures reaching billions of parameters, resulting in significant improvements in their performance [5,13,26,39]. As these complex 'black-box' models, characterized by their high accuracy yet lack of interpretability, continue to evolve, the demand for transparency and understanding of the underlying model processes has intensified [35]. Explainable Artificial Intelligence (XAI) has emerged to address this challenge by enhancing the trustworthiness and transparency of the predictions of complex AI models [18].

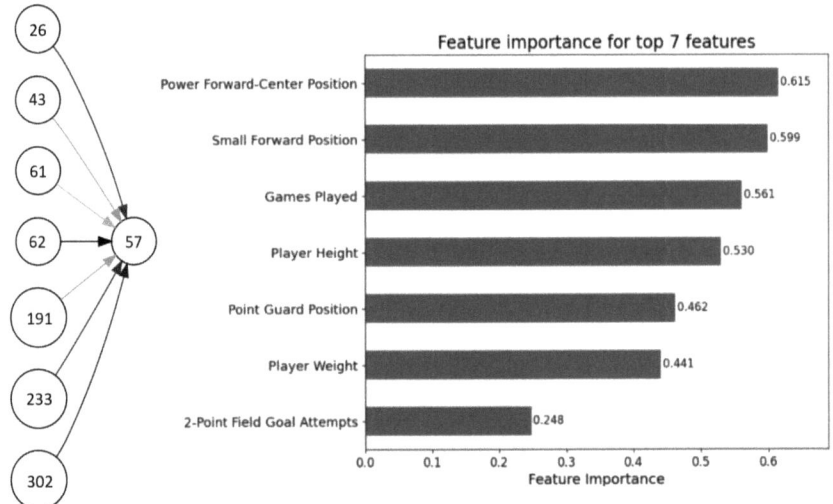

Fig. 1. LLM-generated GraphXAIN (bottom part) complements the explanatory subgraph and feature importance output of GNNExplainer [47] (top part), providing a comprehensive explanation of the GNN's prediction of salary level classification for the NBA player (node 57).

Graph Neural Networks (GNNs) have recently gained notable success and have become state-of-the-art solutions for modelling relational data, characterized by instances (nodes) being connected via edges [21,40,44,46]. However, the need for interpretability of the GNNs' predictions remains [23,25,47].

Existing GNN explanation techniques [25,47] predominantly offer explanatory subgraphs and feature-importance attributions. This is illustrated in the upper section of Fig. 1, which shows the explanation produced by GNNExplainer [47] for a GNN model's prediction on a real-world dataset. The example presents the explanation for the classification of node (player) 57 from the NBA dataset, taking into account the player's attributes, field statistics, and social connections. For a node regression example, which illustrates the explanation for the prediction of the IMDB movie rating for node (movie) 95 based on the movie features and relations to other movies being connected via shared actors, see Fig. 4b in A.1.

GNNExplainer output provides some insights into the prediction process, however, the correct interpretation of the subgraph visualization alongside feature importance metrics alone can pose significant challenges for readers. Without a complementary natural language narrative, practitioners employing this explanation technique to analyse the GNN's prediction must rely solely on subgraphs and feature importance outputs, which can be particularly challenging given the complex nature of GNN models. Despite its limitations, GNNExplainer remains a state-of-the-art graph explainer. Such an approach is not aligned with the *comprehensibility postulate* introduced by Michalski [30], which advocates that computer-generated results should be directly interpretable in natural language. Moreover, effective explanations should enhance the alignment between the user's mental model and the AI model [20,29]. GNNExplainer, among other graph explainers, does not adhere to these principles and exemplifies the phenomenon termed the *"Inmates Running the Asylum"*, where solutions are technical and created primarily for experts, overlooking the needs of less-technical practitioners and end users who prefer natural-language explanations [6,28,33].

Martens et al. [28] proposed the XAIstories framework that employs Large Language Models (LLMs) to generate narratives explaining the AI model's predictions for tabular and image data based on SHAP and counterfactual (CF) explanations. In their survey among data scientists and lay users, over 90% of the general audience found these narratives convincing, while 83% of the surveyed data scientists indicated they would likely use XAIstories to communicate explanations to non-expert audiences. By incorporating narrative communication to technical XAI methods, the model's predictions can be presented in a manner that aligns with human cognitive preferences, elevating explanations beyond mere descriptions and clarifying cause-and-effect relationships [6].

To the best of our knowledge, no previous research proposes the general framework for natural language XAI Narratives to explain Graph Neural Network models' predictions. In this article, we introduce the first method to automatically generate *GraphXAIN*, a natural language narrative, to explain the GNN models. By complementing explanatory subgraphs and feature importances with coherent XAI Narratives (see Fig. 2), we aim to further explain the GNNs' predictions in a more transparent and accessible way. We posit that this method will not only enhance interpretability but also facilitate more effective communication of model predictions across various graph applications.

To summarise, our main contributions are as follows:

- We present the GraphXAIN, a novel model-agnostic and explainer-agnostic method that generates natural language XAI Narratives to enhance the explainability of the model's predictions over graph-structured data.

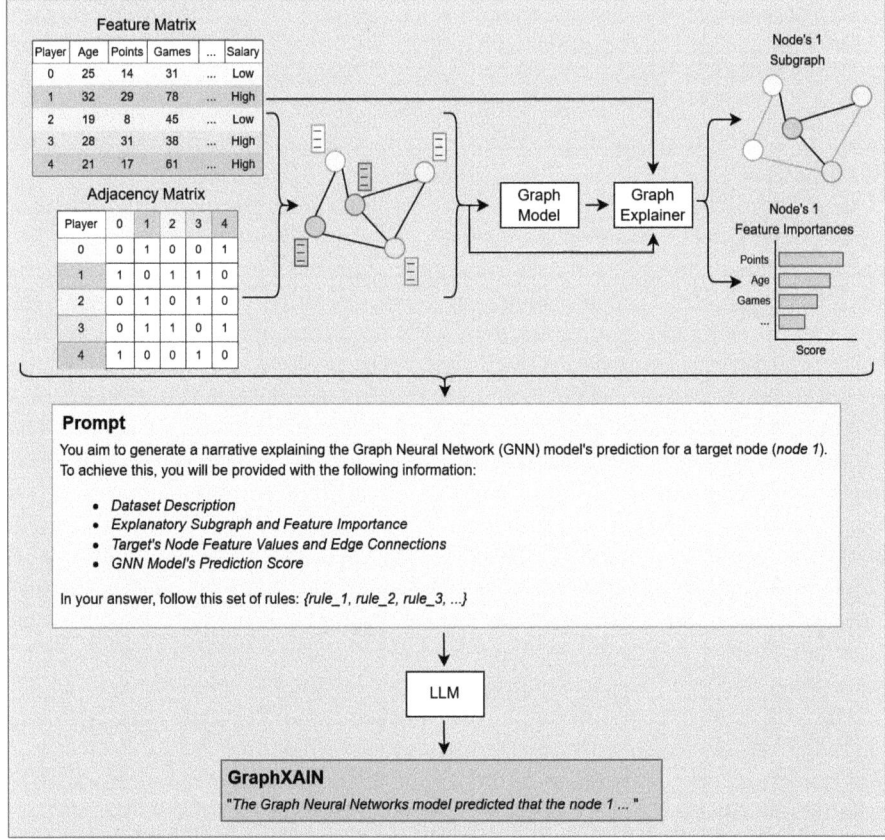

Fig. 2. Workflow diagram of the GraphXAIN method. Graph-structured data, along with its corresponding features, is first processed by a GNN model. Next, a graph explainer generates an explanatory subgraph and corresponding feature importance values for a target node. The dataset description, explanatory subgraph, feature importance values, target node features and edge connections, and final GNN prediction are then incorporated into a prompt. This prompt is processed by the LLM, which generates GraphXAIN, a complementary narrative to explain GNN's prediction.

- We illustrate our approach by integrating GraphXAIN with the existing graph XAI framework (GNNExplainer) for GNNs and demonstrating its explanatory abilities on real-world datasets, both in classification and regression tasks.
- We qualitatively assess the GraphXAIN method with a user study conducted with machine learning practitioners.
- We formalise the concepts of narrative and descriptive explanations within the context of XAI, clarifying their distinctions and discussing their implications for model explainability.

2 Related Work

2.1 Explainability in Machine Learning

Several approaches have been proposed to enhance the explainability of machine learning models across various modalities, including image data [1,16,39,41,43], tabular data [4,26,39], natural language [26,39,43], and unstructured data such as graphs [25,47]. Among the most popular XAI methodologies are post-hoc explanations, which aim to explain the model's prediction after the training stage [35]. The counterfactual explanations indicate what minimal changes in the input data are required to obtain a different predicted class [29,45]. These methods comprise feature importance measures, visualisation techniques, and surrogate models. For instance, SHAP (SHapley Additive exPlanations [26]) and LIME (Local Interpretable Model-agnostic Explanations [39]) estimate the contribution of each feature to a particular prediction.

However, despite these advancements, challenges persist in ensuring that explanations are both methodologically accurate and meaningful for a variety of stakeholders, both for the data scientists and lay users [11,28,36]. Explanations must bridge the gap between technical complexity and the reader's comprehension, necessitating a careful balance between fidelity and interpretability [6,33]. The need for explainability methods that are understandable to less technical users is primarily crucial in sensitive domains such as healthcare, finance, and legal systems, where understanding the model's prediction process is essential for trust and transparency [35,39] for both domain experts and end users. As the conversational AI explanation systems have been studied previously [22,27,42], the LLM's general knowledge presents a promising avenue for enriching targeted explanations with additional insights [48].

2.2 Explainability in Graph Neural Networks

GNNs are increasingly used for modelling relational data in domains such as social networks, molecular structures, and knowledge graphs [21,40,44]. Their complex architectures, however, pose challenges for understanding and interpreting their predictions. GNNExplainer [47] is the first method developed to address GNNs' explanations by identifying an explanatory subgraph and relevant node features which are the most influential for a specific prediction. GNNExplainer formulates the explanation task as an optimisation problem, maximising the mutual information between the explanatory subgraph with a subset of node features and the original graph that is subject to explanation.

Among other graph explanation methods, Lucic et al. [25] introduced CF-GNNExplainer, which alters the GNNExplainer to answer 'what-if' questions using the counterfactual explanation approach. Rather than merely identifying influential features or subgraphs, CF-GNNExplainer searches for minimal perturbations to the original graph that would change the GNN model's prediction by edge deletion. This method demonstrates how small changes in graph structure could impact the outcome, enhancing the understanding of the model's decision-making process.

Although the aforementioned state-of-the-art graph explanation frameworks are methodologically sound, they merely provide users with additional graphs and node feature importance values that are not easily interpretable (see Fig. 1 and Fig. 4b), thereby limiting their practical utility and force practitioners to construct the explanatory narrative themselves.

We posit that incorporating natural language into GNN explanations could bridge the gap between technical outputs and human understanding by translating complex model reasoning into accessible narratives, thereby enhancing comprehension and trust among practitioners. However, previous methods to generate them are not tailored to the popular GNNExplainer output and/or provide descriptive explanations rather than a cohesive narrative (see Subsect. 3.1 for a discussion of the important differences). Giorgi et al. [10] addressed this issue by using LLMs to generate textual explanations for counterfactual graphs. However, their explanations lack contextual information and do not illustrate cause-and-effect relationships, resulting in primarily descriptive communication rather than narrative explanation, the latter being more valuable for conveying more complex information [6] (see Appendix A.2 for examples).

He et al. [15] used LLMs to generate explanations for counterfactual graphs in the context of molecular property prediction. However, since their framework adheres to domain-specific knowledge, it cannot be considered a general method for graph model explanations with natural language explanations. Furthermore, the explanations produced by their method exhibit the same limitation as in Giorgi et al. [10], being more descriptive rather than narrative in their nature (see Appendix A.3 for examples).

The most comparable approach to ours is presented by Pan et al. [36], who developed TAGExplainer, a method for generating natural language explanations for Text-Attributed Graphs (TAGs). Although their explanations incorporate some elements of narrative communication, the examples provided by the authors consist of bullet points of information that can be rearranged without affecting the conveyed message, which is a characteristic aligning with descriptive writing rather than a coherent narrative [6]. Consequently, the proposed explanations remain context-independent. Moreover, the proposed method is limited only to TAGs, which limits the general use of TAGExplainer to broader graph data modelling scenarios, as TAGs represent only a subset of real-world graph data (see Appendix A.4 for examples).

3 Methods

3.1 XAI Narrative and Description

Research in psychology and communication theory indicates that narrative-based explanations are more accessible and memorable than descriptive forms, making them effective for conveying scientific evidence to non-expert audiences [6]. Moreover, narratives are processed more rapidly by individuals without prior knowledge and are more engaging and persuasive, thereby enhancing trust and understanding of AI models [3,28,33].

Further, as narrative communication relies on contextual cause-and-effect relationships, it is considerably more challenging to fragment a narrative into smaller, meaningful segments without either significantly altering the interpretation of these segments or disrupting the coherence of the original narrative [6]. Consequently, narratives are often perceived as storytelling, characterised by a coherent structure comprising an introduction, a main body, and a conclusion. In contrast, descriptive, context-free communication can be readily fragmented into smaller units while still effectively conveying the necessary information [6], however, at the cost of understanding and remembering. The XAIstories method addresses the aforementioned explanation limitations by enhancing the narrative communication of SHAP and CF explanations of models trained on tabular and image data, aligning with the research on human-AI interactions [3,28,33].

Having identified the need to distinguish between narrative and descriptive explanations in XAI and drawing on social science research [6,7,12,33], we propose definitions for both terms:

Definition 1 (XAI Narrative). *A XAI Narrative provides a structured, story-like representation of a model's prediction. Narrative explanations illustrate the relationships between key features in a context-dependent manner, providing a coherent and comprehensive understanding of how the model arrives at specific outcomes.*

Definition 2 (XAI Description). *A XAI Description provides a static presentation of key features or attributes relevant to a model's prediction, delivered in a context-free and fact-based manner.*

In the context of explaining GNN models, a description would just list the most important features and neighbouring nodes. This relates closely to the data-to-text or graph-to-text approaches [9,37]. Figure 3 presents an example of XAI Description for the subgraph and feature importance output provided by GNNExplainer shown in Fig. 1. Clearly, a XAI Description is less valuable than an XAI Narrative, as descriptions are less accessible and memorable than narrative communication methods, making them less effective for conveying scientific evidence to a broader audience [6,28].

From the XAI Description presented in Fig. 3, a clear template may be derived: *Prediction of instance X is Y based on:* x_1 *(importance score of feature* x_1*), feature* x_2 *(importance score of feature* x_2*), feature* x_3 *(importance score of feature* x_3*), ..., feature* x_n *(importance score of feature* x_n*)*. Regarding the connections between the nodes, a XAI Description would just describe which connections appear in the subgraph, however, not reflecting their meaning, which is seen in the bottom of the Fig. 3. In conveying the information to the reader, if the order of the features or connections mentioned in the text were changed, the information conveyed itself would persist, contrary to the assumption of the coherency and context-dependent manner and therefore violates the definition of XAI Narrative. The GraphXAIN examples shown in Fig. 1 and Fig. 4b, provide more coherent story, and are enhanced by LLM's general knowledge cause-and-effect narration as an explanation, which is aligned with the recommendations regarding effective scientific communication [6,12].

> **Example of the XAI Description of GNN's prediction for player (node) 57**
>
> Node 57 is predicted as "High Salary" based on the following features importances: Power Forward-Center Position (0.615), Small Forward Position (0.599), Games Played (0.561), Player Height (0.530), Point Guard Position (0.462), Player Weight (0.441), and 2-Point Field Goal Attempts (0.248). The number of games played significantly influences the model prediction towards "High Salary". The player's height, recorded at 200.66 cm, places them near the median of the height distribution among the players.
>
> The Twitter interaction subgraph reinforces this prediction, with a heavily weighted connection to node 62 (labelled "Low Salary") and additional connections to nodes 302, 233, and 26 (labelled "High Salary").

Fig. 3. LLM-generated XAI Description for the GNNExplainer's [47] subgraph and feature importance explain the GNN's prediction for player (node) 57. Compared to GraphXAIN's output, XAI Description focuses on features and connections in a static and context-free format, which is less valuable than a XAI Narrative.

3.2 From GNNs to Natural Language Narratives

To address the limitations of existing XAI methods for GNNs, which usually produce technical outputs, we propose GraphXAINs, which are natural language explanatory narratives for graphs. We propose the following definition of GraphXAIN, a XAI Narratives for graphs:

Definition 3 (GraphXAIN). *A GraphXAIN is a XAI Narrative tailored for graph-structured data.*

Our solution involves converting subgraph structures and feature importance scores derived from graph explainers, dataset information, and external knowledge of the LLM into GraphXAINs, resulting in coherent natural language explanatory narratives that explain GNN predictions. The detailed workflow to generate the GraphXAINs in presented in Fig. 2.

Following the approach proposed by Fatemi et al. [8], we transform the graph into the textual form for LLM's further inference. Importantly, our framework is agnostic to the graph data type, graph model, performed task (classification and regression), and graph explainer, allowing its application across various graph scenarios and applications.

4 Experiments

4.1 Datasets

We conduct the experiments on two real-world graph datasets, one used in the node classification scenario and the other in the node regression task. The dataset for the node classification, the NBA players' dataset[1], includes players' performance statistics from one basketball season, alongside various personal attributes such as height, weight, age, and nationality. The graph is constructed by linking NBA players based on their relationships and interactions on the Twitter platform. After preprocessing, filtering out disconnected nodes, and ensuring the graph is undirected, the final graph comprised 400 nodes (players), 42 node features, and 21,242 edges (Twitter connections). The node classification involves predicting whether a player's salary exceeds the median salary.

The dataset used to perform node regression, the IMDB movie dataset[2], includes information on 1,000 movies from the IMDB database. The movie's features consist of information on the director, main actors, release year, duration, and genre. The graph is created by connecting nodes (movies) by edges which link movies if at least one actor played in both movies. In total, the graph consists of 1,000 nodes, 12 node features, and 5,608 undirected edges. The node regression task involves predicting the IMDB rating score ranging between 0 and 10, where 10 is the maximum score indicating the general appreciation of the movie by the audience.

4.2 Graph Models

Prior to training, both datasets are randomly divided into separate training, validation, and test sets in a 60/20/20 split. We systematically explore different hyperparameter settings for both classification and regression GNN models, adjusting the number of layers (2–4), number of hidden channels (8, 16, 31, 64, 128), learning rates (0.001, 0.005, 0.01, 0.02, 0.05), weight decay (1×10^{-4}, 5×10^{-4}, 1×10^{-3}), and training epochs (100, 500, 1,000, 5,000, 10,000) to evaluate performance on the held-out test sets. The GNN classification model consists of two Graph Convolutional Network (GCN) layers [21], with 16 hidden channels. For training, we use the Binary Cross-Entropy loss function, the AdamW [24] optimizer with a learning rate of 0.001 and a weight decay of 5×10^{-4}. The training continued for 1,400 epochs, resulting in the GCN classification model that achieved a test AUC of 0.80.

The GNN regressor model consists of two GCN layers with 32 hidden channels. The Root Mean Square Error loss function is used to train the model, with the AdamW optimizer, a learning rate of 0.01 and a weight decay of 5×10^{-4}. The training process continues for 7,500 epochs, with the early stopping of 500 steps, resulting in the RMSE of 0.28 on the test set.

4.3 Graph Explainer

To obtain the explanatory subgraph and feature importance scores, we use GNNExplainer [47], the current state-of-the-art method for explaining GNN

---

[1] https://kaggle.com/noahgift/social-power-nba.
[2] https://kaggle.com/datasets/harshitshankhdhar/imdb-dataset-of-top-1000-movies-and-tv-shows.

models' predictions. The GNNExplainer formulates the explanation task as an optimization problem that maximizes the mutual information between the explanatory subgraph and a subset of node features relative to the input graph under consideration. In both scenarios (classification and regression), the GNNExplainer training process are conducted for 200 epochs, adhering to the default settings recommended by the authors [47]. In the explanatory subgraph, different shades of the edges indicate the strength of the importance of each connection, with darker edges indicating higher strength. However, to generate the GraphXAINs, any graph explainer may be used as long as it provides an explanatory subgraph and feature importance.

4.4 Graphs and Large Language Models

The XAI Narratives are derived from the GNNExplainer output using an LLM. In this work, we use GPT-4o, however, any LLM may be used to generate GraphXAINs. In our method we use LLM in a zero-shot manner with the default hyperparameters. The base of the prompt is inspired by earlier works on narratives aiming to explain machine learning models developed on tabular data [19,28], which we adapt to graphs and then refine through iterative manual adjustments until we achieve reasonable narratives. A thorough prompt engineering process could yield further improvements and help assess sensitivity to minor prompt changes.

The prompt includes the following information (see Fig. 2): dataset information, the target node's feature values, the feature importance, the explanatory subgraph, the feature values of the nodes within the subgraph, and the final GNN model prediction for the target node.

In our visualisations, we use the seven most important features and restrict the subgraph to output seven nodes with the highest importance, aligning with Miller's [31] theory on cognitive limits, which suggests that seven pieces of information represent an optimal amount for receiving, processing and recalling. However, the number of presented nodes in the subgraph and the number of most important features may be changed. Figure 2 presents the generation process in detail. The full prompt used to generate GraphXAINs is available in the article's GitHub repository[3].

5 Results

In the following, we provide examples presenting various automatically generated GraphXAINs to explain the GNN model's prediction for the target node. It is important to clarify that the presented results are not selectively chosen - rather, subsets of five nodes from the test sets (subject to explanation) are randomly drawn from both datasets. The GraphXAINs are subsequently generated for each of the drawn nodes. Figure 1 and Fig. 4b present examples of generated

---

[3] https://github.com/ADMAntwerp/GraphXAIN.

GraphXAINs for node classification and node regression tasks, respectively. For the other GraphXAIN example, see Appendix A.1.

The results of the GraphXAINs show the effectiveness of generating XAI narrative-based explanations from the technical and context-free subgraphs and feature importance values. Unlike other GNN XAI descriptive outputs, which typically present static feature values, the outputs generated by our method provide coherent XAI Narratives. Not only do these narratives articulate which features contributed most to the model's prediction, but they also explain how and why these features combined in a cause-and-effect manner. For instance, the narrative for a high-salary prediction highlights the player's field and performance statistics, such as position and the number of games played, simultaneously contextualising these with, arguably, broader patterns of team dynamics, basketball domain considerations, and social interactions.

GraphXAIN approach ensures that the explanation is not limited to mere numerical and visual descriptions but instead offers a comprehensive, story-like narrative that enables the practitioners to understand the model's decision-making process more intuitively. By conveying the reasoning beyond the sole prediction, the XAI Narrative explanation addresses a primary goal in XAI by bridging the gap between technical model outputs and practitioner's comprehension, thereby reflecting both the principles of narrative communication and the general objectives of explainability research [6].

Note that in the IMDB dataset, movie titles are available and directly mapped to nodes, whereas in the NBA dataset, player names are hashed, preventing their direct mapping. We hypothesize that having actual names would allow GraphXAIN to produce more effective explanations by drawing additional information on specific player information from LLM's knowledge.

6 Evaluation with Human Subjects: A User Study

To evaluate the proposed GraphXAIN method, we conducted an online user study similar to Martens et al. [28] and Baniecki et al. [2]. Twenty active researchers and practitioners from the field of machine learning (ML) and data science (DS) participated in the evaluation survey. Seventy-five percent of the participants are academic ML researchers, and the remaining 25% are industry ML/DS practitioners. Regarding professional experience, 30% of the participants had between 0 and 2 years of experience, 50% had 3 to 5 years, 15% had 6 to 10 years, and 5% had more than 10 years of experience in the domain. The survey was distributed to the authors' network, however, none of the respondents participated in developing the proposed method, ensuring that the responses are valid and unbiased.

The purpose of the survey was to evaluate the impact of the proposed GraphXAIN method in comparison with the current state-of-the-art GNN XAI method, GNNExplainer [47], to explain GNN predictions. Six randomized GNN explanation examples were shown to each participant sequentially. After viewing each singe XAI method, participants are asked to rate their agreement with

Table 1. Survey Questions for Assessing Explainable AI Method Perceptions

Dimension	Question
Understandability	Q1: I find the explanation understandable.
Trustworthiness	Q2: This explanation increased my trust in the model's prediction.
Insightfulness	Q3: The explanation helped me gain insight into the factors influencing the classification/regression.
Satisfaction	Q4: I am satisfied with the explanation's clarity and thoroughness.
Confidence	Q5: I feel confident in the classification/regression after reviewing the explanation.
Convincingness	Q6: I find this explanation convincing in justifying why node X is classified as Y/predicted to have a regression score of Y.
Communicability	Q7: I find this explanation method suitable for communicating the model's predictions to others.
Usability	Q8: If I work with Graph Neural Network models in the future, I am likely to use this explanation method to explain the model's prediction.

eight questions on a five-point Likert scale, ranging from "Strongly disagree" (1) to "Strongly agree" (5), where higher scores indicate stronger agreement or preference. Each participant was presented with three examples drawn from each of the classification and regression scenarios: 1) GNNExplainer [47] explanation comprising a subgraph and feature importance attributions, 2) GraphXAIN, which provides a narrative explanation of the model's prediction, 3) a combined approach that integrates GNNExplainer and GraphXAIN. The order of method presentation was randomized.

Respondents evaluated XAI methods across eight dimensions: understandability, trustworthiness, insightfulness, satisfaction, confidence, convincingness, communicability, and usability. Table 1 presents the survey questions used to measure each dimension. The following section presents the theoretical principles for selecting these evaluation criteria.

- Understandability - In Hoffman et al. [17], Miller [32], and Mohseni et al. [34], the understanding of XAI explanation is declared to be a crucial part of the XAI methods to ensure understandability of the rationale behind the model's predictions.
- Trustworthiness - Hoffman et al. [17] note that fostering appropriate trust is one of the core objectives of explanations, underscoring the need to assess whether an explanation effectively increases trust.

- Insightfulness - Riberio et al. [39] declare that a good explanation should provide additional insights into model predictions.
- Satisfaction - Miller [32] investigates the cognitive and social dimensions that render explanations meaningful to humans, positing that, among others, practitioner and user satisfaction is fundamental to effective explanatory strategies.
- Confidence - Ribeiro et al. [38] argue that explanations should enable individuals to gain confidence in the model.
- Convincingness - Miller [32] underscores that an explanation must be persuasive to the user.
- Communicability - Miller [32] argues that the information exchanged between the explainer and the explainee should align with the general rules of cooperative conversation proposed by Grice [12], ensuring that it remains relevant to the explainee's context and builds upon their prior knowledge.
- Usability - Miller [33] argues that individuals evaluate explanations according to pragmatic influences of causality, which encompass criteria such as usefulness.

Table 2 presents the survey results along with the statistical significance of Wilcoxon signed-rank tests assessing the differences between XAI methods, conducted at the $\alpha = 0.05$ significance level.

In a preference comparison between GNNExplainer (presented in Table 2 as the "GNNExp" method) and GraphXAIN, the latter is preferred in four dimensions (understandability, satisfaction, convincingness, and communicability), while no statistically significant differences are observed in the remaining four dimensions.

Evaluation of the GraphXAIN alone against a combined explanation that integrates GNNExplainer's outputs with the GraphXAIN narratives (presented in Table 2 as the "Combined" method), only one dimension, communicability, shows a statistically significant difference, with the combined method being preferred. For the remaining seven dimensions, no significant differences between GraphXAIN and the combined approach occur, indicating the power and the need of narrative explanations to explain graph models.

Moreover, across all eight investigated dimensions, the combined method is always preferred over the GNNExplainer method. This finding suggests that incorporating GraphXAIN's narrative component into the technical subgraph and feature importance explanations consistently enhances the overall quality of the explanation.

Furthermore, 95% of participants (19/20) answered "Yes" to the question, "Do you think that the narratives are a useful addition to explaining the GNN model's predictions?". This response aligns with the observed advantages of the alone and combined approaches over the stand-alone GNNExplainer outputs.

Additionally, at the $\alpha = 0.05$ significance level, no statistically significant differences are identified between responses over the NBA and IMDB datasets across any condition or question. Overall, these findings indicate that partici-

Table 2. Pairwise post-hoc Wilcoxon signed-rank tests comparing XAI methods for each dimension question. Higher values indicate increased preference on a 5-point Likert scale (1–5). "GNNExp" refers to GNNExplainer [47], while "Combined" refers to combined GNNExplainer and GraphXAIN outputs. Columns M_1 and M_2 report the mean ± standard deviation (SD) of participants' preferences, $\Delta(M_2, M_1)$ is the mean difference (with SD). Bonferroni-corrected p-values are reported (* indicates statistical significance at $\alpha = 0.05$). Bolded methods indicate statistically significant preferences.

Dimension	Method Comparison (M_1 vs M_2)	$M_1 \uparrow$	$M_2 \uparrow$	$\Delta(M_2, M_1)$	p
Understandability	GNNExp vs **GraphXAIN**	3.3±0.8	4.3±0.5	0.95±1.02	0.004*
	GNNExp vs **Combined**	3.3±0.8	4.4±0.6	1.05±0.94	0.003*
	GraphXAIN vs Combined	4.3±0.5	4.4±0.6	0.1±0.58	1.000
Trustworthiness	GNNExp vs GraphXAIN	3.3±0.7	3.8±0.6	0.42±1.03	0.254
	GNNExp vs **Combined**	3.3±0.7	4.2±0.6	0.92±0.94	0.005*
	GraphXAIN vs Combined	3.8±0.6	4.2±0.6	0.5±0.84	0.072
Insightfulness	GNNExp vs GraphXAIN	3.9±0.6	4.2±0.4	0.28±0.62	0.178
	GNNExp vs **Combined**	3.9±0.6	4.4±0.6	0.5±0.63	0.018*
	GraphXAIN vs Combined	4.2±0.4	4.4±0.6	0.22±0.50	0.251
Satisfaction	GNNExp vs **GraphXAIN**	3.0±1.1	3.8±0.6	0.85±1.29	0.045*
	GNNExp vs **Combined**	3.0±1.1	4.0±0.6	1.05±1.0	0.003*
	GraphXAIN vs Combined	3.8±0.6	4.0±0.6	0.2±0.70	0.586
Confidence	GNNExp vs GraphXAIN	3.0±0.9	3.6±0.7	0.62±1.09	0.085
	GNNExp vs **Combined**	3.0±0.9	3.9±0.8	0.88±1.17	0.015*
	GraphXAIN vs Combined	3.6±0.7	3.9±0.8	0.25±1.02	0.786
Convincingness	GNNExp vs **GraphXAIN**	3.2±0.7	3.8±0.8	0.62±0.96	0.030*
	GNNExp vs **Combined**	3.2±0.7	4.1±1.0	0.9±1.15	0.021*
	GraphXAIN vs Combined	3.8±0.8	4.1±1.0	0.28±1.18	0.314
Communicability	GNNExp vs **GraphXAIN**	2.8±1.0	3.8±0.8	1.0±1.39	0.020*
	GNNExp vs **Combined**	2.8±1.0	4.2±0.7	1.45±1.22	0.001*
	GraphXAIN vs **Combined**	3.8±0.8	4.2±0.7	0.45±0.63	0.019*
Usability	GNNExp vs GraphXAIN	3.2±0.9	3.6±1.0	0.35±1.43	0.284
	GNNExp vs **Combined**	3.2±0.9	4.0±0.8	0.78±0.9	0.008*
	GraphXAIN vs Combined	3.6±1.0	4.0±0.8	0.42±1.24	0.541

pants' ratings do not differ between the presented scenarios representing different graph predictive tasks.

Although the sample size is modest, the survey findings demonstrate that GraphXAIN consistently outperforms the current state-of-the-art graph explanation method [47], serving as a valuable addition to improve understanding, trust, insightfulness, satisfaction, confidence, convincingness, communicability, and usability.

7 Conclusion and Future Work

In this work, we introduced GraphXAIN, a novel method that transforms technical subgraph and feature importance explanations into coherent natural language narrative explanations of Graph Neural Network's (GNN) prediction. GraphXAIN is a graph data-agnostic, model-agnostic and explainer-agnostic approach that complements traditional graph explainer outputs with the use of Large Language Models (LLMs). Results of LLM-generated narrative explanations for both classification and regression tasks on real-world datasets demonstrate that these narratives provide clearer insight into the predictive processes of GNN models, making them more accessible to practitioners. GraphXAIN method addresses a significant gap in the current Explainable AI (XAI) field by moving beyond technical and descriptive outputs by offering intuitive, story-like explanations that enhance comprehension and trust.

A user study conducted among practitioners highlights the advantages of GraphXAIN over the current state-of-the-art graph XAI method, GNNExplainer [47]. At the $\alpha = 0.05$ level, the GraphXAIN significantly improves the explanation's understandability, satisfaction, convincingness, and suitability for communicating the model's predictions. Furthermore, when the GraphXAIN narrative is combined with the GNNExplainer output, the all eight measured dimensions of the explanation (understandability, trustworthiness, insightfulness, satisfaction, confidence, convincingness, communicability, and future usability) show significant improvements compared to using GNNExplainer alone, indicating that integration of the XAI Narratives with subgraph and feature importance enhances user's perception of the explanation. Moreover, in seven out of eight measured dimensions, the preferences of GraphXAIN explanations alone do not differ from the combined approach (subgraph, feature importance and the narrative), thereby even more strengthening the power and need for the narrative explanations. Notably, 95% of participants indicate that GraphXAIN is a valuable addition to the explanation of GNN predictions. The study result indicates that explanatory narratives, alone or as a compliment to technical outputs of graph XAI methods, result in the improvement of the general perception of the explanations. Therefore, GraphXAIN may offer a solution not only for AI practitioners but also for domain experts and end users in fields where transparency and understanding are necessary, such as medicine (for clinicians and patients) or finance (for credit analysts and loan applicants).

In future work, the use of quantitative metrics will be essential for a more thorough and objective assessment of the quality of generated narrative explanations, as these narratives may happen to be unfaithful since LLMs are prone to hallucinations [8,19,49]. In particular, an assessment of the prevalence and impact of errors, in conjunction with the completeness and soundness metrics introduced in [49] and the faithfulness and assumptions metrics proposed in [19], could measure the alignment of the generated narratives with the original explanations. The issue of hallucinations can also be addressed by integrating our approach with retrieval-augmented generation (RAG) methods designed for graphs such as G-Retriever [14]. G-Retriever uses a RAG approach on textual graphs, ensuring that the answers are retrieved from the original graph, which decreases the hallucination and leads to a more robust response. However, we also emphasize that the central aim of this study is to demonstrate the strength and feasibility of LLM-generated narratives for graphs as an explanation method and leave their further optimization for future work.

Acknowledgments. This research received funding from the Flemish Government under the "Onderzoeksprogramma Artificiële Intelligentie (AI) Vlaanderen".

Data and Code Availability. The data and code used in this research, as well as the survey results, are available at: https://github.com/ADMAntwerp/GraphXAIN.

Ethical Considerations. This study involved a voluntary and anonymous online survey to evaluate the proposed explainable AI technique. No sensitive and personally identifiable information was collected. Informed consent was obtained via a consent form presented at the beginning of the survey, which informed participants that participation was voluntary and anonymous and that they could withdraw at any time.

Disclosure of Interests. The authors have no competing interests to declare that are relevant to the content of this article.

A Examples of XAI Explanations in Natural Language for GNN Models

A.1 GraphXAIN

In this section, we present more examples generated by the GraphXAIN method. Figure 4a and Fig. 4b provide further insight into the interpretability of the GNN's model prediction by presenting coherence narratives, which demonstrates the GraphXAIN's consistency across a range of randomly sampled nodes for both node classification and node regression tasks. The examples showcase the explanatory depth of GraphXAINs in capturing the reasoning behind the GNN model's predictions.

In the truncated subgraph visualisation presented in Fig. 4a, GNNExplainer is instructed to reduce the subgraph to the seven most influential nodes according to the edges' weight importance. As a result, this process occasionally results in disconnected nodes within the truncated subgraph, as GNNExplainer prioritises node importance over connectivity in the simplified view. Consequently, these subgraph representations can appear more unintuitive or fragmented. A complementary natural language narrative is therefore argued to be essential to bridge these interpretative gaps, providing end users with a coherent understanding of the GNN model's final prediction, regardless of the connectivity of the subgraph.

A.2 Natural Language Counterfactual Explanations for Graphs Using Large Language Models (Giorgi et al., 2024)

This section presents three examples of textual explanations proposed by Giorgi et al. [10] for counterfactual explanations of node classification using a GNN

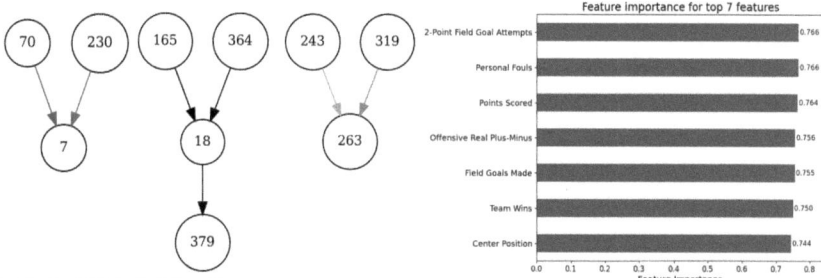

GraphXAIN for node 379

"The model predicted that the NBA player at node index 379 falls into the "Low Salary" category based on key performance metrics and social connections with other players. The player's high number of personal fouls suggested a possible impact on the player's effectiveness within games, which, combined with fewer field goals made and attempted, might indicate lower scoring contributions compared to peers. Notably, the player's offensive real plus-minus was quite high, placing the player in the upper percentile, which would typically indicate a strong offensive presence, but this positive aspect may have been counterbalanced by other factors or perceived inconsistencies. A pivotal role is also played by the player's position, as being a "Small Forward"—which is less frequently associated with a high salary—can shape salary expectations.

The subgraph of related NBA players provides another layer of context for this prediction, showing that the player has substantial Twitter interactions with those labeled as having low salaries. These connections, especially prominent with strongly influential connections like nodes 165 and 18, may suggest similar performance or recognition levels among peers, impacting salary perceptions. The subgraph edges, which measure the weight of influence on the player's salary prediction, highlight how these relationships reinforce the low salary prediction by associating with other low-salary peers. Collectively, these features and relationships paint a comprehensive picture, grounding this prediction in both individual performance and social dynamics within the NBA network."

(a) GraphXAIN for prediction for the NBA player (node 379).

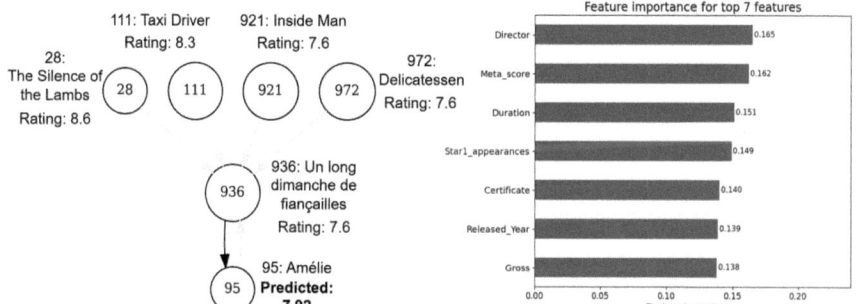

GraphXAIN for node 95

"The Graph Neural Network model predicted a score of 7.92 for the movie "Amélie" (node index 95) in its task of estimating an IMDB rating based on various features and relationships with other movies. "Amélie's" director, Jean-Pierre Jeunet, is a significant factor in the prediction due to his well-regarded filmography, which often yields positive critic reviews. The movie's Metascore also contributes notably, although it is lower than many in the industry, indicating that other factors helped bolster the prediction. The extensive audience engagement, with a high number of votes, underscores the film's popularity, probably influencing the prediction towards a favorable outcome.

The Gross revenue adds weight to the prediction, suggesting commercial success and audience reception aligned with a higher rating. Released in 2001, "Amélie" falls within a time when many classic films emerged, possibly aiding its favorable standing. The film's universal classification (U) suggests widespread accessibility, aligning with the positive prediction. The strongest connection in the movie's network comes from "The Silence of the Lambs," a highly rated film, reflecting the shared actor network's powerful influence—emphasizing the social network effects within this dataset. Overall, "Amélie's" narrative charm, strong industry connections, and these diverse social features collectively contribute to its predicted rating."

(b) GraphXAIN for prediction for the movie "Amélie" (node 95).

Fig. 4. LLM-generated GraphXAINs (bottom parts of the images) complements GNNExplainer's [47] subgraphs and feature importance outputs (top parts) in explaining the GNN's predictions.

model trained on the Cora dataset. The Cora dataset is a citation network dataset in which nodes represent research papers, and edges denote citation relationships, with the task being to classify each paper into one of seven categories. Since the authors do not provide any output examples in their article, the examples presented below are taken from the article's official GitHub repository. These examples are not selectively chosen but represent the first three explanations generated by the best-performing model, as reported in the paper and available in the article's official GitHub repository[4]:

- *"The target node (node 15) was originally classified as 'Probabilistic_ Methods' in the factual graph. However, in the counterfactual graph, the classification changes to 'Reinforcement_ Learning'. Despite the features of node 15 remaining identical, the classification shifts due to changes in the classification of its neighboring nodes. Specifically, nodes 4 and 12, which were previously classified as 'Probabilistic_ Methods', are now reclassified as 'Reinforcement_ Learning'. This change in the neighborhood context strongly influences the classification of node 15, leading to its reclassification as 'Reinforcement_ Learning'. The only neighbor that remains consistent is node 19, but its influence is outweighed by the changes in nodes 4 and 12. Thus, the primary factor driving the change in classification is the altered classification of neighboring nodes, rather than any intrinsic change in the features of node 15 itself."* (Line 4)
- *"In the factual scenario, Node 3 is classified as 'Theory' and is connected to Nodes 0, 9, 10, and 13. In the counterfactual scenario, Node 3 is reclassified as 'Case_ Based' and is only connected to Node 10. The change in classification is influenced by the loss of connections to Nodes 0, 9, and 13, and the retention of a connection to Node 10, which is classified as 'Case_ Based'."* (Line 8)
- *"In the factual scenario, Node 0 is classified as 'Theory' and is connected to both Nodes 1 and 4. Node 1 shares similar features with Node 0 and is also classified as 'Theory'. However, Node 4, which is classified as 'Case_ Based', introduces a conflicting influence. In the counterfactual scenario, the connection to Node 4 is removed, isolating Node 0 from the 'Case_ Based' influence. As a result, Node 0 is reclassified as 'Case_ Based', reflecting the reduced influence of 'Theory' nodes and the absence of conflicting 'Case_ Based' connections. This counterfactual explanation highlights how the removal of a single connection can significantly alter the classification of a node, providing insight into the decision-making process of the graph-based model."* (Line 12)

According to Dahlstrom [6] and our proposed definitions, these examples constitute an XAI Description rather than an XAI Narrative.

---

[4] https://github.com/flaat/llm-graph-cf/blob/main/data/results/cf-gnn_Qwen2.5-14B-Instruct-GPTQ-Int4_cora_Response.json.

A.3 Explaining Graph Neural Networks with Large Language Models: A Counterfactual Perspective for Molecular Property Prediction (He et al., 2024)

Presented below are three examples of textual explanations generated by the method proposed by He et al. [15] for counterfactual explanations in the context of molecular property prediction using a Graph Neural Network (GNN) model trained on a chemical molecule dataset. This dataset comprises molecular structures in which nodes represent atoms and edges signify chemical bonds, with the primary objective being the prediction of specific molecular properties. These three examples are the only instances provided by the authors in their article [15]:

- *"This molecule contains a cyclohexane ring, a dithiane ring, a ketone group, and a thiocarbonyl group, in which the ketone group may be the most influential for AIDS treatment."* (Page 3, Figure 2)
- *"The molecule contains hydroxylamine, cyclohexane, sulfone, and thioether functional groups, in which hydroxylamine may be the most influential for AIDS treatment."* (Page 4, Figure 4)
- *"This molecule contains a cyclohexane ring, a dithiane ring, a ketone group, and a hydrazine group, in which the hydrazine group may be the most influential for AIDS treatment."* (Page 6, Figure 5)

Again, the explanations presented by He et al. [15] are delivered in a context-free and fact-based manner without illustrating underlying relationships or cause-and-effect relationships, thereby categorising them as XAI Descriptions rather than XAI Narratives.

A.4 TAGExplainer: Narrating Graph Explanations for Text-Attributed Graph Learning Models (Pan et al., 2024)

Presented below are three instances of textual explanations proposed by Pan et al. [36] for Text-Attributed Graph (TAG) learning models using their TAGExplainer method. The authors applied TAGExplainer to the Cora, DBLP, and Book-History datasets to generate natural language explanations that incorporate elements of narrative communication. These three examples are the only instances provided by the authors in their article, each corresponding to the aforementioned datasets, respectively [36]:

- *"The classification of the ROOT node into the 'Reinforcement Learning' category can be explained as follows:*
  - *ROOT mentions reinforcement learning, learning algorithms, and hierarchical control structures indicating that it focuses on reinforcement learning methodologies and their applications. - Node-1 discusses transfer learning in reinforcement learning, highlighting how learning agents can adapt to multiple tasks.*

- *Node-1.1–Node-1.8 provide more context about various reinforcement learning architectures and approaches, including modular Q-learning and hierarchical reinforcement learning.*
- *Node-2 focuses on learning in continuous domains with delayed rewards, a pertinent aspect of reinforcement learning, particularly in real-world applications.*
- *Node-2.1 discusses generalization in reinforcement learning using neural networks, which is relevant but less directly tied to the prediction.*
- *Node-3: This node discusses the need for hierarchies within control systems and the improvements in nested Q-learning, which are highly relevant to the classification label.*

    In summary, the classification of the ROOT node into 'Reinforcement Learning' is well-supported by the strong presence of key reinforcement learning terms within the node itself and its direct connections to Nodes 1, 2 and 3, which also focus on reinforcement learning methodologies." (Page 10, Figure 4b)

- *"The classification of the ROOT node into the 'Cloud computing' category can be explained as follows:*
  - *ROOT: The presence of keywords such as 'user', 'interfaces', and 'service-oriented approach' indicates that the paper is focused on topics central to cloud computing, particularly how users interact with cloud services and the modular nature of these services.*
  - *Node-1: While Node 1 discusses 'graphical user interfaces' and 'domain-specific languages', which are relevant to cloud computing, it is slightly less directly related to the core concepts of cloud computing compared to the ROOT node.*
  - *Node-1.1: This node emphasizes 'user interface requirements' and 'requirements analysis', which are crucial for developing effective cloud applications that meet user needs.*
  - *Node-1.2: This node focuses on 'stereotypes' and 'domain-specific terms', highlighting the importance of understanding user interactions and the context in which cloud services are utilized.*

    In summary, the classification of the ROOT node into 'Cloud computing' is well-supported by the presence of key terms related to user interaction and service-oriented architectures. The direct connection to Node 1, which discusses user interfaces, further reinforces this classification, while the additional insights from Nodes 1.1 and 1.2 emphasize the importance of user-centric design in cloud computing applications." (Page 16, Figure 6b)

- *"The classification of the ROOT node into the 'Europe' category can be explained as follows:*
  - *ROOT: The presence of keywords such as 'cambodia', 'year', and 'translation' indicates a context that may involve historical or cultural discussions relevant to Europe, particularly in terms of colonial history and cultural exchanges. The mention of 'english' and 'french' highlights the linguistic dimensions that are significant in European contexts.*

- *Node-1: This node discusses Michael D. Coe, an anthropologist specializing in Southeast Asia and the Khmer civilization. While it provides historical context, the focus on Southeast Asia may dilute its direct relevance to Europe. However, the terms 'civilizations' and 'ancient' could connect to European historical interests.*
- *Node-2: This node is more directly relevant as it discusses the destruction of Cambodia during the Nixon-Kissinger era, a significant historical event that involved European powers' interests in Southeast Asia. The emphasis on 'destruction' and 'cambodia' alongside key historical figures suggests a critical perspective on the geopolitical dynamics involving European countries.*

In summary, the classification of the ROOT node into 'Europe' is supported by the presence of key terms that indicate a historical and cultural context relevant to European interests, particularly through the stronger connection found in Node-2." (Page 16, Figure 7b)

The TAGExplainer approach applies to text-attributed graphs only and does not provide an explanatory subgraph or feature importance scores.

References

1. Adebayo, J., Gilmer, J., Muelly, M., Goodfellow, I., Hardt, M., Kim, B.: Sanity checks for saliency maps. Adv. Neural Inf. Process. Syst. **31** (2018)
2. Baniecki, H., Parzych, D., Biecek, P.: The grammar of interactive explanatory model analysis. Data Min. Knowl. Disc. **38**(5), 2596–2632 (2024)
3. Biecek, P., Samek, W.: Position: explain to question not to justify. In: Forty-First International Conference on Machine Learning (2024)
4. Brughmans, D., Leyman, P., Martens, D.: Nice: an algorithm for nearest instance counterfactual explanations. Data Min. Knowl. Disc. **38**(5), 2665–2703 (2024)
5. Cedro, M., Chlebus, M.: Beyond the black box: do more complex deep learning models provide superior XAI explanations? arXiv preprint arXiv:2405.08658 (2024)
6. Dahlstrom, M.F.: Using narratives and storytelling to communicate science with nonexpert audiences. Proc. Natl. Acad. Sci. **111**, 13614–13620 (2014)
7. Dahlstrom, M.F., Scheufele, D.A.: (Escaping) the paradox of scientific storytelling. PLoS Biol. **16**(10) (2018)
8. Fatemi, B., Halcrow, J., Perozzi, B.: Talk like a graph: encoding graphs for large language models. arXiv preprint arXiv:2310.04560 (2023)
9. Gatt, A., Krahmer, E.: Survey of the state of the art in natural language generation: core tasks, applications and evaluation. J. Artif. Intell. Res. **61**, 65–170 (2018)
10. Giorgi, F., Campagnano, C., Silvestri, F., Tolomei, G.: Natural language counterfactual explanations for graphs using large language models. arXiv preprint arXiv:2410.09295 (2024)
11. Goethals, S., Martens, D., Evgeniou, T.: Manipulation risks in Explainable AI: the implications of the disagreement problem. In: Joint European Conference on Machine Learning and Knowledge Discovery in Databases, pp. 185–200. Springer (2023)
12. Grice, H.: Logic and conversation. Syntax Semant. **3** (1975)

13. Guidotti, R., Monreale, A., Ruggieri, S., Turini, F., Giannotti, F., Pedreschi, D.: A survey of methods for explaining black box models. ACM Comput. Surv. (CSUR) **51**(5), 1–42 (2018)
14. He, X., et al.: G-retriever: retrieval-augmented generation for textual graph understanding and question answering. arXiv preprint arXiv:2402.07630 (2024)
15. He, Y., Zheng, Z., Soga, P., Zhu, Y., Dong, Y., Li, J.: Explaining graph neural networks with large language models: a counterfactual perspective on molecule graphs. In: Findings of the Association for Computational Linguistics: EMNLP 2024, pp. 7079–7096 (2024)
16. Hinns, J., Martens, D.: Exposing image classifier shortcuts with counterfactual frequency (CoF) tables. arXiv preprint arXiv:2405.15661 (2024)
17. Hoffman, R.R., Mueller, S.T., Klein, G., Litman, J.: Metrics for explainable AI: challenges and prospects. arXiv preprint arXiv:1812.04608 (2018)
18. Holzinger, A., Saranti, A., Molnar, C., Biecek, P., Samek, W.: Explainable AI methods-a brief overview. In: International Workshop on Extending Explainable AI Beyond Deep Models and Classifiers, pp. 13–38. Springer (2020)
19. Ichmoukhamedov, T., Hinns, J., Martens, D.: How good is my story? Towards quantitative metrics for evaluating llm-generated XAI narratives. arXiv preprint arXiv:2412.10220 (2024)
20. Kayande, U., De Bruyn, A., Lilien, G.L., Rangaswamy, A., Van Bruggen, G.H.: How incorporating feedback mechanisms in a DSS affects DSS evaluations. Inf. Syst. Res. **20**(4), 527–546 (2009)
21. Kipf, T.N., Welling, M.: Semi-supervised classification with graph convolutional networks. arXiv preprint arXiv:1609.02907 (2016)
22. Kuźba, M., Biecek, P.: What would you ask the machine learning model? Identification of user needs for model explanations based on human-model conversations. In: Koprinska, I., Gulla, J.A. (eds.) ECML PKDD 2020. CCIS, vol. 1323, pp. 447–459. Springer, Cham (2020). https://doi.org/10.1007/978-3-030-65965-3_30
23. Longa, A., et al.: Explaining the explainers in graph neural networks: a comparative study. ACM Comput. Surv. **57**(5), 1–37 (2025)
24. Loshchilov, I.: Decoupled weight decay regularization. arXiv preprint arXiv:1711.05101 (2017)
25. Lucic, A., Ter Hoeve, M.A., Tolomei, G., De Rijke, M., Silvestri, F.: CF-GNNExplainer: counterfactual explanations for graph neural networks. In: International Conference on Artificial Intelligence and Statistics, pp. 4499–4511. PMLR (2022)
26. Lundberg, S.: A unified approach to interpreting model predictions. arXiv preprint arXiv:1705.07874 (2017)
27. Madumal, P., Miller, T., Sonenberg, L., Vetere, F.: A grounded interaction protocol for explainable artificial intelligence. arXiv preprint arXiv:1903.02409 (2019)
28. Martens, D., Hinns, J., Dams, C., Vergouwen, M., Evgeniou, T.: Tell me a story! Narrative-driven XAI with large language models. Decis. Support Syst., 114402 (2025)
29. Martens, D., Provost, F.: Explaining data-driven document classifications. MIS Q. **38**(1), 73–100 (2014)
30. Michalski, R.S.: A theory and methodology of inductive learning. In: Machine Learning, pp. 83–134. Elsevier (1983)
31. Miller, G.A.: The magical number seven, plus or minus two: some limits on our capacity for processing information. Psychol. Rev. **63**(2), 81 (1956)
32. Miller, T.: Explanation in artificial intelligence: insights from the social sciences. Artif. Intell. **267**, 1–38 (2019)

33. Miller, T., Howe, P., Sonenberg, L.: Explainable AI: beware of inmates running the asylum or: how i learnt to stop worrying and love the social and behavioural sciences. arXiv preprint arXiv:1712.00547 (2017)
34. Mohseni, S., Zarei, N., Ragan, E.D.: A multidisciplinary survey and framework for design and evaluation of Explainable AI systems. ACM Trans. Interact. Intell. Syst. (TiiS) **11**(3–4), 1–45 (2021)
35. Molnar, C.: Interpretable Machine Learning, 2 edn. (2022). https://christophm.github.io/interpretable-ml-book
36. Pan, B., Xiong, Z., Wu, G., Zhang, Z., Zhang, Y., Zhao, L.: TagExplainer: narrating graph explanations for text-attributed graph learning models. arXiv preprint arXiv:2410.15268 (2024)
37. Puduppully, R., Dong, L., Lapata, M.: Data-to-text generation with content selection and planning. In: Proceedings of the AAAI Conference on Artificial Intelligence, vol. 33, pp. 6908–6915 (2019)
38. Ribeiro, J., Cardoso, L., Santos, V., Carvalho, E., Carneiro, N., Alves, R.: How reliable and stable are explanations of XAI methods? arXiv preprint arXiv:2407.03108 (2024)
39. Ribeiro, M.T., Singh, S., Guestrin, C.: "Why should I trust you?" explaining the predictions of any classifier. In: Proceedings of the 22nd ACM SIGKDD International Conference on Knowledge Discovery and Data Mining, pp. 1135–1144 (2016)
40. Scarselli, F., Gori, M., Tsoi, A.C., Hagenbuchner, M., Monfardini, G.: The graph neural network model. IEEE Trans. Neural Networks **20**(1), 61–80 (2008)
41. Simonyan, K., Vedaldi, A., Zisserman, A.: Deep inside convolutional networks: Visualising image classification models and saliency maps. arXiv preprint arXiv:1312.6034 (2013)
42. Sokol, K., Flach, P.A.: Conversational explanations of machine learning predictions through class-contrastive counterfactual statements. In: IJCAI, pp. 5785–5786 (2018)
43. Sundararajan, M., Taly, A., Yan, Q.: Axiomatic attribution for deep networks. In: International Conference on Machine Learning, pp. 3319–3328. PMLR (2017)
44. Veličković, P., Cucurull, G., Casanova, A., Romero, A., Lio, P., Bengio, Y.: Graph attention networks. arXiv preprint arXiv:1710.10903 (2017)
45. Wachter, S., Mittelstadt, B., Russell, C.: Counterfactual explanations without opening the black box: automated decisions and the GDPR. Harv. JL Tech. **31**, 841 (2017)
46. Xu, K., Hu, W., Leskovec, J., Jegelka, S.: How powerful are graph neural networks? arXiv preprint arXiv:1810.00826 (2018)
47. Ying, Z., Bourgeois, D., You, J., Zitnik, M., Leskovec, J.: GNNExplainer: generating explanations for graph neural networks. Adv. Neural Inf. Process. Syst. **32** (2019)
48. Yousuf, R.B., Defelice, N., Sharma, M., Xu, S., Ramakrishnan, N.: LLM augmentations to support analytical reasoning over multiple documents. In: 2024 IEEE International Conference on Big Data (BigData), pp. 1892–1901. IEEE (2024)
49. Zytek, A., Pidò, S., Veeramachaneni, K.: LLMs for XAI: future directions for explaining explanations. arXiv preprint arXiv:2405.06064 (2024)

Open Access This chapter is licensed under the terms of the Creative Commons Attribution 4.0 International License (http://creativecommons.org/licenses/by/4.0/), which permits use, sharing, adaptation, distribution and reproduction in any medium or format, as long as you give appropriate credit to the original author(s) and the source, provide a link to the Creative Commons license and indicate if changes were made.

The images or other third party material in this chapter are included in the chapter's Creative Commons license, unless indicated otherwise in a credit line to the material. If material is not included in the chapter's Creative Commons license and your intended use is not permitted by statutory regulation or exceeds the permitted use, you will need to obtain permission directly from the copyright holder.

MSL: Multi-class Scoring Lists for Interpretable Incremental Decision-Making

Stefan Heid[1(✉)], Jaroslaw Kornowicz[2(✉)], Jonas Hanselle[1,3], Kirsten Thommes[2], and Eyke Hüllermeier[1,3,4]

[1] LMU Munich, Geschwister-Scholl-Platz 1, 80539 Munich, Germany
{stefan.heid,jonas.hanselle,eyke}@lmu.de
[2] Paderborn University, Warburger Street 100, 33098 Paderborn, Germany
{jaroslaw.koronowicz,kirsten.thommes}@upb.de
[3] Munich Center for Machine Learning (MCML), Munich, Germany
[4] German Research Center for Artificial Intelligence (DFKI, DSA), Kaiserslautern, Germany

Abstract. A scoring list is a sequence of simple decision models, where features are incrementally evaluated and scores of satisfied features are summed to be used for threshold-based decisions or for calculating class probabilities. In this paper, we introduce a new multi-class variant and compare it against previously introduced binary classification variants for incremental decisions, as well as multi-class variants for classical decision-making using all features. Furthermore, we introduce a new multi-class dataset to assess collaborative human-machine decision-making, which is suitable for user studies with non-expert participants. We demonstrate the usefulness of our approach by evaluating predictive performance and compared to the performance of participants without AI help.

Keywords: machine learning · decision support · scoring systems · user study

1 Introduction

Machine Learning (ML) methods have achieved remarkable accomplishments in various application domains. While complex and powerful methods like deep neural networks offer state-of-the-art predictive accuracy, they lack transparency and inherent explainability, which are key requirements for high-stakes decision-making [3]. In general, there are two competing approaches navigating the accuracy-explainability trade-off in ML [2,4]: On the one hand, complex models may be accompanied by simplistic *post-hoc* explanation methods like LIME [39] and SHAP [28]. These can be applied to any predictive and complex model and help mitigate some lack of transparency by explaining individual predictions. Yet, they fail to provide full transparency.

An alternative approach is the use of less complex models that are genuinely interpretable, also known as *ante-hoc* explanation. Corresponding models have a restricted, simple structure that humans can inspect, offering a global understanding of how different features influence the model predictions without the need for additional explanation. This inherent property of explainability makes them an appropriate choice for decision support in high-stakes domains [42] when human understanding and accountability are required.

One of the most prominent model classes of this kind are scoring systems with a long-standing tradition in clinical decision-making [38]. Simply put, they assign an integer-valued score to each (binary) feature, and a decision is made by comparing the sum of all scores for present features to a threshold. Recently, the need for situation-adapted decision models of such kind has been addressed with Probabilistic Scoring Lists (PSL) [15], for which a prediction can be made with any prefix of features in an ordered list. This allows for adjusting the decision process by stopping the feature acquisition once a prediction can be made with sufficient confidence for the decision context at hand. A PSL is a simple model that can be handled by lay persons [19].

While these methods have shown promising performance for the binary case, they have not yet been adapted to polychotomous decision situations in which three or more options are considered. However, many real-world applications are multi-class problems, at least if there is more than one option available (in addition to "do nothing"). For instance, in many medical situations, there is more than one treatment available in addition to "do nothing", which makes this scenario already a multi-class problem.

In this paper, we introduce *Multi-class Scoring Lists* (MSL), an extension of PSL to accommodate multi-class predictions. We evaluate the MSL's predictive performance against various baselines on benchmark datasets, and we observe a favorable compromise between accuracy and interpretability. Additionally, we introduce a new dataset rooted in the sports domain that is particularly well-suited for studies on human-AI interaction. To this end, we have conducted a first study to compare participants' predictive performance on the dataset with the introduced model class.

2 Related Work

Scoring systems are widely utilized in medical applications, including the assessment of atrial fibrillation [27], pancreatitis [32], pneumonia [21], strokes [12], and infants [52]. While their simplistic architecture may result in reduced accuracy, their transparency and ease of use allow for application without computational support. Additionally, such transparency and interpretability can lead to higher acceptance. However, the potential increase in cognitive load compared to so-called "black-box" decision support systems should be considered to avoid causing the opposite effect [29,36].

Traditionally, scoring systems have been manually designed based on domain expertise. However, recent advancements have introduced data-driven methods, such as Supersparse Linear Integer Models (SLIM) and RiskSLIM, which employ mixed-integer programming (MIP) [46,47], as well as Interval Coded Scoring (ICS) [5,7,8].

Although these models have demonstrated effectiveness in binary decision-making, there remains a need for scoring systems capable of handling multi-class classification. Established scoring systems are either considering the pure binary setting, like the PERC rule [22], or scenarios in which multiple classes exhibit an ordinal structure, most notably risk classes in the clinical setting, e.g., the SAPS or APACHE scores [23,30]. In the first case, the total score is compared to a threshold to make the decision, while in the latter case, the risk classes correspond to predefined intervals, and membership is determined by checking in which interval the total score falls. However, little attention has been paid to the multi-class setting with nominal categories, and only a few proposed methods exist. Rouzot et al. propose a one-versus-rest decomposition on top of SLIM for solving multi-class classification problems [41]. While this is a natural approach to transforming a binary into a multi-class classifier, the resulting decomposition has one classifier per class. The more recent approach, MISS, uses a multinomial approach instead [13]. Many existing multi-class approaches leverage mixed-integer nonlinear programming for model learning [13,41].

Despite their potential, both binary and multi-class scoring models face a critical limitation: they become inapplicable when essential feature data is unavailable. This challenge arises in scenarios where data acquisition is costly or when decision-makers operate under time constraints, limiting the available information [6,45].

To address these constraints, adaptive decision support frameworks are required. One approach involves decision lists, which apply predefined rules for prediction. If no applicable rule is found, the decision-making process is deferred to the next rule in the sequence [40]. Heid et al. [18] propose a framework of complexity-ordered catalogues of models, where each successive model incorporates an additional rule compared to its predecessor, along with a methodology for learning these models. Expanding on this concept, probabilistic scoring lists have been introduced [15]. These systems, structured as sequentially dependent scoring models, function similarly to decision lists but provide probabilistic rather than deterministic predictions, akin to RiskSLIM.

3 Multi-class Scoring List

We consider a decision-making scenario in which decisions have to be made for varying contexts that are specified in terms of binary features $\mathcal{F} = \{f_1, \ldots f_K\}$. Moreover, decisions are incremental in the sense that the concrete values $x_i \in \{0, 1\}$ of these features are acquired in a stagewise fashion, one after another, in a prespecified order. At each of these stages $1, \ldots, K$, the decision-maker (DM) has the option to make a decision immediately or gather additional evidence in terms of further feature values, until all features are exhausted. When learning an arbitrary set of classifiers, e.g., logistic regression models, those models do not share any parameters, which makes it impossible to carry over partial results from previous stages. Decision lists on the other hand are a joint model and can also be interpreted as a sequence of models with coherence constraints.

The multi-class scoring list (MSL) is a decision support model tailored to this scenario and is formally defined as follows:

Definition 1. A *multi-class scoring list* (MSL) over candidate features $\mathcal{F}$ and score set $\mathcal{S} \subset \mathbb{Z}$ is a triple $h = \langle F, S, b \rangle$, where $F = (f_1, \ldots, f_K)$ is a list of (distinct) features from $\mathcal{F}$, $S \in \mathcal{S}^{C \times K}$ is a score matrix and $b \in \mathcal{S}^C$ is a bias term, where $\mathcal{Y}$ is the set of classes and $C = |\mathcal{Y}|$ is the number of elements therein.

At prediction time, stagewise decisions are formed in the following manner.

- Let $s^{(k)} = (s_1^{(k)}, \ldots, s_C^{(k)})$ denote the cumulative score vector at stage k, with $s_c^{(k)}$ the score of class c. At stage $k = 0$, where no features have been evaluated yet, the scores are formed by the bias term

$$s^{(0)} = b$$

that can be interpreted as a general tendency towards a certain decision when no information is available.
- For subsequent stages $k > 0$, the cumulative scores are given by

$$s_c^{(k)} = s_c^{(k-1)} + S_{c,k} \cdot x_k, \quad \forall c \in \mathcal{Y}$$

where $S_{c,k}$ is the score associated with class c at stage k (feature f_k) in the score matrix S.
- After computing the cumulative class scores, the prediction for stage k can be conducted by computing the argmax set of these scores

$$\hat{y} = \arg\max_{c \in \mathcal{Y}} s_c^{(k)} \tag{1}$$

Note that the argmax of the cumulative scores may indeed be ambiguous due to the discrete nature of the scores. Hence, the prediction $\hat{y}$ can be set-valued, if several classes are scored maximally likely. This is a natural way for the predictor to express its uncertainty about a predictive outcome [31].
- Another practical interpretation of the cumulative class scores $s_c^{(k)}$ is to use them as logits for the softmax function. This way, we can obtain probabilistic predictions

$$\hat{p}_c = \frac{\exp\left(s_c^{(k)}\right)}{\sum_{c' \in \mathcal{Y}} \exp\left(s_{c'}^{(k)}\right)}, \quad \forall c \in \mathcal{Y} \tag{2}$$

where $\hat{p}_c$ denotes the estimated probability for class c. Therefore, multiple maximal scores in the discrete decision scenario will be converted into equal predictive probabilities in the probabilistic setting.

– At every stage k, the decision maker can either exit with decision (1) or continue the process and acquire the next feature f_{k+1}. This question will mainly be answered on the basis of the probability estimates (2), which provides information about the confidence in the decision (1).

Table 1. Example of a multi-class scoring list for football player classification. The numerical features have been binarized through thresholding (The binarization thresholds are as follows: *Many shots > 0.55; Long Playing Time > 78.8; High Pass Success Rate > 74.5; Many Aerial Duels Won/Match > 0.65; Tall Player > 183.5.*). The model was trained using a score set $\{0, \pm 1, \pm 2, \pm 3\}$ and L_2 regularization of 10^{-6}.

Feature	Forward	Midfielder	Defender	Goalkeeper
⟨Bias⟩	0	1	1	0
Many Shots	2	2	0	−3
Long Playing Time	−3	−1	2	3
High Pass Success Rate	−1	1	1	−1
Many Aerial Duels Won/Match	2	0	1	−3
Tall Player	−1	−1	−1	2

Table 1 shows an exemplary MSL for classifying positions of football players. The first row corresponds to the bias term: Here, the class *forward* and the class *goalkeeper* have a score of 0, while *midfielder* and *defender* have a score of 1. These bias scores, which are available before acquiring any feature values, hint at the marginal distribution of classes. Overall, there are more midfielders and defenders in a team than there are goalkeepers and forwards. The first feature acquired is the average number of shots per match (second row). This feature carries positive evidence for the classes *forward* and *midfielder*, no evidence for *defender*, and strong negative evidence for *goalkeeper*. Again, this is intuitively reasonable, as most shots are performed by players in offensive positions and definitely not by goalkeepers. This can be continued until all features have been consumed, and the final prediction is formed.

The MSLs score set $\mathcal{S}$ is specified in advance according to the DMs preferences and typically comprises a set of small integers reflecting different levels of "evidence" in favor or against a decision. For example, the score set $\mathcal{S} = \{0, \pm 1, \pm 2, \pm 3\}$ distinguishes three levels of evidence: weak, medium, and strong. Assigning a score of +1 to a feature then means that the presence of that feature provides weak evidence in favor of a decision, whereas a score of −3 means strong evidence against that decision. Restricting the magnitude and number of admissible scores ensures that the resulting model is cognitively tractable for a human expert. The influence of an individual feature can be immediately understood and communicated, and in principle, predictions could even be made without the help of computing devices.

3.1 Connections to Other Interpretable Probabilistic Classifiers

Given the simple and inherently interpretable structure of MSL, one may wonder how it distinguishes itself from other simple probabilistic classifiers. Most notably, MSL resembles a multinomial logistic regression (MLR) with two major differences: First, MLR has unbounded real-valued coefficients which are harder to understand than integer-valued scores that stem from a small, predefined score-set. Secondly, MLR does not provide stagewise predictions but uses the full feature set for all predictions.

Another natural connection can be drawn to the Naïve Bayes (NB) classifier, which models the posterior probability of class c given a feature vector $\boldsymbol{x}$ as

$$P(c \mid \boldsymbol{x}) = \frac{P(c) \prod_{k=1}^{K} P(x_k \mid c)}{P(\boldsymbol{x})}.$$

Taking the logarithm on both sides yields

$$\log P(c \mid \boldsymbol{x}) = \log P(c) + \sum_{k=1}^{K} \log P(x_k \mid c) - \log P(\boldsymbol{x}) \qquad (3)$$

which shows the relation to MSL. The $\log P(c)$ correspond to the bias term b and the log-likelihoods $\log P(x_k \mid c)$ in the sum correspond to the stagewise class scores $s_c^{(k)}$. As $P(\boldsymbol{x})$ is constant across all classes, it only serves to normalize the values to form a valid probability distribution over class labels and can be neglected.

Unlike MSL and MLR, NB can make predictions with any subset of features, even without adhering to a predefined order, making it an interesting choice for situated decision support. However, there are again two major disadvantages compared to MSL: The log-likelihoods in NB are not restricted to a predefined score set, yielding the same disadvantages regarding score complexity as MLR. Additionally, the probability estimates in NB are built upon the naïve assumption of conditional independence and are formed by normalization. MSL can implicitly model feature dependencies by selecting scores that reflect the combined influence of multiple correlated features on the predicted probability.

3.2 Learning Multi-Class Scoring Lists

Consider a standard supervised learning setting in which the data generating process is characterized by a joint probability distribution $P(\boldsymbol{x}, y)$ over $\mathcal{X} \times \mathcal{Y}$. Given a loss function $\ell(\hat{y}, y)$ that quantifies how different a prediction $\hat{y}$ is from the true outcome y, the risk of a classifier $h \colon \mathcal{X} \longrightarrow \mathcal{Y}$ is defined as

$$R(h) = \mathbb{E}\left[\ell\left(h(\boldsymbol{x}), y\right)\right] = \int \ell\left(h(x), y\right) \, dP(\boldsymbol{x}, y). \qquad (4)$$

As the distribution $P(\boldsymbol{x}, y)$ is unknown, the true risk is substituted with the empirical risk on observed training data $\mathcal{D}_{\text{train}} = \{(\boldsymbol{x}, y)\}_{n=1}^{N}$:

$$R_{\text{emp}}(h) = \frac{1}{N} \sum_{n=1}^{N} \ell\big(h(\boldsymbol{x}_n), y_n\big)$$

In our listwise scenario, we are not considering a single model, but rather a sequence of models $h = (h_1, \ldots, h_K) \in \mathcal{H}^K$, where $\mathcal{H}$ is an underlying hypothesis space (in our case the set of scoring systems). The learning objective is to find such a sequence of models, or decision list, that has minimal global risk throughout the stages, i.e.,

$$h^* \in \arg\min_{h \in \mathcal{H}} R(h_1) \oplus R(h_2) \oplus \cdots \oplus R(h_K), \tag{5}$$

where $\oplus$ is a suitable aggregation operator[1] (e.g., the sum).

It is important to note that an optimal decision list (5) does not necessarily consist of elements h_k that have minimal stagewise risk, as the stage-optimal models may not constitute a valid MSL due to conflicting feature selections and score assignments. Hence, the problem is not decomposable in the sense that we could simply identify optimal models for the individual stages and combine them into a decision list.

In the following, we propose a learning algorithm for inferring MSLs from training data $\mathcal{D}_{\text{train}}$. The learning algorithm has to identify three components, that is, the order of features F, the score matrix $\boldsymbol{S}$, and the bias term $\boldsymbol{b}$. Note that this search space is rather large, precisely, the number of candidate MSLs for a score set $\mathcal{S}$, K features, and C classes is

$$K! \cdot |\mathcal{S}|^{(C \cdot (K+1))},$$

as it consists of all possible feature permutations and score assignments. Needless to say, an exhaustive search in such a huge space is not feasible. Thus, a heuristic approach has to be employed, that does not consider all candidate solutions. A natural strategy is to build the model bottom-up and stage by stage, starting with an empty list, first identifying the bias term, and then adding locally optimal features and score assignments for each stage consecutively.

An illustration of such a greedy forward selection procedure is given in Algorithm 1. The function EVALUATE is used to compute a loss value for candidate solutions, fully specified through F, $\boldsymbol{S}$ and $\boldsymbol{b}$, given the training data $\mathcal{D}_{\text{train}}$. The core of the greedy forward selection is the loop starting in line 2, that continues until all available features have been added to the MSL. In the first iteration, the bias term $\boldsymbol{b}$ is identified by considering all possible $\boldsymbol{b} \in \mathcal{S}^C$.

Afterwards, the subsequent stages are constructed: In each iteration, the locally optimal extension of the current MSL is identified by selecting the feature $f \in \bar{F}$ and corresponding score vector $\boldsymbol{s} \in \mathcal{S}^C$ that minimizes the loss achieved on the training data in line 6. As there are $|\mathcal{S}|^C$ many possible score vectors and $|\bar{F}|$ many remaining features, this step takes $|\mathcal{S}|^C \cdot |\bar{F}|$ many calls of EVALUATE. In the beginning, we start with the full feature set and have $|\bar{F}| = K$, which is

---

[1] The learning algorithm we propose below is of heuristic (greedy) nature and does not directly optimize a specific global risk. Therefore, the concrete form of $\oplus$ is not that important. The essential property assumed by the algorithm is the monotonicity of $\oplus$, which is naturally fulfilled by all meaningful candidates.

reduced by 1 in each iteration, as features are being added to the MSL. This results in
$$|\mathcal{S}|^C + \frac{K(K+1)}{2} \cdot |\mathcal{S}|^C \in \mathcal{O}(K^2 \cdot |\mathcal{S}|^C)$$
overall calls of EVALUATE for identifying the entire MSL including the bias term.

The loss function ℓ can be instantiated with any meaningful loss that compares a class label y with probability estimates. We choose the well-established cross-entropy loss
$$\ell(\widehat{\boldsymbol{p}}, y) = -\log \widehat{p}_y, \tag{6}$$
where $\widehat{p}_y$ is the predicted probability for the true class label y.

To further trade-off interpretability and performance, an L_2-loss of all scores can be added to the cross-entropy loss as a regularizer. This yields models with even smaller scores with often little to no expense in performance.

4 Football Player Dataset

Along with the MSL, we introduce a dataset containing the career statistics of football players and their position (*goalkeeper*, *defender*, *midfielder*, and *forward*) as the classification label. Although a classification of players to their positions may not look like a very important problem, it provides distinct advantages in experimental human-(X)AI interaction research.

In human-(X)AI interaction experiments, participants are often assigned classification tasks drawn from various datasets and task types, such as quiz question answering [10], and playing chess moves [9]. While several well-known tabular datasets exist for binary classification and regression in human-(X)AI experiments (e.g., income [24], recidivism [49], or house pricing [43]), there is a lack of comparable datasets for multi-class classification [26]. This gap is partly due to the common practice of recruiting lay participants—often via crowdsourcing platforms like Prolific—which necessitates easy understandable tasks to ensure valid results.

In our view, popular multi-class datasets in the machine learning literature, such as *iris* [11], *wine* [1], and *heart* [20], do not fully meet this criterion and therefore cannot be as readily adapted for human-(X)AI research as the aforementioned binary and regression datasets. Football, as the world's most popular sport, offers a clear advantage in this context. Its universal appeal ensures that a diverse participant pool is already familiar with the game, enhancing both task engagement and the reliability of study outcomes.

Our raw dataset comprises 5,449 active professional football players from eight professional leagues[2]. It includes all players who were on their teams' rosters at the time of data collection. The dataset contains performance statistics spanning each player's entire career up to the time the dataset was compiled

---

[2] England and Germany (1st and 2nd divisions), and the top-tier (1st division) leagues in Spain, France, Italy, Portugal, the Netherlands, Russia, Turkey, and the USA.

Algorithm 1: Greedy MSL

input : dataset $\mathcal{D}_{\text{train}}$, number of classes C,
set of all features $\mathcal{F}$ including the $\emptyset$ for the bias term
the available scores $\mathcal{S}$, loss function ℓ to evaluate a hypothesis
output : MSL model h

1   $F, \boldsymbol{S} \leftarrow (), []$
    # While not all features have been used. For set difference and inequality operators we treat F as a set for ease of notation.
2   **while** $F \neq \mathcal{F}$ **do**
       # In the first iteration compute the bias term
3   **if** $\emptyset \notin F$ **then**
4         $\boldsymbol{b} \leftarrow \arg\min_{\boldsymbol{b} \in \mathcal{S}^C} \{\text{EVALUATE}\left((), [], \boldsymbol{b}\right)\}$
       # Select all remaining features
5      $\bar{F} \leftarrow \mathcal{F} \setminus F$
       # Evaluate remaining features with all comb. of scores per class
6      $f, \boldsymbol{s} \leftarrow \arg\min_{f \in \bar{F}, \boldsymbol{s} \in \mathcal{S}^C} \left\{ \text{EVALUATE}\left(F \parallel (f), \begin{bmatrix} \boldsymbol{S} \\ \boldsymbol{s} \end{bmatrix}, \boldsymbol{b}\right) \right\}$
7      $F \leftarrow F \parallel (f)$
8      $\boldsymbol{S} \leftarrow \begin{bmatrix} \boldsymbol{S} \\ \boldsymbol{s} \end{bmatrix}$
9   **return** $h = \langle F, \boldsymbol{S}, \boldsymbol{b} \rangle$

10 **Function** EVALUATE($F, \boldsymbol{S}, \boldsymbol{b}$):
11     $L \leftarrow 0$
12   **for** $(\boldsymbol{x}, y) \in \mathcal{D}_{train}$ **do**
13        $\boldsymbol{x}_F \leftarrow \boldsymbol{x}[F]$ /* Select features F of instance $\boldsymbol{x}$ */
         # Matrix product of scores and selected features and bias
14        $\boldsymbol{s} \leftarrow \boldsymbol{S}\boldsymbol{x}_F + \boldsymbol{b}$
15        $\widehat{\boldsymbol{p}} \leftarrow \text{SOFTMAX}(\boldsymbol{s})$ /* Softmax probabilities acc. to Eq. 2   */
16        $L \leftarrow L + \ell(\widehat{\boldsymbol{p}}, y)$
17   **return** L

(11th November 2024). In addition to basic information such as *name, nationality, age, height,* and *current team*, the dataset provides a variety of performance metrics, including the *number of matches played, total minutes played, goals, assists, yellow* and *red cards, shots, pass success percentage, aerial duels won percentage,* and each player's primary *playing position*. To our knowledge, no comparable dataset exists. Other publicly available football datasets typically include information from only a single season or provide fewer performance indicators.

Because some players occupy multiple positions (e.g., *central defender* or *defensive midfielder*), various approaches to handling such cases are possible. For our evaluation, we chose four broad categories—*goalkeeper, defender, midfielder,* and *forward*. Players who could be assigned to more than one of these four

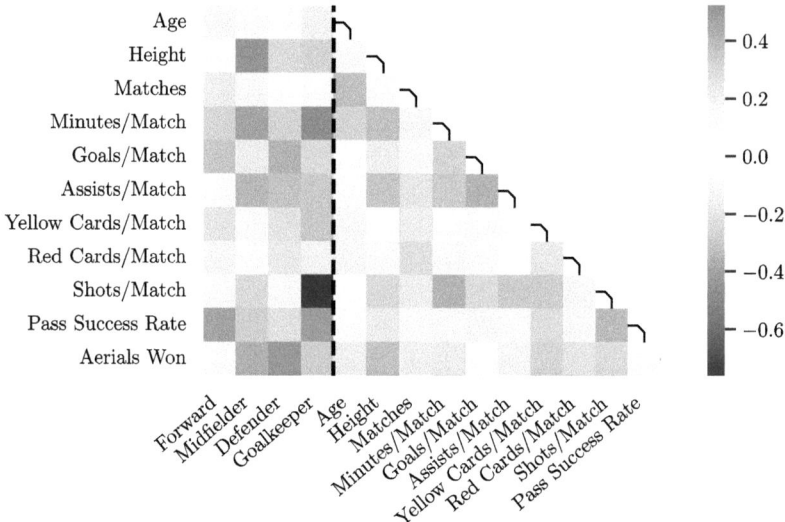

Fig. 1. Correlation of classes and features in football player dataset.

categories were removed, leading to the exclusion of 1,582 players (29%). An additional 256 players (6.6%) were removed due to missing data, resulting in 3,611 players in the cleaned dataset. Figure 1 presents the cross-correlation of the classes and features on the dataset.

5 User Study

We conducted an online user study as a benchmark for the MSL. Our main objectives were to assess how accurately participants perform the classification task and gauge the dataset's comprehensibility. Moreover, to determine the potential for automated decision support, we wanted to compare the performance of human decision-makers with the performance of a data-driven approach, namely a machine learning model.

We recruited 31 participants through the Prolific platform. Each participant was asked to predict the playing positions of football players drawn from our dataset. The study included detailed instructions, which were verified through comprehension checks. Before making their predictions, participants completed four Likert-scale questions assessing their familiarity with football. They were then asked to describe their decision-making process during the classification tasks, after which they received feedback on their responses.

The study included incentives: participants received a fixed payment of € 2 and an additional € 0.40 for each correct prediction. Only UK residents with English as their native language were eligible to participate. Moreover, participants were required to have a Prolific acceptance rate of at least 95% and to have successfully completed more than 10 prior studies on the platform.

The dataset was adapted specifically for this user study: we included only players who had participated in more than 50 games, as those with fewer games were particularly difficult to classify during a pretest. This criterion removed 54% of the 3,611 players, but the remaining total of 1,957 players was still sufficient. Additionally, we included a variable called *Man of the Match*, which cannot be published for legal reasons.

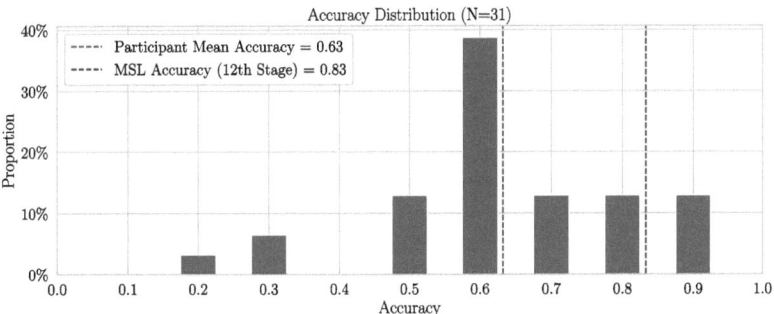

Fig. 2. Distribution of participants' accuracy on the football dataset. The red line shows the mean (63%), and the green line shows the accuracy of the 12th stage of an MSL model (83%).

The remaining dataset contained 1,957 players, which was then split into training and test sets. Only players from the test set were presented to participants to allow a fair comparison. Each participant was randomly assigned 10 players, ensuring the selected positions mirrored the overall class distribution. The participant were not made aware of this stratification.

Figure 2 shows the distribution of participants' classification accuracies compared to the MSL. For a fair comparison, the MSL is trained on the training data and evaluated on the same test samples as the participants. Their average accuracy of 63% fell below that of the MSL model, which achieved up to 83%. These results demonstrate that meaningful classifications are possible from humans (crowd-sourced workers), but also that performance can be improved through data-driven methods based on machine learning. Pearson correlation between accuracy and self-reported football knowledge ($r = 0.246$, $p = 0.165$) suggests that greater familiarity with soccer did not necessarily lead to better performance, although this may be due to self-selection effects in the study or insufficient sample size.

Figure 3 further analyses the classification errors with the help of a confusion matrix. In general, the participants make less precise decisions, however, many of the participants can better judge whether a player plays in the *forward* position. Albeit, this is not due to misclassifications, but is caused by many ties during prediction. Since the MSL implementation is configured to resolve ties at random, this yields to sub-par performance for ambiguous decisions. Yet, this is not an

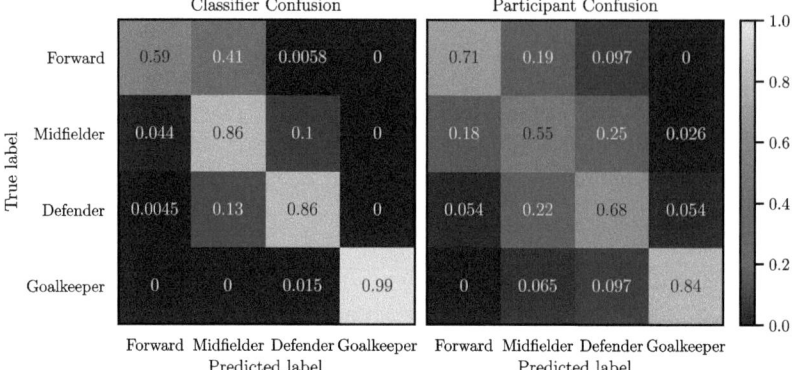

Fig. 3. Confusion matrices for classifier predictions (left) and participant classifications (right). The matrices show the distribution of predicted labels for each true label, with row summing to 1.

issue in a decision-support setting, as the classifier will yield both potential classes, allowing the decision maker to disambiguate.

6 Evaluation

In this section, we provide an evaluation of our newly introduced classifier on various datasets including the football player dataset presented in Sect. 4. The detailed experimental setup and implementation is publicly available[3] as is the implementation of the learning algorithm[4].

6.1 Datasets

To evaluate our classifier, we use well-known binary and multi-class datasets from the UCI repository in addition to our newly introduced dataset.

Table 2 provides an overview of all used datasets. For all datasets we report the entropy with respect to the base of the class count. A uniform class balance will, therefore, yield and entropy of 1. A dataset with 1:2 class-imbalance will yield an entropy of 0.92. The three binary datasets stem from the medical domain. Note, that the `ilp` is therefore relatively unbalanced, with significantly more positive samples (416) than negative samples (167). The multi-class datasets include the previously introduced football player dataset as well as one harder dataset: the customer segmentation dataset, also used in [13].

Since the MSL classifier can only work with binary features, all numerical features have been binarized by calculating a threshold to minimize the expected entropy over the two subsets, similar to splits of a decision stump. Note, that

---

[3] https://github.com/TRR318/pub-msl.
[4] https://github.com/TRR318/scikit-psl.

Table 2. Overview of the datasets used in the evaluation. Entropy is calculated to the base of the number of classes of the dataset.

Name	Classes	Instances	Features	Entropy	Task	OpenML	Ref.
breast	2	116	9	0.99	Breast cancer	42900	[35]
ilp	2	583	10	0.86	Liver disease	41945	[37]
diabetes	2	768	8	0.93	Diabetes	37	[44]
wine	3	178	13	0.99	Wine origin	187	[1]
player	4	3611	11	0.90	Football player position	46764	ours
segmentation	4	6665	9	1.00	Customer category		[48]

binarization will be problematic if features do not exhibit a monotonic relationship with the target classes. The (close-to) optimal split is selected by employing a hierarchical search heuristic introduced in [15]. The categorical features in the `segmentation` dataset were one-hot-encoded. The detailed dataset preparation can be found in the experimental repository.

6.2 Setup and Baselines

To evaluate the out-of-sample performance of the classifiers, all experiments have been conducted using Monte Carlo cross-validation (MCCV) with 20 splits where $\frac{2}{3}$ of the data was used for training and the remainder held back for evaluation. The resulting performances have been aggregated and are reported by mean performance and its 95% confidence interval. All experiments have been executed on a single core of a Intel i7-9750H and parallelized over the folds. The total training time of all experiments was more than 40h when parallelized over 12 cores and mostly dominated by the evaluation of MISS, one of our baselines. All MSL instances were learned without regularization and configured with a score set of $\{0, \pm 1, \pm 2, \pm 3\}$. Some metrics, like accuracy, precision, or informedness, do not rely on probability predictions but on discrete classifications. However, the discrete nature of MSLs small score set will often yields ties, especially in earlier stages of the classifier. For example, if only the bias term is evaluated (ref. Table 1), there might be multiple classes with the same maximal total score. In the case of such a set-valued prediction, we select one of the highest-scoring classes uniformly at random.

In each evaluation, we train the PSL and MSL models on all features of the training dataset. Both classifiers create a decision list, i.e., a sequences of decision models for on a nested sequence of features. We call these models "stages". All other baseline models only create single decision models for a specific set of features. Table 3 provides an overview of the training and evaluation method for each stage and the baseline models. In the following paragraphs, we explain in detail how those baseline models can be adapted to those stages.

In Sect. 3.1, we have shown the connection to NB. Using only the likelihoods $P(x_k \mid c)$ of the features available at stage k, NB can naturally be extended to

Table 3. Overview of all models used in the evaluation. k is the number of features used in the kth stage. $model_k$ is the model at the stage k

Model	Training	Training features	Evaluation per stage	Consistent
PSL	global	all	global	✓
MSL	global	all	global	✓
NB	global	all	features of MSL_k	✓
MISS	local	k	features of $MISS_k$	✗
LR, RF, XGB	local	features of MSL_k	features of MSL_k	✗

the setting of scoring lists. Similarly to the MSL, the NB classifier is trained on all features of the training dataset. At prediction time, we only use the same features that the MSL has selected on that stage.

Grzeszczyk et al. [13] introduced learning algorithm for multinomial scoring systems. Apart from the fact that miss cannot natively produce decision lists, we consider this model closely related to our work. The MISS model at each stage was trained with all features but parametrized to use exactly as many features as the MSL did on this stage. Note, that this will not create a consistent list of models, as selected features and assigned scores can be completely different between each model. We have executed MISS with two different timeouts throughout the experiments. $MISS_{90}$ and $MISS_{1800}$ refers to a training timeout of 90 s, and 30 min vice-versa.

Finally, we have selected three additional models as the baseline that have been trained and evaluated on the same subset of features that the MSL selected on the stage: Logistic Regression (LR), Random Forest (RF), and XGBoost (XGB). Overall, we can see that MISS has the largest amount of freedom of all models with respect to feature selection, as only the *number* of features is dictated by the MSLs stage.

To evaluate our model, we rely on two metrics: accuracy (classification rate) and *expected calibration error* (ECE). While the classification rate (fraction of correct predictions) is a standard measure of the correctness of the learner's final (deterministic) decisions, calibration aims to assess the model's probability estimates. Here, we adopt a standard notion of classifier calibration called confidence-calibration: A probabilistic classifier producing predictions $\hat{p}(x) = (\hat{p}_1(x), \ldots, \hat{p}_C(x))$ is (confidence-)calibrated, if

$$P\big(y = \arg\max_i \hat{p}_i(x) \mid \max_i \hat{p}_i(x) = \alpha\big) = \alpha$$

for all $\alpha \in [0,1]$. In words, if the model reports α-confidence in its decision, i.e., the probability predicted for the (presumably) most probable class is α, then this decision is indeed correct with probability α. For example, among all decisions for which the model reports a confidence of 80%, indeed 80% of the cases are correct. While this notion of calibration can be criticized (e.g., because it does not condition on the instance x itself), it does appear useful from the point of view of explainability and informed decision-making. In particular, it provides reasonable support for the stopping condition: A calibrated confidence at stage k of the decision process provides the decision maker with a clear idea of how safe or risky it might be to stop and make a final decision at that stage.

Practically, as ground-truth probabilities cannot be observed in the data, the calibration of a model is measured in terms of the *expected calibration error* (ECE), which is based on the partitioning of the unit interval into a set of bins (intervals) $B_1, \ldots, B_m$. Formally, ECE is then defined as follows [14]:

$$ECE = \sum_{j=1}^{m} \frac{|B_j|}{N} \left| \text{acc}(B_j) - \text{conf}(B_j) \right|, \qquad (7)$$

where N is the number of data points, $|B_j|$ is the number of points falling in bin B_j, $\text{acc}(B_j)$ is the fraction of points in bin B_j for which the model predicted correctly (i.e., the accuracy in that bin), and $\text{conf}(B_j)$ the average confidence reported by the model for points in B_j. We rely on the implementation of Kumar et al. for an unbiased estimate of the ECE [25].

6.3 Classification Accuracy

Binary classification problems can be interpreted in two ways: Either as the presence of absence of the positive label or as a genuine two class problem. This allows comparing the PSL model, which can only make predictions towards the positive class and the MSL which collects evidence towards all alternative classes. Recall, that Naïve Bayes and MSL operate on the same features at prediction time.

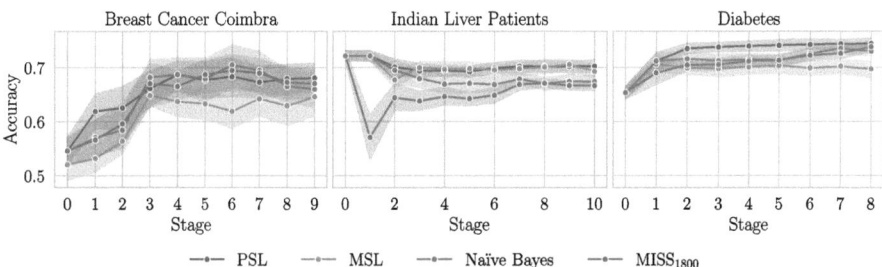

Fig. 4. Classifier accuracy across different stages for all binary datasets. The shaded regions represent confidence intervals of the mean.

Overall, the predictive performance of the compared classifiers yield mixed results on the binary datasets as seen in Fig. 4. While MISS performes good on the `breast` and `diabetes` dataset it exhibits poor accuracy on the unbalanced `ilp` dataset. MSL performes generally sligtly worse than the PSL which is particularly tuned for binary classification problems. On the particularly small

breast dataset 20 MCCV splits appear to have insufficient statistical power to clearly distinguish classifiers performance.

In the multi class setting, we cannot compare to the PSL. Hence, we add multinomial logistic regression and two less interpretable decision models (RF, XGB).

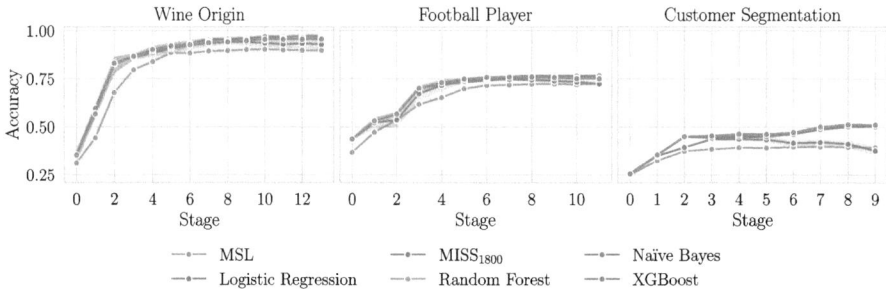

Fig. 5. Classifier accuracy across different stages for all multi-class datasets. The shaded regions represent confidence intervals of the mean.

Figure 5 shows the accuracy of the classifiers across the datasets sorted by sample size. While the MSL performance is worse in general, it must be noted that the MSL and NB construct one list of models that are consistent to each other: Feature subsets form a nested sequence, and the score assigned to a feature remains constant across stages. This is arguably important from an interpretability point of view [18]. The remaining classifiers can create different models for each stage, thereby compromising interpretability. While LR, RF, and XGB at least use the same features that the MSL uses, MISS will only use the same number of features. The parametrizations across those models are not consistent. Still, the MSL performs similarly well to the other classifiers. The performance of MISS declines on the largest dataset (**segmentation**) as more and more features become available. This can only be explained by the 30 min timeout, meaning the models still have a large optimality gap.

6.4 Probability Calibration of the Classifier

In this section we analyze the classifiers probability calibration against the same baselines used in the previous chapter.

Figure 6 shows that all classifiers provide fairly calibrated probability estimates, except for the Naïve Bayes classifier, which is known to be a good classifier but a sub-par probability estimator [51].

On the multi-class datasets (ref. Figure 7) MISS performs slightly worse when only little features are available. In absolute terms, most models exhibit low calibration errors across all stages. The strikingly bad performance of MISS on the **segmentation** can again be explained by the premature terminated training

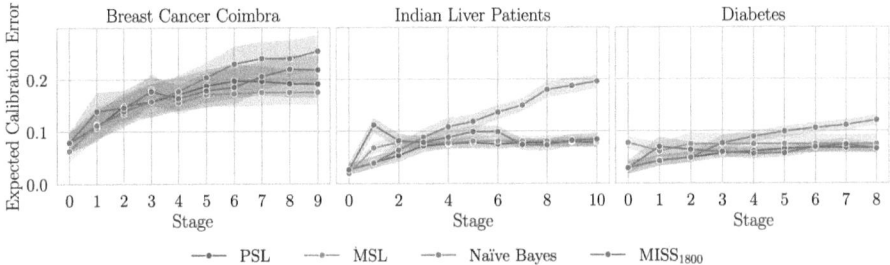

Fig. 6. Expected Calibration Error across different stages for three binary datasets. The plots compare the calibration performance of four models: PSL, MSL, Naïve Bayes, and $MISS_{1800}$. The shaded regions represent confidence intervals.

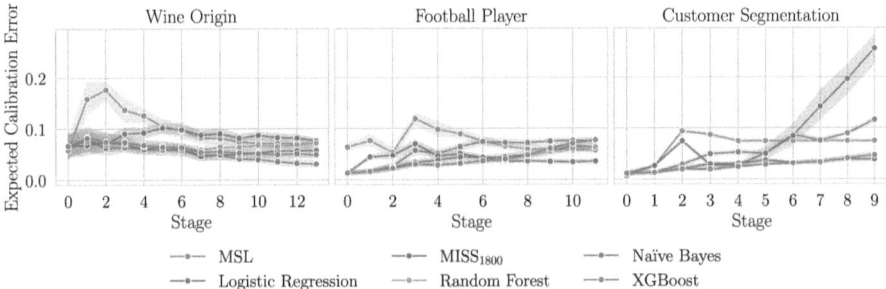

Fig. 7. Expected Calibration Error across different stages for all multi-class datasets. The plots compare the calibration performance of four models: PSL, MSL, Naïve Bayes, and $MISS_{1800}$. The shaded regions represent confidence intervals.

due to timeouts. This can also be seen on the `player` dataset, which is also stopped due to timeouts for stages 8 and following. Fortunately, on this dataset, only a relatively small optimality gap is retained after exhausting the 30 min training budget.

6.5 Runtime Analysis

In the previous sections, we have seen mostly competitive performance of the MISS classifier. However, particularly on the `segmentation` dataset, the performance was often suboptimal, even though the MISS baseline, was the one with the most flexibility as it was only constrained regarding the number of features used.

The MISS classifier is learned by solving a mixed integer program with the help of the `cplex` solver. This can yield provably optimal solutions with respect to the loss function and the training data. However, this training method is also very costly in terms of training time. This is exacerbated in the scenario of decision lists, because many decision models have to be learned independently.

Figure 8 shows the performance of the MSL classifier and two parametrizations of the MISS classifier: one with 90 s and one with 30 min. With only 90 s per stage, the performance of MISS already stagnates after 3 features and hardly exceeds the performance of the MSL, even though the MSL will additionally enforce coherence of the whole decision list. Even with 30 min, stages 6 and following time out, however, with significantly higher performance, which can even be seen in the slight performance decrease after stage 8. For the segmentation dataset, not even 30 min per stage are sufficient and large optimality gaps remain.

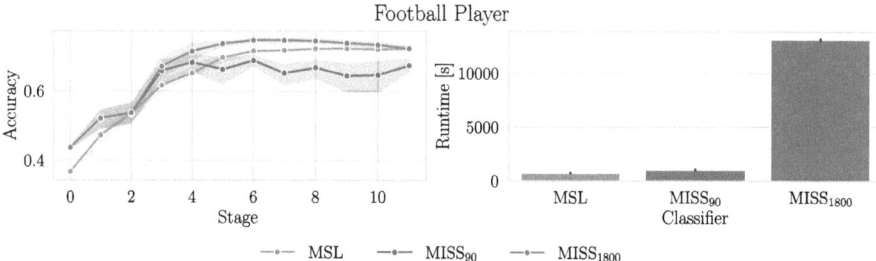

Fig. 8. Accuracy and runtime analysis for the Football Player dataset. The left plot shows accuracy across different stages for MSL and the two 90s and 30min timeout configurations of MISS. The right plot shows the total training time for all stages.

7 Conclusion

In the search for explainable AI, two approaches are currently pursued: post-hoc explaination of complex models and inference of inherently (ante-hoc) explainable models. Although the former approach has been fostered by advances in generative AI, very recent research has shown that explaining complex or even black-box models in easy terms can result in undesirable outcomes, including overreliance on AI if predictions are accompanied by explanations that appear to be comprehensive [17].

In this paper, we therefore pursue a different path to improve the performance of AI in (human) decision-making tasks. We propose a method for learning scoring systems that are commonly used and widely accepted for decision support in real-world applications. In contrast to existing approaches, our method is able to handle problems with more than two choice alternatives. Moreover, by constructing a coherent decision list instead of a single model, MSL supports a stagewise decision-making process, where a decision can be made as soon as enough evidence has been accumulated.

Not less importantly, MSL is inherently explainable due to its restriction to integer scores, its simple additive structure, and the coherence of the models that form a decision list (feature subsets are nested and scores remain unchanged). Admittedly, compared to black-box models or models being less restricted (e.g., additive models with real-valued instead of integer scores, such as logistic regression), MSL may exhibit slightly weaker predictive performance. However, the loss in performance is in general not very high and appears to be acceptable in view of the gain in explainability. Future work should empirically investigate MSL with regard to interpretability and explainability, particularly examining how the stages are used in different decision-making scenarios and how this affects decision quality.

We evaluated human performance on a specific dataset that is especially suited for analyzing AI-human collaborative decision-making, and show that humans perform significantly worse than our approach. Despite this, we believe that a hybrid approach—where a human expert supports a machine learning algorithm in constructing an MSL, or more broadly, engages in an AI-human co-construction of decision models—is a promising direction that we plan to explore in future work, especially given that prior research has shown human-in-the-loop approaches can enhance model performance [34,50], improve decision-making [19], and increase model acceptance [33], even though such methods may be limited when experts are biased [16]. Broadly speaking, the idea is to let the human support or correct decisions about the order of features, the scores assigned to features, etc. This might be beneficial for the learning algorithm, in particular to counteract the heuristic nature of its greedy search strategy. At the same time, a hybrid approach could be appealing for the human expert and increase the acceptance and adoption of automatic decision support—a model that a human expert co-constructed herself will likely increase acceptance, trust, and understanding compared to a model that was constructed in a purely data-driven way and impose on the expert from outside.

Acknowledgements. We gratefully acknowledge funding by the German Research Foundation (Deutsche Forschungsgemeinschaft, DFG): TRR 318/1 2021 – 438445824.

References

1. Aeberhard, S., Forina, M.: Wine. UCI Machine Learning Repository (1992). https://doi.org/10.24432/C5PC7J
2. Ahmed, M.U., Barua, S., Begum, S., Islam, M.R., Weber, R.O.: When a CBR in hand is better than twins in the bush (2023)
3. Barredo Arrieta, A., et al.: Explainable artificial intelligence (XAI): concepts, taxonomies, opportunities and challenges toward responsible AI. Heuristic Optimization **58**, 82–115 (2020). https://doi.org/10.1016/j.inffus.2019.12.012
4. Bell, A., Solano-Kamaiko, I., Nov, O., Stoyanovich, J.: It's just not that simple: an empirical study of the accuracy-explainability trade-off in machine learning for public policy. In: ACM Conference on Fairness, Accountability, and Transparency. pp. 248–266 (2022). https://doi.org/10.1145/3531146.3533090
5. Belle, V.M.C.A.V., et al.: A mathematical model for interpretable clinical decision support with applications in gynecology. PLOS ONE **7**(3), e34312 (2012). https://doi.org/10.1371/journal.pone.0034312

6. Bianchi, F., Piroddi, L., Bemporad, A., Halasz, G., Villani, M., Piga, D.: Active preference-based optimization for human-in-the-loop feature selection. Eur. J. Control. **66**, 100647 (2022). https://doi.org/10.1016/j.ejcon.2022.100647
7. Billiet, L., Huffel, S.V., Belle, V.V.: Interval coded scoring index with interaction effects - A sensitivity study. In: International Conference on Pattern Recognition Applications and Methods (ICPRAM), vol. 2, pp. 33–40 (2016). https://doi.org/10.5220/0005646500330040
8. Billiet, L., Van Huffel, S., Van Belle, V.: Interval coded scoring extensions for larger problems. In: IEEE Symposium on Computers and Communications (ISCC), pp. 198–203 (2017). https://doi.org/10.1109/ISCC.2017.8024529
9. Das, D., Chernova, S.: Leveraging rationales to improve human task performance. In: International Conference on Intelligent User Interfaces (IUI), pp. 510–518 (2020). https://doi.org/10.1145/3377325.3377512
10. Feng, S., Boyd-Graber, J.: What can AI do for me? evaluating machine learning interpretations in cooperative play. In: International Conference on Intelligent User Interfaces (IUI), pp. 229–239 (2019). https://doi.org/10.1145/3301275.3302265
11. Fisher, R.A.: Iris. UCI Machine Learning Repository (1936). https://doi.org/10.24432/C56C76
12. Gage, B.F., Waterman, A.D., Shannon, W., Boechler, M., Rich, M.W., Radford, M.J.: Validation of clinical classification schemes for predicting stroke results from the national registry of atrial fibrillation. JAMA **285**(22), 2864–2870 (2001). https://doi.org/10.1001/jama.285.22.2864
13. Grzeszczyk, M.K., Trzciński, T., Sitek, A.: MISS: multiclass interpretable scoring systems. In: SIAM International Conference on Data Mining (SDM), pp. 55–63 (2024). https://doi.org/10.1137/1.9781611978032.7
14. Guo, C., Pleiss, G., Sun, Y., Weinberger, K.Q.: On calibration of modern neural networks. In: International Conference on Machine Learning (ICML), pp. 1321–1330 (2017)
15. Hanselle, J., Heid, S., Fürnkranz, J., Hüllermeier, E.: Probabilistic scoring lists for interpretable machine learning. Mach. Learn. **114**(3), 55 (2025). https://doi.org/10.1007/s10994-024-06705-w
16. Hanselle, J., Kornowicz, J., Heid, S., Thommes, K., Hüllermeier, E.: Comparing humans and algorithms in feature ranking: a case-study in the medical domain. In: Leyer, M., Wichmann, J. (eds.) Lernen, Wissen, Daten, Analysen (LWDA), vol. 3630, pp. 430–441 (2023)
17. He, G., Aishwarya, N., Gadiraju, U.: Is conversational XAI all you need? Human-AI decision-making with a conversational XAI assistant (2025)
18. Heid, S., Hanselle, J., Fürnkranz, J., Hüllermeier, E.: Learning decision catalogues for situated decision making: The case of scoring systems. Inter. J. Approximate Reas. (IJAR) **171**, 109190 (2024). https://doi.org/10.1016/J.IJAR.2024.109190
19. Heid, S., Kornowicz, J., Hanselle, J., Hüllermeier, E., Thommes, K.: Human-AI co-construction of interpretable predictive models: the case of scoring systems. In: Workshop on Computational Intelligence (CI), pp. 233–252 (2024)
20. Janosi, A., Steinbrunn, W., Pfisterer, M., Detrano, R.: Heart disease. UCI Machine Learning Repository (1989). https://doi.org/10.24432/C52P4X
21. Jeong, B.H., et al.: Performances of prognostic scoring systems in patients with healthcare-associated pneumonia. Clin. Infect. Dis. **56**(5), 625–632 (2013). https://doi.org/10.1093/cid/cis970
22. Kline, J.A., Mitchell, A.M., Kabrhel, C., Richman, P., Courtney, D.M.: Clinical criteria to prevent unnecessary diagnostic testing in emergency department patients with suspected pulmonary embolism. J. Thromb. Haemost. **2**(8), 1247–1255 (2004)

23. Knaus, W.A., et al.: The APACHE III prognostic system: risk prediction of hospital mortality for critically III hospitalized adults. Chest **100**(6), 1619–1636 (1991)
24. Kohavi, R.: Census income. UCI Machine Learning Repository (1996). https://doi.org/10.24432/C5GP7S
25. Kumar, A., Liang, P., Ma, T.: Verified uncertainty calibration. In: Advances in Neural Information Processing Systems (NeurIPS), pp. 3787–3798 (2019)
26. Lai, V., Chen, C., Smith-Renner, A., Liao, Q.V., Tan, C.: Towards a science of human-AI decision making: an overview of design space in empirical human-subject studies. In: Conference on Fairness, Accountability, and Transparency, pp. 1369–1385 (2023). https://doi.org/10.1145/3593013.3594087
27. Lip, G.Y., Nieuwlaat, R., Pisters, R., Lane, D.A., Crijns, H.J.: Refining clinical risk stratification for predicting stroke and thromboembolism in atrial fibrillation using a novel risk factor-based approach: The euro heart survey on atrial fibrillation. Chest **137**(2), 263–272 (2010)
28. Lundberg, S.M., Lee, S.I.: A unified approach to interpreting model predictions. In: Advances in Neural Information Processing Systems (NeurIPS), pp. 4765–4774 (2017)
29. Mahmud, H., Islam, A.K.M.N., Ahmed, S.I., Smolander, K.: What influences algorithmic decision-making? a systematic literature review on algorithm aversion. Technol. Forecast. Soc. Chang. **175**, 121390 (2022). https://doi.org/10.1016/j.techfore.2021.121390
30. Moreno, R.P., et al.: On behalf of the SAPS 3 Investigators: SAPS 3From evaluation of the patient to evaluation of the intensive care unit. Part 2: Development of a prognostic model for hospital mortality at icu admission. Intensive Care Med. **31**(10), 1345–1355 (2005). https://doi.org/10.1007/s00134-005-2763-5
31. Mortier, T., Hüllermeier, E., Dembczynski, K., Waegeman, W.: Set-valued prediction in hierarchical classification with constrained representation complexity. In: Cussens, J., Zhang, K. (eds.) Uncertainty in Artificial Intelligence (UAI), vol. 180, pp. 1392–1401 (2022)
32. Mounzer, R., et al.: Comparison of existing clinical scoring systems to predict persistent organ failure in patients with acute pancreatitis. Gastroenterology **142**, 1476–1482 (2012). https://doi.org/10.1053/j.gastro.2012.03.005
33. Muijlwijk, H., Willemsen, M.C., Smyth, B., IJsselsteijn, W.A.: Benefits of human-AI interaction for expert users interacting with prediction models: a study on marathon running. In: International Conference on Intelligent User Interfaces (IUI), pp. 245–258 (2024). https://doi.org/10.1145/3640543.3645205
34. Nahar, J., Imam, T., Tickle, K.S., Chen, Y.P.P.: Computational intelligence for heart disease diagnosis: a medical knowledge driven approach. Expert Syst. Appl. **40**(1), 96–104 (2013). https://doi.org/10.1016/j.eswa.2012.07.032
35. Patrcio, M., Pereira, J., Crisstomo, J., Matafome, P., Seia, R., Caramelo, F.: Breast cancer coimbra. UCI Machine Learning Repository (2018). https://doi.org/10.24432/C52P59
36. Poursabzi-Sangdeh, F., Goldstein, D.G., Hofman, J.M., Wortman Vaughan, J.W., Wallach, H.: Manipulating and measuring model interpretability. In: Conference on Human Factors in Computing Systems (CHI), pp. 1–52 (2021). https://doi.org/10.1145/3411764.3445315
37. Ramana, B., Venkateswarlu, N.: Indian liver patient. UCI Machine Learning Repository (2022). https://doi.org/10.24432/C5D02C
38. Rapsang, A.G., Shyam, D.C.: Scoring systems in the intensive care unit: a compendium. Indian J. Critical Care Med. **18**(4), 220–228 (2014). https://doi.org/10.4103/0972-5229.130573

39. Ribeiro, M.T., Singh, S., Guestrin, C.: "Why Should I Trust You?": explaining the predictions of any classifier. In: International Conference on Knowledge Discovery and Data Mining (SIGKDD), pp. 1135–1144 (2016). https://doi.org/10.1145/2939672.2939778
40. Rivest, R.L.: Learning decision lists. Mach. Learn. **2**(3), 229–246 (1987). https://doi.org/10.1007/BF00058680
41. Rouzot, J., Ferry, J., Huguet, M.J.: Learning optimal fair scoring systems for multi-class classification. In: International Conference on Tools with Artificial Intelligence (ICTAI), pp. 197–204 (2022). https://doi.org/10.1109/ICTAI56018.2022.00036
42. Rudin, C.: Stop explaining black box machine learning models for high stakes decisions and use interpretable models instead. Nat. Mach. Intell. **1**(5), 206–215 (2019). https://doi.org/10.1038/S42256-019-0048-X
43. Sanyal, S., Biswas, S.K., Das, D., Chakraborty, M., Purkayastha, B.: Boston house price prediction using regression models. In: International Conference on Intelligent Technologies, pp. 1–6 (2022)
44. Smith, J.W., Everhart, J.E., Dickson, W.C., Knowler, W.C., Johannes, R.S.: Using the ADAP learning algorithm to forecast the onset of diabetes mellitus. In: Computational Applications Medical Care, pp. 261–265 (1988)
45. Taheri, E., Wang, C., Zahmat Doost, E.: Emergency decision-making under an uncertain time limit. Inter. J. Disaster Risk Reduct. **95**, 103832 (2023). https://doi.org/10.1016/j.ijdrr.2023.103832
46. Ustun, B., Rudin, C.: Supersparse linear integer models for optimized medical scoring systems. Mach. Learn. **102**(3), 349–391 (2016). https://doi.org/10.1007/S10994-015-5528-6
47. Ustun, B., Rudin, C.: Learning optimized risk scores. J. Mach. Learn. Res. **20**, 150:1–150:75 (2019)
48. Vidhya, A.: Customer segmentation. Kaggle (2020)
49. Wang, C., Han, B., Patel, B., Rudin, C.: In pursuit of interpretable, fair and accurate machine learning for criminal recidivism prediction. J. Quant. Criminol. **39**(2), 519–581 (2023)
50. Yang, Y., Kandogan, E., Li, Y., Sen, P., Lasecki, W.S.: A study on interaction in human-in-the-loop machine learning for text analytics. In: IUI Workshops (2019)
51. Zadrozny, B., Elkan, C.P.: Obtaining calibrated probability estimates from decision trees and naive bayesian classifiers. In: International Conference on Machine Learning (ICML) (2001)
52. Zeng, Z., Shi, Z., Li, X.: Comparing different scoring systems for predicting mortality risk in preterm infants: a systematic review and network meta-analysis. Front. Pediatr. **11**, 1287774 (2023). https://doi.org/10.3389/fped.2023.1287774

Open Access This chapter is licensed under the terms of the Creative Commons Attribution 4.0 International License (http://creativecommons.org/licenses/by/4.0/), which permits use, sharing, adaptation, distribution and reproduction in any medium or format, as long as you give appropriate credit to the original author(s) and the source, provide a link to the Creative Commons license and indicate if changes were made.

The images or other third party material in this chapter are included in the chapter's Creative Commons license, unless indicated otherwise in a credit line to the material. If material is not included in the chapter's Creative Commons license and your intended use is not permitted by statutory regulation or exceeds the permitted use, you will need to obtain permission directly from the copyright holder.

Interpretable World Model Imaginations as Deep Reinforcement Learning Explanation

Nils Wenninghoff[(✉)] and Maike Schwammberger

Karlsruhe Institute of Technology, Karlsruhe 76131, Germany
{wenninghoff,schwammberger}@kit.edu

Abstract. Explainable Deep Reinforcement Learning aims to clarify the decision-making processes of agents. Recent world model-based approaches, such as Dreamer, train agents through "imagination," where the actor learns by interacting with a learned world model that simulates the environment. Consequently, the overall performance of these systems depends not only on the learned actor but also on the fidelity of the world model's representation. Effective explanations should, therefore, incorporate the learned dynamics of the environment.

In this work, we propose a method that leverages the imagination technique from the training process to generate stepwise, contrastive explanations during inference. Our approach systematically compares predicted states, actions, and value and reward estimates to evaluate the observed trajectory. This analysis provides insights into whether failures arise from inaccuracies in the world model, errors in value estimation, or deficiencies in reward prediction. We demonstrate the effectiveness of our method across multiple goal-oriented tasks.

Keywords: Explainable Deep Reinforcement Learning · Reinforcement Learning · Explainability · Contrastive Explanation · World Model

1 Introduction

Deep Reinforcement Learning (DRL) involves sequential decision-making under uncertainty and partial observability, making it inherently complex. Recent advances, such as DreamerV3 [11], have further increased this complexity by using models from the learned world to enable training in imagination. This approach significantly improves sample efficiency and allows the agent to plan its actions based on predicted future states. However, these improvements come at the cost of increased complexity.

Despite their performance, modern DRL agents remain black-box systems, requiring specialized explanation methods to interpret their behavior [28].

Several Explainable Deep Reinforcement Learning (XDRL) approaches have been introduced [19,28], but explaining every aspect of the DRL decision-making process remains a challenge. Unlike supervised learning models, DRL decisions depend not only on the current state but also on the learned policy, the reward function, the value estimation, and the training process itself.

Training in imagination introduces additional challenges for explainability. Since the agent learns from a surrogate world model rather than from the real environment, imperfections in the learned dynamics may influence decision-making in unexpected ways. Existing explanation techniques do not account for discrepancies between the learned world model and the real world, which can lead to misleading or incomplete explanations.

To address these challenges, we propose a method that utilizes DreamerV3's learned world model to generate outcome explanations based on the imagination of the world model. By using the same policy, world model, and imagination process as during training, we ensure that explanations are consistent with the agent's decision-making and build on the dynamics the agent was trained on. We highlight the differences between learned and real dynamics by comparing imagined trajectories with real-world observations. This approach generates explanations that visualize the behavior within the learned world model and compare it to the behavior in the real environment. These explanations reveal whether the agent has learned different dynamics, making the agent's assumptions about future outcomes transparent. This could help experts better understand the agent's behavior, especially when it acts unexpectedly.

We evaluate our approach on five Minigrid benchmark tasks, assessing its correctness and continuity in discrete environments with partial observability. Our results indicate that leveraging the agent's internal world model for explanations can produce contrastive explanations that are based on the learned dynamics during training. The process of accessing the learned dynamics could serve as a foundation for building further explanations.

The contributions of this paper are:

- Identification of the explanatory requirements for *training in imagination* DRL algorithms
- Contrastive explanation, making the learned dynamics and decision-making process transparent
- Adjustable, visual explanation technique for failure analysis and agent behavior understandability
- Extensive technical evaluation

In Sect. 2, we review the key background concepts in DRL and explainable AI, followed by an overview of the current state of the art in Sect. 3. In Sect. 4, we describe our proposed explanation technique that integrates learned world model dynamics into the explanation process. Section 5 outlines our experimental setup and evaluation metrics, while Sect. 6 presents our empirical findings. We discuss our findings and related limitations in Sect. 7. Finally, Sect. 8 concludes the paper and discusses future research directions.

To promote transparency, all additions to the base DreamerV3 implementation, as well as the model checkpoints, are publicly available https://github.com/wnnng/dreamer_explanation.

2 Preliminaries

In this section, we discuss the fundamental concepts on which our work is based. We give a broad overview of reinforcement learning in Sect. 2.1 and explain the Dreamer algorithm in more detail in Sect. 2.2. Finally, we introduce key definitions and concepts in explainable AI in Sect. 2.3, providing the necessary context for evaluating DRL explanations.

2.1 (Deep) Reinforcement Learning

DRL extends traditional reinforcement learning to complex, high-dimensional domains using deep neural networks. In (deep) reinforcement learning, the agent-environment interaction is formalized as a Markov Decision Process (MDP) [27], defined by the tuple

$$(\mathcal{S}, \mathcal{A}, T, R, \gamma), \tag{1}$$

where $\mathcal{S}$ is the set of states, $\mathcal{A}$ is the set of actions, $T(s'|s,a)$ denotes the state transition probability, $R(s,a)$ is the reward function, and $\gamma \in [0,1)$ is the discount factor. The agent aims to learn a policy $\pi(a|s)$ that maximizes the expected cumulative discounted reward:

$$J(\pi) = \mathbb{E}_\pi \left[\sum_{t=0}^{\infty} \gamma^t R(s_t, a_t) \right]. \tag{2}$$

In many real-world scenarios, the environment is only partially observable, leading to the formulation of a Partially observable Markov Decision Process (POMDP) [13]. A POMDP augments the MDP framework by incorporating an observation space Ω and an observation function $O(o|s',a)$, and is defined by the tuple

$$(\mathcal{S}, \mathcal{A}, T, R, \Omega, O, \gamma). \tag{3}$$

Here, the agent receives observations $o \in \Omega$ that provide incomplete information about the underlying state.

The decision-making process in DRL is encapsulated in a policy $\pi(a|s)$, typically trained alongside a value function $V(s)$ that estimates long-term rewards. DRL approaches are broadly categorized into model-free methods, which learn the policy and value function directly from experience, and model-based methods, where the agent either uses a given model or learns a model of the environment's dynamics. The model can be used for planning or to improve sample efficiency [21].

2.2 Dreamer

For our explanation, we use Dreamer [11] as the base algorithm. Since our technique uses the internal models and processes to generate explanations, it is important to understand the Dreamer algorithm. In this section, we give an overview of the relevant techniques introduced by Hafner et al. [9–11].

Dreamer is a model-based DRL algorithm. Model-based reinforcement learning leverages learned environment dynamics to plan ahead, improve data efficiency, and tackle sparse reward settings. In this context, Dreamer serves as a prime example by using a world model to simulate future trajectories and optimize policy updates.

It models the environment via a latent dynamics model, specifically a Recurrent State Space Model (RSSM). Given a sequence of high-dimensional observations $x_{1:T}$ and actions $a_{1:T}$, the RSSM learns to represent the environment in a compact latent space. At each time step t, an encoder network transforms the observation x_t into a discrete latent representation z_t according to:

$$z_t \sim q_\phi(z_t \mid h_t, x_t), \tag{4}$$

where h_t is a hidden recurrent state that summarizes past information. The hidden state is updated with the previous recurrent state, latent state, and action:

$$h_t = f_\phi(h_{t-1}, z_{t-1}, a_{t-1}), \tag{5}$$

with f_ϕ denoting the transition function parameterized by ϕ.

To ensure that the latent representations capture essential aspects of the environment, a decoder network reconstructs the observation:

$$\hat{x}_t \sim p_\phi(\hat{x}_t \mid h_t, z_t). \tag{6}$$

In addition, auxiliary predictors are employed to estimate rewards r_t and continue signals c_t via:

$$\hat{r}_t \sim p_\phi(\hat{r}_t \mid h_t, z_t), \quad \hat{c}_t \sim p_\phi(\hat{c}_t \mid h_t, z_t). \tag{7}$$

Training is achieved by minimizing a composite loss consisting of a reconstruction loss, a dynamics loss (which minimizes the Kullback-Leibler (KL)-divergence between the encoder's posterior $q_\phi(z_t \mid h_t, x_t)$ and the prior $p_\phi(z_t \mid h_t)$), and a representation loss that regularizes the latent space. Techniques such as free bits [14] are applied to the KL-divergence terms to maintain a minimum level of information in each latent dimension, thereby preventing posterior collapse. The model state is defined as $s_t = \{h_t, z_t\}$, combining the recurrent hidden state with the discrete latent representation.

With a well-regularized latent representation, the world model can simulate future trajectories. This process, known as imagination, allows the model to predict future states from a given start state without new observations from the environment:

$$h_{t+1} = f_\phi(h_t, \hat{z}_t, a_t), \tag{8}$$

where a_t is sampled from the current policy. Since the latent z state depends on observations, the world model approximates it from the recurrent h-state:

$$\hat{z}_t \sim p_\phi(\hat{z}_t \mid h_t). \tag{9}$$

The world model also predicts the corresponding rewards and continue signals for each imagined state. This rollout creates an imagined trajectory:

$$s_0, a_0, r_0, c_0, s_1, a_1, r_1, c_1, \ldots, s_T, a_T, r_T, c_T.$$

The agent uses only imagined trajectories to update its policy and value estimates, a process that can be described as *training in imagination*. For the actor-critic, the critic learns to predict the expected return R_t from a given latent state s_t.

The actor is updated by maximizing a surrogate objective derived from the predicted returns of imagined trajectories. In practice, this means the policy is encouraged to select actions that lead to higher predicted returns, while simultaneously incorporating an entropy term to foster exploration. Importantly, the predicted returns are normalized and treated such that gradients do not flow back through them, ensuring a stable update process for the actor.

This design allows the agent to efficiently optimize its policy using internal, model-generated data, significantly improving data efficiency and enabling long-horizon planning in environments with sparse rewards.

2.3 Explainability

The field of Explainable Artificial Intelligence (XAI) seeks to make the decisions of Artificial Intelligence (AI) systems transparent and interpretable [15]. Explaining the sequential decision-making process of DRL agents, which aim to maximize long-term returns despite sparse rewards, poses challenges that traditional XAI techniques do not fully address [4,6,25]. Consequently, recent research has focused on adapting and extending XAI methods specifically for DRL [6,28]. In the following, we define key concepts including interpretability, explainability, and post-hoc and intrinsic explanation approaches, which underpin the understanding of DRL explanations.

In accordance with [28], we adopt the following definitions: An *explanation* is the surface representation of an interpretation that is communicated to the user. An *interpretation* is the explanation content produced by an interpretable model, while *interpretability* refers to the system's capacity to generate such content. *Explainability* denotes the ability to provide these surface representations, and *transparency* describes the system's capability to deliver understandable explanations in the deployment context, accounting for domain-specific constraints.

Explanations for DRL can target different aspects of the agent. For example, *behavioral explanations* focus on the agent's decision-making process, *task explanations* illuminate the underlying objectives, and *reward decompositions* elucidate the structure of the reward function. Moreover, while technical challenges primarily concern model interpretability, explainability must also address the needs of diverse stakeholders, who vary in their expertise and expectations [15].

One challenge in explainability is the evaluation of explanations, as highlighted by Nauta et al. [22]. Explanations that are intuitive and align with users' expectations may be plausible, but not necessarily correct. Therefore, it is important to assess both the plausibility (i.e., how convincing the explanation appears) and the correctness of an explanation. To address these challenges, Nauta et al. propose the Co-12 evaluation criteria [22], which encompass dimensions such as correctness, continuity, contrastivity, compactness, and controllability. For each criterion, specific evaluation methods are suggested. For our explanation technique, we focus on the evaluation of correctness and continuity.

In summary, we have outlined the fundamental concepts of DRL and Dreamer, as well as the key principles of XAI and XDRL, including the definitions and evaluation criteria critical for assessing DRL explanations. With an understanding of the unique challenges associated with sequential decision-making, sparse rewards, and training in imagination, we are now ready to describe our approach. The next section details our methodology, including the architecture of our explanation technique.

3 State of the Art

As AI processes evolve and are applied to new domains, explanation methods must be adjusted to align with these emerging contexts [16]. Consequently, evaluating existing solutions is essential. This section provides an overview of relevant DRL algorithms that incorporate training in imagination. We also give an overview of explainability techniques related to our approach.

World-model-based DRL is a promising and growing research direction for solving complex tasks [8,33]. A key concept in most approaches is training in imagination, where the actor learns from the dynamics predicted by the world model rather than direct environment interactions.

Dreamer, introduced by Hafner et al. [9–11], employs a RSSM as its world model. It represents latent states using two components: a recurrent state, which encodes historical context, and a stochastic state, which captures the current state. Dreamer uses an actor-critic model, and its world model predicts rewards and a continue probability. It is applicable to both discrete and continuous environments. We selected Dreamer because it offers a well-structured latent state representation, a recurrent architecture that supports explanation, and broad applicability.

Recent approaches to world models for DRL have taken diverse directions. For example, Mattes et al. [17] proposed a simplified structured state-space (S5) model that enables parallel sequence prediction, improving efficiency and long-term dependencies but struggling with short-term dynamics and local precision, which complicates the explanation process. Similarly, Micheli et al. [18] use a transformer-based autoregressive model that also has difficulties capturing fine-grained details. In contrast, Alonso et al. [1] presented a diffusion model that yields more visually accurate imaginations, though its computationally expensive denoising step and reduced interpretability limit its applicability. Lastly, Rigter et al. [24] offer a non-autoregressive diffusion model that iteratively denoises a random trajectory to reduce error accumulation, yet it still inherits the inherent limitations of diffusion-based methods. We acknowledge that all these methods could be explored for explanation, since the explanation focuses on the comparison of the imagined state and the observation.

Several methods have been proposed to explain DRL outcomes. Yau et al. [30] showed that post-hoc explanations suffer from value ambiguity, addressing this by learning a belief map during training. Similarly, Saulières et al. [26] used a Q-learning policy to predict three trajectories—the current, best-case, and worst-case outcomes, by modifying environment dynamics to illustrate alternative results. Both approaches provide valuable outcome explanations for Q-learning but are not designed to capture action differences emerging from training in imagination.

Other methods generate counterfactual explanations. Yu et al. [32] construct causal chains using a causal world model, while Olson et al. [23] and Yeh et al. [31] employed counterfactual generation via simulated environments and variational autoencoders, respectively. Although these techniques offer insights into alternative decision paths, they do not incorporate the learned training dynamics into their explanations.

Amitai et al. [2] visually compare an agent's chosen action with a counterfactual alternative, demonstrating improved user understanding through simulation of subsequent steps in the real environment. In contrast, our approach leverages the learned world model dynamics to generate explanations, thereby reflecting the agent's internal representations more faithfully.

Evaluating explanations is inherently challenging, as it requires balancing technical fidelity with user-centric criteria such as clarity and relevance [12,16,22]. While correctness is essential, explanations must also be accessible and useful to end users.

While explainable DRL has advanced, particularly with the growing focus on counterfactual outcome explanations, no existing approach addresses the unique challenges introduced by training in imagination. To the best of our knowledge, this gap remains unaddressed. We address this gap by integrating the learned world model dynamics into the explanation process.

4 Methodology

Explanations in DRL should be contrastive [20], meaning they should explain why one decision was made over another, aligning with human reasoning. However, explanations must also be faithful, accurately reflecting the true decision-making process of the agent.

This is particularly challenging in training-in-imagination DRL, where the agent learns to use a world model rather than direct interaction with the real environment. Existing explanation techniques primarily focus on the agent's interaction with the real environment, which does not capture the dynamics the agent actually trained on. To generate faithful explanations in this setting, we need to incorporate the agent's learned world model dynamics into the explanation process.

Our explanation technique renders the agent's decision-making process interpretable by incorporating the learned dynamics of its internal world model. In our research abstract [29], we introduced the theoretical concept of using world-model imagination as an explanation technique. Building on this foundation, our approach generates alternative imagination trajectories directly from the learned dynamics, eliminating the need for external simulations. These trajectories capture the agent's internal expectations, and the contrast between the imagined and observed trajectories highlights discrepancies between the world model and the real environment.

Specifically, our method compares the agent's imagined experiences with actual observations to pinpoint where its internal expectations deviate from reality. This analysis allows us to differentiate between errors stemming from the actor's policy and those introduced by inaccuracies in the learned world model dynamics. By providing contrastive, outcome-based explanations that mirror human reasoning, our approach enhances transparency and reveals how the agent's expectations shape its decisions.

4.1 Generating Imagination Trajectories

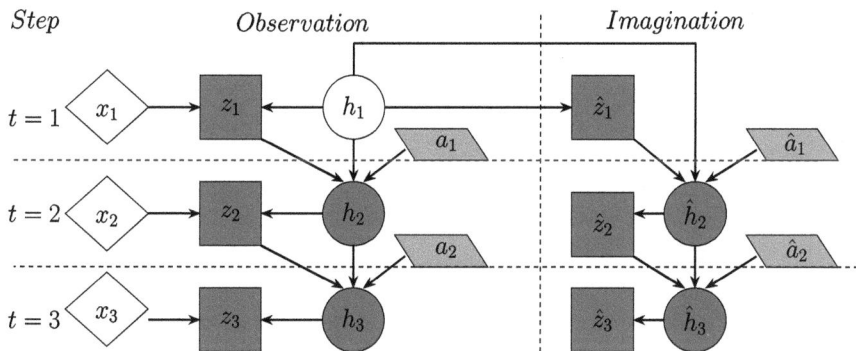

Fig. 1. Stepwise comparison of observed (left) and imagined (right) trajectories. Observations x_t (white), latent states z_t, $\hat{z}_t$ (blue), actions a_t, a'_t (gold), and hidden states h_t, h'_t (purple), are compared at each step. This comparison serves as the basis of our explanation technique and highlights discrepancies between reality and the agent's internal model. (Color figure online)

Figure 1 illustrates the generation of imagination trajectories. For each observation state x_t at time step t in a trajectory of length T, we generate an imagined trajectory of length H, corresponding to the imagination horizon used during training. Hence, the total number of imagined steps is $t + H$.

This procedure replicates the training dynamics by sampling an initial observation from the real environment and subsequently generating imagined rollouts that optimize the actor network. Unlike during training, we do not compute a loss function to optimize decision-making, but instead measure the deviations between imagined trajectories and actual observations. These deviations indicate potential errors in the learned dynamics, which may lead to suboptimal decisions.

Since the imagination process does not automatically terminate at terminal states, we implement a post-processing pruning step. Let $C(s) \in [0, 1]$ denote the continue predictor's output for a model state $s = \{h, z\}$. We prune any state for which $C(s) < \tau$, where τ is a user-defined threshold (guided by the continue loss from training). This step removes invalid imagined states, which would otherwise be hallucinations—predictions made after the environment has terminated, when no new observations or training data are available. Consequently, correctly identifying terminal states is crucial not only to eliminate spurious, hallucinated states but also to ensure that failure states are accurately detected, thereby supporting proper learning of negative consequences.

4.2 Identifying Deviations

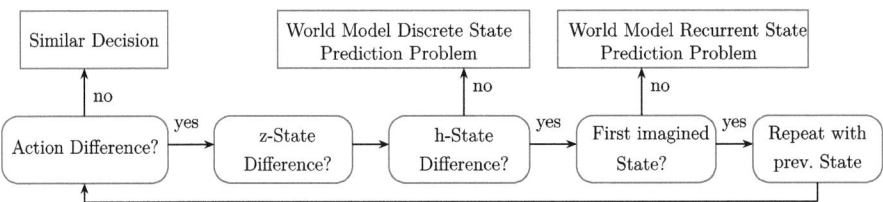

Fig. 2. Sequence of checks for the declaration. Starting with the identification of whether different actions have been selected, followed by the states of the world model.

To explain the action decision-making process, in this work we focus on discrete action spaces. Figure 2 illustrates the explanation process. For each time step t, we compare the observed action with the corresponding imagined action. Unlike imagination processes used during training, which do not inherently perform such a comparison, this method explicitly identifies deviations in the decision-making process.

Because the policy samples actions based on a probability distribution, two input states can produce the same action even if the underlying distributions differ. Furthermore, it is possible for the same distribution to sample two different actions for the same state. To reduce this ambiguity, we also compare the full probability distributions. This dual comparison ensures that even if the final actions appear similar, underlying differences in the agent's confidence or reasoning are not overlooked. While this reduces the risk of ambiguity, it does not fully eliminate it.

To address the ambiguity of similar outputs, we also compare the states within the world model. This includes the recurrent state h and the discrete latent states z. The actor uses the recurrent state and the discrete latent state, which depends on the stochastic latent state. To differentiate the different transformations, we compare them individually. The comparison is done for each time step, aligning the observed state with the corresponding imagined state. For example, when comparing real time step 1, we compare the first observed action with the first action in the imagination. We compare the predicted world model states $\hat{h}_{t+1}, \hat{z}_{t+1}$ with the actual observed states h_{t+1}, z_{t+1}. In Fig. 1, $\hat{h}_{t+1}$ and h_{t+1} are shown in purple, while $\hat{z}_{t+1}$ and z_{t+1} are shown in blue.

The state comparison involves Mean Squared Error (MSE) for the recurrent state, while the discrete latent state is compared using the Hamming distance. The latter is appropriate because the discrete latent state consists of a set of categorical variables, each with a number of possible classes. These comparisons provide insight into the accuracy of the agent's internal world model, highlighting deviations in its understanding of the environment.

Next, we evaluate the value estimation by comparing the critic's estimated value with the actual sum of rewards in the observations, which reveals whether the expected return is accurately predicted. If the agent selects a suboptimal action but imagines a high return, it suggests that the negative consequences of that action are not well learned. In these cases, it is useful to examine the world model's subsequent state predictions. If these predictions differ from the observed states, it suggests that the model may not fully capture the negative outcomes. If they closely match the observations, then the discrepancy likely arises from the critic's evaluation.

Finally, it's important to note that the world model may not always be able to make perfect predictions, especially in stochastic environments. While the model provides plausible predictions, the expert user must assess the validity of these predictions. This means that, in certain cases, deviations identified by the model should be analyzed for uncertainty. We cover this topic further in Sect. 7, where we discuss how to incorporate uncertainty into the explanation framework.

4.3 Explaining the Deviations

To explain the decision-making process, our approach highlights the differences between the imagined and observed trajectories by directly leveraging the agent's inherent world model, the very ground truth used for its optimization. Unlike many existing explanation techniques that rely on external models or surrogate training strategies, our method provides a faithful diagnostic tool that exposes where the learned dynamics diverge from actual behavior. By identifying these deviations, our approach offers domain experts a powerful foundation upon which more detailed causal analyses can later be built. In essence, our evaluation algorithm unfolds in three stages: an action-level analysis, an input-state evaluation, and a reward and value estimation assessment.

Action-Level Analysis. We begin by comparing the discrete actions taken at each time step. To quantify the similarity between two action distributions π_1 and π_2, we use the Jensen-Shannon distance [7], a symmetric and bounded metric defined as:

$$\text{JSD}(\pi_1, \pi_2) = \sqrt{\frac{1}{2} D_{\text{KL}}(\pi_1 \| M) + \frac{1}{2} D_{\text{KL}}(\pi_2 \| M)}, \quad \text{where } M = \frac{1}{2}(\pi_1 + \pi_2) \quad (10)$$

This distance is always finite, lies in $[0, \sqrt{\log 2}]$ (for base-e logarithms), and is well-suited for comparing discrete probability distributions over actions in reinforcement learning. Our dual approach reveals whether similar actions were chosen for similar reasons, or if subtle differences in decision confidence are present.

Input-State Evaluation. Since the policy's decisions are deeply rooted in the internal state generated by the world model, we compare its critical components: the recurrent state h and the stochastic latent state z. For the discrete, categorical components, the Hamming distance is employed to count mismatches, while continuous elements, like the recurrent state h, are compared using the MSE. This analysis pinpoints whether deviations in the world model states have propagated to impact the policy's outputs, directly linking discrepancies in the training process to subsequent decision-making.

Reward and Value Estimation Assessment. Finally, we examine the reward signals and the estimated value function. By comparing the true accumulated rewards with the agent's value estimation, we can identify misalignment in how the learned dynamics translate into expected outcomes. For instance, if a suboptimal action is chosen despite similar action probability profiles, a discrepancy in the value estimation might signal that the policy is not adequately optimized toward the intended goal.

Collectively, these three evaluation stages, tracing from the imagined states, through the action decision, to the downstream value estimation, offer a comprehensive view of where and how the learned dynamics diverge from actual behavior. By directly using the agent's internal world model, our method addresses the unique requirements for understanding decision-making in training-in-imagination deep reinforcement learning. Although our current approach does not yet prove causal relationships, it lays the essential groundwork upon which future causal analyses can be developed, thereby significantly advancing the state of explainable reinforcement learning.

In the chosen benchmark, the agent receives image-based observations that are first encoded into a latent state representation, which is then used for decision-making. Since this latent representation is not easily interpretable for

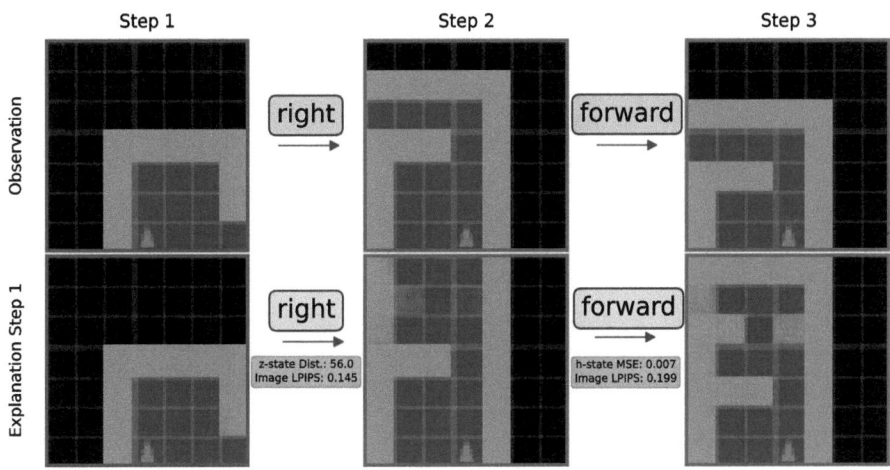

Fig. 3. Exemplary partial visualization of the explanation process. The top row shows a segment of the agent's observation, while the second row displays the explanation for the first step along with its imagination. The first imagined image represents the internal state derived from the observation, and the second image shows the corresponding imagined next state, with measurements provided underneath. From the second step onward, the imagined states diverge from the actual observations. (Color figure online)

human observers, we decode it back into the image space to provide visual explanations. While these decoded images support human understanding, the analytical comparison used to identify differences in behavior operates entirely in the latent space. As described in the preliminaries, Dreamer employs an encoder and a decoder. Although the decoder is not part of the decision-making process, it is critical for the explanations that the reconstructed images look similar to the original observations. To ensure this, we measure the Learned Perceptual Image Patch Similarity (LPIPS) value between the true observation and the decoded latent state. Unlike MSE, LPIPS focuses on structural similarity and is less sensitive to minor color differences or small non-structural changes. A low LPIPS value indicates that the decoded image is similar to the original observation, preserving the fidelity of the explanation. Moreover, the LPIPS error should correspond to the error in the latent state; if the latent space deviates significantly from the true state, the decoded image should reflect this difference to be a faithful explanation for the decision-making process.

To keep the explanations compact, we only display imagined trajectories where at least one state deviates from the observation, based on defined threshold values. By adjusting the variables, the explanation size can be controlled. Figure 3 shows the visualization: green frames highlight states with no deviation, while red frames mark states with deviations. For each deviating state, the corresponding error metrics are displayed below the transition.

In summary, our methodology outlines a comprehensive approach to explaining the decision-making process of DreamerV3, a Model-based Deep Reinforcement Learning (MBDRL) agent. We first generate alternative trajectories using the agent's inherent world model, ensuring that the explanations reflect the same dynamics used during training. Next, we compare observed and imagined trajectories at the action, input-state, and reward levels to identify and quantify deviations. By tracking error propagation over time, our method distinguishes between minor discrepancies and significant deviations that influence performance. Finally, we present these deviations visually through a prototype that uses LPIPS for image fidelity and color-coded frames for clarity. This structured approach not only provides diagnostic insights for domain experts but also lays the groundwork for future causal analyses of explainable reinforcement learning.

5 Evaluation

We use the Minigrid benchmark [5] to evaluate our explanation technique for DreamerV3. Minigrid offers a collection of 2D grid-world environments featuring goal-oriented tasks in which an agent must navigate to a predefined, randomly assigned goal state. Depending on the environment, the task may involve simply solving a maze or interacting with objects such as keys and doors. The observations are provided as $64 \times 64 \times 3$ RGB images, and the environments operate under partial observability with a discrete action space.

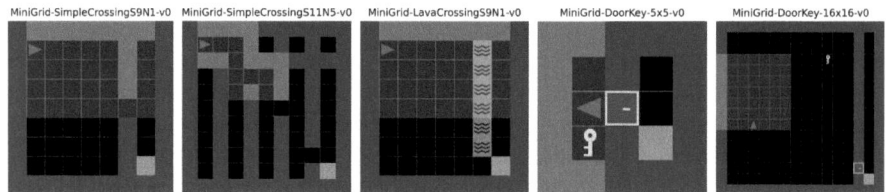

Fig. 4. Example maps for the five Minigrid environments. The green field is the goal, the red triangle the agent. The highlighted fields around the agent represent the agent's visible area. (Color figure online)

For our evaluation, we consider five Minigrid environments. Figure 4 shows an example map for each environment. The first environment, *SimpleCrossing*, consists of a maze divided by a wall with a single opening. The agent must locate the hole in the wall and then proceed to the goal state on the opposite side. There are different variations of this environment that differ in size and the number of walls. We use the 9×9 map with one wall and the 11×11 map with five walls, each with one random opening.

The third environment, *LavaCrossing*, is a modified version of SimpleCrossing, where a lava stream replaces the wall, and falling into the lava results in immediate failure. The fourth environment, *DoorKey*, requires the agent to find a key to open a door, with the goal located in the room beyond. We evaluate the 5×5 and 16×16 versions of the *DoorKey* environment. The increased map size and limited visibility in the 16×16 environment result in additional challenges for navigation and exploration.

In all environments, the reward function is defined as:

$$r = 1 - 0.9 \times \left(\frac{\text{step\_count}}{\text{max\_steps}}\right) \qquad (11)$$

for successful episodes, and 0 for failures. Each environment allows a maximum number of steps per episode (max_steps), relative to its size. The step_count is the number of steps in that episode. The action space for all environments comprises seven possible actions, but only three are utilized in the crossing tasks and five in the key-door tasks.

For each environment, we trained an agent for 800,000 steps, which was sufficient for the agents to reliably solve the tasks.

To assess the fidelity of our explanation technique, we focus on evaluating two key properties from the Co-12 framework [22]: *Correctness* and *Consistency*, using a series of experiments.

Model Replacement Check. In the *Model Replacement Check*, we record a trajectory using an agent trained in a specific Minigrid environment and generate the corresponding explanation. We then produce explanations for the same trajectory using agents trained on different environments, as well as using trajectories recorded from agents trained in alternative settings. Our hypothesis is that an agent's explanation will closely match the ground truth, as indicated by lower MSE, JS-distance, or Hamming distance, when the agent and the trajectory come from the same training task and environment. Qualitatively, the explanation should accurately reflect the key characteristics of the training environment, such as the maze layout, presence of lava, or the key-door mechanism.

Model Parameter Randomization Check. In the *Model Parameter Randomization Check*, we evaluate the correctness of the explanation. We replace the parameters of critical submodels, specifically, the world model, actor, critic, reward predictor, and continue predictor, with random values, while keeping the initial world model prediction unchanged. Our hypothesis is that this randomization will yield increased discrepancies in the generated explanations, as evidenced by higher MSE values. Notably, differences should be observable in the predicted actions, rewards, value estimations, and continue predictions, with subsequent imagination steps exhibiting compounded deviations. For each experiment, we collect quantitative metrics to determine whether the explanations evolve in the expected direction.

6 Results

In this section, we present a comprehensive evaluation of our explanation technique using the Minigrid benchmark. Our primary objective is to assess the technique's fidelity by measuring its *Correctness* and *Consistency* across two distinct experiments: the Model Replacement Check and the Model Parameter Randomization Check.

Quantitative performance is primarily evaluated using the MSE for continuous values, the Jensen-Shannon (JS)-distance for probabilities, and the Hamming distance for categorical values like the discrete latent state. In addition, qualitative assessments are conducted to verify the alignment of the generated explanations with key environmental characteristics. The following subsections detail the outcomes of each experiment.

6.1 Model Replacement Check

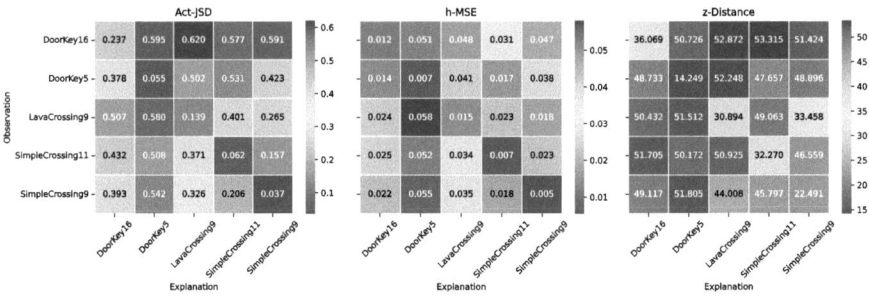

Fig. 5. Heatmap of the MSE for the world model states and JS-distance for the policy outputs. The y-axis corresponds to the observation environment, and the x-axis corresponds to the environment the replaced model was trained on. The diagonal (matched condition) shows the lowest error values, indicating that models trained in the same environment produce the most accurate explanations.

In this experiment, we assess the fidelity of our explanation technique by comparing the generated explanations under two conditions:

1. **Matched Condition:** The agent's models for both the observation and the explanation are trained on the same environment.
2. **Mismatched Condition:** The agent's models for the observation and the explanation are trained on different environments.

Each condition was tested on all five benchmark environments, with 25 independent runs per condition to ensure statistical robustness. The benchmark environments include *SimpleCrossingS9N1*, *SimpleCrossingS11N5*, *LavaCrossingS9N1*, *DoorKey5x5*, and *DoorKey16x16*. We chose *Minigrid* because it is a goal-oriented benchmark with discrete actions that facilitate the evaluation of the explanations..

Table 1. Model Replacement: Aggregated metrics for the matched (top) and mismatched (bottom) conditions across all runs. Metrics include the action JS, the recurrent state MSE (h MSE), and the stochastic state difference ($\hat{z}$ distance).

Matched Env	Act JSD	h-MSE	$\hat{z}$-Distance
DoorKey-16x16	**0.24 ± 0.30**	**0.01 ± 0.01**	**36.07 ± 16.82**
DoorKey-5x5	**0.06 ± 0.20**	**0.01 ± 0.02**	**14.25 ± 12.22**
LavaCrossingS9N1	**0.14 ± 0.28**	**0.01 ± 0.02**	**30.89 ± 17.04**
SimpleCrossingS11N5	**0.06 ± 0.22**	**0.01 ± 0.01**	**32.27 ± 11.58**
SimpleCrossingS9N1	**0.04 ± 0.17**	**0.01 ± 0.01**	**22.49 ± 11.26**
Mismatched Env	**Act JSD**	**h-MSE**	**$\hat{z}$-Distance**
DoorKey-16x16	0.60 ± 0.33	0.04 ± 0.02	52.21 ± 8.57
DoorKey-5x5	0.46 ± 0.38	0.03 ± 0.02	49.38 ± 11.65
LavaCrossingS9N1	0.44 ± 0.32	0.03 ± 0.03	46.15 ± 13.23
SimpleCrossingS11N5	0.38 ± 0.38	0.03 ± 0.02	50.00 ± 11.21
SimpleCrossingS9N1	0.36 ± 0.37	0.03 ± 0.03	47.58 ± 12.67

Quantitative Analysis. For each run, we computed the MSE between the generated explanation and the recorded observation for both the recurrent state h and the stochastic state $\hat{z}$. For the action probability distribution, we calculated the JS-distance (Act JS). Our hypothesis predicted that the matched condition would exhibit significantly lower MSE and JS-distance compared to the mismatched condition.

As shown in Table 1 and Fig. 5, the lowest errors occur when the explainer is trained on the same environment as the agent (matched condition). In mismatched conditions, lower errors are observed when the explainer's training environment shares similar dynamics with the agent's environment (e.g., SimpleCrossing and LavaCrossing) or when the explainer is trained on a larger map. Conversely, an explainer trained on a smaller map cannot fully capture the dynamics of a larger one, resulting in higher errors. These findings support the hypothesis that an explainer trained on the same model can produce high-quality explanations, while explainers from similar environments can only partially bridge the gap.

Aggregating the loss values for the matched and mismatched conditions across all benchmarks, we observe that the mismatched losses are consistently higher than those for the matched condition. This supports our hypothesis that mismatched explanations fail to provide faithful representations, even when the environments differ only in map size or the task defined on that map.

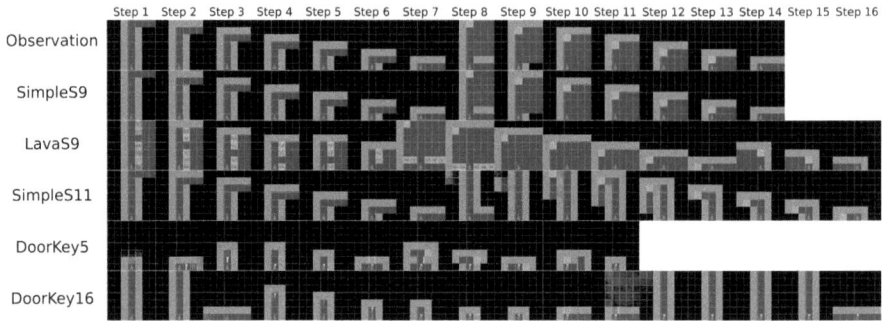

Fig. 6. Comparison of model imaginations. Top row: Simple Crossing environment observation. Second row: matching explanation. Third row: Lava Crossing environment (identified by lava). Fourth row: Simple Crossing S11N5 environment (identified by an additional wall). Fifth row: explanation from an agent trained on the Door Key 5×5 environment (small size, key, door). Bottom row: Door Key 16×16 environment.

Qualitative Analysis. In addition to the quantitative metrics, we performed a qualitative evaluation of the generated explanations to assess their fidelity. Figure 6 provides a representative comparison of the model imaginations under both matched and mismatched conditions.

The top row of Fig. 6 displays the original observation from the Simple Crossing (S9N1) environment. The next row shows the explanation generated by a model trained on the same, matched environment, which accurately captures key features such as the wall opening, present in the observation. In contrast, the following rows illustrate explanations produced by mismatched models. For instance, when a model trained on the Lava Crossing environment is applied to a Simple Crossing observation, its explanation incorrectly incorporates features typical of the Lava Crossing environment, namely, the presence of lava. Similarly, explanations generated by models trained on Simple Crossing (S11N5) and Door Key (5×5, 16×16) reflect the unique structural characteristics of their respective training environments, such as an additional wall or the key-door configuration, even when the input observation originates from a different environment.

These qualitative observations confirm that mismatched models tend to faithfully reproduce the characteristics of their training environments rather than accurately representing the input. This behavior reinforces our quantitative findings, demonstrating that alignment between the training environment and the explanation generation process is critical for producing accurate and meaningful explanations.

6.2 Model Parameter Randomization Check

Inspired by Nauta et al. [22], this experiment evaluates the impact of individual model components on the fidelity of the generated explanations. For each benchmark environment, we conducted 25 independent runs using the corresponding

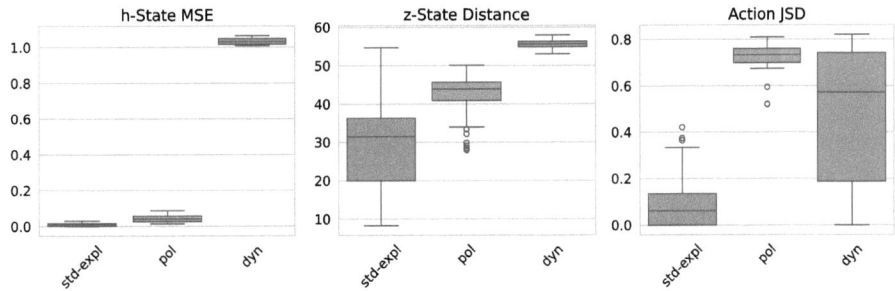

Fig. 7. Box plots comparing the evaluation metrics: h-state MSE, z-state distance, and action probability JS-distance across the five model parameter randomization checks. We compare standard explanation measurements to runs with randomized policy and world model.

trained baseline agent. For each run, we first generated an explanation with the baseline agent and then produced additional explanations by individually replacing the values of one of the following components with random values: the policy, the world model, the reward predictor, the critic, and the continue predictor.

Figure 7 presents box plots that summarize the resulting differences in key metrics—namely, the h-state MSE, z-state Hamming distance, and the action probability JS-distance. The x-axis lists the components that were randomized. As expected, replacing the world model results in the highest MSE for both the recurrent and stochastic states. Notably, randomizing the policy also contributes to increased errors, reflecting the sequential dependency between actions and state predictions. The action probability divergence is primarily influenced by randomization of the world model and the policy, which aligns with our hypothesis that the input quality from the world model directly affects the policy output. In contrast, the critic, reward predictor, and continue predictor each show only increased errors in their specific functions: estimating value, predicting rewards, and determining explanation length.

The impact of randomization on explanation outcomes is also evident in the visualizations. Figure 8 illustrates the expected errors: a random policy results in an agent that lacks goal-oriented behavior, and a randomized world model prevents the generation of plausible state representations.

Overall, these findings validate our hypothesis: every model component is crucial for generating faithful explanations, and randomizing any component leads to measurable deviations from the baseline.

7 Discussion and Limitations

We showed that the world model imagination process used during training can also be leveraged to create local explanations. This can be helpful for debugging or failure analysis. A simple example could be an autonomous vehicle involved in an accident. While the model may have performed well during training and

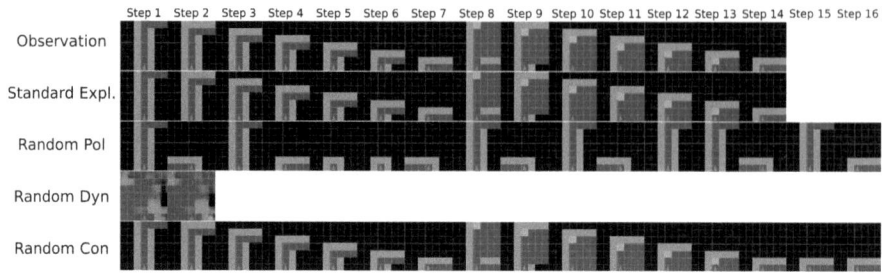

Fig. 8. Comparison of the observation, the standard explanation, and explanations generated by randomized models. With a randomized policy, the agent behaves without clear direction. A randomized world model omits the decoder, resulting in images that resemble the environment but have random internal states. Finally, a randomized continue predictor causes the explanation to persist even after the agent reaches its goal.

evaluation, there might be a shift in dynamics not captured during training. Our explanation technique could provide insights that improve the failure analysis process.

While loss values help to quickly indicate that something is different, they do not reveal what exactly is different. Our approach enables differentiation on a more detailed level.

Previous research [2] demonstrated that contrastive outcome explanations are effective in helping users better understand the decision-making process of DRL. We adapted this idea to DRL trained in imagination, addressing the specific requirements involved in such processes. These explanations can serve as a foundation for integration with other explanation techniques, such as feature attribution to highlight visual differences, or additional counterfactual analyses to provide more contrastive explanations.

Correct interpretation of these explanations is critical. Previous research [3] has shown that world models, especially in Dreamer, tend to overestimate aleatoric uncertainty. Therefore, world models likely cannot be used to reliably predict the future. They represent the learned dynamics of the agent, which may be close to reality but are not guaranteed to match it exactly. This discrepancy is also the motivation for explanations: they should highlight the differences between the learned and actual dynamics.

The explanations presented here primarily target domain experts. However, the information provided by these explanations can also be adapted for other stakeholders. Further research is needed to tailor the explanation format to lay users or specific stakeholder groups. Additionally, as the explanations closely mirror the original training process, further work is required to extend them with additional explainability techniques that help uncover the causal reasons behind agent behavior.

Our results provide an initial exploration into explaining DRL agents trained in imagination. The current evaluation is limited to a discrete environment and a single algorithm (Dreamer). Future research should investigate the applicability of our approach in more complex environments and continuous action spaces. At present, users must manually define threshold values for various measurements; more research is needed to automate this process and reduce reliance on expert input. One potential solution involves generating counterfactuals within imagined trajectories that gradually approach the observation to determine if and when the agent's decision changes. This could be applied to both world model states and policy actions.

With this work, we propose a new explainability approach that can serve as the basis for future, more complex explanation methods based on agent imaginations.

8 Conclusion

In this paper, we presented a novel approach for explaining MBDRL agents by leveraging the capabilities of a learned world model. Our method generates explanations that faithfully capture the underlying dynamics of the environment, as evidenced by both quantitative metrics and qualitative evaluations.

Our approach tailors explanations to the AI model by incorporating *imaginations*, predictive simulations generated by the world model, into the explanation process. Instead of relying on external models, we replicate the training process and use the model's internal representations, resulting in explanations that more accurately reflect the decision-making processes optimized during training.

These results demonstrate the potential of using world models not only for planning and decision-making but also as powerful tools for interpretability. Future work will explore further refinements in explanation techniques and extend our evaluation to more complex environments and real-world applications.

Acknowledgments. This work is supported by the Helmholtz Association Initiative and Networking Fund on the HAICORE@KIT partition, as well as by the Helmholtz Association within the Core Informatics project. The authors acknowledge support by the state of Baden-Württemberg through bwHPC.

References

1. Alonso, E., et al.: Diffusion for world modeling: Visual details matter in atari. arXiv preprint arXiv:2405.12399 (2024)
2. Amitai, Y., Septon, Y., Amir, O.: Explaining reinforcement learning agents through counterfactual action outcomes. In: Proceedings of the AAAI Conference on Artificial Intelligence, pp. 10003–10011 (2024)
3. Becker, P., Neumann, G.: On uncertainty in deep state space models for model-based reinforcement learning. arXiv preprint arXiv:2210.09256 (2022)
4. Bertrand, A., Belloum, R., Eagan, J.R., Maxwell, W.: How cognitive biases affect xai-assisted decision-making: a systematic review. In: Proceedings of the 2022 AAAI/ACM Conference on AI, Ethics, and Society, pp. 78–91 (2022)

5. Chevalier-Boisvert, M., et al.: Minigrid & miniworld: modular & customizable reinforcement learning environments for goal-oriented tasks. CoRR abs/arxiv: 2306.13831 (2023)
6. Dazeley, R., Vamplew, P., Cruz, F.: Explainable reinforcement learning for broad-xai: a conceptual framework and survey. Neural Comput. Appl. **35**(23), 16893–16916 (2023)
7. Endres, D.M., Schindelin, J.E.: A new metric for probability distributions. IEEE Trans. Inf. Theory **49**(7), 1858–1860 (2003)
8. Guan, Y., et al.: World models for autonomous driving: an initial survey. IEEE Trans. Intell. Veh. (2024)
9. Hafner, D., Lillicrap, T., Ba, J., Norouzi, M.: Dream to control: learning behaviors by latent imagination. In: International Conference on Learning Representations (2019)
10. Hafner, D., Lillicrap, T., Norouzi, M., Ba, J.: Mastering atari with discrete world models. arXiv preprint arXiv:2010.02193 (2020)
11. Hafner, D., Pasukonis, J., Ba, J., Lillicrap, T.: Mastering diverse domains through world models. arXiv preprint arXiv:2301.04104 (2023)
12. Hoffman, R.R., Mueller, S.T., Klein, G., Litman, J.: Measures for explainable ai: explanation goodness, user satisfaction, mental models, curiosity, trust, and human-ai performance. Front. Comput. Sci. **5** (2023). https://doi.org/10.3389/fcomp.2023.1096257
13. Kaelbling, L.P., Littman, M.L., Cassandra, A.R.: Planning and acting in partially observable stochastic domains. Artif. Intell. **101**(1–2), 99–134 (1998)
14. Kingma, D.P., Salimans, T., Jozefowicz, R., Chen, X., Sutskever, I., Welling, M.: Improved variational inference with inverse autoregressive flow. Adv. Neural Inform. Proces. Syst. **29** (2016)
15. Langer, M., et al.: What do we want from explainable artificial intelligence (xai)?- a stakeholder perspective on xai and a conceptual model guiding interdisciplinary xai research. Artif. Intell. **296**, 103473 (2021)
16. Longo, L., et al.: Explainable artificial intelligence (xai) 2.0: a manifesto of open challenges and interdisciplinary research directions. Inform. Fusion **106**, 102301 (2024)
17. Mattes, P., Schlosser, R., Herbrich, R.: Hieros: hierarchical imagination on structured state space sequence world models. In: Forty-first International Conference on Machine Learning (2024). https://openreview.net/forum?id=IUBhvyJ9Sr
18. Micheli, V., Alonso, E., Fleuret, F.: Transformers are sample-efficient world models. In: The Eleventh International Conference on Learning Representations (Sep 2022)
19. Milani, S., Topin, N., Veloso, M., Fang, F.: Explainable reinforcement learning: a survey and comparative review. ACM Comput. Surv. **56**(7), 1–36 (2024)
20. Miller, T.: Explanation in artificial intelligence: insights from the social sciences. Artif. Intell. **267**, 1–38 (2019)
21. Moerland, T.M., Broekens, J., Plaat, A., Jonker, C.M.: Model-based reinforcement learning: a survey. Foundat. Trends® Mach. Learn. **16**(1), 1–118 (2023). https://doi.org/10.1561/2200000086
22. Nauta, M., et al.: From anecdotal evidence to quantitative evaluation methods: a systematic review on evaluating explainable ai. ACM Comput. Surv. **55**(13s), 1–42 (2023). https://doi.org/10.1145/3583558
23. Olson, M.L., Khanna, R., Neal, L., Li, F., Wong, W.K.: Counterfactual state explanations for reinforcement learning agents via generative deep learning. Artif. Intell. **295**, 103455 (2021)

24. Rigter, M., Yamada, J., Posner, I.: World models via policy-guided trajectory diffusion. Transactions on Machine Learning Research (2024). https://openreview.net/forum?id=9CcgO0LhKG
25. Rudin, C.: Stop explaining black box machine learning models for high stakes decisions and use interpretable models instead. Nat. Mach. Intell. **1**(5), 206–215 (2019)
26. Saulières, L., Cooper, M., de Saint-Cyr, F.D.: Reinforcement learning explained via reinforcement learning: Towards explainable policies through predictive explanation. In: 15th International Conference on Agents and Artificial Intelligence (ICAART 2023), vol. 2, pp. 35–44. Scitepress (2023)
27. Sutton, R.S., Barto, A.G., et al.: Reinforcement learning: an introduction. MIT Press Cambridge (1998)
28. Vouros, G.A.: Explainable deep reinforcement learning: state of the art and challenges. ACM Comput. Surv. **55**(5), 1–39 (2022)
29. Wenninghoff, N.: Explainable deep reinforcement learning through introspective explanations. In: Joint Proceedings of the xAI 2024 Late-breaking Work, Demos and Doctoral Consortium co-located with the 2nd World Conference on eXplainable Artificial Intelligence (xAI-2024), Valletta, Malta, 17-19 July 2024. Ed.: L. Longo, p. 449 (2024)
30. Yau, H., Russell, C., Hadfield, S.: What did you think would happen? explaining agent behaviour through intended outcomes. Adv. Neural. Inf. Process. Syst. **33**, 18375–18386 (2020)
31. Yeh, E., Sequeira, P., Hostetler, J., Gervasio, M.: Outcome-guided counterfactuals from a jointly trained generative latent space. In: World Conference on Explainable Artificial Intelligence, pp. 449–469. Springer (2023). https://doi.org/10.1007/978-3-031-44070-0_23
32. Yu, Z., Ruan, J., Xing, D.: Explainable reinforcement learning via a causal world model. In: Proceedings of the Thirty-Second International Joint Conference on Artificial Intelligence, pp. 4540–4548 (2023)
33. Zhu, Z., et al.: Is sora a world simulator? a comprehensive survey on general world models and beyond. arXiv preprint arXiv:2405.03520 (2024)

Open Access This chapter is licensed under the terms of the Creative Commons Attribution 4.0 International License (http://creativecommons.org/licenses/by/4.0/), which permits use, sharing, adaptation, distribution and reproduction in any medium or format, as long as you give appropriate credit to the original author(s) and the source, provide a link to the Creative Commons license and indicate if changes were made.

The images or other third party material in this chapter are included in the chapter's Creative Commons license, unless indicated otherwise in a credit line to the material. If material is not included in the chapter's Creative Commons license and your intended use is not permitted by statutory regulation or exceeds the permitted use, you will need to obtain permission directly from the copyright holder.

Unsupervised and Interpretable Detection of User Personalities in Online Social Networks

Alessio Cascione[1(✉)], Laura Pollacci[1,2], and Riccardo Guidotti[1,2]

[1] University of Pisa, Largo Bruno Pontecorvo 3, Pisa, PI 56127, Italy
alessio.cascione@phd.unipi.it,
{laura.pollacci,riccardo.guidotti}@unipi.it
[2] KDD Lab, ISTI-CNR, Via G. Moruzzi 1, Pisa, PI 56124, Italy
{laura.pollacci,riccardo.guidotti}@isti.cnr.it

Abstract. Personalized moderation interventions in online social networks foster healthier interactions by adapting responses to both individual traits and contextual factors. However, implementing such interventions is challenging due to transparency concerns and the lack of ground-truth behavioral data from expert psychologists. Interpretability is crucial for addressing these challenges, as it enables platforms to tailor moderation strategies while ensuring fairness and user trust. In this paper, we present an unsupervised, data-driven framework to build an interpretable predictive model capable of distinguishing between toxic and non-toxic users with different personality traits. We leverage personality representations from an external resource to uncover behavioral profiles through clustering, utilizing embeddings of both toxic and non-toxic users. Then, we model users with features capturing linguistic and affective dimensions, training an interpretable personality detector capable of distinguishing between behavioral profiles in a transparent and explainable manner. A case study on Reddit demonstrates the effectiveness of our approach, highlighting how an interpretable model can achieve competitive performance comparable to a black-box alternative while offering meaningful insights into toxic and non-toxic users behavior.

Keywords: Personality Detection · Interpretable Machine Learning · Data-Driven User Modeling · Unsupervised Learning

1 Introduction

Personality traits play a crucial role in shaping social behaviors in digital spaces, influencing user interactions and adherence to community guidelines. Research shows that online behaviors and language features are closely tied to personality traits, affecting both the nature of interactions and language choices [2]. This link between personality and language patterns provides valuable opportunities to study digital behavior in the context of personality.

A key application of this perspective is in personalized moderation interventions in Online Social Networks (OSNs). Indeed, user responses to moderation efforts differ significantly based on individual characteristics [49]. Thus, implementing personalized moderation strategies can foster greater user engagement, improve compliance with OSNs community guidelines, and enhance the overall effectiveness of moderation by helping to reduce toxic content [10]. However, this approach faces challenges, including the unavailability of ground-truth personality data [15], the need for privacy-preserving techniques [36], and the importance of using interpretable models to ensure fairness and transparency [20].

We address these challenges with TRAITS (Tool for Revealing Attributes and Identifying Toxic and Safe profiles), a framework for building an interpretable personality detection model to analyze toxic and non-toxic user behaviors on OSNs. TRAITS uses semantically transparent features, such as writing style and affective features, alongside latent personality embeddings derived from an external resource. In particular, a clustering method identifies behavioral profiles based on latent embeddings, while linguistic and affective features are aggregated for interpretable user representation. An interpretable model is then trained to predict the cluster labels, linking them to transparent features. By analyzing explanations for prototypical instances, TRAITS identifies the defining characteristics of toxic and non-toxic profiles, enabling experts to design targeted moderation strategies. TRAITS helps prevent harmful counter-reactions or user churn while reducing toxicity more effectively than fixed moderation interventions, by offering a framework where membership in a specific behavioral group is made transparent through an interpretable model. We present a case study applying TRAITS to a dataset of comments from Reddit users. This analysis shows TRAITS' ability to effectively distinguish between toxic and non-toxic data-driven personality profiles. By leveraging language and affective features, TRAITS captures nuanced behavioral patterns within both groups, and through an analysis of the interpretable features and their contributions to these distinctions, we identify and name the profiles as follows: *Aggressive, Provocative, Mildly-Toxic, Constructive, Contentious*, and *Neutral*.

The rest of this paper is organized as follows. After reviewing works in personality detection in Sect. 2, in Sect. 3 we formalize the problem faced, and we describe our proposal to solve it in Sect. 4. In Sect. 5, we present the experimental results. Finally, Sect. 6 summarizes our contributions and outlines potential directions for future research.

2 Related Works

According to psychological trait theory, personality traits are characteristic patterns that reflect individuals' behaviors, thoughts, and emotions [8]. Several psychological frameworks have been proposed to define and categorize personality traits [32], with the two most widely used being the Myers-Briggs Type Indicator (MBTI) and the Five-Factor Model (OCEAN) [17,33,37]. The former framework categorizes personality into 16 unique types through binary assignments across four dimensions: *Introversion* vs. *Extraversion*, *Sensing* vs. *Intuition*, *Thinking* vs. *Feeling*, and *Judging* vs. *Perceiving*. The latter organizes personality traits along five broad dimensions: *Openness, Conscientiousness, Extraversion, Agreeableness*, and *Neuroticism*. The OCEAN model constitutes a widely respected framework in psychology for its empirical reliability and comprehensive scope in personality assessment [9]. A comparison of MBTI and the OCEAN framework is explored in [13], which highlights the structural and conceptual differences between the two models. Based on these frameworks, various datasets have been developed to facilitate personality trait analysis [16,46]. For our purposes, we focus on OCEAN due to its reliability and widespread use in psychology [19], as well as its established role in OSNs users personality analysis [40–42].

Automatic personality detection has been explored across various domains. A comprehensive overview of approaches for text, audio, visual, and multimodal data is presented in [34], where main reference datasets and methodologies for each modality are discussed. For images, in [44] an approach based on Histogram of Oriented Gradients, Eigenfaces and specific face portions for modeling the face and training ML models on top is presented. For the audio-visual domain, [26] introduces a benchmarking framework, which is used to evaluate existing architectures, while [54] integrates a CNN, a Bi-LSTM, and a Transformer model to predict personality traits from audio-visual content. Focusing on audio-based personality detection, the authors of [45] compare different models based on features extracted from audios such as jitter, frame intensity, and loudness. On the other hand, in [43] are employed particle swarm optimization in conjunction with a CNN for speech-based personality recognition.

In our work, we focus on personality detection from textual data, with particular reference to OSNs data. In terms of personality detection on texts, two main approaches can be identified: one based on lexical, linguistic, and psycholinguistic features, and another leveraging Transformers-based methods. Early approaches to personality prediction [29,39] employed psycholinguistic and linguistic features, later advancing through more complex feature aggregation techniques such as CNN-based n-gram extraction and hierarchical NNs [30,52]. An unsupervised method for detecting online personality traits is presented in [6], utilizing an *ad-hoc* clustering technique based on linguistic features. In contrast, Transformer-based models, such as BERT [35], outperform traditional methods, with advancements like the TRANSFORMER-MD architecture [53] enhancing personality detection by integrating dimension-specific attention modules. While we also train models using interpretable linguistic features, our approach focuses on predicting labels identified through unsupervised methods applied to a latent space, aligning with Transformer-based techniques.

Interpretable personality detection methods have been applied to both feature-based and Transformer-based models. In [38], Integrated Gradients are used to explain personality predictions based on OSNs users' activities, while [22] employs BI-LSTM and MENTALROBERTA directly on users' texts, applying LIME and AGRAD to interpret the predictions. Further, [21] refines psychological representations using a Siamese BI-LSTM, providing interpretability by comparing embeddings to baseline personality statements. In [50], the personality detection problem is addressed using affective natural language inference, determining whether the hypothesis, i.e., the personality label description for a speaker, is valid given the affective dialogue content as the premise.

Unlike the aforementioned interpretable approaches, we propose both a globally and locally interpretable model for OSNs comments that identifies data-driven behavioral profiles to differentiate between toxic and non-toxic users.

3 Problem Formulation

This section presents a problem formalization that aims to clarify the differences between supervised and unsupervised personality detection.

Definition 1 (Supervised Personality Detection Problem). *Let $U = \{u_1, \ldots, u_n\}$ be a set of n users of an OSN, and let $Y^* = \{y_1^*, \ldots, y_n^*\}$ be their personality traits with $y_i^* \in \mathcal{Q}^*$ and where $\mathcal{Q}^* = \{1, \ldots, q\}$ is the set of possible personality traits. The* Supervised Personality Detection Problem *consists of learning a personality detection model f that given in input an unlabeled user u_i returns its personality trait y_i^*, i.e., $y_i^* = f(u_i)$.*

Unfortunately, the set of possible personality traits $\mathcal{Q}^*$, and consequentially the ground truth for personality traits Y^*, are typically unknown, and even when based on psychological theories, the specific personality traits y_i^* of a user u_i are typically undisclosed due to privacy concerns or lack of expert validation. This challenge arises despite the fact that users' content on OSNs is publicly accessible. Hence, we face the problem from an unsupervised perspective.

Definition 2 (Unsupervised Personality Detection Problem). *Let $U = \{u_1, \ldots, u_n\}$ be a set of n users of an OSN. The* Unsupervised Personality Detection Problem *consists of the two following parts:*

(i) deriving from the activities of the users U on the OSN a set $\mathcal{K} = \{1, \ldots, k\}$ of data-driven personality traits such that each user $u_i \in U$ is assigned with a data driven personality $Y = \{y_1, \ldots, y_n\}$ with $y_i \in \mathcal{K}$,
(ii) learning a personality detection model f that given in input an unlabeled user u_i returns its data-driven personality y_i, i.e., $y_i = f(u_i)$.

In the rest, we propose an unsupervised method to solve the unsupervised personality detection problem, treating it as an approximation of the supervised personality detection problem, especially useful in scenarios where, as is often the case, ground-truth personality traits for users are unavailable.

4 Methodology

This section presents our framework for deriving an unsupervised, interpretable model to profile OSNs users and distinguish between toxic and safe, i.e., non

Algorithm 1: TRAITS(T)

Input : T - OSN textual comments of users where $t_{i,j} \in T_i$ is the jth comment of user i, and $T_i \in T$ with $T_i = \{t_{i,1}, \ldots, t_{i,n_i}\}$ is the set of n_i comments of user i.
Param : $D_p = \langle T_p, Y_p \rangle$ - external dataset with known personality traits
is_toxic_α - returns 1 if the toxicity score is higher than α, 0 otherwise.
α - text toxicity threshold. β - user toxicity threshold.
Output: f - interpretable personality detection model.

1 $G_p \leftarrow \{g_j | g_j = \mathcal{L}_g(T_p, Y_p^{(j)}) \ \forall j \in [1, p]\}$; // learn pers. detectors on external dataset
2 $X \leftarrow \emptyset$; // init. interpretable user representation
3 $X_{emb}^{toxic} \leftarrow \emptyset; X_{emb}^{safe} \leftarrow \emptyset; A \leftarrow \emptyset$; // init. latent embeddings and user toxicity label set
4 **for** $i \in [1, n]$ **do** // for each user
5 $\quad A \leftarrow A \cup \{\mathbb{1}(\frac{1}{n_i} \sum_{j=1}^{n_i} is\_toxic_\alpha(t_{i,j}) \geq \beta)\}$; // calculate and store user toxicity
6 $\quad X \leftarrow X \cup \{extract\_features(T_i)\}$; // extract interpretable features
7 $\quad \hat{t}_i \leftarrow \bigcup_{j=1}^{n_i} t_{i,j}$; // concatenate all texts of a user
8 $\quad$ **if** $A_i = 1$ **then** $X_{emb}^{toxic} \leftarrow X_{emb}^{toxic} \cup \{emb_{G_p}(\hat{t}_i)\}$; // extract toxic user embedding
9 $\quad$ **else** $X_{emb}^{safe} \leftarrow X_{emb}^{safe} \cup \{emb_{G_p}(\hat{t}_i)\}$; // extract non-toxic user embedding
10 $Y^{toxic} \leftarrow cluster(X_{emb}^{toxic}); Y^{safe} \leftarrow cluster(X_{emb}^{safe})$; // cluster toxic and non-toxic users
11 $Y \leftarrow Y^{toxic} \cup Y^{safe}$; // merge personality traits labels
12 $f \leftarrow \mathcal{L}_f(X, Y)$; // learn interpretable personality detector
13 **return** f;

toxic, behavior patterns. We present here TRAITS, a Tool for Revealing Attributes and Identifying Toxic and Safe profiles in OSNs, our proposal to solve the unsupervised personality detection problem.

The core idea is to leverage latent embeddings learned from an external source to identify personality traits and group users accordingly. Simultaneously, the same users are represented using interpretable linguistic and affective features, which are assigned to the identified groups. An interpretable model is then trained to detect these profiles, revealing the key discriminative factors in terms of the features. The pseudo-code of TRAITS is in Algorithm 1.

Given a set of n users $U = \{u_1, \ldots, u_n\}$ of an OSN, we name $T = \{T_1, \ldots, T_n\}$ the textual comments generated by the users of the OSN in a certain period, where $T_i \in T$ with $T_i = \{t_{i,1}, \ldots, t_{i,n_i}\}$ is the set of n_i texts of user i, while $t_{i,j} \in T_i$ is the jth text of user i. TRAITS is a framework that takes as input T and returns an interpretable personality detection model as f.

We refer to TRAITS as a framework because it relies on external data and pre-trained functions along with their parameters. Indeed, we assume the availability of an external dataset $D_p = \langle T_p, Y_p \rangle$ of texts T_p with attached known personality traits Y_p of the users that generated such texts, where each $t_i \in T_P$ is the concatenation of all the texts written by a user i coming from this external resource and each $y_i \in Y_p$ represents a list of p personality trait scores, i.e., $y_i = \{y_{i,1}, \ldots, y_{i,p}\}$ where each $y_{i,j} \in [1, q]$ can assume q different scores of personality for each one of the p traits. $Y_p^{(j)}$ refers to the j-th personality trait for all the texts in T_p. As first step (line 1), TRAITS learns a set of personality detectors $G_p = \{g_1, \ldots, g_p\}$ for each trait using a predefined learning function $\mathcal{L}_g$ (see Sect. 5 for implementative details). These detectors $g_1, \ldots, g_p$ are trained on the external dataset D_p solving a supervised personality detection problem, and they are used in turn, in a transfer learning fashion [18], for extracting latent embeddings of the users U analyzed by TRAITS. We underline that the set of users U analyzed is not overlapped with the set of users generating the textual comments for which we have the associated personality traits in D_p.

Then, the sets X, X_{emb}^{toxic}, X_{emb}^{safe}, and A are initialized. X stores the interpretable representation of the users U in terms of the attributes revealed by TRAITS; X_{emb}^{toxic} and X_{emb}^{safe} separately store for toxic and safe users the latent embeddings characterizing the users U in terms of some hidden aspects derived from the learning procedure $\mathcal{L}_g$ trained on the external resource D_p; A stores a user toxicity label as 1 for toxic users, 0 for safe users.

For each user in U (loop lines 4-9), the following steps are performed. First, given a function $is\_toxic_\alpha(t)$ that takes a text t as input and returns 1 if the text's toxicity score is α or higher, and 0 otherwise, TRAITS counts[1] the number of toxic comments made by the i-th user. If the proportion of toxic comments relative to the user's total comments meets or exceeds β, the user is classified as toxic, and this information is stored in A (line 5). After that, TRAITS uses the *extract_features* function to retrieve human understandable linguistic and affective features from the set of comments T_i (line 6). Then, TRAITS concatenates[2] all the texts of a user in $\hat{t}_i$ (line 7) and uses it to extract users latent embeddings through a combination of the personality detectors with the function $emb_{G_p}(\hat{t}_i)$. The result is placed in the right set depending on the user toxicity A_i.

After that, assuming the availability of a function *cluster* that takes as input a dataset with n records and assigns a label $Y = \{y_1, \ldots, y_n\}$ to each record, TRAITS groups the toxic users and safe users w.r.t. their latent embedding stored in X_{emb}^{toxic}, X_{emb}^{safe}, respectively (line 10). The labels Y^{toxic}, Y^{safe} identify different behavioral traits for toxic and safe users. However, it is still not possible to describe these profiles in a human understandable way. Thus, Y^{toxic}, Y^{safe} are merged in Y (line 11) and together with the interpretable user representation X are used to train an interpretable personality detection model f (line 12).

Given the set of textual comments from any user T_i, by applying the function f to their interpretable features $x_i = extract\_features(T_i)$, $f(x_i)$ returns the toxic or safe cluster label assigned to user u_i. Since f is interpretable, this decision is justified in terms of the features x_i. Consequently, by analyzing prototypical members of the cluster groups TRAITS allows the user to simultaneously reveal the interpretable features that contribute to their classification and help to characterize the data-driven personality traits in terms of these features. Details about the implementation of the functions $\mathcal{L}_g$, is_toxic, *extract_features*, *cluster* and $emb_{g_1,\ldots,g_p}$ and $\mathcal{L}_f$ are provided in next section as they are attached to and dependent on the specific case study.

Ethical Aspects and Privacy Risk Assessment Discussion. Our proposal mitigates user privacy and anonymity through several mechanisms. Users can be pseudonymized, as only their textual comments are needed, not their real identities. The interpretable features are derived solely from users' texts without

---

[1] The operator $\mathbb{1}(cond)$ returns 1 if the boolean condition $cond$ is satisfied, and 0 otherwise.
[2] The operator $\hat{\cup}$ performs the union as the concatenation of texts.

relying on external data of other users. Data is processed collectively only during clustering and model training phases. In the clustering phase, embeddings make personality traits incomprehensible, and for model training, safeguards like model aggregation can be used to protect user anonymity. In the model training phase, additional safeguards can be applied by aggregating feature values to protect user anonymity [36]. For instance a discretized version of a feature such as "number of posts" can considerably reduce the risk of re-identification from an external attacker. Also, risk assessment studies [31] show that an attacker would need extensive background knowledge to reconstruct a user's full information. Even in such cases, the attacker would not gain access to sensitive data, as the interpretable features only describe writing style and mood, while the target variable reflects group membership based on these features, without referencing psychological or sensitive traits like "depressed", "anxious", or "narcissist".

5 Case Study and Experiments

We apply TRAITS to a Reddit users case study[3], outlining the experimental setup, datasets, and implementation of the functions discussed earlier. We then present the performance of the interpretable models along with the resulting profiles.

5.1 Experimental Setting

We present here the datasets, external functions, and models utilized in our case study to apply the TRAITS framework.

Reddit Dataset. We focus on personality detection within a set U of over 15k Reddit users and their corresponding comments T, based on their activities from April 2020 to January 2021. For a detailed explanation of how users are selected and how the text extraction process is conducted, we refer the reader to [7].

External Personality Dataset. As external dataset with known personality traits $D_p = \langle T_p, Y_p \rangle$, we employ the PANDORA dataset [16], which provides OCEAN scores for approximately 1,6k users derived from explicit mentions of test results or responses to personality tests, with scores ranging from $[0, 100]$ for $p = 5$ personality traits, i.e., *Openness, Consciousness, Extraversion, Neuroticism, Agreeableness*. Since PANDORA also consists of a collection of English-language Reddit comments, similar to our unlabeled dataset T, it serves as a suitable external dataset for training models to generate latent representations of the comments in T. The users' comments in T_p are aggregated into a single text per user by concatenation, while the associated scores are discretized into $q = 5$ values. This approach reduces predictive complexity while retaining distinctions in personality intensity among users. We acknowledge the potential limitations of relying on these scores, as some reported test results may be inaccurate, and some users may have intentionally misrepresented themselves. Nevertheless, we still choose to adopt PANDORA as an external reference dataset for our study, given the

---
[3] The code to replicate the experiments is available at: https://github.com/acascione/traits.

absence of other readily available alternatives, and leave the development of a dataset with validated personality scores to future work.

Supervised Personality Detectors. The supervised personality detectors $G_p = \{g_1, \ldots, g_p\}$ are obtained training a Transformer for each personality trait $j \in [1, p=5]$ on the PANDORA dataset using the OCEAN labels as ground-truth. Given the consistent documents length, due to the concatenation, a LONG-FORMER (LF) architecture [3] is applied as learning function $\mathcal{L}_g$. This allows an efficient processing of up to 4,096 tokens, making it well-suited for lengthy text data[4]. For evaluating the supervised personality detectors, we divided the users in D_p into a 70%/30% train-test split, with an additional hold-out validation on the training set using an 80%/20% split. Details for the hyper-parameters are available in the repository. The weighted F1-score on the test set is reported on the first line in Table 2.

User Toxicity. In order to implement the function is_toxic_α, we use the Perspective API[5], which labels a text as toxic if its toxicity score is greater than or equal to $\alpha = 0.7$. We set $\alpha = 0.7$ to balance sensitivity and specificity in toxicity analysis, reducing false positives without losing relevant data[6]. According to the Perspective API, the toxicity score represents the proportion of readers who would perceive the comment as toxic. For instance, a score of 0.7 indicates that 7 out of 10 readers are likely to find the comment toxic. We consider a user toxic if 10% or more of their comments in T_i are deemed toxic, i.e., $\beta \geq 0.1$.

Interpretable Feature Extraction. The $extract\_features$ function computes linguistic and affective-related features for individual texts[7], and aggregates them into user-level representations using statistical measures such as sum, mean, max, and min. Linguistic features include basic metrics (e.g., counts of stopwords, emojis, and unique words) as well as advanced readability scores. The readability scores assess text complexity based on various linguistic factors: syllable count and sentence length (Flesch Kincaid Grade Level, Flesch Reading Ease, SMOG), word difficulty and frequency (Dale Chall, Spache), letter count and sentence structure (Coleman Liau Index, Automated Readability Index), and the proportion of complex words over the entire text (Gunning Fog, Linsear Write). Furthermore, we use MFD metrics to capture moral intensity [24] and LIWC 2022 language dimensions (such as *Culture* and *politic* highlighting the significance of a text w.r.t these topics). Affective features are extracted using TextBlob's polarity score, NRC-Lex, NRC-EIL, and VAD-Lex for valence,

---

[4] For users whose aggregated texts exceeds the 4,096-token limit, the text is split into batches of up to $4,096 \times 5$ tokens each, with each batch treated as a complete text. If a user has multiple associated texts, the majority predicted class among texts is considered as final label.

[5] https://perspectiveapi.com/.

[6] Both the API documentation [1] and previous studies [11] indicate that higher thresholds, such as 0.9, lower classification errors but exclude cases useful for studying biases in ML models. Furthermore, using 0.7 facilitates the analysis of terms associated with socially targeted groups, mitigating the effect of imbalanced distributions in training data.

[7] For a more detailed description of the features, please refer to the reference repository. Implementations of the tools used are available at: https://pypi.org/project/readability/, https://textblob.readthedocs.io/en/dev, https://pypi.org/project/NRCLex/, https://www.liwc.app/, https://saifmohammad.com/WebPages/lexicons.html,.

Table 1. Cluster sizes and Silhouette scores for different clustering strategies.

Strategy	Type	C1%	C2%	C3%	Silhouette
TRAITS_A	Toxic	9.71	4.15	36.17	0.086
	Safe	19.96	18.02	11.99	0.037
TRAITS_C	Toxic	15.12	13.82	21.08	0.049
	Safe	31.94	14.60	3.40	0.026

arousal, and dominance. We filter out features with a variance lower than 0.2, obtaining 177 total interpretable features. We retain the obtained features without applying any further transformations to preserve their interpretability as much as possible. While feature selection strategies could be explored, we choose to avoid discarding further potentially relevant information that could contribute to a more comprehensive interpretability analysis. Furthermore, our experimental analysis in Sect. 5 demonstrates that methods capable of automatically discarding irrelevant attributes are the most effective for our case study, justifying our previous choice.

Users Embeddings. We leverage the trained models G_p to obtain user embeddings. For each user, the full text $\hat{t}_i$ is processed by averaging token representations from the penultimate layer of each g_j, implementing emb_{G_p}. If a user has multiple documents, their embeddings are further averaged to create a single representation. Two aggregation strategies are explored: *(i)* averaging embeddings from each detector to produce a 768-dimensional vector and *(ii)* concatenating these embeddings for a 3840-dimensional vector, referred in the following as (TRAITS_A) and (TRAITS_C), respectively.

Users Clustering. In our experiments, we adopted a centroid-based approach for clustering users, employing the standard k-means[8] algorithm [47]. We also considered DBSCAN [12] as an alternative density-based clustering strategy, but it yielded poor results in our initial experiments. Consequently, we opted for the k-means approach. Moreover, we also preferred k-means due to its ability to provide a natural identification of exemplar instances, i.e., those closest to the centroid within each cluster, which are valuable for the in-depth interpretability analysis of data-driven personality profiles we present at the end of Sect. 5. We tested values of k ranging from 2 to 10 to avoid generating an excessive number of clusters, which could hinder the subsequent interpretability step. We applied k-means on the entire set of toxic and safe users, i.e., $X_{emb}^{toxic} \cup X_{emb}^{safe}$, as well as separately on toxic and safe user embeddings. To evaluate clustering performance, we considered the Silhouette scores. After testing different approaches, we found that the most effective strategy was to cluster toxic (X_{emb}^{toxic}) and safe (X_{emb}^{safe}) user embeddings separately and apply the k-means *cluster* function with $k = 3$ for both toxic and safe users.

---

[8] https://pypi.org/project/pyclustering/.

Table 2. F1-scores for *(black)* interpretable models trained and applied on transparent features to predict data-driven profiles; *(blue)* supervised pers. detectors trained applied on the external dataset to predict supervised profiles; *(brown)* interpretable models trained and applied on transparent features to supervised profiles; and *(purple)* interpretable models trained and applied on latent embeddings to predict data-driven profiles. Best model in bold, best runner up in italic.

Model	TRAITS$_A$	TRAITS$_C$	Agree.	Consc.	Extra.	Neurot.	Openn.	avg	RTR$_A$	RTR$_C$
LF	-	-	.664	.725	.733	.629	.672	.684	-	-
LGB	.675	**.681**	.431	.508	.448	.447	.478	.462	.453	.480
EBM	.645	*.659*	.405	.493	.434	.433	.464	.446	.468	.493
PT	.283	.259	.338	.448	.351	.337	.381	.371	.455	.473
DT	.478	.491	.360	.449	.366	.345	.397	.383	.318	.337
KNN	.317	.297	.332	.439	.337	.310	.358	.355	.339	.341
LR	.583	.575	.308	.414	.338	.316	.420	.360	.439	.437

Cluster sizes and Silhouette scores for the two embedding aggregation strategies are reported in Table 1. By considering both clustering labels Y^{toxic} and Y^{safe} we obtain the presumed personality traits Y for the users under analysis. We observe that, although the Silhouette scores for the clusters are generally low, the resulting clusters still show a relatively good separation between users with different online behaviors, as we show in Sect. 5.2. Furthermore, our focus is on comparing the performance of the two proposed strategies, rather than on the absolute values of the Silhouette scores. Therefore, we rely on these clustering results for our subsequent evaluations.

Interpretable Personality Detectors. As personality detector models f and respective learning function $\mathcal{L}_f$, we experimented with two gradient boosting algorithms based on Decision Trees (DT) [4]: the Light Gradient Boosting Machine (LGB) and its interpretable variant, the Explainable Boosting Machine (EBM) [27]. As interpretable baselines, we include DT and PivotTree (PT) [5], the latter functioning both as a standalone classifier and a tool for exemplar instances selection. We also consider Logistic Regression (LR) [25] and k-Nearest Neighbor (KNN) [23] as additional interpretable alternatives. We evaluate the performance of each model using a 5-fold cross-validation using the weighted F1-score as evaluation measure[9].

5.2 Results

We present here experimental results from interpretable predictive models. Table 2 presents (in *black*) the experimental results from interpretable predictive

---

[9] Repositories: https://github.com/fismimosa/RuleTree, https://github.com/microsoft/LightGBM, https://interpret.ml/docs/ebm, https://scikit-learn.org. Details for the hyper-parameters are available in the repository. The results reported refer to the best hyper-parameter setting.

models. In column two and three are reported the weighted F1-scores of the interpretable models f trained on transparent features X to predict TRAITS-driven profiles Y. Comparing the two data representation aggregation strategies used for clustering, the *concatenation* (TRAITS$_C$) of embeddings demonstrates superior predictive performance on interpretable features compared to the *average* (TRAITS$_A$) aggregation strategy.

Among predictive models, LGB achieves the highest performance, followed by EBM. Notably, EBM offers a significant interpretability advantage, providing both global and local feature importance for each prediction, as its additive prediction process enables detailed insights [27]. DT, PT, and KNN exhibit unacceptable performance despite their inherent interpretability. The LR model performs slightly better but still falls short of LGB and EBM. Thus, we advocate for EBM as the best model for interpretable data-driven personality traits detection.

To emphasize the importance of the interpretable features X extracted by TRAITS as well as the data-driven personality traits Y, we conducted experiments using a set of baselines. As a primary baseline, the first row of Table 2 presents (in *blue*) the performance of the supervised personality detectors $\{g_1, \ldots, g_p\}$ (LF) on the external dataset D_p for the five OCEAN personality traits, along with their average score. Notably, the performance of EBM and LGB models within the TRAITS framework (reported in black) aligns closely with these significantly more complex LF models (reported in blue), demonstrating the effectiveness of the interpretable models.

As a second baseline, we compare the TRAITS framework against the training of the same interpretable models f on the same interpretable features X, but targeting the recognition of OCEAN personality traits obtained by labeling the texts T_i of Reddit users using supervised personality detectors $\{g_1, \ldots, g_p\}$. The corresponding results are presented (in *brown*) in columns four through nine of Table 2. A clear trend emerges: the interpretable models f trained on the interpretable features X demonstrate poor predictive performance compared to TRAITS alternatives. The only exceptions are PT and KNN, which perform marginally better on this task, though their performance remains subpar and unacceptable overall.

As a third alternative, we experimented by applying *cluster* in the interpretable feature domain X separately for toxic and safe users, instead of using X_{emb}^{toxic} and X_{emb}^{safe}. This was done using k-means with $k = 3$. We then predicted the data-driven labels Y' by training models f on the embeddings X_{emb}^{toxic} and X_{emb}^{safe}, instead of the transparent features X. In essence, this approach is the Reverse process of TRAITS. In Table 2, this method is denoted as RTR$_A$ and RTR$_C$, representing the *average* and *concatenated* versions of the Reverse of TRAITS, respectively. The results, shown in *purple* in the last two columns, indicate better performance for RTR$_C$ than RTR$_A$, except in the case of LR. RTR$_C$ achieves comparable performance compared to OCEAN-label predictions (highlighted in *brown*), with a notable improvement for PT and LR, though overall performance remains unsatisfactory.

Based on these findings, we conclude that the TRAITS$_C$ strategy is the most effective approach for data-driven profile detection for the Reddit case study.

5.3 Analysis of Data-Driven Personality Profiles

We can now utilize the interpretable structure of the trained EBM to analyze the identified behavioral profiles, focusing on exemplar instances from each dataset. We complement these findings with an analysis of the intensity of OCEAN personality traits across clusters, derived from user labeling via LFs.

Interpretable Cluster Analysis. We explain the cluster assignments by considering one representative user from each cluster. As representative users, we select the medoids of the six clusters and interpret their profiles using the EBM.

In Fig. 1, we present radar plots that illustrate the importance of specific features in predicting each representative user's association with their respective behavior group. Among the 177 interpretable features, we visualize a subset of features based on two criteria: the top ten features ranked by the global importance of the EBM (Fig. 1, top), and the top ten features derived from the NRC-Lex and VAD-Lex sentiment lexicons (Fig. 1, bottom). This approach allows us to interpret the assignment of users to behavioral clusters from both an overall feature importance perspective and an affective perspective.

To enhance the readability of the radar plot, we better specify the semantics of the features used in the visualization.

As already described in Sect. 5, given a user u_i with a text collection T_i, each text $t_{i,j} \in T_i$ is analyzed using various tools and attributes. Among many of the features extracted from each text $t_{i,j}$, Perspective API is used to assess $t_{i,j}$'s content in terms of *obscene* (use of offensive or vulgar language), *threat* (expressions of harm or danger), *insult* (derogatory or demeaning language), and *identity_attack* (targeted hostility based on identity) scores. TextBlob evaluates $t_{i,j}$'s *polarity*, which indicates the overall sentiment of the text, ranging from negative to positive. NRC-Lex identifies *positive* sentiment, indicating the presence of emotionally positive expressions. LIWC-extracted features include *swear* (use of profane or offensive language), *politic* (discussion of political topics), and *Culture* (cultural aspects, including ethnicity, technology, and politics).

For each user u_i, the scores of their texts $t_{i,j}$ were aggregated using statistical measures such as sum, mean, max, and min. Based on feature importance results from EBM, the sum operator was the most effective in predicting membership to behavioral clusters. Additional features for each user identified as most relevant are *nbr_posts*, which represents the total number of posts made by a user, and *fuck_sum*, which counts the occurrences of the word in the user's texts, and we report them too in the radar plots.

For affective features, we considered a set of emotional states from the NRC-Lex, including *sadness, surprise, trust, anger, fear, disgust,* and *joy*. These emotions capture a range of human affective responses. Additionally, we incorporated affective dimensions from the VAD-Lex, namely *valence* (emotional value ranging from negative to positive), *arousal* (intensity of emotional response, from calm to excited) and *dominance* (degree of control or power, ranging from submissive to dominant). The extraction and aggregation of these features follow the same approach described above.

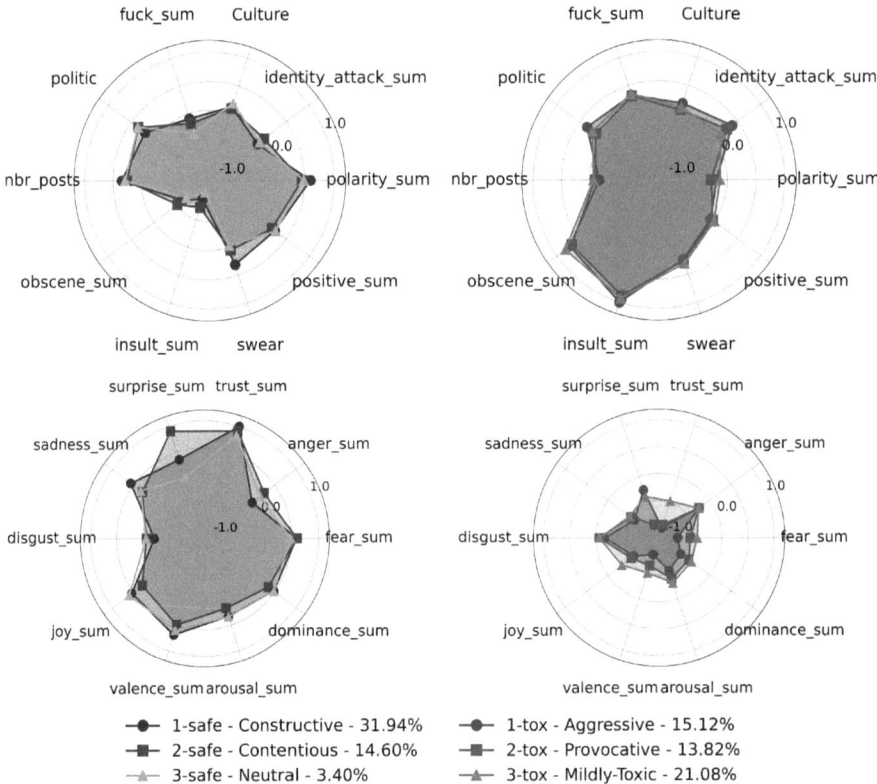

Fig. 1. The plots illustrate the contributions of the top ten most important features (top) and ten affective features (bottom) for the prototype users of safe (left) and toxic (right) clusters. For visualization purposes, feature contribution scores are scaled to the interval $[-1, +1]$, where higher values indicate a greater influence of that feature on the cluster assignment.

Focusing on clusters interpretation, Cluster *1-tox* shows the highest levels of toxicity, with peaks in *identity attacks* and *insult* content. The emotional profile is dominated by *anger, lack of trust,* and *disgust*. We name this group *Aggressive* cluster. Cluster *2-tox* shows slightly more moderate levels of toxic language, with a lower focus on political themes: the user's emotional profile is more oriented toward *arousal, valence,* and *fear*. We name these users *Provocative*. Cluster *3-tox* presents lower overall toxicity, with higher levels of *joy, valence,* and *trust*, and a *reduced* tendency toward *identity attacks*. This can be named as *Mildly-Toxic* cluster. For the safe clusters, Cluster *1-safe* shows peaks of contribution

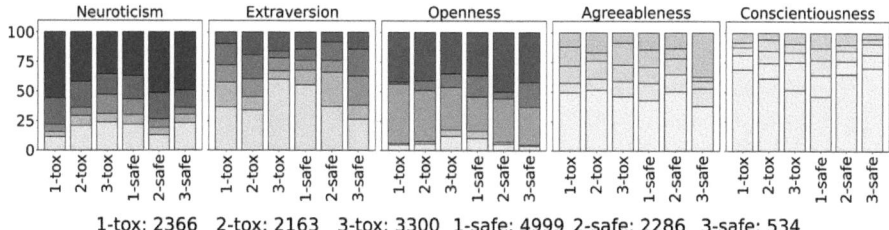

Fig. 2. Stacked bar chart of discretized and normalized OCEAN traits distributed across TRAITS$_C$ clusters and respective cluster sizes. Among the $q = 5$ trait values, deeper shades indicate higher scores.

in *posts number*, *positive polarity comments*, and a low amount of *insults*. The emotional profile is oriented toward *trust* and *valence*, indicating *Constructive* users of the OSN. Users in *2-safe* use slightly harsher language compared to the other ones. They exhibit the highest levels of *anger*, *fear*, and the lowest levels of *joy*, making them *Contentious* users. Cluster *3-safe* is characterized by lower levels of *surprise* and *anger*, as well as slightly lower *polarity*. These users are neutral and less expressive, suggesting they may be considered *Neutral* users.

OCEAN Traits Across Clusters. We complement the previous findings by highlighting how OCEAN personality traits vary in intensity across clusters, as shown in Fig. 2. *1-tox (Aggressive)* stands out with extremely *high Neuroticism* and *low Agreeableness*, aligning with the hostile behaviors seen in Fig. 1. *2-tox (Provocative)* users share many of the traits of *1-tox*, particularly the *elevated Neuroticism*, but also show *higher* levels of *Extraversion* and slightly *higher Agreeableness*. Lastly, *3-tox (Mildly-Toxic)* users display *lower Extraversion* and *moderate Agreeableness* and *Conscientiousness*, suggesting a more reserved behavior. Moving to safe users, *1-safe (Constructive)* ones are characterized by *low* levels of *Neuroticism* and *high* levels of *Agreeableness* and *Conscientiousness*, confirming emotional stability and cooperative tendencies. *2-safe (Contentious)* users share similarities with *1-safe* but with *slightly reduced Agreeableness* and *Conscientiousness*, indicating their more argumentative tendency. In *3-safe (Neutral)* cluster we observe *moderate Openness* and *Agreeableness* levels, reflecting a less expressive disposition.

6 Conclusion

We have introduced TRAITS, an interpretable framework designed for the unsupervised detection of personality traits in both toxic and safe OSN users, explaining user behavior assignments in terms of lexical and affective features. Through a case study on Reddit, we have demonstrated that TRAITS effectively identifies distinct behavioral groups and offers a clearer understanding of users' behavior traits, represented by interpretable feature values, by analyzing the contribution of each feature to the final cluster assignment of a user.

We acknowledge three potential limitations of our approach and propose possible ways to address them. The first concerns the conceptual foundation of our framework, as we assume users' personality traits to be a sufficient basis for evaluating behavior on OSNs. However, users with similar personality traits may exhibit different behavioral tendencies depending on the communication context [48]. Therefore, we plan to extend TRAITS by incorporating contextual variability and emotional intelligence factors, as they significantly influence online social interactions [28]. The second limitation concerns the lack of external validation from experts. To address this, we plan to collect user-generated posts from an OSN while strictly adhering to ethical and privacy-preserving guidelines. These posts will be assessed for toxicity and behavioral tendencies using TRAITS and subsequently reviewed by domain experts. External validation by expert psychologists could further refine behavioral assessments and provide a foundation for more effective targeted moderation strategies. Additionally, we aim to integrate expert knowledge to evaluate aspects more closely associated with toxic personality traits, such as those outlined in the Dark Triad Theory [14]. We also plan to carefully address privacy risks associated with data collection, ensuring proper anonymization. Moreover, we recognize the challenges of human annotation subjectivity and the biases that random user selection may introduce, potentially affecting the representation of various writing styles and personality traits in our analysis. We plan to account for these factors to ensure a more balanced and reliable evaluation. To further enhance the information provided by our interpretable model, we plan to incorporate in our analysis contextual data alongside affective and textual features. In our case-study dataset, the absence of time zone information limited a deeper temporal analysis of posts, which we aim to address in future work. Additionally, considering users' activity within specific communities could provide more specific insights on users' tendencies; however, potential biases must be accounted for to avoid incorrect inferences, as toxic behavior may be more associated with certain communities than others.

Finally, to evaluate the effectiveness of TRAITS in contributing to impactful moderation strategies, we aim to explore its application alongside content generated by large language models. Specifically, we intend to assess whether targeted moderation prompts, tailored to address toxic individuals within specific behavioral groups, lead to more effective behavioral adaptations in simulated users compared to generic, one-size-fits-all moderation approaches. This evaluation will be conducted within OSN-simulated environments [51]. To achieve this, we plan to conduct experiments with different prompt-design strategies, varying aspects such as tone, context, and topic, as well as incorporating leading questions or framing specific issues positively or negatively, while carefully mitigating the introduction of bias, privacy risks, or unfairness in the design.

Acknowledgments. This work has been partially supported by the PRIN 2022 framework project PIANO (Personalized Interventions Against Online Toxicity) under CUP B53D23013290006, by the Italian Project Fondo Italiano per la Scienza FIS00001966 MIMOSA, by the European Community Horizon 2020 programme under the funding schemes ERC-2018-ADG G.A. 834756 "XAI", by the European Commission under the

NextGeneration EU programme âĂŞ National Recovery and Resilience Plan (Piano Nazionale di Ripresa e Resilienza, PNRR) Project: "SoBigData.it" âĂŞ Strengthening the Italian RI for Social Mining and Big Data Analytics" âĂŞ Prot. IR0000013 âĂŞ Av. n. 3264 del 28/12/2021, and M4C2 - Investimento 1.3, Partenariato Esteso PE00000013 - "FAIR" - Future Artificial Intelligence Research" - Spoke 1 "Human-centered AI".

Disclosure of Interests. The authors have no competing interests to declare that are relevant to the content of this article.

References

1. API, P.: Scores – choosing thresholds: Research (nd) (2025). https://developers.perspectiveapi.com/s/about-the-api-score?language=en_US. Accessed: March 28
2. Back, M.D., et al.: Facebook profiles reflect actual personality, not self-idealization. Psychol. Sci. **21**(3), 372–374 (2010)
3. Beltagy, I., et al.: Longformer: the long-document transformer. CoRR **abs/2004.05150** (2020)
4. Breiman, L., et al.: Classification and Regression Trees. Wadsworth (1984)
5. Cascione, A., et al.: Data-agnostic pivotal instances selection for decision-making models. In: ECML-PKDD, vol. 14941, pp. 367–386. Springer (2024)
6. Celli, F., et al.: Unsupervised personality recognition for social network sites. In: ICDS, pp. 59–62 (2012)
7. Cima, L., et al.: Reddit dataset about the Great Ban moderation intervention (2024). https://doi.org/10.5281/zenodo.14034510
8. Costa, P.T., McCrae, R.R.: Trait theories of personality. In: Advanced personality, pp. 103–121. Springer (1998)
9. Costa, P.T., Jr., McCrae, R.R.: Four ways five factors are basic. Pers. Individ. Differ. **13**(6), 653–665 (1992)
10. Cresci, S., et al.: Personalized interventions for online moderation. In: HT-ACM, pp. 248–251. ACM (2022)
11. Dixon, L., Li, J., Sorensen, J., Thain, N., Vasserman, L.: Measuring and mitigating unintended bias in text classification. In: Proceedings of the 2018 AAAI/ACM Conference on AI, Ethics, and Society, pp. 67–73 (2018)
12. Ester, M., et al.: A density-based algorithm for discovering clusters in large spatial databases with noise. In: KDD, pp. 226–231. AAAI Press (1996)
13. Furnham, A.: The relationship between the 30 NEO-PI (R) facets and the four myers-briggs type indicator (MBTI) scores. Psychology **13**(10), 1504–1516 (2022)
14. Furnham, A., et al.: The dark triad of personality: a 10 year review. Soc. Personal Psychol. Compass. **7**(3), 199–216 (2013)
15. Gjurkovic, M., Snajder, J.: Reddit: a gold mine for personality prediction. In: PEOPLES@NAACL-HTL, pp. 87–97. ACL (2018)
16. Gjurkovic, M., et al.: PANDORA talks: personality and demographics on reddit. In: SocialNLP@NAACL, pp. 138–152. ACL (2021)
17. Goldberg, L.R.: The structure of phenotypic personality traits. AP **48**, 26 (1993)
18. Han, X., et al.: Pre-trained models: past, present and future. AIO **2**, 25–50 (2021)
19. John, O.P., et al.: Paradigm shift to the integrative big five trait taxonomy. Handbook Person. Theor. Res. **3**(2), 114–158 (2008)
20. Kasirzadeh, A., Clifford, D.: Fairness and data protection impact assessments. In: AIES-AAAI/ACM, pp. 146–153. ACM (2021)

21. Kazemeini, A., et al.: Interpretable representation learning for personality detection. In: ICDM, pp. 158–165. IEEE (2021)
22. Kerz, E., et al.: Toward explainable AI (XAI) for mental health detection based on language behavior. Front. Psychiatry. **14**, 1219479 (2023)
23. Kramer, O., Kramer, O.: K-nearest neighbors. Dimensionality reduction with unsupervised nearest neighbors, pp. 13–23 (2013)
24. Kwak, H., et al.: Frameaxis: characterizing microframe bias and intensity with word embedding. PeerJ Comput. Sci. **7**, e644 (2021)
25. LaValley, M.P.: Logistic regression. Circulation **117**(18), 2395–2399 (2008)
26. Liao, R., et al.: An open-source benchmark of deep learning models for audio-visual apparent and self-reported personality recognition. IEEE Trans. Affect. Comput. **15**(3), 1590–1607 (2024)
27. Lou, Y., et al.: Accurate intelligible models with pairwise interactions. In: KDD, pp. 623–631. ACM (2013)
28. Madaan, R., et al.: Understanding the role of emotional intelligence in usage of social media. In: Confluence, pp. 586–591. IEEE (2020)
29. Mairesse, F., et al.: Using linguistic cues for the automatic recognition of personality in conversation and text. J. Artif. Intell. Res. **30**, 457–500 (2007)
30. Majumder, N., et al.: Deep learning-based document modeling for personality detection from text. IEEE Intell. Syst. **32**(2), 74–79 (2017)
31. Mariani, G., Monreale, A., Naretto, F.: Privacy risk assessment of individual psychometric profiles. In: Soares, C., Torgo, L. (eds.) DS 2021. LNCS (LNAI), vol. 12986, pp. 411–421. Springer, Cham (2021). https://doi.org/10.1007/978-3-030-88942-5_32
32. Mayer, J.D.: The personality systems framework: current theory and development. JRP **56**, 4–14 (2015)
33. McCrae, R.R., John, O.P.: An introduction to the five-factor model and its applications. J. Pers. **60**(2), 175–215 (1992)
34. Mehta, Y., others Navonil Majumder, Gelbukh, A.F., Cambria, E.: Recent trends in deep learning based personality detection. Artif. Intell. Rev. **53**(4), 2313–2339 (2020)
35. Mehta, Y., et al.: Bottom-up and top-down: Predicting personality with psycholinguistic and language model features. In: ICDM, pp. 1184–1189. IEEE (2020)
36. Monreale, A., Rinzivillo, S., Pratesi, F., Giannotti, F., Pedreschi, D.: Privacy-by-design in big data analytics and social mining. EPJ Data Sci. **3**(1), 1–26 (2014). https://doi.org/10.1140/epjds/s13688-014-0010-4
37. Myers, I.: A Guide to the Development and Use of the Myers-Briggs Type Indicator. CPP Inc. (1998)
38. Panfilova, A.S., et al.: Applying XAI methods to models for diagnosing personal traits and cognitive abilities by social network data. Sci. Rep. **14**(1), 5369 (2024)
39. Pennebaker, J.W., King, L.A.: Linguistic styles: language use as an individual difference. JPSP **77**(6), 1296 (1999)
40. Pratama, B.Y., Sarno, R.: Personality classification based on twitter text using naive bayes, knn and svm. In: ICoDSE, pp. 170–174. IEEE (2015)
41. Qiu, L., et al.: You are what you tweet: personality expression and perception on twitter. JRP **46**(6), 710–718 (2012)
42. Quercia, D., et al.: Our twitter profiles, our selves: Predicting personality with twitter. In: PASSAT-SocialCom, pp. 180–185. IEEE (2011)
43. Rangra, K., et al.: Emotional speech-based personality prediction using NPSO architecture in deep learning. Meas.: Sens. **25**, 100655 (2023)

44. Rojas Q, M., et al.: Automatic prediction of facial trait judgments: Appearance vs. structural models. PloS one **6**(8), e23323 (2011)
45. Srinarong, N., Mongkolnavin, J.: A development of personality recognition model from conversation voice in call center context. In: IAIT, pp. 12:1–12:5. ACM (2021)
46. Stajner, S., Yenikent, S.: A survey of automatic personality detection from texts. In: COLING, pp. 6284–6295. ICCL (2020)
47. Tan, P.N., et al.: Data Mining Introduction. People's Posts and Telecommunications Publishing House, Beijing (2006)
48. Tett, R.P., et al.: Trait activation theory: a review of the literature and applications to five lines of personality dynamics research. Annu. Rev. Organ. Psychol. Organ. Behav. **8**(1), 199–233 (2021)
49. Trujillo, A., Cresci, S.: Make reddit great again: assessing community effects of moderation interventions on r/the_donald. HCI-ACM **6**(CSCW2), 1–28 (2022)
50. Wen, Z., et al.: Affective- NLI: towards accurate and interpretable personality recognition in conversation. In: IEEE PerCom, pp. 184–193. IEEE (2024)
51. Xie, C., et al.: Can large language model agents simulate human trust behavior? In: NeurIPS 2024 (2024)
52. Xue, D., et al.: Deep learning-based personality recognition from text posts of online social networks. Appl. Intell. **48**(11), 4232–4246 (2018). https://doi.org/10.1007/s10489-018-1212-4
53. Yang, F., et al.: Multi-document transformer for personality detection. In: AAAI-IAAI, pp. 14221–14229. AAAI Press (2021)
54. Zhao, X., et al.: Integrating audio and visual modalities for multimodal personality trait recognition via hybrid deep learning. Front. Neurosci. **16**, 1107284 (2023)

Open Access This chapter is licensed under the terms of the Creative Commons Attribution 4.0 International License (http://creativecommons.org/licenses/by/4.0/), which permits use, sharing, adaptation, distribution and reproduction in any medium or format, as long as you give appropriate credit to the original author(s) and the source, provide a link to the Creative Commons license and indicate if changes were made.

The images or other third party material in this chapter are included in the chapter's Creative Commons license, unless indicated otherwise in a credit line to the material. If material is not included in the chapter's Creative Commons license and your intended use is not permitted by statutory regulation or exceeds the permitted use, you will need to obtain permission directly from the copyright holder.

An Interpretable Data-Driven Approach for Modeling Toxic Users via Feature Extraction

Laura Pollacci[1]([✉])[iD], Jacopo Gneri[1], and Riccardo Guidotti[1,2][iD]

[1] University of Pisa, Largo Bruno Pontecorvo 3, Pisa, PI 56127, Italy
`laura.pollacci@unipi.it, j.gneri@studenti.unipi.it`
[2] KDD Lab, ISTI-CNR, Via G. Moruzzi 1, Pisa, PI 56124, Italy
`riccardo.guidotti@isti.cnr.it`

Abstract. Online Social Networks (OSNs) enable large-scale discussions but often suffer from toxic behaviors such as harassment and hate speech. While automated moderation helps manage toxicity, personalized approaches remain challenging due to fairness and transparency concerns. We introduce UTOXIC, a machine-learning framework that detects and analyzes toxic users based on linguistic, affective, and clustering-derived features. It performs binary and multi-class classification while incorporating explainability techniques for transparency. Evaluating UTOXIC on a Reddit dataset with over 8 million comments, we demonstrate its effectiveness in identifying toxic users and specific toxicity types. Our approach enhances automated moderation, offering interpretable insights for fairer and more adaptive interventions.

Keywords: Toxicity Detection · Machine Learning · XAI

1 Introduction

Online Social Networks (OSNs) are a key part of modern digital communication, shaping users' interactions. Platforms like Facebook, X (formerly Twitter), and Reddit enable large-scale, real-time discussions. However, these platforms often suffer from toxic behaviors that harm interactions and degrade discussion quality. Toxic behavior in OSNs includes cyberbullying, harassment, flaming, hate speech, and other harmful actions. To counter this, OSN platforms use content moderation strategies, combining user reports with automated detection methods. While users can report harmful content, automatic machine learning-based approaches, which are typically not interpretable, play a major role in identifying and managing toxic discussions at scale. A major challenge in moderation is implementing personalized strategies that consider user-specific behaviors. Studies show that users respond differently to moderation efforts [19], thus customizing moderation policies based on behavior can improve adherence to community guidelines and enhance moderation effectiveness [4]. However, this approach presents challenges, such as the lack of ground truth, and the importance of interpretable machine learning models to ensure fairness and transparency [9].

In order to pursue this direction, we present UTOXIC[1], a User TOxic eXplainable Identification and Characterization framework for toxic users based on features extracted from their comments and activity. UTOXIC employs linguistic and stylistic, affective-based, and clustering-derived features, aggregating them at the user level to perform binary classification (toxic vs. non-toxic) and multiclass classification (identifying specific toxic behaviors). UTOXIC also incorporates explainability techniques to clarify model decisions at both local (individual cases) and global levels. We evaluate UTOXIC on a Reddit dataset with over 8 million comments from 15,000 users. Our results show that UTOXIC effectively distinguishes toxic from non-toxic users and identifies specific types of toxicity, such as harassment, violence, racism, and profanity. By using *interpretable* linguistic, sentiment-based, and unsupervised features, UTOXIC enhances automated toxicity detection and characterization, potentially enhancing moderation in OSNs.

The rest of the paper is organized as follows. After reviewing the literature in toxicity detection both at a comment and at the user level in Sect. 2, we formalize UTOXIC in Sect. 3. Section 4 presents the Reddit case study together with the experimental results. Finally, Sect. 5 summarizes our contributions and outlines potential directions for future research.

2 Related Works

In the literature, there is not a single and agreed-upon definition of the term "toxicity" or "toxic-speech" but it is often used as an umbrella term indicating negative behaviors. In general, studies in the literature can be grouped into two main lines of research: a first line focuses on identifying and classifying toxicity at the *comment level*, while the second addresses it at the *user level*.

Online toxicity detection at the comment levels often involves analyzing toxic posts and comments, where "toxic" includes rude, vulgar, harmful, or hateful behavior, such as hate speech. In [15], hate-speech detection is performed on tweets by combining textual features with user-related attributes (e.g., demographics, behavior, personality, readability, and writing style), employing models like SVM, Logistic Regression, Random Forest, CatBoost, and XGBoost. Similarly, in [8] multilingual hate speech detection on Facebook posts is investigated, focusing on user demographics. For similar tasks, in [18] and [21], Logistic Regression, SVM, and Multilayer Perceptron are used to classify comments. In these works, the performances of the models involved for the toxicity detection tasks improve considerably thanks to the features extracted from the comments.

Another strand of research in online toxicity detection focuses on analyzing the behaviors of users who post toxic comments, i.e., user level toxicity detection. For instance, in [12] the authors studied users' toxicity on Reddit over time by labeling over 3 million comments with Perspective API and categorizing users into four groups based on toxicity trends, i.e., steady, fickle-minded, pacified, and radicalized. Similarly, in [2] over 500 million comments across eight

---
[1] The code is available on GitHub at https://github.com/LauraPollacci/UTOXIC.

platforms over 30 years are investigated by defining user toxicity as the fraction of toxic comments. The study shows that toxicity arises during interactions between highly polarized users rather than influencing user participation. Factors contributing to toxicity, such as user demographics, posting time, and trolls, are highlighted in [7,10]. For instance, the author in [7] adopts an interdisciplinary approach, combining linguistics and discourse analysis to examine trolling in asynchronous computer-mediated communication. Through a qualitative analysis of user discussions, the study identifies four key characteristics of trolling: aggression, deception, disruption, and success. Also, it presents a structured framework for understanding trolling as a deliberate and socially disruptive behavior in online interactions. The studies in [17] and [16] apply binary classification for toxic user detection. In contrast, [2] and [12] categorize users–using two and four labels, respectively–but without performing a classification task, instead proposing a detailed labeling methodology. In [17], the authors investigate the link between toxic online behavior and Dark Triad personality traits, i.e., narcissism, Machiavellianism, and psychopathy, using classification models such as SVMs, Random Forests, and Naive Bayes on Twitter data. They observe correlations between language use and Dark Triad traits but show low model performance when analyzing individual users.

We propose an interpretable approach for toxic user modeling and classification by exploiting features extracted from their comments and from their activity on the platform like [17] and [16]. Despite our work not being primarily focused on hate speech detection, like [15], we employ textual, such as readability levels, and affective-based features for modeling. In the literature, most of the works that involve XAI focus on the detection of hate speech or similar toxic behaviors, while in our work, we do not employ XAI techniques for the explanation of text classification, but exclusively for the toxicity traits of the users.

3 Methodology

In this section we present UTOXIC, a User TOxic eXplainable Identification and Characterization framework for modeling and classifying toxic users in OSNs. UTOXIC involves extracting interpretable linguistic and behavioral features, and training opaque classification models on top of them to distinguish between toxic and non-toxic users. Finally, we employ explainability techniques on the interpretable features to understand the model's decisions.

We start by formalizing the problem of toxic user identification and classification, distinguishing between binary and multi-class settings.

Definition 1. (Toxic User Detection Problem). *Let $U = \{u_1, \ldots, u_n\}$ represent a set of n users in an OSN, and let $T^* = \{t_1, \ldots, t_n\}$ represent their toxicity levels, where $t_i \in T^*$ and $T^* = \{0, \ldots, c\}$ represent the set of possible toxicity states. The* Toxic User Detection Problem *consists of learning a classification model f that, given an unlabeled user u_i, predicts their toxicity level t_i^*, i.e., $t_i^* = f(u_i)$, where $t_i^* \in T^*$ represents one of the classes in T^*.*

Building on Definition 1, we approach the problem of toxic user identification and characterization by leveraging machine learning models. In particular, we face two problems: the *binary* Toxic User Detection Problem with $c = 2$, i.e., $\mathcal{T}^* = \{0, 1\}$ with 0 for non-toxic and 1 for toxic, and the *multiclass* Toxic User Detection Problem with $c = 5$, i.e., $\mathcal{T}^* = \{0, 1, 2, 3, 4\}$ with 0 for non-toxicity, 1 for harassment, 2 for violence, 3 for racism, and 4 for vulgarity.

However, ground truth labels for user toxicity, such as expert-based annotations, are often unavailable, complicating the direct classification of users. Moreover, the nuanced and context-dependent nature of toxic behavior in OSNs further complicates the task. To address these challenges, we propose a supervised machine learning approach for both the identification (binary classification) and characterization (multi-class classification) of toxic users. This is achieved by extracting features from users' comments and aggregating them.

Definition 2. (Supervised Toxic User Detection Problem). *Let $U = \{u_1, \ldots, u_n\}$ be a set of n users in an OSN. Each user $u_i \in U$ has a set of comments $C_i = \{c_{i_1}, c_{i_2}, \ldots, c_{i_m}\}$, where m denotes the number of comments posted by the user. The set of features $\mathcal{F}(c_{i_j})$ is extracted from each comment $c_{i_j} \in C_i$ for every user u_i. These features are then aggregated using an aggregation function $\mathcal{A}$ (e.g., sum, mean) to represent the user in terms of their commenting activity. The Supervised Toxic User Detection Problem consists of learning a classification model f that, given an unlabeled user $u_i \in U$, predicts their toxicity level t_i^*, i.e., $t_i^* = f(u_i)$, where $t_i^* \in \mathcal{T}^*$ represents one classes in $\mathcal{T}^*$. Specifically, the model assigns a label t_i to each user based on the aggregated features of their comments, where $t_i = f\left(\mathcal{A}\left(\bigcup_{j=1}^{m} \mathcal{F}(c_{i_j})\right)\right)$.*

We apply Definition 2 to both the *Binary* Supervised Toxic User Detection Problem with $c = 2$, i.e., $\mathcal{T}^* = \{0, 1\}$ with 0 for non-toxic and 1 for toxic, and to the *Multi-class Single-label* Supervised Toxic User Detection Problem with $c = 5$, i.e., $\mathcal{T}^* = \{0, 1, 2, 3, 4\}$ with 0 for non-toxicity, 1 for harassment, 2 for violence, 3 for racism, and 4 for vulgarity.

In the rest, we present the UTOXIC framework, aimed at improving the detection and classification of toxic users in OSNs. This framework addresses the challenge of toxicity detection in situations where ground truth data on user toxicity is often unavailable. In Fig. 1 is summarized the core idea of UTOXIC that extracts interpretable and meaningful features from user comments and behaviors to identify and characterize toxic users. The process begins with a two-level feature extraction *(1)*: first, from the comments themselves *(1.a)*, and second, from the users' profiles *(1.b)*, which also include aggregated features from the comments. These features are then used to model user toxicity *(2)*, with both binary *(2.a)* and multi-class *(2.b)* classification models. Finally, we apply an explainability technique *(3)* to interpret and provide insights into the classification models, making the decision process transparent and understandable.

Through the interpretable features UTOXIC framework can help not only in identifying toxic users but also in understanding the factors behind the toxicity

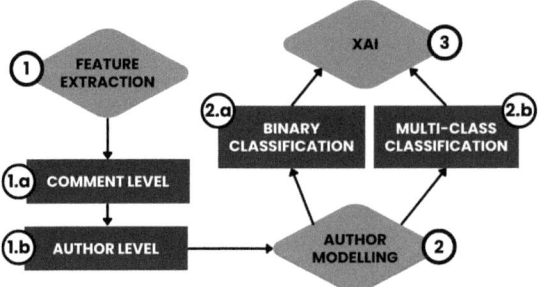

Fig. 1. Workflow of the user toxicity identification and characterization process. The pipeline includes ground truth definition, feature extraction at both comment and user levels, user toxicity modeling (binary and multi-class), and an explainability step.

classification, enhancing the interpretability of the underlying machine learning models.

The pseudo-code of UTOXIC is in Algorithm 1. Given a set $U = \{u_1, \ldots, u_n\}$ of n users in an OSN we consider $T = \{T_1, \ldots, T_n\}$ the textual comments generated by the users of the OSN in a certain period, where $T_i \in T$ with $T_i = \{t_{i,1}, \ldots, t_{i,n_i}\}$ is the set of n_i texts of user i, while $t_{i,j} \in T_i$ is the jth text of user i. UTOXIC takes as input T and returns f as the interpretable users' toxicity classification model by employing α, that is the threshold for determining whether a comment is considered toxic based on its toxicity score, derived by D_p, an external dataset containing comments (T_p) and their corresponding toxicity annotations (Y_p) (used for training and model validation), and β that is the threshold for classifying a user as toxic based on the percentage of toxic comments.

As a first step (line 1), we establish the ground truth for comments (G_t) by using external toxicity annotations, specifically from the Perspective API. Perspective API provides scores indicating the likelihood that a reader would perceive a given comment as toxic or as exhibiting a specific toxicity-related attribute. While Perspective API is not fully transparent regarding its annotation process and may introduce biases, its behavior has been widely investigated, and performances and biases are-at least partially-quantified in the literature [6,11,12,14]. Moreover, prior research [5,20] has provided insights into its application, including recommendations on threshold settings for toxicity detection [1]. In contrast, human annotation would not only entail significant costs given the vast number of comments to be evaluated but would also introduce biases that are inherently more difficult to analyze and quantify. Toxicity and its associated attributes are not entirely objective constructs, and their perception may at least in part depend on individual sensitivity. Thus, human annotation could have introduced biases driven by subjective judgment or prejudice, which, unlike those of Perspective API, would have been challenging to identify, measure, or control. The ground truth helps train the model by associating comments with known toxicity labels. This is done by creating a set of toxicity labels, G_t,

Algorithm 1: UTOXIC(T)

Input : T - OSN textual comments of users where $t_{i,j} \in T_i$ is the jth comment of user i, and $T_i \in T$ with $T_i = \{t_{i,1}, \ldots, t_{i,n_i}\}$ is the set of n_i comments of user i.
Param : α - toxicity threshold for comment-level toxicity scoring
β - toxicity threshold for user-level toxicity classification
$D_p = \langle T_p, Y_p \rangle$ - external dataset with known toxicity annotations
Output: f - toxicity classification model for users.

1 $G_t \leftarrow \{g_j \mid g_j = Y_p(t_{i,j})\ \forall t_{i,j} \in T\}$; // Ground truth for comments from Perspective API
2 $y_{i,j} \leftarrow 1$ if $Y_p(t_{i,j}) \geq \alpha$ else $y_{i,j} \leftarrow 0$; // Assign label (1 if score >= alpha, else 0)
3 $Y_c[i,j] \leftarrow y_{i,j}$; // Assign the label to each comment
4 **for** $i \in [1,n]$ **do** // For each user
5 $\quad n_{toxic} \leftarrow count\_toxic\_comments(T_i, Y_c[i])$; // Define users' ground truth from Y_c
$\quad p_{toxic} \leftarrow \frac{n_{toxic}}{n_i}$; // Compute the percentage of toxic comments for user i if $p_{toxic} \geq \beta$
   then
6 $\quad\quad G_u[i] \leftarrow T$; // Classify user as T if $\geq \beta$ of their comments are toxic
$\quad\quad G_u^M[i] \leftarrow tox\_label(X_{users,i})$; // Multi-label ground truth for toxic users
7 **else**
8 $\quad\quad G_u[i] \leftarrow NT$; // Otherwise, classify the user as non-toxic
9 $\quad\quad G_u^M[i] \leftarrow NT$; // Classify the user as non-toxic in multi-label classification
10 $X_c \leftarrow \emptyset$; // Initialize comment-level features
11 **for** $t_{i,j} \in T$ **do** // For each comment
12 $\quad x_{lexical} \leftarrow extract\_lexical\_features(t_{i,j})$; // Extract lexical and syntactic features
13 $\quad x_{affective} \leftarrow extract\_sentiment\_emotion(t_{i,j})$; // Extract affective-based features
14 $\quad x_{toxic\_words} \leftarrow extract\_toxic\_lemmas(t_{i,j})$; // Identify toxic lemmas in the comment
15 $\quad x_{cluster} \leftarrow extract\_cluster\_features(t_{i,j})$; // Cluster comments to identify toxicity
16 $\quad X_c \leftarrow X_c \cup \{x_{lexical}, x_{affective}, x_{toxic\_words}, x_{cluster}\}$; // Aggregate comments' features
17 $X_u \leftarrow \emptyset$; // Initialize user-level features
18 **for** $i \in [1,n]$ **do** // For each user
19 $\quad x_u \leftarrow aggregate\_features(X_{c,i})$; // Aggregate comment-level features
20 $\quad x_{activity} \leftarrow extract\_activity\_features(T_i)$; // Extract users' activity features
21 $\quad X_u \leftarrow X_u \cup \{x_u, x_{activity}\}$; // Combine all features for user
22 $A_{binary} \leftarrow binary\_classification(X_u, G_u)$; // Classify users as T or NT
$A_{multi} \leftarrow multi\_classification(X_u, G_u^M)$; // Classify users into categories
$f_{explanation} \leftarrow XAI(A_{binary}, A_{multi}, X_u)$; // Apply explainability to all models **return**
$f_{explanation}$; // Return the interpretable toxicity model with explanations

where each label g_j corresponds to a comment $t_{i,j}$ in the dataset T. Thus, for each comment $t_{i,j}$, the toxicity label g_j is directly obtained from the Perspective API score, as represented by $g_j = Y_p(t_{i,j})$. The ground truth G_t is populated by the toxicity labels for all comments in the dataset, where j ranges from 1 to n, the total number of comments. This step is crucial to set the benchmark for labeling toxicity in the data, which is then used for training the model. Once a continuous toxicity score is assigned to each comment from the Perspective API, the algorithm assigns a binary label (toxic or non-toxic) based on whether the score $(Y_p(t_{i,j}))$ is greater than or equal to the threshold α. Specifically, if the score meets or exceeds the threshold, the label $y_{i,j}$ is set to 1; otherwise, it is set to 0 (lines 2 and 3).

Next, at the user level (lines 4–12), the algorithm defines the ground truth by computing the toxicity scores of each user's comments. For each user $i \in [1,n]$ (line 4), the number of toxic comments (n_{toxic}) is computed (line 5) by counting how many of the user's comments are labeled as toxic in the ground truth G_t. The percentage of toxic comments for user i is then calculated (line 6) by dividing the number of toxic comments by the total number of comments the user made.

If a user has at least β toxic comments (line 7), they are classified as toxic (T) in the binary ground truth (G_u) (line 8). For toxic users, a multi-label ground truth (G_u^M) is created based on the average toxicity values of their comments, providing deeper insight into their behavior (line 9). Otherwise, a user is classified as non-toxic (NT) for both binary and multi-label classification (lines 11–12).

Moving to the feature extraction process (lines 13-19), the algorithm initializes comment-level features X_c (line 13). Then, for each comment $t_{i,j} \in T$ (line 14), the following functions are called:

- The function *extract_lexical_features* (line 15) is called to capture textual characteristics, such as the number of unique words, the frequency of specific word types (nouns, verbs, adjectives), and readability indices.
- The function *extract_sentiment_emotion* (line 16) analyzes sentiment polarity (whether the comment is positive, negative, or neutral), tone, through measures like valence, arousal, and dominance, end emotions.
- The function *extract_toxic_lemmas* (line 17) identifies toxic-related lemmas appearing in the comment.
- The function *extract_cluster_features* (line 18) applies clustering techniques to capture patterns or types of toxicity based on how similar comments are grouped together.

Once these features are extracted for each comment, they are aggregated into the set X_c (line 19), which holds all the features for every comment in the dataset.

After extracting the features at the comment level, the algorithm moves to extract features at the user level. It starts by initializing the set X_u (line 20) to store the aggregated features for each user. For each user $i \in [1, n]$ (line 21), the algorithm performs the following steps:

- The individual comment-level features for all comments posted by the user are aggregated into a single vector for the user using the function *aggregate_features* (line 22). This aggregation involves computing statistics such as the sum, mean, maximum, and minimum for each feature across all comments made by the user.
- The function *extract_activity_features* (line 23) is used to capture features related to the user's commenting activity. This includes information such as the total number of comments made, the number of toxic comments, and the number of different subreddits or topics the user has participated in.

Finally, the aggregated comment-level features are combined with the activity features (line 24) to form a comprehensive feature set for the user. With the feature set for each user, the algorithm then models toxicity at the user level. A binary classification algorithm (line 25) is applied to classify each user as either toxic or non-toxic, based on the features extracted from their comments and activity. For users classified as toxic, the algorithm further categorizes them into different toxicity types (line 26). This is done through a multi-class classification, where users are classified into distinct toxicity types based on the features extracted from their comments. The final step of the algorithm is to apply Explainable AI techniques (line 27) to interpret the classification results and understand which features contributed the most to the model's decisions. The algorithm generates explanations for both binary and multi-class toxicity classifications, at a local and global level, providing insights into how different features impacted the classification decisions for users (line 28).

4 Case Study

To evaluate the effectiveness of our framework, we apply UTOXIC to a case study of Reddit users. This section details the experimental setup and the feature extraction process. We then present the classification model performance and insights derived from applying XAI.

4.1 Experimental Setting

We apply the methodology described in Sect. 3 to a Reddit case study by first defining the ground truth, then extracting features from comments and users to model and characterize toxicity, and finally applying explanation techniques. In this study, we employ the Reddit dataset[2] presented in [3], covering the period from April 2020 to January 2021. The dataset represents comments through 16 properties, including *toxicity*, *severe toxicity*, *obscene*, *threat*, *insult*, and *identity attack* scores. These scores capture toxicity-related information extracted using the Perspective API[3]. To define our target variables for multi-class classification, we map *identity attack* to `racism`, *threat* to `violence`, *obscene* to `vulgarity`, and *insult* to `harassment`, using the corresponding scores from the dataset. Together with these, the comments are described by the user, the subreddit where they are posted, the identifiers of the parent comment and the submission, the timestamp (without timezone information), their score, and any potential awards or gildings. After an initial phase of data preparation, which comprises the removal of duplicate comments and irrelevant features, i.e., *awardings*, *gildings*, *parent_id* and *submission*, the dataset includes 8,724,581 comments, produced by 15,721 unique users, and belonging to 45,334 unique subreddits. To define whether a comment is toxic or not, we set a threshold α on the `toxicity` score. We chose $\alpha >= 0.7$ to ensure a broader inclusion of cases, rather than restricting the analysis to only the most clearly toxic ones, as would happen with a higher threshold, as suggested by the documentation [1][4]. As a result, we obtained 961,251 toxic comments and 7,763,330 non-toxic comments. Before the feature extraction, we perform an initial text-cleaning phase in which

---
[2] https://doi.org/10.5281/zenodo.14034510.
[3] Perspective API: https://perspectiveapi.com/.
[4] While ML research often employs stricter thresholds (e.g., 0.9), a lower threshold balances inclusivity and precision, capturing a broader range of cases while maintaining reliability. According to prior research [1,5], ensuring a more comprehensive and representative dataset for analysis.

double spaces, URLs, special characters, and punctuation are removed using regular expressions. Further, to avoid losing useful information, emojis are decoded into the corresponding textual definition by using Emoji[5], and contractions are expanded by using Contractions[6].

4.2 Feature Extraction

Once the comments were cleaned, we focused on the feature extraction phase at the comment level (Algorithm 1, lines 14-18). As described in Algorithm 1 (line 15), we extracted text-related features, capturing the linguistic and stylistic characteristics of the comments. These include, among others, the total number of words and the count of uppercase words, extracted using NLTK[7], and the scores of nine readability tests (See Appendix A.1), obtained from Readability[8]. Regarding the affective-based features (Algorithm 1, line 16), we used TextBlob[9] to obtain the `polarity` score, NRC-Lex[10] for the eight basic emotions[11] by Plutchik [13], and the NRC Lexicon[12] for `valence`, `arousal`, and `dominance` average values in each comment. To obtain additional toxicity-based information, we focused exclusively on the toxic comments to extract their most relevant and frequent words (Algorithm 1, line 17). Specifically, we used the Wordcloud[13] Python library to identify the most frequent terms, selecting the top 150,000 comments for each of the six types of toxicity, and we applied Term Frequency-Inverse Document Frequency[14] (TF-IDF) to detect the key terms in the same set of comments analyzed in the wordclouds. The combination of the two approaches provides a set of 27 words that have been lemmatized and then individually added as binary features in a one-hot encoding fashion: 1 if the lemma is present in the comment, 0 otherwise. Moreover, we add the `toxic_words` feature, representing the total number of toxic lemmas per comment. By following this approach, we obtained a set of 59 features that allow to fully describe textual, affective, and toxic traits in comments. Moreover, we applied a centroid-based clustering analysis (Algorithm 1, line 18) using K-means and taking into consideration the six toxicity-related features. We applied the Elbow Method to determine the optimal number of clusters, which was found to be 5. We started from the assumption that the values of the centroids of each cluster define the type of toxicity of each comment. Thus, the centroid of Cluster 0, labeled "extreme toxic", shows high values for toxicity, obscenity,

---

[5] Emojis: https://pypi.org/project/emoji/.
[6] Contractions: https://pypi.org/project/contractions/.
[7] NLTK: https://www.nltk.org/.
[8] Readability: https://pypi.org/project/readability/.
[9] TextBlob: https://textblob.readthedocs.io/en/dev/.
[10] NRC-Lex: http://saifmohammad.com/WebPages/NRC-Emotion-Lexicon.html.
[11] Namely, anger, fear, sadness, disgust, surprise, anticipation, trust, and joy.
[12] NRC VAD-Lexicon: http://saifmohammad.com/WebPages/nrc-vad.html.
[13] Wordcloud: https://pypi.org/project/wordcloud/.
[14] TF-IDF is a numerical statistic that reflects the importance of a word in a document relative to a collection, balancing word frequency with its rarity across documents.

and insult. The centroids of Clusters 2 and 3 show elevated levels of toxicity and both toxicity and insult, respectively, and are referred to as "moderate toxic" and "obscene toxic". In contrast, the centroids of Clusters 1 and 4 show low values across all toxicity types, indicating that comments in these clusters are generally non-toxic. As a result, they are labeled "polite" and "non-toxic", respectively.

After extracting features from the comments, we focused on the users to identify the features that will be used in the classification tasks. Firstly, we grouped the comments per user, then we extracted user-based features also aggregating the comment-based ones (Algorithm 1, lines 22-24). In addition to the textual-related features, we considered users' activity-related features (Algorithm 1, line 24). These include the number of comments, number and percentage of toxic comments, list and number of toxicity type above average, number of distinct subreddits the user is active in, list and number of emotions above average, number of comments per cluster, ratio of non-toxic comments and number of subreddits, and the ratio of toxic comments and number of subreddits. Additionally, we defined a set of features representing the number of comments of the users belonging to each cluster, i.e., extreme toxic, polite, moderated toxic, obscene toxic, and low toxic. By following the described approach, each user is characterized by 184 features - listed and described in Appendix A.2 - encompassing linguistic aspects, sentiment and emotion attributes, textual complexity, and activity-related metrics.

4.3 Classification

Ground Truth and Experimental Setting. To accomplish the classification tasks, we first set two different ground truths for users, i.e., G_u and G_u^M. The first annotation (G_u) identifies a user as toxic (T) or non-toxic (NT). This is achieved by setting a threshold β on the feature that indicates the percentage of toxic comments per user (Algorithm 1, line 7-9, 11). The a threshold β is set at 10%, meaning a user is classified as toxic if at least 1 over 10 of their comments are toxic. This threshold is based on the idea that even a small percentage of toxic behavior can have a significant impact on the online discussion environment[15]. The 10% threshold allows for the identification of harmful behaviors without over-classifying users who contribute minimally to toxic content. As a result of the binary annotation, we obtain a balanced dataset including 7,843 toxic and 7,878 non-toxic users.

The second annotation (G_u^M) focuses exclusively on the toxic users, and it is based on the average of the toxicity-related features derived from the Perspective API, i.e., threat, insult, obscene, and identity attack, respectively translated as *violence*, *harassment*, *vulgarity*, and *racism* (Algorithm 1, line 9). The multi-class annotation led to an imbalanced dataset composed of 16 violent users, 297 molesters, 7,496 vulgar users, and 34 racists.

---

[15] Toxicity, can negatively affect other users' experiences and the overall climate of the community and research in OSNs have explored how relatively low levels of negative content can create a harmful environment, emphasizing the importance of identifying and mitigating such behavior early.

Table 1. Binary classification. Best results in bold.

		NT				T			
Model	Acc.	Prec.	Rec.	F1	AuC	Prec.	Rec.	F1	AuC
LR	**93.6%**	**0.925**	0.953	**0.939**	0.98	0.950	**0.920**	**0.935**	0.98
RF	92.8%	0.911	0.953	0.931	**0.99**	0.949	0.903	0.926	**0.99**
SVM	92.7%	0.889	**0.980**	0.932	0.98	**0.977**	0.874	0.922	0.98
DT	90.6%	0.888	0.933	0.910	0.95	0.927	0.879	0.902	0.95
KNN	89%	0.859	0.939	0.897	0.97	0.930	0.841	0.883	0.97

Table 2. Multiclass classification before SMOTE. Best results in bold.

Model	Acc.	harassment	non-toxic	racism	violence	vulgarity
RF	90%	**0.491**	0.921	**0.110**	**0.402**	**0.901**
SVM	90%	0.282	**0.943**	0.000	0.000	**0.901**
DT	89%	0.256	0.912	0.000	0.000	0.881
KNN	88%	0.000	0.904	0.000	0.000	0.872
LR	84%	0.361	0.902	0.021	0.012	0.871

Both the binary and multi-class single-label classification tasks are carried out using Hold-out Test Set (with a 70-30 split) and testing five different models DT, RF, KNN, LR, and SVM whose parameters have been tuned through random search[16]. Given the variety of features extracted, a preliminary feature selection allowed to find the best set of features for the classification tasks. The feature selection combines boxplot analysis and Mutual Information[17] and led to a set of 33 features (highlighted in bold in the complete list in Appendix A.2).

Binary Classification. The performance are reported in Table 1. Every model shows a high overall accuracy, ranging around 90%, with Logistic Regression achieving the highest (93.6%), and KNN the lowest (89%). All models show similar and comparative performances on both classes (NT and T) and for all considered metrics, with values between 0.89 and 0.99, except KNN which shows precision on NT and recall on T slightly lower (0.86 and 0.84, respectively).

Multi-Class Single-Label Classification. After the binary classification task, we experimented with multi-label single-class classification, which takes

---

[16] Scikit Learn RandomizedSearchCV: https://scikit-learn.org/stable/modules/generated/sklearn.model_selection.RandomizedSearchCV.html.

[17] Mutual information is a statistical measure that quantifies the amount of information shared between two variables, indicating how much knowing one variable reduces the uncertainty of the other.

Table 3. Multiclass classification before SMOTE. Best results in bold.

Model	Acc.	harassment	non-toxic	racism	violence	vulgarity
RF	**89%**	**0.419**	**0.920**	0.068	0.000	**0.895**
LR	85%	0.325	0.918	0.053	0.017	0.866
DT	84%	0.256	0.897	0.071	**0.133**	0.861
SVM	84%	0.261	0.902	**0.175**	0.081	0.833
KNN	78%	0.151	0.895	0.030	0.000	0.780

into account four types of toxicity, i.e., *harassment, violence, racism,* and *vulgarity*, plus *non-toxicity*. Since, as mentioned in Sect. 4.3, the dataset is highly imbalanced, we applied the SMOTE oversampling algorithm.

Tables 2 and 3 present Accuracy and the five F1-scores for the classifiers before and after applying SMOTE, respectively. Starting from the performances on the imbalanced dataset in Table 2, every model shows high accuracy, with also high F1-scores for the most represented classes, i.e., *non-toxicity*, and *vulgarity*. Instead, for the classes *racism* and *violence* the values are close to 0 for every classifier except for RF, which has 0.11 and 0.40, respectively. In terms of F1-score, model performance varies significantly, especially depending on the types of toxicity. However, RF seems to outperform the other classifiers for every class except non-toxic, where SVM achieves the best performance. After oversampling, as shown in Table 3, the accuracy scores slightly decrease for each classifier (ranging from −1% to −5%), and the F1-scores for the least represented classes (*racism* and *violence*) show no improvement. In general, the oversampling shows only slight improvements, particularly for the least represented classes (*racism* and *violence*). However, in most cases, including RF, SMOTE tends to worsen the F1-scores across all other classes.

4.4 Explainable AI

We applied the SHAP[18] explainer, using TreeExplainer, to the Random Forest model to analyze feature importance and impact across both classification tasks. Our analysis considers both local and global explanations, highlighting key similarities and differences between the two approaches.

Local Explanation of Binary Classification. For the local explanation, the points considered correspond to the medoids of the SHAP value clusters, computed for each class. Here we show in Fig. 2, for illustrative purposes, only two medoids: one for the non-toxic class and one for the toxic class. With regards to the *non-toxic* medoids (Fig. 2a), the feature `tox_over`, representing the number of toxicity types above average, has a high importance in every case, even if in one case-here not showed-, it contributes negatively to the classification.

---
[18] SHAP: https://shap.readthedocs.io/en/latest/index.html.

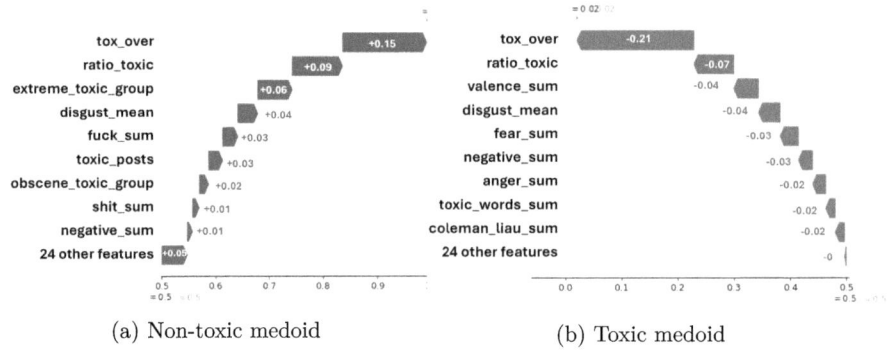

Fig. 2. Local binary classification explanation.

Among the emotion-based features, `disgust_mean` has a positive impact in every medoid, while `fear_mean` has a positive impact for three medoids. The feature `extreme_toxic_group` is always present as an important feature and in most cases contributes positively to the classification. `fuck_sum` and `shit_sum`, representing the sum number of occurrences of "fuck" and "shit" terms per comment, are the only two features based on toxic-related terms that appear as the most important, although with different contributions.

Considering the toxic medoids (Fig. 2b), the feature `tox_over` is by far the most important one in every case, but for a medoid it determines a misclassification. The attributes `ratio_toxic`, i.e., the ratio between the number of toxic comments and the number of subreddits for each user, and `extreme_toxic_group`, i.e., the number of comments from cluster 0 - which has high values for the features `toxicity`, `obscene` and `insult`, appear as important features for three medoids. In general, for the binary classification task the most important features are `tox_over` and `ratio_toxic`, followed by the information about the clusters that contain toxic comments. Among the features representing emotions, `disgust` and `fear` are present in most cases with different impacts.

Local Explanation of Multi-Class Single-Label Classification. The bar charts of the local explanation for the multi-class classification are shown in Fig. 3. Focusing on the *non-toxic* class (Fig. 3a), `tox_over` is again the most impactful feature, followed by `valence_sum`, i.e., the sum of the valence score per comment. In one case, `ratio_toxic` shows a positive contribution, and the emotion `disgust` consistently plays a role, albeit with varying degrees of influence. For the *harassment* class (Fig. 3b), the most impactful features are `tox_over` and the cluster-related attributes, which generally show a positive contribution. Also, features linked `disgust` appear in two medoids but with a negative contribution, while toxic terms, such as "fuck", "shit", and "idiot" show a small positive contribution. In the case of *racism* (Fig. 3c), only one medoid is classified

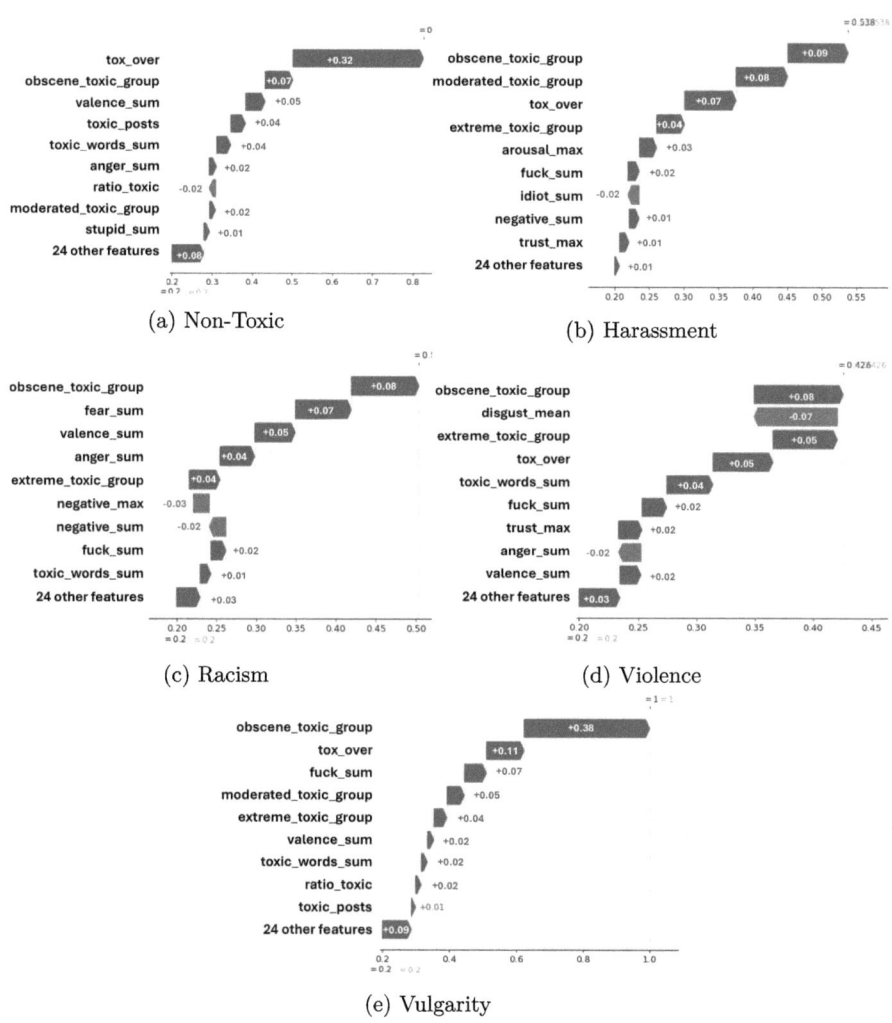

Fig. 3. Local multi-class classification explanation.

correctly. Here, the most relevant feature is `obscene_toxic_group`, i.e., the number of comments from Cluster 3, that is characterized by high values for `toxicity` and `insult`, followed by `ratio_toxic` and `valence_sum`. However, in the misclassified medoids, the importance of features changes significantly. Although `obscene_toxic_group` always provides a small positive contribution, features like `tox_over`, `arousal_max`, and `extreme _toxic_group` show higher impact, although depending on the case. Regarding *violence* (Fig. 3d), we analyzed a well-classified medoid and one that was misclassified. For the correctly classified medoid, `disgust_mean` contributes negatively, while `obscene_toxic_group`, `extreme_toxic_group`, and `tox_over` play a positive role. Conversely, in the misclassified medoid, obscene_toxic_group and extreme_toxic_group still provide a positive contribution, but trust_max and toxic_words_sum have a negative impact on the classification. Finally, for *vulgarity* (Fig. 3e), all medoids are classified correctly, showing consistent patterns in feature contributions. The most significant attribute is obscene_toxic_group, which is complemented by tox_over – although in one case it has a negative contribution – and other cluster-related features. Moreover, ratio_toxic provides a small positive contribution, and toxic-related terms such as "fuck", "shit", and "toxic_words" rank among the most relevant for this class. In general, for every class the most relevant features appear to be the ones related to the clusters of the comments and to the toxic activity of the user, like tox_over and ratio_toxic.

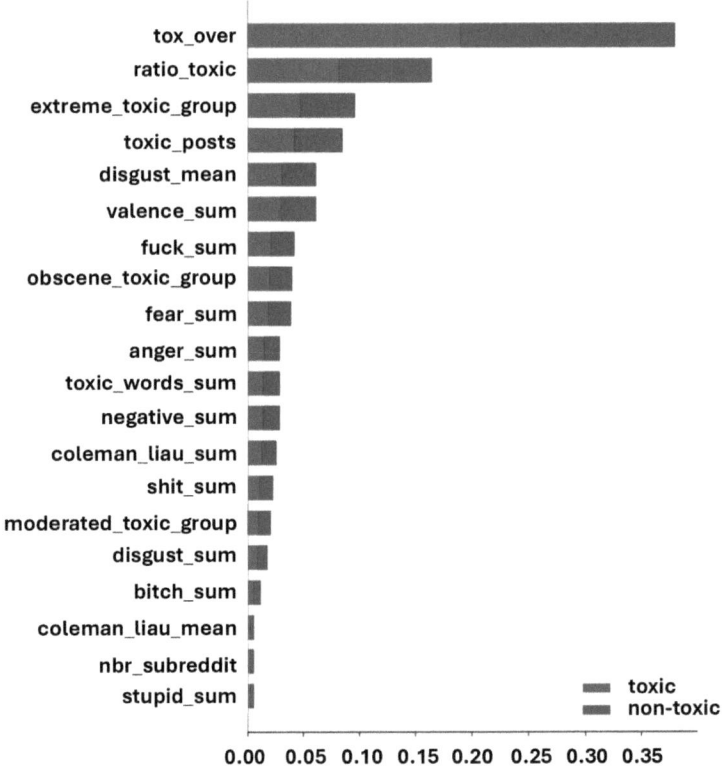

Fig. 4. Global binary classification explanation with SHAP.

Global Explanation of Binary Classification. For the binary classification, we compared the relevance of the features calculated by the SHAP Explainer (Fig. 4) with the features' importance directly derived from the Random Forest classifier (Fig. 5). The importance of the features for the two

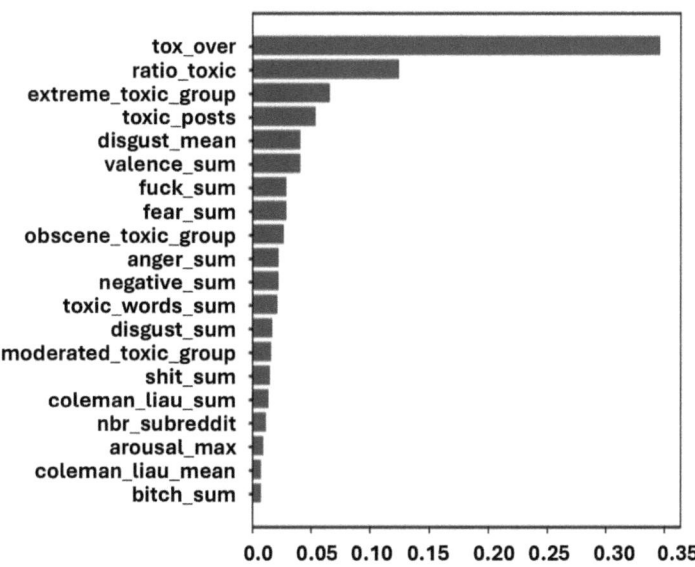

Fig. 5. Global binary classification explanation with RF feature importance.

approaches is almost identical, with tox_over is by far the most important one, followed by ratio_toxic and extreme_toxic_group. According to SHAP, obscene_toxic_group is slightly more important than fuck_sum, while for RF feature importance it is the opposite. Both approaches identify two features as important, based on readability tests: coleman_liau_sum and dale_chall_mean. These features estimate readability by considering word and sentence length, as well as familiar vocabulary and sentence structure, respectively. On the other hand, the approaches differ in terms of the features stupid_sum and arousal_max, which are important for SHAP and RF feature importance, respectively.

Global Explanation of Multi-Class Single-Label Classification. The global explanation of the multi-class single-label RF classifier highlights that the six most important features remain the same before and after oversampling, although their impact differs. Moving to the SHAP explainer (Fig. 6), before SMOTE (Fig. 6a), tox_over is the most important feature, particularly for the most represented classes (*non-toxicity* and *vulgarity*). After balancing (Fig. 6b), obscene_toxic_group becomes the most important feature, with a greater impact on the *racism* class. In both cases, these two features are by far the most relevant for this classification task. ratio_toxic is the third most important feature in both scenarios, with a greater impact on the *racism* and *violence* classes after SMOTE. In the balanced dataset, extreme_toxic_group and moderated_toxic_group have a bigger importance, while valence_sum decreases its relevance for every class. While the top six features remain simi-

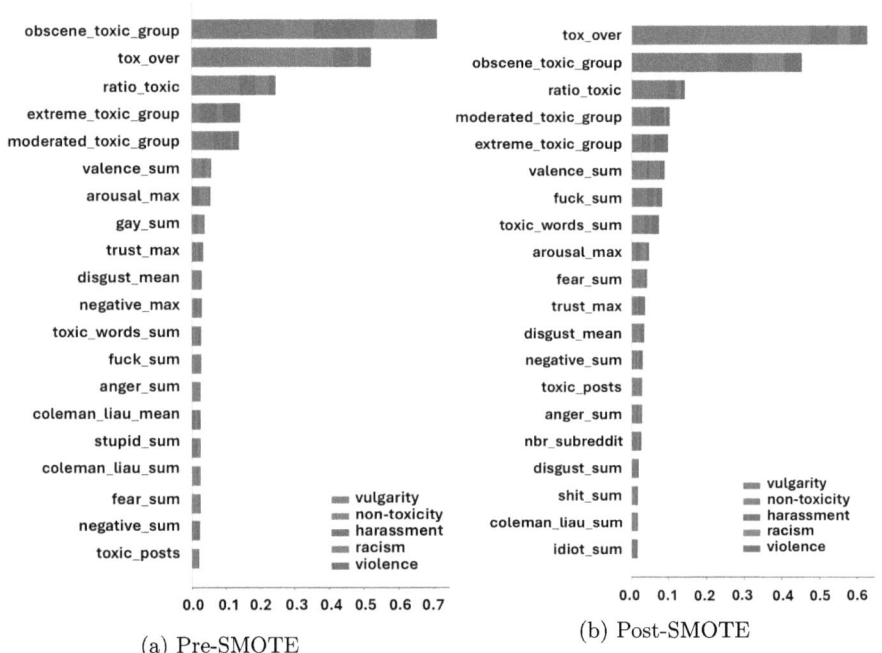

Fig. 6. Global multi-class classification explanation pre and post SMOTE.

lar before and after SMOTE balancing, the remaining fourteen features play a different role in the classification and have a smaller impact, with their SHAP values close to 0 in both cases.

4.5 Explanation Comparison

Local Explanation Comparison. At the local level, both binary and multi-class classification tasks highlight the importance of features related to user toxicity and comment clusters. For the binary classification, key features such as tox_over, ratio_toxic, and extreme_toxic_group are identified as the most impactful across various medoids, indicating that the overall toxicity of a user or their comments plays a significant role in the classification. In multi-class classification, this trend persists for classes such as *harassment* and *vulgarity*, where features like tox_over and those related toxic clusters show consistent contributions. Also, emotion-related, like disgust and fear appear in some cases, but their influence varies in terms of polarity (positive/negative). In cases of *racism* or *violence*, the impact of emotion-related features becomes more pronounced, but again, with variations in their contribution. Specific toxic terms such also show some level of positive contribution, particularly for the *vulgarity* class.

Global Explanation Comparison. In the global explanation, both SHAP and RF approaches align closely in terms of identifying the most important features for binary classification. Features like `tox_over`, `ratio_toxic`, and `extreme_toxic_group` are consistently ranked as highly influential in both methods. However, minor differences arise, such as the importance of `obscene_toxic_group` and `fuck_sum`, where SHAP ranks `obscene_toxic_group` slightly higher than `fuck_sum`, while the opposite is true for Random Forest. For the multi-class classification, especially after SMOTE, the feature `obscene_toxic_group` becomes more prominent, particularly for the *racism* class, whereas `tox_over` maintains its importance across most classes. These two features dominate the classification, with `ratio_toxic` also remaining significant, particularly in classes such as *racism* and *violence* post-balancing. The global analysis thus reinforces the helpful impact of these toxicity-related features, particularly after that the dataset is balanced.

Local Vs. Global Explanation. When comparing the findings from local and global explanations, we observe both overlapping and distinct aspects in feature importance and behavior. Both approaches identify key toxicity-related features such as `tox_over`, `ratio_toxic`, and `extreme_toxic_group` as the most significant across both binary and multi-class classification tasks. However, local explanations provide a more nuanced, case-specific perspective, revealing that features linked to emotions, like disgust and fear, have variable impact depending on the specific medoid and class. For example, `disgust` shows a positive contribution in *harassment* but a negative one in *violence*. In contrast, global explanations, fails to capture such class-specific variations. Another key difference is in how dataset balancing affects feature importance. Local explanations do not account for oversampling techniques like SMOTE, leading to consistent feature importance across instances. On the other hand, global explanations show how the distribution of classes shifts the relative importance of features after balancing, as seen in the increased significance of `obscene_toxic_group` for identifying *racism* post-SMOTE.

5 Conclusions

Toxic behavior in Online Social Networks poses a significant challenge to maintaining healthy digital interactions. In this work, we introduced UTOXIC, a ML framework designed to detect and analyze toxic users by leveraging linguistic, stylistic, affective-based, and clustering-derived features. By aggregating these features at the user level, UTOXIC performs both binary and multi-class classification, distinguishing toxic users from non-toxic ones and further categorizing specific toxic behaviors such as harassment, violence, racism, and profanity. Our results demonstrate that UTOXIC effectively identifies toxic users and provides interpretable insights into their behavior. The use of explainability techniques ensures transparency in model decisions, addressing key concerns in AI-driven moderation. Additionally, our analysis confirms that even without directly incorporating toxicity-related features, our approach maintains strong classification performance, highlighting the robustness of the extracted user features. By offering an explainable and behavior-driven approach to toxicity detection, UTOXIC can serve as a valuable tool for improving content moderation in OSNs. Future work could explore personalized moderation strategies, integrating adaptive interventions to mitigate toxic behavior while maintaining fair and transparent moderation policies.

Acknowledgments. This work has been partially supported by the PRIN 2022 framework project PIANO (Personalized Interventions Against Online Toxicity) under CUP B53D23013290006, by the Italian Project Fondo Italiano per la Scienza FIS00001966 MIMOSA, by the European Community Horizon 2020 programme under the funding schemes ERC-2018-ADG G.A. 834756 "XAI", by the European Commission under the NextGeneration EU programme - National Recovery and Resilience Plan (Piano Nazionale di Ripresa e Resilienza, PNRR) Project: "SoBigData.it" - Strengthening the Italian RI for Social Mining and Big Data Analytics" - Prot. IR0000013 - Av. n. 3264 del 28/12/2021, and M4C2 - Investimento 1.3, Partenariato Esteso PE00000013 - "FAIR" - Future Artificial Intelligence Research" - Spoke 1 "Human-centered AI".

Disclosure of Interests. The authors have no competing interests to declare that are relevant to the content of this article.

A Appendix

A.1 Readablity Tests

- Flesch Kincaid Grade Level: Measures the readability of a text based on the average number of syllables per word and the average number of words per sentence. The result corresponds to a U.S. grade level, indicating the minimum education level required to understand the text.
- Flesch Reading Ease: Another readability measure that rates text on a 0-100 scale. Higher scores indicate easier readability, with 60-70 being considered plain English, and scores below 30 indicating very difficult text.
- Dale Chall Readability: Estimates the reading level of a text by counting difficult words not commonly found in elementary school-level texts.
- Automated Readability Index (ARI): Calculates the readability of a text based on its word and sentence length, yielding a score corresponding to the U.S. grade level required to understand the text.
- Coleman Liau Index: Similar to ARI, it assesses readability based on the average number of letters per 100 words and the average number of sentences per 100 words.
- Gunning Fog: Measures the readability of English writing based on sentence length and the percentage of complex words.
- SMOG: "Simple Measure of Gobbledygook". It estimates the years of education a person needs to understand a piece of writing, based on the number of words with three or more syllables.

- Spache: Evaluates the readability of children's books by considering the number of words per sentence and the number of unfamiliar words.
- Linsear Write: Calculates readability by considering the number of words of more than two syllables per sentence.

A.2 User's Features List

user: ID of the user
nbr_posts: Number of comments
toxic_posts: Number of toxic comments
nbr_subreddit: Number of subreddits where the user comments
extreme_toxic_group: Number of comments from cluster 0
polite_group: Number of comments from cluster 1
moderated_toxic_group: Number of comments from cluster 2
obscene_toxic_group: Number of comments from cluster 3
low_toxic_group: Number of comments from cluster 4

Aggregated Metrics (sum, mean, max, min):
score: Aggregated score of the comments
toxicity: Aggregated toxicity
severe_toxicity: Aggregated severe toxicity
obscene: Aggregated obscenity
threat: Aggregated threat
insult: Aggregated insult
identity_attack: Aggregated identity attack
emoji_count: Number of emojis per comment
num_unique_words: Unique words per comment
num_words_upper: Uppercase words per comment
num_full_words: Full words per comment

Emotion Metrics (sum, mean, max, min):
fear, **anger**, anticipation, **trust**, surprise, joy, **disgust**, positive, **negative**

Readability Scores (sum, mean, max, min):
flesch_kincaid, flesch, **coleman_liau**, **dale_chall**, ari, **linsear_write**, smog, **spache**, gunning_fog

Valence-Arousal-Dominance (sum, mean, max, min):
valence, **arousal**, dominance

Occurrences of each word per comment:
'ass', **'bitch'**, 'black', 'bootlicker', 'die', **'dumb'**, **'fuck'**, 'fuckin', 'fucking', **'gay'**, 'get', 'go', **'holy'**, **'idiot'**, 'just', 'kill', 'like', 'oh', 'people', **'racist'**, **'shit'**, 'shut', **'stupid'**, 'think', 'want', 'white', 'would'

Additional Features:
toxic_words_sum: Aggregated number of toxic words per comment
tox_over: Number of toxicities above average
tox_list: List of toxicities above average

emotion_over: Number of emotions above average
emotion_list: List of emotions above average

User Behavior Ratios:
ratio: Ratio between the number of comments and the number of subreddits for each user, in [0,1]
ratio_toxic: Ratio between the number of toxic comments and the number of subreddits for each user, in [0,1]
perc: Percentage of toxic comments
toxic_annotation: User's toxic label

References

1. API, P.: Scores – choosing thresholds: Research (nd). https://developers.perspectiveapi.com/s/about-the-api-score?language=en_US, Accessed 28 Mar 2025
2. Avalle, M., et al.: Persistent interaction patterns across social media platforms and over time. Nature **628**(8008), 582–589 (2024)
3. Cima, L., Trujillo, A., Avvenuti, M., Cresci, S.: The great ban: Efficacy and unintended consequences of a massive deplatforming operation on reddit. In: WebSci (Companion), pp. 85–93. Websci '24, ACM (2024)
4. Cresci, S., Trujillo, A., Fagni, T.: Personalized interventions for online moderation. In: HT, pp. 248–251. ACM (2022)
5. Dixon, L., Li, J., Sorensen, J., Thain, N., Vasserman, L.: Measuring and mitigating unintended bias in text classification. In: AIES, pp. 67–73. ACM (2018)
6. Gargee, S., Gopinath, P.B., Kancharla, S.R.S., Anand, C., Babu, A.S.: Analyzing and addressing the difference in toxicity prediction between different comments with same semantic meaning in google's perspective API. In: ICT Systems and Sustainability: Proceedings of ICT4SD 2022, pp. 455–464. Springer (2022)
7. Hardaker, C.: Trolling in asynchronous computer-mediated communication: from user discussions to academic definitions (2010)
8. Hilte, L., Markov, I., Ljubesic, N., Fiser, D., Daelemans, W.: Who are the haters? a corpus-based demographic analysis of authors of hate speech. Front. Artif. Intell. **6** (2023)
9. Kasirzadeh, A., Clifford, D.: Fairness and data protection impact assessments. In: AIES-AAAI/ACM, pp. 146–153. ACM (2021)
10. Komaç, G., Çağıltay, K.: An overview of trolling behavior in online spaces and gaming context. In: 2019 1st International Informatics and Software Engineering Conference (UBMYK), pp. 1–4. IEEE (2019)
11. Lees, A., et al.: A new generation of perspective api: Efficient multilingual character-level transformers. In: Proceedings of the 28th ACM SIGKDD Conference on Knowledge Discovery and Data Mining, pp. 3197–3207 (2022)
12. Mall, R., Nagpal, M., Salminen, J., Al-Merekhi, H.A., Jung, S., Jansen, B.J.: Four types of toxic people: characterizing online users' toxicity over time. In: NordiCHI, pp. 37:1–37:11. ACM (2020)
13. Plutchik, R.: The nature of emotions: human emotions have deep evolutionary roots, a fact that may explain their complexity and provide tools for clinical practice. Am. Sci. **89**(4), 344–350 (2001)

14. Pozzobon, L., Ermis, B., Lewis, P., Hooker, S.: On the challenges of using black-box apis for toxicity evaluation in research. In: EMNLP, pp. 7595–7609. Association for Computational Linguistics (2023)
15. Raut, R., Spezzano, F.: Enhancing hate speech detection with user characteristics. Int. J. Data Sci. Anal. **18**(4), 445–455 (2024)
16. Seah, C., Chieu, H.L., Chai, K.M.A., Teow, L., Yeong, L.W.: Troll detection by domain-adapting sentiment analysis. In: FUSION, pp. 792–799. IEEE (2015)
17. Sumner, C., Byers, A., Boochever, R., Park, G.J.: Predicting dark triad personality traits from twitter usage and a linguistic analysis of tweets. In: ICMLA (2), pp. 386–393. IEEE (2012)
18. Teng, T.H., Varathan, K.D.: Cyberbullying detection in social networks: a comparison between machine learning and transfer learning approaches. IEEE Access **11**, 55533–55560 (2023)
19. Trujillo, A., Cresci, S.: Make reddit great again: assessing community effects of moderation interventions on r/The_Donald. HCI-ACM **6**(CSCW2), 1–28 (2022)
20. Welbl, J., et al.: Challenges in detoxifying language models. In: EMNLP (Findings), pp. 2447–2469. Association for Computational Linguistics (2021)
21. Wulczyn, E., Thain, N., Dixon, L.: Ex machina: personal attacks seen at scale. In: WWW, pp. 1391–1399. ACM (2017)

Open Access This chapter is licensed under the terms of the Creative Commons Attribution 4.0 International License (http://creativecommons.org/licenses/by/4.0/), which permits use, sharing, adaptation, distribution and reproduction in any medium or format, as long as you give appropriate credit to the original author(s) and the source, provide a link to the Creative Commons license and indicate if changes were made.

The images or other third party material in this chapter are included in the chapter's Creative Commons license, unless indicated otherwise in a credit line to the material. If material is not included in the chapter's Creative Commons license and your intended use is not permitted by statutory regulation or exceeds the permitted use, you will need to obtain permission directly from the copyright holder.

Assessing and Quantifying Perceived Trust in Interpretable Clinical Decision Support

Mohsen Abbaspour Onari[1,2(✉)], Isel Grau[1,2], Chao Zhang[3], Marco S. Nobile[4], and Yingqian Zhang[1,2]

[1] Information Systems, Eindhoven University of Technology, Eindhoven, The Netherlands
[2] Eindhoven Artificial Intelligence Systems Institute, Eindhoven University of Technology, Eindhoven, The Netherlands
[3] Human-Technology Interaction, Eindhoven University of Technology, Eindhoven, The Netherlands
{m.abbaspour.onari,i.d.c.grau.garcia,c.zhang.5,yqzhang}@tue.nl
[4] Computational Biology, Bioinformatics and Biomedicine, Department of Environmental Sciences, Informatics and Statistics, Ca' Foscari University of Venice, Venice, Italy
marco.nobile@unive.it

Abstract. Technical and ethical concerns impede the establishment of trust among healthcare professionals (HCPs) in developing artificial intelligence (AI)-based decision support. Yet, our understanding of trust models is constrained, and a standard accepted approach to evaluating trust in AI models is still lacking. We introduce a novel methodology to assess and quantify HCPs' perceived trust in an interpretable machine learning model that serves as clinical decision support for diagnosing COVID-19 cases. Our approach leverages fuzzy cognitive maps (FCMs) to elicit and quantify HCPs' trust mental models for understanding trust dynamics in clinical diagnosis. Our study reveals that HCPs rely predominantly on their own expertise when interacting with the developed interpretable clinical decision support. Although the model's interpretations offer limited assistance in diagnostic tasks, they facilitate the HCPs' utilization of it. However, the impact of these interpretations on the establishment of perceived trust varies among HCPs, which can lead to an increase in trust for some while decreasing it for others. To validate quantified perceived trust, we employ the degree of agreement metric, which quantitatively assesses whether HCPs lean more towards their own expertise or rely on the model's recommendations in diagnostic tasks. We found significant alignment between the conclusions of the two metrics, indicating successful modeling and quantification of perceived trust. Plus, a moderate to strong positive correlation between the two metrics confirmed this conclusion. This means that FCMs can quantify HCPs' perceived trust, aligning with their actual diagnostic advice shift after interacting with the model.

Keywords: Perceived Trust · User Study · Explainable AI · Interpretable AI · Clinical Decision Support

1 Introduction

The need for trustworthy artificial intelligence (TAI) systems is clear in driving the integration of AI into healthcare, primarily due to the limited measurable benefits observed in real-world patient care, despite the promising results demonstrated by an increasing number of AI-driven clinical decision support systems in preclinical and in silico studies [37]. The European Ethics Guidelines for TAI [11] outlines specific criteria to establish trustworthiness that AI systems must comply with. The existing literature reveals a scarcity of prospective studies to validate proposed AI solutions in real-world settings [12]. This scarcity has resulted in diminished trust from healthcare professionals (HCPs) towards the developed solutions. Therefore, in the current study, we propose a methodology to assess and quantify *perceived trust* of HCPs in interpretable clinical decision support. We aim to adhere to the guidelines set forth by the General Data Protection Regulation (GDPR) [10], emphasizing the critical role of transparency and explainability in establishing TAI. Miller [23] recommends incorporating interpretable machine learning (IML) models, particularly in high-stakes tasks, to enhance the comprehensibility and reliability of AI systems. Doshi-Velez and Kim [9] presented a taxonomy of IML model evaluation methodologies, including application-based assessments that involve domain experts using the IML model. Aligned with the goals of this study, which aim to assess and quantify HPCs' perceived trust in the developed clinical decision support, and considering the problem's high sensitivity, we involve HCPs to develop our methodology. Our proposed methodology considers perceived trust as a dynamic entity affected by different elements. Hence, we aim to elicit and quantify HCPs' perceived trust mental model.

Initially, IML serves as clinical decision support, recommending and interpreting diagnostic advice. This helps categorize suspected COVID-19 patients into positive or negative cases. Then, we have structured a diagnostic task that engages the HCPs in diagnosing the COVID-19 status of selected patients under two distinct scenarios: (i) relying on their expertise and (ii) interacting with the IML model. Then, they will express their satisfaction with the effectiveness of interpretations in the diagnostic task, using the Explanation Satisfaction Scale (ESS) proposed by Hoffman *et al.* [13] using fuzzy linguistic variables. This phase seeks four main objectives: (i) its efficacy in assisting HCPs in diagnosing the disease, (ii) the effectiveness of interpretations in diagnosing the disease, (iii) the impact of interpretations on establishing HCPs' trust, and (iv) incorporating HCPs' subjectivity and uncertainty through the use of fuzzy variables. In the next phase of the research, HCPs will contribute to eliciting their mental models of perceived trust in the IML model based on the influence of ESS on their perceived trust using fuzzy cognitive maps (FCM) [19] using fuzzy linguistic variables. FCMs model and simulate dynamic systems with complex interactions, allowing decision-makers to forecast future system states through scenario-making, learning algorithms, and current state analysis [1]. Upon constructing FCMs by HCPs, a distinctive perceived trust mental model will be established for each HCP and we can derive a quantified value indicative of perceived trust. To validate the results, we measure the *degree of agreement (DoA)* between the diagnostic advice of HCPs when relying on their expertise and after interaction with the IML model. This measure can elucidate whether HCPs exhibit reliance on their expertise or lean toward the IML model's recommendations. Considerable alignment and correlation between the two metrics can indicate whether FCMs could successfully measure HCPs' perceived trust. In undertaking this research, we contribute to the literature in several ways by addressing the following gaps.

- Prospective studies validating AI solutions remain limited, as noted by Nauta *et al.* [26], revealing a gap in the literature on eXplainable AI (XAI) with respect to application-based performance assessments of IML models. The contribution of medical experts is crucial to this study, as their involvement is essential for establishing the realism and reliability of a trust analysis. Although the number of participating experts is limited to 15, their input plays a vital role in understanding trust behaviors toward AI models.
- Trust in AI models is often evaluated using Hoffman's trust scale [13], which relies on Likert-scale questions to provide a simplified representation of users' trust perception. To better model this perception, we utilize FCM to extract mental models of HCPs, capturing their trust perception following their interaction with the XAI model.
- Existing methodologies overlook the role of transparency, interpretability, and explainability in shaping trust [22]. By embedding the model's interpretability into the diagnostic decision-making process and leveraging FCM's capability to model the impact of interpretability on trust, we emphasize the critical role of interpretability in modeling and measuring perceived trust.

The subsequent sections of this paper are structured as follows. In Sect. 2, we investigate the XAI literature, reviewing studies that address trust in XAI models. Section 3 encompasses the primary definition of trust and used methods to develop the proposed methodology. The experimental task designed to measure and quantify perceived trust is described in Sect. 4. In Sect. 5, we will validate the proposed methodology. Lastly, Sect. 6 encompasses the discussion of the results and outlines potential avenues for future research.

2 Background

Nauta *et al.* [26] found that a minority of XAI papers engage users in evaluating model explanations, a trend consistent even when domain experts are involved in assessments. Also, Vereschak *et al.* [38] conducted a comprehensive study revealing a lack of organized research on modeling decision-makers' trust, inspiring us to assess the impact of model interpretations on the trust levels of

HCPs. Lakkaraju and Bastani [20] conducted groundbreaking research aimed at empirically establishing how user trust in black box models can be manipulated through misleading explanations. However, the study did not compare the results with users' own perceptions regarding the efficacy of explanations in decision-making and their trust levels to elicit their mental models. Zhang et al. [42] underscored that local explanations for AI-assisted decision-making struggle to accurately calibrate human trust in AI. Nonetheless, they did not also directly assess users' perceptions regarding the effectiveness of explanations in facilitating the decision-making process.

In their empirical evaluation of XAI methods, Wang and Yin [39] conducted a comparison of established XAI techniques, analyzing their impact on AI-assisted decision-making and user trust. However, their study did not delve into users' perceptions regarding the effectiveness of these explanations in shaping their decision-making processes. Bansal et al. [4] conducted mixed-method user studies on three datasets. In these studies, participants were assisted by an AI system, with accuracy comparable to humans, in completing tasks. The AI system explained itself in some conditions, and the researchers studied whether users trusted the XAI model or not. However, the results may not be generalizable to high-stakes domains with expert users, such as medical diagnosis. Yang et al. [41] investigated the effects of example-based explanations for an ML classifier on end users' appropriate trust. However, we contend that they primarily measured agreement rather than trust. Additionally, their focus was solely on the efficacy of explanations in terms of helpfulness, neglecting other essential aspects of ESS. In Huber et al.'s study [14], which explored the impacts of global and local explanation methods on reinforcement learning agents, the methodology primarily focuses on assessing users' agreement rather than their trust. The interpretable decision support interface for sepsis treatment proposed by Sivaraman et al. [35] predominantly examines the influence of AI model explanations on HCPs' confidence in their diagnoses, yet it only marginally addresses their trust in the IML model.

Wysocki et al. [40] introduced a pragmatic evaluation framework for XAI within clinical decision support in a separate study. However, their approach merely assesses HCPs' trust with a simplistic survey, lacking a systematic method to assess trust in the AI model. In an extensive study, Mehrotra et al. [21] showed the impact of various integrity-based explanations made by an AI agent on the appropriateness of human trust in that agent. However, their evaluation focused solely on the usefulness of the provided explanations in decision-making tasks and corresponding trust, neglecting other essential factors of ESS. Joshi et al. [18] presented a Wizard of Oz study comparing low- and high-explainability versions of a vacation planning chatbot in a between-subjects design, examining the effect of explainability on users' understanding, trust, and acceptance. Chanda et al. [6] developed an XAI model to generate domain-specific, interpretable explanations to support melanoma diagnosis. In this study, medical experts assessed their trust in the model using a 10-point Likert scale. Perlmutter et al. [32] also investigated the impact of an example-based XAI interface on trust, understanding, and performance in highly technical populations using a 10-point Likert scale.

Therefore, the main shortcomings of existing studies in the literature can be summarized as follows: misdefining the concept of trust, conducting studies at a general user level without involving domain experts, and neglecting to assess the efficacy of explanations in facilitating decision-making tasks and their impact on users' trust, which causes overlooking the elicitation of users' trust mental models.

3 Methodology

In this section, we outline the foundational concepts of this study. Sub-sect 3.1 explores the definition of trust, while Subsect. 3.2 introduces FCM.

3.1 XAI and Perceived Trust

Trust is generally defined as "the willingness of a party to be vulnerable to the actions of another party based on the expectation that the other will perform a particular action important to the trustor, regardless of the ability to monitor or control that other party [36]." In the same way, when a user trusts the AI model, the anticipation depends on whether the model can fulfill its expectations. Here, we refer to the definition of Jacovi et al. [16] for Human-AI trust:

"If H (human) perceives that M (AI model) is trustworthy to contract C and accepts vulnerability to M's actions, then H trusts M contractually to C. The objective of H in trusting M is to anticipate that M will maintain C in the presence of uncertainty; consequently, trust does not exist if H does not perceive risk."

Ribeiro *et al.* [33] asserted the importance of trust for effective human interaction with ML systems, emphasizing the importance of explaining individual predictions as a key factor in assessing trust. By hypothesis, effective and satisfying explanations enable users to construct a good mental model. So, this sound mental model can facilitate the development of trust in AI and enhance user performance when using it [13]. Miller [22] states that trust as a mental attitude must be measured in field studies, lab experiments, and surveys/interviews with human participants. The main reason is that trust can rapidly deteriorate when subjected to factors such as time constraints, noticeable system defects, high error rates, or frequent false alarms [13]. Like the diverse forms of trust, various manifestations of negative trust exist, including mistrust and distrust [13]. The proposed trust continuum by Cho et al. [7] can demonstrate this behavior (see Fig. 1).

In the XAI domain, the trust assessment is based mainly on the trust scale proposed by Hoffman et al. [13]; however, Miller [22] declares that the trust scale presented does not explicitly measure the effect of trust. In fact, this scale measures users' trust through a set of Likert scale questions, primarily focusing on

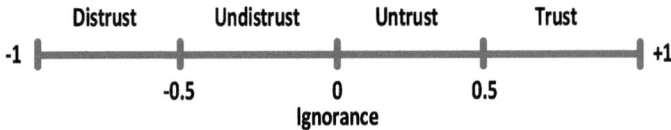

Fig. 1. Trust continuum [7].

the users' perception of trust rather than their demonstrated trust when interacting with an XAI model. Besides, the existing techniques do not measure the impact of transparency, interpretability, and explainability methods on human participants' trust [22]. In essence, trust measurement efforts have often focused on precisely defining the elements of trust to measure perceived trust, often overlooking the underlying mental models that shape users' perceptions. Therefore, it is imperative to introduce a methodology that delves into the influence of explanations on trust establishment and examines how they can impact users' perceived trust.

3.2 Eliciting Perceived Trust Mental Models by FCM

The ESS proposed by Hoffman et al. [13] serves as the foundational elements of HCPs' perceived trust mental models in this study so that we can analyze the contribution of interpretation in building trust. We slightly modified the ESS for our specific context by adding a "Functionality" scale, as outlined in Table 1. In this study, trust is considered a dynamic entity with intricate interactions among ESS, and we model it using FCM.

Table 1. Explanation Satisfaction Scale and description

ESS	Description
Understandability (US)	The interpretation was understandable in diagnosing the disease.
Sufficiency of details (SD)	The interpretation had sufficient details to help me diagnose the disease.
Completeness (CL)	The interpretation was complete enough to diagnose the disease.
Feeling of satisfaction (FS)	I am satisfied with the quality of the interpretation for diagnosing the disease.
Accuracy (AC)	The interpretation was accurate enough to diagnose the disease.
Usability (US)	Interpretation is easy to use to diagnose the disease.
Functionality (FC)	In general, the interpretation helped me diagnose the disease.

Kosko [19], for the first time, introduced FCMs to mitigate the limited ability of cognitive maps [3] to represent causal beliefs in social scientific knowledge [25]. Multiple domain experts who have knowledge in a particular area contribute as knowledge engineers to manually develop an FCM or a mental model [30]. They start by identifying key domain components or concepts (C) and then determine the influence (edges) of concepts, including their strength on each other or weight (w) [30]. A semantic representation of an FCM (including concepts, edges, and weights) is shown in Fig. 2. In our study, ESS serves as FCM concepts, and their initial value, edges, and weights are determined by HCPs.

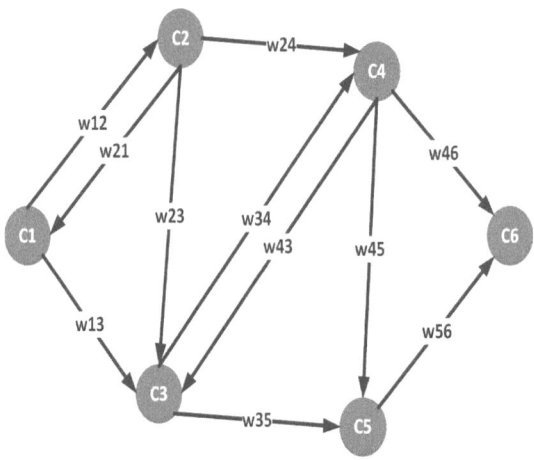

Fig. 2. A semantic representation of an FCM.

There are three types of relationships between concepts in the FCM [28]:

- $w_{ij} > 0$, direct influence between concepts C_i and C_j,
- $w_{ij} < 0$, inverse influence between concepts C_i and C_j,
- $w_{ij} = 0$, no relationship between concepts C_i and C_j.

The established reasoning process of an FCM [19, 25, 28, 30], uses the following simple mathematical formula:

$$C_i^{(k)} = f\left(C_i^{k-1} + \sum_{j=1, j \neq i}^{N} C_j^{(k-1)} \cdot w_{ji}\right), \qquad (1)$$

where, $C_i^{(k)}$ represents the value of concept i at iteration k of the reasoning process. w_{ji} indicates the weight of the edge from C_j to C_i, and N is the number of entered edges to C_i. Our study utilizes a state vector of size 1×8, encompassing ESS and a target concept denoted as perceived trust (PT).

The initial values of these concepts reflect HCP's subjective satisfaction with ESS effectiveness in diagnostic tasks, employing fuzzy linguistic variables detailed in Table 2. With this approach, we achieve two primary objectives: firstly, we gain insight into the satisfaction level of HCP with interpretations; secondly, we embed HCP's satisfaction impact in establishing the perceived trust, which, in fact, models their trust mental model based on the model's interpretability. To convert these linguistic variables into actionable data to develop FCM, defuzzification is applied to convert them into crisp numbers (see Table 2), employing the center of gravity (CoG) method [31]. Due to its high accuracy, the CoG defuzzification method is the most widely used in practice [2]. It effectively satisfies important criteria such as continuity, disambiguity, and plausibility, contributing to its reliability and interoperability [2]. These initial values fall within the interval [0, 1], with proximity to 1 indicating higher importance.

w is an 8×8 weighted matrix defining relationships between ESS and PT, determined by HCPs using the linguistic variables outlined in Table 3. In the same way, defuzzification is applied to weights as well (see Table 3), transforming them within the range [-1, 1], with values closer to 1 indicating stronger influence and the sign denoting direct or inverse influence between concepts. Following this approach, we integrate the influence of each individual ESS on one another, ultimately culminating in their collective impact on the perceived trust of HCP. The activation function $f(x)$, typically sigmoid or hyperbolic tangent, is employed to constrain the state vector's values within [0, 1] and [-1, 1], respectively. Our study adopts the hyperbolic tangent function to align perceived trust values with the trust continuum outlined in Fig. 1. According to FCM literature, interaction among concepts persists until one of the following states occurs [5]:

- stable state: The model reaches an equilibrium fixed point, with output values settling at constant numerical levels.
- limit cycle: The concept values fall in a loop of numerical values.
- chaotic behavior: The model exhibits non-deterministic, random fluctuations in concept values.

We set a maximum iteration limit for the algorithm, ensuring that it terminates after this number of iterations, regardless of convergence status. Finally, the ultimate value of PT in the state vector quantifies the corresponding HCP's perceived trust level. This process will be repeated for all HCPs to elicit a unique mental model for each participant involved in this study.

Table 2. Linguistic variables for the initial values of C.

	Linguistic variables	Membership function	Defuzzified value
1	I disagree strongly	(0, 0, 0.25)	0
2	I disagree somewhat	(0, 0.25, 0.5)	0.25
3	I'm neutral about it	(0.25, 0.5, 0.75)	0.5
4	I agree somewhat	(0.5, 0.75, 1)	0.75
5	I agree strongly	(0.75, 1, 1)	1

4 Experimental Design

This section outlines the step-by-step process used to quantify perceived trust in this study. Subsect. 4.1 introduces the implemented dataset, the training of the

Table 3. Linguistic variables to determine w.

	Linguistic variables	Membership function	Defuzzified value
1	Inversely high	(-1, -1, -0.5)	-1
2	Inversely low	(-1, -0.5, 0)	-0.5
3	No influence	(-0.5, 0, 0.5)	0
4	Directly low	(0, 0.5, 1)	0.5
5	Directly high	(0.5, 1, 1)	1

IML model, and its interpretation. Subsect. 4.2 explains how HCPs were selected for the study. Subsect. 4.3 analyzes the shift in diagnostic advice during the decision-making task before and after interaction with the IML model. Subsect. 4.4 evaluates HCPs' satisfaction with the model's interpretability. Subsect. 4.5 presents the elicited mental models of HCPs' using FCM, followed by presenting the quantified perceived trust for each HCP based on FCM implementation in Subsect. 4.6.

4.1 Clinical Setting and Exploited IML Model

Data Set: The data set comprises the results of blood sample tests obtained from suspected patients with COVID-19 upon their arrival in the emergency department, encompassing a minimum of 30 distinct clinical measurements. The data set comprises 12873 patients with 32 clinical features derived from blood samples. We followed the ethical aspects of the AI application by signing written agreements regarding the limited use of data. Second, we adhered to security measures to protect data privacy per the agreements. Third, patients' identities were removed. The data set includes missing values in both the features and labels. Certain observations collected before the COVID-19 outbreak were classified as negative cases. Observations with no labels and missing values exceeding 40% were discarded as they offer no meaningful information for the IML model. Patients under the age of 18 years were also excluded. Ultimately, the data set comprises 8781 observations, of which 8461 are negative and 320 are positive.

IML Model: Repeated Incremental Pruning to Produce Error Reduction (RIPPER) [8] is an IML algorithm that operates on rules directly learned from the data. Abbaspour Onari *et al.* [27] showed its high predictive performance compared to other ML models in COVID-19 prediction. RIPPER produces IF-THEN classification rules using the separate-and-conquer technique and the reduced-error pruning approach. Afterward, a set of rules is returned, which can be applied to classify new objects [27]. Before implementing RIPPER, KNN data imputation is applied to correct 2563 missing values in the data set. Then, the correlation between the features is calculated, and features with a higher correlation value of 0.7 with each other are dropped from the data set, leaving 27 features to build the IML model. The data set is split into training and test data sets with 80%–20% partition, respectively. Although RIPPER shows high capability in unbalanced data set classification, we implement the SMOTE oversampling technique to have the same number of positive and negative cases in the training phase. Furthermore, the model's hyperparameters are optimized using grid search. The model undergoes 5-fold cross-validation on the training data set to validate its performance. The results on the test dataset demonstrate performance metrics of 0.9841 for accuracy, 0.8667 for precision, 0.6393 for recall, and 0.7358 for the F1 score.

Interpretations: To interpret the prediction's logic, RIPPER generates three rules on the test data set represented in Table 4. The instances that satisfy either of these rules are classified as positive cases, and all others are considered as negative cases. Building upon the insights of Huysmans et al. [15], which demonstrated that representing decision rules in decision tables enhances respondents' understanding of the rules, we will present RIPPER rules in the same format. We represented RIPPER's logic in correctly diagnosing a truly affected patient in Table 5 as a visual representation in Fig. 3. The legend in the figure explains the colors used: orange indicates that the conditions based on the patient's clinical features are not verified in the RIPPER's conditions, blue shows that the patient's features are verified in the RIPPER's conditions, and purple highlights when all conditions are satisfied, and the rule is applied to the patient. In cases where only a single rule is satisfied in RIPPER, that specific rule becomes the sole basis for the classification decision.

Table 4. Rules generated by RIPPER to classify patients into positive cases.

Feature	Rule 1	Rule 2	Rule 3
Albumin	≤ 37.9	-	-
Alkaline Phosphatase	≤ 82	≤ 83.6	-
Calcium	≤ 2.28	-	-
Erythrocytes	≥ 3.94	-	≥ 4.29
Glucose	≥ 5.66	-	-
Lactate Dehydrogenase	≥ 302	-	≥ 320
Basophils	-	≤ 0.01	-
C-Reactive Protein	-	≥ 19.62	-
Leukocytes	-	≤ 7.69	≤ 7.68
Lipase	-	≥ 30.5	-
Mean Cellular Haemoglobin	-	-	≥ 1.85

4.2 Selection of Participants

In the current study, we use an IML model to recommend and interpret diagnostic advice to HCPs due to the high-stakes nature of decision-making. Inter-

Table 5. Blood sample test results of a patient diagnosed as a positive case by RIPPER.

	Features	Test result
1	Albumin	37
2	Alkaline phosphatase	70
3	Basophils	0.03
4	Calcium	2.09
5	C-reactive protein	1.43
6	Erythrocytes	4.75
8	Glucose	10.36
9	Lactate dehydrogenase	392
10	Leukocytes	7.13
11	Lipase	47.8
12	Mean Cellular Haemoglobin	1.895

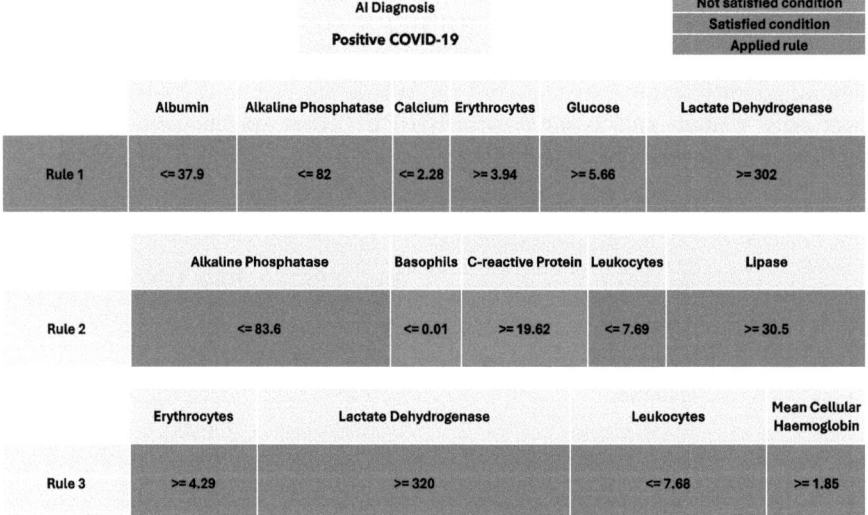

Fig. 3. Representation of RIPPER's rules as decision tables.

pretable models rely on a limited set of features characterized by a low complexity. The underlying assumption is that the model encompasses the necessary explanatory information due to its interpretability [23]. This study will focus on understanding how interpretability can build perceived trust among HCPs in the IML model. The university's ethical board granted ethical approval for this research project[1]. The participants in our study, including HCPs, were identi-

---
[1] This study has been approved by Ethical Board of the university with reference number: ERB2023IEIS10.

fied by snowball sampling. Initially, we contacted our network of clinically active HCPs with practical experience in healthcare centers during the COVID-19 pandemic. Subsequently, we requested them to send our participation request to individuals who meet our criteria and might be interested. Our research involved a total of N=15 HCPs. While this sample size classifies the study as a pilot, the valuable contributions of the HCPs make it highly insightful and meaningful. We used Qualtrics software as our main tool to design the user study. First, the HCPs responded to three questions about their professional background, professional tenure, and whether they wanted to participate in this research voluntarily. This question is apart from the ethical consent forms sent to them. If they had opted not to participate, their survey would have been terminated immediately. HCPs are general practitioners, senior medical students, cardiovascular imaging specialists, medical specialists in infectious diseases, and internal medicine specialists. Our participants have at least two years of professional work experience in healthcare centers and, at most, 13 years. HCPs from diverse geographic locations participated: Iran (10), Italy (2), Canada (1), Australia (1) and the UK (1). The gender distribution comprised 7 men and 8 women.

4.3 Diagnostic Task: Diagnostic Advice Shift

Four instances were selected from the test data set to present to all HCPs. In two cases, the ground truth status aligns with the recommendation of the IML model, while in the remaining two, there are contradictions. In the first sub-task, the clinical blood sample test results (As shown in Table 5) are presented to HCPs, and they are asked to offer their diagnostic advice relying on their expertise. The same question is asked in the next sub-task, including generated rules by IML and recommendations (see Fig. 3) functioning as clinical decision support to diagnose the disease. For both sub-tasks, HCPs can choose an option between "Positive COVID-19," "Negative COVID-19," and "Not possible to diagnose." The results of the diagnostic task have been outlined in Fig. 4. Using Sankey diagram, we show how HCPs change their diagnostic advice after interaction with the clinical decision support.

In Case 1, following their interaction with the IML model, seven HCPs adjusted their diagnostic advice. Remarkably, six of them aligned their advice with the model's recommendation. Notably, one HCP revised their initial diagnosis from "Negative COVID-19" to "Not possible to diagnose." This adjustment can be deemed a positive impact of the model, revealing the HCP's initial lack of confidence in their initial diagnostic advice. Moving on to Case 2, four HCPs modified their diagnostic advice to "Negative COVID-19" after engaging with the model. Regarding Case 3, there was no discernible shift in the diagnostic advice patterns of HCPs. It appears that the clinical features recommended by the model lacked sufficient information for the HCPs. It is plausible that these features resembled those of a patient with "Positive COVID-19," prompting HCPs to err on caution. In Case 4, six HCPs followed the model's recommended advice after interacting with it. In conclusion, we assert that the IML model can influ-

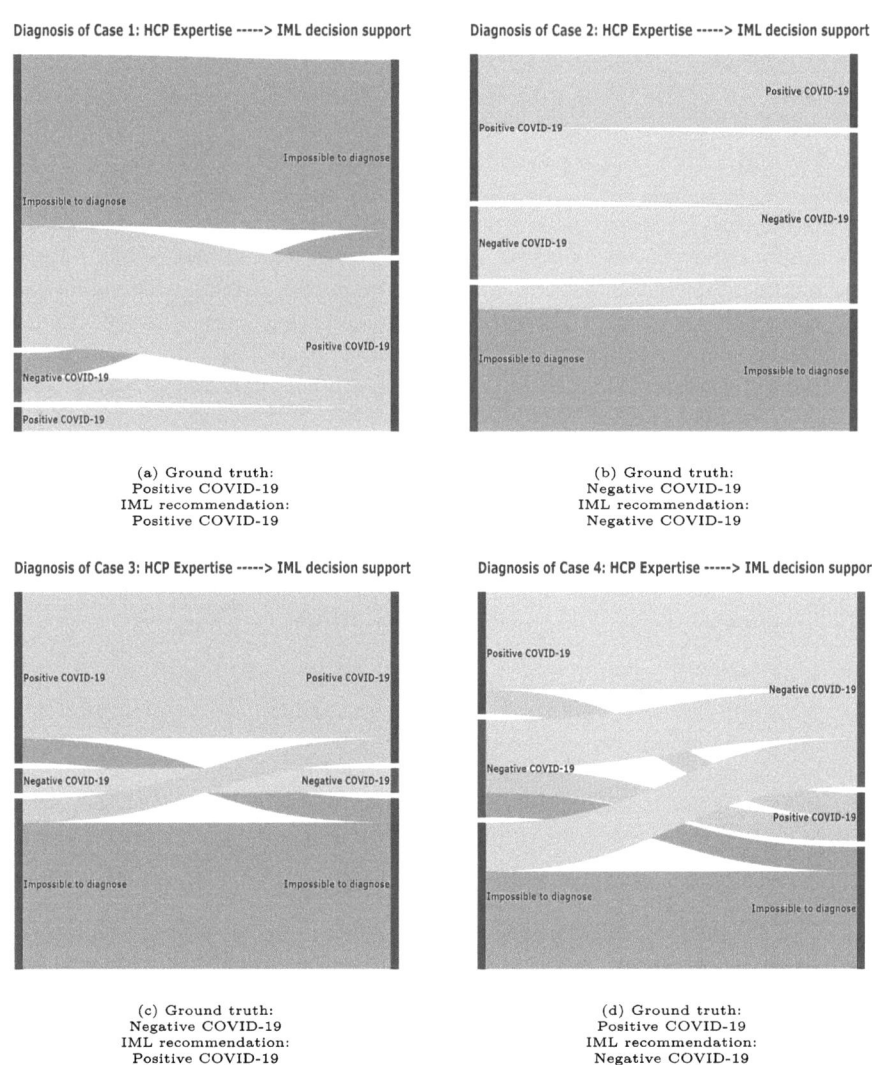

Fig. 4. Diagnostic advice shift of HCPs before and after interaction with IML model's recommendations and interpretation.

ence HCPs' diagnostic advice in at least three tasks to some extent, though not drastically.

4.4 HCPs' Satisfaction with Interpretations

After completing the diagnostic tasks, the HCPs expressed their satisfaction with the effectiveness of the model's interpretation as outlined in Sect. 3.2. The results have been demonstrated in Fig. 5. The results indicate that HCPs perceived the model's interpretations as insightful across three scales: understandability, satisfaction, and usability. However, regarding completeness and accuracy, HCPs did not deem the model's interpretations sufficiently informative. This observation might help explain why HCPs were inclined to refrain from providing precise diagnostic advice on the diagnostic task and prefer to rely on their expertise. Finally, when it comes to evaluating the sufficiency of details and functionality, a notable lack of meaningful consensus among HCPs is apparent. Consequently, no informative conclusion can be drawn from these aspects. In conclusion, the utility of the model's interpretability appears more evident when HCPs intend to utilize it for their understanding rather than as a significant source of information for offering diagnostic advice.

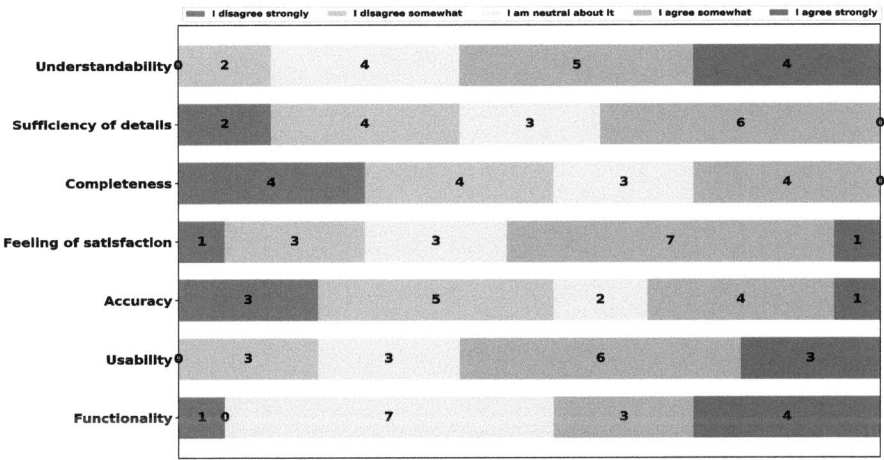

Fig. 5. HCPs' satisfaction with model's interpretations.

4.5 Eliciting HCPs' Mental Models Using FCM

In the conclusive phase of the experiment, HCPs contributed to eliciting their perceived trust mental models, as detailed in Sect. 3.2. Using FCMExpert tool [24] to semantically visualize mental models as FCMs, we identified four discernible patterns: trust, distrust, neutrality, and unknown, as illustrated in Fig. 6. The positive-weighted edges that originate from the ESS and enter PT in Fig. 6a represent a direct influence of ESS on HCP trust. An elevation in ESS values corresponds to an increase in perceived trust in them. In contrast, the negative-weighted edges from ESS to PT in Fig. 6b indicate that an increase in ESS values leads to a decreased perceived trust of HCPs. This observation may stem from the realization that the model falls short of meeting their expectations when its interpretability is increased. The neutrality behavior emerges when the cumulated weight in PT converges to zeros, signifying that edges' weights neutralize each other, and HCPs feel neutral about the IML model (see Fig. 6c). Finally, the solitary unknown pattern indicates that the HCP perceives no influence from ESS on PT and vice versa (see Fig. 6d). Extracting meaningful information from this pattern regarding HCP's perceived trust is challenging. To keep the paper concise, we present mental models for four HCPs to illustrate key patterns.

Table 6. Quantified perceived trust and DoA results. The "Alignment" column shows whether both metrics converge in a common conclusion.

HCP	PT	DoA	Alignment
HCP1	0.8098	1.1660	✓
HCP2	−0.7619	0.6111	✓
HCP3	0.9992	0.7849	×
HCP4	unk	0.9668	-
HCP5	0.9836	0.8876	×
HCP6	0.0	0.8326	✓
HCP7	−0.7805	0.6489	✓
HCP8	0.5884	1.0694	✓
HCP9	−0.0746	0.7849	✓
HCP10	0.9997	1.1660	✓
HCP11	0.2061	0.6111	✓
HCP12	0.9997	1.1660	✓
HCP13	0.9999	1.6988	✓
HCP14	0.9942	1.0694	✓
HCP15	−0.4631	1.0694	×

4.6 Quantified Value of Perceived Trust for Each HCP

The FCM for each HCP was implemented following the reasoning process outlined in Sect. 3.2. The reasoning process is terminated once the algorithm reaches its maximum iteration limit ($k = 35$). To determine this value, we began by testing smaller iteration counts (e.g., 10) and observed whether FCM demonstrates triple stop criteria. If it did not, we incrementally increased k and reassessed it. Eventually, at $k = 35$, all concepts either reached steady state convergence or showed chaotic behavior, thereby satisfying the stop criteria outlined in Subsect. 3.2.

Upon completing the FCM implementation, we derived the quantified PT values for each HCP, as presented in Table 6. Comparing the results obtained with the trust continuum illustrated in column "PT" of Fig. 1 reveals distinctive patterns. Two HCPs (2 and 7) demonstrate distrust towards the model, while two others (9 and 15) exhibit an undistrusting stance. HCP6 expresses a neutral

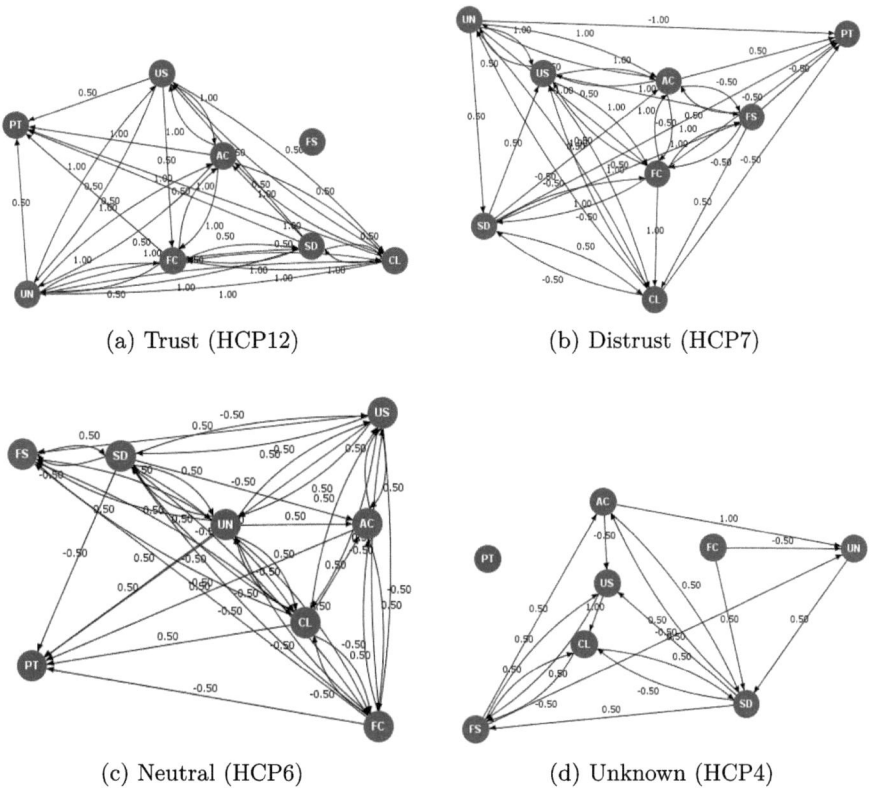

Fig. 6. Semantic representation of mental models (FCMs) of four HCPs representing trust, distrust, neutrality, and unknown behavior.

stance towards the model, and HCP11 displays an untrusting disposition. Also, the quantified value of trust for HCP4 is unknown, as depicted in Fig. 6d, and we exclude it in our future analysis. While the remaining HCPs express trust in the model, the extent of trust varies among them.

5 Validation of the Quantified Perceived Trust

Formal validation of FCMs is challenging due to their subjective nature. The difficulty lies in the fact that FCMs represent different interpretations of the system, and assessing their accuracy requires comparing them against yet another interpretation of reality [29]. To achieve this, we adopted the approach outlined by Schmidt and Biessmann [34], who introduced a metric to quantify trust by incorporating the concept of mutual information. However, Miller [22] believes that the metric primarily measures the agreement of users with the ML model's recommendations rather than trust. So, we have adjusted the terminology to refer to this metric as DoA. This metric measures the shift of diagnostic advice among HCPs after interacting with the IML model, indicating reliance on it. To do so, using the information collected in Sect. 4.3, the mutual information between the IML model recommendation and the diagnostic advice of each HCP after interacting with it is measured using the following formula:

$$I(\widehat{y}_{IML}, \widehat{y}_{HI}) = \sum_{\widehat{y}_{IML}, \widehat{y}_{HI}} p(\widehat{y}_{IML}, \widehat{y}_{HI}) \log_2 \frac{p(\widehat{y}_{IML}, \widehat{y}_{HI})}{p(\widehat{y}_{IML})p(\widehat{y}_{HI})} \qquad (2)$$

In Eq. 2, the result is measured in bits. Similarly, $I(\widehat{y}_{GT}, \widehat{y}_{HE})$ indicates the mutual information between the ground truth status and HCP's diagnostic advice based on their expertise. Hence, the following equation can be used to measure DoA of each HCP with IML recommendations:

$$DoA = \frac{I(\widehat{y}_{IML}, \widehat{y}_{HI})}{I(\widehat{y}_{GT}, \widehat{y}_{HE})}, \qquad (3)$$

where $DoA < 1$ represents that HCP does not have a high agreement with the model's recommendation and prefers to rely on its own expertise. $DoA > 1$ shows the HCP relies on the model's recommendation. The perfect agreement between the HCP and the IML model is established when the $DoA = 1$. The measured DoA for all HCPs is presented in DoA column of Table 6, showing eight HCPs rely on their expertise ($DoA < 1$). This tendency may be influenced by factors such as confirmation bias, general skepticism toward AI models, and the way IML rules are presented. HCPs found the rules lacking in completeness and accuracy, with no clear consensus on their sufficiency in terms of detail and functionality. While these factors are important and warrant further investigation to understand the underlying reasons for this behavior, they fall outside the scope of this research.

The results indicate that seven HCPs exhibit reliance on the model's diagnostic advice ($DoA > 1$), which is a sign of over-reliance on it. Possible factors contributing to this preference include the level of expertise, and general optimism toward AI. However, we acknowledge that further studies are needed to better understand the underlying causes of this over-reliance. The "Alignment" column of Table 6 evaluates whether both metrics lead to consistent conclusions regarding PT and DoA. Apart from three HCPs (3, 5, 15), all others adhere to the trust continuum pattern depicted in Fig. 1 and DoA. For instance, HCP3's PT is 0.9992, suggesting near-perfect perceived trust. However, during the diagnostic task, they relied on their own expertise ($DoA < 1$). These discrepancies may stem from inaccuracies in how their mental models were elicited. Weights and edges in an FCM reflect the subjective perspectives of HCPs, which is an advantage because it incorporates domain-specific expertise, but it is a limitation due to its inherent subjectivity. This highlights the need for further analysis in future studies.

Finally, we further analyze the obtained results by calculating the Pearson correlation between PT and DoA in Table 6. The correlation coefficient is 0.6851, indicating a moderate to strong positive correlation between the two metrics. Thus, FCM demonstrates a high level of confidence in quantifying the perceived trust of HCPs, aligning closely with their propensity to adjust diagnostic advice after interaction with the IML model.

6 Discussion and Conclusions

This study introduces a novel methodology to measure the perceived trust of HCPs in interpretable clinical decision support by eliciting their mental models. Our findings suggest that while clinical decision support can somewhat influence HCPs' diagnostic advice, its impact is limited. Additionally, HCPs did not find interpretations very useful for diagnosing diseases; instead, they were more helpful in implementing them in the diagnostic task. This finding resonates with Jin et al.'s [17] conclusion that existing XAI algorithms often fall short of meeting clinical needs. The study validates the quantified perceived trust obtained via FCMs by comparing it with the DoA measure, which shows in most cases, both metrics converge to the same conclusion about the behavior of HCPs. Finally, the moderate to strong correlation between perceived trust and DoA suggests that FCM can effectively measure HCPs' perceived trust.

Our developed methodology is applicable across all realms in which domain experts are accessible. The pivotal aspect of this research lies in identifying key components that contribute to trust establishment within the domain of interest. This can be achieved by involving experts to pinpoint the principal elements of their trust. The strength of the proposed methodology lies in its ability to model the trust mechanisms of participants and reflect their subjectivity. Leveraging the high interpretability of FCMs, we can detect crucial aspects contributing to participants' trust refinement. Subsequently, this understanding enables us to refine and improve the IML model to increase trust. Furthermore, FCMs offer the flexibility to be updated or modified based on new information or changes in the system, allowing for continuous refinement and improvement.

This study is limited by its small sample size, which categorizes it as a pilot study and potentially renders the results statistically unreliable. While a larger sample might reveal a greater discrepancy between PT and DoA, it is important to note that the core contribution of modeling perceived trust through FCM remains unaffected. Because FCM is a subjective model grounded in each HCP's mental model, the quantified perceived trust precisely reflects what HCPs report and how they conceptualize their mental models due to the mathematical basis of FCM is robust. Despite these limitations, the insights gained—particularly from user studies involving HCPs—remain valuable. Trust, though central to this study, is a nuanced concept encompassing multiple facets beyond the scope of ESS alone. Future research will involve participants in identifying and articulating these broader trust elements.

Acknowledgments. I. Grau and C. Zhang are supported by the European Union's HORIZON Research and Innovation Program under grant agreement No. 101120657, project ENFIELD (European Lighthouse to Manifest Trustworthy and Green AI).

Disclosure of Interests. All authors declare that they have no conflicts of interest.

References

1. Abbaspour Onari, M., Jahangoshai Rezaee, M.: Implementing bargaining game-based fuzzy cognitive map and mixed-motive games for group decisions in the healthcare supplier selection. Artif. Intell. Rev. 1–34 (2023)
2. Arun, N., Mohan, B.: Modeling, stability analysis, and computational aspects of some simplest nonlinear fuzzy two-term controllers derived via center of area/gravity defuzzification. ISA Trans. **70**, 16–29 (2017)
3. Axelrod, R.: The cognitive maps of political elites (1976)
4. Bansal, G., et al.: Does the whole exceed its parts? the effect of AI explanations on complementary team performance. In: Proceedings of the 2021 CHI Conference on Human Factors in Computing Systems, pp. 1–16 (2021)
5. Beena, P., Ganguli, R.: Structural damage detection using fuzzy cognitive maps and Hebbian learning. Appl. Soft Comput. **11**(1), 1014–1020 (2011)
6. Chanda, T., et al.: Dermatologist-like explainable AI enhances trust and confidence in diagnosing melanoma. Nat. Commun. **15**(1), 524 (2024)
7. Cho, J.H., Chan, K., Adali, S.: A survey on trust modeling. ACM Comput. Surv. (CSUR) **48**(2), 1–40 (2015)
8. Cohen, W.W.: Fast effective rule induction. In: Machine Learning Proceedings 1995, pp. 115–123. Elsevier (1995)
9. Doshi-Velez, F., Kim, B.: Towards a rigorous science of interpretable machine learning. arXiv preprint arXiv:1702.08608 (2017)
10. Regulation (eu) 2016/679 (general data protection regulation) (2016). https://eur-lex.europa.eu/eli/reg/2016/679/oj
11. Ethics guidelines for trustworthy AI (2019). https://digital-strategy.ec.europa.eu/en/library/ethics-guidelines-trustworthy-ai
12. González-Gonzalo, C., et al.: Trustworthy AI: closing the gap between development and integration of AI systems in ophthalmic practice. Prog. Retin. Eye Res. **90**, 101034 (2022)
13. Hoffman, R.R., Mueller, S.T., Klein, G., Litman, J.: Measures for explainable AI: explanation goodness, user satisfaction, mental models, curiosity, trust, and human-AI performance. Front. Comput. Sci. **5**, 1096257 (2023)
14. Huber, T., Weitz, K., André, E., Amir, O.: Local and global explanations of agent behavior: integrating strategy summaries with saliency maps. Artif. Intell. **301**, 103571 (2021)
15. Huysmans, J., Dejaeger, K., Mues, C., Vanthienen, J., Baesens, B.: An empirical evaluation of the comprehensibility of decision table, tree and rule based predictive models. Decis. Support Syst. **51**(1), 141–154 (2011)
16. Jacovi, A., Marasović, A., Miller, T., Goldberg, Y.: Formalizing trust in artificial intelligence: Prerequisites, causes and goals of human trust in AI. In: Proceedings of the 2021 ACM conference on fairness, accountability, and transparency, pp. 624–635 (2021)
17. Jin, W., Li, X., Hamarneh, G.: Evaluating explainable AI on a multi-modal medical imaging task: Can existing algorithms fulfill clinical requirements? In: Proceedings of the AAAI Conference on Artificial Intelligence, vol. 36, pp. 11945–11953 (2022)

18. Joshi, R., Graefe, J., Kraus, M., Bengler, K.: Exploring the impact of explainability on trust and acceptance of conversational agents–a wizard of OZ study. In: International Conference on Human-Computer Interaction, pp. 199–218. Springer (2024)
19. Kosko, B.: Fuzzy cognitive maps. Int. J. Man Mach. Stud. **24**(1), 65–75 (1986)
20. Lakkaraju, H., Bastani, O.: "How do I fool you?". manipulating user trust via misleading black box explanations. In: Proceedings of the AAAI/ACM Conference on AI, Ethics, and Society, pp. 79–85 (2020)
21. Mehrotra, S., Jorge, C.C., Jonker, C.M., Tielman, M.L.: Integrity-based explanations for fostering appropriate trust in AI agents. ACM Trans. Interact. Intell. Syst. **14**(1), 1–36 (2024)
22. Miller, T.: Are we measuring trust correctly in explainability, interpretability, and transparency research? CHI TRAIT Workshop (2022)
23. Miller, T.: Explainable AI is dead, long live explainable AI! hypothesis-driven decision support using evaluative AI. In: Proceedings of the 2023 ACM Conference on Fairness, Accountability, and Transparency, pp. 333–342 (2023)
24. Nápoles, G., Espinosa, M.L., Grau, I., Vanhoof, K.: FCM Expert: software tool for scenario analysis and pattern classification based on fuzzy cognitive maps. Int. J. Artif. Intell. Tools **27**(07), 1860010 (2018)
25. Nápoles, G., Grau, I., Bello, R., Grau, R.: Two-steps learning of fuzzy cognitive maps for prediction and knowledge discovery on the HIV-1 drug resistance. Expert Syst. Appl. **41**(3), 821–830 (2014)
26. Nauta, M., et al.: From anecdotal evidence to quantitative evaluation methods: a systematic review on evaluating explainable AI. ACM Comput. Surv. **55**(13s), 1–42 (2023)
27. Onari, M.A., et al.: Comparing interpretable AI approaches for the clinical environment: an application to Covid-19. In: 2022 IEEE Conference on Computational Intelligence in Bioinformatics and Computational Biology (CIBCB), pp. 1–8. IEEE (2022)
28. Onari, M.A., Yousefi, S., Rezaee, M.J.: Risk assessment in discrete production processes considering uncertainty and reliability: Z-number multi-stage fuzzy cognitive map with fuzzy learning algorithm. Artif. Intell. Rev. **54**(2), 1349–1383 (2021)
29. Özesmi, U., Özesmi, S.L.: Ecological models based on peoples knowledge: a multi-step fuzzy cognitive mapping approach. Ecol. Model. **176**(1–2), 43–64 (2004)
30. Papageorgiou, E.I.: A new methodology for decisions in medical informatics using fuzzy cognitive maps based on fuzzy rule-extraction techniques. Appl. Soft Comput. **11**(1), 500–513 (2011)
31. Pedrycz, W.: Fuzzy control and fuzzy systems. Research Studies Press Ltd. (1993)
32. Perlmutter, M., Gifford, R., Krening, S.: Impact of example-based XAI for neural networks on trust, understanding, and performance. Int. J. Hum Comput Stud. **188**, 103277 (2024)
33. Ribeiro, M.T., Singh, S., Guestrin, C.: " why should i trust you?" explaining the predictions of any classifier. In: Proceedings of the 22nd ACM SIGKDD International Conference on Knowledge Discovery and Data Mining, pp. 1135–1144 (2016)
34. Schmidt, P., Biessmann, F.: Quantifying interpretability and trust in machine learning systems. In: AAAI-19 Workshop on Network Interpretability for Deep Learning (2019)
35. Sivaraman, V., Bukowski, L.A., Levin, J., Kahn, J.M., Perer, A.: Ignore, trust, or negotiate: understanding clinician acceptance of AI-based treatment recommendations in health care. In: Proceedings of the 2023 CHI Conference on Human Factors in Computing Systems, pp. 1–18 (2023)

36. Ueno, T., Sawa, Y., Kim, Y., Urakami, J., Oura, H., Seaborn, K.: Trust in human-AI interaction: scoping out models, measures, and methods. In: CHI Conference on Human Factors in Computing Systems Extended Abstracts, pp. 1–7 (2022)
37. Vasey, B., et al.: Reporting guideline for the early-stage clinical evaluation of decision support systems driven by artificial intelligence: decide-AI. Nat. Med. **28**(5), 924–933 (2022)
38. Vereschak, O., Bailly, G., Caramiaux, B.: How to evaluate trust in AI-assisted decision making? a survey of empirical methodologies. Proc. ACM Hum. Comput. Interact. **5**(CSCW2), 1–39 (2021)
39. Wang, X., Yin, M.: Are explanations helpful? a comparative study of the effects of explanations in AI-assisted decision-making. In: 26th International Conference on Intelligent user Interfaces, pp. 318–328 (2021)
40. Wysocki, O., et al.: Assessing the communication gap between AI models and healthcare professionals: explainability, utility and trust in AI-driven clinical decision-making. Artif. Intell. **316**, 103839 (2023)
41. Yang, F., Huang, Z., Scholtz, J., Arendt, D.L.: How do visual explanations foster end users' appropriate trust in machine learning? In: Proceedings of the 25th International Conference on Intelligent user Interfaces, pp. 189–201 (2020)
42. Zhang, Y., Liao, Q.V., Bellamy, R.K.: Effect of confidence and explanation on accuracy and trust calibration in AI-assisted decision making. In: Proceedings of the 2020 Conference on Fairness, Accountability, and Transparency, pp. 295–305 (2020)

Open Access This chapter is licensed under the terms of the Creative Commons Attribution 4.0 International License (http://creativecommons.org/licenses/by/4.0/), which permits use, sharing, adaptation, distribution and reproduction in any medium or format, as long as you give appropriate credit to the original author(s) and the source, provide a link to the Creative Commons license and indicate if changes were made.

The images or other third party material in this chapter are included in the chapter's Creative Commons license, unless indicated otherwise in a credit line to the material. If material is not included in the chapter's Creative Commons license and your intended use is not permitted by statutory regulation or exceeds the permitted use, you will need to obtain permission directly from the copyright holder.

Benchmarking and XAI Evaluation Measures

When Can You Trust Your Explanations? A Robustness Analysis on Feature Importances

Ilaria Vascotto[1](✉) , Alex Rodriguez[1,2] , Alessandro Bonaita[3], and Luca Bortolussi[1]

[1] Department of Mathematics, Informatics and Geosciences, University of Trieste, Trieste, Italy
ilaria.vascotto@phd.units.it,
{alejandro.rodriguezgarcia,lbortolussi}@units.it
[2] The Abdus Salam International Center for Theoretical Physics, Trieste, Italy
[3] Assicurazioni Generali Spa, Milan, Italy
alessandro.bonaita@generali.com

Abstract. Recent legislative regulations have underlined the need for accountable and transparent artificial intelligence systems and have contributed to a growing interest in the Explainable Artificial Intelligence (XAI) field. Nonetheless, the lack of standardized criteria to validate explanation methodologies remains a major obstacle to developing trustworthy systems. We address a crucial yet often overlooked aspect of XAI, the robustness of explanations, which plays a central role in ensuring trust in both the system and the provided explanation. To this end, we propose a novel approach to analyse the robustness of neural network explanations to non-adversarial perturbations, leveraging the manifold hypothesis to produce new perturbed datapoints that resemble the observed data distribution. We additionally present an ensemble method to aggregate various explanations, showing how merging explanations can be beneficial for both understanding the model's decision and evaluating the robustness. The aim of our work is to provide practitioners with a framework for evaluating the trustworthiness of model explanations. Experimental results on feature importances derived from neural networks applied to tabular datasets highlight the importance of robust explanations in practical applications.

Keywords: XAI · Robustness · Feature Importance · Neural Networks · Tabular Data · Trustworthy AI

1 Introduction

The popularity of neural networks and their application to high-risk scenarios has recently raised questions on their accountability and trustworthiness. The rapid expansion of the field of Artificial Intelligence (AI) has stimulated legislative discussions and a series of novel regulations and guidelines has been proposed. In the European Union, the *AI Act* [10] and parts of the *General Data Protection Regulation* (GDPR) [9] have stressed the need for a fairer and more transparent approach to artificial intelligence. Similarly, the United States of America have proposed the new *Blueprint for an AI bill of rights* [31] that strives for a fair development and deployment of AI systems.

Modern AI systems are increasingly complex due to the elevated number of parameters involved to solve challenging tasks and are often referred to as *black boxes* given the opaque nature of their predictions. Transparency is, instead, a fundamental property that AI systems should guarantee, aiming to provide detailed descriptions of the model reasoning, even in natural language. Imagine that a model is being used in healthcare for patient diagnosis. If doctors can understand how it reached a given prediction, they gain a valuable tool for evaluating the correctness of such diagnosis and grow confidence in the AI system, even if they don't fully comprehend the technical aspects of the *black box* model.

The field of Explainable Artificial Intelligence (XAI) has proposed a variety of approaches to *open the black box* and provide explanations addressing the model inner reasoning, for example in the form of feature importances. While not explicitly referred to from a legislative standpoint, XAI can act as a powerful tool in enhancing transparency of AI-based systems. Understanding the reasoning behind a model decision is an asset from a technical standpoint, allowing experts to validate the predictions and detect possible biases before a model is deployed. Additionally, end-users may benefit from explanations as the *right to explanation* cited in the GDPR explicitly requires the user to receive an explanation when the decision is entirely subject to an automated decision system.

Despite their usefulness, the lack of standardized criteria to validate explainability approaches is still a major obstacle towards transparent and trustworthy systems. Although it is a critical aspect, the robustness of explanations remains an often underexplored facet of the development of explanation approaches. Robustness can be defined as an explainer's ability to provide consistent explanations for similar inputs. It can be evaluated through both non-adversarial perturbations, showing intrinsic weaknesses even under small changes, and adversarial attacks, implying a malicious nature of manipulating explanations.

Another complex characteristic of the XAI field is the disagreement problem [14], which occurs in scenarios where multiple explanation methods applied to the same datapoint return contrasting results. The debate over which explanation to choose (or *trust*) is still open, as explanation disagreement posits practical impediments to trustable AI systems.

Our contribution explores the following points:

- We propose a set of desirable properties that a robustness estimator should satisfy and show that our proposal, tailored for feature importance methods, satisfies them all.
- We address the disagreement problem on neural network explanations by proposing an ensemble of explanations focused on the ranking of the features.

- We introduce a framework to test explanation robustness to non-adversarial perturbations and assess their trustworthiness in practical applications.
- We propose a novel validation assessment of the robustness estimation, to tackle the lack of a ground truth.

We have tested our proposal on eight publicly-available tabular datasets and three neural network-specific feature importance methods. Our analysis demonstrates the need for evaluation tools to assess explanation robustness, supporting transparency and accountability in real-world applications.

2 Related Work

LIME [23] and SHAP [16] are among the most widely used XAI techniques in real-world applications. LIME works by fitting an inherently transparent model (such as a linear model or a decision tree) around the datapoint which is being explained. A neighbourhood is constructed from a fixed data distribution, generating a set of points on which the model, which acts as a local explanation, is fitted. SHAP makes use of Shapley values to explain predictions, measuring how the prediction changes when a feature is included or excluded in the feature set. It then averages these changes across all possible combinations of features, producing a vector of feature importances.

Despite their wide use, both methods lack *robustness* (or *stability*), which in this context represents the ability of an explanation method to produce similar and consistent explanations when different conditions change. LIME is an unstable method by design, as the neighbourhood generation step yields different sets of datapoints at each call of the method. This implies that, at each time the method is applied to the same datapoint, a different model is fitted, resulting in explanations whose coefficients differ feature-wise by magnitude or even by sign. SHAP is instead susceptible to feature correlations, sampling variability and data distribution shifts due to the way Shapley values are approximated. The instability of these approaches was first proved in [28], where the authors showed how an adversarial model could easily be defined to mask biased classifiers though unbiased explanations. Their untrustworthiness, along with other model-agnostic additive methods, has also been investigated in [12]. Their theoretical assumptions on feature independence are hardly met in practice, rendering them unable to correctly detect feature interactions when present.

According to [19], explanation robustness can be tested along three directions: robustness to input perturbations, to model changes and to hyperparameter selection. The first one includes the scenarios where the input may be modified by random perturbations or by adversarial attacks to the explanations themselves. The second one refers to manipulations of the model, such as fine-tuning of the parameters with a modified loss function, and the last one considers the influence of technique-specific hyperparameters.

An adversarial attack in the context of XAI is a perturbation of the input such that the model prediction is unchanged but the explanation marks different features as important or not [6]. An evaluation is provided in [11], in which attacks to interpretations provided by neural networks aim at maximising the change in the explanations (according to different change functions) under the constraint that the perturbation is small and the prediction is unchanged. [8] explores how model manipulation, in particular with the introduction of a penalty term in the loss function, can damage explanations. They call for a rigorous test of robustness to limit the effects of such manipulations. In [4] the authors note that it is possible, for any classifier g, to construct a classifier $\hat{g}$ that exhibits the same behaviour on seen data but presents biased explanations. They propose a version of the presented gradient-based explanations ([5,30]) robust to model manipulation by projecting the explanations on the tangent space of the data manifold.

While random perturbations and adversarial attacks to explanations in the context of images (as in [11]) can be easily examined by human experts, as the changes are often evident even to the naked eye, it is not sufficient to rely on non-quantitative evaluations. Robustness analysis must be supported by an adequate robustness estimation and agreed-upon metrics must be defined. To this end, [13] proposes a robustness score to evaluate explanation robustness when the data generation process is known, but this assumption makes it difficult to adapt to real-world datasets, where a ground truth is hardly available. In [2] the authors propose a formalization of local robustness based on the estimate of the local Lipschitz continuity. They test their proposal on explanations applied to images and show that gradient-based approaches are much more robust than their perturbation counterparts (LIME and SHAP).

The work of [20] presents an in-depth survey on the evaluation of XAI techniques and identifies different metrics that can be used to assess explanation robustness. Similarities can be computed with metrics such as: rank order correlations, top-k intersections, rule matching and structural similarity indexes. [25] proposes similar metrics for evaluating stability, as the Jaccard similarity, additionally requiring that stability tests should be performed using perturbations that do not change the class label and that introduce small amounts of resampling noise to ensure the stability of the explanations.

Robust-by-construction approaches have emerged as an interesting area of research. For example, [3] proposes self-explaining neural networks, a class of models for which faithfulness and robustness are enforced by construction through a specific regularization, aided by a generalization of the above-mentioned local Lipschitz continuity. Similarly, ROPE [15] is a framework based on adversarial training that generates explanations which are robust to both changes in the input and in the data distribution.

We aim at investigating the robustness of explanations to non adversarial perturbations on tabular datasets, presenting a robustness metric that addresses limitations of the previously mentioned methods (recalled within brackets in this paragraph). In particular we define a metric that can be computed even in absence of a ground truth [13], considering practitioners needs (for example, deploying a model without requiring a retraining [8]) and keeping in mind the limitations derived from theoretical assumptions [12]. Importantly, our metric is bounded within the [0, 1] range, allowing for comparability among methods, datasets and used models [2].

Alongside robustness analysis, we seek to explore the efficacy of an ensemble approach on explanations. [14] presents an overview of the disagreement problem according to practitioners: while it is underlined that the problem is of non-negligible size, the authors do not propose solutions or good practices. In the context of adversarial attacks, [24] showcases the efficacy of ensemble methods as defences on explanations. They test their aggregated explanation on image data and show that it is more resilient to attacks, when a composing explanation method or the model itself is being fooled. Aggregations can also be performed leveraging multiple explanations from the same method: [7] derives a more robust Shapley-value explanation by aggregating the explanations computed on a carefully crafted neighbourhood, minimizing explanation sensitivity. We will consider these characteristics when devising our ensemble and considering the robustness estimator.

3 Background

This section introduces key terminology related to the XAI field and describes the techniques used in the experimental analysis.

3.1 Terminology

While there is not an agreed-upon taxonomy to classify XAI techniques, we follow the proposal of [1], which identifies the following axes of interest:

- Scope of the explanation: a local approach aims at explaining how a given individual prediction is made while a global one focuses on the model as a whole, analysing its overall reasoning.
- Model of interest: model-specific techniques are tailored to the structure of the model under investigation, while model-agnostic ones can be applied to any model.
- Transparency: intrinsically transparent models are interpretable by construction (and are also known as *glass boxes*) while post-hoc techniques are applied after the model is fully trained.

As we will be discussing results obtained from neural networks, we can further distinguish between perturbation-based and gradient-based approaches [26]. Perturbation-based approaches are often model-agnostic and rely either on neighbourhood generation or combinatorial aspects, as in LIME [23] or SHAP [16]. Gradient-based methods, instead, are specific to neural networks and harness their inner structure, mainly taking advantage of the backpropagation mechanisms [5,27,30].

The broader category of approaches we will be considering is that of feature attributions. Having an input $\mathbf{x} = (x_1, \ldots x_m)$ with m features, a feature attribution is a vector $\mathbf{a} = (a_1, \ldots, a_m)$ of size m where each entry represents the importance of the corresponding feature towards the model's prediction. According to the specific datatype of **x**, the attributions may refer to individual variables (tabular data), words or bag of words (natural language), pixels or superpixels (images - in this case explanations are often called *heatmaps*). A positive (negative) sign usually represents a positive (negative) contribution of the feature and its relevance in the prediction. In the following, we will use the terms *feature importances* and *attributions* interchangeably.

3.2 Considered Techniques

We focus on local post-hoc approaches specific to neural networks and that are applicable to nets trained on tabular datasets. We have not considered model-agnostic approaches such as LIME [23] and SHAP [16] due to their known instability [2,12,28], as presented in Sect. 2. Model-specific approaches, such as Saliency and Input X Gradient [26] are also known for being unstable [2,11] and have therefore been excluded from the analysis.

Note that neural network explanations require the selection of the output neuron to be explained: this is more relevant in classification problems where one may want to investigate the features that contributed to any of the classes probability scores. In the following, the target neuron will be chosen as the one associated with the model's predictions, that is, the one with the largest output score.

DeepLIFT. DeepLearning Important Features (DeepLIFT) [27] computes feature importances with respect to their difference from a given reference. In particular, the differences between the two outputs are explained in terms of the differences among the two inputs. Each neuron is analysed with respect to the difference between its activation and that of the reference input. DeepLIFT makes use of contribution scores and multipliers to backpropagate the difference in output through the network. It requires a single forward-backward pass through the net, making it efficient. The propagations are computed through appropriate chain rules, defined according to the neuron's type and its activations.

Integrated Gradients. Integrated Gradients (IG) [30] satisfies the axioms of sensitivity and implementation invariance. It computes the integral of the gradients of a net f along the straight-line path from a baseline x' to the input x, considering a series of linearly separated instances along the path from the baseline to the point of interest. In practice, it takes advantage of an approximation of s steps such that, for the j-th dimension, it holds:

$$\text{IG}_j^{approx} = \frac{x_j - x'_j}{s} \sum_{k=1}^{s} \frac{\partial f(x' + (x - x') \cdot k/s)}{\partial x_j} \qquad (1)$$

The authors of [30] found that $s \in (20, 300)$ produced satisfactory approximations but the computation can nonetheless be expensive when the number of steps is large.

Layerwise Relevance Propagation Layerwise Relevance Propagation (LRP) [5] is based on the backpropagation principle. It defines a series of rules to propagate the output score (or *relevance*) $f(x)$ through the net's layers, according to the architecture at hand. The conservation property holds: with R_j the relevance for neuron j, for each pair of layers $\sum_j R_j = \sum_k R_k$ and globally it holds that summing over all layers $\sum_i R_i = f(x)$. Two common propagation rules are the epsilon and the gamma rules:

$$\text{LRP-}\epsilon : R_j = \sum_k \frac{a_j \cdot w_{jk}}{\epsilon + \sum_{0,j} a_j \cdot w_{jk}} R_k$$
$$\text{LRP-}\gamma : R_j = \sum_k \frac{a_j \cdot (w_{jk} + \gamma \cdot w_{jk}^+)}{\epsilon + \sum_{0,j} a_j \cdot (w_{jk} + \gamma \cdot w_{jk}^+)} R_k \quad (2)$$

where a_j is the activation of neuron j, w_{jk} is the weight linking neuron j to neuron k in the following layer (w_{jk}^+ is a positive weight), $\sum_{0,j}$ is the sum over all lower-layer activations.

Missingness Property. DeepLIFT, Integrated Gradients and LRP satisfy the missingness property: if $x_j = 0 \Rightarrow a_j = 0$. The features corresponding to the null entries in the feature vector will have null coefficients in the attribution vector, representing a lack of importance towards the prediction. This property is particularly relevant when dealing with categorical variables, preprocessed with one-hot encoding.

4 Methodology

Our approach is applied to tabular datasets and classification problems. Let us introduce the following notation: let $\mathcal{D} = (\mathbf{X}, \mathbf{y})$ be a dataset with N datapoints and m features such that $(\mathbf{x}^i, y^i) = (x^{(i,1)}, \ldots, x^{(i,j)}, \ldots, x^{(i,m)}, y^i)$ with y^i a class label. The dataset is split into a training, validation and test datasets, identified by $\mathcal{D}_{train}$, $\mathcal{D}_{valid}$ and $\mathcal{D}_{test}$ respectively. Let $f(\cdot)$ be a neural network trained on $\mathcal{D}_{train}$ and t be a target class. Let e be an explanation method (or explainer) and $e(\mathbf{x}^i) := e(\mathbf{x}^i, f)$ the explanation of model f prediction of point $\mathbf{x}^i$. More specifically, let the feature attribution vector of the l-th method be $\mathbf{a}_l^i = (a_l^{(i,1)}, \ldots, a_l^{(i,m)})$.

4.1 Robustness Estimator

We define the robustness of an explanation as a measure of its variability when the input is modified. If we consider $\mathbf{x}$ the original datapoint, $\tilde{\mathbf{x}}$ a perturbation, e an explanation method and $e(\mathbf{x})$ the corresponding explanation, then:

$$\mathbf{x} \to \tilde{\mathbf{x}}, e(\mathbf{x}) \to e(\tilde{\mathbf{x}}) \Rightarrow r(\mathbf{x}, e) = g(\mathbf{x}, \tilde{\mathbf{x}}, e) \quad (3)$$

that is, the robustness r of $e(\mathbf{x})$ is a function of the chosen explanation method, the original datapoint and the perturbed one.

Further considering a constraint of the form $dist(\mathbf{x}, \tilde{\mathbf{x}}) < \epsilon$ with $\epsilon > 0$ and $dist$ a distance metric (such as the euclidean distance), we can introduce the notion of local robustness.

Definition 1. *An explanation method e is locally robust if perturbing the input results in a similar explanation. If $\mathbf{x} \to \tilde{\mathbf{x}}$ with $dist(\mathbf{x}, \tilde{\mathbf{x}}) < \epsilon$ ($\epsilon > 0$) $\Rightarrow e(\mathbf{x}) \approx e(\tilde{\mathbf{x}})$.*

Given a robustness estimator $\hat{\mathcal{R}}(\mathbf{x}^i, \mathcal{N}^i) := \hat{\mathcal{R}}(\mathbf{x}^i, \mathcal{N}^i, e, f)$ that measures the robustness of the explanation method e applied to the neighbourhood $\mathcal{N}^i$ of the point $\mathbf{x}^i$ over the model f, we can define the following set of *desiderata*.

Property 1. If $r(\mathbf{x}^i, \tilde{\mathbf{x}}^i) := r(\mathbf{x}^i, \tilde{\mathbf{x}}^i, e, f)$ is the robustness of $e(\mathbf{x}^i)$ with respect to the perturbation $\tilde{\mathbf{x}}^i$, then the robustness $\mathcal{R} = \mathbb{E}[r]$ is estimated by:

$$\hat{\mathcal{R}}(\mathbf{x}^i, \mathcal{N}^i) = \frac{1}{|\mathcal{N}^i|} \sum_{\tilde{\mathbf{x}}^i \in \mathcal{N}^i} r(\mathbf{x}^i, \tilde{\mathbf{x}}^i) \qquad (4)$$

where $\mathcal{N}^i = \{\tilde{\mathbf{x}}^i | \tilde{\mathbf{x}}^i = \mathbf{x}^i + \lambda \text{ with } dist(\mathbf{x}^i, \tilde{\mathbf{x}}^i) < \epsilon \ (\epsilon > 0), \lambda \in \mathbb{R}^m\}$.

Two points which are close to each other within the dataspace will produce explanations with comparable robustness scores.

Property 2. If $\hat{\mathcal{R}}$ is a local robustness estimator, then for two distinct points $\mathbf{x}^i, \mathbf{x}^j$ such that $dist(\mathbf{x}^i, \mathbf{x}^j) < \epsilon$ ($\epsilon > 0$) it holds that:

$$\exists \delta > 0 \text{ s.t. } |\hat{\mathcal{R}}(\mathbf{x}^i, \mathcal{N}^i) - \hat{\mathcal{R}}(\mathbf{x}^j, \mathcal{N}^j)| < \delta \qquad (5)$$

Robustness estimation is intrinsically linked to uncertainty in the estimates, due to errors in the explanations themselves and the lack of a ground truth for the robustness.

Property 3. $\hat{\mathcal{R}}$ is such that $\hat{\mathcal{R}} = \mathcal{R} + \theta_\epsilon$ where $\mathcal{R} = \mathbb{E}[r]$ is the true robustness and $\theta_\epsilon \neq 0$ is an error term.

By definition, the neighbourhood generation is highly influential in the robustness estimation process when non-adversarial perturbations are considered. On-manifold perturbations better reflect the true data distribution and the manifold learned by the model, therefore exhibit greater robustness scores than random perturbations which may be off-manifold.

Property 4. If $\mathcal{N}^i$ is an on-manifold neighbourhood and $\bar{\mathcal{N}}^i$ an off-manifold one, then $\hat{\mathcal{R}}(\mathbf{x}^i, \mathcal{N}^i) > \hat{\mathcal{R}}(\mathbf{x}^i, \bar{\mathcal{N}}^i)$.

The robustness of an aggregation of explainers is bounded by the robustness of the individual components.

Property 5. If the explainer $\bar{e}$ is an aggregation of explainers, $\bar{e} = agg(e_1, \ldots, e_l)$, then, if $\hat{\mathcal{R}}(e) := \hat{\mathcal{R}}(\mathbf{x}^i, \mathcal{N}^i, e, f)$, it holds that $\hat{\mathcal{R}}(\bar{e}) \leq \max(\hat{\mathcal{R}}(e_1), \ldots, \hat{\mathcal{R}}(e_l))$.

Two equivalent models predicting the same class for a datapoint will be related to explanations with comparable robustness scores. The data manifold learned by the models influences the robustness score.

Property 6. Let $f(\cdot)$ and $g(\cdot)$ be two models with comparable accuracy on the dataset $\mathcal{D}$. If the point $\mathbf{x}^i$ is predicted to belong to the same class by both models, say $\hat{y}^i_f = \hat{y}^i_g$, and let $\hat{\mathcal{R}}(f) := \hat{\mathcal{R}}(\mathbf{x}^i, \mathcal{N}^i, e, f)$, then:

$$|\hat{\mathcal{R}}(f) - \hat{\mathcal{R}}(g)| < \delta \text{ with } \delta > 0 \qquad (6)$$

We propose the robustness r to be computed as $r(\mathbf{x}^i, \tilde{\mathbf{x}}^i) = \rho(e(\mathbf{x}^i, f), e(\tilde{\mathbf{x}}^i, f))$, where ρ is the Spearman's rho rank correlation coefficient and $e(\mathbf{x}^i, f)$ the explanation of model f prediction of point $\mathbf{x}^i$. By Property 1, it then holds that the robustness $\mathcal{R}$ can be estimated via:

$$\hat{\mathcal{R}}(\mathbf{x}^i, \mathcal{N}^i, e, f) = \frac{1}{|\mathcal{N}^i|} \sum_{\tilde{\mathbf{x}}^i \in \mathcal{N}^i} \rho(e(\mathbf{x}^i, f), e(\tilde{\mathbf{x}}^i, f)) \qquad (7)$$

where $\mathcal{N}^i = \{\tilde{\mathbf{x}}^i | \tilde{\mathbf{x}}^i = \mathbf{x}^i + \lambda \text{ with } \lambda \in \mathbb{R}^m, \ dist(\mathbf{x}^i, \tilde{\mathbf{x}}^i) < \epsilon \ (\epsilon > 0) \text{ and } \hat{y}^i = \hat{y}^{\tilde{i}}\}$. By definition, it holds that $0 \le \hat{\mathcal{R}}(\mathbf{x}^i, \mathcal{N}^i, e, f) \le 1$.

We will show in Sect. 5 that our estimator also satisfies Properties 2-6.

4.2 Neighbourhood Generation

As remarked in Property 4, neighbourhood generation is an influential step in the estimation of the robustness, as the score is averaged over the set $\mathcal{N}^i$. In the previous subsection, we have limited the constraints of the neighbourhood to only consider perturbed points $\tilde{\mathbf{x}}^i$ which are close to the original datapoint $\mathbf{x}^i$ and for which the model's prediction is the same, $\hat{y}^i = \hat{y}^{\tilde{i}}$. We will consider two possible neighbourhood generation mechanisms which deeply influence the robustness computation. Let us distinguish between numerical and categorical variables, x^i_{num} and x^i_{cat} respectively, as they require different perturbations by construction.

Random Neighbourhood ($\mathcal{N}_R$). A first naive approach is the random generation of the neighbourhood, consisting of the addition of random white noise to numerical variables and a random flip of the categorical ones:

$$\begin{cases} \tilde{x}^i_{num} = x^i_{num} + \delta^i \text{ with } \delta^i \leftarrow \mathcal{N}(0, \sigma^2) \\ \tilde{x}^i_{cat} = \text{flip}(x^i_{cat}) \text{ with probability } \gamma_{cat} \end{cases} \qquad (8)$$

The flip of a categorical variable entails a random sampling among the possible modalities associated with that variable, the observed value of x^i_{cat} being excluded.

Medoid-Based Neighbourhood ($\mathcal{N}_M$). We propose a more refined mechanism that leverages the manifold hypothesis to generate perturbed datapoints which are still on-manifold, as our interest lies in testing non-adversarial perturbations consistent with the observed data distribution. Consider a k-medoid clustering on $\mathcal{D}_{valid}$, with $k_{medoids}$ selected so that each cluster is, on average, of size $n_k = 10$. For each cluster, the medoid $\mathbf{x}^c$ is used as a representative and its k_M nearest neighbours among the other cluster centres are stored in the set $NN^c = (\mathbf{x}^1, \ldots, \mathbf{x}^{k_M})$. For each point $\mathbf{x}^i \in \mathcal{D}_{test}$ we want to test, the associated cluster c is retrieved. From the corresponding cluster centre neighbours list NN^c, one of the medoids is randomly chosen, say $\mathbf{x}^M$. With α and α_{cat} the probabilities of perturbing a numerical and a categorical variable respectively, a perturbation is performed according to the following scheme:

$$\begin{cases} \tilde{x}^i_{num} = (1 - \bar{\alpha}) \cdot x^i_{num} + \bar{\alpha} \cdot x^M_{num} \text{ with } \bar{\alpha} \leftarrow Beta(\alpha \cdot 100, (1-\alpha) \cdot 100) \\ \tilde{x}^i_{cat} = \begin{cases} x^i_{cat} \text{ with probability } 1 - \alpha_{cat} \\ x^M_{cat} \text{ with probability } \alpha_{cat} \end{cases} \end{cases} \quad (9)$$

With both generating schemes, the resulting neighbourhood should be of at least size $n = 100$ to ensure statistical significance. A filtering step is then performed to remove the perturbations for which the model prediction is different from $f(\mathbf{x}^i)$. Hyperparameter tuning is performed on $\theta_1 = (\sigma, \gamma_{cat})$ and $\theta_2 = (\alpha, \alpha_{cat}, k_M)$ to ensure that, on average, at least 95% of the points are kept.

The main differences among the two approaches are presented in Fig. 1, where the Swiss roll dataset is used as an example. Both schemes were applied to the same datapoint: the left most column represents a 3D visual of the dataset (in the shape of a rolled piece of paper), while the middle one is a view from above. It is easy to note that the random neighbourhood is expanded beyond the Swiss roll spiral shape. This is more evident in the right-most column, where a zoomed-in visualization is proposed: while the random neighbourhood does not follow the data manifold even when a small perturbation is applied ($\sigma = 0.05$), the medoid-based one remains constantly within bounds despite a larger coefficient being used ($\alpha = 0.3$).

4.3 Ensemble

We present a novel aggregation approach that aims at dealing with the disagreement problem [14] by merging feature importances, focusing on the ranking of the features according to their absolute value. Let L be the number of methods which are being aggregated and let $\mathbf{r}^i_l$ be the l-th ranking, a vector of size m storing the indices that would sort the array $|\mathbf{a}^i_l|$ in decreasing order. Then, let an average attribution $\mathbf{a}^i_{ens}$ be defined by:

$$a^{(i,j)}_{ens} = \frac{\sum_{l=1}^{L} r^{(i,j)}_l \cdot w^{(i,j)}_l}{\sum_{l=1}^{L} w^{(i,j)}_l} \cdot (1 + \lambda \bar{n}^{(i,j)}) \quad (10)$$

where w_l is the weight corresponding to the l-th feature attribution vector, $\lambda = 0.15$ is a penalization term and $\bar{n}^{(i,j)}$ is the number of methods for which there is

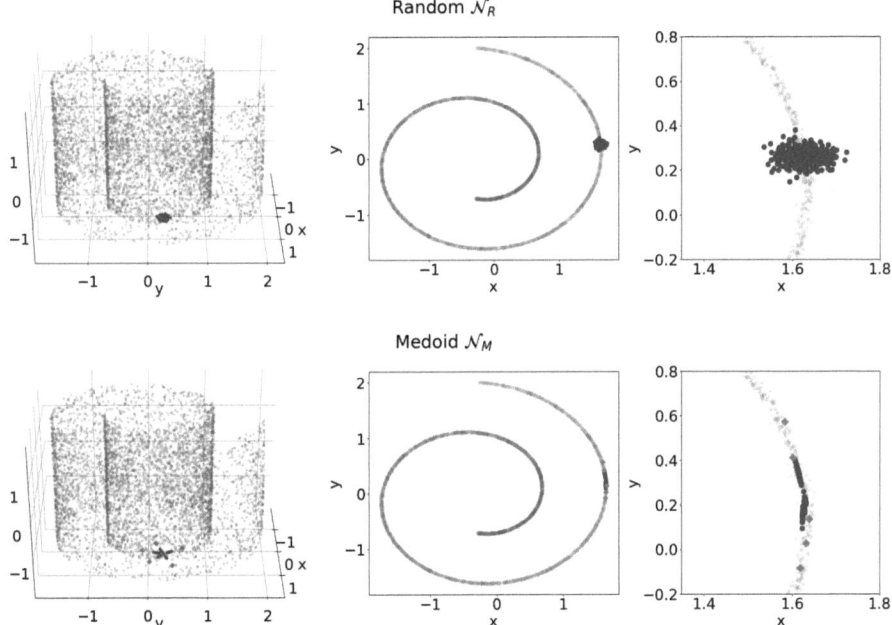

Fig. 1. An example of neighbourhood generation ($n = 500$) on the Swiss roll dataset: the top row depicts the random neighbourhood generation $\mathcal{N}_R$ ($\sigma = 0.05$) while the bottom one the medoid-based generation $\mathcal{N}_M$ ($\alpha = 0.3$ and $k_M = 5$). Blue datapoints represent the generated perturbations while the orange ones in the bottom row are the k_M neighbouring cluster centres.

a disagreement on the sign of the attribution $a_l^{(i,j)}$ for $l = 1, \ldots, L$. The ranking $\mathbf{r}_{ens}^i$ storing the indices that would sort the attribution vector $\mathbf{a}_{ens}^i$ in increasing order is the results of our approach.

This aggregation method is able to deal with practical issues that emerge when considering multiple explanations altogether. First of all, attributions may result in coefficients very close, but not equal, to zero. A zero coefficient implies that the feature is not important towards the prediction, but the lack of a common scale for feature attributions makes it difficult to discriminate between important and unimportant features only based on the absolute value of the corresponding coefficient. We aim at limiting this issue by considering the following weighting scheme where, for the l-th methods, i-th point and j-th feature, it holds:

$$w_l^{(i,j)} = \frac{\sigma(\mathbf{a}_l^i)}{\sqrt{|\overline{\mathbf{a}_l^i}| \cdot |a_l^{(i,j)}|}} \qquad (11)$$

with $\mathbf{a}_l^i$ the feature importance vector, $\overline{\mathbf{a}_l^i}$ its average and $\sigma(\mathbf{a}_l^i)$ the standard deviation.

Smaller values of the feature importance coefficients translate into larger weights, that contribute to moving a feature into the set of non-informative ones of our ranking, effectively capturing the scarcer importance towards the prediction. As coefficients may differ greatly in magnitude between multiple methods, a normalization is then introduced with the consideration of the average and standard deviation within the weighting scheme.

The ensemble is computed as the weighted average of the $L = 3$ rankings and a penalization term λ is introduced to penalize features that exhibit sign disagreement among the L methods, as we consider it a symptom of feature instability. The penalization term allows us to favour the features for which there is sign concordance ($\bar{n}^{(i,j)} = 0$), either positive or negative, and when the attribution magnitude is non negligible. Considering how larger weights move features towards the set of non influential ones, the penalization contributes to a lower attribution value for concordant features, effectively capturing their (absolute) relevance and importance towards the prediction.

We will compare our ensemble to another aggregation method in Sect. 5. Inspired by [24], we will simply consider the average of the attributions, when the vectors have norm 1. If $\mathbf{a}_l^i$ is such that $\|\mathbf{a}_l^i\|_2 = 1$, then

$$a_{mean}^{(i,j)} = \frac{1}{L} \sum_{l=1}^{L} a_l^{(i,j)} \tag{12}$$

with $\mathbf{a}_{mean}^i$ such that $\|\mathbf{a}_{mean}^i\|_2 = 1$.

One of the disadvantages of using the mean as aggregation is that it may assign a zero attribution even when all L coefficients are non-null. Assume that, for the j-th feature, the $L = 3$ coefficients derived from the corresponding methods are $(v, v, -2v)$ with $v > 0$. The mean will be equal to zero, implying that the feature is non relevant towards the prediction, but the importance for each of the L method highlights a relevance of magnitude at least v. Our ensemble is, instead, able to take this into account, penalizing the disagreement but still considering the feature to have some level of relevance towards the prediction.

While we have computed both aggregations with the feature attributions derived from DeepLIFT, Integrated Gradients and LRP (as presented in Subsect. 3.2), both approaches can be easily extended to include a higher number of feature attribution methods.

4.4 When Can You Trust Your Explanations?

Assessing the trustworthiness of explanations on previously unseen datapoints is a non trivial task. While it is possible to compute an estimate of the robustness via Eq. 7, we argue that the result may not reflect the true robustness of the considered datapoint, as it may lay in an unstable area of the feature space. We want to verify not only if a datapoint is robust, but also if it lies in a robust area of the feature space: knowing that the neighbourhood is non robust allows us to *doubt* the robustness score of a previously-unseen datapoint. To tackle this issue, we propose the usage of a k-nearest neighbours regressor fitted on $\mathcal{D}_{valid}$ robustness scores. For $\mathbf{x}^i \in \mathcal{D}_{test}$, we compute both the robustness score $\hat{\mathcal{R}}(\mathbf{x}^i) := \hat{\mathcal{R}}(\mathbf{x}^i, \mathcal{N}^i, e, f)$ via 7 and the regressor's prediction $\mathcal{R}_{knn}(\mathbf{x}^i)$. According to a selected threshold value r_{th}, it is possible to discriminate between three scenarios:

1. if $\hat{\mathcal{R}}(\mathbf{x}^i) \geq r_{th}$ and $\mathcal{R}_{knn}(\mathbf{x}^i) \geq r_{th}$ then $\mathbf{x}^i$ is a robust point;
2. if $\hat{\mathcal{R}}(\mathbf{x}^i) \geq r_{th}$ and $\mathcal{R}_{knn}(\mathbf{x}^i) < r_{th}$ then $\mathbf{x}^i$ is an uncertain point, as it lies in an uncertain area of the feature space and its robustness should be carefully considered;
3. if $\hat{\mathcal{R}}(\mathbf{x}^i) < r_{th}$ then $\mathbf{x}^i$ is a non robust point.

The second scenario represents a set of conditions that practitioners should carefully evaluate: despite the robustness score being greater than the selected threshold, the local information derived from the neighbours suggests otherwise. This scenario aims at ringing a bell in the practitioner evaluating a given explanation: knowing that it may be misleading, the analysis will be more careful and require a more detailed human-evaluation of both the prediction and its explanation.

The usage of a knn regressor instead of a knn classifier allows for independence from the selected robustness threshold r_{th}, requiring the model be fitted only once. The number of neighbours k_R is a dataset-dependent hyperparameter and relies on the goodness of approximation of the robustness score by the regressor.

The selection of the threshold r_{th} is a delicate step of the procedure: as the robustness estimator is bounded by construction in the $[0, 1]$ range, it is possible to select a case-specific threshold to discriminate between robust and non robust datapoints. As it will be seen in Subsect. 5.1, in which hyperparameter selection is discussed in detail, a default value of $r_{th} = 0.80$ works well on most of the datasets.

4.5 A Complete Pipeline

With the considerations presented up to this point, we can discuss the complete framework (Fig. 2) for robustness evaluation and explanation trustworthiness.

1. Split the dataset into $\mathcal{D}_{train}, \mathcal{D}_{valid}, \mathcal{D}_{test}$ and perform the required preprocessing steps.
2. Train a neural network on $\mathcal{D}_{train}$.
3. Perform k-medoid clustering on $\mathcal{D}_{valid}$ and compute the k_M nearest neighbours among the medoids.
4. For each point $\mathbf{x}^j \in \mathcal{D}_{valid}$, generate a neighbourhood $\mathcal{N}^j$ of size n.
5. Compute the attributions of DeepLIFT, Integrated Gradients and LRP and merge them following the ensemble aggregation scheme.
6. Compute the robustness score via Eq. 7 for each point $\mathbf{x}^j \in \mathcal{D}_{valid}$.
7. Use the previously computed robustness scores to train a k-nearest neighbours regressor and select an appropriate threshold r_{th}.

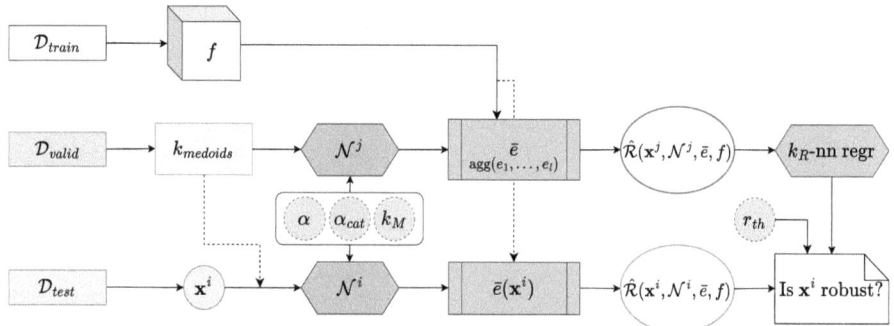

Fig. 2. The complete pipeline.

8. For each datapoint $\mathbf{x}^i \in \mathcal{D}_{test}$, predict the medoid cluster it belongs to and generate a neighbourhood $\mathcal{N}^i$.
9. Compute the L feature attribution vectors and the resulting aggregation.
10. Compute then the robustness score via Eq. 7 and the predicted robustness via the $k$nn regressor.
11. Assess the trustworthiness following Subsect. 4.4.

Note that the computational cost of the procedure is dominated by the computation of the individual attributions, as a pass through the network is required for each datapoint, for each perturbation and for each of the three methods. The scaling of the underlying robustness method inherits this complexity.

The advantages of using this framework include the leveraging of an ensemble-based explanation, which captures the signals of L individual explanation methods, and the estimation of the robustness on a carefully constructed neighbourhood. The pipeline is designed to point out possibly non robust points, even when they appear so, ensuring greater trustworthiness in the system and a more aware analysis from a practitioners perspective.

The presented framework is applicable to datasets entirely made of numerical variables, but to correctly consider also categorical ones a small adjustment is required. Categorical features are often preprocessed with a one-hot encoding before a neural network is trained. For example, a feature x_{cat} with four modalities is represented by a vector of the form $(0, 0, 1, 0)$, where the non zero-entry corresponds to the observed modality. A feature attribution method applied to the one-hot encoded feature vector returns a set of importances of the form $(0, 0, u, 0)$: the non-zero entry is the only one associated with a non-null value. This is to be expected as the attribution methods we are evaluating satisfy the missingness property (Subsect. 3.2). To limit the effects of zero-entries in the Spearman's rho computation, we propose a *reverse encoding* of categorical variables. They are represented by the observed modality and the variable x_{cat} is associated with an attribution $a_l = u$. This allows us to consider feature vectors of size m, as in the original feature vector, and to perform a more effective comparison of the robustness. The *reverse encoding* is applied in steps 5 and 9, prior to the ensemble's computation.

4.6 Validation

Robustness estimation is often subject to the lack of a ground truth, as the data generation process is not known in real-world applications and comparison against expert-provided explanations can be unfeasible due to the large amount of data being examined. We argue that robust (explanation-wise) points lie in a robust area of the feature space and can be deemed robust even when passed though different models. Our assumption implies that non robust points will exhibit differences both in the explanations and in the predictions of multiple models, as their lack of robustness is a somewhat intrinsic characteristic of the area of the manifold in which they lie.

Let us consider three neural networks, say f_1, f_2 and f_3, which have comparable accuracy over $\mathcal{D}_{train}$ and that differ either in the number of hidden layers or neurons per layer. Let $\mathcal{D}_{agree}$ be the subset of datapoints for which models f_1, f_2, f_3 predict the same class and $\mathcal{D}_{disagree}$ the subset for which one of the models predicts a different class. Consider a point to be robust if $\hat{\mathcal{R}}(\mathbf{x}^i) \geq r_{th}$ and non-robust otherwise.[1] We propose the validation to follow a ROC/AUC analysis, where the True Positive Rate (TPR) and False Positive Rate (FPR) are defined as:

$$\text{TPR} = \frac{\#\{\text{Robust \& Agree}\}}{\#\{\text{Agree}\}} \quad \text{FPR} = \frac{\#\{\text{Robust \& Disagree}\}}{\#\{\text{Disagree}\}} \quad (13)$$

Varying the threshold value r_{th}, it is possible to plot the ROC curve and compute the corresponding AUC value.

5 Experimental Evaluation

5.1 Experimental Setting

We have selected the following publicly-available datasets from the UC Irvine Machine Learning Repository: `beans`, `cancer`, `mushroom`, `white wine`, `adult` and `bank marketing`. We have additionally used the `heloc` and `ocean` datasets, following the work of [21,29] respectively. The first four represent toy examples, as the classification tasks are easier to tackle even with non-neural models and present an overall lower number of both features and datapoints. All the datasets propose binary or multiclass classification tasks and contain both numerical and categorical variables.

We have relied on the Python libraries `pytorch` and `captum` for the implementation of our approach. The former was used for the training and usage of

---

[1] Note that, in this case, we are not considering the classification presented in Subsect. 4.4, but only if the robustness score $\hat{\mathcal{R}}$ is above the selected threshold r_{th}.

the nets while the latter, a `pytorch`-compatible explainability framework developed by Meta, was applied for the retrieval of the attribution vectors. The full implementation is available on Github.[2]

For all datasets, the following preprocessing steps were performed:

- Standardization of numerical variables and one-hot encoding of the categorical ones.
- Removal of correlated features. Spearman's rank correlation coefficient was used for numerical variables while the normalized mutual information criterion for the categorical ones. The removal of highly correlated features ensures that neighbourhood generation is more aligned with the data distribution and that the computed attributions are non distorted by unconsidered correlations among the features.
- Softmax in the final layer of the net, also for binary classification examples. It ensures stability during attribution computations, as higher relevances are backpropagated. This also reduces the effects of the vanishing gradient problem, when the attribution is returned as a zero-vector, as the signal is lost when the output score is propagated through the net.
- Selection of the `gamma` rule for LRP attributions. It was chosen as it was the rule minimizing the vanishing gradient problem, and it was applied to all the layers of the nets (as they are all linear layers).

As anticipated in Subsect. 4.6, we trained three neural networks per dataset, say Model 1, 2 and 3, with comparable accuracy scores (Appendix A, Table 4). Model 1 represents the baseline model, model 2 has more layers and more neurons in each layer while model 3 is a more compact version, with fewer layers and neurons. The ReLU activation function was used in all cases, with the exception of the `ocean` dataset, where tanh was used, following the structure in [29].

Hyperparameter Selection. Default values for the neighbourhood generation hyperparameters are $\theta_1 = (\sigma = 0.05, \gamma_{cat} = 0.05)$ for the random generation $\mathcal{N}_R$ and $\theta_2 = (\alpha = 0.05, \alpha_{cat} = 0.05, k_M = 5)$ for the medoid-based one $\mathcal{N}_M$. In both cases, the neighbourhood should be of size at least $n = 100$ (we have set $n = 100$ in our experiments) and dataset-specific hyperparameters are set via a grid search, ensuring that at least 95% of the generated datapoints are kept within the neighbourhood, i.e. they are predicted to belong to the same class as the original datapoint.

The number of neighbours k_R to be used in the $k$nn regressor is chosen as the one minimizing the approximation error over the robustness scores derived from all three nets in each dataset. A good default value is $k_R = 7$.

The robustness threshold r_{th} is selected by looking at the distribution of robust, non robust and uncertain datapoints at varying levels of the threshold. In particular, it is chosen as the threshold value that corresponds to the first inflection point of the robust percentage curve. The default value $r_{th} = 0.80$ works well in most scenarios.

---

[2] https://github.com/ilariavascotto/XAI_robustness_analysis

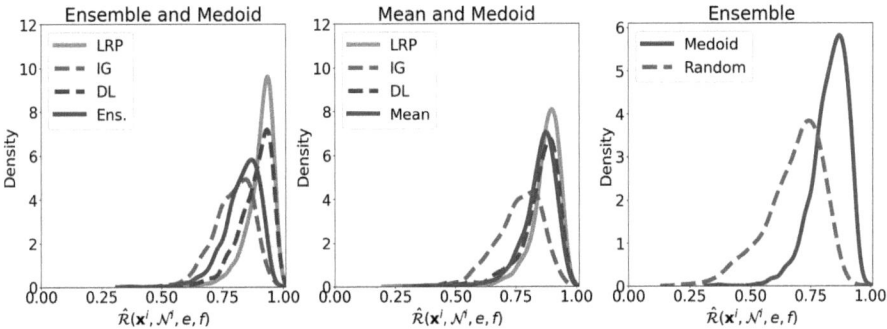

Fig. 3. The robustness score distribution for `adult` dataset of the ensemble (left) and of the mean (centre) with medoid-based neighbourhood generation; random and medoid-based neighbourhood generations are compared for the ensemble aggregation (right).

Dataset-specific hyperparameters can be found in Appendix A, Table 5.

5.2 Results

We will begin the discussion focusing on the results derived from Model 1, that acts as our baseline, on the test set $\mathcal{D}_{test}$.

Figure 3 depicts the robustness score distribution derived from the ensemble (left) and the mean (centre) aggregations with the medoid-based neighbourhood generation mechanism on the `adult` dataset. They are compared with the robustness scores derived from the individual XAI approaches, taking into account the nature of the aggregation. In particular, the ensemble is compared to the robustness computed on the feature importance vectors in absolute value, to mimic the reasoning of the ensemble's construction, while the mean is compared to the feature vectors with sign. As stated by Property 5, in both cases the aggregated explanation robustness acts as an average of the robustness of the individual approaches and is limited by their span. In this example, Integrated Gradients is on average the least robust method while DeepLIFT and LRP present grater values of the estimated robustness. Note that this behaviour is dataset dependent: Integrated Gradients is not, in general, the least robust method. The aggregated explanations, either with the ensemble or the mean, represent an advantage over the use of individual approaches. In particular, the aggregation acts as a conservative explanation, that takes into account the individual method's robustness and their feature-wise agreement. While the average robustness may be lower than that of some of the considered approaches, it is able to take into account the possible undesirable effects of a less robust and disagreeing method, flagging possible untrustworthiness for a given datapoint.

The rightmost part of Fig. 3 depicts the comparison between the effects of two neighbourhood generating schemes on the ensemble non-adversarial robustness. As previously shown in Fig. 1, the random neighbourhood consists of datapoints which are off-manifold, while the medoid-based one is constructed to remain on-

Table 1. When can you trust your explanations? Comparison of the robustness scores with ensemble and mean aggregations with $r_{th} = 0.80$.

Dataset	$\mathcal{D}_{test}$	Ensemble			Mean		
		Robust	Uncertain	Non Robust	Robust	Uncertain	Non Robust
beans	500	74.6%	7.2%	18.2%	93.0%	2.2%	4.8%
cancer	50	62.0%	12.0%	26.0%	100.0%	0.0%	0.0%
mushroom	400	0.0%	1.2%	98.8%	0.0%	0.0%	100.0%
white wine	200	7.5%	26.5%	66.0%	56.5%	11.0%	32.5%
adult	1000	63.4%	7.1%	29.5%	72.6%	7.3%	20.1%
bank	1000	65.2%	7.1%	27.7%	44.6%	16.4%	39.0%
heloc	500	62.8%	9.2%	28.0%	60.6%	14.0%	25.4%
ocean	10000	79.1%	5.6%	15.3%	53.5%	16.0%	30.5%

manifold, mimicking the effects of non-adversarial perturbations. This reflects into larger average robustness over the test set of the latter neighbourhood over the random one, validating that the robustness estimator with the ensemble consistently satisfies Property 4. The same property is satisfied also by the mean aggregation and the individual XAI methods when tested individually.

Table 1 presents the classification of the test set into robust, uncertain and non robust datapoints (as per Subsect. 4.4). For comparability, we set $r_{th} = 0.80$ for all datasets and both aggregation methods, even if the ensemble often requires lower values of r_{th} compared to the mean (see Appendix A). Medoid-based neighbourhoods were used, as it was shown in Fig. 3 that they produce larger robustness scores.

For almost all the datasets, robust datapoints are the majority, with the exception of the `white wine` dataset with the ensemble and `mushroom` dataset with both aggregations. This is due to the selection of the threshold value equal for all datasets, as carefully selected dataset-specific thresholds would be lower than 0.80. The percentages of uncertain and non robust datapoints are non-negligible. In particular, we consider uncertain datapoints to be the most interesting ones to investigate. They represent areas of the feature space where the robustness estimation is uncertain (as per Property 3) and should be carefully considered during a practical evaluation.

In Fig. 4 we present a two dimensional visualization of the UMAP [18] projections of the validation set $\mathcal{D}_{valid}$, clustered with HDBSCAN algorithm [17], where each cluster is coloured by its mean robustness score. UMAP is a dimensionality reduction technique that allows us to visualize a lower dimensional projection of the data. We applied the density-based clustering algorithm HDBSCAN to such projections, producing clusters without the need of setting hyperparameters for the desired number of clusters, as in k-means for example. As can be seen in the figure, the projected data space may be more or less complex according to the dataset being analysed. Robustness homogeneity within the derived clusters

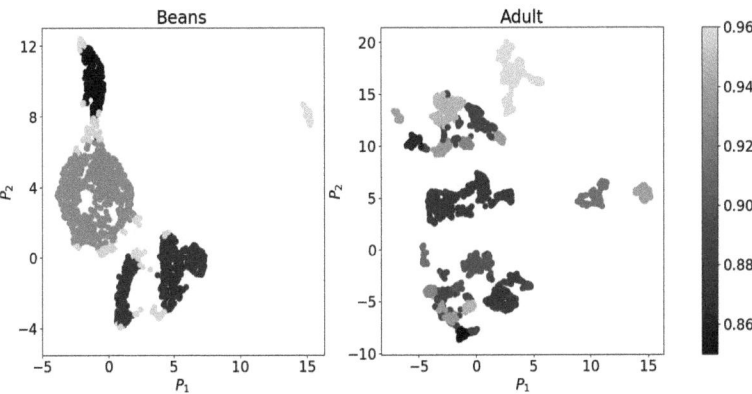

Fig. 4. HDBSCAN clusters, coloured by mean robustness scores, over the two dimensional UMAP projections (P_1, P_2): **beans** dataset (left) and **adult** dataset (right).

Table 2. Comparison of ensemble's robustness classification (with $r_{th} = 0.80$) according to Model 1,2,3 concordance in the prediction.

Dataset	Robust			Non Robust		
	Agree	Disagree	N. points	Agree	Disagree	N. points
beans	95.35%	4.65%	409	95.60%	4.40%	91
cancer	91.89%	8.11%	37	92.31%	7.69%	13
mushroom	100.00%	0.00%	5	100.00%	0.00%	395
white wine	94.11%	5.88%	68	92.42%	7.58%	132
adult	93.76%	6.24%	705	80.68%	19.32%	295
bank	95.99%	4.01%	723	90.25%	9.75%	277
heloc	82.22%	17.78%	360	56.43%	43.57%	140
ocean	85.21%	14.8%	8475	80.33%	19.67%	1525

support the claims of Property 2, in which close points are expected to exhibit smaller differences between their robustness scores. This allows us to support the use of the $k$nn regressor to estimate local robustness scores as points are naturally grouped in clusters with similar robustness scores.

As introduced in Subsect. 4.6, the validation of robustness estimations is subject to the lack of a ground truth. Table 2 shows how the percentage of points over which the three models (Model 1, 2 and 3) (dis)agree varies according to the predicted robustness of the datapoints, with $r_{th} = 0.80$ for all datasets. The ensemble robustness is computed with the medoid-based neighbourhood. Note that the **mushroom** dataset is a particular case, as all three methods reach 100% accuracy and are, therefore, always agreeing. It can be seen that the percentage of disagreeing points within the non-robust ones is, for most datasets, greater than that of the robust ones. This supports our validation proposal, as we consider

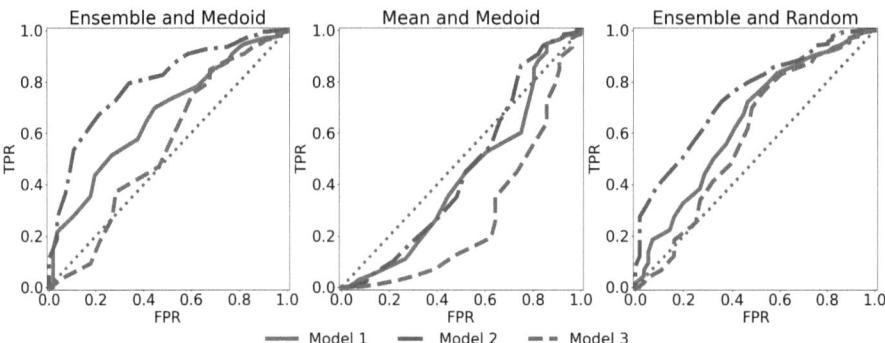

Fig. 5. ROC curves on the **bank** dataset with ensemble aggregation and medoid-based neighbourhood (left), mean aggregation and medoid-based neighbourhood (centre) and ensemble aggregation with random neighbourhood (right). The gray dotted line represents the bisecting line.

Table 3. Average AUC value of Model 1, 2, 3 for both aggregation types and neighbourhoods. For each dataset, the largest average AUC is presented in bold.

	Medoid		Random	
Dataset	Ensemble	Mean	Ensemble	Mean
beans	**0.5711**	0.4854	0.4842	0.4067
cancer	0.7346	**0.7400**	0.6766	0.6612
mushroom	0.0000	0.0000	0.0000	0.0000
white wine	0.4762	0.5931	0.4819	**0.6614**
adult	0.7018	0.6695	**0.8284**	0.8077
bank	**0.6670**	0.3883	0.6612	0.4696
heloc	0.6640	**0.6673**	0.6262	0.5875
ocean	**0.5194**	0.5128	0.4350	0.4053

the disagreement in the predictions to be a symptom of non robustness, as per Property 6.

The ROC/AUC analysis presented in Subsect. 4.6 allows us to jointly consider the aggregation method and the neighbourhood generation scheme which better fit the dataset at hand. Figure 5 depicts the ROC curves of the three models in varying scenarios: Model 2 is consistently associated with the highest ROC curve, suggesting that, for the **bank** dataset, a deeper net is better able to propose robust explanations. Moreover, the ROC curves are preferable for all three models with the ensemble aggregation and the medoid-based neighbourhood, while the mean aggregation (as shown in the central plot) presents ROC curves even below the bisecting line.

This is further confirmed by the results presented in Table 3, where the average AUC is computed for the four possible combinations of aggregation method and neighbourhood generation. The dataset-wise maximum values of AUC are presented in bold, showing how the ensemble is, on average, preferable with respect to the mean aggregation and how the medoid-based neighbourhood is related to larger AUC values in most examples. The `mushroom` dataset represents, as in Table 2, a peculiar case: having only agreeing datapoints the ROC and AUC cannot be computed and are therefore exempt from this analysis.

6 Conclusions and Future Work

We presented a novel framework to test explanation robustness, introducing a new neighbourhood generation mechanism, an ensemble approach to merging explanations and a validation test. We have shown that our robustness estimator satisfies the *desiderata* 1-6 and it overcomes the limitations of other metrics (Sect. 2). In practical applications, our approach would aid practitioners in understanding the quality of an explanation in terms of its robustness, allowing questioning on the proposed results when the framework flags a datapoint as *uncertain*.

We have proposed our work targeting neural networks, but the approach is agnostic in nature with respect to both the investigated model and the XAI techniques being applied. Future steps include a first generalization of the proposal on different classes of machine learning models, such as tree-based ones, assuming that local feature importance approaches are available for testing. Future work will also aim at better investigating the relationship between robustness and adversarial attacks. In particular, we aim at assessing the defence ability of our ensemble - as aggregated explanations have proved to be more resilient to adversarial attacks in numerous contexts - and to validate whether our robustness estimator is able to detect attacks. Lastly, we wish to investigate how our explanations could be used to increase the robustness of classifiers, as in [22].

Acknowledgments. This study was partially carried out within the PNRR research activities of the consortium iNEST funded by the European Union Next-GenerationEU (PNRR, Missione 4 Componente 2, Investimento 1.5âĂŞ D.D. 1058 23/06/2022, ECS 00000043).

Disclosure of Interests. The authors have no competing interests to declare that are relevant to the content of this article.

A Dataset Description and Hyperparameters

Table 4. Dataset description and model accuracy.

Dataset	Dataset details							Accuracy (%) - $\mathcal{D}_{train}$		
	Classes	#Num	#Cat	$\mathcal{D}_{train}$	$\mathcal{D}_{valid}$	$\mathcal{D}_{test}$	$k_{medoids}$	Model 1	Model 2	Model 3
beans	7	7	0	10888	2223	500	225	93.41	93.44	89.47
cancer	2	15	0	397	121	50	10	99.5	99.75	99.24
mushroom	2	0	21	6498	1225	400	120	100.00	100.00	100.00
white wine	2	9	0	3918	780	200	80	89.23	89.10	86.55
adult	2	5	7	36177	8045	1000	1000	91.39	91.38	91.09
bank	2	5	9	36168	8043	1000	1000	91.99	91.76	91.45
heloc	2	14	2	8367	1592	500	130	85.50	85.57	85.01
ocean	6	8	0	109259	30328	10000	3000	92.04	87.88	92.27

Table 5. Dataset-specific hyperparameter selection.

	$\mathcal{N}_M$									$\mathcal{N}_R$			
	Neighbourhood			Ensemble		Mean				Neighbourhood		Ensemble	Mean
Dataset	α	α_{cat}	k_M	k_R	r_{th}	k_R	r_{th}	σ	γ_{cat}	k_R	r_{th}	k_R	$r_{th}-$
beans	0.10	–	10	9	0.85	9	0.90	0.02	–	5	0.75	7	0.80
cancer	0.10	–	4	11	0.85	9	0.90	0.10	–	5	0.55	7	0.65
mushroom	–	0.15	10	7	0.70	11	0.60	–	0.15	9	0.70	11	0.60
white wine	0.15	–	5	11	0.85	7	0.80	0.03	–	9	0.45	7	0.65
adult	0.05	0.05	5	9	0.80	9	0.80	0.05	0.05	5	0.70	5	0.70
bank	0.05	0.10	5	7	0.80	11	0.80	0.05	0.10	7	0.75	9	0.75
heloc	0.05	0.05	5	15	0.80	13	0.80	0.03	0.10	11	0.45	5	0.60
ocean	0.05	–	5	5	0.65	5	0.75	0.001	–	5	0.75	5	0.65

References

1. Adadi, A., Berrada, M.: Peeking inside the black-box: a survey on explainable artificial intelligence (xai). IEEE Access **6**, 52138–52160 (2018). https://doi.org/10.1109/ACCESS.2018.2870052
2. Alvarez-Melis, D., Jaakkola, T.: On the robustness of interpretability methods (June 2018). https://doi.org/10.48550/arXiv.1806.08049
3. Alvarez-Melis, D., Jaakkola, T.S.: Towards robust interpretability with self-explaining neural networks. In: Proceedings of the 32nd International Conference on Neural Information Processing Systems, NIPS 2018, pp. 7786–7795. Curran Associates Inc., Red Hook (2018). https://hdl.handle.net/1721.1/137669

4. Anders, C., Pasliev, P., Dombrowski, A.K., Müller, K.R., Kessel, P.: Fairwashing explanations with off-manifold detergent. In: III, H.D., Singh, A. (eds.) Proceedings of the 37th International Conference on Machine Learning. Proceedings of Machine Learning Research, 13–18 Jul, vol. 119, pp. 314–323. PMLR (2020), https://proceedings.mlr.press/v119/anders20a.html
5. Bach, S., Binder, A., Montavon, G., Klauschen, F., Müller, K.R., Samek, W.: On pixel-wise explanations for non-linear classifier decisions by layer-wise relevance propagation. PLoS ONE **10(7)** (2015). https://doi.org/10.1371/journal.pone.0130140
6. Baniecki, H., Biecek, P.: Adversarial attacks and defenses in explainable artificial intelligence: a survey. Inform. Fusion **107**, 102303 (2024). https://doi.org/10.1016/j.inffus.2024.102303
7. Bhatt, U., Weller, A., Moura, J.M.F.: Evaluating and aggregating feature-based model explanations. In: Proceedings of the Twenty-Ninth International Joint Conference on Artificial Intelligence, IJCAI 2020 (2021). https://dl.acm.org/doi/abs/10.5555/3491440.3491857
8. Dimanov, B., Bhatt, U., Jamnik, M., Weller, A.: You shouldn't trust me: learning models which conceal unfairness from multiple explanation methods. In: ECAI 2020 - 24th European Conference on Artificial Intelligence, 29 August-8 September 2020, Santiago de Compostela, Spain, - Including 10th Conference on Prestigious Applications of Artificial Intelligence (PAIS 2020). Frontiers in Artificial Intelligence and Applications, vol. 325, pp. 2473–2480. IOS Press (2020). https://doi.org/10.3233/FAIA200380
9. European Commission: Regulation (EU) 2016/679 of the European Parliament and of the Council of 27 April 2016 on the protection of natural persons with regard to the processing of personal data and on the free movement of such data, and repealing Directive 95/46/EC (General Data Protection Regulation) (Text with EEA relevance) (2016). https://eur-lex.europa.eu/eli/reg/2016/679/oj
10. European Commission: Proposal for a Regulation of the European Parliament and of the Council laying down harmonised rules on artificial intelligence (Artificial Intelligence Act) and amending certain union legislative acts (COM(2021) 206 final) (2021). https://eur-lex.europa.eu/legal-content/EN/TXT/?uri=celex%3A52021PC0206
11. Ghorbani, A., Abid, A., Zou, J.: Interpretation of neural networks is fragile. In: Proceedings of the AAAI Conference on Artificial Intelligence, vol. 33(01), pp. 3681–3688 (2019). https://doi.org/10.1609/aaai.v33i01.33013681
12. Gosiewska, A., Biecek, P.: Do not trust additive explanations. arXiv: Learning (2019). https://doi.org/10.48550/arXiv.1903.11420
13. Kantz, B., et al.: Robustness of explainable artificial intelligence in industrial process modelling. In: ICML 2024 Workshop ML for Life and Material Science: From Theory to Industry Applications (2024). https://doi.org/10.48550/arXiv.2407.09127
14. Krishna, S., Han, T., Gu, A., Wu, S., Jabbari, S., Lakkaraju, H.: The disagreement problem in explainable machine learning: A practitioner's perspective. Trans. Mach. Learn. Res. (2024). https://doi.org/10.21203/rs.3.rs-2963888/v1
15. Lakkaraju, H., Arsov, N., Bastani, O.: Robust and stable black box explanations. In: Proceedings of the 37th International Conference on Machine Learning, ICML 2020, JMLR.org (2020). https://proceedings.mlr.press/v119/lakkaraju20a/lakkaraju20a.pdf

16. Lundberg, S.M., Lee, S.I.: A unified approach to interpreting model predictions. Adv. Neural Inform. Process. Sys. **2017**, 4766—-4775 (2017). https://dl.acm.org/doi/10.5555/3295222.3295230
17. Malzer, C., Baum, M.: A hybrid approach to hierarchical density-based cluster selection. In: 2020 IEEE International Conference on Multisensor Fusion and Integration for Intelligent Systems (MFI), pp. 223–228 (2020). https://doi.org/10.1109/MFI49285.2020.9235263
18. McInnes, L., Healy, J., Saul, N., Großberger, L.: Umap: uniform manifold approximation and projection. J. Open Source Softw. **3**(29), 861 (2018). https://doi.org/10.21105/joss.00861
19. Mishra, S., Dutta, S., Long, J., Magazzeni, D.: A survey on the robustness of feature importance and counterfactual explanations (2023). https://arxiv.org/abs/2111.00358
20. Nauta, M., et al.: From anecdotal evidence to quantitative evaluation methods: a systematic review on evaluating explainable ai. ACM Comput. Surv. **55**(13s), 1–42 (2023). https://doi.org/10.1145/3583558
21. Pawelczyk, M., Broelemann, K., Kasneci, G.: Learning model-agnostic counterfactual explanations for tabular data. In: Proceedings of The Web Conference, WWW 2020, p. 3126–3132. Association for Computing Machinery, New York (2020). https://doi.org/10.1145/3366423.3380087
22. Rasouli, P., Yu, I.C.: Analyzing and improving the robustness of tabular classifiers using counterfactual explanations. In: 2021 20th IEEE International Conference on Machine Learning and Applications (ICMLA), pp. 1286–1293 (2021). https://doi.org/10.1109/ICMLA52953.2021.00209
23. Ribeiro, M.T., Singh, S., Guestrin, C.: "Why should i trust you?" explaining the predictions of any classifier. In: NAACL-HLT 2016 - 2016 Conference of the North American Chapter of the Association for Computational Linguistics: Human Language Technologies, Proceedings of the Demonstrations Session, pp. 97—-101 (2016). https://doi.org/10.18653/v1/n16-3020
24. Rieger, L., Hansen, L.K.: A simple defense against adversarial attacks on heatmap explanations (2020). https://arxiv.org/abs/2007.06381
25. Rosenfeld, A.: Better metrics for evaluating explainable artificial intelligence. In: Proceedings of the International Joint Conference on Autonomous Agents and Multiagent Systems, AAMAS. vol. 1, pp. 45–50 (2021). https://dl.acm.org/doi/abs/10.5555/3463952.3463962
26. Samek, W., Montavon, G., Lapuschkin, S., Anders, C.J., Müller, K.R.: Explaining deep neural networks and beyond: a review of methods and applications. Proc. IEEE **109**(3), 247–278 (2021). https://doi.org/10.1109/JPROC.2021.3060483
27. Shrikumar, A., Greenside, P., Kundaje, A.: Learning important features through propagating activation differences. In: 34th International Conference on Machine Learning, ICML 2017, vol. 7, pp. 4844–4866 (2017). https://dl.acm.org/doi/10.5555/3305890.3306006
28. Slack, D., Hilgard, S., Jia, E., Singh, S., Lakkaraju, H.: Fooling lime and shap: adversarial attacks on post hoc explanation methods. In: AIES 2020 - Proceedings of the AAAI/ACM Conference on AI, Ethics, and Society, p p. 180–186 (2020). https://doi.org/10.1145/3375627.3375830
29. Sonnewald, M., Lguensat, R.: Revealing the impact of global heating on north atlantic circulation using transparent machine learning. J. Adv. Model. Earth Syst. **13** (2021). https://doi.org/10.1029/2021MS002496

30. Sundararajan, M., Taly, A., Yan, Q.: Axiomatic attribution for deep networks. In: 34th International Conference on Machine Learning, ICML 2017 **7**, 5109–5118 (2017). https://dl.acm.org/doi/10.5555/3305890.3306024
31. The White House: Blueprint for an AI Bill of Rights: Making Automated Systems Work for the American People (2022). https://www.whitehouse.gov/ostp/ai-bill-of-rights/

Open Access This chapter is licensed under the terms of the Creative Commons Attribution 4.0 International License (http://creativecommons.org/licenses/by/4.0/), which permits use, sharing, adaptation, distribution and reproduction in any medium or format, as long as you give appropriate credit to the original author(s) and the source, provide a link to the Creative Commons license and indicate if changes were made.

The images or other third party material in this chapter are included in the chapter's Creative Commons license, unless indicated otherwise in a credit line to the material. If material is not included in the chapter's Creative Commons license and your intended use is not permitted by statutory regulation or exceeds the permitted use, you will need to obtain permission directly from the copyright holder.

XAIEV – A Framework for the Evaluation of XAI-Algorithms for Image Classification

Carsten Knoll[1]($\boxtimes$), Julian Ullrich[2], Thomas Manjooran[1], Kilian Göller[1], Haadia Amjad[1], Ronald Tetzlaff[1], and Steffen Seitz[1]

[1] Fundamentals of Electrical Engineering, TUD Dresden University of Technology, Dresden, Germany
{carsten.knoll,thomas.manjooran,kilian.goler,haadia.amjad,
ronald.tetzlaff,steffen.seitz}@tu-dresden.de
[2] Faculty of Mathematics and Natural Sciences – Institute of Computer Science, Heinrich Heine University Düsseldorf, Düsseldorf, Germany

Abstract. Convolutional Neural Networks (CNNs), such as VGG and ResNet, have been widely used for image classification for several years. Numerous explainable AI (XAI) algorithms, including Grad-CAM and XRAI, have been proposed to enhance interpretability in this domain. However, a persistent challenge lies in quantitatively comparing different XAI algorithms, variants of the same algorithm, or combinations of CNN models and XAI algorithms. In this work, we introduce XAIEV – a versatile framework for computationally evaluating the quality of saliency-map-based XAI algorithms. This framework includes (A) a benchmark dataset (traffic sign recognition) with a known ground truth and (B) a software toolbox designed to facilitate the evaluation pipeline. The pipeline consists of four steps: (1) model training, (2) applying XAI algorithms to generate weighted saliency maps, (3) generating new test images with varying percentages of "important" pixels removed or retained, and (4) statistically evaluating accuracy changes on these test images and comparison to the ground truth. Based on this statistical evaluation, we define an Accuracy-Sensitivity Quotient (ASQ) as a novel quality metric for XAI algorithms applied to image classification. Using the XAIEV framework, we compare various combinations of CNN architectures ("SimpleCNN" (custom model), VGG, ResNet, ConvNext) with multiple XAI algorithms (Grad-CAM, XRAI, LIME, PRISM). Our numerical results reveal that the performance of XAI algorithms is highly dependent on the underlying CNN model.

Keywords: XAI-evaluation · CNN · Image Classification · Quality Metric · Accuracy Sensitivity Quotient

1 Introduction

Along with the success of deep neural networks (DNN) in the field of image classification there is a growing interest in explaining the outputs of such models.

Since more than a decade (as of 2025) researchers have proposed a multitude of "explainable artificial intelligence" (XAI) methods to cater this need, see e. g. [14, 20] and the references therein. These methods typically yield "explanations" in the form of suitable visualizations which are often superimposed on the original image in order to make the classification process comprehensible for humans. An illustrative example (taken from [18]) is that a dysfunctional Wolf-vs-Husky classifier could be uncovered by using XAI: The classifier achieved good accuracy on the test set but actually (due to missing variability in the dataset from which both train and test split were taken) learned to associate snow-related features with the "wolf"-class. As the XAI method highlights mainly the snowy areas on the (correctly classified) wolf-pictures a human can then easily recognize the trained model as flawed.

The development of these various XAI methods, however, raised the issue of how to objectively measure and compare the performance of those different methods or even of one method with different parametrizations. In principle there are two different types of approaches: a) human-based evaluation (i. e. user studies) and b) algorithmic evaluation.

Because *explainability* is a human-oriented objective the first category of approaches is obviously reasonable, see e. g. [14]. However, user studies also have some disadvantages: They require considerable effort to prepare, conduct and evaluate and additionally rely on (many) voluntary participants spending their time which is a limited and costly resource. Additionally, the results of those studies might be systematically influenced by the selection of those participants.

Thus, algorithmic evaluation methods are desirable to provide fast and cost-efficient quantification of XAI performance, at least as a complement to user studies.

However, designing and implementing such evaluation methods comes with its own challenges: Different XAI methods produce different kinds of results which are nontrivial to compare and an objective ground truth does not exist. Also, there are degrees of freedom (design parameters) with a certain range of plausible values, which nevertheless affects the resulting performance score. Furthermore, it should be noted that the suitability of an XAI method might depend on the downstream task [7], which justifies the existence of various XAI methods as well as evaluation methods and metrics. Previously presented evaluation metrics include e. g. [1,2,6,11].

In this contribution we present the XAI evaluation framework XAIEV [10] which focuses on simplicity w. r. t. understandability, usability and reproducibility, to ease algorithmic evaluation and to facilitate comparative studies. This framework allows to algorithmically generate a quantitative performance metric (so-called Accuracy-Sensitivity Quotient, ASQ) for combinations of a trained Convolutional Neural Networks (CNNs) model and a XAI-method. This score is based on how much the classification accuracy changes if different quantities of importance-ranked pixels (according to the saliency map produced by the respective XAI-method) are occluded or revealed. To eliminate the influence of the input data, the framework includes a dataset tailored to the evaluation task.

Note that, while drawing inspiration from earlier occlusion-sensitivity based approaches such as [28] our approach has a different goal: We use occlusion (and revelation) based on the importance values of XAI saliency maps to *evaluate* them, whereas that method uses a sliding occlusion window to *generate* a saliency map.

2 Material and Methods

2.1 XAI Methods

In this study we consider four different XAI methods: Grad-CAM, XRAI, LIME and PRISM. However, it should be noted that due to the modular structure of the XAIEV framework further methods could be added straightforwardly, provided they are compatible with the used classification models.

Grad-CAM. The Grad-CAM [21] method is a generalization of the CAM algorithm [29]. It extracts localization information for features from the last *convolutional* layer in a network. Thereby Grad-CAM is able to operate on CNNs, which do not meet the special requirements set by CAM for the structure of the classification head: It uses the gradients of the feature maps of the final convolutional layer with respect to the desired output class as weights. The outcome is a saliency map with the dimensions of the original image. Due to upsampling the important pixels form relatively large connected regions.

XRAI. The XRAI method proposed by [9] is based on the Integrated Gradients (IG) method introduced by [23]. Among other features it addresses a major issue of IG-generated saliency maps: They usually contain scattered important pixels with neighboring seemingly unimportant pixels, making the output less interpretable for humans and harder to compare to other XAI methods [15].

Thus, XRAI uses precomputed segments of the input image generated by the Felzenszwalb's segmentation algorithm [4]. In particular, using six different parameter settings a so-called oversegmentation is produced, where a singular pixel in the original image is part of multiple segments.

Importance values are given to each segment by calculating the mean attribution value for the contained pixels with IG. The segment with the highest value is moved to a separate list, and its pixels are excluded from other segments. This process repeats, ranking segments by importance until the entire image is covered. The ranked segments are then combined into a weighted heatmap using their mean attribution values.

LIME. The LIME-method ("Local Interpretable Model-agnostic Explanations") proposed by [18] uses perturbations of the input data to explore the behavior of the model for a certain local area. When applied to CNNs, so-called super-pixel segments, which are essentially larger areas of the input image, are perturbed.

The perturbed instances are fed into the CNN to receive the outputs. Using these outputs, a new interpretable model (sparse linear classifier as suggested in [18]) is trained with the goal of approximating the behavior of the CNN for each image. The importance of the regions/super-pixels in the original input image can directly be derived from the weights of the sparse linear classifier. This allows for a ranking of the features.

To use the results for the comparisons, a heatmap is derived using only the most important feature. Thus, this variant of LIME only highlights the feature and does not include any weighting within the important/unimportant area. This results in a binary heatmap which, in the context of this study smoothened in order to achieve a gray scale saliency map.

PRISM. Principal Image Sections Mapping (PRISM) unlike many other methods does not depend on backpropagation [25]. PRISM, similar to Grad-CAM, assumes that the features in the final convolutional layer have a high spatial correlation to relevant areas in the input image. PRISM derives its importance heatmap, by performing Principal Component Analysis (PCA) for the last convolutional layer, which for this purpose has to be reshaped from 4D to 2D.

The PCA results are truncated to the three most important components and reshaped to the original spatial dimensions (batchsize, height and width). These three channels are now considered as the color channels of an RGB-image. As final step upsampling is achieved with so-called Gradual Extrapolation [24].

PRISM thus produces an RGB image which mostly contains gray base color, where important regions can visually be identified by a bright saturated color. To extract a 2D saliency map for comparison with the other XAI-methods, the gray base color is subtracted and the highest value of the three channels is selected as the importance value of a pixel.

2.2 CNN Models

In this study we investigate the different XAI Methods for four different CNN models. Although in recent times transformer-based classification models such as Swin Transfomer [12] are considered state of the art CNNs remain widely used for various reasons: They typically have fewer parameters and require less computational resources for training and inference [13]. Also, they perform better when training data is scarce, while transformers require larger datasets to achieve comparable or superior results [17]. Additionally, due to their longer existence, they are better covered by XAI literature.

As for the XAI methods due to the modular structure of the XAIEV framework further CNN models could be added straightforwardly.

Simple CNN. The "Simple CNN" is a custom model by the authors, designed to allow observations of XAI methods on basic building blocks. It starts with a 7×7 convolutional layer (stride 2) that reduces spatial dimensions while increasing channels from 3 to 32. This is followed by a 3×3 convolution, increasing filters to 64. A max pooling layer reduces spatial dimensions to 55 × 55, followed by two more 3×3 convolutional layers, increasing channels to 128 and 256 respectively. The single max pooling layer maintains larger feature maps, which could be interesting for XAI methods deriving heatmaps from the last convolutional layer. ReLU activation is applied after each convolutional layer. The model ends with Global Average Pooling, creating a 1 × 256 feature vector mapped to 19 classes. To combat overfitting, Batch Normalization is applied after every convolutional layer, and 25% dropout before the global average pooling. This simple architecture was iteratively developed to achieve over 90% training accuracy while maintaining good generalization.

VGG. The VGG architecture proposed by [22] over a decade ago is still very popular today. While its accuracy on the ImageNet benchmark is not as good as that of more recent models, VGG16 (also used in this study) still achieves state of the art performance on other datasets, for example outperforming many more recent CNN designs on the InDL [26] dataset, while matching the performance of ConvNeXt.

Despite being a much deeper network with a large amount of parameters as compared to the proposed Simple CNN, it still consists of very basic building blocks, utilizing only simple convolutional filters, the ReLU activation function and max-pooling layers for the feature extraction.

ResNet. Residual Networks (ResNets) were proposed in [5] and introduced so-called "residual connections" (also: "shortcut connections"). These consist of a signal path which adds the input of a block (typically comprising two or three convolutional layers) directly to its output. The input-output-relation of such a "residual block" is thus $y = x + f(x)$ instead of the usual $y = f(x)$, which significantly improves the gradient flow and thus alleviates the problem of vanishing gradients during the training of very deep CNNs. In this study the ResNet50 is used. It offers a reasonable trade-off in terms of computational demand and performance which makes it a popular choice in the field of XAI [20].

ConvNeXt. The ConvNeXt architecture, proposed by [13], is based on ResNet but updated in several aspects inspired by the Swin Transformer [12] design and training methodology. In particular these updates include modified block designs, larger kernels sizes, GeLU instead of ReLU activation functions, replacing batch normalization by layer normalization and using so-called LayerScale regularization during the training. With this architecture, [13] showed that a model consisting only of classical CNN components can compete with state of the art Transfomer architectures. In this study the "ConvNeXt-Tiny" variant is used.

2.3 Augmented Traffic Sign Dataset (ATSDS): Dataset Creation and Properties

Large and well designed datasets like ImageNet [3] have been very important for the progress made in the field of computer vision. However, such diverse datasets are not optimally suited for our study because their images often contain many relevant features with varying degree of importance that are distributed over multiple locations.

For a given input image we expect the XAI algorithm to identify those pixels which are decisive for the classification of the image by a chosen CNN model. Thus, we require the dataset images to have a clearly distinguishable "important area" whose size is limited and similar across the whole dataset[1]. To perform sanity checks of the XAI results, the dataset should contain annotations of the exact position of that important area (i. e. partial image segmentation). Furthermore, each image should include a "natural substitution background" which can be used to (partially) replace the important area in occlusion and revelation scenarios (see Sect. 2.4). Finally, the dataset should be simple enough to allow the chosen CNN models to achieve classification accuracy close to 100% in order to rule out incorrect assignments caused by a poor model as far as possible.

To meet these characteristics we decided to artificially generate a new dataset taylored to the task of evaluating saliency-map based XAI algorithms: the **"Augmented Traffic Sign Dataset" (ATSDS)** as follows: From the over 60K Google Street View images published along with [27] depicting urban road traffic infrastructure, we randomly chose 9500 and cropped them to a size of 512×512. From the "German Traffic Sign Detection Benchmark" [8] we chose those 19 classes for which at least 500 distinct images are available and from these classes we chose the first 500 images. For each of them we produced a cutout patch by using the available bounding box annotation and the known shape of the respective traffic sign (round, triangular, etc.). Finally each patch was overlayed on top of one of the 9500 background images at a random position (with sufficient margin to prevent protruding). The patch position was saved as a binary mask which enables to access the *initial background pixels* of the classification-relevant area – i. e. the overlayed traffic sign – for the occlusion-based evaluation (see Sect. 2.4). Figure 1 shows some random examples of this dataset. In total it consists of 9500 images, divided into 19 classes each with a train-test-split of 450:50.

2.4 XAI-Evaluation: Incrementally (Un)Occluded Test Images

The actual evaluation of a combination of an XAI algorithm and a CNN model is performed in four steps (summarized in Fig. 2).

Step (1) consists of training the chosen CNN model on the ATSDS. In **step (2)** for each image of the dataset the XAI method is applied to generate

---

[1] This is motivated by our earlier observations [15,16] where saliency map generating XAI methods performed well on image classes like "lighthouse" or "windmill" whereas the saliency maps for image classes like "dining room" or "desert" are less plausible.

Fig. 1. ATSDS example images for four (out of 19) classes.

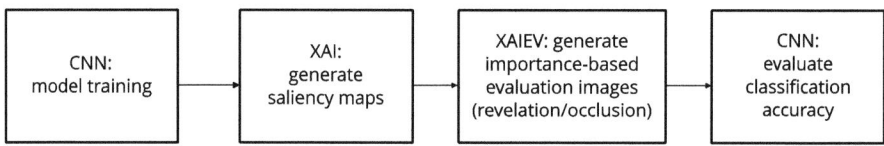

Fig. 2. XAIEV evaluation pipeline.

a saliency map (sometimes also called "heatmap" [19]). This 2D array has the same resolution as the input images i. e. 512×512 and associates an "importance value" $i(x,y) \in [0,1]$ to each pixel (with coordinates x,y)[2].

Step (3): For each image of the dataset a series of 10 additional images is created, both for the *occlusion* and *revelation* method. More precisely, for every threshold value $T \in \{1\%, 2\%, \ldots 10\%\}$ a binary mask (2D array) $m_T(x,y) \in 0,1$ is created. Those pixels (x,y) of the map whose corresponding importance value is greater or equal to the $(1-T)$-quantile of the overall saliency map are assigned to 1, while all other pixels of the map are set to 0. With each of those 10 binary masks two evaluation images are generated: The occlusion-image consists of the original ATSDS-image but with the top T most important pixels replaced by the initial background pixels (see Sect. 2.3). On the other hand, the revelation-image consists of the whole initial background (before the traffic sign overlay) but with the top T most important pixels replaced by the original ATSDS-image.

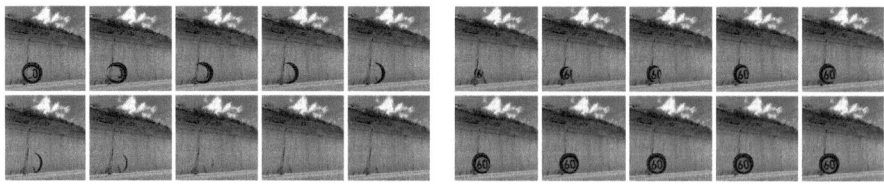

Fig. 3. Examples for the evaluation images for different values of T. Left: Occlusion. Right: Revelation.

---

[2] For Grad-CAM this saliency map is the direct result, for the other XAI-methods some post-processing such as Gaussian blur is necessary to obtain a comparable saliency map.

In **step (4)** the CNN model is applied to classify all of the evaluation-images from step (3). Thereby, the accuracy is calculated for a given threshold value T and for occlusion/revelation separately which results in two accuracy-sensitivity curves, $a_{oc}(T)$ and $a_{re}(T)$, like schematically depicted in Fig. 4. Qualitatively, a monotone dependency is to be expected because the occlusion of (presumably) relevant pixels should decrease the probability of correct classification for a single image and thus reduce the accuracy when classifying the whole dataset. An analogous consideration holds for the revelation case. Since the most relevant pixels are associated with low T-values, it is plausible that the curvature of the curves has the opposite sign of the slope. In other words: both curves start steep and then flatten out.

2.5 Proposed Metric: Accuracy-Sensitivity Quotient (ASQ)

Based on the accuracy-sensitivity curves from step (4) we can define the areas $A_{oc1}, A_{oc1}, A_{re1}, A_{re2}$ below and above the curves as shown in Fig. 4. Thereby, the left and right bounds of these areas are determined by the threshold values $T = 0$ and $T = T_{\max}$ (chosen to $T_{\max} = 10\%$). The upper and lower bounds of these areas are given by $a_{\max}$ (accuracy achieved on the unchanged ATSDS images) and $a_{\min}$ (inverse of the number of classes, i.e. accuracy achieved by randomly guessing).

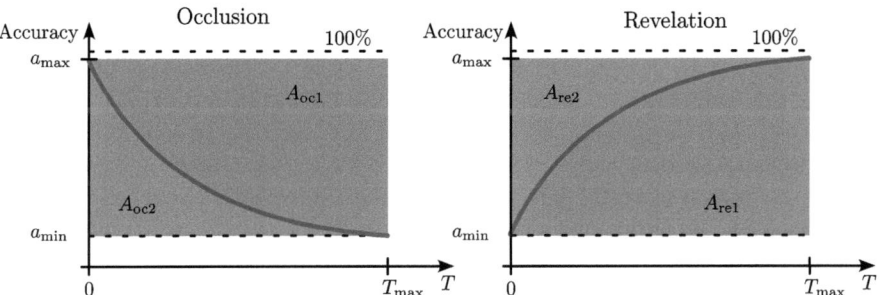

Fig. 4. Schematic depiction of expected accuracy curves (blue) in dependence of the importance threshold T. Left (occlusion): For $T = 0\%$ we have maximum accuracy, then it drops. Right (revelation): For $T = 0\%$ we have minimum accuracy (random guessing), then it rises. The colored areas below and above the curve are used to calculate the ASQ in Eq. (1) (Color figure online).

While these areas by themselves have no obvious interpretation, their share of the total colored area (for each respective diagram) has: The expression $\frac{A_{oc1}}{A_{oc1}+A_{oc2}} \in [0,1]$ represents the loss of accuracy due to occluding presumably relevant pixels while $\frac{A_{re1}}{A_{re1}+A_{re2}} \in [0,1]$ represents the gain of accuracy due to revealing those pixels. In both cases a higher number, i.e. closer to 1, means a higher sensitivity of the accuracy and thus a higher share of accuracy-relevant pixels which are occluded or revealed, respectively.

By symmetrically combining these two quantities we can now define the Accuracy-Sensitivity Quotient

$$\text{ASQ} := \frac{1}{2}\left(\frac{A_{\text{oc1}}}{A_{\text{oc1}} + A_{\text{oc2}}} + \frac{A_{\text{re1}}}{A_{\text{re1}} + A_{\text{re2}}}\right) \in [0,1] \qquad (1)$$

as a measure how much the classification accuracy changes if the important pixels (according to the chosen XAI method) are gradually revealed or occluded.

This formula follows the rationale that a good XAI method should identify those pixels as important which significantly influence the classification result. Thus, if the accuracy curve strongly depends on the importance threshold T the areas A_{oc1} and A_{re1} (both green) take up a large fraction of the total area which results in a high ASQ value.

2.6 Software Toolbox xaiev

While the individual steps of the evaluation pipeline described in Sect. 2.4 can be implemented without too much effort the total amount of work is still not negligible. To facilitate the quantitative evaluation of XAI methods, we preset xaiev, an easy-to-use Python toolbox, which provides the necessary evaluation infrastructure. It is available on github [10] and the Python package index.

The toolbox offers a simple command line interface with a main command for each of the pipeline steps, i.e. xaiev train, xaiev create-saliency-maps, xaiev create-eval-images and xaiev eval. This main command is followed by options such as --model simple_cnn_1_1 or --xai-method gradcam. The full range of commands and options is available via xaiev --help.

To facilitate the first steps for users of the toolbox is equipped with a --bootstrap command and an extensive README.md file. Also, the functioning of the system is ensured by deploying continuous integration which at the same time specifies a verified runtime environment and thus significantly supports the reproducibility of the results.

3 Results

According to step (1) the four CNN models from Sect. 2.2 where trained on the ATSDS dataset until achieving at least 97% accuracy on the test fraction (Simple CNN: 98.9%, VGG16: 99.3%, ResNet50: 98.6%, ConvNeXt Tiny: 97.7%).

After applying the other steps of the pipeline we obtain 32 accuracy-sensitivity curves which are displayed in Fig. 5. From those curves the ASQ-values for the 16 model-XAI-combinations are calculated according to (1), see Table 1.

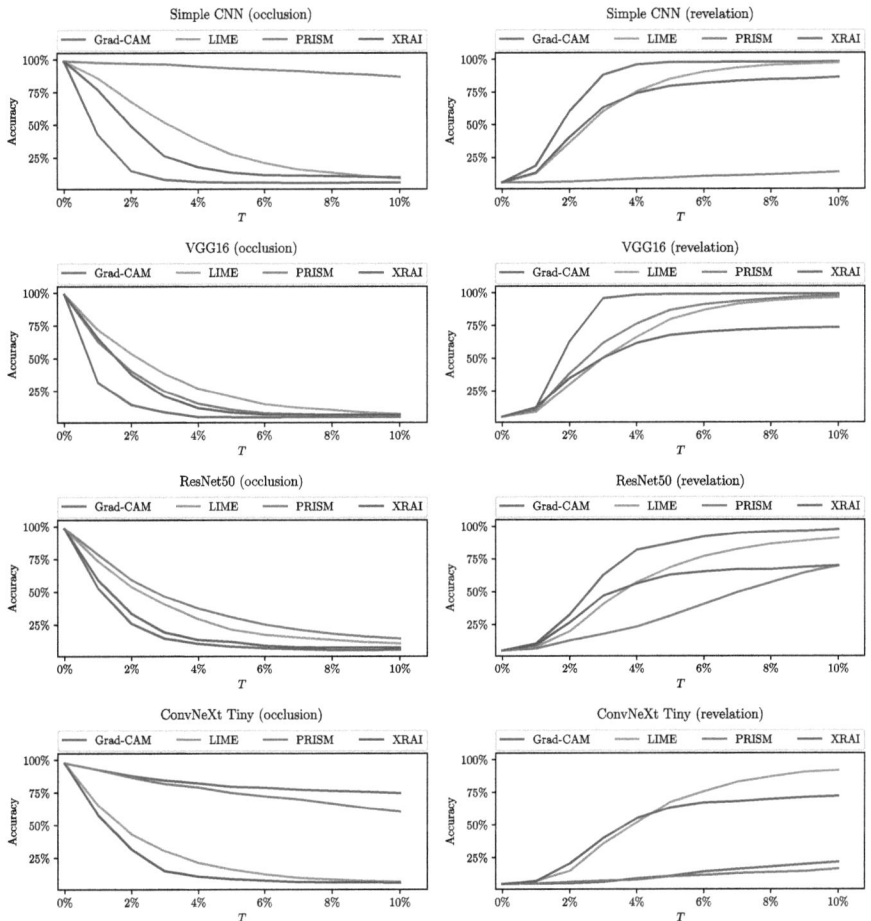

Fig. 5. Accuracy-Sensitivity curves for all CNN models and XAI-methods.

4 Discussion

The results from Sect. 3 allow for the following conclusions: (1) The classification accuracy in dependence of T behaves qualitatively as expected (cf. Fig. 4). (2) The exact shape of the curve strongly depends on the specific combination of CNN model and XAI method. (3) The proposed quantity ASQ seems to be a suitable scalar measure for the "quality" of the curves. (4) In most cases the revelation curves are similar to a flipped version of the occlusion curves. This is plausible because the relevant features of the ATSDS images are locally concentrated. However, for XRAI the revelation method results in significantly less

Table 1. Resulting ASQ values according to (1).

	Grad-CAM	LIME	PRISM	XRAI
Simple CNN	0.85	0.67	0.05	0.70
VGG16	0.86	0.68	0.75	0.67
ResNet50	0.78	0.63	0.47	0.65
ConvNeXt Tiny	0.12	0.66	0.14	0.66

accuracy dependency. Especially for higher T-values there is almost no additional accuracy gain. This means that those pixels whose importance value is in the top 90% to 95% of our XRAI saliency maps in average do not contain enough information to enable the correct classification of more images. On the other hand they do prevent correct classification if they are occluded together with the more important pixels.

Note that the focus of this work is the development of an easy to use algorithmic XAI *evaluation method* – not the evaluation of the used *XAI methods*. The latter would require a broader study where each XAI method should be investigated with different parameter settings and each model should be trained with different initializations.

Nevertheless, our results indicate that the ASQ-performance strongly depends on the used CNN model. This is noteworthy because all investigated XAI methods are "model-agnostic" but this obviously does not mean that they perform equally (w.r.t ASQ) on different CNNs.

5 Summary and Outlook

In this paper we presented a framework to evaluate the performance of saliency map generating XAI methods on CNNs. Apart from the theoretical background (cf. Sect. 2.4 – 2.6) the framework consist of a dedicated dataset and an open source toolbox [10].

For the future the availability of this framework significantly simplifies studies to answer e. g. the following research questions: How much does the XAI performance depend on the (random) initial weight distribution of a CNN? How does the training progress (i. e. test accuracy) influence ASQ? How sensitive is the XAI performance on changes to the model architecture or training process?[3]

Another interesting research direction is to compare ASQ-results to user studies and search for scenarios where it can serve as a proxy for such – or under which circumstances both approaches yield contradicting results. A related question is, how helpful a metric like ASQ is in selecting the adequate XAI method for a given task.

---

[3] This question is motivated by the observation that the ASQ value for Grad-CAM drastically improved when the so-called "Layer Scale"-regularization (used in [13]) is removed from the training process.

Finally, it should be stated that the XAIEV framework itself still bears significant potential for improvements, e. g. more XAI-methods, more datasets, more flexible configuration or more modularization. For example, currently it is an open question how generalizable the presented approach is when applied to more complex datasets.

Nevertheless, despite its imperfections we are convinced that sharing version 1.0 of the framework with the community is the right way to generate feedback and foster XAI research.

Acknowledgments. This study was partially supported by DFG (grant number TE257/37-1) and by the Konrad Zuse School for Embedded Composite Artificial Intelligence, SECAI (BMBF Project Nr. 57616814). We warmly thank Romy Müller and Timo Dickscheid for inspiring discussions during the preparation of this study. The authors gratefully acknowledge the computing time made available to them on the high-performance computer at the NHR Center of TU Dresden. This center is jointly supported by the Federal Ministry of Education and Research and the state governments participating in the NHR (https://www.nhr-verein.de/unsere-partner).

Disclosure of Interests. The authors have no competing interests to declare that are relevant to the content of this article.

References

1. Agarwal, C., et al.: OpenXAI: towards a transparent evaluation of post hoc model explanations. Adv. Neural. Inf. Process. Syst. **35**, 15784–15799 (2022)
2. Arras, L., Osman, A., Samek, W.: CLEVR-XAI: a benchmark dataset for the ground truth evaluation of neural network explanations. Inform. Fusion **81**, 14–40 (2022)
3. Deng, J., Dong, W., Socher, R., Li, L.-J., Li, K., Fei-Fei, L.: ImageNet: a large-scale hierarchical image database. In: 2009 IEEE Conference on Computer Vision and Pattern Recognition, pp. 248–255 (2009)
4. Felzenszwalb, P.F., Huttenlocher, D.P.: Efficient graph-based image segmentation. Inter. J. Comput. Vis. **59**(2), 167–181 (2004)
5. He, K., Zhang, X., Ren, S., Sun, J.: Deep Residual Learning for Image Recognition. CoRR arXiv: 1512.03385 (2015)
6. Hedström, A., et al.: Quantus: an explainable AI toolkit for responsible evaluation of neural network explanations and beyond. J. Mach. Learn. Res. **24**(34), 1–11 (2023)
7. Hesse, R., Schaub-Meyer, S., Roth, S.: Funnybirds: a synthetic vision dataset for a part-based analysis of explainable AI methods. In: Proceedings of the IEEE/CVF International Conference on Computer Vision, pp. 3981–3991 (2023)
8. Houben, S., Stallkamp, J., Salmen, J., Schlipsing, M., Igel, C.: Detection of traffic signs in real-world images: the german traffic sign detection benchmark. In: International Joint Conference on Neural Networks, vol. 1288 (2013)
9. Kapishnikov, A., Bolukbasi, T., Viégas, F., Terry, M.: XRAI: better attributions through regions. In: Proceedings of the IEEE/CVF International Conference on Computer Vision, pp. 4948–4957 (2019)

10. Knoll, C., Ullrich, J., Manjooran, T.: Framework for the Evaluation of XAI Algorithms (XAIEV) - Source Repository on GitHub (2025). https://github.com/cknoll/xaiev/
11. Kokhlikyan, N. et al.: Captum: A unified and generic model interpretability library for PyTorch. arXiv: 2009.07896 (2020)
12. Liu, Z. et al.: Swin Transformer: Hierarchical Vision Transformer using Shifted Windows. arXiv: 2103.14030 (2021)
13. Liu, Z., Mao, H., Wu, C.-Y., Feichtenhofer, C., Darrell, T., Xie, S.: A ConvNet for the 2020s. In: Proceedings of the IEEE/CVF Conference on Computer Vision and Pattern Recognition, pp. 11976–11986 (2022)
14. Müller, R.: How explainable AI affects human performance: a systematic review of the behavioural consequences of saliency maps. In: International Journal of Human–Computer Interaction, pp. 1–32 (2024)
15. Müller, R., Dürschmidt, M., Ullrich, J., Knoll, C., Weber, S., Seitz, S.: Do humans and convolutional neural networks attend to similar areas during scene classification: effects of task and image type. Appli. Sci. **14**(6) (2024)
16. Müller, R., Ullrich, M.T.J., Seitz, S., Knoll, C.: Interpretability is in the eye of the beholder: human versus artificial classification of image segments generated by humans versus XAI. Inter. J. Hum. Comput. Interact. **41**(4), 2371–2393 (2025)
17. Nanni, L., Loreggia, A., Barcellona, L., Ghidoni, S.: Building ensemble of deep networks: convolutional networks and transformers. IEEE Access **11**, 124962–124974 (2023)
18. Ribeiro, M. T., Singh, S., Guestrin, C.: Why Should I Trust You?": Explaining the Predictions of Any Classifier. arXiv: 1602.04938 (2016)
19. Samek, W., Binder, A., Montavon, G., Lapuschkin, S., Müller, K.-R.: Evaluating the visualization of what a deep neural network has learned. IEEE Trans. Neural Netw. Learn. Syst. **28**(11), 2660–2673 (2016)
20. Saranya, A., Subhashini, R.: A systematic review of explainable artificial intelligence models and applications: recent developments and future trends. Decision Analytics J. **7** (2023)
21. Selvaraju, R. R., Das, A., Vedantam, R., Cogswell, M., Parikh, D., Batra, D.: Grad-CAM: Why did you say that? Visual Explanations from Deep Networks via Gradient-based Localization. arXiv: 1610.02391 (2016)
22. Simonyan, K., Zisserman, A.: Very Deep Convolutional Networks for Large- Scale Image Recognition. arXiv: 1409.1556 (2014)
23. Sundararajan, M., Taly, A., Yan, Q.: Axiomatic Attribution for Deep Networks, arXiv: 1703.01365 (2017)
24. Szandaa, T.: Enhancing Deep Neural Network Saliency Visualizations with Gradual Extrapolation. arXiv: 2104.04945 (2021)
25. Szandaa, T., Maciejewski, H.: PRISM: principal image sections mapping. In: Groen, D., de Mulatier, C., Paszynski, M., Krzhizhanovskaya, V.V., Dongarra, J.J., Sloot, P.M.A. (eds.) Computational Science – ICCS 2022, pp. 749–760. Springer International Publishing, Cham (2022). https://doi.org/10.1007/978-3-031-08751-6_54
26. Yang, H., Wang, W., Cao, Z., Duan, Z., Liu, X.: InDL: A New Dataset and Benchmark for In-Diagram Logic Interpretation based on Visual Illusion (2023). arXiv: 2305.17716
27. Zamir, A.R., Shah, M.: Image geo-localization based on multiple nearest neighbor feature matching using generalized graphs. IEEE Trans. Pattern Anal. Mach. Intell. **36**(8), 1546–1558 (2014)

28. Zeiler, M.D., Fergus, R.: Visualizing and understanding convolutional networks. In: Fleet, D., Pajdla, T., Schiele, B., Tuytelaars, T. (eds.) ECCV 2014. LNCS, vol. 8689, pp. 818–833. Springer, Cham (2014). https://doi.org/10.1007/978-3-319-10590-1_53
29. Zhou, B., Khosla, A., Lapedriza, À., Oliva, A., Torralba, A.: Learning Deep Features for Discriminative Localization. arXiv: 1512.04150 (2015)

Open Access This chapter is licensed under the terms of the Creative Commons Attribution 4.0 International License (http://creativecommons.org/licenses/by/4.0/), which permits use, sharing, adaptation, distribution and reproduction in any medium or format, as long as you give appropriate credit to the original author(s) and the source, provide a link to the Creative Commons license and indicate if changes were made.

The images or other third party material in this chapter are included in the chapter's Creative Commons license, unless indicated otherwise in a credit line to the material. If material is not included in the chapter's Creative Commons license and your intended use is not permitted by statutory regulation or exceeds the permitted use, you will need to obtain permission directly from the copyright holder.

From Input to Insight: Probing the Reasoning of Attention-Based MIL Models

Paulina Tomaszewska[1](), Michał Gozdera[1], Elżbieta Sienkiewicz[1], and Przemysław Biecek[1,2]

[1] Warsaw University of Technology, Warsaw, Poland
paulina.tomaszewska3.dokt@pw.edu.pl
[2] University of Warsaw, Warsaw, Poland

Abstract. Despite their critical applications in healthcare, particularly in digital pathology, Multiple Instance Learning (MIL) models have been poorly investigated with regard to their properties, vulnerabilities, and reasoning. To address this research gap, we propose rule-based synthetic datasets SyntheticSMIL, and ReasonSMIL protocol, for the investigation of the attention-based MIL models. The datasets are generated on a rule basis to enable easy manipulation of their difficulty level. Moreover, they are designed in such a way that the model has to pay attention to multiple locations within the images to perform correct classification (spatial context). The ReasonSMIL consists of two parts: (1) ReasonSMIL-R, which checks if models reason according to ground truth and (2) ReasonSMIL-A, which measures the agreement between models trained on different subsets (stability). We used the proposed SyntheticSMIL and ReasonSMIL to analyse CLAM and TransMIL models. These tools offer a novel way to address the challenges of investigating model properties without relying on expert knowledge, as the ground truth is given during the dataset generation.

Keywords: Synthetic datasets · Model evaluation · Multiple Instance Learning · Spatial context

1 Introduction

By 2030, most data used in AI is expected to be artificially generated through rules, simulations, or models [19]. While the focus is typically on generating realistic data [4], an alternative approach is to create simplified datasets to shed some light on model behavior. Such datasets allow for precise evaluation of whether models are learning the correct relationships. Though simplified, these datasets are crucial for testing model reasoning, particularly in complex tasks like medical imaging. By using clearly defined rules, they enable targeted investigations, help identify model weaknesses, and ensure models are reasoning correctly rather than relying on shortcuts [6,12,31]. In this work, the term 'reasoning' is used in a distinct sense compared to its use in Large Language Models.

Our approach is a reverse of *'garbage in, garbage out'* in the form of *'understandable input, understandable output'* – making synthetic datasets an effective tool in explainable AI (XAI) research and for early-stage model development, ensuring transparency, scalability, and reproducibility before deployment.

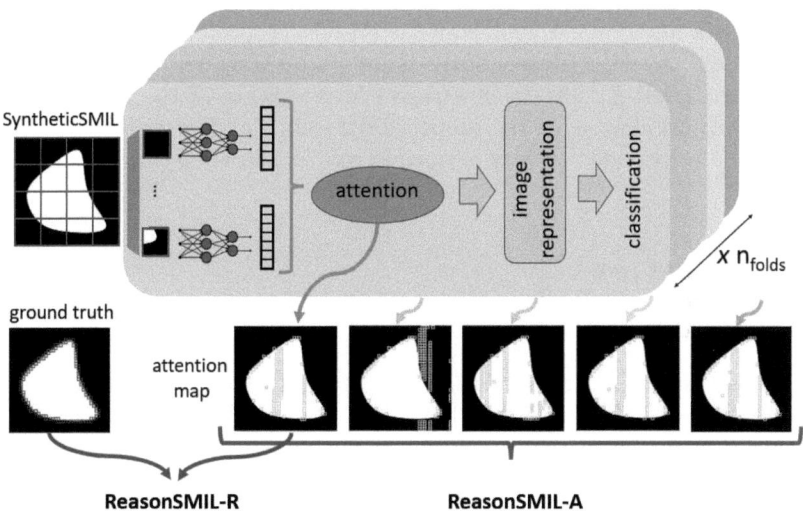

Fig. 1. The proposed ReasonSMIL protocol evaluates the reasoning ability of attention-based MIL models trained e.g. on the SyntheticSMIL dataset. ReasonSMIL-R compares the model's patchwise attention scores against ground truth, while ReasonSMIL-A checks the agreement between attention maps from models trained on different cross-validation folds. Ground truth and model-identified important patches are highlighted in green and yellow, respectively. (Color figure online)

In our work, we focus on attention-based Multiple Instance Learning (MIL) models [16] which are often applied to large, high-resolution images with single global label, such as Whole Slide Images (WSIs) in pathology. Such medical application makes them an important area for research investigation. These models aggregate information extracted from image patches to make an overall prediction. Note that in real high-resolution images, more than one patch can be crucial in the decision-making process.

Our goal is to quantitatively investigate if the models truly capture all important patches instead of relying on just a few, i.e. shortcuts. The assumption that each image can contain multiple important patches leads to the concept of spatial context (relationships between the patches in the space), which is in line with a notion of spatial XAI [29]. Our proposed pipeline is shown in Fig. 1. We address the need to investigate the behavior of the attention-based MIL models in regards to their spatial reasoning capabilities (SMIL) which are important e.g. in the analysis of histopathological images [1,7]. We propose a term Spatial Multiple Instance Learning (SMIL). It is an extension of traditional Multiple Instance Learning (MIL) models by incorporating spatial context and relationships between instances (patches) in a bag. This makes it a powerful approach for tasks that require understanding of spatial patterns, such as in medical imaging. The notion is inspired by 'correlated MIL' [26].

Our main contributions are: (1) a set of configurable datasets (Synthetic-SMIL) where multiple patches are essential for correct classification (spatial context), (2) a fine-grained, multi-criteria evaluation protocol to analyze if MIL models reason correctly (ReasonSMIL-R) and are stable within cross-validation folds (ReasonSMIL-A), (3) an illustrative investigation of the popular CLAM and TransMIL models using the proposed datasets and protocol.

The code is provided at https://github.com/gozderam/synth_reason_smil.git.

2 Related Work

2.1 Multiple Instance Learning

In Multiple Instance Learning (MIL), images of extremely high resolution with only global labels (weakly annotated) are processed. This approach is widely used in Whole Slide Images in digital pathology. Such images are analysed as bags of instances (here understood as patches). Each patch can be either with tumour cells or without. One patch with a tumour is enough to label the whole lesion as a tumour. In MIL, the samples (patches) from images are often first analysed individually and later the information from them is aggregated within attention-based modules to make a final decision about a bag. Common attention-based MIL models used for WSI analysis include CLAM [21], TransMIL [26], ProtoMIL [25].

Our work focuses on analysing the reasoning of the attention-based MIL vision models, used for instance, in digital pathology for Whole Slide Images. Typically, such models are evaluated by global performance metrics (e.g., accuracy, AUC) and visualizations of attention scores via heatmaps. However, spatial context understanding through attention scores has rarely been studied, with only a few exceptions [14,30]. In the first, the coexistence of some instances (MNIST images) within bags is evaluated (only even/odd numbers in a bag or only adjacent pairs of numbers in a bag). In the latter, the spatial regression is used to quantify the role of context in a form of neighborhood in WSIs.

2.2 Model Evaluation on Synthetic Data

Synthetic datasets have been used in machine learning mainly to address data sensitivity and privacy issues [24]. The rise of Generative Adversarial Networks [13] and diffusion models [15] has further popularized the use of synthetic datasets, including text-to-image generation [17] and 3D environments for dataset sampling [8,22]. These methods aim to create realistic images for training models, ensuring good performance in real-world scenarios.

However, synthetic datasets can also be used to evaluate models by testing hypotheses, such as understanding spatial relationships [27], or vulnerability to adversarial attacks [5]. Such datasets can also serve for explainable AI (XAI) study [3,28]. The MIL models were challenged under the adversarial attack [32, 33] and other synthetic tile modifications [2]. Yet, no rule-based datasets were used to investigate the MIL model's reasoning, vulnerabilities or properties.

The model testing using rule-based datasets in our work is inspired by the notion of unit tests for symbolic conceptual reasoning in Deep Learning using synthetic datasets [20] that are based on the theory of concepts by [11] where one of the arguments is a significant role of compositionality in reasoning. The ability of abstract reasoning is also evaluated in visual IQ tests i.e. based on Ravens Matrices [23].

3 SyntheticSMIL Datasets

We propose a set of three synthetic datasets, SyntheticSMIL, to test MIL models' ability to reason using spatial context, where distinguishing classes depends on multiple patches. MIL is often used to analyse images of non-standardized size larger than typical 224×224, with weak labels, and valuable role of spatial relationships e.g. WSIs in digital pathology.

The SyntheticSMIL datasets were inspired by histopathological images that are input to the analysed MIL models. Key features in histopathological images are shapes, textures, and densities [18]. Their analysis is critical for detecting abnormalities and classifying tissue samples: (1) shape—irregular or enlarged nuclei often indicate malignancy, (2) texture—coarser chromatin texture is a common marker in cancerous nuclei, (3) density—increased cellular density typically signals high-grade tumors. We wanted to create datasets checking one data characteristic to make models' explanations as firm and straightforward as possible. Hence, to isolate the understanding of spatial context, we designed datasets with pure signal, free from distractors, ensuring straightforward interpretation without the need for disentanglement.

Inspired by configurable 3D environments [8,22], the datasets allow flexible adjustments thanks to parametrization. The SyntheticSMIL implementation enables the generation of images of different sizes (Fig. 3). We describe the generation process of the synthetic binary datasets, their configurable parameters, and methods to define important patches (ground truth). The goal is to create a flexible, diverse dataset generation framework with adjustable difficulty levels. The key values of the parameters used for the generation of datasets for the experiments are provided in Sect. 5.

Concavity. The *concavity* dataset focuses on differences among concave shapes. The task is to distinguish structures based on the ratio of a given structure's area to its convex hull area. Specifically, structures with a ratio below a given threshold ('more' concave) must be separated from those with a ratio above it ('less' concave).

Algorithm 1. *Concavity* dataset generation (single image).

$a_f \leftarrow -1$
while $a_f \notin [a_{f_{min}}, a_{f_{max}}]$ **do**
    $b_{pts} \leftarrow$ gen_points($n_{pmin}, n_{pmax}, d_m, d_s, d_{var}$)
    $s_{pts} \leftarrow$ get_spline_points(b_{pts})
    $c_{hull} \leftarrow$ convex_hull(s_{pts})
    $a_f \leftarrow$ pol_area(s_{pts}) / pol_area(c_{hull})
end while
$pts_{scaled} \leftarrow$ scale($s_{pts}, sf_{min}, sf_{max}$)
draw_polygon(pts_{scaled})

In Algorithm 1:

- gen_points($n_{pmin}, n_{pmax}, d_m, d_s, d_{var}$) generates base points for spline creation. The number of points n_p is an integer sampled from $\{n_{pmin}, n_{pmin} + 1, \ldots, n_{pmax} - 1\}$ with equal probabilities for each value. Later, for each point i, $i \in \{0, 1, \ldots, n_p - 1\}$ a distance d_p (from the origin of the coordinate system) is sampled from a normal distribution $d_i \sim \mathcal{N}(d_m, d_s)$. Therefore, each point i can be placed on a circle with a radius d_i. The points are placed on the corresponding circles so that the angle between the y axis of the coordinate system and the line from the origin of the coordinate system to the point i is $rot_i = 2\pi i/n_p + shift_i \pi/n_p$ where $shift_i \sim \mathcal{U}(0, 1)$ is a noise factor.
- get_spline_points(b_{pts}) generates the B-spline based on points b_{pts}.
- convex_hull(s_{pts}) returns a list of points that are the convex hull of points s_{pts}.
- pol_area(*) returns the areas of polygons formed by s_{pts} and c_{hull} respectively.
- Generation algorithm keeps repeating as long as the resulting area ratio a_f (computed for a generated shape) does not fall into the range $[a_{f_{min}}, a_{f_{max}}]$.
- scale($s_{pts}, sf_{min}, sf_{max}$) scales generated points with a scaling factor $sf \sim \mathcal{U}(sf_{min}, sf_{max})$.

The graphical explanation of Algorithm 1 is shown in Fig. 2.

The classes differ in the allowed values of a_f – the ratio of the polygon area to its convex hull area. For class 1, the allowed values ($[a_{f_{min_1}}, a_{f_{max_1}}]$) are lower than for class 0 ($[a_{f_{min_0}}, a_{f_{max_0}}]$). The ranges for different classes are disjoint – 'more' concave belong to class 1, whereas the 'less' concave to class 0. The smaller and closer a_f ranges for classes, the more difficult it is to classify a dataset.

In *concavity*, key patches (ground truth, GT) for class distinction can be defined in three ways: (1) background only, (2) foreground – polygon area (without the edge), and (3) polygon edge (Fig. 3d). Each method provides enough information for classification.

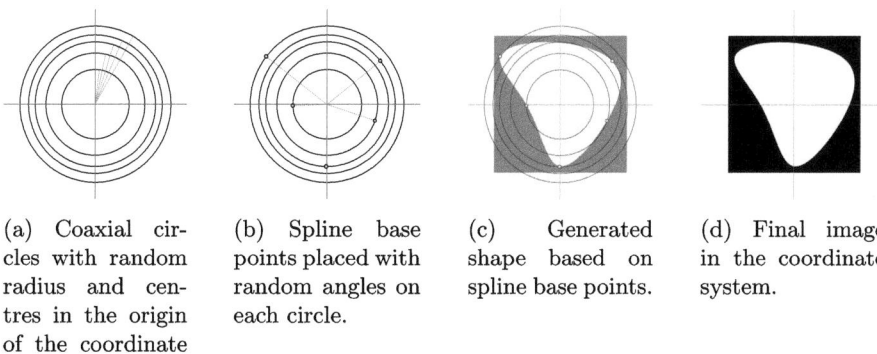

(a) Coaxial circles with random radius and centres in the origin of the coordinate system.

(b) Spline base points placed with random angles on each circle.

(c) Generated shape based on spline base points.

(d) Final image in the coordinate system.

Fig. 2. *Concavity* images generation process.

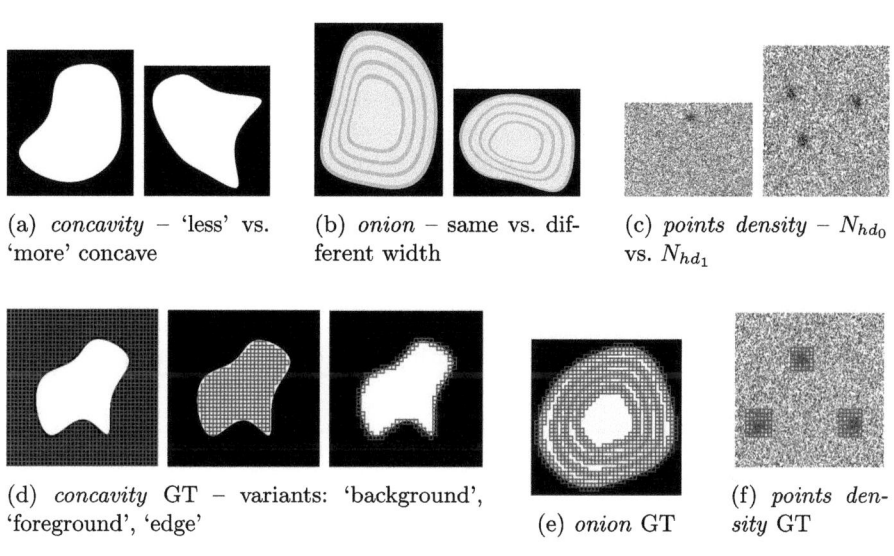

(a) *concavity* – 'less' vs. 'more' concave

(b) *onion* – same vs. different width

(c) *points density* – N_{hd_0} vs. N_{hd_1}

(d) *concavity* GT – variants: 'background', 'foreground', 'edge'

(e) *onion* GT

(f) *points density* GT

Fig. 3. Samples from two different classes of the *concavity*, *onion*, and *points density* datasets (a–c), along with exemplary ground truth patches outlined (d–f). The size of images can be different – width and height can be sampled from normal distribution given mean and standard deviation.

Onion. An image from the *onion* dataset consists of a series of nested, light-grey regions, referred to as *layers*, surrounding a central area. Each layer is enclosed by a dark-grey boundary (called *edge*). In class 0, the layers are coaxial and share the exact same shape, differing only in scale. In class 1, however, the shapes vary across layers.

In Algorithm 2:

- get_edge(e_{pts_i}, e_w) returns a set of points constituting an edge shape that is constructed based on e_{pts_i}. The edge has a width of e_w.

Algorithm 2. *Onion* dataset generation (single image).

$edges \leftarrow \emptyset$
$epts_0 \leftarrow s_{pts}$
for each $i \in \{0, 1, \ldots, l_c - 1\}$ **do**
    $edges \leftarrow edges \cup \texttt{get\_edge}(epts_i, e_w)$
    $epts_{i+1} \leftarrow \texttt{transform}(epts_i, l_w, noise_{std})$
end for
`draw_layers`($edges$)

- `transform`($epts_i, l_w, noise_{std}$) returns transformed points being the input points for the next (inner) edge. The transformation is based on layer width (l_w) and the normally distributed noise factor ns applied to points location, $ns \sim \mathcal{N}(1, noise_{std})$ ($ns = 1$ means no noise is applied).
- s_{pts} are generated as for *concavity* dataset (Algorithm 1).

The key parameter in the generation scheme is $noise_{std}$. When $noise_{std} = 0$, the noise is not applied to the subsequent layers and all layers on a single image are of the same shape disregarding a scale (class 0). With $noise_{std} \neq 0$, subsequent layers differ both in a scale and shape (class 1). The lower $noise_{std}$, the more difficult it is to properly classify images.

The important patches (ground truth) are all the patches that include pixels comprising layer edges (Fig. 3e).

Points Density. The *points density* dataset refers to images where the distinguishing factor is the number of areas with a high density of points (Fig. 3c).

Algorithm 3. *Points density* dataset generation (single image).

$r \leftarrow \texttt{discrete\_uniform}(\{r_{min}, 2r_{min}, \ldots, wr_{min}\})$
$pts_{bg} \leftarrow \texttt{get\_background\_points}(n_{bg})$
$centers_{hd} \leftarrow \texttt{get\_high\_density\_centers}(N_{hd})$
$pts_{hd} \leftarrow \emptyset$
for each $c_{hd} \in centers_{hd}$ **do**
    $pts_{c_{hd}} \leftarrow \texttt{get\_hd\_neigh}(c_{hd}, n_{hd}, r)$
    $pts_{hd} \leftarrow pts_{hd} \cup pts_{c_{hd}}$
end for
`draw`(pts_{bg}), `draw`(pts_{hd})

In Algorithm 3:

- `get_background_points`(n_{bg}) returns n_{bg} points (x_{bg}, y_{bg}) uniformly distributed across the entire image, $x_{bg}, y_{bg} \sim \mathcal{U}(0, 1)$.
- `get_high_density_centers`(N_{hd}) returns N_{hd} points (x_{hdc}, y_{hdc}) that constitute the centers of areas with high densities and are uniformly distributed across the image without border parts, $x_{hdc}, y_{hdc} \sim \mathcal{U}(0.15, 0.85)$. A given

minimal distance between centers ($c_{d_{min}}$) is preserved in order not to generate high-density areas in the same regions.
- get_hd_neigh(c_{hd}, n_{hd}, r) returns n_{hd} points (x_{hd}, y_{hd}) that define the dense area around point $c_{hd}(x_{hdc}, y_{hdc})$ and are normally distributed with scale r, $x_{hd} \sim \mathcal{N}(x_{hdc}, r)$, $y_{hd} \sim \mathcal{N}(y_{hdc}, r)$. For each image, r is randomly sampled from the discrete uniform distribution, $r \sim \mathcal{U}_d(\{r_{min}, 2r_{min}, \ldots, wr_{min}\})$ where w - maximal multiplicity parameter.

In the *points density* dataset, classes are distinguished by the number of dense areas (N_{hd}). The dataset difficulty can be controlled by adjusting n_{hd} – lower values increase difficulty.

The key patches (ground truth) for decision-making in *points density* dataset are the ones that cover regions of a high density (Fig. 3f).

4 ReasonSMIL Protocol

We propose the ReasonSMIL evaluation protocol to investigate the attention-based MIL models in a fine-grained manner to understand the model's internal reasoning. The ReasonSMIL evaluation protocol has two components for the investigation of: (1) alignment between model reasoning and the important patches (ground truth) and (2) consistency across models.

4.1 Investigation of Model Reasoning

The goal of ReasonSMIL-Reasoning (ReasonSMIL-R) is to verify if the model's decision is based on the correct patches. Since the datasets are synthetic, we know the key rules for class distinction. The process involves (1) defining a ground truth (GT), (2) extracting attention scores per patch from the trained model for each image, (3) using evaluation metrics to compare attention scores with the GT, (4) averaging the metric values across all images.

Metrics. We propose using diverse metrics from two domains for a comprehensive analysis – segmentation (Dice score) and classification (with binarization: balanced accuracy (BAC), Matthew's correlation; without binarization: AUC, PR AUC, Relevance Mass Accuracy (RMA) [3]). The Dice, BAC and Matthew's coefficient scores are applied after binarizing the attention scores, while metrics like AUC and PR AUC handle continuous values. BAC and Matthew's correlation are useful for imbalanced datasets. Here, a dataset is a set of patches within an image where in the case of weakly annotated data, a region of interest is often small.

Binarization. To binarize the attention scores, we select the same number of top-scoring patches as there are important patches in the ground truth. Recall and precision are not used as they yield the same values as the Dice score with this binarization method.

4.2 Investigation of Models' Agreement

The ReasonSMIL-Agreement (ReasonSMIL-A) compares models trained on different data subsets during cross-validation, focusing on internal reasoning rather than global metrics like accuracy or AUC. It analyzes the correspondence of attention scores, similar to inter-annotator agreement, using Fleiss' kappa [10] (0 = no agreement, 1 = full agreement) and RMSE for attention score maps.

5 Experiments

The ReasonSMIL protocol is versatile and applicable to any attention-based vision MIL model. We use CLAM and TransMIL to illustrate how ReasonSMIL and SyntheticSMIL can be employed to analyse a specific MIL architecture. Additionally, to demonstrate how these methods can facilitate the comparison of different architectures, we conduct a comparative analysis between CLAM and TransMIL.

For CLAM, we used default hyperparameters (except switching from Resnet-50 to Resnet-32 due to datasets simplicity). In TransMIL, we used the same patch features as in CLAM, with default parameters except for *points density*, where the learning rate was set to 1e-5.

We generated 3 versions of each of the datasets – *concavity, onion, points density*, for the experiments. The versions differ in difficulty level which was achieved by manipulation of dataset parameters: *concavity* (*easy*: $area_{fmin_0} = 0.90, area_{fmax_1} = 0.89, area_{fmin_1} = 0.80$, *medium*: 0.93, 0.92, 0.86, *hard*: 0.97, 0.96, 0.94); *onion* (*easy*: $noise_{std} = 0.07$, *medium*: 0.06, *hard*: 0.05); *points density* (*easy*: $n_{hd} = 200$, *medium*: 110, *hard*: 90) are specified in Table 10 (Sect. A.2). Each image is of size 8960×8960 pixels (40×40 patches of size 224×224). More statistics on data is provided in Table 11 (Sect. A.2). We fixed the image size as one degree of freedom to focus on dataset difficulty. In total, the dataset used during 5-fold cross-validation contains 300 images and the test set (same for all folds) comprises 100 images. The number of samples in the datasets were inspired by the setup of the widely-used CAMELYON16 [9] dataset in digital pathology research on MIL models which consists of 270 training and 130 test samples.

6 Results CLAM

We provide the results (on test sets) of an illustrative investigation of the CLAM model trained on the proposed SyntheticSMIL datasets.

6.1 Global Performance

The global classification performance of CLAM model trained on SyntheticSMIL datasets of various difficulty levels (defined by a set of parameters) are in Table 1. As expected, easier datasets yield higher global performance (accuracy and AUC), with models showing stability across cross-validation folds (small standard deviations). The exception is the onion dataset (*medium*), where the standard deviation of accuracy is 0.16. Next, we apply the fine-grained ReasonSMIL protocol for further investigation.

Table 1. The performance of the CLAM model on SyntheticSMIL datasets. Performance metrics are reported as mean and standard deviation. Hereinafter red color means the most difficult dataset/the worst metric value within a given dataset; green – the easiest dataset/the best metric value; yellow – in between.

dataset	level	accuracy	AUC
concavity	hard	$0.66_{\pm 0.03}$	$0.73_{\pm 0.03}$
	medium	$0.77_{\pm 0.02}$	$0.88_{\pm 0.01}$
	easy	$0.86_{\pm 0.02}$	$0.93_{\pm 0.01}$
onion	hard	$0.59_{\pm 0.04}$	$0.62_{\pm 0.03}$
	medium	$0.82_{\pm 0.16}$	$0.91_{\pm 0.06}$
	easy	$0.93_{\pm 0.03}$	$0.98_{\pm <0.01}$
points density	hard	$0.55_{\pm 0.05}$	$0.60_{\pm 0.02}$
	medium	$0.66_{\pm 0.05}$	$0.73_{\pm 0.01}$
	easy	$0.99_{\pm 0.02}$	$1.0_{\pm <0.01}$

6.2 ReasonSMIL-R

The results of ReasonSMIL-R for the CLAM model are shown in Table 2. The highest values occur in the *concavity* dataset when the ground truth is 'foreground'. Lower values are found in the 'edge' variant of *concavity* and in *points density*, both of which have sparse ground truth. Negative Matthew's correlation coefficients appear only in *concavity* when the ground truth is 'background'.

Points Density. There is a clear link between higher global performance and higher fine-grained metrics, indicating that models are better at assigning correctly attention scores to important patches in easier datasets. However, in these easiest cases, despite near-maximal global performance, fine-grained metrics remain unsatisfactory, suggesting that models may focus on unimportant patches.

Onion. For the most difficult *onion* dataset, the fine-grained metrics are significantly lower than for other variants (i.e. Dice score equals 0.04). However, in easier dataset variants, fine-grained metrics remain similar to each other despite varying *global performance: (in contrary to points density dataset)*. Therefore, here the reasoning metrics are not in line with global accuracy. This can be attributed to two aspects. Firstly, sometimes there are more and less important

Table 2. ReasonSMIL-R on CLAM. In the first column, different datasets ('d') are pointed out ('c' – *concavity*, 'o' – *onion*, 'p' – *points density*). In the 'variant' column, different methods for defining the ground truth are indicated ('back' – background, 'fore' – foreground, 'edge').

d.	level	variant	PR AUC	AUC	BAC	Dice	M. coeff.	RMA
	hard	back	$0.69_{\pm 0.16}$	$0.31_{\pm 0.37}$	$0.42_{\pm 0.31}$	$0.51_{\pm 0.26}$	$-0.16_{\pm 0.62}$	$0.58_{\pm 0.03}$
	medium	back	$0.78_{\pm 0.18}$	$0.47_{\pm 0.45}$	$0.57_{\pm 0.36}$	$0.66_{\pm 0.29}$	$0.14_{\pm 0.73}$	$0.63_{\pm 0.04}$
	easy	back	$0.66_{\pm <0.01}$	$0.14_{\pm 0.01}$	$0.3_{\pm <0.01}$	$0.45_{\pm <0.01}$	$-0.40_{\pm 0.01}$	$0.60_{\pm 0.02}$
	hard	fore	$0.84_{\pm 0.27}$	$0.8_{\pm 0.40}$	$0.83_{\pm 0.32}$	$0.77_{\pm 0.41}$	$0.65_{\pm 0.64}$	$0.35_{\pm 0.03}$
c.	medium	fore	$0.69_{\pm 0.34}$	$0.62_{\pm 0.49}$	$0.69_{\pm 0.37}$	$0.57_{\pm 0.51}$	$0.37_{\pm 0.74}$	$0.30_{\pm 0.04}$
	easy	fore	$0.95_{\pm 0.01}$	$0.98_{\pm 0.01}$	$0.96_{\pm 0.01}$	$0.95_{\pm 0.01}$	$0.92_{\pm 0.02}$	$0.33_{\pm 0.02}$
	hard	edge	$0.21_{\pm 0.02}$	$0.21_{\pm 0.02}$	$0.56_{\pm 0.01}$	$0.18_{\pm 0.02}$	$0.11_{\pm 0.02}$	$0.07_{\pm <0.01}$
	medium	edge	$0.26_{\pm 0.06}$	$0.27_{\pm 0.04}$	$0.58_{\pm 0.03}$	$0.22_{\pm 0.06}$	$0.16_{\pm 0.07}$	$0.07_{\pm <0.01}$
	easy	edge	$0.24_{\pm 0.05}$	$0.27_{\pm 0.03}$	$0.57_{\pm 0.03}$	$0.2_{\pm 0.05}$	$0.14_{\pm 0.06}$	$0.07_{\pm <0.01}$
	hard	-	$0.46_{\pm 0.06}$	$0.46_{\pm 0.18}$	$0.52_{\pm 0.13}$	$0.48_{\pm 0.14}$	$0.04_{\pm 0.25}$	$0.50_{\pm 0.05}$
o.	medium	-	$0.53_{\pm 0.02}$	$0.63_{\pm 0.01}$	$0.57_{\pm <0.01}$	$0.53_{\pm <0.01}$	$0.14_{\pm <0.01}$	$0.58_{\pm 0.03}$
	easy	-	$0.53_{\pm 0.01}$	$0.63_{\pm <0.01}$	$0.57_{\pm <0.01}$	$0.53_{\pm <0.01}$	$0.14_{\pm <0.01}$	$0.60_{\pm <0.01}$
	hard	-	$0.06_{\pm <0.01}$	$0.57_{\pm 0.01}$	$0.52_{\pm <0.01}$	$0.08_{\pm 0.01}$	$0.03_{\pm 0.01}$	$0.04_{\pm <0.01}$
p.	medium	-	$0.11_{\pm 0.02}$	$0.6_{\pm 0.01}$	$0.55_{\pm 0.01}$	$0.13_{\pm 0.02}$	$0.09_{\pm 0.02}$	$0.05_{\pm <0.01}$
	easy	-	$0.29_{\pm <0.01}$	$0.66_{\pm 0.01}$	$0.62_{\pm <0.01}$	$0.28_{\pm <0.01}$	$0.24_{\pm <0.01}$	$0.07_{\pm <0.01}$

patches within ground truth. There are patches with a central density peak, as well as those scattered toward the periphery – potentially less relevant. However, some metrics in ReasonSMIL-R expect a binary decision if a patch is important or not. This could be mitigated by more selective choice of GT patches. Secondly, the feed-forward layers may make wrong predictions even though the assigned attention scores to patches are reasonable.

Concavity. All models achieve very weak values in 'edge' variant in comparison with other GT variants. Adding to this very low standard deviations (stdevs), we can conclude that models tend to not choose 'edge' variant in its reasoning. For the two hardest versions of the dataset, we observe varying metric values and significant standard deviations for both the 'back' and 'fore' GT variants. Such high standard deviations suggest that different cross-validation models select different GT variants, which can be further analyzed using ReasonSMIL-A. Notably, for the 'back' variant, the best metric values are observed for the medium dataset variant, while for the 'fore' variant, the worst metrics appear in the medium variant. For the easiest dataset variant, we see low metric values for the 'back' variant and very high ones for 'fore', both with low standard deviations–leading to the conclusion that the reasoning of all cross-validation models aligns with the 'fore' GT variant. Additionally, there is no clear relationship between global accuracy and ReasonSMIL-R metrics for this dataset.

For datasets with one possible definition of ground-truth important patches (such as *points density*, *onion*), the low ReasonSMIL-R metric value means the model does not reason in a correct way. For datasets with multiple possible ground truth variants (*concavity*), ReasonSMIL-R analysis becomes more complex and insightful. Firstly, if a model for a given GT variant achieves a poor metric value, it does not necessarily mean that it reasons in an incorrect way – it could have learnt a pattern matching a different GT variant. Secondly, models trained on different cross-validation folds can reason in line with different GT variant which directly impacts ReasonSMIL-R metrics calculated as averages of values from models trained on different cross-validation folds. To detect such phenomena, we calculate the standard deviations for all ReasonSMIL-R metrics and introduce another component of ReasonSMIL – ReasonSMIL-A.

6.3 ReasonSMIL-A

The results on reasoning stability are shown in Table 3. There is no clear relationship between ReasonSMIL-A metrics (Fleiss' kappa, RMSE) and dataset difficulty: for *points density* and *concavity* the Fleiss' kappa values are not in line with global accuracy, for *onion* such a relation can be observed. For *concavity*, models achieve the lowest Fleiss' kappa values for *medium* dataset in all GT variants. The small Fleiss' kappa values in the *medium* dataset and mediocre in *hard* suggest that the models tend to reason in line with different ground truth variants (Fig. 4 and Appendix B). The analysis of RMSE metric gives perspective on the topic of stability which does not depend on the definition of the ground truth variant (does not require binarization). Note that in the case of *points density* and *onion*, there is an alignment that the Fleiss' kappa and RMSE for the easiest dataset are the most favorable.

7 Results – TransMIL

Global Performance. The results for TransMIL are provided in Table 4. In the case of *concavity* CLAM achieves better or similar performance than TransMIL unlike in the case of *onion*. In *points density*, in a hard variant, CLAM outperforms TransMIL which is contrary to the situation in the medium variant. For the detailed comparative study between CLAM and TransMIL, we select datasets on which the models achieved similar performance (*concavity*: medium, *onion*: easy, *points density*: easy). In the following analyses, we used the attention scores from the first multi-head self-attention module of TransMIL.

ReasonSMIL-R. TransMIL outperforms CLAM in the *concavity* 'back' variant in all metrics. In the 'edge' variant it is observed for all metrics except PR AUC and RMA. However, CLAM performs better than TransMIL in the *concavity* 'fore' variant and across all metrics in *onion* and *points density*. The exact results are in Table 5.

Table 3. ReasonSMIL-A on CLAM.

dataset	level	v.	Fleiss' ↑	RMSE ↓
concavity	hard	back	$0.41_{\pm 0.11}$	
	hard	fore	$0.40_{\pm 0.08}$	$0.11_{\pm 0.02}$
	hard	edge	$0.50_{\pm 0.09}$	
	medium	back	$0.16_{\pm 0.15}$	
	medium	fore	$0.14_{\pm 0.12}$	$0.07_{\pm 0.02}$
	medium	edge	$0.35_{\pm 0.05}$	
	easy	back	$0.93_{\pm 0.04}$	
	easy	fore	$0.94_{\pm 0.01}$	$0.12_{\pm 0.02}$
	easy	edge	$0.69_{\pm 0.14}$	
onion	hard	-	$0.69_{\pm 0.06}$	$0.10_{\pm 0.01}$
	medium	-	$0.84_{\pm 0.03}$	$0.14_{\pm 0.02}$
	easy	-	$0.88_{\pm 0.02}$	$0.06_{\pm 0.01}$
points density	hard	-	$0.78_{\pm 0.05}$	$0.14_{\pm 0.01}$
	medium	-	$0.70_{\pm 0.05}$	$0.13_{\pm 0.01}$
	easy	-	$0.81_{\pm 0.04}$	$0.03_{\pm <0.01}$

Table 4. The performance of the TransMIL model on SyntheticSMIL datasets.

dataset	level	accuracy	AUC
concavity	hard	$0.55_{\pm 0.05}$	$0.61_{\pm 0.06}$
	medium	$0.78_{\pm 0.06}$	$0.84_{\pm 0.09}$
	easy	$0.80_{\pm 0.11}$	$0.86_{\pm 0.10}$
onion	hard	$0.94_{\pm 0.03}$	$0.99_{\pm 0.01}$
	medium	$0.96_{\pm 0.02}$	$0.99_{\pm <0.01}$
	easy	$0.96_{\pm 0.01}$	$0.99_{\pm 0.01}$
points density	hard	$0.50_{\pm <0.01}$	$0.76_{\pm 0.02}$
	medium	$0.84_{\pm 0.02}$	$0.96_{\pm 0.01}$
	easy	$0.95_{\pm 0.01}$	$0.99_{\pm <0.01}$

Table 5. ReasonSMIL-R on TransMIL where the model achieved similar performance metrics as CLAM.

d.	level	variant	PR AUC	AUC	BAC	Dice	M. coeff.	RMA
c.	medium	back	$0.79_{\pm 0.07}$	$0.67_{\pm 0.21}$	$0.79_{\pm 0.21}$	$0.85_{\pm 0.14}$	$0.58_{\pm 0.41}$	$0.67_{\pm 0.05}$
		fore	$0.39_{\pm 0.13}$	$0.33_{\pm 0.22}$	$0.44_{\pm 0.18}$	$0.23_{\pm 0.26}$	$-0.13_{\pm 0.35}$	$0.26_{\pm 0.05}$
		edge	$0.10_{\pm 0.03}$	$0.46_{\pm 0.09}$	$0.64_{\pm 0.13}$	$0.32_{\pm 0.25}$	$0.27_{\pm 0.27}$	$0.07_{\pm <0.01}$
o.	easy	-	$0.41_{\pm 0.02}$	$0.37_{\pm 0.03}$	$0.23_{\pm 0.07}$	$0.16_{\pm 0.08}$	$-0.54_{\pm 0.15}$	$0.42_{\pm 0.02}$
p.	easy	-	$0.07_{\pm <0.01}$	$0.51_{\pm 0.01}$	$0.57_{\pm 0.01}$	$0.19_{\pm 0.01}$	$0.14_{\pm 0.01}$	$0.06_{\pm <0.01}$

ReasonSMIL-A. The results are in Table 6. In the case of *concavity*, TransMIL exhibits higher RMSE values compared to CLAM, which favors CLAM since, for RMSE, lower values indicate better performance. Regarding Fleiss' kappa for *concavity*, the results are inconsistent and heavily influenced by the GT variant. In the 'back' and 'fore' variants, TransMIL achieves higher Fleiss' kappa scores than CLAM, which is favorable as higher Fleiss' kappa values are better. However, in the 'edge' variant, TransMIL's Fleiss' kappa scores are lower than CLAM's, giving an advantage to the CLAM model.

For *onion*, TransMIL yields lower Fleiss' kappa scores and higher RMSE values than CLAM. In terms of *points density*, Fleiss' kappa scores are comparable between TransMIL and CLAM, while TransMIL shows a higher RMSE.

Table 6. ReasonSMIL-A on TransMIL.

dataset	level	att	Fleiss' ↑	RMSE ↓
concavity	medium	back	$0.32_{\pm 0.25}$	$0.50_{\pm 0.07}$
		fore	$0.21_{\pm 0.22}$	
		edge	$0.16_{\pm 0.09}$	
onion	easy	-	$0.62_{\pm 0.06}$	$0.11_{\pm 0.04}$
points density	easy	-	$0.82_{\pm 0.06}$	$0.08_{\pm 0.11}$

(a) fold 1

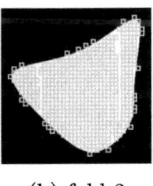
(b) fold 2

Fig. 4. The important patches in the same test image, identified by the CLAM model but trained on different cross-validation folds. We selected the same number of patches as the ground truth in the 'fore' variant.

8 Under the Lens

Along with the analysis of ReasonSMIL metrics, we inspected visualizations of the important patches identified by CLAM and TransMIL models in the case when multiple GT variants are possible (*concavity*).

For the analysis of TransMIL in Sect. 7, we picked the attention scores from the first attention layer (*att0*) as their visualizations seem less noisy than the ones from the consecutive layer (*att1*) (Appendix – Fig. 5), It may be due to some additional high-level patch interactions (Appendix). The 'edge' variant is very rarely observed in reasoning (both in *att0* and *att1*). Note that it may happen that in *att0* the model follows another GT variant than in *att1* (Appendix – Fig. 7). From now on, we focus only on *att0*. **TransMIL tends to alternate its reasoning for different samples within the same cross-validation fold**. It is observed mainly between the 'fore' and 'back' variants (Fig. 8b –Appendix). However, there are a few exceptions. In one fold in each of the dataset difficulty levels (*easy*, *medium*, *hard*), TransMIL reasons mostly in line with just one GT – the 'back' variant.

The empirical analyses showed that the **CLAM model reasons in general in line with one GT variant within one cross-validation fold** (Fig. 8a – Appendix). **However, it turns out that the model tends to choose a different reasoning scheme across different folds** (Fig. 4). From 5 different cross-validation folds CLAM learnt to reason in line with the following GT variants depending on the dataset difficulty: *hard* (4/5 models – 'fore', 1/5 – 'back'), *medium* (3/5 models – 'fore', 2/5 – 'back'), *easy* (5/5 models – 'fore'). In general, the most popular is 'fore' GT variant.

Overall, we can conclude that the TransMIL model is less consistent than CLAM, as it shows less ability to consistently focus on a specific GT variant within a given fold. These observations are reflected in standard deviations of ReasonSMIL metrics averaged within each cross-validation fold.

9 Role of Position Encoding

In order to check the benefit of positional encoding (PE) in TransMIL, we run additional experiments. In TransMIL, the positional encoding is created in the PPEG module where convolutional layers with different kernel sizes are applied to input patch features to catch the information on neighbourhood at different granularities. We ran our evaluation pipeline on TransMIL with PE turned off meaning no convolutional kernels are applied and only identity operation is preserved.

The global performance values in case with and without positional encoding are given in Table 7. In general, positional encoding in all analysed cases improved global accuracy slightly (the biggest difference is in the case of *concavity*). The fact that the differences are small aligns with the ablation study conducted by the authors of TransMIL on Whole Slide Images.

ReasonSMIL-R. The results are provided in Table 8. For *concavity* in the 'back' and 'edge' variants, PE improves most metrics, particularly PR AUC, AUC, and balanced accuracy (BAC). In contrast, the 'fore' variant experiences a decline in most metrics. The *onion* variant shows minimal improvement in PR AUC and AUC, while balanced accuracy, Dice, and Matthew's coefficient slightly degrade. For *points density*, all metrics exhibit slight but consistent improvements with PE, indicating that PE generally enhances model alignment with ground truth patches.

Table 7. Performance comparison of TransMIL with and without positional encoding (PE).

dataset	w/o PE		w/ PE		difference	
	accuracy	AUC	accuracy	AUC	accuracy	AUC
concavity (medium)	$0.73_{\pm 0.06}$	$0.83_{\pm 0.09}$	$0.78_{\pm 0.07}$	$0.84_{\pm 0.09}$	+0.042	+0.008
onion (easy)	$0.94_{\pm 0.02}$	$0.99_{\pm 0.01}$	$0.96_{\pm 0.01}$	$0.99_{\pm 0.01}$	+0.012	+0.001
points density (easy)	$0.94_{\pm 0.01}$	$0.98_{\pm 0.01}$	$0.95_{\pm 0.01}$	$0.99_{\pm 0.01}$	+0.006	+0.006

Table 8. ReasonSMIL-R comparison for *concavity* (medium) with and without positional encoding (PE).

metric	w/o PE	w/ PE	difference
back variant			
PR AUC	$0.79_{\pm 0.11}$	$0.80_{\pm 0.07}$	+0.005
AUC	$0.66_{\pm 0.28}$	$0.67_{\pm 0.21}$	+0.008
BAC	$0.78_{\pm 0.28}$	$0.79_{\pm 0.21}$	+0.010
Dice	$0.84_{\pm 0.22}$	$0.85_{\pm 0.14}$	+0.010
Matthews Coeff.	$0.56_{\pm 0.57}$	$0.58_{\pm 0.41}$	+0.019
Relevant Mass Acc.	$0.68_{\pm 0.09}$	$0.67_{\pm 0.05}$	−0.007
edge variant			
PR AUC	$0.09_{\pm 0.03}$	$0.10_{\pm 0.03}$	+0.005
AUC	$0.44_{\pm 0.08}$	$0.46_{\pm 0.09}$	+0.015
BAC	$0.60_{\pm 0.14}$	$0.64_{\pm 0.13}$	+0.036
Dice	$0.25_{\pm 0.26}$	$0.32_{\pm 0.25}$	+0.068
Matthews Coeff.	$0.20_{\pm 0.28}$	$0.27_{\pm 0.27}$	+0.072
Relevant Mass Acc.	$0.07_{\pm 0.01}$	$0.07_{\pm 0.01}$	+0.001
fore variant			
PR AUC	$0.40_{\pm 0.19}$	$0.39_{\pm 0.13}$	−0.014
AUC	$0.34_{\pm 0.30}$	$0.33_{\pm 0.22}$	−0.013
BAC	$0.47_{\pm 0.30}$	$0.44_{\pm 0.18}$	−0.031
Dice	$0.28_{\pm 0.41}$	$0.23_{\pm 0.26}$	−0.043
Matthews Coeff.	$-0.07_{\pm 0.60}$	$-0.13_{\pm 0.35}$	−0.062
Relevant Mass Acc.	$0.25_{\pm 0.08}$	$0.26_{\pm 0.05}$	+0.006

ReasonSMIL-A. The results are provided in Table 9. The shift from the 'without PE' to the 'with PE' scenario reveals that Fleiss' kappa improves for *concavity* (all GT variants), while RMSE is worse (Table 11). In the *onion* variant, Fleiss' kappa slightly drops, but RMSE improves significantly. For *points density*, Fleiss' kappa shows a notable improvement, suggesting better agreement, while RMSE remains stable (Table 9).

Table 9. ReasonSMIL-A comparison of *concavity* (medium) with and without positional encoding.

variant	Fleiss' Kappa		
	w/o PE	w/ PE	difference
back	$0.27_{\pm 0.15}$	$0.32_{\pm 0.25}$	+0.05
edge	$0.12_{\pm 0.08}$	$0.16_{\pm 0.09}$	+0.04
fore	$0.16_{\pm 0.12}$	$0.21_{\pm 0.22}$	+0.05
	RMSE		
variant	w/o PE	w/ PE	difference
back/edge/fore	$0.45_{\pm 0.04}$	$0.50_{\pm 0.07}$	+0.05

10 Conclusions

We propose a set of configurable synthetic datasets (SyntheticSMIL) complemented with a comprehensive evaluation protocol (ReasonSMIL) for the investigation of the attention-based vision MIL models. To justify their usefulness, we provide an illustrative investigation of the CLAM and TransMIL models.

The results show that there is no straightforward mapping between the models' global performance metrics and the models' reasoning correctness evaluated using ReasonSMIL-R. It is observed that the maximal global performance metrics do not lead to maximal fine-grained metrics. It turns out that the reasoning of models in cases when they can base their prediction on different valid reasoning schemes ('foreground', 'background', 'edge') is surprising. CLAM model seems to reason consistently across all images when trained on a particular cross-validation fold. However, this reasoning scheme may not be the same across folds. TransMIL in turn follows different reasoning patterns (GT) for different images even within a single model, trained on a given cross-validation fold. We can therefore conclude that the reasoning of the CLAM model is more consistent than the TransMIL's.

The proposed tools give valuable insights into model's internals and reasoning which may be useful in the early stage of SMIL architecture development (analogy to unit tests to explore program properties).

Acknowledgements. We would like to thank Małgorzata Hadasz, Aleksandra Nawrocka, Dominika Umiastowska, Arkadiusz Zalas for their contributions in the early stage of the project and reviewers for useful comments. This research was financially supported by the Warsaw University of Technology within the Excellence Initiative: Research University (IDUB) programme (grant: 1820/97/Z01/2023). The work was carried out with the support of the Laboratory of Bioinformatics and Computational Genomics and the High Performance Computing Center of the Faculty of Mathematics and Information Science, Warsaw University of Technology.

A Datasets

A.1 Ground truth definitions

Concavity Let p_{ij} be the patch of a given image, $i \in \{1, 2, \ldots, N\}$, $j \in \{1, 2, \ldots, M\}$, and pts_{scaled} - as in Algorithm 1 (main paper). The procedure of selecting ground-truth important patches in the *concavity* dataset is described in Algorithm 4.

Algorithm 4. Setting ground-truth for a given image from *concavity* dataset.

$pol \leftarrow \texttt{polygon}(pts_{scaled})$
$bg \leftarrow \texttt{background}(pts_{scaled})$
$gt_{patches_{bg}} \leftarrow \{p_{ij} | p_{ij} \cap pol = \emptyset\}$
$gt_{patches_{pol}} \leftarrow \{p_{ij} | p_{ij} \cap bg = \emptyset\}$
$gt_{patches_{edge}} \leftarrow \{p_{ij} | p_{ij} \cap pol \neq \emptyset \wedge p_{ij} \cap bg \neq \emptyset\}$

In Algorithm 4:

- $\texttt{polygon}(pts_{scaled})$ returns a region determined by pts_{scaled} (together with the edges).
- $\texttt{background}(pts_{scaled})$ returns the background of the region determined by pts_{scaled} (a complement of $\texttt{polygon}(pts_{scaled})$ in the context of the entire image).

Onion Let p_{ij} be the patch of a given image, $i \in \{1, 2, \ldots, N\}$, $j \in \{1, 2, \ldots, M\}$. The procedure of selecting important patches (ground-truth) in *onion* dataset is described in Algorithm 5.

Algorithm 5. Setting ground-truth for a given image from *onion* dataset.

$gt_{patches} \leftarrow \emptyset$
for each $i \in \{1, 2, \ldots, N\}$ **do**
  for each $j \in \{1, 2, \ldots, M\}$ **do**
    $n_{colors} \leftarrow \texttt{get\_n\_colors}(p_{ij})$
    if $n_{colors} > 1$ **then**
      $gt_{patches} \leftarrow gt_{patches} \cup \{p_{ij}\}$
    end if
  end for
end for

In Algorithm 5:

- $\texttt{get\_n\_colors}(p_{ij})$ returns the number of different colors (pixel RGB values) present in a patch p_{ij}.

Points density Let p_{ij} be the patch of a given image, $i \in \{1, 2, \ldots, N\}$, $j \in \{1, 2, \ldots, M\}$, and $centers_{hd}$, $pts_{c_{hd}}$ - as in Algorithm 3 (main paper). The procedure of selecting important patches (ground-truth) in *points density* dataset is described in Algorithm 6.

Algorithm 6. Setting ground-truth for a given image from *points density* dataset.

$gt_{patches} \leftarrow \emptyset$
for each $c_{hd} \in centers_{hd}$ **do**
    $x_{min}, x_{max} \leftarrow \text{min\_x}(pts_{c_{hd}}), \text{max\_x}(pts_{c_{hd}})$
    $y_{min}, y_{max} \leftarrow \text{min\_y}(pts_{c_{hd}}), \text{max\_y}(pts_{c_{hd}})$
    $center_{neigh} \leftarrow \text{rect}(x_{min}, x_{max}, y_{min}, y_{max})$
    $gt_{patches} \leftarrow gt_{patches} \cup \{p_{ij} | p_{ij} \cap center_{neigh} \neq \emptyset\}$
end for

In Algorithm 6:

- $\text{min\_x}(pts_{c_{hd}})$, $\text{max\_x}(pts_{c_{hd}})$, $\text{min\_y}(pts_{c_{hd}})$, $\text{max\_y}(pts_{c_{hd}})$ return minimal and maximal x and y coordinates of a set of points $pts_{c_{hd}}$.
- $\text{rect}(x_{min}, x_{max}, y_{min}, y_{max})$ returns a rectangular area determined by vertical (x_{min}, x_{max}) and horizontal (y_{min}, y_{max}) lines.

A.2 Generation parameters

Table 10. The parameters of the SyntheticSMIL datasets used in the experiments. The values of the parameters in bold were modified to create datasets of different difficulty levels.

param	value
n_{pmin}	4
n_{pmax}	10
d_m	1.5
d_s	0.4
d_{var}	0.5
$a_{f_{max_0}}$	0.99
$a_{f_{min_0}}$	**0.97/0.93/0.90**
$a_{f_{max_1}}$	**0.96/0.92/0.89**
$a_{f_{min_1}}$	**0.94/0.86/0.80**
sf_{min}	0.6
sf_{max}	1.0

(a) *concavity*

param	value
e_w	0.0555
l_w	0.1111
c	4
$noise_{std}$	**0.05/0.06/0.07**

(b) *onion*

param	value
r_{min}	0.025
w	1
$c_{d_{min}}$	0.15
N_{hd_0}	1
N_{hd_1}	3
n_{hd}	**90/110/200**
n_{bg}	20000

(c) *points density*

Table 11. The number of ground truth patches (min, max, mean with standard deviation) across datasets of different difficulty levels. The whole size of the image within the datasets is 1600 patches (40 × 40).

dataset	level	variant	min	max	mean
concavity	hard	back	464	1282	$948_{\pm 202}$
	medium	back	445	1288	$1003_{\pm 177}$
	easy	back	672	1289	$1002_{\pm 175}$
	hard	fore	227	990	$536_{\pm 185}$
	medium	fore	220	1013	$483_{\pm 162}$
	easy	fore	221	794	$480_{\pm 159}$
	hard	edge	84	149	$116_{\pm 18}$
	medium	edge	84	148	$115_{\pm 17}$
	easy	edge	90	153	$117_{\pm 18}$
onion	hard	-	657	783	$732_{\pm 24}$
	medium	-	644	783	$730_{\pm 26}$
	easy	-	645	783	$728_{\pm 28}$
points density	hard	-	25	121	$70_{\pm 35}$
	medium	-	25	139	$74_{\pm 38}$
	easy	-	30	160	$86_{\pm 46}$

B Patches visualisations

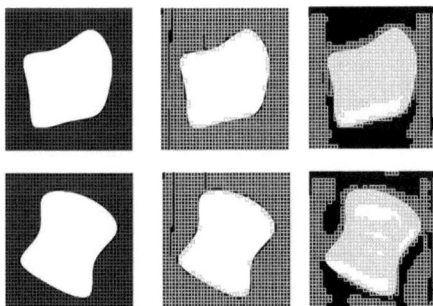

Fig. 5. TransMIL vs. 'back' GT variant green patches (first column). In the second column, there are visualisations of important patches based on *att0* from TransMIL, whereas, the third column – *att1*. Dataset difficulty: *hard*, upper image: class 0; lower image: class 1, cross-validation fold: 0. In this case for the same image, the reasoning in *att0* follows 'edge' whereas in *att0* it is 'foreground'. (Color figure online)

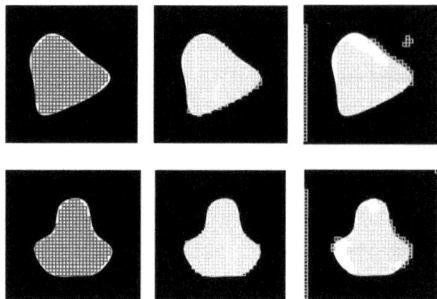

Fig. 6. The comparison of important patches selected by TransMIL against the 'fore' GT variant in green (first column). In the second column, there are visualisations of important patches based on *att0* from TransMIL, whereas, the third column – *att1*. Dataset difficulty: *medium*, upper image: class 0; lower image: class 1, cross-validation fold: 0. It is visible that for *att0*, the choice of important patches is more reasonable. (Color figure online)

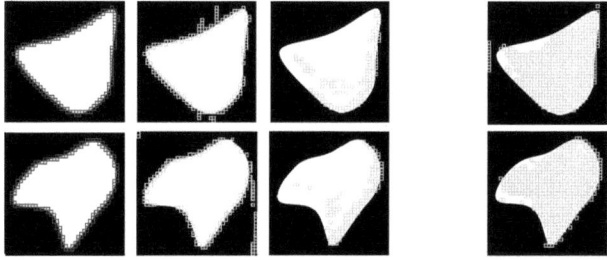

Fig. 7. TransMIL vs. 'edge' GT variant (green patches, yellow patches - selected by TransMIL: *att0* – second column, *att1* – third column). Dataset difficulty: *medium*, upper images: class 0; lower images: class 1, cross-validation fold: 0. GT 'edge' is rarely chosen in the performed experiments, here only visible in *att0*. When checking the 'fore' variant in the case of *att1* (fourth column), it seems that indeed this is the reasoning in this model layer. (Color figure online)

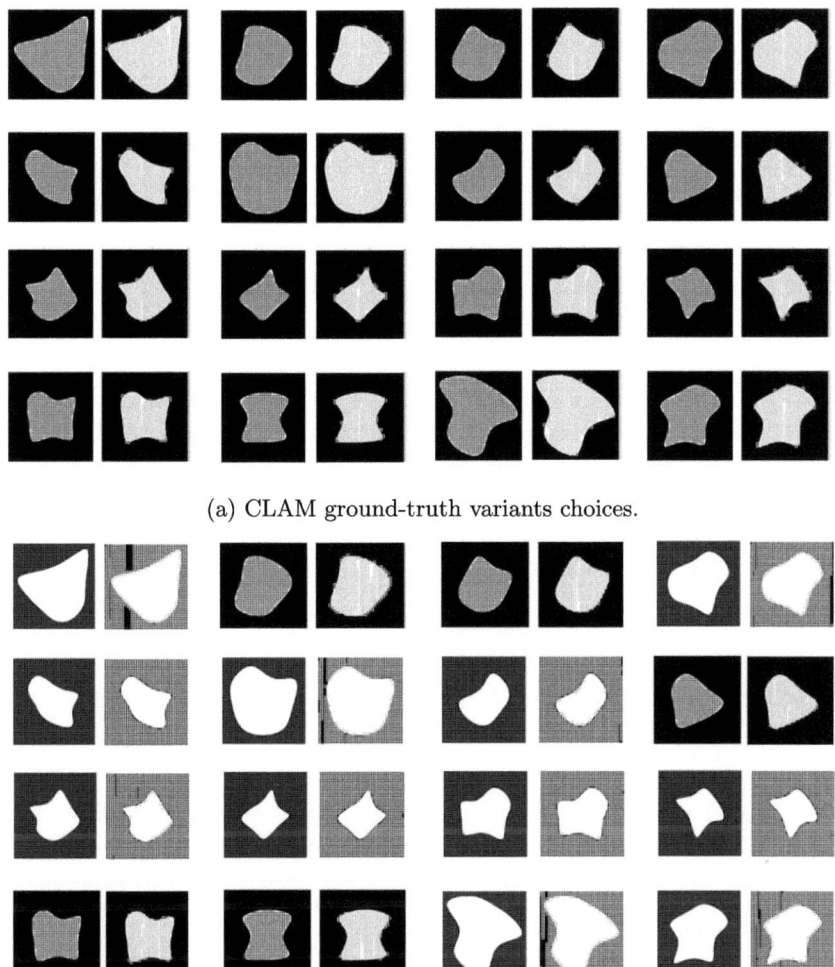

(a) CLAM ground-truth variants choices.

(b) TransMIL ground-truth variants choices.

Fig. 8. The choices of GT variants in the case of a model trained on a given cross-validation fold shown on few samples (green patches – GT, yellow patches – selected by CLAM (a)/TransMIL - *att0* (b)). Dataset difficulty: *medium*, two upper rows: class 0; two lower rows: class 1, cross-validation fold: 0. GT patches visualizations were selected to match models' choices ('fore' or 'back'). In all experiments, a given CLAM model trained on a given fold chooses a single GT variant in all test images. When trained on a particular fold, TransMIL tends to alternate with different reasoning schemes for different images. (Color figure online)

References

1. Abousamra, S., Gupta, R., Kurc, T., Samaras, D., Saltz, J., Chen, C.: Topology-guided multi-class cell context generation for digital pathology. In: IEEE/CVF Conference on Computer Vision and Pattern Recognition (CVPR), pp. 3323–3333 (2023)
2. Albuquerque, T., Yüce, A., Herrmann, M.D., Gomariz, A.: Characterizing the interpretability of attention maps in digital pathology (2024)
3. Arras, L., Osman, A., Samek, W.: CLEVR-XAI: a benchmark dataset for the ground truth evaluation of neural network explanations. Info. Fusion **81**, 14–40 (2022)
4. Bauer, A., et al.: Comprehensive exploration of synthetic data generation: a survey. Arxiv (2024)
5. Costa, J.C., Roxo, T., Proença, H., Inácio, P.R.M.: How deep learning sees the world: a survey on adversarial attacks & defenses. IEEE Access **12**, 61113–61136 (2024)
6. Dagaev, N., Roads, B.D., Luo, X., Barry, D.N., Patil, K.R., Love, B.C.: A too-good-to-be-true prior to reduce shortcut reliance. Pattern Recogn. Lett. **166**, 164–171 (2023)
7. Dee, E., et al.: Determinants of widespread metastases and of metastatic tropism in patients with prostate cancer: a genomic analysis of primary and metastatic tumors. Int. J. Rad. Oncol. Biol. Phys. **117**(2, Supplement), e375–e376 (2023). aSTRO 2023: 65th Annual Meeting
8. Eftekhar, A., Sax, A., Malik, J., Zamir, A.: Omnidata: a scalable pipeline for making multi-task mid-level vision datasets from 3D scans. In: Proceedings of the IEEE/CVF International Conference on Computer Vision (ICCV), pp. 10786–10796 (2021)
9. Ehteshami Bejnordi, B., et al.: The CAMELYON16 consortium: diagnostic assessment of deep learning algorithms for detection of lymph node metastases in women with breast cancer. JAMA **318**(22), 2199–2210 (2017)
10. Fleiss, J.L.: Measuring nominal scale agreement among many raters. Psychol. Bull. **76**, 378–382 (1971)
11. Fodor, J.A.: Concepts: Where Cognitive Science Went Wrong. Oxford University Press (1998)
12. Geirhos, R., et al.: Shortcut learning in deep neural networks. Nature Mach. Intell. **2**, 665–673 (2020)
13. Goodfellow, I., et al.: Generative adversarial nets. In: Advances in Neural Information Processing Systems (NeurIPS), vol. 27 (2014)
14. Hense, J., et al.: xMIL: insightful explanations for multiple instance learning in histopathology. In: The Thirty-eighth Annual Conference on Neural Information Processing Systems (NeurIPS) (2024)
15. Ho, J., Jain, A., Abbeel, P.: Denoising diffusion probabilistic models. In: Proceedings of the 34th International Conference on Neural Information Processing Systems. NeurIPS, Curran Associates Inc., Red Hook, NY, USA (2020)
16. Ilse, M., Tomczak, J., Welling, M.: Attention-based deep multiple instance learning. In: Proceedings of the 35th International Conference on Machine Learning (ICML), vol. 80, pp. 2127–2136 (2018)
17. Kandwal, S., Nehra, V.: A survey of text-to-image diffusion models in generative AI. In: 2024 14th International Conference on Cloud Computing, Data Science & Engineering (Confluence), pp. 73–78 (2024)

18. Kumar, V., Abbas, A.K., Aster, J.C.: Robbins Basic Pathology. Elsevier - Health Sciences Division, 10th Edn. (2017)
19. Ramos, L., Subramanyam, J.: Maverick Research: Forget About Your Real Data – Synthetic Data Is the Future of AI. Gartner (2024). Online 12 February 2024
20. Lovering, C., Pavlick, E.: Unit testing for concepts in neural networks. Trans. Assoc. Comput. Ling. **10**, 1193–1208 (2022)
21. Lu, M.Y., Williamson, D.F., Chen, T.Y., Chen, R.J., Barbieri, M., Mahmood, F.: Data-efficient and weakly supervised computational pathology on whole-slide images. Nature Biomed. Eng. **5**(6), 555–570 (2021)
22. Martinez-Gonzalez, P., et al.: UnrealROX+: an improved tool for acquiring synthetic data from virtual 3D environments. In: 2021 International Joint Conference on Neural Networks (IJCNN), pp. 1–8 (2021)
23. Małkiński, M., Mańdziuk, J.: A review of emerging research directions in abstract visual reasoning. Info. Fusion **91**, 713–736 (2023)
24. Rubin, D.B.: Discussion: statistical disclosure limitation. J. Off. Stat. **9**, 462–468 (1993)
25. Rymarczyk, D., Pardyl, A., Kraus, J., Kaczyńska, A., Skomorowski, M., Zieliński, B.: ProtoMIL: multiple instance learning with prototypical parts for whole-slide image classification. In: Machine Learning and Knowledge Discovery in Databases, pp. 421–436. Springer International Publishing (2023)
26. Shao, Z., et al.: TransMIL: transformer based correlated multiple instance learning for whole slide image classification. In: Advances in Neural Information Processing Systems (NeurIPS) (2021)
27. Swingler., K., Bath., M.: Learning spatial relations with a standard convolutional neural network. In: Proceedings of the 12th International Joint Conference on Computational Intelligence (IJCCI 2020), pp. 464–470 (2020)
28. Tjoa, E., Guan, C.: Quantifying explainability of saliency methods in deep neural networks with a synthetic dataset. IEEE Trans. Artif. Intell. **4**, 858–870 (2020)
29. Tomaszewska, P., Biecek, P.: Position: do not explain vision models without context. In: Proceedings of the 41st International Conference on Machine Learning (ICML), vol. 235, pp. 48390–48403 (2024)
30. Tomaszewska, P., Sienkiewicz, E., Hoang, M.P., Biecek, P.: Deep spatial context: when attention-based models meet spatial regression (2024). https://link.springer.com/chapter/10.1007/978-3-031-95838-0_43
31. Wu, S., Chen, S., Xie, C., Huang, X.: One-pixel shortcut: on the learning preference of deep neural networks. In: The Eleventh International Conference on Learning Representations (ICLR) (2023)
32. Yao, G.: Combating extreme adversarial vulnerabilities in WSI classification. In: The 2022 ICML Workshop on Computational Biology (2022)
33. Zhang, Y.X., Meng, H., Cao, X.M., Zhou, Z., Yang, M., Adhikary, A.R.: Interpreting vulnerabilities of multi-instance learning to adversarial perturbations. Pattern Recog .**142** (2023)

Open Access This chapter is licensed under the terms of the Creative Commons Attribution 4.0 International License (http://creativecommons.org/licenses/by/4.0/), which permits use, sharing, adaptation, distribution and reproduction in any medium or format, as long as you give appropriate credit to the original author(s) and the source, provide a link to the Creative Commons license and indicate if changes were made.

The images or other third party material in this chapter are included in the chapter's Creative Commons license, unless indicated otherwise in a credit line to the material. If material is not included in the chapter's Creative Commons license and your intended use is not permitted by statutory regulation or exceeds the permitted use, you will need to obtain permission directly from the copyright holder.

Uncovering the Structure of Explanation Quality with Spectral Analysis

Johannes Maeß[1,2(✉)], Grégoire Montavon[1,3], Shinichi Nakajima[1,2,6], Klaus-Robert Müller[1,2,4,5], and Thomas Schnake[1,2]

[1] BIFOLD – Berlin Institute for the Foundations of Learning and Data, Berlin, Germany
[2] Machine Learning Group, TU Berlin, Berlin, Germany
{maess,nakajima,klaus-robert.mueller,t.schnake}@tu-berlin.de
[3] Charité – Universitätsmedizin Berlin, Berlin, Germany
gregoire.montavon@charite.de
[4] Department of Artificial Intelligence, Korea University, Seoul, Korea
[5] Max-Planck Institute for Informatics, Saarbrücken, Germany
[6] RIKEN AIP, Tokyo, Japan

Abstract. As machine learning models are increasingly considered for high-stakes domains, effective explanation methods are crucial to ensure that their prediction strategies are transparent to the user. Over the years, numerous metrics have been proposed to assess quality of explanations. However, their practical applicability remains unclear, in particular due to a limited understanding of which specific aspects each metric rewards. In this paper we propose a new framework based on spectral analysis of explanation outcomes to systematically capture the multifaceted properties of different explanation techniques. Our analysis uncovers two distinct factors of explanation quality–*stability* and *target sensitivity*–that can be directly observed through spectral decomposition. Experiments on both MNIST and ImageNet show that popular evaluation techniques (e.g., pixel-flipping, entropy) partially capture the trade-offs between these factors. Overall, our framework provides a foundational basis for understanding explanation quality, guiding the development of more reliable techniques for evaluating explanations.

Keywords: Explainable AI · Spectral Analysis · Stability · Sensitivity · Interpretability · Explanation Quality · Transparency · Machine Learning

1 Introduction

Machine learning (ML) models are being adopted in critical domains such as healthcare, finance, and media, often surpassing human capabilities in various tasks. However, their internal decision-making processes–particularly in artificial neural networks–are notoriously opaque, effectively making them 'black boxes'. As these models permeate high-stakes domains, the need for robust transparency and interpretability has grown. This lack of transparency has spurred the development of Explainable AI (XAI), a field that focuses on extracting explanations for the predictions of complex ML models.

A range of explanation methods have been proposed (see, e.g., [5,6,11,21, 34,35,41,46,47]), each of which has been shown to be useful in specific domains. Yet, with the large number of XAI methods, users face the challenge of selecting an appropriate method and assessing its quality. Additionally, evaluating the quality of XAI methods is essential not only for improving human interpretability but also because heat maps have been reported to mislead users, a concern heightened by their recent use in sensitive domain such as healthcare [18] and industry [25]. For instance, adversarial attacks can manipulate explanation methods [15], and models may base their predictions on spurious correlations rather than meaningful patterns, a phenomenon known as the 'Clever-Hans' effect [23].

Previous work [29,43] highlights that evaluating an explanation's quality is inherently multifaceted. While numerous evaluation techniques have been proposed (e.g., [1,13,32]) to assess explanation quality, there is still limited clarity about which specific aspects each technique rewards. There has been longstanding effort to holistically assess explanations (e.g., [17,43]), yet this remains largely empirical. In contrast, we aim to develop a deeper theoretical understanding of how evaluation techniques are interconnected.

In this paper, we seek a better theoretical understanding of the question of explanation quality. We propose a novel spectral analysis approach that applies Singular Value Decomposition (SVD) to a matrix containing input-neuron contributions for each output neuron, thereby characterizing explanations via their singular values. We demonstrate that these singular values can reveal whether an explanation meets specific desired properties: Sensitivity to the model's output (termed *target sensitivity*) or distinct identification of salient features (termed *stability*).

Our spectral analysis is tested on two image datasets, MNIST and ImageNet. Specifically, we investigate how the explanation techniques and their hyperparameters relate to the sensitivity and stability properties identified in our spectral analysis. Our analysis also allows us to check whether parameters that perform well on both properties are consistent with those identified by pixel-flipping and other commonly used evaluation techniques. Our results provide further support for existing approaches for evaluating explanations.

In summary, our work unifies previously disparate explanation quality metrics and proposes a framework to guide the development of more robust evaluation techniques.

2 Related Work

In this section, we review two areas of XAI that are most related to the problem studied here, namely, the problem of evaluation, and the spectral analyses that operate on explanation techniques. For a broader discussion of XAI and its applications, we refer to the review papers [4,20,33].

2.1 Evaluation of Explainable AI Methods

Evaluating XAI methods has become a pressing concern, prompting the development of a wide range of approaches (cf. [29] for a review). In the context of expert systems, [43] identifies a number of desiderata aimed at holistically characterizing what constitutes a good explanation. Other research efforts have focused on mathematically defining what makes an explanation desirable, establishing specific axioms or unit tests that any effective explanation should satisfy [1,8,27,37].

Another category of work addresses the question of evaluating explanations by performing direct tests on the model, specifically testing whether removing features deemed relevant by the explanation results in a substantial change in the output of the model. These methods include pixel-flipping and its many variants [2,5,9,31,32]. Pixel-flipping tracks the change in the target prediction as individual pixels are removed (flipped) in order of relevance, from most to least relevant. Denoting $i_1, \ldots, i_d$ the feature indices sorted by relevance, and $x_{\{i_1,\ldots,i_k\}}$ a data point where the k most relevant features have been replaced with a placeholder value, a 'pixel-flipping curve' $\{\phi(x_{\{i_1,\ldots,i_k\}})\}_{k=1}^d$ is created, where ϕ is the ML-model. The smaller the area under the pixel-flipping curve (PF-AUC), the more successful the explanation was at identifying the truly relevant features.

Another category of methods evaluates the consistency of an explanation against established 'ground-truth' knowledge, such as leveraging the outputs of a high-performing vision model. Several studies have proposed verifying whether the spatial distribution of relevance scores aligns with the regions corresponding to visual objects detected by the model [13,49].

In [45,48], the authors suggest using *Shannon entropy* to assess whether the explanation is free of highly entropic noise patterns, which is a prerequisite for these explanations to be faithful and interpretable. The entropy can be quantified by first converting the explanation into a probability vector $\overline{R} = |R|/1^\top |R|$ and then calculating the entropy as $-\sum_i \overline{R}_i \cdot \log(\overline{R}_i)$.

Efforts have been made to develop benchmarks and software tools to enable a comprehensive, multifaceted evaluation of explanation techniques [17]. Finally, [16,36] describes end-to-end evaluation settings where a human recipient is actively involved and where performance metrics can be more easily defined.

2.2 Spectral Methods for Explainable AI

Spectral methods have interacted with the field of XAI in several ways. Spectral Relevance Analysis (SpRAy) [23] generates a collection of explanations from a dataset and uses spectral clustering to identify clusters of prototypical decision strategies. While both SpRAy and our approach rely on singular values, our approach differs by focusing on characterizing the explanation for a single data point, rather than analyzing the broader decision strategies of an entire model.

Spectral methods are also employed in [12], where eigenvalues of a cross-covariance matrix, which links model activations to responses, are used to assess the complexity of a decision strategy. While the techniques used are related, our work focuses on the distinct problem of evaluating an explanation.

The authors of [38] analyze the rank of explanations in propagation-based methods and observe a rank collapse under certain conditions, causing explanations to lose their task specificity. While it shares the same general goal as our work of evaluating and better understanding explanation techniques, our work differs in that it looks at the globality of the explanation spectrum and makes connections to other properties of explanations, such as their stability.

3 Spectral Analysis of Explanation Quality

In this section, we present our spectral analysis framework for analyzing model explanations. Its purpose is to gain better insight into the structure of explanation quality, by uncovering underlying factors that contribute to it.

Our analysis will apply to ML models, typically neural networks, that map some input vector $x \in \mathbb{R}^d$ to some output $z \in \mathbb{R}^h$ via some function $\phi : \mathbb{R}^d \to \mathbb{R}^h$ learned from the data. The model's output may consist of h class logits or an abstract h-dimensional representation, suitable for linear readouts. We focus on attribution-based explanation techniques, which assign a relevance score to each input feature, indicating its importance in the model's prediction.

Our framework begins by encoding the attribution from each output to each input in a $d \times h$ redistribution matrix $R_{\cdot|\cdot}$. Each column is defined as:

$$R_{\cdot|j} = \frac{\mathcal{E}(z_j)}{1^\top \mathcal{E}(z_j)}$$

for all $j = 1 \ldots h$. Here $\mathcal{E}(z_j) \in \mathbb{R}^d$ denotes the attribution of the model's output z_j at class j to the input features, given by the explanation method of interest at one specific data point. The matrix $R_{\cdot|\cdot}$ satisfies the property $1^\top R_{\cdot|\cdot} = 1$. In particular, when its entries are non-negative, it acquires a probabilistic interpretation, where its elements correspond to the percentage of each output that is redistributed to each input of the network.

This redistribution matrix is particularly useful because it enables any quantity $y \in \mathbb{R}^h$ at the network output to be propagated backward via matrix-vector multiplication $\mathcal{E}(y) = R_{\cdot|\cdot} y$, producing the desired explanation. For example, if the output of the network represents class logits, we can explain evidence for class j by defining $y = e_j \odot z$ where e_j is a one-hot vector of the jth dimension, and then matrix multiplying by $R_{\cdot|\cdot}$. Likewise, defining $y = (e_j - e_{j'}) \odot z$ enables to explain the log-likelihood ratio between two classes. In a general case, when the output of the network is an abstract representation, defining $y = w \odot z$ enables to explain the readout with the weights w.

We now would like to characterize general properties of the explanation process in a way that is independent on the exact prediction task. In particular, we analyze the inherent behavior of the multiplication of y by $R_{\cdot|\cdot}$, and whether it amplifies or attenuates the magnitude of the vector y it multiplies to. These amplification/attenuation properties can be characterized by the spectrum of $R_{.|.}$, that is, the collection of singular values extracted by singular value decomposition (SVD):

$$R_{.|.} \stackrel{(\text{SVD})}{=} \sum_{i=1}^{K} \sigma_i u_i v_i^\top \qquad (1)$$

with $K = \min(d, h)$ and $\sigma_1 \geq \sigma_2 \geq \cdots \geq \sigma_K \geq 0$ are the singular values. The largest singular value σ_1 is equivalent to the spectral norm of the redistribution matrix $\|R_{.|.}\|_2$ and corresponds to the maximum amplification that can be experienced during the explanation process. In turn, $\sigma_2, \sigma_3, \ldots$ represent second, third, etc. largest amplification factors along orthogonal directions $u_2, u_3, \ldots$ and $v_2, v_3, \ldots$ in both input and output space, respectively.

3.1 Stability of an Explanation

The *stability* of an explanation technique is defined by its ability to produce consistent explanations that remain unaffected by factors irrelevant to the model's prediction strategy. One manifestation of irrelevant factors in the context of deep neural networks is the shattered gradient effect [7], where strong variations of the ML-model manifest themselves only locally. Simple gradient-based explanation techniques such as Gradient × Input (see [3]) are strongly affected by them and tend to produce noisy explanations that perform poorly on explanation benchmarks (e.g., [8]).

Thus, the content of an explanation should be limited to what is strictly necessary to support the prediction y. Assuming our explanations $\mathcal{E}(y)$ satisfy the conservation property ($\mathbf{1}^\top \mathcal{E}(y) = \mathbf{1}^\top y$), such an objective can be enforced with a small norm $\|\mathcal{E}(y)\|$, where $\|\cdot\|$ represents any operator norm. If $\|\mathcal{E}(y)\|$ is small, we can generally assume that the heat map is rather smooth or stable.

Our spectral analysis is especially useful to quantify this property as it gives an upper bound on the norm of the explanation in terms of the first singular value σ_1 of the redistribution matrix $R_{.|.}$, i.e.:

$$\frac{\|\mathcal{E}(y)\|_2}{\|y\|_2} \leq \sigma_1 \qquad (2)$$

In other words, it is desirable for an explanation technique to have a low σ_1. Similar relations to Eq. (2) can be stated beyond the spectral norm $\sigma_1 = \|R_{.|.}\|_2$ for other norms of $\|R_{.|.}\|_p$. We show in Sect. 3.4, in the context of the Layerwise Relevance Propagation (LRP) explanation method [5,28], how $\|R_{.|.}\|_1$ (and the resulting explanation *stability*) can be controlled by an appropriate choice of the LRP parameter γ.

It should be noted, however, that a stable explanation like the aforementioned is not sufficient to ensure high quality explanations. A uniform redistribution matrix of the type $R_{.|.} = 1/d$, has a very small σ_1, but this results in a uniform redistribution over the input features, which is undesirable since it lacks any *sensitivity* to the output, and thus fails to discriminate between features contributing to different predicted outputs.

3.2 Sensitivity of an Explanation

Sensitivity of the explanation to different outputs, in other words, the ability to distinguish attributions between classes, is an important additional property of an explanation, and its importance has been highlighted in several works (e.g., [1,8,29]). To illustrate how *sensitivity* can be related to the spectral properties of the explanation, let us consider two different output neurons j and j', accessed by the readout functions $y = e_j \odot z$ and $y' = e_{j'} \odot z$. If the two output neurons encode different concepts, and the latter are supported by different input features, it is fair to say that the two explanations should be different. Using our spectral analysis, we can express these two explanations and decompose them in terms of the singular values extracted by our spectral analysis:

$$\mathcal{E}(y) = R_{.|.}\, y = \sum_i \sigma_i u_i v_i^\top y \tag{3}$$
$$\mathcal{E}(y') = R_{.|.}\, y' = \sum_i \sigma_i u_i v_i^\top y' \tag{4}$$

A key observation in these equations is that the explanations of y and y' are tightly controlled by the spectra of the network. In the extreme case, when $\sigma_2 = \cdots = \sigma_K = 0$, $\mathcal{E}(y)$ and $\mathcal{E}(y')$ become mere rescalings of each other–the rapid decay of the singular value spectrum severely limits the capacity to generate explanations that accurately capture the diverse concepts present at the output. This phenomenon has also been observed in [38] for certain backpropagation-based techniques in deep networks. Maintaining large values for all singular values, which can be quantified by the norm $\|(\sigma_k)_{k=1}^K\|_2$, is, therefore, essential to ensure the *sensitivity* of explanations.

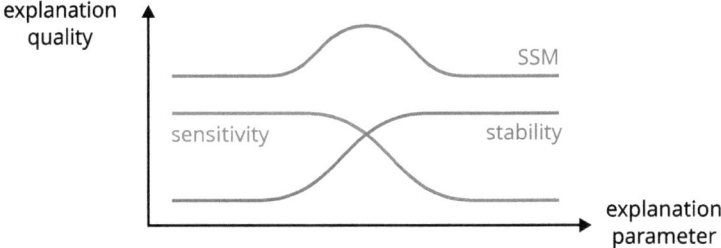

Fig. 1. Cartoon depiction of the two factors of explanation quality that can be derived from our spectral analysis and the SSM metric (Eq. (5)) that aggregates them. We postulate the existence of a 'sweet spot' where both explanation *stability* and *sensitivity* can be achieved. This can be reached by a subtle adjustment of explanation parameters such as LRP's γ and SmoothGrad's standard deviation (as later shown in Figs. 3 and 4).

3.3 Stability-Sensitivity Metric

Having singled out σ_1, or more precisely its inverse $1/\sigma_1$, as a factor of explanation *stability*, and $\|(\sigma_k)_{k=1}^K\|_2$ as a factor of explanation *sensitivity*, it comes quite natural to combine them into a single score, which we define as the 'stability-sensitivity metric' (SSM):

$$\text{SSM} = \frac{1}{\sigma_1} \cdot \|(\sigma_k)_{k=1}^K\|_2 \quad (5)$$

The SSM and the two factors on which it depends are sketched in Fig. 1 for a hypothetical explanation parameter that interpolates between a stable but insensitive explanation and a sensitive but unstable explanation. This explanation quality metric and the two factors that make it up will be compared to existing evaluation metrics such as pixel-flipping in later experiments. The computational complexity of evaluating the *stability*, *sensitivity*, and the *SSM* is discussed in Appendix C.

3.4 Linking LRP Parameters to Stability and Sensitivity

To demonstrate how the parameters of an explanation technique can influence the *stability-sensitivity* profile of an explanation method, we perform a theoretical analysis for the case of the LRP [5,28] explanation technique. LRP is an explanation technique that operates by propagating the output of a neural network layer-by-layer to the input features, where each propagation step consists of the application of a purposely designed propagation rule. Extending the framework of Sect. 3, we can characterize the LRP explanation process as a composition of multiple redistribution steps. In other words, it is achieved through a sequence of multiplications with redistribution matrices defined at each layer:

$$R^{\text{LRP}}_{\cdot|\cdot} = R^{(1)}_{\cdot|\cdot} \cdot R^{(2)}_{\cdot|\cdot} \cdot \ldots \cdot R^{(L)}_{\cdot|\cdot} \quad (6)$$

We specifically consider the case where the propagation rule LRP-γ (cf. [27]) is applied at each layer. At a given layer, let j and k denote the indices of input and output neurons, respectively. The LRP-γ rule then defines the resulting redistribution scheme:

$$R^{(l)}_{j|k} := \frac{a_j \cdot (w_{jk} + \gamma w_{jk}^+)}{\sum_{j'} a_{j'} \cdot (w_{j'k} + \gamma w_{j'k}^+)} \quad (7)$$

where a_j and a_k are the neuron activations and w_{jk} are the weights connecting these neurons. The parameter γ emphasizes positive contributions, which is instrumental in controlling the explanation behavior of LRP.

Next, to analyze the *stability* of $R^{\text{LRP}}_{\cdot|\cdot}$, we combine matrix norm identities and the form of Eq. (6), to derive the following chain of inequalities:

$$\frac{\|\mathcal{E}(y)\|_p}{\|y\|_p} \leq \|R^{\text{LRP}}_{\cdot|\cdot}\|_p \leq \prod_{i=1}^{L} \|R^{(l)}_{\cdot|\cdot}\|_p \quad (8)$$

which hold for any p. In the case of $p = 2$ the expression reduces to an expression involving spectral norms computed either globally or individually for each layer.

If, instead, we choose $p = 1$, we get a closed-form expression where the layer-wise terms can be written analytically as $\|R^{(l)}_{\cdot|\cdot}\|_1 = 1 + 2c^{(l)}/(1 - c^{(l)} + \gamma)$ with $c^{(l)} = \max_k |\sum_j [h_j w_{jk}]^-|/\sum_j [h_j w_{jk}]^+ \in [0, 1)$ (the proof is given in the Appendix). This leads to the closed-form relation:

$$\frac{\|\mathcal{E}(y)\|_1}{\|y\|_1} \leq \prod_{l=1}^{L} \left(1 + \frac{2c^{(l)}}{1 - c^{(l)} + \gamma}\right) \quad (9)$$

This shows that increasing γ tightens the bound on the operator norm, promoting *stability*. As observed in prior work (e.g., [12,30]), small γ values result in noisy explanations and poor benchmark performance. Notably, both noise reduction and explanation *stability* are achieved rapidly, as Eq. (9) saturates relatively quickly with increasing γ.

4 Experiments

In this section, we empirically evaluate our proposed XAI framework on neural networks trained for the MNIST [24] and ImageNet [14] vision tasks, using four different explanation methods. We then compare our results to established metrics, highlighting the strengths and insights offered by our spectral analysis approach.

4.1 Experimental Setup

Machine Learning Models. We evaluate our approach on two established datasets of different sizes and characteristics. MNIST, containing gray-valued 28×28 images for the task of digit classification, and ImageNet, with colored images of size 224×224 picturing everyday objects of 1000 classes. For ImageNet, we download a pre-trained VGG16 model, specifically the `IMAGENET1K_V1` weights from the torchvision library [26]. The model achieves a Top-5 accuracy of 90% on images sampled from the ILSVRC 2012 validation set [14], meaning in 90% of the the predictions the correct class is within the most probable 5 class predictions. For MNIST, we use a Convolutional Neural Network (CNN) (11 layers; Top-1 accuracy 98%) whose artificially deep architecture makes it challenging to explain. For more information on the training and architecture of the model on MNIST we refer to Appendix D.

Explanation Techniques. We employ multiple explanation techniques to compare our framework against existing evaluation techniques. Below, we detail how we apply and parameterize the different explanation techniques.

Layer-wise Relevance Propagation (LRP): For the LRP explanation method [5], we follow the approach of [28]. Specifically, on the VGG-16 ImageNet model, we use the LRP-γ rule in the first three blocks of the architecture, and the $z^\mathcal{B}$-rule in the first layer. For the small MNIST-CNN, we use LRP-γ for all layers except the last one. In our experiments, we analyze the effect of varying γ on the different measures of explanation quality.

SmoothGrad (SG): For SG [39], we calculate the gradient of the model 10 times, each time under a zero-mean Gaussian noise perturbation of the input. In our experiments, we analyze the impact of different smoothing parameters s (i.e. standard deviation values for the noise).

Integrated Gradient (IG): In the explanation method IG [42], we approximate the integral by 10 equidistant evaluations of the model. The reference point in the integral is a black image.

Shapley Value Sampling (Shapley): We use the Shapley method [40] as an additional baseline, and limit the number of feature removal cycles to 25. The scheme we use for removing pixels and patches consists of filling them with uniform black color.

XAI Evaluation Metrics. We compare our spectral analysis framework with the evaluation methods pixel-flipping [5,32] and Shannon entropy. In pixel-flipping, we remove increasing sets of the most relevant features. We stop after 5% of the total features are flipped, and calculate the area under the curve (PF-AUC) as a summary of how faithful the explanation is to the model. The lower the PF-AUC, the better the truly relevant features have been identified. Placeholder values for flipped pixels in the input image are in-painted using the OpenCV [10] implementation of the Fast-Marching algorithm [44], utilizing 3 and 5 pixels around the deleted section for MNIST and ImageNet inputs, respectively.

We then compare our spectral analysis to Shannon entropy, which is commonly used to detect noise and evaluate the overall readability of heat maps. We calculate the Shannon entropy according to the formula given in Sect. 2.1. Explanations are evaluated on 100 different input images each.

4.2 Comparison of XAI Evaluation Methods with Spectral Analysis

We first provide an qualitative description of heat maps that fulfill *stability* or *sensitivity* to build an intuition of how either manifest visually, and then show a quantitative analysis of the different properties we are interested in on a variety of explanation methods.

Qualitative Assessment of Stability and Sensitivity. In Fig. 2, we see how the γ parameter in the LRP method influences the heat maps and how each heat map corresponds to specific properties, such as *stability* and *sensitivity*. For a small γ parameter (i.e., $\gamma = 0.005$), *stability* is low but the *sensitivity* is high. This means that the explanation may vary with small output perturbation, yet is distinguishable from different classes. Effectively, we see that the heat map looks relatively noisy and irregular, which aligns with our expectation, since a small σ_1^{-1} does not limit the growth of noise in the explanation phase. The other extreme is when γ is high (i.e., $\gamma = 0.3$), where we observe high *stability* but low *sensitivity*. The absence of noise in the explanation gives it high *stability*. However, its low *sensitivity* suggests that heat maps may not be

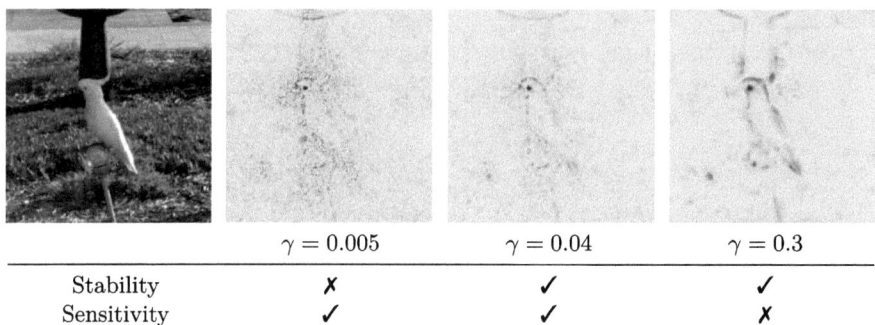

	$\gamma = 0.005$	$\gamma = 0.04$	$\gamma = 0.3$
Stability	✗	✓	✓
Sensitivity	✓	✓	✗

Fig. 2. Examples of explanations produced by the LRP explanation technique using the rule LRP-γ with different values of the parameter γ. An increase in γ is associated with an increase in explanation *stability* (visible here as the vanishing noise pattern in the explanation). On the other hand, choosing too large a value for γ results in a decrease in target *sensitivity*.

able to distinguish features specific to each class, thereby reducing its overall usefulness as an explanation. For the case when $\gamma = 0.04$, a 'sweet spot' is reached where both *stability* and *sensitivity* are high. The noise remains small and the heat map is easy to interpret, while the *sensitivity* measure indicates that heat maps are specific to each class.

Quantitative Comparison with Different Evaluation Methods. We consider in our quantitative analysis the MNIST and ImageNet models described above, and apply to each model different explanation techniques and evaluations of these explanations. In addition to the LRP and SG explanation techniques, each of which come with a hyperparameter, we also include results for IG and Shapley value sampling for comparison. Note that we do not include the Shapley value sampling method in the ImageNet experiments for computational reasons. Results of our comparison are shown in Figs. 3 and 4. Exact numerical values are reported in Appendix A.

For the LRP method, we observe in both models that as the γ parameter increases, the explanation *stability* increases while its *sensitivity* decreases. Our analysis suggests the existence of a 'sweet spot', where *stability* and *sensitivity* can be both achieved, as indicated by a high value for the sensitivity-stability metric (SSM). In the LRP case, this sweet spot corresponds to choosing an intermediate value of the γ parameter ($\gamma = 0.04$ for ImageNet and MNIST, cf. Appendix A). For the SG explanation method, we observe a trend similar to LRP, where increasing the smoothing hyperparameter s results in higher *stability* but lower *sensitivity*. For the ImageNet model, SSM exhibits a clear preference for a specific parameter, whereas on MNIST, the smoothing hyperparameter seems to have no effect on SSM.

Comparing the result of our stability-sensitivity analysis with the pixel-flipping evaluation, specifically, the PF-AUC score described above, we see that

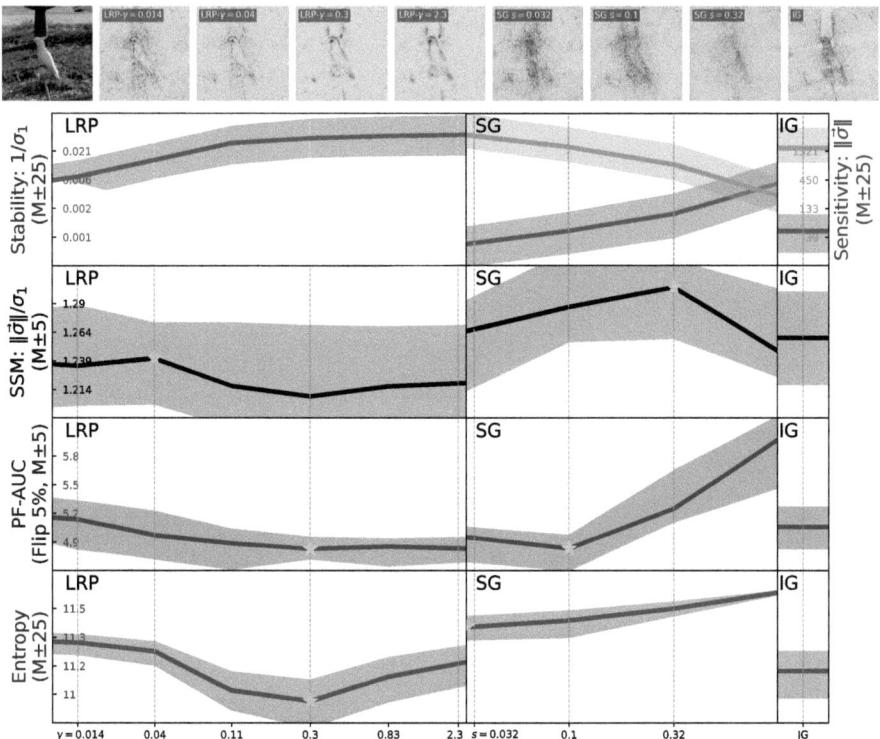

Fig. 3. Quantitative analysis of evaluation metrics for explanation methods on an ImageNet-trained model using 100 images. The top row shows exemplary heat maps for the class 'sulphur-crested cockatoo', one per method and parameter choice per dashed vertical line drawn in the main plot. Below, we present evaluation metrics (top to bottom): *stability* & *sensitivity* (ours), SSM (ours), PF-AUC, and entropy. Explanation methods (left to right) include LRP, SG, and IG. For LRP, results for 11 γ values are shown, and for SG, 4 different noise levels. PF-AUCs are calculated after deleting 5% of the image. Thick lines indicate the median, with shaded areas showing variability: 5% for SSM and PF-AUC, 25% for *stability*, *sensitivity*, and entropy. The star indicates where explanation quality under the given metric is maximized.

both methods reveal a preference for intermediate values of γ. Extending the comparison to the entropy-based evaluation, we see that the *entropy* expresses a similar preference for intermediate values of the γ parameter in LRP. This close relation between SSM and *entropy* is particularly intriguing as the *entropy* was originally intended as a test for the presence of noise in the explanation, in other words, a measure of *stability* only. It turns out that the *entropy* metric does more than that: Stable but insensitive explanations are also highly entropic due to the spreading of relevance scores onto excessively many pixels. Thus, our analysis suggests that *entropy* is a fairly holistic measure of explanation quality.

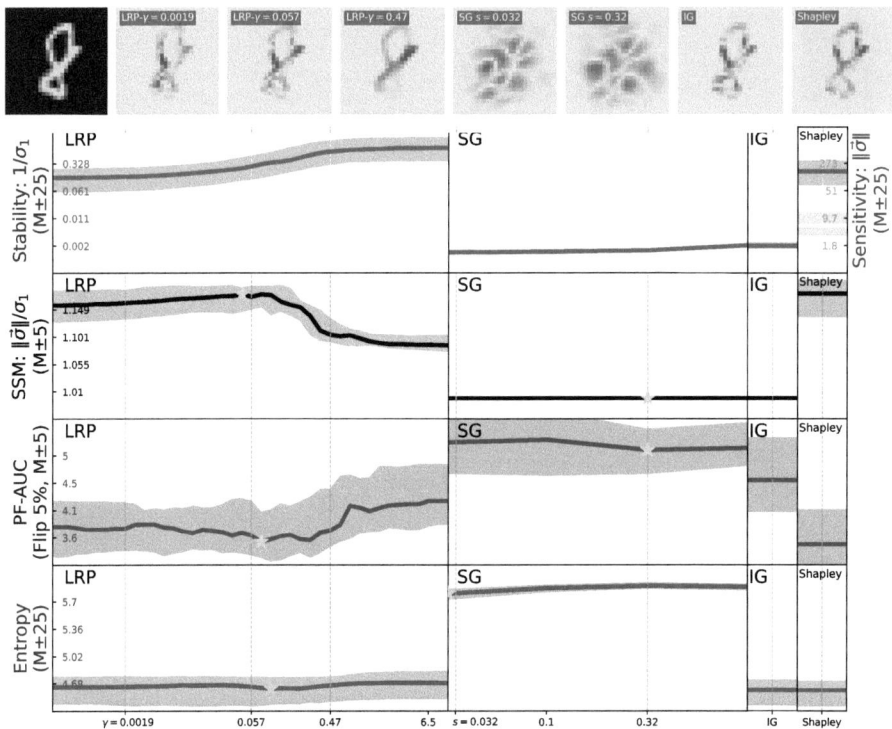

Fig. 4. Quantitative analysis of evaluation metrics for explanation methods on an MNIST-trained model using 100 images. The top row shows exemplary heat maps for the class '8', one per method and parameter choice per dashed vertical line drawn in the main plot. The structure of this figure follows Fig. 3, with the following difference: The rightmost column includes results for the Shapley methods. The LRP curve was obtained using 80 different γ parameters.

Furthermore, we observe that entropy fails in some cases in its original aim to characterize explanation stability (i.e. absence of noise). The SG explanation with low smoothing, which is objectively highly instable, appears not to be so when looking at its low entropy score. This discrepancy can be traced to the normalization step before the entropy computation, which tends to ignore the magnitude of noise patterns, causing noise to be neglected when it is collocated with very strong noise occurring only on few pixels.

Overall, our analysis has revealed that the SSM metric and most evaluation methods witness a subtle interplay between different factors of explanation quality such as stability and sensitivity. Explanation hyperparameters are shown to be effective in influencing those factors of explanation quality. However, these evaluation methods disagree on what precise hyperparameter values are optimal. This imposes caution in drawing general conclusions from the results of specific explanation evaluations.

4.3 Expanded Explanations with Spectral Analysis

In this section, we show another use of our spectral analysis, which follows from the decomposition of the explanations it offers in terms of singular values; in particular, we recall that the explanation $\mathcal{E}(y)$ can be rewritten as:

$$\mathcal{E}(y) = \sum_{i=1}^{K} \underbrace{\sigma_i u_i v_i^\top y}_{\mathcal{E}(y;\,\sigma_i)} \tag{10}$$

Each term $\mathcal{E}(y;\sigma_i)$ of the sum has the same shape as the original $\mathcal{E}(y)$ and can therefore also be rendered as a heat map. Furthermore, the collection of heat maps sums to the original heat map and can thus be seen as a sum-decomposition of the original explanation. This analysis is shown in Fig. 5 for an image predicted by the same model, but explained by two versions of LRP (with different γ parameters).

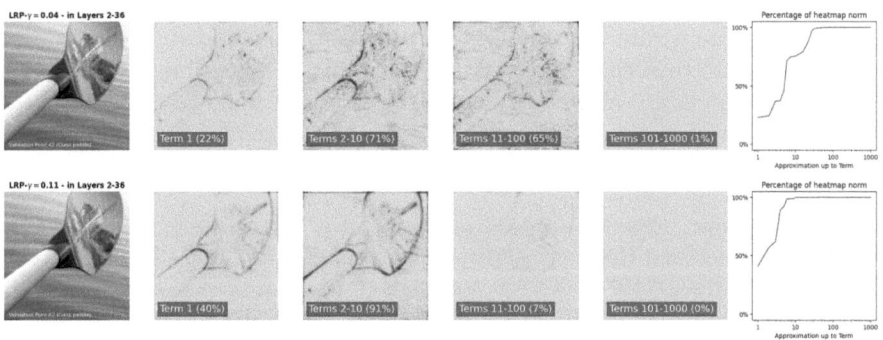

Fig. 5. LRP explanations for the class 'paddle' decomposed into contributions of different singular values (cf. Eq. (10)). Heat maps visualize how bins of singular values, namely, the ranges $(1,1)$, $(2,10)$, $(11,100)$, and $(101,1000)$ contribute, with the norm of this partial result (as a percentage of the norm of the full heat map) denoted in brackets. The top row of heat maps corresponds to LRP with $\gamma = 0.04$ and the bottom row uses $\gamma = 0.11$. The plots on the right visualize the rise in the heat maps norm as it is produced with approximations of $R_{\cdot|\cdot}$ with increasing rank k: $\|\sum_{i=1}^{k} \mathcal{E}(y;\sigma_i)\|_2 \cdot \|\mathcal{E}(y)\|_2^{-1}$. Depending on the choice of γ, small singular values contribute little to heat maps and their norm, indicating that explanations are sensitive to only a low number of patterns in the data.

As the γ parameter increases, the bulk of the explanation is shifted to a smaller number of leading singular values. These are also associated with less noisy singular vectors. As a result, this shift–associated with an increase in γ– causes both a denoising of the explanations and the effective degree of freedom in which explanations vary to drop.

5 Conclusion

XAI was originally conceived to increase the transparency of complex, nonlinear machine learning methods. Over time, a wide array of evaluation metrics has emerged to assess the quality of explanations, yet this diversity has created new challenges in determining which metric is most appropriate for a particular application and in correctly interpreting the resulting scores. Consequently, it is crucial to develop a better theoretical understanding of the underlying factors that determine explanation quality, as well as how these factors are weighted in different evaluation metrics.

In this work, we propose a novel formal analysis framework that elucidates the multifaceted nature of explanation quality. By applying a spectral analysis of the explanation-generating process, our approach mathematically characterizes two distinct evaluation factors, explanation *stability* and explanation *sensitivity*, which jointly contribute to achieving high-explanation quality.

Moreover, extensive simulations on MNIST and ImageNet models illustrate how the factors of explanation quality align with popular explanation metrics such as pixel-flipping or the explanation's entropy.

We also demonstrate how to operationalize our framework by decomposing explanations into their spectral components, distinguishing primary explanation factors from secondary effects or noise. Overall, these findings underscore the potential of our conceptual framework to guide the search for better, more consistent explanations.

Acknowledgment. This work was in part supported by the Federal German Ministry for Education and Research (BMBF) under Grants BIFOLD24B, BIFOLD25B, 01IS14013A-E, 01GQ1115, 01GQ0850, and 031L0207D. KRM was partly supported by the Institute of Information & communications Technology Planning & Evaluation (IITP) grants funded by the Korea government (MSIT) (No. RS-2019-II190079, Artificial Intelligence Graduate School Program, Korea University and No. RS2024-00457882, AI Research Hub Project). We thank Stefan Blücher and Adrian Hill for suggestions of experiments and valuable discussions. We thank Nicole Trappe for proofreading of the manuscript.

A Numerical results of explanation quality

Table 1 provides numerical values for the stability-sensitivity metric (SSM), Pixel Flipping (PF-AUC), and Shannon Entropy metric displayed in Figs. 3 and 4. On the LRP-γ and SG methods, we report the values for the optimal parameter choice γ or σ (shown in brackets).

Table 1. Explanation quality metrics for the ImageNet and MNIST datasets. We report the median score over 100 validation images. The values correspond to the best parameter setting for each method; parameter choices for LRP-γ and SmoothGrad are denoted in brackets. ($\uparrow$) The higher the better, and ($\downarrow$) the lower the better.

	LRP (γ)	SG (s)	IG	Shapley
ImageNet				
SSM ($\uparrow$)	1.24 (0.04)	1.31 (0.32)	1.26	—
PF-AUC (5%) ($\downarrow$)	4.81 (0.3)	4.81 (0.1)	5.03	—
Shannon Entropy ($\downarrow$)	10.99 (0.30)	11.38 (0.03)	11.14	—
MNIST				
SSM ($\uparrow$)	1.18 (0.04)	1.00 (0.32)	1.00	1.18
PF-AUC (5%) ($\downarrow$)	3.53 (0.07)	5.10 (0.32)	4.58	3.49
Shannon Entropy ($\downarrow$)	4.61 (0.10)	5.80 (0.03)	4.60	4.60

B   Analytical form of LRP-γ operator norms

The LRP-γ rule leverages the preference towards positive contributions in reassigning relevance as a stabilizing effect in the creation of heat maps [28]. We now provide an analytical perspective on this heuristic, demonstrating that γ has a domain-specific regularization effect on the explanation process, reducing the operator norm of the conditional relevance matrix $R_{\cdot|\cdot}$. In this section, we define $p_k := \sum_j [a_j w_{j,k}]^+$ and $n_k := \sum_j [a_j w_{j,k}]^-$ as the sum of all positive or negative inputs to the neuron k. We then focus on ReLU-activated neurons, denoting their activation value by $0 \leq |n_k| < p_k$.

We first observe that every element of the conditional relevance matrix decreases monotonically in magnitude as γ increases, ultimately favoring smaller outputs in the matrix multiplication. Negative entries in the matrix have $R_{j|k} = [a_j w_{j,k}]^- / ((1+\gamma)p_k + n_k)$; the conditional relevance goes towards 0 because the denominator increases with γ. Positive entries of the matrix have $R_{j|k} = (1+\gamma)[a_j w_{j,k}]^+ / ((1+\gamma)p_k + n_k)$ and the derivative $\partial R_{j|k}(\gamma)/\partial \gamma = [a_j w_{j,k}]^+ \cdot n_k / ((1+\gamma)p_k + n_k)^2 < 0$ is negative (because $n_k < 0$). The conditional relevance decrease monotonically towards $\lim_{\gamma \to \infty} R_{j|k} = \frac{a_j [w_{j,k}]^+}{p_k}$.

Moreover, we establish a precise relationship between the L1 operator norm of LRP explanation steps and the γ parameter. The key observation is that LRP normalizes the total relevance leaving each neuron: while both positive and negative values of any magnitude are allowed, they must cancel each other so that each column sums to 1, c.f. Section 2.1. This requirement aligns with the L1 operator norm's role of measuring the sum of all *absolute* relevances going out of a neuron. Leveraging these parallels, we derive an analytical expression for the L1 operator norm in terms of γ.

First, the L1 norm of a column k of the conditional relevance matrix is:

$$\|R_{\cdot|k}(\gamma)\|_1 = \sum_j |R_{j|k}(\gamma)| = \sum_j \left| \frac{(1+\gamma)a_j[w_{j,k}]^+ + a_j[w_{j,k}]^-}{(1+\gamma)p_k + n_k} \right|$$

$$= \frac{\sum_j |(1+\gamma)a_j[w_{j,k}]^+ + a_j[w_{j,k}]^-|}{(1+\gamma)p_k + n_k}$$

Then, using the fact that $([a_j w_{j,k}]^+ = 0) \vee ([a_j w_{j,k}]^- = 0)$ for a given (j,k) we can pull the absolute value operation into the terms of the denominator and use our definition of the summed negative and positive contributions to a neuron as p_k and n_k:

$$\|R_{\cdot|k}(\gamma)\|_1 = \frac{\sum_j |(1+\gamma)[a_j w_{j,k}]^+| + |[a_j w_{j,k}]^-|}{(1+\gamma)p_k + n_k}$$

$$= \frac{|\sum_j (1+\gamma)[a_j w_{j,k}]^+| + |\sum_j [a_j w_{j,k}]^-|}{(1+\gamma)p_k + n_k}$$

$$= \frac{(1+\gamma)p_k + |n_k|}{(1+\gamma)p_k - |n_k|} = 1 + \frac{2|n_k|}{(1+\gamma)p_k - |n_k|} = 1 + \frac{2\frac{|n_k|}{p_k}}{1 - \frac{|n_k|}{p_k} + \gamma}$$

By defining $c_k := \frac{|n_k|}{p_k}$, we obtain a compact expression for the L1 column norm in dependence of γ:

$$\|R_{\cdot|k}(\gamma)\|_1 = 1 + \frac{2c_k}{1 - c_k + \gamma}$$

The induced L1 operator norm is then simply the maximum over all columns k' norms. While all column norms decrease with γ, the column index k of the column that is largest stays constant across the whole domain of γ. This allows us to define a constant 'coefficient' c for the entire operator and write the operator norm in a compact form. With $c := \max_{k', |n_{k'}| < p_{k'}} \frac{|n_{k'}|}{p_{k'}}$ and k as the *argmax* of the expression,

$$\|R_{\cdot|\cdot}(\gamma)\|_1 = \max_{k'} \|R_{\cdot|k'}(\gamma)\|_1 = \|R_{\cdot|k}(\gamma)\|_1 = 1 + \frac{2c}{1 - c + \gamma}. \quad (11)$$

When $\gamma = 0$, the L1 norm $\|R_{\cdot|\cdot}(0)\|_1$ can become large if there is an activated neuron k in the layer, whose negative inputs are almost as large as it's negative input: $|n_k| \lesssim p_k \Rightarrow c \lesssim 1$. The LRP-$\gamma$ rule outweighs the positive contributions when assigning relevance. If the positive inputs already dominate in every neuron, the operator norm is not significantly changed by increasing the γ-parameter.

Finally, we can **bound the operator norms of the entire explanation method** as a function of the LRP-γ parameters in the layers that use the rule.

Simplifying to the case that every layer $0 \leq t < T$ of the network uses the LRP-γ rule, and that the measured $c^{(t)}$ is the same for all layers t, we find that the operator norm of the entire explanation process is bounded by

$$\|A_{\cdot|\cdot}^{(0\leftarrow T)}(\gamma)\|_1 \leq \prod_{t=0}^{T} \|A_{\cdot|\cdot}^{(t)}(\gamma)\|_1 = \left(1 + \frac{2c}{1-c+\gamma}\right)^T = \sum_{t=0}^{T} \binom{T}{t} \left(\frac{2c}{1-c+\gamma}\right)^T$$

The operator norm bound decreases monotonically with γ. In fact, for large $c \approx 1$, the bound can shrink rapidly, at a rate up to γ^{-T}. Practitioners commonly observe this effect in deep networks explained with the LRP-γ rule across multiple consecutive layers (e.g. [28,30]). Specifying too high γ quickly leads to very high *Stability* and low *Sensitivity*. The explanations have a coarse-grained nature and can not distinguish between classes anymore, as visualized in Sect. 4.3 (bottom).

C Computational Complexity of the Evaluation Methods

Stability, as the largest singular value, can be computed efficiently using iterative methods such as the power iteration or Lanczos algorithms [22]. Assuming a network with d inputs and h outputs, and its redistribution matrices as described in Sect. 3, these methods have a computational cost of $\mathcal{O}(dh)$ per iteration. The number of iterations until the first singular value and vector are found depend on the desired precision and the spectral gap of the matrix. *Sensitivity* can be calculated as the square root of the sum of the squared entries of the redistribution matrix, which is equivalent to its Frobenius norm. The computational complexity for this calculation is $\mathcal{O}(dh)$.

Complexity of Constructing the Redistribution Matrix. In perturbation-based methods (such as Shapley), heatmaps for all classes–and thus the entire redistribution matrix–can be created simultaneously by collecting each class's output for every perturbed input. Therefore the complexity to create the redistribution matrix is equivalent to the complexity of the explanation for one target output.

Propagation-based methods such as LRP and SmoothGrad require both forward and backward passes per (perturbed) input to generate a heatmap. However, the forward computation can be reused to compute gradients for multiple classes. In summary, LRP scales with $\mathcal{O}(h)$ per input image, while SmoothGrad with k noise perturbations scales with $\mathcal{O}(hk)$.

D MNIST CNN architecture

The convolutional neural network (CNN) architecture used for the MNIST dataset is a small network with 6 convolutional layers containing ReLU activation functions. The full sequence includes 3 convolutional layers with kernel sizes 3×3, 3×3, and 5×5 using 8 filters each, followed by a max-pooling layer with kernel size 2. This is followed by convolutional layers of kernel sizes 5×5, 3×3, and 3×3 and 16 filters each. After a second max-pooling layer (with a kernel size of 2), the output is flattened and passed through a fully connected layer to compute the 10 logit scores. The network is trained using the SGD optimizer and a learning rate of 0.1 until convergence.

The data from the Kaggle Digit Recognizer dataset [19] is randomly split into a training and test set with a ratio of 80% to 20%. The network is trained on the 33,600 training data points using the SGD optimizer and a learning rate of 0.1 until convergence. 100 images are drawn from the test set for the evaluation of the explanation methods.

References

1. Adebayo, J., Gilmer, J., Muelly, M., Goodfellow, I., Hardt, M., Kim, B.: Sanity checks for saliency maps. In: Proceedings of the 32nd International Conference on Neural Information Processing Systems, pp. 9525–9536. NIPS'18, Curran Associates Inc., Red Hook, NY, USA (2018)
2. Ancona, M., Ceolini, E., Öztireli, C., Gross, M.: Towards better understanding of gradient-based attribution methods for deep neural networks. In: ICLR (Poster). OpenReview.net (2018)
3. Ancona, M., Ceolini, E., Öztireli, C., Gross, M.H.: Gradient-based attribution methods. In: Explainable AI, Lecture Notes in Computer Science, vol. 11700, pp. 169–191. Springer (2019)
4. Arrieta, A.B., et al.: Explainable artificial intelligence (XAI): concepts, taxonomies, opportunities and challenges toward responsible AI. Inf. Fusion **58**, 82–115 (2020)
5. Bach, S., Binder, A., Montavon, G., Klauschen, F., Müller, K.R., Samek, W.: On pixel-wise explanations for non-linear classifier decisions by layer-wise relevance propagation. PLoS ONE **10**(7), e0130140 (2015)
6. Baehrens, D., Schroeter, T., Harmeling, S., Kawanabe, M., Hansen, K., Müller, K.R.: How to explain individual classification decisions. J. Mach. Learn. Res. **11**, 1803–1831 (2010)
7. Balduzzi, D., et al.: The shattered gradients problem: if resnets are the answer, then what is the question? In: International Conference on Machine Learning, pp. 342–350. PMLR (2017)
8. Binder, A., Weber, L., Lapuschkin, S., Montavon, G., Müller, K.R., Samek, W.: Shortcomings of top-down randomization-based sanity checks for evaluations of deep neural network explanations. In: Proceedings of the IEEE/CVF Conference on Computer Vision and Pattern Recognition, pp. 16143–16152 (2023)
9. Bluecher, S., Vielhaben, J., Strodthoff, N.: Decoupling pixel flipping and occlusion strategy for consistent XAI benchmarks. In: Transactions on Machine Learning Research (2024)
10. Bradski, G.: The OpenCV Library. Dr. Dobb's Journal of Software Tools (2000)
11. Caruana, R., Lou, Y., Gehrke, J., Koch, P., Sturm, M., Elhadad, N.: Intelligible models for healthcare: predicting pneumonia risk and hospital 30-day readmission. In: KDD, pp. 1721–1730. ACM (2015)
12. Chormai, P., Herrmann, J., Müller, K.R., Montavon, G.: Disentangled explanations of neural network predictions by finding relevant subspaces. IEEE Trans. Pattern Anal. Mach. Intell. **46**(11), 7283–7299 (2024)

13. Dabkowski, P., Gal, Y.: Real time image saliency for black box classifiers. In: NIPS, pp. 6967–6976 (2017)
14. Deng, J., Dong, W., Socher, R., Li, L.J., Li, K., Fei-Fei, L.: Imagenet: a large-scale hierarchical image database. In: 2009 IEEE Conference on Computer Vision and Pattern Recognition, pp. 248–255 (2009)
15. Dombrowski, A.K., Alber, M., Anders, C., Ackermann, M., Müller, K.R., Kessel, P.: Explanations can be manipulated and geometry is to blame. Adv. Neural Info. Process. Syst. **32** (2019)
16. Doshi-Velez, F., Kim, B.: A roadmap for a rigorous science of interpretability. CoRR **abs/1702.08608** (2017)
17. Hedström, A., et al.: Quantus: an explainable AI toolkit for responsible evaluation of neural network explanations and beyond. J. Mach. Learn. Res. **24**(34), 1–11 (2023)
18. Hense, J., et al.: XMIL: insightful explanations for multiple instance learning in histopathology (2025). https://arxiv.org/abs/2406.04280
19. Kaggle: Digit recognizer dataset (2017). https://www.kaggle.com/competitions/digit-recognizer/data. Accessed 01 April 2025
20. Klauschen, F., et al.: Toward explainable artificial intelligence for precision pathology. Annu. Rev. Pathol. **19**(1), 541–570 (2024)
21. Koh, P.W., Liang, P.: Understanding black-box predictions via influence functions. In: ICML. Proceedings of Machine Learning Research, vol. 70, pp. 1885–1894. PMLR (2017)
22. Lanczos, C.: An iteration method for the solution of the eigenvalue problem of linear differential and integral operators. J. Res. Natl. Bur. Stand. **45**(4), 255–282 (1950)
23. Lapuschkin, S., Wäldchen, S., Binder, A., Montavon, G., Samek, W., Müller, K.R.: Unmasking clever HANs predictors and assessing what machines really learn. Nat. Commun. **10**(1), 1096 (2019)
24. LeCun, Y., Cortes, C.: MNIST handwritten digit database (2010). http://yann.lecun.com/exdb/mnist/
25. Letzgus, S., Müller, K.R.: An explainable AI framework for robust and transparent data-driven wind turbine power curve models (2024)
26. Marcel, S., Rodriguez, Y.: Torchvision the machine-vision package of torch (2010). https://pypi.org/project/torchvision/
27. Montavon, G.: Gradient-based vs. propagation-based explanations: An axiomatic comparison. In: Explainable AI: Interpreting, Explaining and Visualizing Deep Learning, pp. 253–265 (2019)
28. Montavon, G., Binder, A., Lapuschkin, S., Samek, W., Müller, K.R.: Layer-wise relevance propagation: an overview. In: Explainable AI: Interpreting, Explaining and Visualizing Deep Learning, pp. 193–209 (2019)
29. Nauta, M., et al.: From anecdotal evidence to quantitative evaluation methods: a systematic review on evaluating explainable AI. ACM Comput. Surv. **55**(13s) (Jul 2023)
30. Pahde, F., Yolcu, G.Ü., Binder, A., Samek, W., Lapuschkin, S.: Optimizing explanations by network canonization and hyperparameter search. In: Proceedings of the IEEE/CVF Conference on Computer Vision and Pattern Recognition, pp. 3818–3827 (2023)
31. Petsiuk, V., Das, A., Saenko, K.: RISE: randomized input sampling for explanation of black-box models. In: BMVC, p. 151. BMVA Press (2018)

32. Samek, W., Binder, A., Montavon, G., Lapuschkin, S., Müller, K.R.: Evaluating the visualization of what a deep neural network has learned. IEEE Trans. Neural Netw. Learn. Syst. **28**(11), 2660–2673 (2016)
33. Samek, W., Montavon, G., Lapuschkin, S., Anders, C.J., Müller, K.R.: Explaining deep neural networks and beyond: a review of methods and applications. Proc. IEEE **109**(3), 247–278 (2021)
34. Schnake, T., et al.: Higher-order explanations of graph neural networks via relevant walks. IEEE Trans. Pattern Anal. Mach. Intell. **44**(11), 7581–7596 (2022)
35. Schnake, T., et al.: Towards symbolic XAI – explanation through human understandable logical relationships between features. Info. Fusion **118**, 102923 (2025)
36. Selvaraju, R.R., Cogswell, M., Das, A., Vedantam, R., Parikh, D., Batra, D.: Grad-Cam: visual explanations from deep networks via gradient-based localization. Int. J. Comput. Vis. **128**(2), 336–359 (2020)
37. Shapley, L.S.: A Value for n-Person Games, pp. 307–318. Princeton University Press (1953)
38. Sixt, L., Granz, M., Landgraf, T.: When explanations lie: why many modified BP attributions fail. In: International Conference on Machine Learning, pp. 9046–9057. PMLR (2020)
39. Smilkov, D., Thorat, N., Kim, B., Viégas, F.B., Wattenberg, M.: Smoothgrad: removing noise by adding noise. CoRR **abs/1706.03825** (2017)
40. Štrumbelj, E., Kononenko, I.: An efficient explanation of individual classifications using game theory. J. Mach. Learn. Res. **11**, 1–18 (2010)
41. Strumbelj, E., Kononenko, I.: Explaining prediction models and individual predictions with feature contributions. Knowl. Inf. Syst. **41**(3), 647–665 (2014)
42. Sundararajan, M., Taly, A., Yan, Q.: Axiomatic attribution for deep networks. In: International Conference on Machine Learning, pp. 3319–3328. PMLR (2017)
43. Swartout, W.R., Moore, J.D.: Explanation in Second Generation Expert Systems, pp. 543–585. Springer Berlin Heidelberg (1993)
44. Telea, A.: An image inpainting technique based on the fast marching method. J. Graph .Tools **9**(1), 23–34 (2004)
45. Tseng, A., Shrikumar, A., Kundaje, A.: Fourier-transform-based attribution priors improve the interpretability and stability of deep learning models for genomics. In: Advances in Neural Information Processing Systems, vol. 33, pp. 1913–1923. Curran Associates, Inc. (2020)
46. Xiong, P., Schnake, T., Gastegger, M., Montavon, G., Müller, K.R., Nakajima, S.: Relevant walk search for explaining graph neural networks. In: Proceedings of the 40th International Conference on Machine Learning. Proceedings of Machine Learning Research, vol. 202, pp. 38301–38324. PMLR (2023)
47. Xiong, P., Schnake, T., Montavon, G., Müller, K.R., Nakajima, S.: Efficient computation of higher-order subgraph attribution via message passing. In: Proceedings of the 39th International Conference on Machine Learning. Proceedings of Machine Learning Research, vol. 162, pp. 24478–24495. PMLR (2022)
48. Yu, H., Varshney, L.R.: Towards deep interpretability (MUS-ROVER II): learning hierarchical representations of tonal music. In: 5th International Conference on Learning Representations, ICLR 2017, Toulon, France, April 24-26, 2017, Conference Track Proceedings. OpenReview.net (2017)
49. Zhang, J., Bargal, S.A., Lin, Z., Brandt, J., Shen, X., Sclaroff, S.: Top-down neural attention by excitation backprop. Int. J. Comput. Vis. **126**(10), 1084–1102 (2018)

Open Access This chapter is licensed under the terms of the Creative Commons Attribution 4.0 International License (http://creativecommons.org/licenses/by/4.0/), which permits use, sharing, adaptation, distribution and reproduction in any medium or format, as long as you give appropriate credit to the original author(s) and the source, provide a link to the Creative Commons license and indicate if changes were made.

The images or other third party material in this chapter are included in the chapter's Creative Commons license, unless indicated otherwise in a credit line to the material. If material is not included in the chapter's Creative Commons license and your intended use is not permitted by statutory regulation or exceeds the permitted use, you will need to obtain permission directly from the copyright holder.

Consolidating Explanation Stability Metrics

Jeremie Bogaert[1(✉)], Antonin Descampe[2], and François-Xavier Standaert[1]

[1] Crypto Group, ICTEAM Institute, UCLouvain, Ottignies-Louvain-la-Neuve, Belgium
`jeremie.bogaert@uclouvain.be`
[2] ORM/PCOM, ILC Institute, UCLouvain, Ottignies-Louvain-la-Neuve, Belgium

Abstract. The explanations of large language models (e.g., where each word is assigned a relevance score) have recently been shown to be sensitive to the randomness used during model training, creating a need to evaluate this sensitivity. While simple visualization tools such as box plots can provide a qualitative characterization, exploring the design space of the parameters influencing the explanation's sensitivity to the training randomness may benefit from a more quantitative approach. First attempts in this direction explored simple (word-level univariate, first-order) explanations and proposed tentative information theoretic metrics such as the explanation's signal, noise and Signal-to-Noise Ratio (SNR). They left the suitability of such metrics as an open question, which we tackle in this work. For this purpose, we start by identifying corner cases where they appear unable to capture intuitively desirable features of explanations corresponding to a different training randomness. Namely, the SNR does not reflect well the relative differences of relevance (between words). We next put forward that the correlation with a mean explanation provides a better treatment of these corner cases, at the cost of being unable to reflect absolute differences of relevance (for single words). We then discuss how to turn these observations into a consolidated approach for analyzing the explanations' sensitivity to the training randomness. While there is no silver bullet that perfectly deals with the full complexity of this sensitivity problem, we argue that design space exploration with the correlation metric and individual model analysis with box plots provides a good tradeoff. Besides, we put forward additional desirable features of the correlation metric (e.g., unbiased estimation thanks to cross-validation and simple confidence intervals).

1 Introduction

In recent years, Large Language Models (LLM) like BERT [8] or GPT [9] have led to significant performance improvements for a vast amount of Natural Language Processing (NLP) tasks [1]. These improvements generally come from more complex architectures with more parameters, of which the training relies on randomized optimization techniques. As a result, it has been consistently observed that the explainability of LLMs is a major challenge [14], which is especially important for applications implying critical (e.g., medical or legal) decisions.

At high level, the explainability of LLMs relates to broad and hard-to-define concepts like faithfulness [12,16] and plausibility [11,12]. Informally, faithfulness requires that an explanation accurately reflects the algorithmic reasoning process behind a model's predictions, and plausibility requires explanations to be understandable and convincing to the target audience. In this paper, we are concerned with a more specific issue which has connections with both concepts. Namely, the sensitivity of the explanations to the randomness used to train models, recently put forward by Bogaert et al. [3,6]. The main observation of this paper is that it is sometimes possible to produce many models of which the training only differs by the (indistinguishable) random seeds they use, that are "equivalent" from the accuracy viewpoint and nevertheless lead to different explanations.[1] The authors then argue that this sensitivity to the training randomness must at least be characterized, since in the extreme case where the explanations would be uniformly distributed, any selection of explanation would be completely arbitrary.

The explanations' sensitivity to randomness has for now been exhibited in the case of "simple" explanations, defined in [5] as word-level, univariate (i.e., assigning a single relevance value per word) and first-order (i.e., assuming readers are interested by mean explanations in case of sensitivity to randomness). We will use Chefer et al.'s Layerwise Relevance Propagation (LRP) method as our running example [7]. Such simple explanations, next denoted as (1,1,1), are of course not expected to be perfectly faithful, although we assume they reflect the models' reasoning to a sufficient extent. They are not expected to be the only plausible ones either. Yet, they provide a useful theoretical framework to answer the question: *how stable can the simple explanations of complex models be?*

Evaluating the sensitivity to the training randomness of LLMs can be done qualitatively. For example, visualization tools like box plots provide a good intuitive understanding of single texts. Yet, more quantitative tools become useful to explore the explanations' design space. For example, one could be interested to compare the randomness' sensitivity of different texts, and for explanations assigning relevance scores for various number of words. One could also be interested to compare the randomness' sensitivity of bigger vs. smaller models, for various tasks, datasets or languages, or for different explanation methods. First steps in this direction were made in [5], where the explanations' signal, noise and Signal-to-Noise Ratio (SNR) are proposed as tentative explanation stability metrics. In this paper, we consolidate these investigations in three directions.

First, we highlight the limited ability of the SNR to reflect the relative differences of relevance (between words) in a set of explanations corresponding to different (random) training seeds. We additionally show that the correlation with a mean explanation mitigates this issue, as to cost of being unable to reflect absolute differences of relevance (for single words), which are better captured by the

---

[1] Equivalent meaning that there is no statistically significant difference in their accuracies, implying that there is no "better" model from the accuracy viewpoint.

SNR. Second, we discuss the consequence of these observations and argue that combining a design space exploration with the correlation metric and a more qualitative analysis thanks to box plots appears as a good tradeoff. The first one better captures relative differences within explanations, whereas the second one reflects absolute differences at the individual word level, exhibiting possibly interesting intuitions that the (quantitative) SNR metric may hide. We finally put forward additional desirable features of the correlation metric such as easier interpretation, unbiased estimation thanks to cross-validation and simple confidence intervals thanks to a well-known statistical distribution.

Related Works. The quantitative evaluation of the sensitivity to the training randomness is quite related to the problem of inter-annotator agreement – see for example [2,10]. One difference is that the explanations of LLMs provide continuous relevance scores (vs. more discretized ones for human annotators). The other is that, due to the (1,1,1) restriction, we can replace pairwise correlations, which are frequently used in the inter-annotator agreement literature but can become expensive as the number of random seeds under investigation increases in our context, by the correlation with a mean explanation. Our study is also related to [18] which, among others, performed an experiment to test whether the words' relevance obtained thanks to four different types of explanations were impacted by the random seeds used for model initialization. They used Pearson's correlation for this purpose, but only considered two random seeds and did not ensure model equivalence (nor input compatibility, as we define next).

2 Background

2.1 Dataset, Model and Explanation Method

We run our experiments on the InfOpinion dataset [4], composed of 10,000 french texts belonging to the *information* and *opinion* journalistic genres. This binary categorization relies solely on the articles' annotation by their authors as either *information* or *opinion*. The dataset is split in 3 parts: a training set (80%), a validation set (10%) and a test set (10%). The classes are balanced among each of these sets. The task is to predict the binary category of a given text.

The model we consider is the French pre-trained transformer model CamemBERT [15], in the two different setups presented in [8]. In the first one, that we denote as *fine-tuned*, we jointly train all the weights of the encoder blocks and the classification head during 2 epochs. In the second one, that we denote as *frozen*, we only train the classification head while freezing the encoder blocks (i.e., the model learns to use the embeddings without modifying them). We note that the model's training randomness can be controlled via a seed parameter that rules the initialization of the layers, the order of the training dataset and the neurons that are deactivated by the dropout layers during the training.

Once our model is trained, we use Chefer et al.'s LRP method to generate word-level explanations for every text [7]. It back-propagates the relevance from the last layer of the network using conservation constraints, so that the relevance of each neuron is redistributed to the neurons of the previous layer based on their respective gradient. This principle is then followed through the whole network up to the input layer in order to obtain word-level explanations.[2]

2.2 Equivalent Models' Explanations

In a previous work [3,6], Bogaert et al. showed that the training randomness of LLMs can have an impact on their explainability. To do so, and as illustrated in Fig. 1, they trained many models with the same settings and on the same dataset, but with different random seeds. The accuracy of these models was then evaluated on a test set, and a subset of m most accurate models was selected, such that the difference between the best (a) and worst (b) accuracies of the models in the subset was not statistically significant. For this purpose, one can computed the z statistic [13], which can detect whether two proportions (here, the accuracies a and b) are different:

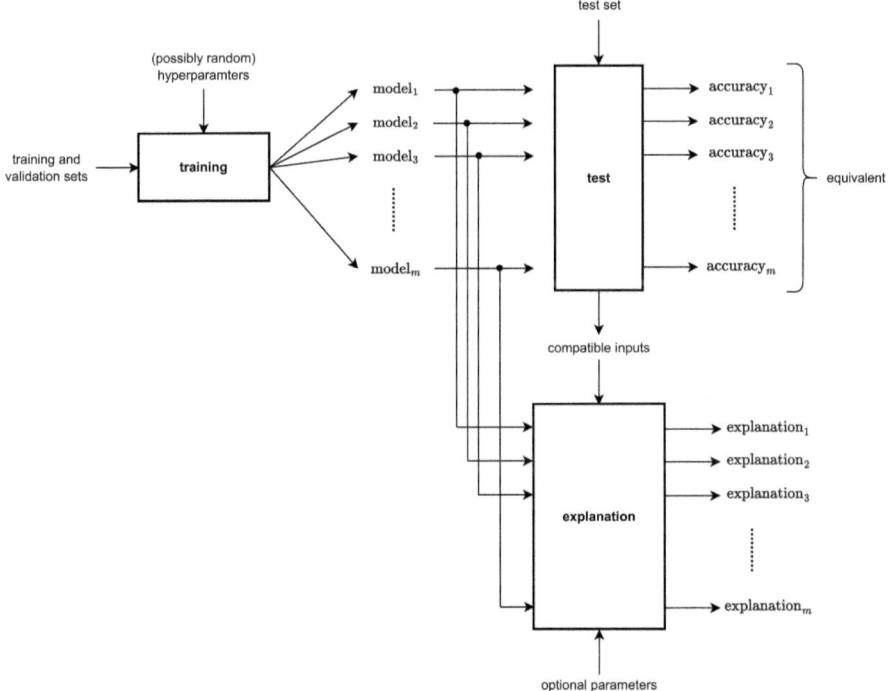

Fig. 1. Setup for the generation of equivalent models and compatible inputs.

---

[2] CamemBERT uses the roBERTa tokenization to work with word pieces. We post-process explanations to get one weight per word instead of one per word piece.

$$z = \left| \frac{a-b}{\sqrt{\frac{\frac{a+b}{2}*(1-\frac{a+b}{2})}{t}}} \right|.$$

As Bogaert et al., we next consider that z values greater than 1.96 ($p < 0.025$) mean that the accuracies of the best and the worst models in a subset are different. For lower z values, we conclude that these accuracies do not differ significantly and therefore, we consider the models in the subset as equivalent from the performance viewpoint. Starting from 200 models (see Sect. 2.1), a restriction to $m = 100$ was sufficient to reach model equivalence in the subset. We then selected so-called compatible inputs for which all models predict the same class, and we computed explanations for each model on such inputs.

2.3 Explanation Stability

The main observation in [3,6] is that the explanations of equivalent models on compatible inputs can differ, raising a need to characterize their sensitivity to the training randomness. For this purpose, one can construct an explanation matrix of m rows (corresponding to different random seeds) and n columns (corresponding to different words), where each $a_{s,w}$ corresponds to the relevance value assigned by the s-th model (seed) to the word at the w-th position, as showed in Fig. 2. The left part of the figure additionally shows the average curve which corresponds to the "simple" (word-level, univariate and first-order) explanations introduced in [5]. Word-level means that all m explanations of an n-word text display a weight for each word independently. Univariate means that each of these weights is a single value. First-order means that variable explanations are summarized by their mean (i.e., a first-order statistical moment).

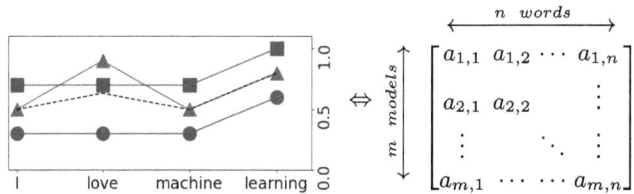

Fig. 2. Explanations of $n = 4$-word texts for $m = 3$ seeds and mean (dotted).

2.4 k-Words Explanations

To capture the possibility that shorter explanations are more plausible, we can evaluate so-called k-word explanations, obtained by keeping only the $0 \leq k \leq n$ highest relevance values of each explanation. To further simplify the individual explanations, one can also use k-word binary explanations, where only the k top words are considered relevant, without any distinction among them:

$$a_{s,w} = \begin{cases} a_{s,w} & \text{if } a_{s,w} \in TOP_k(a_{s,:}), \\ 0 & \text{oth.} \end{cases} \qquad a_{s,w} = \begin{cases} 1 & \text{if } a_{s,w} \in TOP_k(a_{s,:}), \\ 0 & \text{oth.} \end{cases}$$

2.5 Signal, Noise and SNR

Simple (word-level, univariate and first-order) explanations naturally suggest simple quantities to capture their sensitivity to randomness. In [5], the explanations' signal (S), noise (N) and Signal-to-Noise Ratio (SNR) were suggested as tentative metrics for this purpose. Intuitively, the signal reflects the flatness of the average explanation, the noise reflects the variation of the relevance scores for each word (averaged) and the SNR is simply the ratio between both:

$$S = \hat{\text{Var}}_{n \text{ words}} \left(\hat{\mathbb{E}}_{m \text{ seeds}} (a_{s,w}) \right), \qquad N = \hat{\mathbb{E}}_{n \text{ models}} \left(\hat{\text{Var}}_{m \text{ seeds}} (a_{s,w}) \right), \qquad SNR = \frac{S}{N}.$$

3 Metrics' Corner Cases

We next discuss the adequacy of the SNR metric to reflect the stability of explanations in the setting of Fig. 2. For this purpose, we use illustrative hand-made examples and compare how the stability of some explanations is captured by the SNR and by an alternative simple metric, namely the (average) correlation with a mean explanation. We are in particular interested in the ability of these metrics to reflect the relative differences of relevance between words and the absolute differences of relevance for single words in a set of variable explanations.

3.1 Relative Differences (Between Words)

Figure 3 illustrates two pairs of explanations such that the relevance of some words are swapped when moving from the left to the right plots. As a result, these left and right plots show quite disparate relative differences of relevance between words. Interestingly, the SNR metric is unable to reflect these relative differences. This is because the swaps do not affect the mean explanations (which are the same on the left and right plots, leading to the same signal) nor the absolute difference between words (hence the noise). By contrast, the correlation metric captures these relative differences: the explanations of the left plot are highly correlated with the mean explanation; the ones of the right plot are not.

3.2 Absolute Differences (for Single Words)

A complementary situation is illustrated in Fig. 4, in which an offset δ was added to all the relevance values of one explanation and subtracted for the other. As a result, the left and right plots show disparate absolute differences. This time,

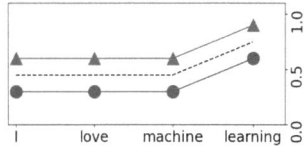 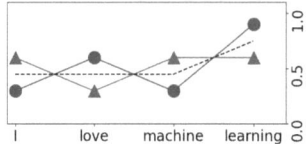

Fig. 3. Two pairs of explanations (△ and ○), with the same absolute differences and different relative differences, with the mean explanation in dotted line.

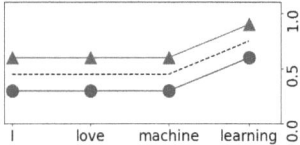 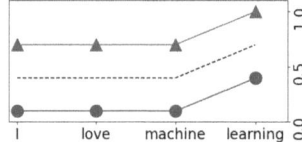

Fig. 4. Two pairs of explanations (△ and ○), with the same relative differences and different absolute differences, with the mean explanation in dotted line.

the correlation metric is unable to reflect the discrepancy between the left and right plots (because the correlation is invariant to the δ offset). By contrast, the SNR reflects it because the noise of the left and right plots differs.

3.3 Discussion

The two examples above suggest a quite natural tradeoff between the SNR and correlation metrics: the first one better captures absolute differences, the second one better captures relative differences. While this may encourage using both metrics in parallel, Fig. 5 highlights additional limitations of the (noise component of the) SNR metric. Namely, it illustrates that the noise metric is averaged over (possibly dependent) words, which may hide important intuition regarding which word is causing the noise. (By contrast, the correlation can be averaged over independent seeds). As a result, we suggest using the correlation metric for design space exploration and box plots for a qualitative analysis of the noise. As will be experimented next, this appears as a relevant combination to characterize the explanations' sensitivity to the training randomness, capturing both the absolute and relative differences within these explanations.[3]

Besides, the SNR is also slightly less convenient to manipulate from the statistical viewpoint. First, it is a biased metric since small estimation errors in the mean explanations are considered as signal by definition. Second, its interpretation in case of small noise levels is not always intuitive (e.g., the SNR tends to infinity when the noise tends to zero). Despite these drawbacks do not lead to fundamental issues (i.e., the SNR bias decreases with the amount of seeds and

---

[3] In Appendix A, we give additional arguments why the noise metric alone cannot be used for design space exploration. In appendix B, we give additional arguments why the signal metric alone is making undesirable implicit plausibility assumptions.

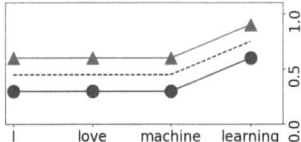 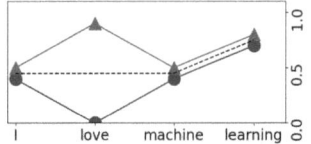

Fig. 5. Two pairs of explanations (△ and ○), with the same (average) relative differences but distributing these differences differently among the words of a sentence.

can be corrected, intuition is just less direct), we show next that the correlation coefficient also comes with advantages in this respect. It can be estimated without bias thanks to cross-validation, benefits from a well-known sample distribution leading to easy-to-obtain confidence intervals and its interpretation is direct.

4 Application to Case Studies

We now apply the methodology proposed above to the classification case study described in Sect. 2. First, we detail how to estimate the correlation metric in Sect. 4.1. Next, we show how it can be used for design space exploration in Sect. 4.2. Finally, we illustrate how such a quantitative analysis is nicely combined with a more qualitative one using box plots in Sect. 4.3.

4.1 Estimation and Confidence Interval

The examples of Sect. 3 suggest using the correlation of different explanations with their mean as a good way to quantify the explanations' sensitivity to the training randomness.[4] We next detail how correlation samples can be estimated without bias thanks to 10-fold cross validation, and possibly averaged.

For this purpose, the average explanation is first repeatedly computed using 90% of the explanation matrix's rows and the remaining 10% of the rows are repeatedly compared to these means in order to compute correlation samples (one per explanation). Figure 6 shows a scatter plot of all the correlations to the mean (i.e., one per trained model, so 100 in our case study), highlighting the high disparity of the results depending of the training randomness.

Different quantities of the correlation distribution could then be considered to summarize the explanations' stability. In the following, and for simplicity purposes, we suggest to use the average correlation. We note that while it is in general better to estimate the correlation between two variables based on a large set of samples than averaging correlations estimated from several smaller sets of samples, this approach can serve as a useful heuristic in our context, if interpreted carefully. Namely, as a way to capture a global tendency for many

---

[4] Under the assumption of simple explanations formalized in [5] as (1,1,1) explanations, computing the average correlation to a mean explanation rather than the average pairwise correlation allows significant speedups without intuition loss.

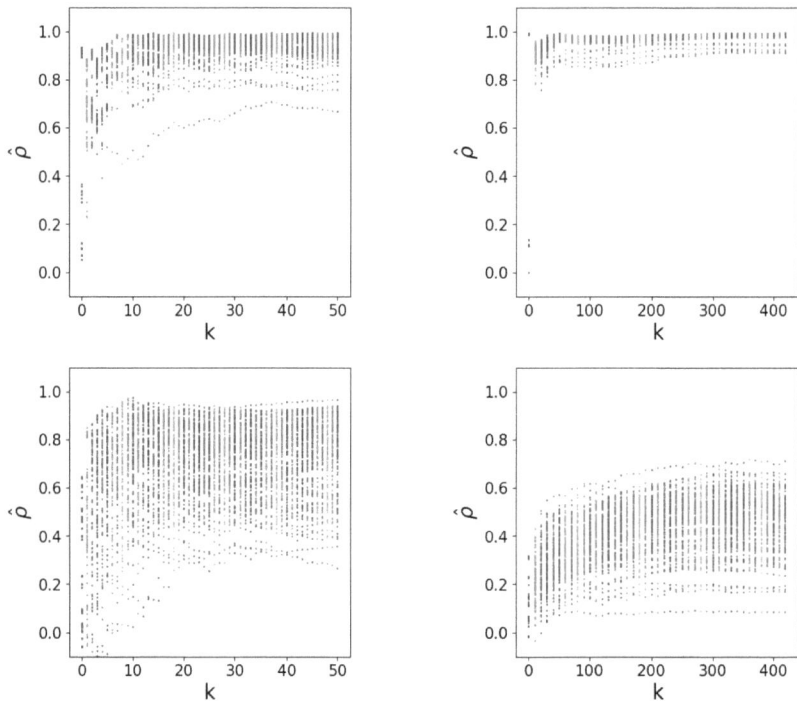

Fig. 6. Scatter plot of the correlation to the mean for LRP explanations corresponding to the *frozen* (top) and *fine-tuned* (bottom) models in function of the number of words used per explanation, illustrated for a short (left) and a long (right) text. For readability, only the values $k = 10, 20, 30, ...$ are displayed for the long text.

explanations, possibly leading to different correlation values. For this purpose, we follow [17] and first use the following "Fisher Z transformation":

$$F(\hat{\rho}) = \frac{1}{2}\ln(\frac{1+\hat{\rho}}{1-\hat{\rho}}) = \text{arctanh}(\hat{\rho}),$$

which projects the correlation samples in a space where they are normally distributed. We can then compute the average Fisher value $\bar{F}$, as well as its sample variance $\hat{\sigma}^2$. A confidence interval on the estimation of $\bar{F}$ (e.g., 96%) is obtained by adding or removing $2\frac{\hat{\sigma}}{\sqrt{m}}$ to $\bar{F}$. Applying the inverse function $\rho = \tanh(F(\rho))$ finally leads to 96% confidence interval for the average correlation:

$$\left[\tanh\left(\bar{F} - \frac{2\hat{\sigma}}{\sqrt{m}}\right); \tanh\left(\bar{F} + \frac{2\hat{\sigma}}{\sqrt{m}}\right)\right].$$

This interval indicates that the average correlation is better estimated with more models (i.e., large m values). By contrast, longer texts (i.e., large n values) lead

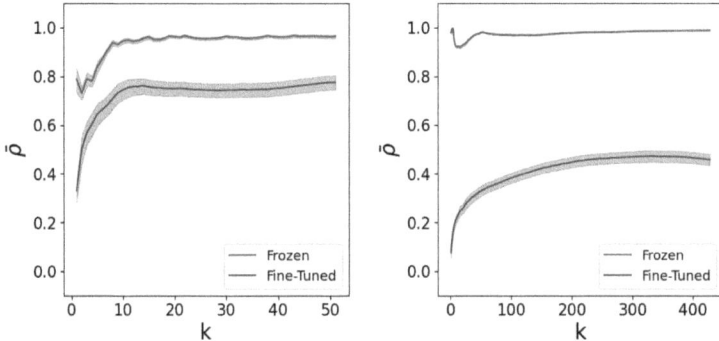

Fig. 7. Average correlation to the mean (with confidence intervals) for LRP explanations corresponding to the *frozen* and *fine-tuned* models in function of the number of words used per explanation, illustrated for a short (left) and a long (right) text.

to better estimated correlation samples, but do not necessarily decrease the variance $\hat{\sigma}$, since the correlations of different explanations may differ.

4.2 Quantitative Analysis

Figure 7 shows the average correlation to the mean for k-word explanations. Positing that shorter and more aligned explanations are more plausible, such an exploration can lead to identify relevant parameters to investigate more qualitatively. For example, we can see on the left plot that the average correlation to the mean increases up to $k = 7$ and then reaches a plateau . Hence, larger values of k (i.e., longer explanations) may not lead to a reduced sensitivity to the training randomness. We next complete this observation with a qualitative analysis for the explanations obtained for $k = 7$ and the maximum $k = 51$.

4.3 Qualitative Analysis

Starting with the box plot for $k = 7$ displayed on Fig. 8, we can observe that, qualitatively as well, the LRP explanations of the frozen model are significantly less sensitive to the training randomness than the ones of the fine-tuned model. This is quite expected since the amount of network weights that are trained in these two models vastly differ. What is maybe less expected is that the the variability per word is also distributed very differently for both models. Namely, 7-word explanations across the 100 seeds only consider 10 different words in the frozen case, while most words are considered by the fine-tuned models. This tends to justify our proposed methodology, where we do not analyze the absolute difference with the noise metric (which is averaged over the words).

More interestingly, Fig. 9 shows the box plots obtained for the same models and $k = 51$. Its upper part is particularly relevant: it confirms that increasing

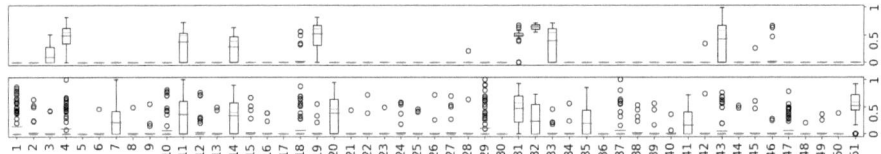

Fig. 8. Box plot for $k = 7$ and the *frozen* (top) and *fine-tuned* (bottom) models.

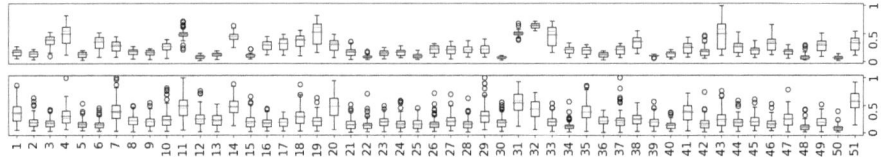

Fig. 9. Box plot for $k = 51$ and the *frozen* (top) and *fine-tuned* (bottom) models.

the explanations' length beyond $k = 7$ is not only discouraged by the correlation metric, it actually also leads to harder to interpret first-order explanations assigning non-zero relevance scores to most words, as the fine-tuned model.

5 Conclusions

Our results provide consolidated tools for analyzing the sensitivity of the explanations of LLMs to the training randomness, hopefully opening a path to their better understanding and leading to various interesting open problems.

First, and maybe most importantly, the extent to which the stability of the explanations of LLMs is a requirement for their plausibility remains unknown. While we posit in the paper that shorter and more aligned explanations are easier to understand, it could also be that human explanations show variations that are similar to the ones observed in this paper. Designing a real-world experiment with human annotators would be interesting to contribute to this question.

Second, even if explanations appear unstable when considering their average correlation to a mean explanation as in this paper, it is possible that some clusters exist within these explanations. This would mimic a situation where a few groups of human annotators share very similar explanations within the groups and have very different ones between the groups. In order to stimulate research in this direction, Fig. 10 shows a TSNE visualization of 100 explanations used in our experiments. It would be interesting to investigate whether clusters an be extracted from such plots and lead to more stable/aligned explanations.

Third, it would be interesting to investigate whether more complex explanations (e.g., assigning relevance scores to tuples of words) or more complex models (e.g., generative ones) may lead to different outcomes, and whether a sensitivity to the training randomness is observed for other tasks or data sets.

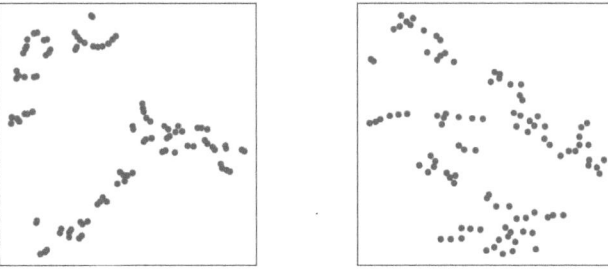

Fig. 10. TSNE for $k = 51$ and the *frozen* (left) and *fine-tuned* (right) models.

Finally, our conclusion may also differ for other modalities than texts. For example, image explanations may be more stable due to the more correlated nature of adjacent pixels (compared to consecurive words in a text).

Acknowledgments. François-Xavier Standaert is a research director of the Belgian fund for scientific research (FNRS-F.R.S.). This work has been supported by the Service Public de Wallonie Recherche, grant no2010235-ARIAC.

A The Noise Is Not Good for Design Space Exploration

As illustrated in Fig. 11, we cannot use the signal or the noise alone to explore our design space, as their range is directly impacted by the amount of top words k. This is the case even for deterministic/random explanations, which lead to an hypothesis that selecting a certain ratio of word leads to more stable explanations, even if all the models perfectly agree on the relevance of every token. This is not the case for the correlation metric that is always at its maximum for the deterministic model, and at its minimum for the random one.

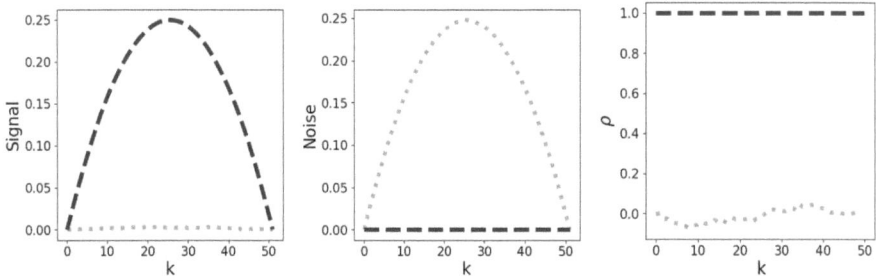

Fig. 11. Signal (left), noise (middle) and correlation (right) of deterministic (-) and random (.) explanations, for the binary variant of k-word explanations.

B Implicit Assumption of the Signal Metric

As illustrated in Fig. 12, it is possible to obtain explanations such that their absolute and relative differences are identical, but their signal differs, because the signal is focused on the flatness of the mean explanation. It implicitly suggests that more relative differences within this mean explanation lead to better explainability, which may not be connected to a definition of plausibility.

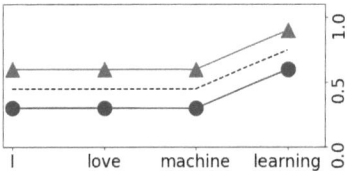 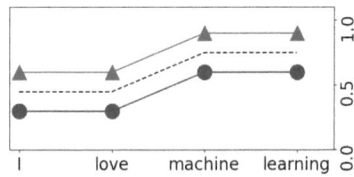

Fig. 12. Two pairs of explanations ($\triangle$ and $\bigcirc$), with the same absolute and relative differences and different signal, with the mean explanation in dotted line.

References

1. Acheampong, F.A., Nunoo-Mensah, H., Chen, W.: Transformer models for text-based emotion detection: a review of BERT-based approaches. *Artif. Intell. Rev.* **54**(8), 5789–5829 (2021)
2. Artstein, R.: Inter-Annotator Agreement. *Handbook of linguistic annotation*, pp. 297–313 (2017)
3. Bogaert, J., et al.: Explanation sensitivity to the randomness of large language models: the case of journalistic text classification. CoRR, abs/2410.05085 (2024)
4. Bogaert, J., Escouflaire, L., de Marneffe, M., Descampe, A., Standaert, F., Fairon, C.: TIPECS: a corpus cleaning method using machine learning and qualitative analysis. In: International Conference on Corpus Linguistics (JLC) (2023)
5. Bogaert, J., Standaert, F.: A question on the explainability of large language models and the word-level univariate first-order plausibility assumption. *Responsible Language Models (ReLM)*, p. 7 (2024)
6. Bogaert, J., de Marneffe, M., Descampe, A., Escouflaire, L., Fairon, C., Standaert, F.: Sensibilité des Explications à l'Aléa des Grands Modèles de Langage: le Cas de la Classification de Textes Journalistiques, TAL (Traitement Automatique des Langues), vol. 64, no. 3, pp. 15–40 (2024)
7. Chefer, H., Gur, S., Wolf, L.: Transformer interpretability beyond attention visualization. In: *CVPR*, pp. 782–791. Computer Vision Foundation / IEEE (2021)
8. Devlin, J., Chang, M., Lee, K., Toutanova, K.: BERT: pre-training of deep bidirectional transformers for language understanding. In: *NAACL-HLT (1)*, pp. 4171–4186. Association for Computational Linguistics (2019)
9. Brown, T.B., et al.: Language models are few-shot learners. In: *NeurIPS* (2020)
10. Hayes, A.F., Krippendorff, K.: Answering the call for a standard reliability measure for coding data. Commun. Methods Meas. **1**(1), 77–89 (2007)

11. Herman, B.: The promise and peril of human evaluation for model interpretability. CoRR, abs/1711.07414 (2017)
12. Jacovi, A., Goldberg, Y.: Towards faithfully interpretable nlp systems: how should we define and evaluate faithfulness? In: *ACL*, pp. 4198–4205. Association for Computational Linguistics (2020)
13. Lehmann, E.L., Romano, J.P.: *Testing Statistical Hypotheses, Third Edition*. Springer texts in statistics. Springer (2008)
14. Lyu, Q., Apidianaki, M., Callison-Burch, C.: Towards faithful model explanation in NLP: a survey. CoRR, abs/2209.11326 (2022)
15. Martin, L., et al.: CamemBERT: a tasty french language model. CoRR, abs/1911.03894 (2019)
16. Ribeiro, M., Singh, S., Guestrin, C.: "Why Should I Trust You?": explaining the predictions of any classifier. In: *KDD*, pp. 1135–1144. ACM (2016)
17. Clayton Silver, N., Dunlap, W.P.: Averaging correlation coefficients: should Fisher's Z transformation be used? *J. Appl. Psychol.* **72**(1), 146 (1987)
18. Wu, Z., Ong, D.C.: On explaining your explanations of BERT: an empirical study with sequence classification. CoRR, abs/2101.00196 (2021)

Open Access This chapter is licensed under the terms of the Creative Commons Attribution 4.0 International License (http://creativecommons.org/licenses/by/4.0/), which permits use, sharing, adaptation, distribution and reproduction in any medium or format, as long as you give appropriate credit to the original author(s) and the source, provide a link to the Creative Commons license and indicate if changes were made.

The images or other third party material in this chapter are included in the chapter's Creative Commons license, unless indicated otherwise in a credit line to the material. If material is not included in the chapter's Creative Commons license and your intended use is not permitted by statutory regulation or exceeds the permitted use, you will need to obtain permission directly from the copyright holder.

XAI for Representational Alignment

Latent Space Interpretation and Mechanistic Clipping of Subject-Specific Variational Autoencoders of EEG Topographic Maps for Artefacts Reduction

Taufique Ahmed[1]($^{\boxtimes}$), Przemyslaw Biecek[2], and Luca Longo[1]

[1] The Artificial Intelligence and Cognitive Load Research Lab, The Centre of Explainable Artificial Intelligence, Technological University Dublin, Grangegorman Lower, Dublin D07H6K8, Ireland
taufique.ahmed@tudublin.ie
[2] Faculty of Mathematics and Information Science, Warsaw University of Technology, Warsaw, Poland
przemyslaw.biecek@pw.edu.pl

Abstract. Electroencephalographic (EEG) recordings are often contaminated with artefacts, such as eye blinks, which complicate their analysis. While various methods exist to address, identify, and mitigate artefacts, many require human intervention. This study introduces a novel, self-supervised, fully automated approach for identifying and reducing artefacts in EEG signals using a Variational Autoencoder (VAE) architecture. In detail, subject-specific VAEs, with convolutional layers, are trained from spatially preserved EEG topographic maps. A sample-wise strategy based on the negative log-likelihood of activated latent vectors from training data is proposed to identify anomalous topomaps. This assigns an anomaly score to each model's input. The vectors of input topomaps above a chosen threshold are automatically clipped with a percentile-based approach of activated latent space components. Eventually, the reconstructed EEG signals are compared with a baseline built upon an offline ICA method with automatic detection of artefactual components inspired by the FASTER methodology. Results show that the signal-to-noise ratio (SNR) and the peak signal-to-noise ratio (PSNR) of the FP1, FP2, and other channels were higher, while the remaining channels were similar to ICA Fast. Similarly, mean absolute error (MAE), normalised root mean square error (NRMSE), and correlation coefficients indicated comparable signals from both methods. In addition, findings demonstrate the method's strength in avoiding signal updates in non-artefactual segments, preserving their neural dynamics. The contribution to the body of knowledge is a fully automated, subject-specific method for identifying and denoising EEG signals.

Keywords: Electroencephalography · Spectral topographic maps · Subject-specific · Variational autoencoder · Latent space ·

interpretability · Artefacts removal · Deep learning · full automation · explainable AI

1 Introduction

Electroencephalography (EEG) serves as a technique for capturing brain activity by employing electrodes positioned on the scalp [14]. EEG signals are important because they can convey crucial information about brain functioning across frequency, temporal, and spatial domains. While they have proven valuable in diagnosing various mental disorders, the analytical process is challenging, and decision-making poses difficulties due to factors such as low amplitude, intricate data collection setups, and significant noise [29]. EEG noise sources include physiological artefacts such as eye blinks, muscle movement, and artefacts from the EEG equipment itself. The superimposition of these artefacts on the EEG data may obscure its interpretation. This is especially important in the medical industry, where EEG signals might be employed as the sole diagnostic source, and failure to recognise artefacts can seriously impact clinical judgements. Consequently, artefact identification is the first and most important stage in EEG signal processing before its mitigation.

It is widely recognized that EEG signals encompass crucial information across frequency, temporal, and spatial domains. EEG topography mapping is a neuroimaging approach using visual-spatial depiction to map the EEG signal [54]. The EEG data from the electrodes is collected and processed into topographical maps (topomaps). A topomap usually depicts raw EEG data of voltage or power amplitude to topographic head visualisations [4]. Other studies have generated spectral topographic head maps for various EEG bands, aiming to preserve spatial information while capitalising on the insights from the frequency domain [49]. Topographic maps have also recently been used with deep learning for various tasks. For example, a 2D Convolutional Neural Network (CNNs) to autonomously learn EEG features across diverse mental tasks without prior knowledge has been designed in [5]. Similarly, a tensor decomposition-based algorithm reduces the CNN input into a concise set of slices to improve computational efficiency and enhance the extraction of relevant EEG features for categorising epileptic seizures. Another example of works employing deep learning with EEG data is Variational Autoencoders (VAEs) [32]. Autoencoders (AE) are self-supervised deep-learning neural network architectures that leverage unsupervised learning to acquire efficient features without labelled inputs. These features, part of a latent space, are often of lower dimension than the original input and are employed to reconstruct it with high fidelity [8]. A variational autoencoder (VAE) is a specific version of AE that learns a probabilistic model of the input sample and subsequently reconstructs it based on that model, essentially generating synthetic data [15]. For example, convolutional VAEs were used with topographic maps to learn prominent high-level features of a lower dimension of EEG signals [1–3]. However, limited exploration exists to use autoencoders with

EEG topography and understand the meaning of their latent representations for artefact identification and reduction.

This research tackles this problem and focuses on developing an offline, self-supervised approach using subject-specific VAEs trained with spatially preserved EEG topographic maps to detect and minimize artefacts in EEG signals fully automatically, specifically of an ocular nature. The proposed method is a novel contribution to the body of knowledge for reducing the amplitude of EEG signals during artefactual intervals. The detailed research question being addressed is: Can a fully automated, offline denoising architecture for EEG signals using Variational Autoencoders trained with EEG topographic maps perform better or equal to traditional ICA-based methods for artefact detection and mitigation?

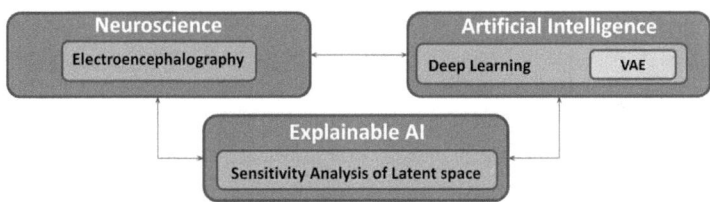

Fig. 1. The scope of this research is at the intersection of electroencephalography from the discipline of neuroscience, variational autoencoders (VAEs) from deep learning, a sub-discipline of artificial intelligence, and sensitivity analysis of the latent space of such VAEs from the new discipline of explainable.

This research is at the intersection of neuroscience, Artificial Intelligence (AI), and Explainable AI (XAI) to address the problem of identification and mitigation of artefacts in EEG signals (Fig. 1). In detail, explainable AI techniques are used to perform sensitivity analysis on their latent components to better understand person-specific models trained using a deep variational autoencoder. It follows similar work on sensitivity analysis, where Receiver Operating Characteristic (ROC) curves and Area Under the Curve (AUC) metrics were used to assess the discriminated performance of individual latent components involved in capturing eye blink artefacts [18]. Similarly, interpreting the latent space could facilitate the generation of realistic, plausible representations of EEG dynamics, potentially paving the way for a more in-depth understanding [13].

The subsequent sections are structured as follows: Sect. 2 delves into prior research on VAE-based methods for handling EEG artefacts and the interpretation of their latent spaces. Section 3 outlines the empirical study and its methodology to address the earlier research question. Section 4 presents the experimental results, findings, and discussion. Finally, Sect. 5 concludes the manuscript, summarizing the contribution to the body of knowledge and outlining potential directions for future research.

2 Literature Review

EEG data is widely used in research, including neuroscience, cognitive science, cognitive psychology, neurolinguistics, and psycho-physiological studies [53]. Unfortunately, various internal and external artefact sources overlap neural data in laboratory-based or naturalistic settings, hampering its analysis. Artefacts can be classified according to their origin. If the source is within the subject's body, they are called physiological artefacts; outside, they are called external artefacts. Physiological artefacts are caused by electrical activity in other regions of the subject's body that disguise EEG signals. These include ocular or muscle artefacts among others. Ocular artefacts are generated by eye blinks or saccades inducing a voltage change in the electrodes near the eyes, especially at the Fp1-Fp2 (Fronto Parietal) electrode locations on the scalp. They generate high-amplitude signals many times greater than the amplitude of the EEG signals of interest [20], especially in low-frequency EEG bands (0–12 Hz). Muscle artefacts are generated, for example, by chewing, swallowing, tongue movements, and grimacing, to mention a few. They mainly contaminate the high-frequency EEG bands (110–140 Hz) and occur less frequently in sleep, overlapping with the beta band (15–30 Hz) [7,50]. Cardiac artefacts are generated by the heart and are visible from an electrocardiogram (ECG) signal in the temporal left area. They are more prominent in subjects with short necks, overlapping with neural frequency around 1 Hz, with amplitudes in the millivolt range [50]. External artefacts are derived from electronic devices, transmission lines, and environmental lines, among other things. For example, phone artefacts are caused by a cell phone signal overlapping with the high-frequencies of EEG signals in a spurious way [50]. Electrode artefacts are low-frequency types of noise caused by poor contact with the scalp. They are short transients localised to one electrode, for example, caused by respiration that might move it [50]. Physical movement artefacts are generated by electrode contact loss caused by the sudden physical movement of a subject. Its morphology differs from that of an EEG [50].

Several methods exist to remove the above types of artefacts. Regression methods are the most basic and widely used to remove them from EEG signals by modelling and subtracting the unwanted components based on their linear relationship with reference signals [10,19,25]. Adaptive filtering is based on the assumption that there is no relationship between the true EEG signal and artefactual activities [46]. The objective of an adaptive filter is to adapt the coefficients of a selected linear filter and, therefore, of its frequency response to generate a signal similar to the noise present in the actual EEG signal to be filtered. Blind source separation (BSS) refers to a group of techniques to separate mixed signals into their original, independent sources without prior knowledge of the mixing process or the sources themselves. In EEG signal processing, BSS methods include independent component analysis (ICA), principal component analysis (PCA), and canonical correlation analysis (CCA) primarily. ICA separates multichannel EEG data from several sources into independent components (ICs). The selection of artefactual independent components is usually done by visualising topographic maps and time series of ICs and hence is largely dependent on the researcher's experience [42]. PCA is a statistical method that uses an orthogonal transformation to turn time-domain observations of possibly correlated variables into values of linearly uncorrelated variables [42]. It has been reported that PCA outperforms regression-based artefact reduction [9]. In contrast to the ICA approach, which uses higher-order statistics, canonical correlation analysis employs second-order statistics, requiring less processing effort. CCA distinguishes components from uncorrelated sources, whereas ICA distinguishes components from statistically independent sources. Empirical Mode Decomposition (EMD) is well-suited for analyzing and processing EEG signals due to its ability to handle non-stationary, non-linear, and stochastic processes. It breaks down the signal into a series of intrinsic mode functions (IMFs), each representing simple oscillatory modes, which facilitates the analysis of complex EEG data [27]. In recent years, researchers have increasingly focused on leveraging the strengths of various techniques by combining them into a single, hybrid method for artefact detection and removal [27]. Artefact reduction methods are manual, automatic, offline and online [36]. Manual methods often require manual detection of artefact-contaminated EEG, typically performed by a panel of experts. They can be challenging and time-consuming, especially for large amounts of data [31]. Therefore, classifying independent components (ICs) may be the most challenging step in manually removing EEG artefacts [31]. Several methods improved this by the proposal of automatic or semi-automatic IC classification. For example, using spectrum properties, topographic map properties, or an analysis of each IC's contribution [38]. Offline methods are those applied only when the whole observation dataset is available. Online methods are more challenging because they need to denoise EEG signals in real time, thus requiring sophisticated strategies that humans cannot supervise.

Recent advances in deep learning with applications in neuroscience and electroencephalography have demonstrated how offline automatic methods can be developed with high accuracy. These methods are like source separation methods. They take advantage of the recorded EEG data and learn high-level representations through training neural networks similar to independent and principal components analysis [37]. However, like source separation methods, they suffer from the understanding of the high-level representations [35], the latent components, and which of these are responsible for artefacts, or not [2,3]. Human intervention is often required, and like source separation methods, such higher-level representations require a degree of interpretation. This is also because they can be lower in number than the number of original EEG channels. Examples include the family of autoencoders (AEs), with variational (VAEs) being the most adopted with EEG data [1,3,12,17,18,24,57]. Similarly, recent research on VAE with EEG has focused chiefly on data augmentation, emotion prediction, and feature representation. In most research, VAE is employed as an EEG data generator and provides classification models with a substantial amount of data [16,21,56]. VAE is also utilized in other investigations to extract features such as influential elements from EEG data [33,55]. A VAE model gives a closed-form latent space representation of the distribution underlying the input data, which is ideal for unsupervised learning to understand the impact and importance of each latent component for capturing the number of true generative factors. Research towards establishing the ideal dimension of the latent space of an autoencoder trained with EEG data is still in its infancy. For example, the preliminary study conducted in [1] focused on examining various latent space dimensions of person-specific autoencoders trained with spectral topographic maps of different frequency bands from different overlapping EEG time windows [1]. Similarly, research on understanding the reconstruction capacity of autoencoders is preliminary. For example, the analysis conducted in [22] was focused on visualising the disentangled representation of VAE to grasp its decision towards reconstruction capacity. The disentanglement is a condition of the latent space in which each latent variable is sensitive to changes in only one feature while insensitive to changes in the others [8]. The disentangled latent variables have been applied successfully in various applications, including face recognition, video prediction, and anomaly detection [26]. Here, the disentangled representations of the VAE are mainly interpreted to determine which one helps capture data artefacts. An example of such an interpretation method is based on determining the latent variable's out-of-order distribution (OOD) [43]. Employing the KL divergence metric, the OOD latent components of a variational autoencoder's latent space are determined. This is the difference between the generated latent distribution and the standard normal distribution ($\mu = 0, \sigma = 1$). Therefore, manually adjusting the VAE's latent space component enables a user to examine how different latent values affect the model's outcome. Scholars also illustrated how a VAE model's latent space might be more explainable by utilising latent space regularisation to force some selected dimensions of the latent space to map to meaningful musical qualities [6]. Similarly, a sensitivity analysis of the VAE latent space is conducted using Receiver Operating Characteristic (ROC) curves and Area Under the Curve (AUC) metrics to assess the discriminating performance of individual latent components involved in capturing eye blink artefacts [17].

Despite the increasing use of VAE with EEG signals, designing an offline and automatic method for EEG artefact identification and reduction using the spatial information of EEG data is not a trivial task. This is because of two main challenges. The first is determining the smallest size of topographic maps that can preserve spatial information concerning the number of electrodes employed while achieving maximum dimensionality reduction without losing meaningful information. The second approach manipulates the latent space of a subject-specific VAE, trained on spatially preserved EEG topographic maps. Boundaries for each component can be set using the standard approach on normal distribution, since 99.7% of data in it lies within ±3 standard deviations, thus identifying values likely associated with irregularities in the data [45]. The above gaps motivated this research study and informed the design of a VAE trained with spatially preserved topographic maps extracted from raw signals to leverage spatial information and mechanistic, automatic interpretation and manipulation of its latent components for artefact reduction.

3 Methodology

This research aims to design, develop and test an offline, fully automated, self-supervised approach using VAEs trained with spatially preserved EEG topographic maps. This is tested against detecting and minimising artefacts, with a special focus on blink-related artefacts in EEG signals. A high-level design of the layers of this research is illustrated in Fig. 2, and the following sections describe its components.

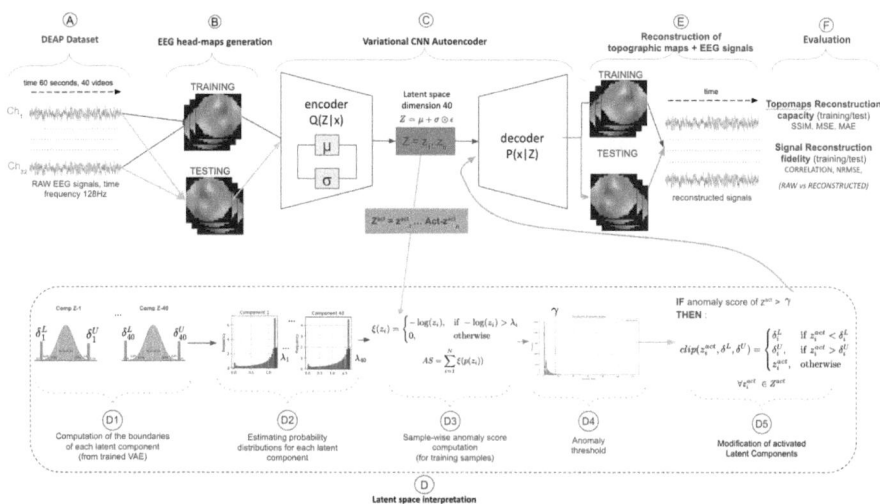

Fig. 2. A novel fully automated method for identifying and reducing artefacts from EEG signal based on convolutional variational autoencoders. (**A**) Multi-variate EEG recordings are selected; (**B**) Spatially-preserved EEG topographic head maps of size 40 × 40 are formed for the entire EEG recording, at each time step; (**C**) A convolutional, variational autoencoder architecture is trained with topographic maps; (**D**) An automated analysis of the variational autoencoder (VAE)'s latent space is performed after training, and a clipping strategy is implemented for anomalous input via a sample-wise strategy; (**E**) A reconstruction of anomalous topographic maps and their transformation into the time domain is performed for each original electrode recording; (**F**) The model's performance (EEG topomaps reconstruction capacity and signals reconstruction fidelity) is evaluated.

The specific research hypothesis is:

IF a person-specific VAE is trained with spatially preserved EEG topographic maps, achieving a high SSIM and lower MSE, MAE, and MAPE, **AND** a procedure to manipulate the latent components based on percentile-clipping
THEN the SNRs and PSNRs of EEG channels are expected to be equal to

or higher than the ICA-Fast (baseline), reflecting similar or improved artefact suppression, especially for ocular artefacts **AND** the mean absolute error (MAE), normalised root mean square error (NRMSE), and correlation coefficients (Corr) are expected to have equal or higher signal fidelity compared to the baseline, indicating effective artefact reduction without significant distortion of the underlying EEG signals.

3.1 Dataset

The DEAP dataset was chosen to train the proposed method for detecting and reducing artefacts because it contains multi-channel EEG recordings with many participants and tasks. EEG data were collected from 32 people who watched 40 one-minute music video clips [30]. The 10–20 electrode position system was applied with the following channels: Fp1, AF3, F7, F3, FC1, FC5, T7, C3, CP1, CP5, P7, P3, Pz, PO3, O1, Oz, O2, PO4, P4, P8, CP6, CP2, C4, T8, FC6, FC2, F4, F8, AF4, Fp2, Fz, and Cz. Data was acquired with a sampling rate of 500 Hz and downsampled to 128 Hz for ease of subsequent computations. A low/high-pass filter with a frequency range of 0.1 to 50 Hz was applied to remove slow drifts and DC offsets, and average channel referencing was executed to create a more electrically neutral reference point [40].

3.2 Spatially Preserved EEG Topographic Maps Generation

Raw EEG signals are employed to construct spatially preserved EEG topographic maps, 128 per second, as the sampling rate. Empirical evaluations were conducted to ascertain the minimum dimension of such maps and reduce the computational time required for model training. This preserved the spatial distance between EEG electrodes in proportion to the distance as per the 10–20 electrode position standard. In other words, the goal was to transform EEG signals into plausible, spatially preserved topographic maps of minimal dimension. The conversion of the electrode recordings over time into topographic maps involves, firstly, transforming 3D polar coordinates to 2D cartesian coordinates. Such transformation can distort the original distance among electrodes as set by the 10/20 electrode placement standard if topomps are small. Thus, a grid search was performed among varying square-size topomaps, and the one that minimises such size but with closer average Euclidean distances among all the pairs of electrodes to those of the 10/20 standard was chosen. Such a grid search indicates that the ideal resolution of a topomaps with 32 electrodes resulted in a 40×40 pixels topomap (Fig. 3). Subsequently, such a 40×40 map of initial zeros was filled with the power magnitude of each of the 32 electrodes at their specific locations. Eventually, cubic interpolation was performed to fill all the other empty pixels, creating the final full topographic maps as illustrated in Fig. 2, B.

3.3 Designing and Training a Variational Autoencoder (VAE)

After generating the topographic maps, a VAE is trained. This turns input data into probability distribution parameters, including the mean and standard devi-

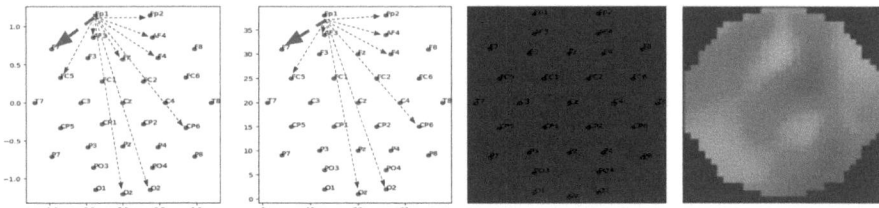

Fig. 3. Electrodes placement of the 10/20 standard in the 2D coordinate space (left) Electrodes coordinates in a topomap of 40 × 40 (middle left) Scattered power values at each electrode position in the 40 × 40 topomap (middle right) Cubic interpolated topomap (right).

ation of Gaussian distributions. It provides a continuous, structured latent space. The VAE architectural design is made up of two networks. First, the encoder is a neural network that takes an input tensor (as in Fig. 2, C). It defines the approximate posterior distribution $Q(Z \mid x)$, where x is the input tensor and Z is the latent space. The architecture (Fig. 2, C) consists of four 2D convolutional layers, each of which is followed by a max pooling layer to reduce the dimensions of the feature maps. ReLU is used as the activation function in each convolutional layer. Second, the decoder of the VAE is a generative network that takes a latent space Z as input and outputs the parameters for the conditional distribution $P(x \mid Z)$ of the observation (as shown in the right part of Fig. 2, C). Similarly, like the encoder network, the decoder consists of four 2D convolutional layers, each followed by an up-sampling layer to reconstruct the data to the shape of the original input. Such a VAE is trained using topographic maps generated with the procedure described in Sect. 3.2, based on a randomly selected 70% (28 out of 40) of 1-minute videos from a single participant. The remaining 30% of videos are split equally into validation and testing sets (15% each). The latent space dimension of the VAE must be carefully tuned to maximise reconstruction quality while capturing the true generative factors in the data. However, identifying the minimum sufficient latent dimensionality remains an open challenge [34]. Following the approach in [1,11], the VAEs were trained on EEG topographic maps to preserve spatial information, using latent dimensions ranging from 25 to 800. Reconstruction performance is measured using SSIM, MSE, MAE, and MAPE. Findings show that such metrics improve as latent dimensionality gets closer to 40 (with 40 × 40 images). Beyond this threshold, additional dimensions yield minimal reconstruction improvement. Therefore, a latent dimension of 40 is selected as optimal, offering a balance between reconstruction accuracy and preserved essential information.

3.4 Latent Space Interpretation and Update

This section details the strategy for automatically and globally interpreting the latent space of a person-specific variational autoencoder (VAE) model. It also presents a percentile-based clipping strategy for EEG artefact denoising. The goal is to understand which parts of each latent component are rare and thus potentially corresponding to an anomalous input, and to manipulate such a latent component accordingly.

By design, each latent space's component is a Gaussian distribution. After training a person-specific VAE model, the topographic maps in the training set are re-input, and the activated latent space Z is read for each of them (Fig. 2 - D1). This leads to 40 distributions, for each latent component z_i, with a mean and standard deviation. A parametric density estimator is then used to estimate probability distributions for each latent component, leading to 40 probability distributions (Fig. 2 - D2). For each input topographic map in the training set, its activated latent space Z (a vector of N=40 activated z_i scores) is read. The probability of each of such z_i is extracted from the related probability distribution, and inputted to a ξ function (Eq. 1). Such a function returns the negative log of the input z_i if such negative log is above a threshold λ_i, otherwise zero. This process is repeated for all the z_i scores and their sum is taken to compute an anomaly score AS for an input topomap (2). A threshold λ_i is set to each latent component's 98th percentile of each probability distribution. This high percentile was chosen to ensure that only the most extreme outliers, the tail of the distribution (anomalies), would contribute to the computation of the anomaly score. Such a threshold is often used in outlier detection to minimise false positives while capturing rare and potentially meaningful anomalies [52].

$$\xi(z_i) = \begin{cases} -\log(z_i), & \text{if } -\log(z_i) > \lambda_i \\ 0, & \text{otherwise} \end{cases} \quad (1)$$

The anomaly score for a given sample is then obtained by summing the retained log-likelihood values across all N activated latent vectors (Fig. 2 - D3, equation, similarly to the approach in [39]. This method provides a cumulative measure of how strongly a sample's latent representation deviates from the average, based on the behaviour of its individual component activations. A final threshold γ is set to the 98th percentile to discriminate average topomaps from those anomalous. Intuitively, the higher this percentile, the less the anomalous topomaps, and vice versa. This threshold is fixed, and can now be used for any input topomaps, even those from the test set (unseen).

$$AS = \sum_{i=1}^{N} \xi(p(z_i)) \quad (2)$$

After identifying the anomalous topomaps via the above strategy, that means those with an anomaly score exceeding γ is passed through a *clipping strategy*. Such a strategy is implemented, using the standard procedure of ±3 standard deviations of the distribution of the activations of each latent component. In detail, two boundaries are set, δ_i^L and δ_i^U, corresponding respectively to 0.03% and 99.7%, (Fig. 2, step D1). If every component z_i^{act} of an anomalous topomap exceeds the upper boundary δ_i^U of its latent space distribution, then it is *clipped* to such boundary, otherwise is left intact. Likewise, if it falls below the lower boundary δ_i^L, it is clipped to it. This procedure is mathematically described by the function $clip(z_i^{act}, \delta^L, \delta^U)$, as shown in Eq. 3 (Fig. 2, D5).

$$clip(z_i^{act}, \delta^L, \delta^U) = \begin{cases} \delta_i^L & \text{if } z_i^{act} < \delta_i^L \\ \delta_i^U, & \text{if } z_i^{act} > \delta_i^U \\ z_i^{act}, & \text{otherwise} \end{cases} \quad \forall z_i^{act} \in Z^{act} \quad (3)$$

This ensures that the latent variables contributing to extreme deviations are constrained within the boundaries established, thereby enhancing the model's robustness in mitigating anomalous input topomaps, likely the noisy inputs containing artefacts.

3.5 Artefacts Identification and Removal Using an Automatic Baseline

The FASTER pipeline, used primarily for ERP-based studies, systematically identifies artefactual trials (epochs) and try to corrects, or discard EEG portions containing artefacts [41]. It is built upon five data dimensions: channels, epochs, independent components (ICs), single-channel single-epochs, and aggregated datasets (for example across participants). The methodology involves computing statistical parameters for each dimension and flagging artefacts based on outlier detection, defined as a z-score beyond ±3 standard deviations [41,44]. This threshold was selected after comparing several alternatives.

EEG channel artefacts often result from poor electrode contact, movement during recording, or hardware issues like damaged wires. Such artefacts can introduce irregularities into the signal. To detect these, three statistical features were computed for each channel:

- Spatial Kurtosis - This metric quantifies the 'tailedness' of the component's amplitude distribution over time. High kurtosis may indicate sharp, transient artefacts (for example, muscle bursts or eye blinks), whereas lower values suggest more regular, brain-related activity.
- Spectral slope from Power Spectrum (SL-F) - The power spectrum is computed using the real value Fast Fourier Transform (rFFT), and the spectral slope is estimated by averaging the gradient of the resulting spectrum. This feature captures how power decreases across frequencies. Flatter slopes may reflect noise or artefactual components.
- Correlation with EOG - This metric assesses how strongly an independent component (IC) aligns with eye movement activity. In the DEAP dataset, EOG signals are estimated by combining the signals from two electrodes, one placed above and one below the right eye (EXG3 and EXG4). Their absolute sum provides a measure of eye activity. A high correlation between this signal and an IC suggests that the component may represent ocular artefacts, such as blinks or vertical eye movements.

- Median Gradient (MG): This feature was calculated by first computing the gradient of the component's time series, which estimates the rate of change between successive time points. The median of these gradient values was then taken to summarize the typical rate of change in a way that is robust to noise and outliers.
- Hurst Exponent - This parameter captures long-range temporal dependencies in EEG signals. Normal EEG activity usually yields a Hurst exponent around 0.7; significant deviations suggest artefacts.

Such a baseline method, now referred to as ICA-F, was implemented because ICA is the reference method for EEG denoising, but it requires visual human inspection of components. However, the metrics borrowed from the FASTER methodology fully automate artefactual component selection, thus avoiding human intervention. In such methodology, parameters were corrected for reference offset as described [28]. Channels identified as noisy were excluded and replaced through spherical spline interpolation (with EEGLAB), ensuring continuity and signal integrity.

3.6 Evaluating the Performance of Trained Person-Specific VAEs

The proposed training architecture is evaluated at two different stages. Firstly, the reconstruction capacity of VAE for generated EEG topo maps is assessed using the SSIM, MSE, and MAE metrics. SSIM is a perceptual metric that measures how much image quality is lost due to processing, including data compression. It is an index of structural similarity (in the real range $[0, 1]$ between two images, the topographic maps) [47]. Values close to 1 indicate that the two topographic maps are very structurally similar, whereas values close to 0 suggest they are exceptionally dissimilar and structurally different. MAE is the average variance between the significant values in the dataset and the projected values in the same dataset and is defined as the mean absolute error (MAE) [48]. MSE is defined as the mean (average) of the square of the difference between the actual and reconstructed values: the lower value indicates a better fit. In this case, the MSE involves the comparison, pixel by pixel, of the original and reconstructed topographic maps [47].

Secondly, SNR, PSNR, MAE, NRMSE, and the correlation coefficient are applied to the architecture's final output (topographic maps) after being converted back into the time domain (reconstructed EEG signals) for evaluation to assess how well the reconstructed EEG signals align with the signal produced by the baseline method. In order to identify artefactual segments containing eye-blinks, an offline semi-automatic threshold-based approach is employed [51]. In detail, a peak detection algorithm has been adopted to identify the peak locations of eye-blinks, which requires a threshold. This threshold value is automatically computed using the algorithm described in [23]. The pseudo-code of this approach is presented in algorithm 1. In such algorithm, the K-value is a hyperparameter, and its tuning is required because varying it can lead to more or less true positives and false positives peaks. To improve the accuracy of correctly identified peak locations, another strategy is employed by computing the Z-scores of each electrode's values at a particular location in time, and then ranked.

Algorithm 1. Algorithm for threshold identification for ocular artefact locations.

Require: Array of pre-processed Fp1 and Fp2 EEG channels, [data]
Ensure: Threshold for detecting the ocular artefacts
1: [data $_{abs}$] ← abs([data])
2: [data $_{sqrt}$] ← sqrt ([data $_{abs}$])
3: [data $_{max}$] ← max ([data $_{sqrt}$])
4: std ← std([data])
5: Threshold ← data $_{max}$ − std/k

In EEG signal recordings, eye-blinks are captured primarily by the frontal electrodes, Fp1 and Fp2, due to their proximity to the eyes. If the Z-scores of Fp1 and Fp2 are top-ranked, followed by AF3 and AF4 when compared to the z-scores of the remaining electrodes, then such location in time can be safely considered as containing a true, plausible blink peak. In other words, this process generates a list of locations where plausible blink peaks likely exist in the time domain.

4 Results and Discussion

This section outlines the empirical findings for hypothesis testing grouped by the previous two stages: model reconstruction capacity and ocular artefact mitigation.

4.1 VAE Model's Reconstruction Capacity

The VAE's reconstruction capacity is evaluated based on the reconstructed topographic maps and EEG signals. Tables 1 and 2 presents the SSIM, MSE, MAE, and MAPE scores for the both training and unseen test data. The SSIM values approach close to one, while the MSE, MAE, and MAPE values approach close to zero. Furthermore, the evaluation incorporates an analysis focused exclusively on the reconstructed topographic maps at the 32 electrode positions in 2D space, offering additional insight into the VAE's effectiveness. Figure 4 presents a selection of original and corresponding reconstructed topographic maps from the test data of a randomly chosen participant. The visual similarity between the reconstructions and the originals demonstrates the VAE's ability to preserve spatial patterns effectively. Furthermore, the reconstructed EEG topomaps are converted back into time series to evaluate the temporal reconstruction performance of the trained VAE. As illustrated in Fig. 5 for the Fp1 and Fp2 channels, also summarized in Tables 1 and 2, the reconstructed signals exhibit a perfect positive correlation (close to 1) with the originals.

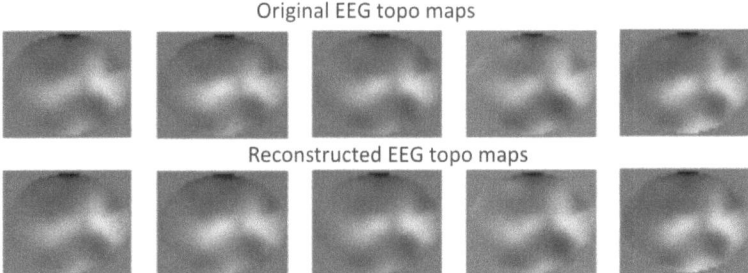

Fig. 4. Original and reconstructed topographic maps from the VAE models trained with topographic maps from a random participant.

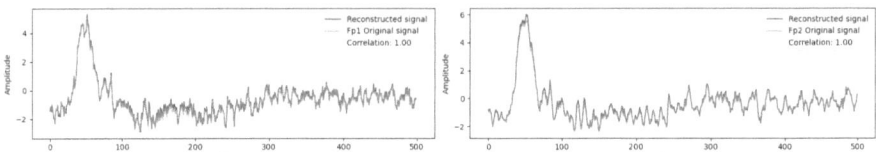

Fig. 5. The reconstruction capacity of the Variational Autoencoder model of a random subject for Fp1 and Fp2 channels.

Table 1. Reconstruction capacity of 10 Variational Autoencoder models from random participants using SSIM, MSE, MAE, MAPE on topographic maps and 32 coordinate values (c), and correlation coefficient (Training Data).

Part	SSIM	MSE	MAE	MAPE	SSIM (C)	MSE (C)	MAE (C)	MAPE (C)	CORR
1	0.999	5.69E−09	5.40E−05	8.65E−05	1	2.26E−14	9.81E−08	0.139	0.999
2	0.999	1.04E−08	7.71E−05	401.9231	1	3.91E−14	1.34E−07	0.154	0.999
3	0.999	6.29E−09	6.14E−05	0.0002	1	4.30E−14	1.58E−07	0.107	0.999
4	0.998	1.52E−08	4.56E−05	402.0	1	3.27E−14	7.19E−08	0.345	0.999
5	0.999	7.91E−09	0.002	259.13	1	5.866E−15	5.98E−08	0.099	0.99
6	0.999	1.52E−08	5.15E−05	215.95	1	6.18E−13	3.33E−07	0.347	0.999
7	0.999	5.74E−09	6.66E−05	0.0002	1	5.06E−14	1.89E−07	0.145	0.998
8	0.998	1.62E−08	9.91E−05	314.007	1	1.213E−14	8.791E−08	0.099	0.998
9	0.999	7.80E−09	5.66E−05	249.163	1	5.66E−15	5.28E−08	0.103	0.999
10	0.991	1.01E−07	0.001	153.565	1	1.99E−12	8.71E−07	1.284	0.996

4.2 Identifying and Reducing the Artefacts

As mentioned in the design Sect. 3.6, this experiment specifically considered the Fp1 and Fp2 channels, given that ocular artefacts are predominantly captured in the frontal electrodes [20]. A random segment of EEG signals was selected for the FP1 and FP2 channels to evaluate the impact of manipulating the VAE's latent space and compare it with the existing baseline approach. This included the raw

Table 2. Reconstruction capacity of Variational Autoencoder models using SSIM, MSE, MAE, MAPE on topographic maps and 32 coordinate values, along with correlation coefficient (Test Data).

Part	SSIM	MSE	MAE	MAPE	SSIM (C)	MSE (C)	MAE (C)	MAPE (C)	CORR
1	0.999	5.57E−09	5.19E−05	8.30E−05	1	3.93E−14	9.48E−08	0.204	0.999
2	0.999	1.883E−08	8.026E−05	9.94E−05	1	8.17E−14	1.41E−07	0.194	0.998
3	0.999	2.08E−08	7.81E−05	0.002	1	1.74E−13	2.11E−07	0.118	0.998
4	0.999	1.78E−08	6.02E−05	0.002	1	3.16E−13	4.67E−07	0.170	0.995
5	0.997	2.34E−08	5.31E−05	0.005	1	2.54E−13	1.03E−07	0.096	0.999
6	1	4.38E−09	4.09E−05	9.84E−05	1	2.16E−13	2.67E−07	0.270	0.996
7	0.999	1.67E−08	7.04E−05	0.002	1	2.78E−13	2.03E−07	0.126	0.999
8	0.998	2.23E−08	0.001	0.001	1	1.98E−14	9.21E−08	0.102	0.999
9	0.999	7.91E−09	5.54E−05	0.001	1	6.70E−15	5.19E−08	0.0712	0.999
10	0.995	6.12E−08	0.001	0.005	1	1.21E−12	8.02E−07	0.603	0.999

data, the baseline output, the modified VAE latent space (VAEm), and the standard VAE (VAE, no latent space manipulation) reconstructions, as illustrated in Fig. 6. In contrast to the raw and regular VAE signals, both the VAEm and the baseline's outputs exhibit a noticeable reduction in amplitude during periods of ocular artefacts. Outside these artefact intervals, the signals closely resemble the original data, suggesting that latent space modification selectively targets artefactual information while preserving the integrity of the neural signal.

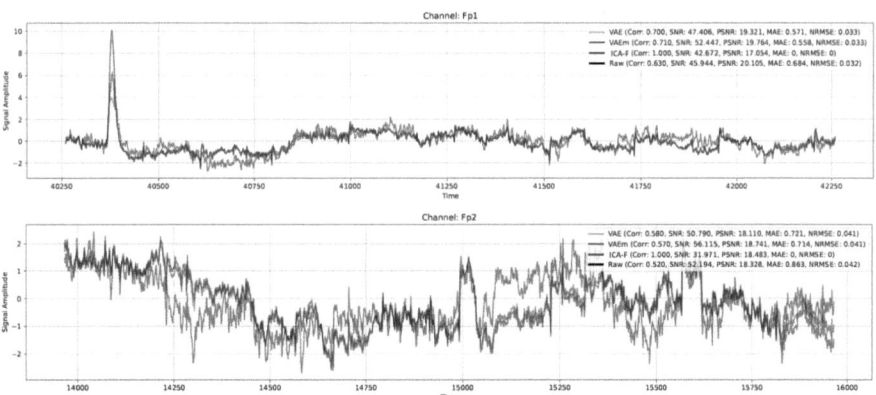

Fig. 6. An illustration of a random segment from the Fp1 and Fp2 channels and their reconstructions by the baseline method, the VAEm, and VAE autoencoders.

Subsequently, SNR and PSNR metrics were computed individually across all channels for the raw, baseline VAEm, and standard VAE signals to support a more detailed evaluation. The results, illustrated in Fig. 7, demonstrate noticeably higher SNR and PSNR values for the FP1, FP2, and few other channels, while the remaining channels exhibited performance comparable to the baseline. These findings suggest that the proposed approach effectively suppresses the artefacts without compromising signal quality elsewhere.

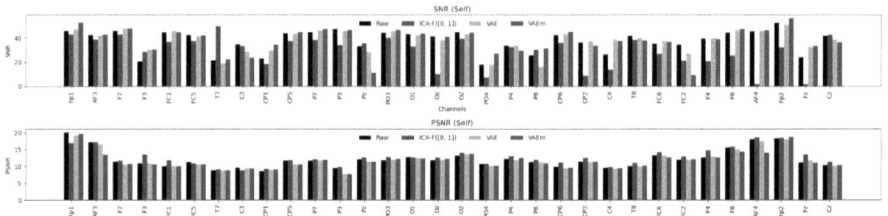

Fig. 7. SNR and PSNR computed for Raw and reconstructed signals outputed from ICA Faster, VAEm, and VAE for all channels.

Additionally, to assess the impact of latent space manipulation, MAE, NRMSE, and correlation coefficients were computed between the original signal test data and those reconstructed using ICA-Faster, VAEm, and VAE. The results, presented in Fig. 8, show that VAEm yields lower MAE and NRMSE values for most channels, suggesting it effectively preserves the signal while reducing artefacts. In contrast, ICA-F reduces artefacts but also introduces distortions in other parts of the signal, as indicated by the higher MAE and NRMSE values for several channels. Correlation coefficients were computed for the FP1 and FP2 and the average of all channels for each combination of signals. As shown in Fig. 9, the correlation between the raw and VAEm signals is consistently higher than between the raw and ICA-F signals, with VAEm closely resembling the original data. This indicates that latent space manipulation in VAEm significantly improves signal reconstruction, maintaining more of the original content than ICA-F, which reduces artefacts and distorts other parts of the signal. This supports the notion that latent space manipulation enhances signal quality while effectively reducing ocular artefacts.

Subsequently, for enhanced analysis, a specific segment of the ocular artefacts in the Fp1 and Fp2 signals, spanning from -0.2 ms before to $+0.5$ ms after the blink peak, was plotted for both original and reconstructed EEG signals. This interval captures the temporal dynamics of ocular related distortions and their reconstruction through latent space manipulation. Figure 10 displays four rows, each corresponding to different percentile thresholds used to define the lower and upper bounds of each latent component distribution. In each row, the original topographic map at blink peak (top-left) is compared with the reconstructed map (top-right), while the corresponding original and reconstructed Fp1 and Fp2 signals are shown below. In the first row, with bounds set at the $\delta^L =$

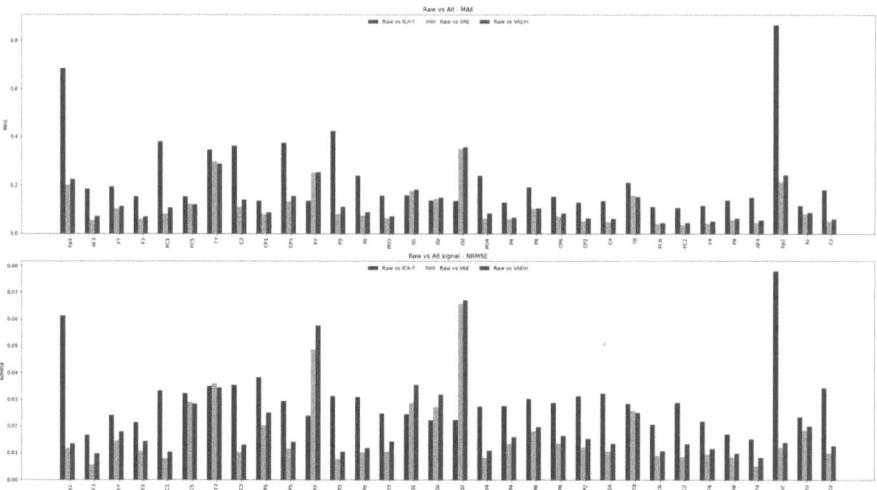

Fig. 8. MAE, NRMSE, and correlation coefficient computed for between the original signal and those reconstructed using ICA-Faster, VAEm, and VAE.

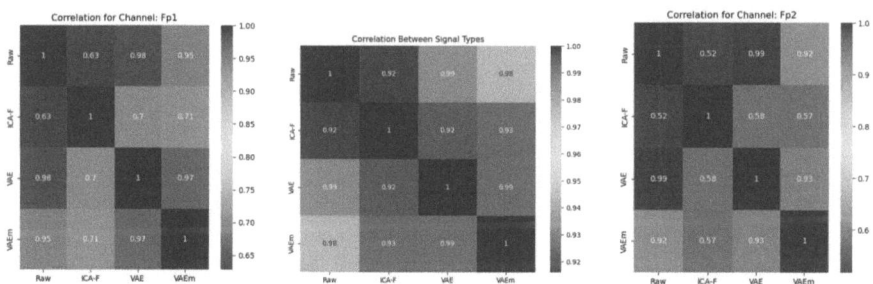

Fig. 9. Correlation coefficients between the raw and reconstructed EEG signals for Fp1 (left), Average of all channels (middle), and Fp2 (right), illustrating the effect of latent space manipulation.

0.25^{th} and $\delta^U = 99.75^{\text{th}}$ percentiles (approximately ± 3 standard deviations), the impact of latent space modification is minimal on reducing the artefacts, as evidenced by the near identical topographic maps and signal amplitudes. Reducing the percentile spread to $\delta^L = 1.0^{\text{st}}$ and $\delta^U = 99.0^{\text{th}}$ percentiles in the second row does not introduce any noticeable changes in the reconstructed outputs, indicating that the latent space modification has little to no effect. More pronounced effects begin to emerge when narrowing the thresholds to $\delta^L = 2.0^{\text{nd}}$ and $\delta^U = 98.0^{\text{th}}$ percentiles, where only subtle and mild changes are observed. Further tightening to $\delta^L = 3.0^{\text{rd}}$ and $\delta^U = 97.0^{\text{th}}$ results in noticeable alterations in the reconstructed topographic maps, particularly around the frontal electrodes, and the Fp1/Fp2 signals exhibit clearer attenuation during the blink interval. However, additional restriction to $\delta^L = 4.0^{\text{th}}$ and $\delta^U = 96.0^{\text{th}}$ does not yield further improvement, suggesting a saturation point where increased latent space modification no longer significantly enhances artefact suppression. These findings highlight that percentile-based manipulation of the latent space can selectively modulate reconstruction behaviour, with tighter bounds enhancing artefact removal while preserving overall spatial and temporal signal integrity. Changing percentile values through latent space manipulation impacts the reconstructed signals by progressively improving artefact reduction, with a saturation effect observed at higher constraints.

Figure 11 presents MNE topographic maps across the blink peak in six rows. The first row displays the original maps, while the remaining five rows show reconstructions under progressively narrower latent space percentile boundaries. The second row, with $\delta^L = 0.25^{\text{th}}$ and $\delta^U = 99.75^{\text{th}}$, shows reconstructed maps that closely resemble the originals, indicating virtually no impact from latent space modification. Similarly, the third row ($\delta^L = 1.0^{\text{st}}$, $\delta^U = 99.0^{\text{th}}$) exhibits minimal to no noticeable change. Subtle and mild changes begin to appear in the fourth row using $\delta^L = 2.0^{\text{nd}}$ and $\delta^U = 98.0^{\text{th}}$, suggesting a mild influence of latent constraint. In the fifth row ($\delta^L = 3.0^{\text{rd}}$, $\delta^U = 97.0^{\text{th}}$), the reconstructed outputs display noticeable differences, particularly around the frontal electrodes, with clearer attenuation in the Fp1/Fp2 signals during the blink interval. Finally, in the sixth row ($\delta^L = 4.0^{\text{th}}$, $\delta^U = 96.0^{\text{th}}$), the impact is comparable to that of the previous setting, indicating a saturation point where further tightening of the percentile thresholds does not yield substantial additional improvements in artefact suppression.

Table 3. Performance metrics for Raw (SNR and PSNR only), and all metrics for ICA-F and VAEm across participants

Participant	Raw		ICA-F					VAEm				
	SNR	PSNR	SNR	PSNR	Corr	MAE	NRMSE	SNR	PSNR	Corr	MAE	NRMSE
P1	33.07	18.26	34.05	17.56	0.8	0.36	0.024	43.48	13.66	0.89	0.20	0.02
P2	41.36	13.04	32.47	13.32	0.93	0.25	0.028	41.70	11.89	0.98	0.10	0.017
P3	37.60	12.14	29.12	12.71	0.92	0.22	0.029	37.89	11.71	0.98	0.11	0.019
P4	35.63	14.91	30.09	15.58	0.86	0.22	0.02	41.00	12.72	0.87	0.24	0.03
P5	42.68	12.91	23.46	12.75	0.97	0.12	0.023	45.69	12.46	0.95	0.13	0.02
P6	41.35	13.81	27.87	13.88	0.96	0.17	0.02	41.76	13.21	0.98	0.09	0.01
P7	35.83	14.02	33.45	13.570	0.90	0.11	0.05	37.48	13.29	0.97	0.06	0.01
P8	39.44	14.78	13.96	14.72	0.89	0.28	0.02	40.62	13.55	0.98	0.09	0.00
P9	38.66	13.01	28.99	13.23	0.87	0.23	0.02	39.73	12.53	0.94	0.14	0.01

The findings illustrate that training a person-specific VAE with (40, 40) topographic maps derived from 32 electrode values, resulting in a tensor of 1600

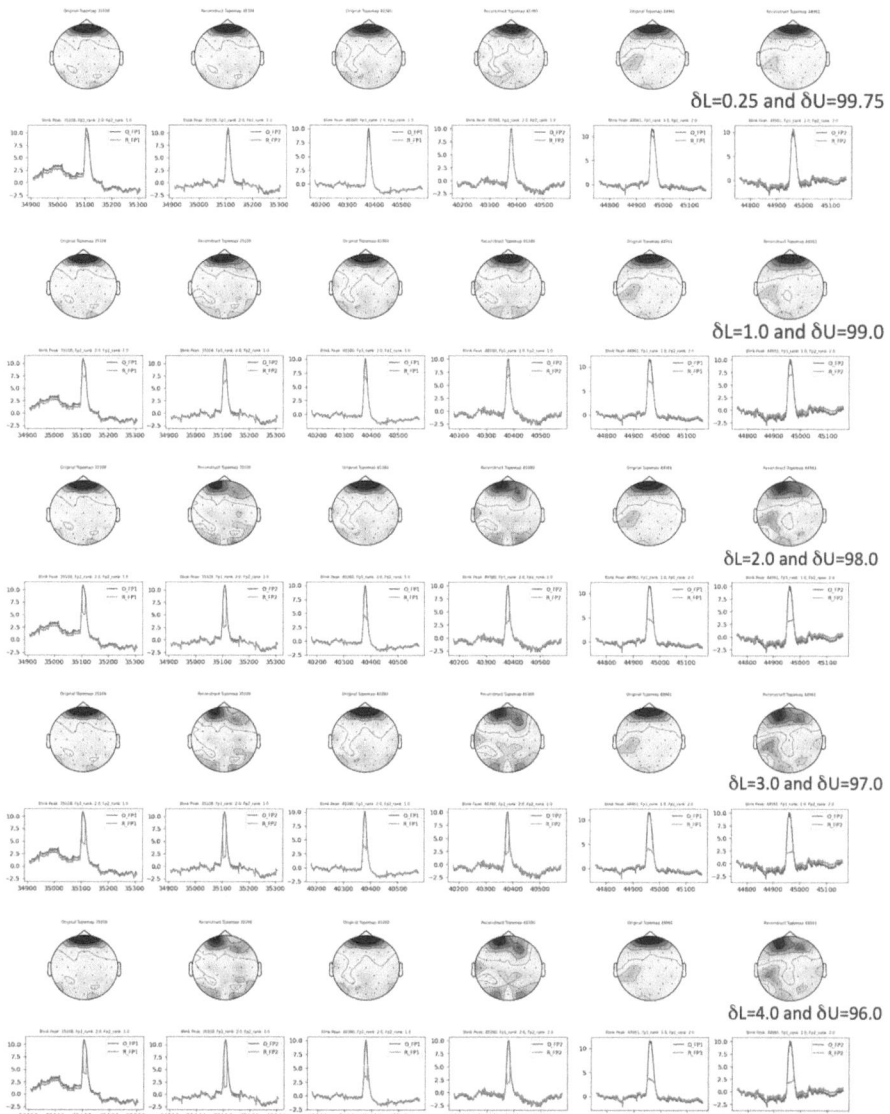

Fig. 10. Original and reconstructed MNE topomaps and Fp1/Fp2 signals from −0.2 ms to 0.5 ms around the blink peak, using different percentile thresholds. Each row shows the original (left) and reconstructed (right) data.

values, enables a significant reduction in map size—up to 99%—without losing essential information. The VAE learns a latent space representation by encoding 1600 values into a compact form, preserving essential features. This is validated through metrics such as MSE, MAE, RMSE, and MAPE, confirming the accu-

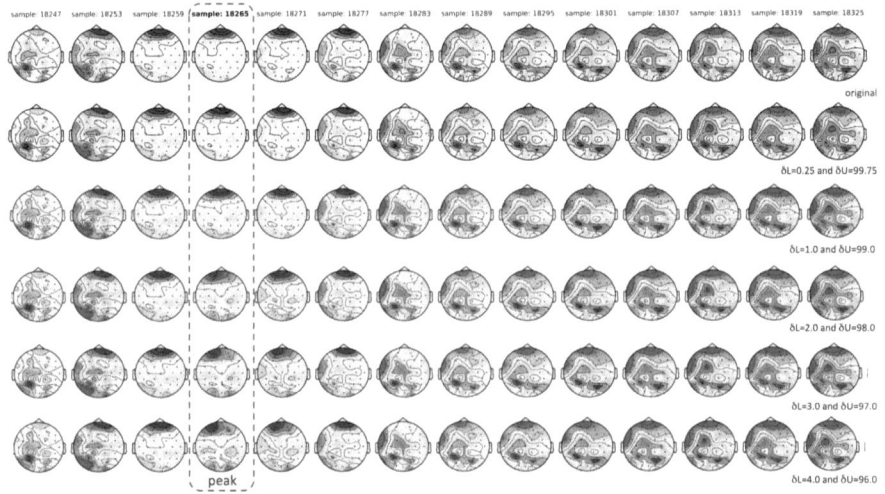

Fig. 11. Original and reconstructed topographic maps from −0.2 ms to 0.5 ms around the blink peak, using different percentile thresholds.

racy between the original and reconstructed tensors. The impact of latent space modification is further explored using SNR, PSNR, MAE, NRMSE, and correlation coefficients. The VAEm method shows higher SNR and PSNR values for FP1 and FP2 signals than ICA-F, suggesting a better reduction of ocular artefacts while maintaining signal integrity. The correlation coefficient between the raw and reconstructed signals further supports the effectiveness of the latent space manipulation in artefact suppression. Data from 9 randomly selected participants were used to assess the model's generalizability. Table 3 shows the average channel-wise metrics across these subjects. VAEm yields higher SNR than Raw and ICA-Faster, with a stronger correlation to the original signal. Additionally, the lower MAE and NRMSE values indicate that VAEm better preserves the non-artefactual portions of the signal, maintaining closer resemblance to the original data. In contrast, ICA-F tends to alter other parts of the signal. This method also offers flexibility, adapting to datasets with different electrode configurations and generating topographic maps of various sizes. The ability to interpret the latent space enhances understanding of the VAE's has learnt salient high-level representations of multi-variate EEG data, helping to identify artefactual components. Importantly, the model is trained on the training data, with distribution boundaries computed from it, ensuring robustness when applied to unseen data. Regarding the effect of modifying latent space boundaries, Figs. 10 and 11 shows that noticeable changes in the reconstructed topomaps only occur after reducing the distribution to $\delta^L = 3.0^{\text{rd}}$ and $\delta^U = 97.0^{\text{th}}$ (fifth row). These results highlight that tighter latent space boundaries lead to more significant reductions in ocular artefacts.

5 Conclusion

Electroencephalogram (EEG) recordings are often contaminated with artefacts that hinder analysis. This study introduces a novel, subject-specific VAE-based automated artefact identification and reduction method within a self-supervised framework, minimising the need for human intervention. Unlike traditional approaches relying on vector representations, this method leverages spatially structured EEG topographic maps to retain spatial information during reconstruction. A key approach component involves analysing the latent space after training a VAE. Boundaries for each latent component were estimated using percentile-based thresholds, and probability distributions from training data were used to compute anomaly scores. Test samples were flagged as anomalous if their scores exceeded the 98th percentile of training scores. These samples were then corrected by clipping and adjusting their activated latent values within the established boundaries. Results demonstrate that person-specific VAE models effectively reduce artefacts while preserving signal structure and spatial integrity. Modifying latent space boundaries using percentiles further improves artefact suppression, especially ocular artefacts, with noticeable improvements seen at narrower thresholds. In summary, the proposed method offers a practical and generalizable solution for EEG artefact reduction, maintaining signal fidelity while minimising human input. Future work will aim to validate the technique across datasets with varying electrode configurations and explore more profound insights into latent components responsible for different artefact types, enhancing interpretability and robustness.

References

1. Ahmed, T., Longo, L.: Examining the size of the latent space of convolutional variational autoencoders trained with spectral topographic maps of EEG frequency bands. IEEE Access **10**, 107575–107586 (2022)
2. Ahmed, T., Longo, L.: Interpreting disentangled representations of person-specific convolutional variational autoencoders of spatially preserving EEG topographic maps via clustering and visual plausibility. Information **14**(9), 489 (2023)
3. Ahmed, T., Longo, L.: Latent space interpretation and visualisation for understanding the decisions of convolutional variational autoencoders trained with EEG topographic maps (2023)
4. Anderson, E.W., Preston, G.A., Silva, C.T.: Using python for signal processing and visualization. Comput. Sci. Eng. **12**(4), 90–95 (2010)
5. Anwar, A.M., Eldeib, A.M.: EEG signal classification using convolutional neural networks on combined spatial and temporal dimensions for BCI systems. In: 2020 42nd Annual International Conference of the IEEE Engineering in Medicine & Biology Society (EMBC), pp. 434–437. IEEE (2020)
6. Banar, B., Bryan-Kinns, N., Colton, S.: A tool for generating controllable variations of musical themes using variational autoencoders with latent space regularisation. In: Proceedings of the AAAI Conference on Artificial Intelligence, vol. 37, pp. 16401–16403 (2023)

7. Barlow, J.S.: Computerized clinical electroencephalography in perspective. IEEE Trans. Biomed. Eng. **7**, 377–391 (1979)
8. Bengio, Y., Courville, A., Vincent, P.: Representation learning: a review and new perspectives. IEEE Trans. Pattern Anal. Mach. Intell. **35**(8), 1798–1828 (2013)
9. Berg, P., Scherg, M.: Dipole modelling of eye activity and its application to the removal of eye artefacts from the EEG and MEG. Clin. Phys. Physiol. Meas. **12**(A), 49 (1991)
10. Van den Berg-Lenssen, M., Van Gisbergen, J., Jervis, B.: Comparison of two methods for correcting ocular artefacts in EEGS. Med. Biol. Eng. Compu. **32**, 501–511 (1994)
11. Bergstra, J., Bengio, Y.: Random search for hyper-parameter optimization. J. Mach. Learn. Res. **13**(2), 281–305 (2012)
12. Bethge, D., et al.: Eeg2vec: Learning affective EEG representations via variational autoencoders. In: 2022 IEEE International Conference on Systems, Man, and Cybernetics (SMC), pp. 3150–3157. IEEE (2022)
13. Biedebach, L., et al.: Towards a deeper understanding of sleep stages through their representation in the latent space of variational autoencoders (2023)
14. Binnie, C., Prior, P.: Electroencephalography. J. Neurol. Neurosurgery Psychiatry **57**(11), 1308–1319 (1994)
15. Bornschein, J., Bengio, Y.: Reweighted wake-sleep. arXiv preprint arXiv:1406.2751 (2014)
16. Chikkankod, A.V., Longo, L.: On the dimensionality and utility of convolutional autoencoder's latent space trained with topology-preserving spectral eeg headmaps. Mach. Learn. Knowl. Extract. **4**(4), 1042–1064 (2022)
17. Criscuolo, S., Apicella, A., Prevete, R., Longo, L.: Interpreting the latent space of a convolutional variational autoencoder for semi-automated eye blink artefact detection in EEG signals. Comput. Stand. Interfaces **92**, 103897 (2025)
18. Criscuolo, S., Prevete, R., Apicella, A., Longo, L.: Interpreting the latent space of a convolutional variational autoencoder for fully automated eye blink artefact detection in EEG signals. Available at SSRN 4761327
19. Croft, R.J., Barry, R.J.: EOG correction: a new perspective. Electroencephalogr. Clin. Neurophysiol. **107**(6), 387–394 (1998)
20. Egambaram, A., Badruddin, N., Asirvadam, V.S., Fauvet, E., Stolz, C., Begum, T.: Unsupervised eye blink artifact identification in electroencephalogram. In: TENCON 2018-2018 IEEE Region 10 Conference, pp. 2148–2152. IEEE (2018)
21. Elbattah, M., Loughnane, C., Guérin, J.L., Carette, R., Cilia, F., Dequen, G.: Variational autoencoder for image-based augmentation of eye-tracking data. J. Imaging **7**(5), 83 (2021)
22. Fortuin, V., Hüser, M., Locatello, F., Strathmann, H., Rätsch, G.: SOM-VAE: interpretable discrete representation learning on time series. In: 7th International Conference on Learning Representations (ICLR). ICLR (2019). https://openreview.net/pdf?id=rygjcsR9Y7
23. Gramfort, A., et al et al.: MEG and EEG data analysis with MNE-Python. Front. Neurosci. **7**, 267 (2013)
24. Hagad, J.L., Kimura, T., Fukui, K.i., Numao, M.: Learning subject-generalized topographical EEG embeddings using deep variational autoencoders and domain-adversarial regularization. Sensors **21**(5), 1792 (2021)
25. He, P., Wilson, G., Russell, C., Gerschutz, M.: Removal of ocular artifacts from the EEG: a comparison between time-domain regression method and adaptive filtering method using simulated data. Med. Biol. Eng. Comput. **45**, 495–503 (2007)

26. Hsieh, J.T., Liu, B., Huang, D.A., Fei-Fei, L.F., Niebles, J.C.: Learning to decompose and disentangle representations for video prediction. In: Advances in Neural Information Processing Systems, vol. 31 (2018)
27. Islam, M.K., Rastegarnia, A., Yang, Z.: Methods for artifact detection and removal from scalp EEG: a review. Neurophysiologie Clinique/Clin. Neurophys. **46**(4–5), 287–305 (2016)
28. Junghöfer, M., Elbert, T., Tucker, D.M., Rockstroh, B.: Statistical control of artifacts in dense array EEG/MEG studies. Psychophysiology **37**(4), 523–532 (2000)
29. Khare, S.K., March, S., Barua, P.D., Gadre, V.M., Acharya, U.R.: Application of data fusion for automated detection of children with developmental and mental disorders: a systematic review of the last decade. Inf. Fus. **99**, 101898 (2023)
30. Koelstra, S., et al.: DEAP: a database for emotion analysis; using physiological signals. IEEE Trans. Affect. Comput. **3**(1), 18–31 (2011)
31. Lawhern, V., Hairston, W.D., McDowell, K., Westerfield, M., Robbins, K.: Detection and classification of subject-generated artifacts in EEG signals using autoregressive models. J. Neurosci. Methods **208**(2), 181–189 (2012)
32. Li, K., et al.: Feature extraction and identification of Alzheimer's disease based on latent factor of multi-channel EEG. IEEE Trans. Neural Syst. Rehabil. Eng. **29**, 1557–1567 (2021)
33. Liu, S., et al.: Discovering influential factors in variational autoencoders. Pattern Recogn. **100**, 107166 (2020)
34. Locatello, F., et al.: Challenging common assumptions in the unsupervised learning of disentangled representations. In: International Conference on Machine Learning, pp. 4114–4124. PMLR (2019)
35. Longo, L., et al.: Explainable artificial intelligence (XAI) 2.0: a manifesto of open challenges and interdisciplinary research directions. Inf. Fus. **106**, 102301 (2024)
36. Longo, L., Reilly, R.B.: onEEGwaveLAD: a fully automated online EEG wavelet-based learning adaptive denoiser for artefacts identification and mitigation. PLOS ONE **20**(1), 1–25 (01 2025). https://doi.org/10.1371/journal.pone.0313076
37. Mahajan, K., Vargantwar, M., Rajput, S.M., et al.: Classification of EEG using PCA, ICA and neural network. Int. J. Eng. Adv. Technol. **1**(1), 80–83 (2011)
38. Mayeli, A., et al.: Automated pipeline for EEG artifact reduction (appear) recorded during FMRI. J. Neural Eng. **18**(4), 0460b4 (2021)
39. Naval Marimont, S., Tarroni, G.: Anomaly detection through latent space restoration using vector-quantized variational autoencoders. arXiv e-prints pp. arXiv–2012 (2020)
40. Niedermeyer, E., da Silva, F.L.: Electroencephalography: Basic Principles, Clinical Applications, and Related Fields. Lippincott Williams & Wilkins (2005)
41. Nolan, H., Whelan, R., Reilly, R.B.: Faster: fully automated statistical thresholding for EEG artifact rejection. J. Neurosci. Methods **192**(1), 152–162 (2010)
42. Plöchl, M., Ossandón, J.P., König, P.: Combining EEG and eye tracking: identification, characterization, and correction of eye movement artifacts in electroencephalographic data. Front. Hum. Neurosci. **6**, 278 (2012)
43. Ramakrishna, S., Rahiminasab, Z., Karsai, G., Easwaran, A., Dubey, A.: Efficient out-of-distribution detection using latent space of β-VAE for cyber-physical systems. ACM Trans. Cyber-Phys. Syst. (TCPS) **6**(2), 1–34 (2022)
44. Raufi, B., Longo, L.: An evaluation of the EEG alpha-to-theta and theta-to-alpha band ratios as indexes of mental workload. Front. Neuroinform. **16**, 861967 (2022)
45. Reimann, C., Filzmoser, P.: Normal and lognormal data distribution in geochemistry: death of a myth. consequences for the statistical treatment of geochemical and environmental data. Environ. Geol. **39**, 1001–1014 (2000)

46. Romero, S., Mañanas, M.A., Barbanoj, M.J.: A comparative study of automatic techniques for ocular artifact reduction in spontaneous EEG signals based on clinical target variables: a simulation case. Comput. Biol. Med. **38**(3), 348–360 (2008)
47. Sara, U., Akter, M., Uddin, M.S.: Image quality assessment through FSIM, SSIM, MSE and PSNR–a comparative study. J. Comput. Commun. **7**(3), 8–18 (2019)
48. Schneider, P., Xhafa, F.: Chapter 3—anomaly detection: concepts and methods. In: Anomaly Detection and Complex Event Processing Over IoT Data Streams, pp. 49–66 (2022)
49. Sudaryat, Y., Nurhadi, J., Rahma, R.: Spectral topographic brain mapping in EEG recording for detecting reading attention in various science books. J. Turkish Sci. Educ. **16**(3), 440–450 (2019)
50. Tandle, A., Jog, N., D'cunha, P., Chheta, M.: Classification of artefacts in EEG signal recordings and overview of removing techniques. Int. J. Comput. Appli. **975**, 8887 (2015)
51. Tran, D.K., Nguyen, T.H., Nguyen, T.N.: Detection of EEG-based eye-blinks using a thresholding algorithm. Eur. J. Eng. Technol. Res. **6**(4), 6–12 (2021)
52. Tun, M.T., Nyaung, D.E., Phyu, M.P.: Network anomaly detection using threshold-based sparse autoencoder (2020)
53. Urigüen, J.A., Garcia-Zapirain, B.: EEG artifact removal–state-of-the-art and guidelines. J. Neural Eng. **12**(3), 031001 (2015)
54. Valdes-Sosa, P.: Topographic time-frequency decomposition of the EEG. Neuroimage **14**(2), 383–390 (2001)
55. Vogelsanger, C., Federau, C.: Latent space analysis of VAE and intro-VAE applied to 3-dimensional MR brain volumes of multiple sclerosis, leukoencephalopathy, and healthy patients. arXiv preprint arXiv:2101.06772 (2021)
56. Yang, J., Yu, H., Shen, T., Song, Y., Chen, Z.: 4-class MI-EEG signal generation and recognition with CVAE-GAN. Appl. Sci. **11**(4), 1798 (2021)
57. Zhao, T., et al.: VAEEG: variational auto-encoder for extracting EEG representation. Neuroimage **304**, 120946 (2024)

Open Access This chapter is licensed under the terms of the Creative Commons Attribution 4.0 International License (http://creativecommons.org/licenses/by/4.0/), which permits use, sharing, adaptation, distribution and reproduction in any medium or format, as long as you give appropriate credit to the original author(s) and the source, provide a link to the Creative Commons license and indicate if changes were made.

The images or other third party material in this chapter are included in the chapter's Creative Commons license, unless indicated otherwise in a credit line to the material. If material is not included in the chapter's Creative Commons license and your intended use is not permitted by statutory regulation or exceeds the permitted use, you will need to obtain permission directly from the copyright holder.

Metric-Guided Synthesis for Class Activation Mapping

Alejandro Luque-Cerpa[1]($\boxtimes$), Elizabeth Polgreen[2], Ajitha Rajan[2], and Hazem Torfah[1]

[1] Chalmers University of Technology and University of Gothenburg, Gothenburg, Sweden
{luque,hazemto}@chalmers.se
[2] University of Edinburgh, Edinburgh, UK
{elizabeth.polgreen,arajan}@ed.ac.uk

Abstract. Class activation mapping (CAM) is a widely adopted class of saliency methods used to explain the behavior of convolutional neural networks (CNNs). These methods generate heatmaps that highlight the parts of the input most relevant to the CNN output. Various CAM methods have been proposed, each distinguished by the expressions used to derive heatmaps. In general, users look for heatmaps with specific properties that reflect different aspects of CNN functionality. These may include similarity to ground truth, robustness, equivariance, and more. Although existing CAM methods implicitly encode some of these properties in their expressions, they do not allow for variability in heatmap generation following the user's intent or domain knowledge. In this paper, we address this limitation by introducing SyCAM, a metric-based approach for synthesizing CAM expressions. Given a predefined evaluation metric for saliency maps, SyCAM automatically generates CAM expressions optimized for that metric. We specifically explore a syntax-guided synthesis instantiation of SyCAM, where CAM expressions are derived based on predefined syntactic constraints and the given metric. Using several established evaluation metrics, we demonstrate the efficacy and flexibility of our approach in generating targeted heatmaps. We compare SyCAM with other well-known CAM methods on three prominent models: ResNet50, VGG16, and VGG19.

Keywords: Explainability · Class activation mappings · Oracle-guided inductive synthesis

1 Introduction

Convolutional Neural Networks (CNNs) have enabled the development of efficient solutions for a wide range of challenging vision problems, such as object

---

This work was partly supported by the Wallenberg AI, Autonomous Systems and Software Program funded by the Knut and Alice Wallenberg Foundation, a Royal Academy of Engineering Research Fellowship and a Royal Society Industry Fellowship.

detection in autonomous vehicles [11], facial recognition through semantic segmentation [19], and medical image analysis [18,28]. Despite their advantages, CNNs, like other neural models, suffer from an opaque decision-making process, making it challenging to build trust in their predictions. For instance, physicians using a CNN for X-ray classification require more than just a diagnosis; they need to understand which specific part of the X-ray led to that diagnosis. Similarly, in autonomous vehicles, debugging and employing CNN-based object detectors requires insight into which parts of an image triggered a classification. The growing need to explain CNN behavior has led to the development of various explainability techniques [4,6,32,36]. However, with each new method, it is becoming increasingly clear that more systematic approaches are needed to generate explanations that adapt to the specific intents and needs of end users [14].

In this paper, we address the challenge of incorporating intent by proposing a metric-based approach to generating explanations for CNNs, i.e., where explanations are optimized for a predefined metric. Specifically, we study this problem in the context of explainability methods based on *class activation mappings* (CAM) [37]. CAM methods are one of the most adopted methods for generating saliency maps, i.e., heatmaps that highlight the regions of an input most relevant to the CNN's prediction. The definition of relevance differs from one method to another, and thus, each method may result in different heatmaps. Figure 1, shows example heatmaps generated by a set of different CAM methods. In the figure, the heatmaps highlight slightly different image regions across the different techniques. Heatmaps produced by CAM are the result of computing a linear combination of the feature maps from the convolutional layers of a CNN. CAM methods generate heatmaps by weighting feature maps based on their contribution to the class score. They differ in how they calculate the weights, each offering a unique expression for computing them. Selecting the most appropriate CAM method depends on the specific application and the level of detail in the activation map.

For example, GradCAM [32] tends to favor larger activation regions in the activation maps, highlighting the most prominent part of an image that influences classification. In an image with multiple swans (see Fig. 1, first row), GradCAM primarily highlights the two more visible swans on the right. However, if these swans are removed, the model may still classify the image correctly based on the partial swan. In contrast, GradCAM++ [4] incorporates all activation regions, highlighting also the partial swans as influential in the CNN's decision. Depending on the user's intent, whether they seek to understand the model's overall behavior or identify the most influential part of a specific image, they may prefer one method over the other. Choosing the right CAM method is, therefore, often a complex task, traditionally relying on human intuition and empirical experimentation. A non-expert user may not know which CAM expression is most suitable for their application, and a systematic approach to guide the generation of optimal CAM expressions, with respect to certain predefined metrics, is missing.

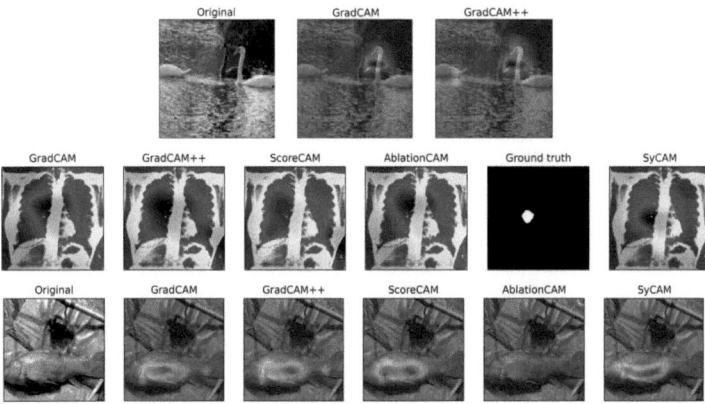

Fig. 1. Saliency maps generated using different CAM methods (GradCAM [32], GradCAM++ [4], ScoreCAM [36], AblationCAM [6], and one using an expression synthesized by our SYCAM framework) for three models different CNNs trained on three different data sets ImageNet [5], COVID-QU-Ex [34] and ImageNette [13]. The first row of images shows heatmaps for GradCAM and GradCAM++. The second row of images shows how SYCAM guided by a ground truth metric, captures the ground truth more accurately than the other methods. The last row shows how SYCAM guided by the insertion metric generates a heatmap that closely mimics that of the dominant CAM method, ScoreCAM in this case.

Our framework, SYCAM, presents a metric-based framework for the automatic synthesis of CAM expressions. From a given class of expressions, SYCAM can synthesize expressions tailored to specific properties captured via a fitting evaluation metric. For instance, metrics capturing the overlap between a heatmap and the ground truth mask [33] or the pixel intensity of the heatmap in such overlap [9] guide towards the generation of CAM expressions that generate heatmaps with higher similarity to ground truth. Metrics like the Deletion or Insertion metrics [27] lead to CAM expressions that generate heatmaps highlighting what the model is truly paying attention to (independent of the correctness of the prediction).

Consider the heatmaps shown in the second row in Fig. 1, where different saliency methods have been applied to explain why a CNN classified an X-ray image as a COVID case. Here, we used SYCAM to synthesize an expression optimized toward the ground truth, i.e., during synthesis, expressions are evaluated based on whether they highlight pixels that also match the ground truth. From the figure, we can see that the heatmap generated according to the SYCAM synthesized expression captured the ground truth more accurately. In contrast, all other methods failed to do so, producing significantly less accurate representations of the ground truth region.

We applied SYCAM using different metrics to study their impact on heatmap generation. In Fig. 1, in the last row, we present another example where SYCAM was applied using the insertion metric [27]. The insertion metric evaluates how the highest-scoring pixels in the heatmap influence image classification. In this case, ScoreCAM achieved the highest score compared to GradCAM, GradCAM++, and AblationCAM. SYCAM generated an expression that closely resembled ScoreCAM and achieved a very similar score. This demonstrates that when a particular method outperforms others based on a given evaluation metric, SYCAM produces expressions that align with the dominant approach.

Our results are based on an instantiation of SYCAM, adapting techniques from the syntax-guided synthesis literature (SyGuS) [2], which searches a space defined by a grammar of potential CAM expressions. This is done via an *oracle-guided inductive synthesis* (OGIS) approach [15]. In OGIS, a learner explores the space of possible solutions, guided by oracles that give feedback and evaluate the correctness of solutions generated by the learner. Here, the learner is a synthesis process that searches the space of possible CAM expressions, guided by two oracles: one that can remove equivalent solutions and another that evaluates the candidate solution according to a given evaluation metric. We show that, while a monolithic enumerative approach can be used to synthesize CAM expressions, it comes with the limitation of not taking into account any of the image properties, such as the image class. To overcome this limitation, we present an adaptation of the synthesis approach leveraging a class-based decomposition of the problem. Specifically, our approach allows for case splits, thereby synthesizing a set of CAM expressions for each class of properties. This is showcased in our experiments, where we use SYCAM to synthesize CAM expressions for three prominent models: ResNet50, VGG16, and VGG19 [22], and compare them with those of established methods like GradCAM, GradCAM++, ScoreCAM, and AblationCAM.

In summary, SYCAM provides a general framework for the systematic generation of CAM methods, with flexibility in two dimensions: first, the user can provide an evaluation metric to suit their use case; and second, the user can provide a syntactic template or grammar that defines the space of possible expressions, giving the potential to provide user intuition to the search algorithm. SYCAM will then find an expression that is dominant with respect to the given evaluation metric. Our primary contributions can be summarized as follows:

- We introduce the problem of synthesizing CAM expressions for CNNs optimized for specific evaluation metrics.
- We present a framework for solving the problem following the OGIS approach, adapting enumerative techniques from SyGuS.
- We present a thorough experimental evaluation demonstrating the efficacy of our framework in synthesizing CAM-expressions for the prominent classification models ResNet50, VGG16, and VGG19.
- We evaluate our framework over a COVID-19 benchmark, where the expressions incorporate metrics that favor expert knowledge.

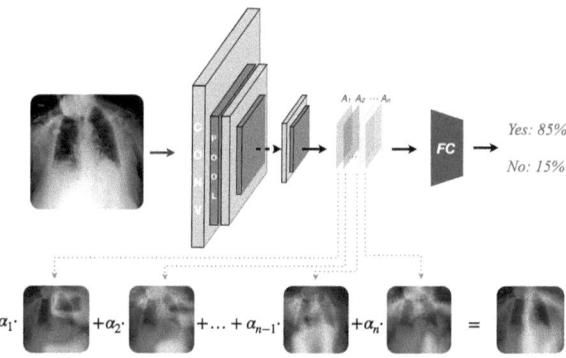

Fig. 2. Overview of a CNN-based model that classifies X-ray images into COVID-19 positive or negative, and a CAM-based method that explains each classification.

2 Background

2.1 Convolutional Neural Networks

Convolutional Neural Networks (CNNs) have proven highly effective in pattern recognition tasks, especially in image processing [11,17,19]. The typical architecture of a CNN is illustrated in Fig. 2. The fundamental building blocks of a CNN are the convolutional layers, which are used for identifying features within an image. These layers work by iteratively applying filters, so-called kernels, to the input image. These filters are learned during the training phase. Each layer applies multiple filters to the output of the previous layer, starting with the input image. The output produced by applying a filter is known as a feature map. As the network deepens, the feature maps define increasingly complex features. While the initial layers may focus on basic elements, such as colors and edges, deeper layers recognize larger patterns. In classification tasks, these higher-level features are usually passed to a fully connected layer used for classifying the image. To reduce the size of these feature maps while preserving critical information, pooling layers are introduced after each convolutional layer. Common pooling methods include average pooling and max pooling, which reduce a portion of a feature map into its average or maximum value, respectively.

2.2 Class Activation Mapping

Saliency maps are visual artifacts that highlight the regions of an image most relevant to a model's prediction. Class Activation Mapping (CAM) is a prominent set of methods for generating these saliency maps. The core idea of CAM is to compute a saliency map, the class activation map, via a weighted linear combination of the feature maps of the last convolutional layer [37]. This layer is chosen because it captures high-level features that are most relevant for the classification. The map is always generated for a certain class and points to the parts of an image the network focuses on when predicting that particular class.

The general concept of CAM is illustrated in Fig. 2. Formally, for an output class c and a convolutional layer l, the saliency map L^c can be defined as: $L^c = \sum_k \alpha_k^c A_k^l$, where A_k^l denotes the k-th feature map of the layer l, i.e., the two-dimensional array resulting from applying the k-th convolutional filter of the layer l to its input, and the weights α_k^c depend on the CAM method chosen.

Each feature map highlights specific aspects of the image. High values in a feature map point to the presence of a feature; low values hint at its absence. Since each feature map contributes differently to the scores of individual classes, the linear combination is weighted to reflect the influence of each feature map in producing the final class activation map. These influences are represented by the weights $\alpha_1, \ldots, \alpha_n$.

Different CAM methods are distinguished by how they calculate the weights. In the original CAM, the weights were defined via the learned weights corresponding to different classes. Methods like GradCAM or GradCAM++ [21] compute the weights by using the gradients of the score for a specific class with respect to the feature maps of a convolutional layer. Further gradient-based approaches building on the latter two include SMOOTH GRADCAM++ [26], AUGMENTED GRADCAM [24], and XGRADCAM [10]. Gradient-free approaches determine the importance of different regions in the input image for a specific class without relying on gradients. These include perturbation-based approaches like SCORECAM [36] and ABLATIONCAM [6], attention-based methods like Attention-Guided CAM [20], and methods like EIGENCAM [25], that apply principal component analysis to create the class activation map. For a comprehensive survey, we refer the reader to [14]. So far, no systematic approach has been used to determine the optimal weight expression for a given task. Our work addresses this challenge by introducing an automated approach capable of synthesizing both gradient-based and gradient-free expressions if the grammar allows it.

2.3 Heatmaps Evaluation Metrics

Several metrics have been introduced in the literature to evaluate saliency methods [16]. Some of these methods are perturbation-based, i.e., they evaluate the effect of masking regions highlighted by CAM methods on the model's performance. Examples of such metrics include Average Drop % [4], AOPC [31], ROAD [30], IROF [29], and the Deletion and Insertion [27] metrics. Another category of metrics is ground-truth-based. These metrics measure the distance of the explanation to the ground-truth explanation data. Some examples of these metrics are the m_{GT} metric defined in [33], the Segmentation Content Heatmap (SCH) metric [9], CEM [7], and CLEVR-AI [3]. SYCAM is agnostic to the chosen metric, and CAM-weight expressions can be synthesized by SYCAM with respect to any of the aforementioned metrics. Each evaluation metric focuses on different properties of the heatmaps, e.g., similarity to ground truth, robustness, and more. The synthesized expressions are, in consequence, based on well-founded criteria, guided by quantitative evaluation metrics. The resulting expressions generate optimized saliency maps according to these metrics, thus allowing us to eliminate any human biases and to select a CAM method more suitable for a given context. An extensive study on the correctness of XAI techniques in generating the true explanations, the so-called fidelity, can be found in [23].

In the following, we provide a detailed introduction to key evaluation metrics that we also use later in our experiments.

Average Drop %: The intuition behind this metric is one that checks whether removing parts not highlighted by the heatmap of an image reduces the classification confidence of the model. Removing parts of an image that are not relevant shouldn't heavily impact the confidence drop. To check if the most relevant parts of an image i are preserved, the product of the heatmap and the image is computed. Then, the resulting image h is classified to measure the confidence drop. A low confidence drop implies that the heatmap contains the most relevant features of the image, so the lower the metric value, the better.

Given a dataset $\mathcal{I}$, the Average Drop % is expressed as $\sum_{i \in \mathcal{I}} \frac{\max(0, y_i^c - h_i^c)}{y_i^c} \cdot 100$, where y_i^c is the classification score for image $i \in \mathcal{I}$ and class c, and h_i^c is the classification score for the product of image i and the generated heatmap for such image, and class c.

Deletion and Insertion Metrics: The Deletion metric measures the drop in the classification score when the most relevant pixels of the image are *gradually* removed, while the Insertion metric measures the rise in the classification score when they are iteratively added to a blank image. In this paper, we use modified versions of the Deletion and the Insertion metrics. Given a model M, an image x, a limit on the number of perturbations P, and a saliency map $\mathcal{H}$ over x, the process recursively modifies the image according to the following formula:

$$x^{(0)} = x \qquad \forall\, 1 \leq j \leq P \;:\; x^{(j)} = g(x^{(j-1)}, \bar{x}, r_j)$$

For the Deletion metric, the function g gradually replaces the most relevant pixels r_j, ordered by the saliency map $L_M^c[e]$, and their neighborhoods with the corresponding parts of a highly blurred version of x, denoted by $\bar{x}$. The neighborhood of a pixel is given by the feature maps used to compute the saliency map. If the feature maps A_k have size $w \times h$, we split the image into a grid of $w \times h$ neighborhoods. For the Insertion metric, the process is analogous, but the most important pixels are added to the highly blurred version of the image instead. The metrics are then defined by:

$$\mu_{deletion} = \frac{1}{|I|} \sum_{x \in I} \frac{1}{P+1} \left(\sum_{j=0}^{P} M(x^{(0)})^{c_0} - M(x^{(j)})^{c_0} \right)$$

$$\mu_{insertion} = \frac{1}{|I|} \sum_{x \in I} \frac{1}{P+1} \left(\sum_{j=0}^{P} M(x^{(j)})^{c_0} - M(x^{(0)})^{c_0} \right)$$

where c_0 is the output class of $M(x^{(0)})$, $M(x)^{c_0}$ is the output score for class c_0, and $|I|$ is the number of images in the set I. Unlike for other similar metrics [12], no artifacts are added through this procedure, and $\bar{x}$ is generated using deterministic filters, so the influence of random perturbations over the metric is also avoided. The purpose of using these versions instead of the originals [27] is to avoid adding artifacts, to make sure that the computed scores are relative to the initial score of the model M over the base image, and to make them work so that the higher the values, the better.

Intuitively, higher values of the metrics imply higher variations in the classification score during the perturbation process, i.e., higher relevance of the pixels highlighted by the saliency map. We may get some insights about the datasets employed using these metrics. For example, when the confidence drop for the Deletion metric is much lower for a subset than for the others, it means that the model is still confident in its classification even after masking portions of the objects. This may imply that the objects occupy most of the image or that the model identifies the objects through the background. In such cases, it is important to improve the dataset.

Ground Truth Similarity Metrics: Some evaluation metrics are focused on measuring the similarity of the heatmap to a ground-truth mask.

Given a heatmap H and a ground-truth mask H_{GT} with p pixels, the m_{GT} metric takes the p most relevant pixels of H and counts how many of those pixels are part of the ground-truth mask. This is, if n of the p most relevant pixels of H are part of the mask H_{GT}, then $m_{GT}(H, H_{GT}) = n/p$. While the m_{GT} metric measures the similarity between a heatmap and the ground truth, it doesn't provide information about the intensity of the heatmap pixels. The SCH metric, on the other hand, solves this problem. The SCH metric is given by:

$$SCH(H, H_{GT}) = \frac{\sum_{i,j} H_{i,j} \cdot M_{i,j}}{\sum_{i,j} H_{i,j}}$$

Intuitively, the SCH metric measures how concentrated the heatmap is in the ground-truth mask. The more concentrated the pixels are and the higher their relevance, the higher the metric will be, so the higher, the better.

Notice that a strong assumption of ground-truth similarity metrics is that the models are making classifications based on the ground-truth part of the image. If the models are not doing so, and are making decisions based on other information found in the input data, these metrics would return low values independently of how well the heatmaps are explaining what the models are paying attention to.

2.4 Syntax-Guided Synthesis

Syntax-Guided Synthesis (SyGuS) [2] is the problem of generating a function that both satisfies a semantic specification and is contained within a language described in a context-free grammar (CFG).

Definition 1 (Context-Free Grammar). *A context-free grammar G is defined as as a set of terminal symbols T and a set of nonterminal symbols NT, a start symbol S, and a set of production rules $R \subseteq NT \times (T \cup NT)^*$ which describe the way programs may be constructed iteratively from the grammar.*

Definition 2 (SyGuS problems). *Formally, a SyGuS problem is a 4-tuple $\langle T, G, \phi, F \rangle$ such that T is a first-order theory, G is a context-free grammar, ϕ is a first-order formula, and F is a function symbol that may occur in ϕ. A solution to a SyGuS problem $\langle T, G, \phi, F \rangle$ is a function f such that $T \models \phi[F \mapsto f]$ and $f \in \mathcal{L}(G)$, where $\phi[F \mapsto f]$ denotes replacing all occurrences of F in ϕ with f.*

Later in the paper, we study a SyGuS instantiation of CAM expression synthesis, where the specification is that the resulting CAM method must perform better than a given threshold function. This is described in detail in Sect. 4. The most common approach for solving SyGuS problems is Oracle Guided Inductive Synthesis (OGIS) [15]; a family of algorithms that alternate between a learner, which attempts to learn a solution to the synthesis problem, and an oracle, which guides the learner via means of queries and responses, the simplest of which is a correctness query (the learner asks "is this candidate program correct?", and the oracle replies with "yes" or "no"). There is a broad variety of learners in the literature, but the most common are enumerative techniques. We take inspiration from some of the most common enumerative learners [1] when implementing our approach.

3 CAM Expression Synthesis

3.1 Problem Statement

Let $t[?]$ define an expression with holes, known as a *template*, where holes in the expression are marked by the symbol ?. For an expression e, the expression $t[e]$ results from replacing every appearance of the symbol ? in t with e. Following the definition of CAM as given in Sect. 2.2, we define a CAM template as $L^c[?] = \sum_k ? \cdot A_k^l$. The ? is a placeholder for an expression that defines how the weights α_k^c are computed for a class c. We refer to such expressions as CAM-weight expressions. We refer to the set of all instantiations of $L^c[?]$ by $\mathcal{F}_{CAM}$.

Problem 1 (CAM expression synthesis) *Let $\mathcal{M} = (\mathcal{I} \to \mathbb{R}^{|\mathcal{C}|})$ be a set of CNN-based classifiers defined over a space of images $\mathcal{I}$ and a set of classes $\mathcal{C}$. Given $M \in \mathcal{M}$, a set of images $I \subseteq \mathcal{I}$, a threshold function $\lambda: \mathcal{M} \times \mathcal{I} \to \mathbb{R}$, a set of CAM-weight expressions $\mathcal{E}$, and an evaluation function $\mu: \mathcal{F}_{CAM} \times \mathcal{M} \times \mathcal{I} \to \mathbb{R}$, synthesize an expression $e \in \mathcal{E}$ s.t. $\mu(L^c[e], M, I) > \lambda(M, I)$.*

In our problem statement, the role of the threshold function λ is to set a lower bound on the quality of synthesized expressions with respect to the evaluation function μ. As we will see in our experiments, the threshold function can be given as a fixed number or as a function of any other CAM function. The evaluation function μ defines a metric for evaluating CAM functions and can be realized by implementing known CAM evaluation metrics from the literature.

3.2 Oracle-Guided Synthesis of CAM-Weight Expressions

Now that we have a formally defined problem statement, we can discuss the SYCAM framework, an oracle-guided synthesis approach for the synthesis of CAM-weight expressions. Let us initially assume we have access to two oracles:

- an equivalence oracle: this oracle receives as input a set of expressions ϵ, which may contain semantically equivalent expressions, and returns a set of expressions $\epsilon' \subseteq \epsilon$ such that no two expressions in ϵ' are semantically equivalent; and
- a correctness oracle: this oracle receives a single CAM-weight expression as input, and returns a boolean which is true if the CAM-weight expression results in a saliency map that scores above a pre-defined threshold on a pre-defined metric, for a given set of images and classification model.

We will define the SYCAM framework assuming access to these oracles, but we should note that these oracles are performing tasks that are, in general, undecidable (equivalence checking) or at least computationally expensive (evaluating a given CAM weight expression across a large set of images). We will address the practical implementation of each of these oracles in Sect. 4.

The general workflow of SYCAM is depicted below. SYCAM is composed of two main procedures, the synthesis phase (which is guided by the equivalence oracle) and the evaluation phase (the correctness oracle). Candidate expressions produced by the synthesis procedure are generated from a space of expressions defined by an input grammar G, as described in Sect. 4. The expressions are then forwarded one by one to the evaluation process. An expression is evaluated using a correctness oracle, defined in terms of the given evaluation metric μ and a threshold function r, over a set of images I. If a candidate passes the evaluation process, it is returned as a solution to the overall synthesis process. If the evaluation fails, another expression is selected out of the current list of candidate expressions, and the same evaluation process is repeated for the new expression. If all candidate expressions have been evaluated with no success, the synthesizer is triggered again to generate a new set of candidates.

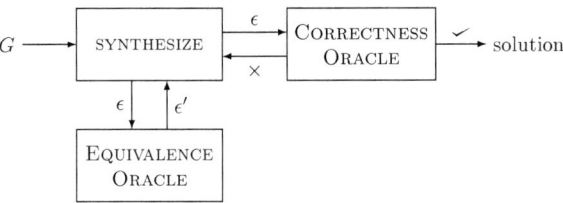

Synthesis Phase: The task of the synthesis phase is to enumerate expressions using the feedback given by the oracles. The algorithm we use is based on a classical program synthesis technique: the bottom-up search algorithm [1]. For the algorithm, we require an input grammar G, which defines an initial set of expressions (*terminals*) and production rules R that allow us to combine

Algorithm 1. Bottom-up Search

```
function SEARCH(G, λ, M, I, μ)           function EXPAND(E, G)
    exprs ← ∅                                 E' ← ∅
    exprs' ← G.Term                           for r ∈ G.R do
    while True do                                 if r is 1-ary then
        solution ← EVAL(exprs', λ, M, I, μ)           for e₁ ∈ E do
        if solution ≠ nil then                            E' ← E' ∪ r{e₁}
            return solution                       else if r is 2-ary then
        exprs ← exprs ∪ exprs'                        for e₁, e₂ ∈ PROD(E, E) do
        exprs' ← EXPAND(expr, G)                          E' ← E' ∪ r{e₁, e₂}
        exprs' ← ELIMEQUIV(exprs, exprs', I)      return E'
```

expressions to synthesize new ones (*synthesize* block). The synthesis phase calls the equivalence oracle, ELIMEQUIV, in order to reduce the exponential growth in expressions. This bottom-up search algorithm is shown in Algorithm 1.

Initially, we populate *exprs* with all expressions for *Term*. At each iteration of the Algorithm 1, the search process deploys the EXPAND function to iterate through the production rules of the grammar, and generates all possible new expressions that use the elements in *exprs* to replace the non-terminals in each production rule and adds them to *exprs*. We use $r\{e_1, \ldots, e_n\}$ to indicate the result of taking the rule $r \in R$ and replacing the first nonterminal symbol occurring in r with e_1, the second with e_2, and so on.

Oracles: The equivalence oracle ELIMEQUIV then reduces the set of expressions, by removing all semantically equivalent expressions. At each iteration, the correctness oracle EVAL checks the current list of programs to see if it contains a program that it deems correct (i.e., a program that performs above a given threshold on the evaluation metric). If so, the program is returned as a solution.

4 An Instantiation of SyCAM

Our approach is customizable to any grammar. In this section, we give an instantiation of our framework for a grammar defining gradient-based expressions, and expressions based on ScoreCAM and AblationCAM. We use a grammar with non-terminals $NT = \{Expr, Term, Grads\}$, and starting category $S = \{Expr\}$. The set of production rules R is defined as follows:

$Expr := Term \mid Expr + Expr \mid 2 \cdot Expr + Expr \mid Expr \cdot Expr \mid ReLU(Expr)$

$Term := Grads \mid top_5(Grads) \mid top_{10}(Grads) \mid top_{20}(Grads) \mid top_{50}(Grads)$
$\mid CICScores \mid AblScores$

$Grads := GP(\frac{\partial Y^c}{A_k})$ for any $c \in C$ and $k \in K$.

where $ReLU$ is the element-wise function $\max\{\cdot, 0\}$. Inspired by algorithms like GradCAM, we use as terminals the *gradients*, denoted by *Grads*, of the score for the predicted class c with $Y^c = \mathcal{M}(x)$ with respect to the feature map activations A_k of the last convolutional layer, i.e. $GP(\frac{\partial Y^c}{\partial A_k})$ where GP denotes the global average pooling operation, for each feature map k in the set of feature maps K and for each class c in the set of classes C. We also include as terminals the functions $top_n(Grads)$ that nullify all but the highest n elements of $Grads$ and are denoted by top_n.

Inspired by ScoreCAM, we include as terminals ($CICScores$) the *channel-wise Increase of Confidence (CIC)* [36]. For each feature map k, each image x, a baseline input image x_b, and a model $\mathcal{M}$, the CIC is defined as $CIC(A^k) = \mathcal{M}(x \circ H^k) - \mathcal{M}(x_b)$ where $H^k = s(Up(A^k))$, Up denotes the upsample operation that upsamples A^k into the input image size, and $s(\cdot)$ is a normalization function to the range $[0,1]$. We assume that $\exists x_b : \mathcal{M}(x_b) = 0$, and use $C(A^k) = \mathcal{M}(x \circ H^k)$.

AblScores represent the weights used in the definition of AblationCAM [6]. For each feature map k of a model $\mathcal{M}$, and each image x, these weights w are defined by $w_k^c = \frac{y^c - y_k^c}{y^c}$, where $y^c = \mathcal{M}(x)$ and y_k^c is the result of setting all the activation cell values of A_k to zero and classifying again the x.

Notice that the terminals of the grammar are vectors with number of elements equal to feature maps in the last convolutional layer of $\mathcal{M}$, and every expression generated by this grammar produces vectors with the same size as the terminals.

4.1 Equivalence Oracle

In general, determining the equivalence between two expressions is undecidable. We thus use an approximation, referred to as observational equivalence.

Definition 3 (Observational Equivalence). *Formally, two expression e_1 and e_2 are observational equivalent on a finite set of images I, according to an evaluation metric μ and a model M iff $\mu(L^c[e_1], M, I) = \mu(L^c[e_2], M, I)$.*

If two expressions are observationally equivalent, we can remove one of these expressions from the pool of expressions used to build subsequent programs *provided* the semantics of the program fragment do not depend on context. That is, given two expressions e_1 and e_2, and a set of images I, if e_1 and e_2 give the same result on the set of images, then so will $C[e_1]$ and $C[e_2]$ where $C[e_1]$ is a program that uses e_1 as a subexpression, and $C[e_2]$ is the same program but with e_2 in place of e_1.

CAM-weight expressions are arithmetic expressions so this property is true, *for the set of images I*. However, since evaluating the expression on all the images in our dataset is time-consuming and impractical, our observational equivalence oracle uses a smaller subset of the full dataset. Thus, if this set is not representative of the full dataset, the observational equivalence oracle may remove expressions that we subsequently may need. As a consequence of this approximation of equivalence, SyCAM may fail to find some possible solutions, but this trade-off is worth it to prune the exponential growth of the search space.

4.2 Correctness Oracle

Recall that we wish to synthesize an expression e such that the following is true; $\mu(L^c[e], M, I) > \lambda(M, I)$, for a given I and M. Unlike many domains where OGIS is used, it is not possible for us to reason about this expression symbolically using techniques like SMT solvers, since this would require us to reason about the weights of the model and the pixels of each image. We must therefore use testing, executing each generated CAM method on the images in the set I. Expressions are then checked one by one for their correctness. If an expression passes the correctness test, the overall synthesis process terminates, returning this expression as a solution. As we will see in the experiments, this process is modified to run for a fixed amount of time and then return the best expression synthesized instead.

4.3 Class-Based Decomposition

A limitation of the algorithm presented in the previous section is that the grammar we use does not contain any expressions that can perform case splits, e.g., an "if" expression, or any logical expressions that can define when to apply a specific CAM method to a particular image. This means that the function we synthesize is applied uniformly to all images, regardless of the properties of that image. In this section, our goal is to extend this grammar to permit case splits. One obvious way of doing this would be to introduce an "if-then-else" statement into the grammar G, as well as expressions for identifying features or characteristics of different images. This, however, results in a significantly expanded search space, and an intractable synthesis problem. In this section, thus, we break down the synthesis method into two parts: a *classification* model $\mathcal{M}$, and a set of CAM-weight expressions, synthesized using the enumeration approach described previously, that should be applied to each class. Thus, for a given set of classes, the end CAM-weight expression will be an expression in the grammar given by G extended with the following production rule:

$$Expr := (Y^{c_i} = max(Y^{c_1}, \ldots Y^{c_n}))\,?\,Expr : Expr$$

where Y^{c_i} is the confidence score for class c_i, and $\{c_1, \ldots c_n\}$ is the set of classes generated by the model $\mathcal{M}$. It would be possible to use any classifier in this step, but we take advantage of having a classifier that can choose the expression for each image: the model $\mathcal{M}$.

One advantage of this approach is that it prevents the rejection of good expressions that do not perform well only for small subsets of images. However, an important disadvantage is that the algorithm has to be executed once for each output class. If the number of output classes of a model is in the order of thousands, this method requires considerable computing power.

5 Experiments

In this section, we present three sets of experiments that show the efficacy of SYCAM:

– **E1 - Sanity check:** We show the ability of SyCAM to synthesize known dominant CAM expressions for a given metric, or better ones if the grammar allows for more expressive expressions. We apply SyCAM to one Pytorch model, VGG16 trained over the PASCAL VOC 2007 dataset [8].
– **E2 - Enumeration vs class-based decomposition:** We compare SyCAM to the classical approaches of GradCAM, GradCAM++, ScoreCAM, and AblationCAM. Here, we particularly compare the enumerative and class-based decomposition approaches and show how the latter improves over the former. SyCAM is applied to three PyTorch models: ResNet50, VGG16, and VGG19, trained over the Imagenette dataset [13].
– **E3 - Incorporating ground truth:** This experiment is an application of SyCAM to show that, in contrast to standard methods, SyCAM allows us to incorporate expert knowledge into the generation of saliency maps, resulting in better saliency maps. SyCAM is applied to a ResNet50 model trained over COVID-19 X-ray images from the COVID-QU-Ex dataset [34].

All experiments were run using an NVIDIA T4 with 16 GB RAM. The code used can be found in https://github.com/starlab-systems/SyCAM. The computations were enabled by resources provided by the National Academic Infrastructure for Supercomputing in Sweden (NAISS), partially funded by the Swedish Research Council through grant agreement no. 2022-06725.

5.1 Experimental Setup

As established in Sect. 3.1, the goal is to find an expression e such that $\mu(L^c[e], M, I) > \lambda(M, I)$, for a given image set I and a model M by following Algorithm 1. We adapt Algorithm 1, to one that instead of stopping the computation the moment we find an expression e that beats a threshold λ, to one that continues the search, always saving the so-far best expression found, and taking the value $\mu(L^c[e], M, I)$ for the best expression as the new threshold λ. We start with $\lambda = 0$. We let the experiments run for a fixed amount of time and return the best expression synthesized during that time.

Grammar: The grammar used for the experiments is defined in Sect. 4. Computing the weights generated by terminals *CICScores* and *AblScores* is computationally expensive. In the case of ResNet50, VGG16, and VGG19, they are required to compute 512 classifications per image. To reduce the computation overhead, for each dataset and evaluation metric, we precompute the weights produced by these terminals beforehand for each image in the dataset.

Synthesis Phase: The set of expressions generated grows exponentially. Because we have 7 terminals in the grammar, and we are enumerating solutions that can be produced with the rules defined, more than 1000 expressions were generated in only three applications of the EXPAND function (see Algorithm 1) even after discarding equivalent expressions using observational equivalence (Sect. 4.1). By the fourth application of the EXPAND function, we would generate more than

10^6 expressions. To prevent spending too much time just discarding equivalent expressions without evaluating them, instead of generating a whole new set of expressions with EXPAND before evaluating, we generate and yield expressions one by one. Each expression is evaluated just after being generated by the equivalence oracle and, if not discarded, by the correctness oracle.

Equivalence Oracle: The function ELIMEQUIV of Algorithm 1 employs a subset with 10 images, one of each class of the dataset, to ensure this subset is as representative as possible. We also tested subsets of size 20 and 30 of the Imagenette dataset, and we confirmed that the number of expressions discarded decreases (by 1.5% and 7.2%, respectively) with the number of images in the subset. However, the expressions synthesized were the same, and there is a trade-off with the computation time dedicated to generating expressions and discarding those equivalents, so we maintained the original size of 10 images.

Correctness Oracle: It would be time-consuming to test every generated CAM method on every image in the dataset I. For example, it takes around 18 min to compute the Deletion metric for ResNet50 and a single expression over a dataset of 4000 images. To overcome this computation overhead, we implement the correctness oracle as follows, aiming to discard expressions as early as possible.

The evaluation is done by applying an evaluation procedure on the candidate expression defined in terms of an evaluation metric μ and over increasingly large sets of images $I_1 \subset I_2 \subset \ldots \subset I$. If a candidate expression e is evaluated over the set I_i and results in a score larger than that computed by a threshold function λ over at least half of the images in I_i, and the average score is better, i.e. $\mu(L^c[e], M, I_i) > \lambda(M, I_i)$, it is then evaluated over the next largest set of images, I_{i+1}. Otherwise, the candidate is discarded. If a candidate expression e is evaluated on the set I and achieves a score higher than that computed by the threshold function over at least half of the images, and the average score is higher, then e is the best expression found, and λ is updated with the new threshold defined by e. With this multi-layered approach, we can quickly eliminate programs that already fail evaluation on smaller sets of data, thus speeding up the search for solutions. It is possible that a candidate may perform poorly on a subset I_i and then perform better than the threshold function on a subset I_{i+1}, and thus be discarded early. This risk is small since our subsets are relatively large and are uniformly sampled from the full set of images, so likely to be representative.

The oracle checks if the candidate expression e is better than the best solution found for at least half of the images because the goal is to find an expression that works well for as many images as possible, i.e., that generalizes well, and at the same time has a higher score.

Lastly, we set a timeout of 6 h for experiment E1 and 24 h for E2 and E3, i.e., the returned expression is the best expression found within these time bounds. We note that within this timeout, we were able to reach the fourth iteration of the algorithm, but despite the optimizations, we are not able to cover all the 10^6 expressions of that iteration. This results in a limitation on the size of the expressions that can be synthesized. However, we show later that SYCAM manages to synthesize better expressions than widely known CAM methods. Furthermore, once the SYCAM expression is synthesized, the computational cost of generating saliency maps is similar to that of other CAM expressions, so it is reasonable to spend time on generating the best possible expression. The cost depends on the terminals used. For example, the cost of generating saliency maps for an expression that computes the *CICScores* as part of the expression is similar to the cost of ScoreCAM.

5.2 Experiments E1: Sanity Check

"Show the ability of SYCAM to synthesize known CAM expressions if they are dominant for a given metric, or even better ones if the grammar allows for more expressive expressions"

In this experiment, we applied SYCAM to a VGG16 model trained over the training subset of the PASCAL VOC 2007 dataset, and using the Average Drop % metric: one of the settings described in the original GradCAM++ paper [4]. The dataset I contains 2510 images distributed in 20 classes. For the correctness oracle, we use three subsets of images, $I \supset I_2 \supset I_1$. The set I_2 is a subset of 1000 randomly chosen images, and I_1 contains 100 randomly chosen images.

We applied SYCAM using two grammars for a fixed time of 6 h each:

- G1: A grammar defined by:

$$Expr := Term \mid Expr + Expr \mid 2 \cdot Expr + Expr \mid Expr \cdot Expr \mid ReLU(Expr)$$
$$Term := Grads \mid top_5(Grads) \mid top_{10}(Grads) \mid top_{20}(Grads) \mid top_{50}(Grads)$$
$$Grads := GP(\frac{\partial Y^c}{\partial A_k}) \text{ for any } c \in C \text{ and } k \in K.$$

- G2: The grammar G1 adding the terminals *CICScores* and *AblScores*. This is, the grammar described in Sect. 4.

Using grammar G1, SYCAM can only synthesize expressions that employ gradients, so SYCAM can't synthesize ScoreCAM, AblationCAM, or other similar expressions. By incorporating the *CICScores* and *AblScores* terminals into G2, SYCAM can generate more diverse expressions. Figure 3 illustrates the results obtained by SYCAM using both G1 and G2. When G1 was used, SYCAM managed to synthesize GradCAM++, represented by $ReLU(Grads)$ [21], guided by the Average Drop % metric, and did not synthesize a better expression before the timeout. However, when G2 was used, SYCAM was able to synthesize even better expressions, with a reduction of the Average Drop % metric of 5%. This shows that SYCAM can synthesize the dominant known expression, or even better expressions if there is a possibility of doing so, and the grammar allows it.

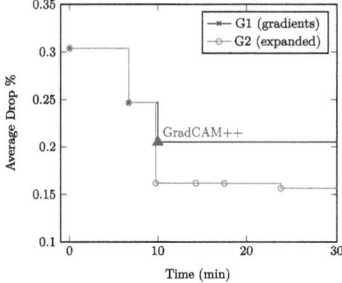

	Grammar G1		Grammar G2	
	SyCAM exp.	Avg.Drop	SyCAM exp.	Avg.Drop
	GradCAM	0.3038	GradCAM	0.3038
	top_{50}	0.2468	top_{50}	0.2468
	GradCAM++	**0.2049**	ScoreCAM	0.1617
			Grads + CICScores	0.1616
			2 · Grads + CICScores	0.1614
			CICScores + AblScores	**0.1563**

Fig. 3. SyCAM application to a VGG16 model trained over the PASCAL VOC 2007 dataset and the Average Drop % metric (lower is better). If only gradients-related terminals are included in the grammar, SyCAM synthesizes GradCAM++. Better CAM expressions are synthesized for an expanded grammar.

5.3 Experiments E2: Enumerate & Class-Based Decomposition

"Show the efficacy of SyCAM, and that the class-based decomposition approach can perform better than the enumerate approach."

We use this set of experiments to show the efficacy of SyCAM in comparison to other well-known CAM methods: GradCAM, GradCAM++, ScoreCAM, and AblationCAM. We also show how the class-based decomposition allows us to obtain better results than the simple enumerative approach.

In general, whilst the average value-wise improvement in the score obtained by SyCAM in each experiment may look only marginally better than the base methods, this marginally better score already results in more targeted saliency maps for a significant number of images. In Fig. 4, while the SyCAM score shows minor improvement, SyCAM gets a better saliency map that does not highlight the right dog as GradCAM and GradCAM++ do and highlights the body of the left dog more than ScoreCAM and AblationCAM. This implies that the model is making the classification of the image mostly based on the left dog, specifically the head and the upper body.

In the following, we give more details about our findings for both the enumerative and class-based decomposition approaches.

Results for the Enumerative Approach. We use a reduced version of *ImageNet*, namely the *Imagenette* dataset [13] that includes images for 10 classes out of the 1000 classes of *ImageNet*. Specifically, we use the validation dataset, with 3925 images distributed evenly into the 10 output classes. The evaluation metric in all the experiments is the Deletion or the Insertion metric. The experiments run for a fixed time of 24 h. Then, they return the best expression found. For the correctness oracle, we use three subsets of images, $I \supset I_2 \supset I_1$. The set I_2 is a subset of 1000 images: 100 from each class. I_1 contains 100 images: 10 per class.

As explained in Sect. 5.1, the evaluation of each candidate over the whole dataset can lead to scalability issues. Around 1020 candidate expressions are

Fig. 4. Saliency maps generated by GradCAM, GradCAM++, ScoreCAM, AblationCAM, and the SYCAM expression for ResNet50, the class "2. English springer", and the Deletion metric ($P = 30$, higher is better). The scores for each method are 0.2141, 0.2414, 0.2419, 0.2343, and 0.2441, respectively. SYCAM gets a better score and a saliency map that does not highlight the right dog as much as GradCAM and GradCAM++ do and highlights the body of the left dog more than ScoreCAM and AblationCAM.

generated in three iterations of Algorithm 1, and it takes ~0.3s to evaluate the Deletion or the Insertion metric ($P = 10$) over a single image. The computation time of the evaluation of a candidate expression over each subset for the Deletion and Insertion metrics ($P = 10$) is ~18 m, ~5 m, and ~27s, respectively.

In Table 1, we present our results for all three models. We show the expressions synthesized by SYCAM, and provide a comparison with GradCAM, GradCAM++, ScoreCAM, and AblationCAM, showing the average scores for each method when evaluated using the Deletion and the Insertion metrics. In general, SYCAM synthesizes expressions better than the base methods. In some cases, SYCAM synthesizes GradCAM (*Grads*), ScoreCAM (*CICScores*), or AblationCAM (*AblScores*). We point to the fact that AblationCAM performs better than the rest of the base methods for the Deletion metric, but not for the Insertion metric, for which it is almost always surpassed by ScoreCAM. This emphasize the necessity of using a framework like SYCAM to synthesize the best expression for each context. For $P = 15$ and $P = 30$, the computation time grows proportionally to P. There are some exceptions because of the correctness oracle. In the worst case, every expression is better than the threshold for I_1 and I_2 but worse than I and must be evaluated over the three sets. Note that both metrics depend on the ratio between P and the size of the feature maps in the last convolutional layer. Because the feature maps are bigger in VGG-16 and VGG-19 (14×14) than in ResNet50 (7×7), this dependency makes the values obtained by both metrics larger for ResNet50 than for VGG-19 and VGG-16 when comparing the same CAM methods. Larger values of P are correlated with better metric scores when comparing the same CAM methods.

Results for the Class-based Decomposition Approach. For each of the ten classes, the correctness oracle will use a subset I, which contains approximately 390 images each, and $I_1 \subset I$, which contains 100 images each. The time needed for evaluating an expression over each subset is ~2 m 10 s and ~30 s, respectively.

To make a fair comparison between the enumerate and the class-based decomposition approach, we established a timeout of 2.4 h per class. Although this limits the size of the expressions synthesized for each class, we can see in Table 2

Table 1. Enumerative approach for the models ResNet50, VGG-16, and VGG-19 over the Imagenette dataset using our variants of the Deletion and Insertion metrics (higher is better). G=GradCAM, G+=GradCAM++, S=ScoreCAM, A=AblationCAM.

Model	Deletion metric (P=10)						Insertion metric (P=10)					
	G	G+	S	A	SYCAM	SYCAM Exp.	G	G+	S	A	SYCAM	SYCAM Exp.
ResNet50	0.3559	0.3479	0.3523	0.3601	**0.3619**	$5 \cdot Grads$ $+ top_{50}$ $+ ReLU(Grads)$ $+ AblScores$	0.2287	0.2204	0.2243	0.2219	**0.2296**	top_{50} $* CICScores$
VGG-16	0.1722	0.1718	0.1727	0.1836	**0.1883**	$2 \cdot Grads$ $+ top_5$ $+ CICScores$ $+ AblScores$	0.0167	0.0185	**0.0320**	0.0204	**0.0320**	$CICScores$
VGG-19	0.1736	0.1713	0.1744	0.1824	**0.1825**	top_{10} $+ AblScores$	0.0260	0.0210	**0.0346**	0.0237	**0.0346**	$CICScores$

Model	Deletion metric (P=30)						Insertion metric (P=30)					
	G	G+	S	A	SYCAM	SYCAM Exp.	G	G+	S	A	SYCAM	SYCAM Exp.
ResNet50	0.6075	0.6010	0.6017	0.6049	**0.6079**	$Grads$ $+top_{10}$	**0.5435**	0.5289	0.5349	0.5402	**0.5435**	$Grads$
VGG-16	0.3344	0.3382	0.3385	0.3523	**0.3579**	$4 \cdot Grads$ $+ top_5$ $+ CICScores$ $+ AblScores$	0.0957	0.1075	**0.1422**	0.1160	**0.1422**	$CICScores$
VGG-19	0.3337	0.3364	0.3340	**0.3454**	**0.3454**	$AblScores$	0.0996	0.1105	0.1422	0.1146	**0.1424**	$2 \cdot Grads$ $+ ReLU(Grads)$ $+ CICScores$

that, for ResNet50, the average scores of SYCAM per class show improvement over the enumerative approach except for the Deletion metric for L = 10 case. For certain images, SYCAM resulted in scores higher than those of GradCAM, GradCAM++, ScoreCAM, and AblationCAM. In other cases, SYCAM was outperformed. This is because other methods may get much higher scores for a small subset of the data, but not for the rest. As explained in Sect. 5.1, our goal is to find expressions that are better than the best one found in at least half of the images and that have a higher average score.

5.4 Experiments E3: Incorporating Ground Truth

"Show how to incorporate expert knowledge into the generation of saliency maps."

We use the COVID-QU-Ex dataset [34], which consists of 5826 chest X-ray images with infection segmentation data distributed between 1456 normal (healthy) images, 2913 COVID-19 images, and 1457 non-COVID images with other diseases. Ground-truth COVID-19 segmentation masks are provided. We fine-tuned a ResNet50 model to correctly classify the test dataset with accuracy higher than 95%, and precision and recall higher than 92% for each class.

We consider a set I with only the 2913 COVID-19 X-ray images and the associated ground-truth COVID-19 segmentation masks. For the correctness oracle,

Table 2. Class-based decomposition approach for ResNet50 over the Imagenette dataset using the Deletion and Insertion metrics (higher is better). G=GradCAM, G+=GradCAM++, S=ScoreCAM, A=AblationCAM.

Model	Deletion metric (P=10)						Insertion metric (P=10)					
	G	G+	S	A	SYCAM	SYCAM Exp.	G	G+	S	A	SYCAM	SYCAM Exp.
1.Tench	0.4329	0.4286	0.4203	0.4258	**0.4358**	$Grads + top_5$	0.2307	0.2209	0.2188	0.2346	**0.2367**	$CICScores * AblScores$
2.English springer	0.4293	0.4193	0.4413	**0.4513**	0.4406	$Grads^2 + top_{50} * CICScores$	0.1741	0.1639	**0.1786**	0.1706	0.1741	$Grads$
3.Cassette player	0.2755	0.2719	0.2698	0.2577	**0.2766**	top_{50}	0.1584	0.1517	0.1514	0.1201	**0.1663**	top_{10}
4.Chain saw	0.4360	0.4301	**0.4439**	0.4432	0.4404	top_{10}	0.2524	0.2425	**0.2536**	0.2327	0.2524	$Grads$
5.Church	0.2634	0.2468	0.2505	**0.2799**	0.2640	$2 \cdot Grads + top_{20}$	0.0859	0.0803	0.0880	0.0862	**0.0891**	top_{20}
6.French horn	0.3891	0.3849	0.3831	**0.3972**	0.3891	$Grads$	0.2550	0.2441	0.2460	**0.2693**	0.2550	$Grads$
7.Garbage truck	0.3757	0.3643	0.3650	**0.3779**	0.3757	$Grads$	0.2411	0.2390	0.2412	0.2328	**0.2438**	$Grads + top_{20} + Grads^2$
8.Gas Pump	0.3405	0.3262	0.3369	**0.3470**	0.3405	$Grads$	0.0508	0.0472	**0.0570**	0.0464	0.0508	$Grads$
9.Golf ball	0.3309	0.3272	0.3206	0.3279	**0.3356**	top_{10}	0.4149	0.4047	0.3953	**0.4200**	0.4167	top_{50}
10.Parachute	0.2855	0.2805	**0.2918**	0.2897	0.2858	$2 \cdot Grads + top_{10}$	**0.4343**	0.4205	0.4231	0.4129	**0.4343**	$Grads$
Average	0.3559	0.3480	0.3523	**0.3598**	0.3584		0.2287	0.2215	0.2253	0.2226	**0.2308**	

Model	Deletion metric (P=30)						Insertion metric (P=30)					
	G	G+	S	A	SYCAM	SYCAM Exp.	G	G+	S	A	SYCAM	SYCAM Exp.
1.Tench	0.7215	0.7170	0.7120	0.7148	**0.7236**	$top_{50} * CICScores$	0.6415	0.6310	0.6297	0.6398	**0.6415**	$Grads$
2.English springer	0.6360	0.6290	0.6365	**0.6447**	0.6416	$top_{50} * CICScores$	0.4815	0.4672	0.4746	**0.4855**	0.4815	$Grads$
3.Cassette player	0.4374	0.4336	0.4323	0.4169	**0.4385**	top_{10}	0.3404	0.3256	0.3324	0.2932	**0.3427**	$Grads + top_5$
4.Chain saw	0.6711	0.6667	0.6694	0.6504	**0.6730**	top_{10}	0.5896	0.5698	0.5863	0.5678	**0.5896**	$Grads$
5.Church	0.4677	0.4548	0.4580	**0.4755**	0.4692	$2 \cdot Grads + top_{20}$	0.3488	0.3319	0.3442	**0.3632**	0.3501	$2 \cdot Grads + top_{20}$
6.French horn	0.6464	0.6412	0.6363	**0.6527**	0.6476	top_{50}	0.5968	0.5816	0.5867	**0.6126**	0.5968	$Grads$
7.Garbage truck	0.6676	0.6619	0.6622	**0.6681**	0.6676	$Grads$	0.6072	0.5972	0.6030	**0.6091**	0.6072	$Grads$
8.Gas Pump	0.6286	0.6223	0.6288	**0.6341**	0.6286	$Grads$	0.4049	0.3862	0.4008	0.4045	**0.4050**	$2 \cdot Grads + top_5$
9.Golf ball	0.5865	0.5791	0.5649	0.5875	**0.5895**	top_{10}	0.7158	0.7072	0.6987	**0.7224**	0.7158	$Grads$
10.Parachute	0.6041	0.5972	**0.6090**	0.5930	0.6041	$Grads$	0.7084	0.6924	0.6928	0.6982	**0.7084**	$Grads$
Average	0.6075	0.6010	0.6017	0.6049	**0.6091**		0.5435	0.5289	0.5349	0.5402	**0.5438**	

we use three subsets of images, $I \supset I_2 \supset I_1$. The set I_2 is a subset of 1000 images, while I_1 contains 100 images. We apply SYCAM using two metrics: the m_{GT} and the SCH metrics defined in Sect. 2.3. Because these metrics give importance to the ground truth COVID-19 masks, the SYCAM expressions incorporate expert knowledge into the saliency maps generated. Since we are only considering a binary classification, we employ the enumerative approach. For both metrics defined above, we let the experiments run for 24 h. In this experiment, evaluating m_{GT} or SCH takes around 0.05s per image.

The results are presented in Table 3. We can observe that, for both metrics, SYCAM synthesizes expressions whose basis is of the form exp^n, with exp a terminal and $n \in \mathbb{N}$: $CICScores^4$ for the m_{GT} metric, and $Grads^5$ for the SCH metric. This may indicate that dominant expressions have this form, which highly reduces the values lower than 1 and gives more importance to the high values.

Examples of saliency maps generated by SYCAM are included in Figs. 1, 5a and 5b. We can observe in the X-ray images of Fig. 1 that the saliency map generated by SYCAM is more concentrated on the ground-truth mask, while the rest of the CAM methods fail to do so. In fact, we can see that GradCAM++ and ScoreCAM give high importance to a region outside of the body in the bottom right. Something similar happens in Fig. 5a. In Fig. 5b, because the SYCAM expression is $2 \cdot Grads^5$, the heatmap obtained is a more compact version of the GradCAM heatmap. This reduces the importance of areas outside of the ground truth, achieving a higher SCH score.

Table 3. Enumerative approach for the fine-tuned model ResNet50 over the COVID-19 benchmark. The metrics used are the m_{GT} and the SCH metrics (higher is better).

Metric	GradCAM	GradCAM++	ScoreCAM	AblationCAM	SYCAM	SYCAM Exp.
m_{GT}	0.1861	0.1712	0.1512	0.1876	**0.1972**	$Grads * top_{20} * CIC^4$
SCH	0.1567	0.1491	0.1458	0.1524	**0.1610**	$2 \cdot Grads^5$

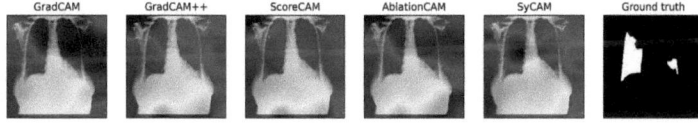

(a) Heatmaps generated for the m_{GT} metric (higher is better). The score for each method is 0.0 for every method except for SYCAM, for which it is 0.3389. The SYCAM heatmap is more concentrated on the ground truth mask.

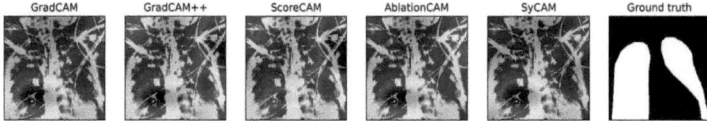

(b) Heatmaps generated for the SCH metric (higher is better). The scores for each method are 0.3474, 0.2874, 0.2650, 0.3377, and 0.3803, respectively. The SYCAM heatmap is a more compact version of GradCAM.

Fig. 5. Saliency maps generated by GradCAM, GradCAM++, ScoreCAM, AblationCAM, and the SYCAM expression synthesized for ResNet50.

6 Discussion and Future Work

We presented SYCAM, a metric-based synthesis framework for automatically generating CAM expressions. SYCAM offers advantages in tailoring CAM expressions to specific syntactic restrictions, datasets, and evaluation metrics. However, our approach still has limitations that we plan to address in future work. One key limitation is the high computation time required to generate expressions, which stems from the complexity of the synthesis algorithms. Improvements in synthesis methods will directly enhance our approach. However, we emphasize that generating a SYCAM expression is a one-time process, and the computation time for generating saliency maps remains reasonable. Additionally, the SYCAM framework relies on enumerating expressions and verifying their validity. Future work will explore ways to guide this search process more efficiently, thereby reducing computation time. Lastly, we also aim to extend our study to multi-objective settings [35], incorporating multiple evaluation metrics simultaneously and identifying Pareto-optimal expressions as solutions.

References

1. Albarghouthi, A., Gulwani, S., Kincaid, Z.: Recursive program synthesis. In: Sharygina, N., Veith, H. (eds.) CAV 2013. LNCS, vol. 8044, pp. 934–950. Springer, Heidelberg (2013). https://doi.org/10.1007/978-3-642-39799-8_67
2. Alur, R., et al.: Syntax-guided synthesis. In: Formal Methods in Computer-Aided Design, FMCAD 2013, Portland, OR, USA, 20–23 October 2013, pp. 1–8. IEEE (2013), https://ieeexplore.ieee.org/document/6679385/
3. Arras, L., Osman, A., Samek, W.: CLEVR-XAI: a benchmark dataset for the ground truth evaluation of neural network explanations. Inf. Fusion **81**, 14–40 (2022). https://doi.org/10.1016/J.INFFUS.2021.11.008
4. Chattopadhyay, A., Sarkar, A., Howlader, P., Balasubramanian, V.N.: Grad-CAM++: generalized gradient-based visual explanations for deep convolutional networks. In: 2018 IEEE Winter Conference on Applications of Computer Vision, WACV 2018, Lake Tahoe, NV, USA, 12–15 March 2018, pp. 839–847. IEEE Computer Society (2018). https://doi.org/10.1109/WACV.2018.00097
5. Deng, J., Dong, W., Socher, R., Li, L., Li, K., Fei-Fei, L.: Imagenet: a large-scale hierarchical image database. In: 2009 IEEE Computer Society Conference on Computer Vision and Pattern Recognition (CVPR 2009), 20–25 June 2009, Miami, Florida, USA, pp. 248–255. IEEE Computer Society (2009). https://doi.org/10.1109/CVPR.2009.5206848
6. Desai, S., Ramaswamy, H.G.: Ablation-CAM: visual explanations for deep convolutional network via gradient-free localization. In: IEEE Winter Conference on Applications of Computer Vision, WACV 2020, Snowmass Village, CO, USA, 1–5 March 2020, pp. 972–980. IEEE (2020). https://doi.org/10.1109/WACV45572.2020.9093360

7. Dhurandhar, A., Chen, P., Luss, R., Tu, C., Ting, P., Shanmugam, K., Das, P.: Explanations based on the missing: towards contrastive explanations with pertinent negatives. In: Bengio, S., Wallach, H.M., Larochelle, H., Grauman, K., Cesa-Bianchi, N., Garnett, R. (eds.) Advances in Neural Information Processing Systems 31: Annual Conference on Neural Information Processing Systems 2018, NeurIPS 2018, 3–8 December 2018, Montréal, Canada, pp. 590–601 (2018), https://proceedings.neurips.cc/paper/2018/hash/c5ff2543b53f4cc0ad3819a36752467b-Abstract.html
8. Everingham, M., Van Gool, L., Williams, C.K.I., Winn, J., Zisserman, A.: The PASCAL visual object classes challenge 2007 (VOC2007) Results. http://www.pascal-network.org/challenges/VOC/voc2007/workshop/index.html
9. Fletcher, L., van der Klis, R., Sedláček, M., Vasilev, S., Athanasiadis, C.: Reproducibility study of "LICO: Explainable models with language-image consistency" (2024), https://doi.org/10.48550/arXiv.2410.13989
10. Fu, R., Hu, Q., Dong, X., Guo, Y., Gao, Y., Li, B.: Axiom-based grad-CAM: towards accurate visualization and explanation of CNNs. In: 31st British Machine Vision Conference 2020, BMVC 2020, Virtual Event, UK, 7–10 September 2020. BMVA Press (2020), https://www.bmvc2020-conference.com/assets/papers/0631.pdf
11. Girshick, R., Donahue, J., Darrell, T., Malik, J.: Rich feature hierarchies for accurate object detection and semantic segmentation. In: 2014 IEEE Conference on Computer Vision and Pattern Recognition (CVPR), pp. 580–587. IEEE Computer Society, Los Alamitos, CA, USA, June 2014. https://doi.org/10.1109/CVPR.2014.81
12. Hooker, S., Erhan, D., Kindermans, P., Kim, B.: A benchmark for interpretability methods in deep neural networks. In: Wallach, H.M., Larochelle, H., Beygelzimer, A., d'Alché-Buc, F., Fox, E.B., Garnett, R. (eds.) Advances in Neural Information Processing Systems 32: Annual Conference on Neural Information Processing Systems 2019, NeurIPS 2019, 8–14 December 2019, Vancouver, BC, Canada, pp. 9734–9745 (2019), https://proceedings.neurips.cc/paper/2019/hash/fe4b8556000d0f0cae99daa5c5c5a410-Abstract.html
13. Howard, J.: Imagenette, https://github.com/fastai/imagenette/
14. Ibrahim, R., Shafiq, M.O.: Explainable convolutional neural networks: a taxonomy, review, and future directions. ACM Comput. Surv. **55**(10), 206:1–206:37 (2023). https://doi.org/10.1145/3563691
15. Jha, S., Seshia, S.A.: A theory of formal synthesis via inductive learning. Acta Informatica **54**(7), 693–726 (2017). https://doi.org/10.1007/S00236-017-0294-5
16. Kadir, M.A., Mosavi, A., Sonntag, D.: Evaluation metrics for XAI: a review, taxonomy, and practical applications. In: 2023 IEEE 27th International Conference on Intelligent Engineering Systems (INES), pp. 000111–000124 (2023). https://doi.org/10.1109/INES59282.2023.10297629
17. Karpathy, A., Toderici, G., Shetty, S., Leung, T., Sukthankar, R., Fei-Fei, L.: Large-scale video classification with convolutional neural networks. In: 2014 IEEE Conference on Computer Vision and Pattern Recognition, pp. 1725–1732 (2014). https://doi.org/10.1109/CVPR.2014.223
18. Khalil, H., et al.: Classification of diabetic retinopathy types based on convolution neural network (CNN). Menoufia J. Electron. Eng. Res. **28**(ICEEM2019-Special Issue), 126–153 (2019). https://doi.org/10.21608/mjeer.2019.76962
19. Lawrence, S., Giles, C., Tsoi, A.C., Back, A.: Face recognition: a convolutional neural-network approach. IEEE Trans. Neural Networks **8**(1), 98–113 (1997). https://doi.org/10.1109/72.554195

20. Leem, S., Seo, H.: Attention guided CAM: visual explanations of vision transformer guided by self-attention. In: Wooldridge, M.J., Dy, J.G., Natarajan, S. (eds.) Thirty-Eighth AAAI Conference on Artificial Intelligence, AAAI 2024, Thirty-Sixth Conference on Innovative Applications of Artificial Intelligence, IAAI 2024, Fourteenth Symposium on Educational Advances in Artificial Intelligence, EAAI 2014, 20–27 February 2024, Vancouver, Canada, pp. 2956–2964. AAAI Press (2024). https://doi.org/10.1609/AAAI.V38I4.28077
21. Lerma, M., Lucas, M.: Grad-CAM++ is equivalent to Grad-CAM with positive gradients (2022). https://doi.org/10.48550/ARXIV.2205.10838
22. Marcel, S., Rodriguez, Y.: Torchvision the machine-vision package of torch. In: Bimbo, A.D., Chang, S., Smeulders, A.W.M. (eds.) Proceedings of the 18th International Conference on Multimedia 2010, Firenze, Italy, 25–29 October 2010, pp. 1485–1488. ACM (2010). https://doi.org/10.1145/1873951.1874254
23. Miró-Nicolau, M., i Capó, A.J., Moyà-Alcover, G.: Assessing fidelity in xai post-hoc techniques: a comparative study with ground truth explanations datasets. Artif. Intell. **335**, 104179 (2024). https://doi.org/10.1016/j.artint.2024.104179
24. Morbidelli, P., Carrera, D., Rossi, B., Fragneto, P., Boracchi, G.: Augmented Grad-CAM: heat-maps super resolution through augmentation. In: 2020 IEEE International Conference on Acoustics, Speech and Signal Processing, ICASSP 2020, Barcelona, Spain, 4–8 May 2020, pp. 4067–4071. IEEE (2020). https://doi.org/10.1109/ICASSP40776.2020.9054416
25. Muhammad, M.B., Yeasin, M.: Eigen-CAM: visual explanations for deep convolutional neural networks. SN Comput. Sci. **2**(1), 47 (2021). https://doi.org/10.1007/S42979-021-00449-3
26. Omeiza, D., Speakman, S., Cintas, C., Weldemariam, K.: Smooth Grad-CAM++: an enhanced inference level visualization technique for deep convolutional neural network models (2019), http://arxiv.org/abs/1908.01224
27. Petsiuk, V., Das, A., Saenko, K.: RISE: randomized input sampling for explanation of black-box models. In: British Machine Vision Conference 2018, BMVC 2018, Newcastle, UK, 3–6 September 2018, p. 151. BMVA Press (2018), http://bmvc2018.org/contents/papers/1064.pdf
28. Rafferty, A., Ramaesh, R., Rajan, A.: Transparent and clinically interpretable AI for lung cancer detection in chest X-rays (2024), https://arxiv.org/abs/2403.19444
29. Rieger, L., Hansen, L.K.: IROF: a low resource evaluation metric for explanation methods (2020), https://arxiv.org/abs/2003.08747
30. Rong, Y., Leemann, T., Borisov, V., Kasneci, G., Kasneci, E.: A consistent and efficient evaluation strategy for attribution methods. In: Chaudhuri, K., Jegelka, S., Song, L., Szepesvári, C., Niu, G., Sabato, S. (eds.) International Conference on Machine Learning, ICML 2022, 17-23 July 2022, Baltimore, Maryland, USA. Proceedings of Machine Learning Research, vol. 162, pp. 18770–18795. PMLR (2022), https://proceedings.mlr.press/v162/rong22a.html
31. Samek, W., Binder, A., Montavon, G., Lapuschkin, S., Müller, K.: Evaluating the visualization of what a deep neural network has learned. IEEE Trans. Neural Networks Learn. Syst. **28**(11), 2660–2673 (2017). https://doi.org/10.1109/TNNLS.2016.2599820
32. Selvaraju, R.R., Cogswell, M., Das, A., Vedantam, R., Parikh, D., Batra, D.: Grad-cam: visual explanations from deep networks via gradient-based localization. In: 2017 IEEE International Conference on Computer Vision (ICCV), pp. 618–626 (2017). https://doi.org/10.1109/ICCV.2017.74

33. Szczepankiewicz, K., et al.: Ground truth based comparison of saliency maps algorithms. Sci. Rep. **13**(1), 16887 (2023). https://doi.org/10.1038/s41598-023-42946-w
34. Tahir, A.M., et al.: Covid-qu-ex. Kaggle (2021). https://doi.org/10.34740/3122958
35. Torfah, H., Shah, S., Chakraborty, S., Akshay, S., Seshia, S.A.: Synthesizing pareto-optimal interpretations for black-box models. In: Formal Methods in Computer Aided Design, FMCAD 2021, New Haven, CT, USA, 19–22 October 2021, IEEE (2021), https://doi.org/10.34727/2021/isbn.978-3-85448-046-4_24
36. Wang, H., et al.: Score-CAM: score-weighted visual explanations for convolutional neural networks. In: 2020 Conference on Computer Vision and Pattern Recognition, CVPR Workshops 2020, Seattle, WA, USA, 14–19 June 2020, pp. 111–119. Computer Vision Foundation/IEEE (2020). https://doi.org/10.1109/CVPRW50498.2020.00020
37. Zhou, B., Khosla, A., Lapedriza, À., Oliva, A., Torralba, A.: Learning deep features for discriminative localization. In: 2016 IEEE Conference on Computer Vision and Pattern Recognition, CVPR 2016, Las Vegas, NV, USA, 27–30 June 2016, pp. 2921–2929. IEEE Computer Society (2016). https://doi.org/10.1109/CVPR.2016.319

Open Access This chapter is licensed under the terms of the Creative Commons Attribution 4.0 International License (http://creativecommons.org/licenses/by/4.0/), which permits use, sharing, adaptation, distribution and reproduction in any medium or format, as long as you give appropriate credit to the original author(s) and the source, provide a link to the Creative Commons license and indicate if changes were made.

The images or other third party material in this chapter are included in the chapter's Creative Commons license, unless indicated otherwise in a credit line to the material. If material is not included in the chapter's Creative Commons license and your intended use is not permitted by statutory regulation or exceeds the permitted use, you will need to obtain permission directly from the copyright holder.

Which Direction to Choose? An Analysis on the Representation Power of Self-Supervised ViTs in Downstream Tasks

Yannis Kaltampanidis[✉], Alexandros Doumanoglou, and Dimitrios Zarpalas

Information Technologies Institute, Centre for Research and Technology Hellas,
1st Km Charilaou - Thermi Road, Thessaloniki, Greece
{ykalt,aldoum,zarpalas}@iti.gr
https://www.iti.gr

Abstract. Self-Supervised Learning (SSL) for Vision Transformers (ViTs) has recently demonstrated considerable potential as a pre-training strategy for a variety of computer vision tasks, including image classification and segmentation, both in standard and few-shot downstream contexts. Two pre-training objectives dominate the landscape of SSL techniques: Contrastive Learning and Masked Image Modeling. Features (or tokens) extracted from the final transformer attention block –specifically, the keys, queries, and values– as well as features obtained after the final block's feed-forward layer, have become a common foundation for addressing downstream tasks. However, in many existing approaches, these pre-trained ViT features are further processed through additional transformation layers, often involving lightweight heads or combined with distillation, to achieve superior task performance. Although such methods can improve task outcomes, to the best of our knowledge, a comprehensive analysis of the intrinsic representation capabilities of unaltered ViT features has yet to be conducted. This study aims to bridge this gap by systematically evaluating the use of these unmodified features across image classification and segmentation tasks, in both standard and few-shot contexts. The classification and segmentation rules that we use are either hyperplane based (as in logistic regression) or cosine-similarity based, both of which rely on the presence of interpretable directions in the ViT's latent space. Based on the previous rules and without the use of additional feature transformations, we conduct an analysis across token types, tasks, and pre-trained ViT models. This study provides insights into the optimal choice for token type and decision rule based on the task, context, and the pre-training objective, while reporting detailed findings on two widely-used datasets.

Keywords: ViT · SSL · DiNO · MAE · Directions · Hyperplane · Cosine Similarity

1 Introduction

Vision transformers [14,18,21,23,37], have shown exceptional performance in addressing complex computer vision and multi-modal tasks [8,32,39,40]. However, their effectiveness is highly dependent on the size of the training dataset, requiring an extensive amount of data to generalize effectively and avoid overfitting. Training these models from scratch is resource-intensive, both in terms of computational power and processing time. Given that related tasks, such as classification and segmentation, often share foundational knowledge, training separate models for each task from scratch is inefficient. Therefore, it has been proposed to train a large model once, using substantial data and resources to capture general knowledge, and then specialize or distill this model for specific downstream tasks by leveraging the knowledge acquired during the initial training phase.

Self-supervision, based on Masked Image Modeling (MIM) [2,7,19] or Contrastive Learning (CL) [6,7,11], has been proposed as a way for ViTs to capture this general knowledge from large datasets without the need for explicit labels. However, to achieve top performance, in most approaches [17,20,42,43] the pretrained ViT features undergo further transformations before the final prediction, in order to align the feature representations with the solution of the downstream task. Moreover, different methods utilize various feature types –such as query-key-value pairs from the last attention block, or the output tokens of the final feed forward layer– and employ diverse decision rules, being either hyperplane-based or direction similarity-based. Even though these approaches have demonstrated their effectiveness in solving downstream tasks, yet to our knowledge, a comprehensive evaluation of the intrinsic representation capabilities of unaltered self-supervised ViT features is missing from the literature.

In this work, we present a comprehensive analysis of the representational power of unaltered features from two self-supervised ViTs, pre-trained on a large dataset [35] using the previously mentioned self-supervision objectives [6,19]. To the best of our knowledge, this is the first study to examine all of the following aspects simultaneously: a) two ViTs pre-trained with different **self-supervised objectives** b) the five possible **token types** from the last transformer layer – keys, queries, values, and features before and after the final feed-forward block– c) two downstream **tasks**: image classification and segmentation, across both standard and 1-way-k-shot **contexts** and d) two commonly used prediction methods (or, as otherwise mentioned, **decision rules**), based on either hyperplane separation (linear probing) or cosine similarity.

We find that the hyperplane decision rule is more effective in semantic separability across most experiments, indicating that the cosine similarity between the tokens of these pretrained models is a suboptimal semantic proximity metric. Furthermore, our experiments indicate that the optimal token type depends heavily on the pre-training objective, task, context and decision rule –with some previously overlooked tokens proving to be the most effective. Beyond practical guidelines, our work challenges existing intuitions about ViT token interpretations and underscores the need for a deeper understanding of the role of each computational block within ViT layers.

2 Related Work

Self-Supervised Pre-Training. Self-supervised pre-training [44] stands out as the leading method towards developing vision, vision-language, and various multi-modal foundation models [5,39,48]. The core strategies in this field involve CL, MIM, or an integration of both. On the one hand, CL methods [7,10,11, 41] utilize image augmentation techniques to generate views with similar or dissimilar semantic content, which, in turn, are considered for feature alignment. On the other hand, representation learning in MIM methods [2,30,40] is driven by masking patches and then reconstructing pixels or features.

Within ViTs, MIM approaches, largely represented by Masked Autoencoders (MAEs) [19,45], typically **require** supervised **fine-tuning** to achieve competitive performance on downstream tasks [2,19,27,45,50,53]. These models tend to exhibit narrow self-attention receptive fields [49] and capture texture-based features, making them best suited for dense prediction tasks such as object detection [29]. They also tend to exhibit great scaling with an increasing number of parameters which can be attributed to the high attention-map variance between transformer heads, meaning that a larger portion of the network can being utilized during fine-tuning [29].

ViTs trained with a CL framework, such as DiNO [6], generate semantic-level feature representations [1], allowing them to serve as universal feature extractors **without further fine-tuning** [38]. Similar to other contrastive learning methods, the self-attention maps of a ViT pre-trained with a DiNO objective, have a broad receptive field, effectively capturing global patterns, but CL also faces the challenge of *collapse into homogeneity* [29], leading to similar self-attention maps for all heads. This limitation has motivated the development of hybrid SSL techniques that combine MIM and CL learning objectives to address their respective limitations [24,28,29,31].

Transfer-Learning Self-Supervised ViTs on Downstream Tasks. In dense prediction tasks, the *patch* tokens of the final encoder layer are commonly used as regional embeddings [19,39,47], while the corresponding *class* token ([CLS]) remains the standard representation for image classification [6,14,50]. The ability of DiNO to induce discriminative saliency maps in the self-attention mechanism of ViTs [6] has inspired the extraction of features directly from the self-attention blocks. Beyond the vanilla approach that uses the class token for image classification tasks, various techniques have been explored that leverage the *key* tokens in the self-attention block of a frozen DiNO backbone (a ViT pre-trained with the DiNO objective), to tackle unsupervised segmentation and localization tasks [36,42,43], often employing a cosine similarity-based signal. Alternative methods that utilize a similar backbone seek to distill its knowledge in both standard [17] and few-shot [20] contexts through lightweight heads, using the backbone as a means to detect semantic similarities within the data.

Unlike CL which is able to build strong frozen backbones, MIM pre-training is best capitalized with task-specific fine-tuning. In [50], a MAE is pre-trained on a face dataset and subsequently fine-tuned on a dataset with facial expressions for facial affective analysis. In the medical domain, where annotated data are more scarce, self-pre-training [53] has been proposed as the paradigm of pre-training a MAE directly on the data of the downstream task. Subsequently, the learned encoder can be combined with a trainable linear head or a convolutional decoder to demonstrate superior performance compared to supervised baselines or baselines pre-trained on out-of-domain data. Beyond masking pixels, the MIM objective can be utilized to train lightweight student models that learn to reconstruct masked features from a larger state-of-the-art teacher, providing efficient solutions to solve the downstream segmentation task [46].

Relation to the Present Work. In contrast to other studies that shed light on self-supervised ViTs from varying perspectives [11,26,29,33,49], our research adopts a latent space probing approach, regularly explored in mechanistic interpretability [13,15,16,34,51]. To our knowledge, this study is the first to rigorously evaluate the effectiveness of tokens derived from a frozen MAE to solve downstream tasks. This is even without taking into account the extensive breadth of this study on variation in token types, decision rules, and downstream tasks and contexts. Instead, previous work tends to prefer DiNO features for segmentation tasks with works considering frozen MAE features being almost non-existent, possibly due to the known fact that MIM works better when fine-tuned. Yet, a quantitative evaluation of the effectiveness of MAE's features compared to DINO's is currently missing, and our work addresses this gap with a detailed analysis. Our findings suggest that for semantic segmentation, while the downstream performance of MAE's features is inferior to DINO's, in some aspects the gap between them is not as large as one might initially believe.

Regarding DiNO, methods such as [1,17,20,36,42,43] address the unsupervised segmentation task using token feature transformations derived from a frozen backbone. In our work, we differentiate and take a step back to meticulously assess the effectiveness of DiNO's **vanilla** tokens (without any transformations or extra processing) on downstream tasks using annotations, revealing to some extent the best starting point of those previous approaches. Furthermore, many previous approaches [17,20,36,42,43] have applied the cosine similarity rule to the tokens of a frozen DINO backbone, utilizing it as an implicit supervisory signal for semantic similarities. However to our knowledge, a rigorous assessment of its potential is missing from the literature and our work aims to address this, by being the first to assess the effectiveness of DiNO's features with the cosine rule on semantic tasks with ground-truth labels. Our work is also unique in providing a thorough study over the representation power of different token types, being either the attention layer's queries, keys, values, or tokens from either side of the final feed forward transformer block, expanding on the shallow analysis of [6]. In principle, our findings are aligned with previous work that prefers to use the attention layer's key tokens for semantic segmentation [1,36,42,43] but also highlights a detailed comparison with the alternative tokens. Finally, image classification based on the two SSL approaches is also less explored in the literature [6,20], and our work provides a detailed analysis, in terms similar to the segmentation task.

3 Approach

As briefly stated in the preface, our work aspires to address the following questions that innately arise when employing pre-trained ViTs in downstream tasks:

- Which self-supervised **pre-training objective** (MIM, CL, implemented by MAE and DiNO respectively) produces frozen backbones, which are more aligned to each **downstream task** (classification, segmentation)?
- Which ViT **token types** (queries q, keys k, values v from the final ViT's self-attention block or tokens x_1, x_2 from either side of the transformer feed forward block) provide semantically meaningful representations?
- Which **decision rule** (hyperplane based, cosine similarity based) should be utilized to separate the feature space into semantic regions?

Additionally, we also consider two downstream contexts: standard (where a plethora of labeled examples are available for learning a decision rule) and few-shot (where only a limited number of samples are available for the same purpose). In the following subsections, we aim to clarify these research questions by conducting experiments with combinatorial variability across pre-trained models, tasks, contexts, decision rules, and token types.

3.1 Self-supervised Pre-Training Objectives

This study concentrates on two well-known SSL ViT architectures: MAE [19] and DiNO [6]. MAE is part of the group of pre-training techniques focused on masked image modeling, whereas DiNO aligns with self-distillation and contrastive learning approaches. For the sake of computational efficiency, we opted for the smallest pre-trained ViT models accessible to the public (DiNO: ViT-S/8 21M parameters, MAE: ViT-B/16 86M parameters).

3.2 Downstream Tasks

We investigate the semantic representation power of ViT tokens in two exemplary downstream tasks: image classification and semantic segmentation. In the context of image classification, we develop a subset of ImageNet [35] resembling ImageNet-Tiny [22], constructed by randomly selecting 550 samples for each of ImageNet-Tiny's 200 classes. For image segmentation, we utilize the Broden dataset [3], which consolidates multiple datasets that are densely annotated [4,9,12,25,52]. Broden encompasses 1197 concepts distributed across approximately $63K$ images within 5 distinct concept categories (object, part, material, texture, color). In this research, we have excluded the color category to focus on the remaining categories which are deemed to hold greater semantic significance. Figure 1 demonstrates the extensive annotations present in Broden, which incorporate low-level concept categories, such as material and texture, alongside high-level concepts, such as object and scene.

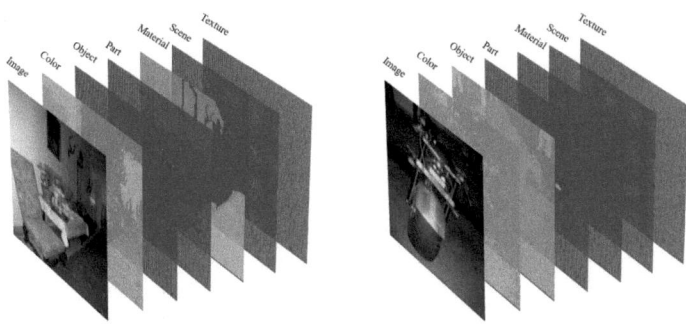

Fig. 1. Broden samples. Each image in the dataset is associated with multiple segmentation maps, covering six primary categories (color, object, part, material, scene, texture). For instance, the image in the left has a *color* and a *material* category-mapping whereas the image on the right a *color* and an *object* segmentation map.

We address **both** tasks through a unified binary classification framework, taking inspiration from [51]. Using independent binary classifiers offers a straightforward yet effective learning scheme suited for Broden's multilabel annotation structure. For image classification, we use the [CLS] token as a global feature representation of the entire image, whereas for semantic segmentation, we leverage the corresponding patch tokens to represent individual regions. Consequently, each object –whether the entire image for classification or an image-region for segmentation– is represented by a single feature vector, which serves as input to a set of binary classifiers. In other words, beyond the typical image classification task, the segmentation task is tackled by treating it as a patch classification problem.

3.3 Token Types

In our analysis we account for various token types derived from the final transformer layer to address the downstream tasks. We consider the query q, key k, and value v tokens of the self-attention block (Fig. 2 top), the output of the self-attention block, denoted as x_1 and the output tokens of the feed forward block (MLP), referred to as x_2 (Fig. 2 bottom).

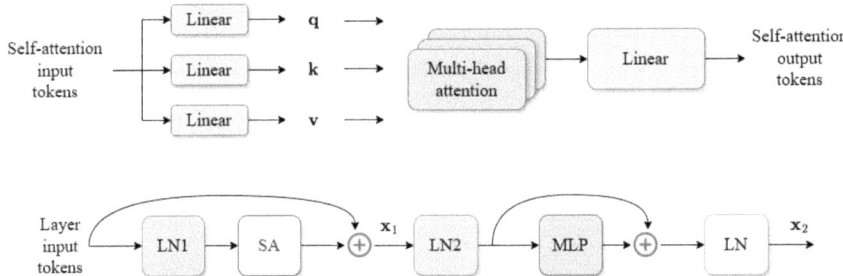

Fig. 2. (Top) Multi-head attention schematic diagram. $q, k, v \in \mathbb{R}^D$ depict the *queries, keys, values* tokens respectively, with D representing the ViT's embedding dimension. (Bottom) Schematic diagram of the transformer's final layer, where LN denotes layer normalization and SA represents the multi-head self-attention mechanism. Note that the final normalization layer (LN) is applied exclusively at the last transformer layer. We denote $x_1 \in \mathbb{R}^D$ the transformer tokens prior to the MLP and the second layer normalization layer, while $x_2 \in \mathbb{R}^D$ the output-tokens after the MLP (layer output).

3.4 Classifier Decision Rules

We examine the semantic separability of ViT tokens using two different decision rules: hyperplane-based and cosine similarity-based. As illustrated in Fig. 3, each classification rule is associated with a distinct decision boundary, dissecting the feature space into two disjoint subspaces.

Specifically, the hyperplane rule is comprised of a normal vector w and a bias term b, defining the orientation and position of the hyperplane respectively. A feature vector z is classified positively if $w^T z - b \geq 0$. In contrast, the cosine decision rule defines a convex cone via a conical axis vector α and an angular threshold θ, such that z is positively classified if $\arccos(\frac{z}{\|z\|_2} \cdot \frac{\alpha}{\|\alpha\|_2}) \leq \theta$, with $\cdot$ denoting the dot product.

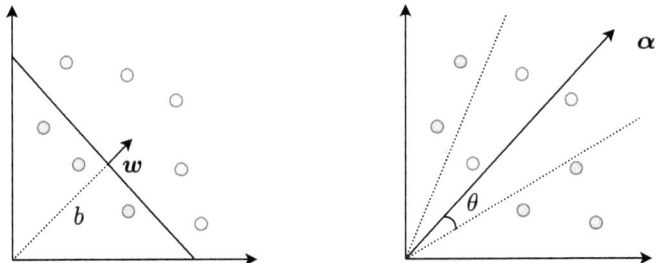

Fig. 3. Classifier decision rules. (Left) Hyperplane classifier (w, b). (Right) Cosine similarity classifier (α, θ). Each classifier dissects the feature space into two disjoints subspaces. Positively classified samples are depicted in blue, while negatively classified samples are illustrated in red. (Color figure online)

Concept Templates: Both decision rules are associated with a class-specific (in image classification) or concept-specific (in semantic segmentation) *directional* vector, a *threshold* and a *projection function*, which altogether may be utilized to classify a feature vector for the downstream task. We use the term *concept template* to encompass these attributes and also refrain from making explicit distinction regarding the label type of each downstream task (*image class* vs *patch concept*) as we treat both tasks within a common framework of similar principles. In the rest of the paper we will mostly refer to the downstream task's labels as *concept labels*, when in fact for image classification these labels correspond to image classes.

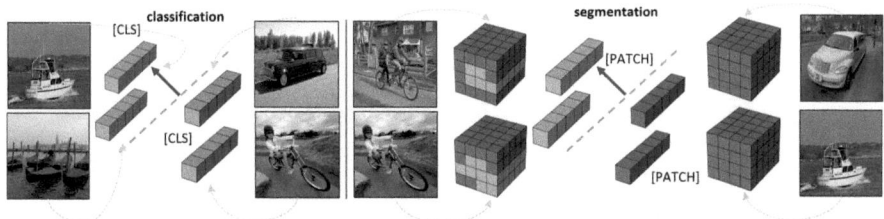

Fig. 4. Hyperplane decision rule: The class token represents the global image content, while individual image regions are represented by their corresponding patch tokens. A hyperplane is learned for each image class or semantic concept to distinguish positive samples from negative ones.

Formally, given the dimensionality of the embedding space D, a feature vector $z \in \mathbb{R}^D$ and a concept $c \in \mathbb{N}$, the concept template is a triplet $\tau_c := (d, t, f)$, where $d \in \mathbb{R}^D$ is the directional vector, $t \in \mathbb{R}$ is the threshold and $f(z; d) : \mathbb{R}^D \to \mathbb{R}$ is the projection function.

The concept template τ_c detects the existence of concept c in the feature vector z (positive classification) if:

$$f(z; d) \geq t \tag{1}$$

In the case of a hyperplane decision rule: $d := w, t := b$ and $f(z; w) := w^T z$, while for a cosine decision rule: $d := \alpha$, $t := \cos(\theta)$ and $f(z; \alpha) := \frac{1}{\|\alpha\|_2 \|z\|_2} \alpha^T z$. Based on the underlying decision rule, we distinguish two cases of concept templates: **hyperplane-templates** and **cosine-templates**.

3.5 Analysis Framework

This section provides details on how we learn the concept templates. In this and the rest of the sections, we often use the terms *concept template* and *classifier* interchangeably, preferring the former to emphasize its geometric interpretation and the latter to focus on its functional application.

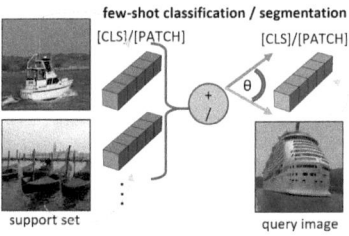

Fig. 5. Cosine similarity decision rule: In the few-shot context, the concept template's direction is derived by averaging intra-class token representations extracted from the support set. Specifically, a token originating from the query image set is classified positively if the cosine similarity between the token and the template's direction exceeds a threshold θ.

Hyperplane Templates: To compute hyperplane templates, for each concept, we learn a hyperplane classifier $(\boldsymbol{w}, b)$ with the process illustrated in Fig. 4. Given a training feature dataset $D_f : \{(\boldsymbol{z}_i, c_i), i = 1, \ldots, N\}$, where $\boldsymbol{z}_i \in \mathbb{R}^D$ represents the feature vector of an object (image/image-region) and $c_i \in \mathbb{N}$ represents its ground-truth label, we construct a positive sample pool for each concept c, denoted as $D_c^+ = \{\boldsymbol{z}_i \mid (\boldsymbol{z}_i, c_i) \in D_f,\ c_i = c\}$, and a corresponding negative sample pool, $D_c^- = \{\boldsymbol{z}_i \mid (\boldsymbol{z}_i, c_i) \in D_f,\ c_i \neq c\}$, where $|D_c^-| \gg |D_c^+|$. In semantic segmentation, when forming the negative sample pool for a concept c_i, we only consider concepts within the same primary category as c_i. To manage the significant class imbalance between the two sample pools, we initially limit the size ratio of $D_c^- : D_c^+$ to be no more than 20 : 1 by random subsampling. During template learning, we conduct five rounds of hard negative mining, following [51]. In each of these rounds, the hyperplane template is fitted to the mined dataset over 3 epochs, ensuring a positive-to-negative sample ratio of 1 : 2. The evaluation of **each** learned template is performed on a reserved test-set (approximately $10K$ image samples for ImageNet and $18K$ image samples for Broden from its validation split) via a set of **balanced** binary classification metrics.

Cosine Templates: Since the cosine decision rule is frequently utilized in unsupervised settings [17,20,36,42,43] including few-shot contexts, we **explicitly** consider learning cosine-templates in a few-shot regime by constructing support-query image sets for template learning and evaluation. The directional vector $\boldsymbol{\alpha}$ and similarity threshold $t \doteq \cos(\theta)$ of cosine templates, are computed in a non-parametric 1-way-k-shot setting. For a concept $c \in \mathbb{N}$, we construct a *support image set* $S_{c,k}$ by randomly sampling k training images that contain c. $S_{c,k}$ is further processed to construct the respective positive and negative *support feature pools* $D_{c,k}^+, D_{c,k}^-$; Notice that for image classification $D_{c,k}^- = \emptyset$, as every image in the support set is mapped to a single feature vector ([CLS] token).

The cosine template's directional vector $\boldsymbol{\alpha}$ is then computed by averaging the positive support features:

$$\boldsymbol{\alpha} = \frac{1}{|D_{c,k}^+|} \sum_{z \in D_{c,k}^+} z \qquad (2)$$

while the angular threshold θ is computed by maximizing the F1-score of the classifier τ_c on the *support feature set*:

$$\theta = \underset{\hat{\theta}}{\mathrm{argmax}}(F1(\hat{\theta}, D_{c,k}; \boldsymbol{\alpha}, f)) \qquad (3)$$

where $F1$ is the F1 score of a classifier $\tau_c = (\boldsymbol{\alpha}, t, f)$ computed on the support feature set $D_{c,k} = D_{c,k}^+ \cup D_{c,k}^-$, given the directional vector $\boldsymbol{\alpha}$ and the cosine-similarity projection function as f. Due to the fact that we use an empty $D_{c,k}^-$ for image classification, in Eq. (3) we consider the smallest possible angle θ that maximizes F1 score. The overall process is illustrated in Fig. 5. Furthermore, we vary $k \in \{1, 5, 10, 50, 100, 500\}$, leveraging different proportions of the available data. Finally, the templates are evaluated on a balanced randomly sampled query test set of 50 positive and 50 negative images using the same set of balanced binary classification metrics as in the hyperplane templates. Due to the stochastic nature of this 1-way-k-shot setting, we average and present the results from $N = 10$ independent trials reporting mean scores and their standard deviation.

4 Experimental Results

The subsequent subsections detail the outcomes of our comprehensive experimental evaluation, structured by downstream task and decision rule. In our analysis, the term *token performance* is used to denote the efficacy of concept templates that incorporate a particular token. It is important to highlight that for image classification tasks, the mentioned tokens refer to the [CLS] tokens, while for image segmentation, they pertain to patch tokens. Lastly, we underline that all the binary performance metrics presented in this work are **balanced**.

4.1 Task: Classification. Rule: Hyperplane

TLDR: We observe a substantial disparity in the classification performance of the hyperplane template between the pre-trained MAE and DiNO models. While MAE tokens resemble the performance of random classifiers, DiNO demonstrates exceptional classification capacity. Specifically, DiNO's x_2 token is particularly well-suited for classification tasks via linear probing, while MAE should not be considered in this context.

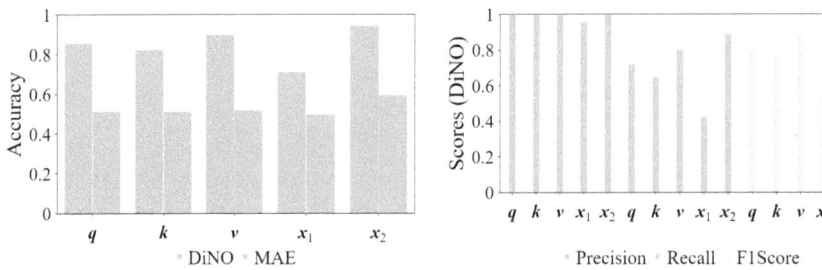

Fig. 6. Hyperplane-template classification: (Left) Accuracy between DiNO and MAE tokens. (Right) Precision, recall and F1 metrics for DiNO tokens.

Details: Figure 6 (Left) compares MAE and DiNO tokens in terms of accuracy. Most of MAE tokens approximately score an accuracy of 0.5, which is equivalent to a random classifier. This may be attributed to the fact that the [CLS] token is not participating in the MAE's loss function. In contrast, DiNO attains its maximum accuracy with x_2 (0.946). A detailed analysis of DiNO's token performance is presented in Fig. 6 (Right). We observe near-perfect precision for q, k, v, and x_2 (> 0.99), while x_1 achieves a precision of 0.96. This enables the construction of a hyperplane with minimal false positives (FP) across all tokens. Furthermore, x_2 exhibits the highest recall (0.89), followed by v (0.80), q (0.72) and k (0.65). These results indicate that x_2 provides the optimal linear separability of semantic concepts.

Notably, x_1 demonstrates the lowest performance across all evaluated metrics. To better understand this phenomenon, we also assess the performance of x_1 after layer normalization, which we denote as x_n. Table 1 presents the impact of the normalization layer on DiNO's x_1 hyperplane classification metrics. Layer normalization positively affects the semantic linear separability of the feature space. However, a more detailed analysis of the effects of layer normalization is beyond the scope of this work.

Table 1. Layer normalization effects on DiNO's x_1 performance metrics.

DiNO	Accuracy	Precision	Recall	F1
x_1	0.714	0.959	0.427	0.550
x_n	0.940	**0.997**	0.884	0.935
x_2	**0.946**	**0.997**	**0.894**	**0.941**

4.2 Task: Classification. Rule: Cosine

TLDR: Similar to hyperplane-based classification, DINO outperforms MAE under the cosine similarity decision rule. Notably, DINO's x_1 token achieves the highest accuracy and F1 scores. Furthermore, MAE shows substantial improvement with cosine templates compared to the hyperplane decision rule, with its k token yielding the highest accuracy and F1 score in this context. Finally, increasing the support set size beyond 50 samples results in diminishing gains in average accuracy and F1 scores for both models.

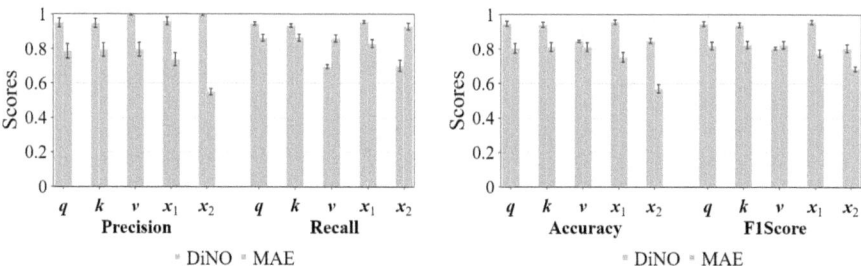

Fig. 7. Cosine-template classification with $k = 500$ support samples per concept. (Left) Precision and recall comparison between MAE and DiNO tokens. (Right) Accuracy and F1 score comparison. The error bars denote the standard deviation across 10 independent trials.

Details: Figure 7 shows the classification metrics for DiNO and MAE tokens using the cosine decision rule, averaged over 10 independent trials with $k = 500$ support images per concept. DiNO's x_1 emerges as the optimal token, achieving the highest accuracy (0.958 ± 0.01) and F1 score (0.958 ± 0.01), while q and k perform similarly. Although all DiNO tokens demonstrate high precision, v and x_2 exhibit the lowest recall in this setting. For MAE, k achieves the highest accuracy (0.812 ± 0.03) and F1 score (0.824 ± 0.02), while q and v demonstrate similar performance. Notably, x_2 exhibits the highest recall (0.929 ± 0.02), making it particularly well-suited for critical risk detection applications where minimizing false negatives (FN) is essential.

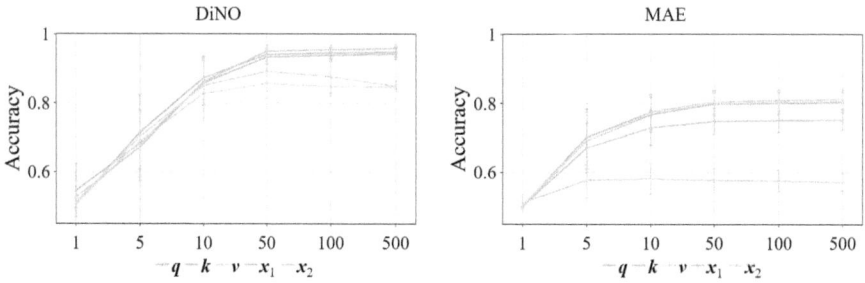

Fig. 8. Cosine-template classification accuracy for $k \in \{1, 5, 10, 50, 100, 500\}$ support samples per concept, for DiNO (Left) and MAE (Right). Error bars denote standard deviation across 10 independent trials.

Figure 8 illustrates the impact of k (number of support samples used to compute cosine-templates) on model accuracy. Notably, performance gains diminish significantly beyond 50 samples. However, increasing the number of support samples leads to a more representative support set, thereby reducing the standard deviation across trials.

4.3 Task: Segmentation. Rule: Hyperplane

TLDR: Both MAE and DINO demonstrate strong and comparable hyperplane-template accuracy, yet inferior to the scores for image classification. Between the two pre-trained models, DINO achieves a higher overall F1 score. Notably, k is the optimal token in terms of overall accuracy and F1 score for both models. However, while k consistently yields the highest F1 score across all concept categories in DINO, MAE shows a slight advantage for x_2 over k when considering textures, objects, or scenes.

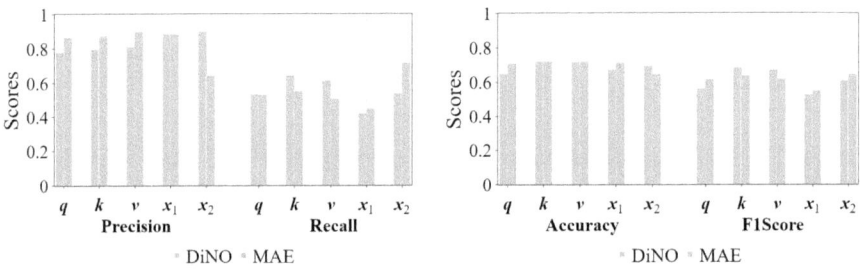

Fig. 9. Hyperplane-template segmentation: (Left) Precision and recall comparison between MAE and DiNO tokens. (Right) Accuracy and F1 score comparison between MAE and DiNO tokens.

Details: Figure 9 presents the overall hyperplane-template segmentation performance of DiNO and MAE tokens. Among DiNO tokens, k achieves the highest accuracy (0.721) and F1 score (0.684), while v attains similar accuracy (–0.001) but a slightly lower F1 score (–0.01). DiNO's x_2 exhibits the highest precision (0.899) making it particularly well-suited for quality assurance applications where minimizing false positives (FP) is essential. MAE's k achieves the highest accuracy (0.721), while x_2 attains the highest F1 score (0.645). Comparing the two, k appears to be the optimal choice, with a significantly higher accuracy (+0.07) and only a slight reduction in F1 score (–0.01). On the other hand, v demonstrates the highest precision (0.899), while x_2 excels in recall (0.716). Notably, x_2 shows a substantial precision drop compared to x_1 (–0.24), coupled with a significant recall increase (+0.27). This suggests that critical semantic information may be lost in x_2, likely in favor of low-level textural patterns, as x_2 tokens are processed through a decoder for masked patch reconstruction.

Figure 10 presents the F1 scores of hyperplane templates, grouped by semantic category. DiNO's k token consistently outperforms others regardless of the semantic category. Among all concept categories, DiNO performs better in part (0.817), material (0.786), and texture (0.765) but is less effective in object (0.682) and scene (0.637) categories. This pattern suggests that DiNO's k token excels at segmenting fine-grained semantic concepts, aligning with prior findings [1]. For MAE, the k token achieves the highest F1 scores in part (0.734) and material (0.727), whereas x_2 leads in object (0.606), scene (0.676), and texture (0.734). Notably, the most significant disparity occurs in the part category, where k significantly outperforms x_2 (+0.08). Interestingly DiNO achieves higher F1 score compared to MAE, in all categories except for scene (–0.13).

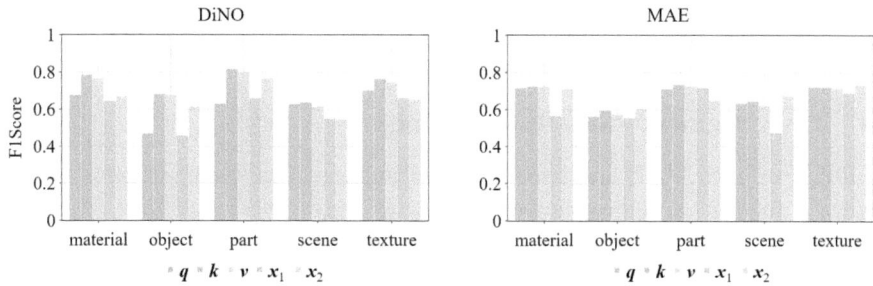

Fig. 10. F1 score for DiNO (Left) and MAE (Right) templates, grouped by label category. The scores for each concept template, are grouped and averaged according to their Broden primary semantic category (material, object, part, scene, texture).

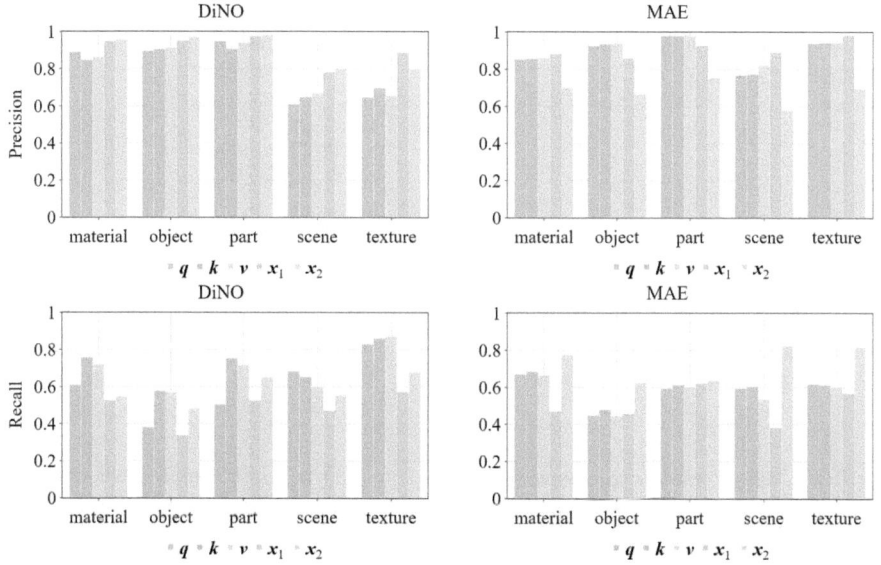

Fig. 11. Precision (Top) and recall (Bottom) for DiNO (Left) and MAE (Right) tokens, grouped by label category.

Figure 11 further examines precision and recall across concept categories. In terms of precision, DiNO's x_2 token achieves the highest overall score (Fig. 9), a trend that persists across most categories, except for texture, where x_1 exhibits superior precision (+0.09). For MAE, v achieves the highest precision in object and part categories, while x_1 is the most precise in material, scene, and texture. Notably, MAE's x_1 consistently outperforms x_2 in precision across all Broden categories. When analyzing recall, DiNO's k token demonstrates the best performance in material, object, and part categories, whereas q and v emerge as the top-performing tokens for scene and texture, respectively. Regarding recall for MAE, x_2 consistently performs best across all categories.

Cross-model comparisons reveal that MAE's v or x_1 tokens achieve higher precision than DiNO in part, scene, and texture categories, while DiNO tokens exhibit superior precision in material and object categories, reinforcing its strength in segmenting individual structures.

4.4 Task: Segmentation. Rule: Cosine

TLDR: For both MAE and DiNO, the utilization of the cosine-decision rule is evidently inferior to hyperplane-templates, as their overall accuracy across all concepts is not significantly superior to a random-classifier (≈ 0.6). However, both models can achieve notable accuracy and F1 scores for textural concepts.

Details: Figure 12 presents the overall segmentation metrics for DiNO and MAE tokens under the cosine decision rule, averaged over 10 trials with $k = 500$ support images per concept. In both models, q tokens achieve the highest accuracy (DiNO: 0.574, MAE: 0.622) and F1 scores (DiNO: 0.419, MAE: 0.464). While MAE outperforms DiNO, both models perform significantly worse compared to the hyperplane decision rule, highlighting the limitations of the cosine decision rule in this setting.

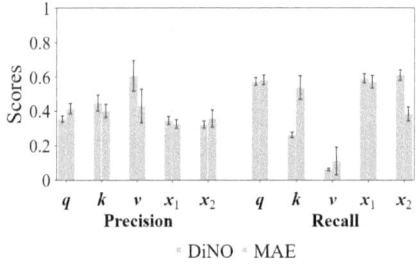
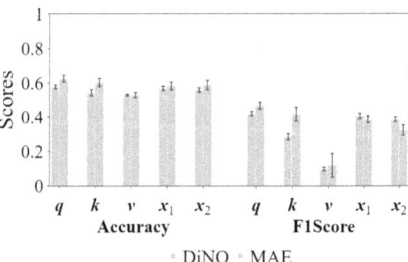

Fig. 12. Cosine-template segmentation with $k = 500$ support samples per concept. (Left) Precision and recall comparison between MAE and DiNO tokens. (Right) Accuracy and F1 score comparison. The error bars denote the standard deviation across 10 independent trials.

Figure 13 shows the accuracy and F1 scores for cosine templates, grouped by semantic category. Notably, both models perform well on textural concepts, and partially well (low accuracy, but higher F1 score) on scenes. MAE's q token achieves an average accuracy of 0.840 and an F1 score of 0.844, while DiNO's x_2 token reaches an average accuracy of 0.744 and an F1 score of 0.765. Figure 14 illustrates the impact of k (number of support samples used to compute cosine-templates) on model accuracy. Similar to cosine-template classification, performance gains diminish significantly beyond 50 samples.

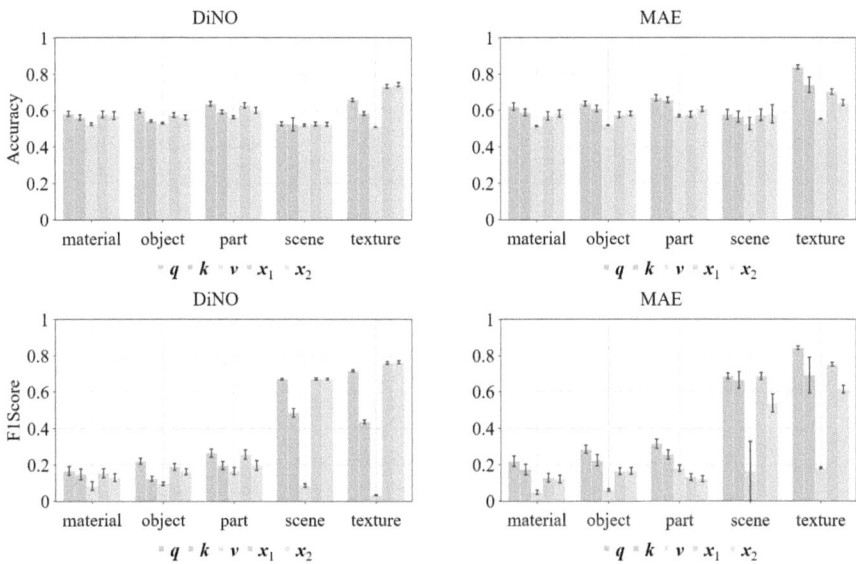

Fig. 13. Cosine-template segmentation with $k = 500$ support samples per concept. (Top) Accuracy for DiNO (Left) and MAE (Right) tokens, grouped by label category. (Bottom) F1 score for DiNO (Left) and MAE (Right) tokens, grouped by label category. The error bars denote the standard deviation across 10 independent trials.

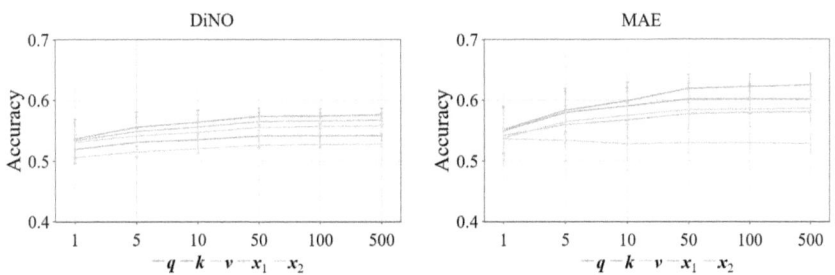

Fig. 14. Cosine-template segmentation accuracy for $k \in \{1, 5, 10, 50, 100, 500\}$ support samples per concept, for DiNO (Left), MAE (Right). Error bars denote standard deviation across 10 independent trials.

4.5 Qualitative Results

In the following subsection, we qualitatively examine the segmentation capabilities of learned concept templates on **unseen** image samples. Based on our previous analysis, we use the k tokens for hyperplane templates and the q tokens for cosine templates for both DiNO and MAE.

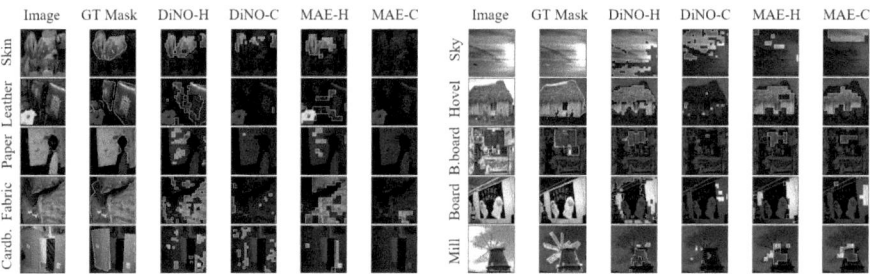

(a) Material: Skin, leather, paper, fabric, cardboard.

(b) Object: Sky, hovel, bulletin-board, board, windmill.

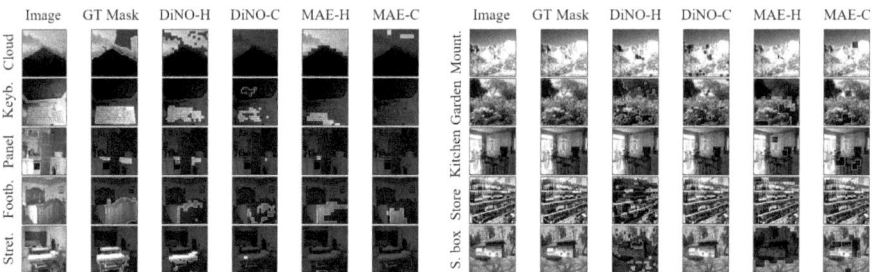

(c) Part: Cloud, keyboard, button-panel, footboard, stretcher.

(d) Scene: Snowy mountain, cottage garden, kitchen, liquor store, signal box.

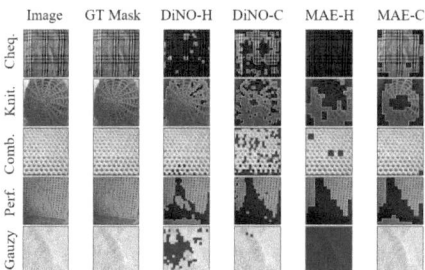

(e) Texture: Chequered, knitted, honeycombed, perforated, gauzy.

Fig. 15. Segmentation visualizations for DiNO and MAE templates using cosine (DiNO-C, MAE-C) and hyperplane (DiNO-H, MAE-H) decision rules. Each figure showcases five unseen images from a specific concept category (material, object, part, scene, texture).

In Fig. 15, we present image samples organized by their primary category (material, object, part, scene, texture). Within each category, we select five representative concepts, and examine one image sample per concept. The selected concepts are chosen to ensure a balanced representation of DiNO hyperplane template performance, incorporating both the highest and lowest F1 scores. To improve visualization clarity, the representative image is selected from the test set based on the largest area coverage of the corresponding concept. Additionally, for each image sample, we provide its ground truth segmentation mask (GT Mask) alongside the predicted masks generated by hyperplane-based (DiNO-C, MAE-C) and cosine decision rule-based (DiNO-C, MAE-C) template models.

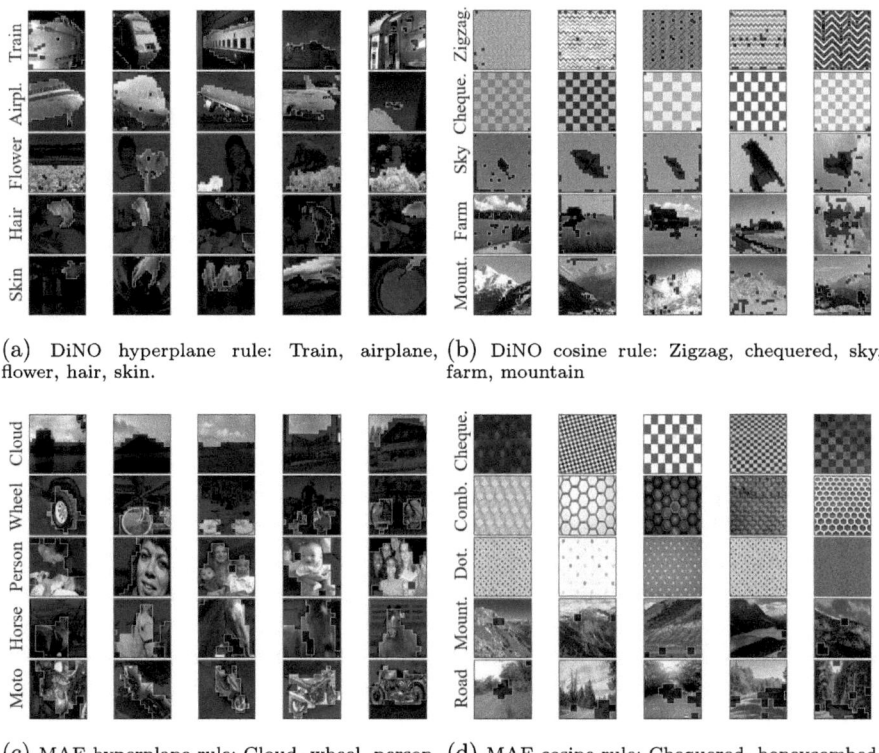

(a) DiNO hyperplane rule: Train, airplane, flower, hair, skin.

(b) DiNO cosine rule: Zigzag, chequered, sky, farm, mountain

(c) MAE hyperplane rule: Cloud, wheel, person, horse, motorcycle.

(d) MAE cosine rule: Chequered, honeycombed, dotted, mountain, forest road

Fig. 16. Segmentation visualizations for DiNO and MAE utilizing cosine and hyperplane decision rules. Each figure presents segmentation masks of unseen samples, produced by a particular model (DiNO, MAE) and decision rule (cosine, hyperplane). We showcase five samples per concept, highlighting the top five concepts with the highest F1 scores.

In Fig. 16, we present segmentation visualizations for the concept labels with the highest F1 scores. Specifically, for each model (DiNO, MAE) and decision rule (hyperplane, cosine), we identify the top-five concept labels based on their F1 scores. For each selected concept, we showcase segmentation masks for five image samples where the template achieves the highest intersection over union (IoU).

4.6 Summary

Our post-hoc concept direction analysis provides insights into the representation power of pretrained DiNO and MAE models, offering guidelines for practical applications while raising questions for future work. A key observation is that the hyperplane classification rule consistently delivers better semantic separability than the cosine counterpart in both classification and segmentation downstream tasks. While MAE's [CLS] tokens seem to be an exception to this finding, we demonstrated that cosine distance between tokens is a suboptimal intra-class similarity metric.

Additionally, we showed that depending on the downstream task, context, and pretraining objective, different ViT tokens –some of which had not been extensively explored in the literature– yield better semantic separability. This challenges current intuitions regarding the interpretation of query, key, and value tokens within transformer architectures and highlights the importance of understanding the role of each block within a transformer layer.

Furthermore, when utilizing pretrained DiNO and MAE models in downstream tasks, the following observations should be mentioned: For image classification, DiNO's x_2 token combined with the hyperplane classification rule results in optimal classification results. Respectively, MAE's tokens should not be considered in this context as they produce random image classifiers. When labels are sparse and a few-shot context is required, DiNO's x_1 is better aligned with the cosine classification rule compared to other token types. We also observe that a support set size of 50 samples represents the point at which performance gains begin to significantly diminish.

For semantic segmentation tasks, the models achieve their highest scores when leveraging their respective k tokens and the hyperplane decision rule. While DiNO outperforms MAE, the latter's strong performance in this context highlights that masked image modeling could serve as an important pretext (sub)task in the development of foundational vision transformers. Furthermore, DiNO's k tokens achieve the highest performance across all object categories, a trend that's not evident in MAE. Finally, in a few-shot context, both models' overall performance across all concept categories is inadequate. However, the q token for both DiNO and MAE provides excellent separability for textural concepts.

5 Limitations

While our study provides a thorough analysis of self-supervised ViT properties across various pre-training objectives, token types, decision rules, downstream tasks, and contexts, it has certain limitations. A primary constraint was computational resources, which restricted our evaluation solely to ViT tokens extracted from the final transformer layer. Additionally, we treat image segmentation as a non-overlapping patch-level classification rather than pixel-level classification. Since ViT-based segmentation methods using frozen backbones [17] perform spatial interpolation of the feature maps to restore the spatial dimensionality of the input space prior to classification, our approach does not significantly deviate from this norm. Finally, regarding classification via the cosine decision rule, we did not account for feature-space centering prior to the computation of cosine-similarity between features. While it would be interesting to investigate its effects, we will consider it in future works.

6 Conclusion

Our work conducted an in-depth post-hoc concept direction analysis to evaluate the representational power of pretrained DiNO and MAE token types in classification and segmentation downstream tasks. We examined their performance in both standard and few-shot learning contexts, utilizing hyperplane and cosine-similarity decision rules. Our findings show that the cosine decision rule –often used in unsupervised learning approaches– consistently results in inferior semantic separability compared to its hyperplane counterpart. We also demonstrate that the optimal token type selection is highly dependent on these factors, while confirming that masked modeling effectively constructs competent backbones for image segmentation tasks.

Future research toward the development of foundational vision architectures should focus on deepening our understanding and interpretation of ViT tokens (arising from the unintuitive and possibly unexpected efficiency of key and query tokens, disproving the hypothesis that value tokens possess superiority), as well as assessing the efficacy of transformer layers, particularly under self-supervised pretraining objectives. Additionally, in unsupervised learning applications –where the cosine distance between ViT tokens is commonly used as an intra-class similarity metric– exploring semantic proximity metrics beyond cosine similarity could enhance downstream task performance. Alternatively, a possible future research direction could be to work towards pre-training methods that will enforce interpretable concept alignment through the cosine rule, offering imminent enhancement of many existing unsupervised works that rely on a self-supervised backbone.

Acknowledgement. This work has been supported by the EC funded Horizon Europe Framework Programme: CAVAA Grant Agreement 101071178.

References

1. Amir, S., Gandelsman, Y., Bagon, S., Dekel, T.: Deep vit features as dense visual descriptors. ArXiv arXiv:2112.05814 (2021)

2. Bao, H., Dong, L., Piao, S., Wei, F.: Beit: bert pre-training of image transformers (2022), https://arxiv.org/abs/2106.08254
3. Bau, D., Zhou, B., Khosla, A., Oliva, A., Torralba, A.: Network dissection: quantifying interpretability of deep visual representations. In: 2017 IEEE Conference on Computer Vision and Pattern Recognition (CVPR), pp. 3319–3327 (2017)
4. Bell, S., Bala, K., Snavely, N.: Intrinsic images in the wild. ACM Trans. Graph. (TOG) **33**, 1–12 (2014)
5. Bommasani, R., et al.: On the opportunities and risks of foundation models (arXiv:2108.07258), July 2022. https://doi.org/10.48550/arXiv.2108.07258, http://arxiv.org/abs/2108.07258, arXiv:2108.07258 [cs]
6. Caron, M., Touvron, H., Misra, I., Jégou, H., Mairal, J., Bojanowski, P., Joulin, A.: Emerging properties in self-supervised vision transformers. In: Proceedings of the IEEE/CVF International Conference on Computer Vision (ICCV), pp. 9650–9660, October 2021
7. Chen, T., Kornblith, S., Norouzi, M., Hinton, G.: A simple framework for contrastive learning of visual representations. In: International Conference on Machine Learning, pp. 1597–1607. PMLR (2020)
8. Chen, X., et al.: Pali: a jointly-scaled multilingual language-image model. ArXiv arXiv:2209.06794 (2022)
9. Chen, X., Mottaghi, R., Liu, X., Fidler, S., Urtasun, R., Yuille, A.L.: Detect what you can: Detecting and representing objects using holistic models and body parts. 2014 IEEE Conference on Computer Vision and Pattern Recognition, pp. 1979–1986 (2014)
10. Chen, X., Fan, H., Girshick, R., He, K.: Improved baselines with momentum contrastive learning (arXiv:2003.04297), March 2020. https://doi.org/10.48550/arXiv.2003.04297, http://arxiv.org/abs/2003.04297, arXiv:2003.04297 [cs]
11. Chen, X., Xie, S., He, K.: An empirical study of training self-supervised vision transformers. In: 2021 IEEE/CVF International Conference on Computer Vision (ICCV), pp. 9620–9629 (2021)
12. Cimpoi, M., Maji, S., Kokkinos, I., Mohamed, S., Vedaldi, A.: Describing textures in the wild. 2014 IEEE Conference on Computer Vision and Pattern Recognition pp, 3606–3613 (2013)
13. Cunningham, H., Ewart, A., Riggs, L., Huben, R., Sharkey, L.: Sparse autoencoders find highly interpretable features in language models. arXiv preprint arXiv:2309.08600 (2023)
14. Dosovitskiy, A., et al.: An image is worth 16x16 words: transformers for image recognition at scale. ArXiv arXiv:2010.11929 (2020)
15. Doumanoglou, A., Asteriadis, S., Zarpalas, D.: Unsupervised interpretable basis extraction for concept–based visual explanations. IEEE Trans. Artif. Intell. (2023)
16. Fel, T., et al.: Craft: concept recursive activation factorization for explainability. In: Proceedings of the IEEE/CVF Conference on Computer Vision and Pattern Recognition, pp. 2711–2721 (2023)
17. Hamilton, M., Zhang, Z., Hariharan, B., Snavely, N., Freeman, W.T.: Unsupervised semantic segmentation by distilling feature correspondences. ArXiv arXiv:2203.08414 (2022)
18. Han, K., et al.: A survey on vision transformer. IEEE Trans. Pattern Anal. Mach. Intell. **45**(1), 87–110 (2022)
19. He, K., Chen, X., Xie, S., Li, Y., Dollár, P., Girshick, R.: Masked autoencoders are scalable vision learners. In: Proceedings of the IEEE/CVF Conference on Computer Vision and Pattern Recognition (CVPR), pp. 16000–16009, June 2022

20. Kang, D., Koniusz, P., Cho, M., Murray, N.: Distilling self-supervised vision transformers for weakly-supervised few-shot classification & segmentation. In: 2023 IEEE/CVF Conference on Computer Vision and Pattern Recognition (CVPR), pp. 19627–19638 (2023)
21. Khan, S., Naseer, M., Hayat, M., Zamir, S.W., Khan, F.S., Shah, M.: Transformers in vision: a survey. ACM Comput. Surv. (CSUR) **54**(10s), 1–41 (2022)
22. Le, Y., Yang, X.S.: Tiny imagenet visual recognition challenge (2015)
23. Liu, Y., et al.: A survey of visual transformers. IEEE Trans. Neural Netw. Learn. Syst. (2023)
24. Mishra, S.K., et la.: A simple, efficient and scalable contrastive masked autoencoder for learning visual representations. ArXiv arXiv:2210.16870 (2022)
25. Mottaghi, R., et al.: The role of context for object detection and semantic segmentation in the wild. In: 2014 IEEE Conference on Computer Vision and Pattern Recognition, pp. 891–898 (2014)
26. Naseer, M.M., Ranasinghe, K., Khan, S.H., Hayat, M., Shahbaz Khan, F., Yang, M.H.: Intriguing properties of vision transformers. Adv. Neural. Inf. Process. Syst. **34**, 23296–23308 (2021)
27. Nguyen, H.H., Yamagishi, J., Echizen, I.: Exploring self-supervised vision transformers for deepfake detection: a comparative analysis. ArXiv arXiv:2405.00355 (2024)
28. Oquab, M., et al.: Dinov2: learning robust visual features without supervision. ArXiv arXiv:2304.07193 (2023)
29. Park, N., Kim, W., Heo, B., Kim, T., Yun, S.: What do self-supervised vision transformers learn? ArXiv arXiv:2305.00729 (2023)
30. Peng, Z., Dong, L., Bao, H., Ye, Q., Wei, F.: Beit v2: Masked image modeling with vector-quantized visual tokenizers (arXiv:2208.06366), October 2022. https://doi.org/10.48550/arXiv.2208.06366, http://arxiv.org/abs/2208.06366, arXiv:2208.06366 [cs]
31. Qian, Y., Wang, Y., Lin, J.: Enhancing the linear probing performance of masked auto-encoders. In: International Conference on Pattern Recognition, pp. 289–301. Springer (2022)
32. Radford, A., et al.: Learning transferable visual models from natural language supervision. In: International Conference on Machine Learning (2021), https://api.semanticscholar.org/CorpusID:231591445
33. Raghu, M., Unterthiner, T., Kornblith, S., Zhang, C., Dosovitskiy, A.: Do vision transformers see like convolutional neural networks? Adv. Neural. Inf. Process. Syst. **34**, 12116–12128 (2021)
34. Rao, S., Mahajan, S., Böhle, M., Schiele, B.: Discover-then-name: task-agnostic concept bottlenecks via automated concept discovery. In: European Conference on Computer Vision, pp. 444–461. Springer (2024)
35. Russakovsky, O., et al.: Imagenet large scale visual recognition challenge. Int. J. Comput. Vision **115**, 211–252 (2014)
36. Siméoni, O., et al.: Localizing objects with self-supervised transformers and no labels. ArXiv arXiv:2109.14279 (2021)
37. Touvron, H., Cord, M., Douze, M., Massa, F., Sablayrolles, A., J'egou, H.: Training data-efficient image transformers & distillation through attention. In: International Conference on Machine Learning (2020)
38. Vanyan, A., Barseghyan, A., Tamazyan, H., Huroyan, V., Khachatrian, H., Danelljan, M.: Analyzing local representations of self-supervised vision transformers. ArXiv arXiv:2401.00463 (2023)

39. Wang, P., et al.: One-peace: Exploring one general representation model toward unlimited modalities. ArXiv arXiv:2305.11172 (2023)
40. Wang, W., et al.: Image as a foreign language: beit pretraining for all vision and vision-language tasks. ArXiv arXiv:2208.10442 (2022)
41. Wang, X., Zhang, R., Shen, C., Kong, T., Li, L.: Dense contrastive learning for self-supervised visual pre-training. In: 2021 IEEE/CVF Conference on Computer Vision and Pattern Recognition (CVPR), pp. 3023–3032. IEEE, Nashville, TN, USA, June 2021. https://doi.org/10.1109/CVPR46437.2021.00304, https://ieeexplore.ieee.org/document/9578497/
42. Wang, X., Girdhar, R., Yu, S.X., Misra, I.: Cut and learn for unsupervised object detection and instance segmentation. In: 2023 IEEE/CVF Conference on Computer Vision and Pattern Recognition (CVPR), pp. 3124–3134 (2023)
43. Wang, Y., Shen, X., Hu, S.X., Yuan, Y., Crowley, J.L., Vaufreydaz, D.: Self-supervised transformers for unsupervised object discovery using normalized cut. 2022 IEEE/CVF Conference on Computer Vision and Pattern Recognition (CVPR), pp. 14523–14533 (2022)
44. Wu, H., et al.: Self-supervised models are good teaching assistants for vision transformers. In: Proceedings of the 39th International Conference on Machine Learning, pp. 24031–24042. PMLR, June 2022, https://proceedings.mlr.press/v162/wu22c.html
45. Xie, Z., et al.: Simmim: a simple framework for masked image modeling. In: 2022 IEEE/CVF Conference on Computer Vision and Pattern Recognition (CVPR), pp. 9643–9653 (2021)
46. Xiong, Y., et al.: Efficientsam: leveraged masked image pretraining for efficient segment anything. In: Proceedings of the IEEE/CVF Conference on Computer Vision and Pattern Recognition, pp. 16111–16121 (2024)
47. Yang, L., Kang, B., Huang, Z., Xu, X., Feng, J., Zhao, H.: Depth anything: unleashing the power of large-scale unlabeled data. In: 2024 IEEE/CVF Conference on Computer Vision and Pattern Recognition (CVPR), pp. 10371–10381 (2024)
48. Yu, J., Wang, Z., Vasudevan, V., Yeung, L., Seyedhosseini, M., Wu, Y.: Coca: contrastive captioners are image-text foundation models. Trans. Mach. Learn. Res. **2022** (2022)
49. Yue, X., et al.: Understanding masked autoencoders from a local contrastive perspective. ArXiv arXiv:2310.01994 (2023)
50. Zhang, W., Ma, B., Qiu, F., qiong Ding, Y.: Multi-modal facial affective analysis based on masked autoencoder. In: 2023 IEEE/CVF Conference on Computer Vision and Pattern Recognition Workshops (CVPRW), pp. 5793–5802 (2023)
51. Zhou, B., Sun, Y., Bau, D., Torralba, A.: Interpretable basis decomposition for visual explanation. In: European Conference on Computer Vision (2018)
52. Zhou, B., Zhao, H., Puig, X., Fidler, S., Barriuso, A., Torralba, A.: Scene parsing through ade20k dataset. 2017 IEEE Conference on Computer Vision and Pattern Recognition (CVPR), pp. 5122–5130 (2017)
53. Zhou, L., Liu, H., Bae, J., He, J., Samaras, D., Prasanna, P.: Self pre-training with masked autoencoders for medical image classification and segmentation (arXiv:2203.05573), April 2023. https://doi.org/10.48550/arXiv.2203.05573, http://arxiv.org/abs/2203.05573, arXiv:2203.05573 [eess]

Open Access This chapter is licensed under the terms of the Creative Commons Attribution 4.0 International License (http://creativecommons.org/licenses/by/4.0/), which permits use, sharing, adaptation, distribution and reproduction in any medium or format, as long as you give appropriate credit to the original author(s) and the source, provide a link to the Creative Commons license and indicate if changes were made.

The images or other third party material in this chapter are included in the chapter's Creative Commons license, unless indicated otherwise in a credit line to the material. If material is not included in the chapter's Creative Commons license and your intended use is not permitted by statutory regulation or exceeds the permitted use, you will need to obtain permission directly from the copyright holder.

XpertAI: Uncovering Regression Model Strategies for Sub-manifolds

Simon Letzgus[1](✉), Klaus-Robert Müller[1,2,3,4], and Grégoire Montavon[2,5](✉)

[1] Machine Learning Group, Technische Universität, Berlin, Germany
simon.leszek@tu-berlin.de
[2] BIFOLD – Berlin Institute for the Foundations of Learning and Data, Berlin, Germany
[3] Department of Artificial Intelligence, Korea University, Seoul, Korea
[4] Max Planck Institute for Informatics, Saarbrücken, Germany
[5] Charité – Universitätsmedizin, Berlin, Germany
gregoire.montavon@charite.de

Abstract. In recent years, Explainable AI (XAI) methods have facilitated profound validation and knowledge extraction from ML models. While extensively studied for classification, few XAI solutions have addressed the challenges specific to regression models. In regression, explanations need to be precisely formulated to address specific user queries (e.g. distinguishing between '*why is the output above 0?*' and '*why is the output above 50?*'). They should furthermore reflect the model's behaviour on the relevant data sub-manifold. In this paper, we introduce *XpertAI*, a framework that disentangles the prediction strategy into multiple output range-specific sub-strategies and allows the formulation of precise queries about the model as a linear combination of those sub-strategies. *XpertAI* is formulated generally to work alongside popular XAI attribution techniques, based on occlusion, gradient integration, or reverse propagation. Qualitative and quantitative results demonstrate the benefits of our approach.

Keywords: XAI · Post-hoc attributions · Regression · Mixture of experts · Contrastive explanations

1 Introduction

Machine learning has provided powerful predictive models for numerous scientific and industrial applications. As the use of ML models for critical autonomous decisions increases, there is a growing demand for establishing trust while maintaining their predictive capabilities. Explainable artificial intelligence (XAI) has emerged as a step towards enhancing transparency and allows for insights into the inner workings of these highly complex AI models [5,40]. XAI can be utilized for both, model validation against expert intuition as well as for obtaining new insights into the data-generating processes under investigation [23,24].

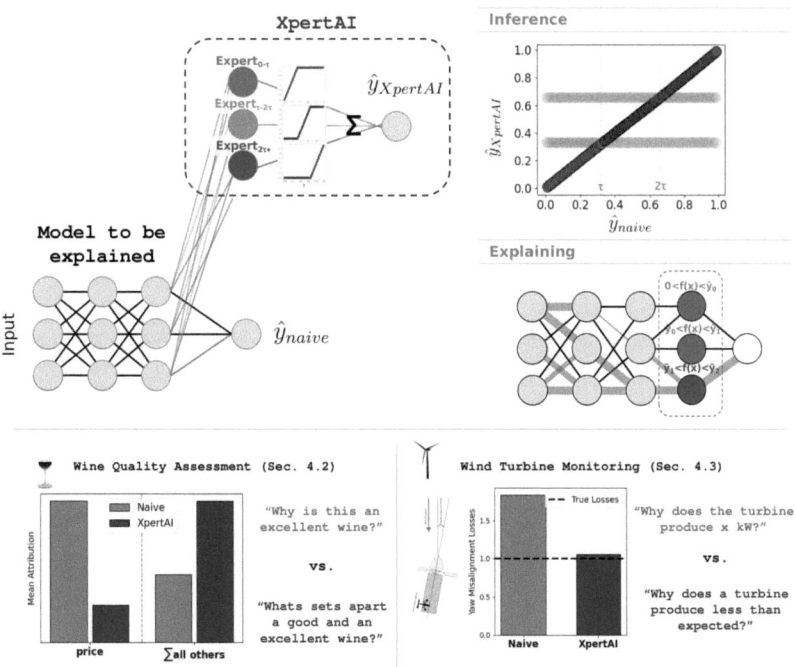

Fig. 1. Top: Conceptual overview of our proposed *XpertAI* approach. We add a layer of *range expert* neurons, each responsible for mimicking the original model behaviour on a range-specific sub-manifold of the data. During inference, the outputs of all range experts are added up and result in the original model output. When explaining, we isolate output-range-specific effects by querying only the respective or a combination of range experts. **Bottom:** While the naive application of attribution methods typically answers questions from a generic point of view (grey) our approach enables answers to more nuanced questions as defined by the user (red). For the tasks of wine quality prediction and attributing losses of a wind turbine, we see significant structural changes in the explanations. For details see Sects. 4.2 and 4.3. (Color figure online)

So far, the predominant focus within XAI has been placed on understanding the decisions made by classification models [6,7,38,49,51]. The widely used family of post-hoc attribution methods aims to achieve this by allocating evidence for a particular class across the corresponding input features. In doing so, they indicate the extent to which each feature has contributed to the model output. In this process, the model's decision boundary serves as a natural point of reference for the explanation. In regression, on the other hand, the equivalent to the decision boundary needs to be defined for every single query, since it is a priori unknown which of the two questions '*why is the output above 50?*' or '*why is the output above 0?*' is most relevant for the user [26]. Moreover, in non-linear problems, sub-manifolds on which the model builds specific responses are to be expected, for example, for different output values.

To address these challenges, we propose our *XpertAI* framework. The basic idea is to decompose the output of the regression model into a set of additive basis functions, the so-called *range experts* (compare Fig. 1, top). Each range expert is dedicated to capturing the model behavior within a specific, output-range-dependent sub-manifold. Subsequently, the user can query the range experts with *any* state-of-the-art attribution method to obtain explanations that are contextualized to the individual explanatory needs. We demonstrate the benefits of our method on several (controlled and real-world) problems (see Fig. 1, bottom). We, for example, find that a model considered the price the most important input feature to distinguish an excellent wine from a bad one. But when explaining with respect to decent alternatives (close-by-reference values), other quality-related features become much more important. In another case study, we used attributions to monitor the performance of a wind turbine. There, we find that our contextualized explanations more faithfully capture the performance losses, which enables better maintenance decisions in practice. In addition to these qualitative insights, we report improved faithfulness through better contextualization with *XpertAI*. An implementation is available online.[1]

2 Related Work

Our proposed method relates to several specific areas of XAI, which we will briefly discuss within this chapter (see e.g. [5,40] for XAI reviews).

2.1 Mixture of Experts

The Mixture of Experts (MoE) framework [14,20,35] follows a divide-and-conquer strategy, commonly used to enhance model performance. Recent work has applied MoEs for transparency by combining interpretable linear experts [19]. In contrast, our approach utilizes MoEs for explaining models in a post-hoc manner, without restriction on the structure of the model, and steering the expert to become 'range experts' focusing on specific value ranges. This is achieved by dividing the data into sub-manifolds according to the output range of a regression model, a way of domain-informed gating, and explaining the model strategy within these specific regions.

2.2 Context in XAI Attribution Methods

Generally speaking, every explanation requires context to be meaningful. When explaining the outcome of a classification model, the decision boundary serves as a natural point of reference. Contrastive explanations have been proposed to better incorporate user-specific context into the explanation [21,28,43]. For regression models, on the other hand, explanations depend on the reference output relative to which we seek an explanation [26]. XAI attribution methods

---
[1] https://github.com/sltzgs/XpertAI.

allow for the incorporation of context through baselines, which depending on the method have to be chosen in input space [29,45] or latent space [26,31,41]. Each baseline then corresponds to a respective reference value ($\widetilde{y}$). In practice, the choice of baselines represents a challenge with fundamental impact on the outcome of the explanation. In this work, we therefore propose a practical solution that ensures contextualization by design for regression models and, as a result, increases robustness against suboptimal baseline choices.

2.3 Disentangled XAI and Virtual Layers

While refining the question to be asked is essential in a regression setting, many works have focused on independently refining the explanation itself (mainly in a classification context). Specifically, enriching explanations by identifying its multiple components, associated with distinct abstract concepts. These can be obtained in a supervised manner [22,50], in an unsupervised manner [9,46], or by directly inspecting neurons [2,49,51]. This kind of analysis often involves an informed transformation of latent representations to obtain a meaningful or relevant 'concept space', followed by the inverse transformation to leave the overall model behaviour intact [48]. Therefore, these approaches are referred to as *virtual layers*. [9], for example, extract sub-concepts that jointly contribute to the explanation of an overall class concept. Likewise, [47] generates a Fourier basis on which the prediction of speech samples can be analyzed more efficiently, and [27] introduces a virtual PCA layer, which disentangles verified from unverified factors of variation and subsequently prune the latter for increased robustness. We extend these efforts to the broad domain of regression, by introducing a novel technique that aims to disentangle global phenomena that exert influence consistently across the entire range of potential regression outputs from more localized context-specific patterns (see Fig. 1, top).

3 Our Method: XpertAI

In the following, we introduce our novel method, called *XpertAI* for explaining neural network regression models. Our approach is inspired by the MoE concept and consists of appending *range experts* to a given ML model, thus allowing the user to formulate precise *queries* for which range they need an explanation. This appendage can be seen as a virtual layer inserted in the neural network, which – while leaving the overall prediction function intact – enriches it by providing the basis for query formulation and explanation. Figure 2 conceptually depicts the method and its notation, with details in the following sections.

3.1 Adding Range Experts

We abstract the ML model as a function f mapping the input x to a real-valued output y. The model may either be a pure black-box or a neural network

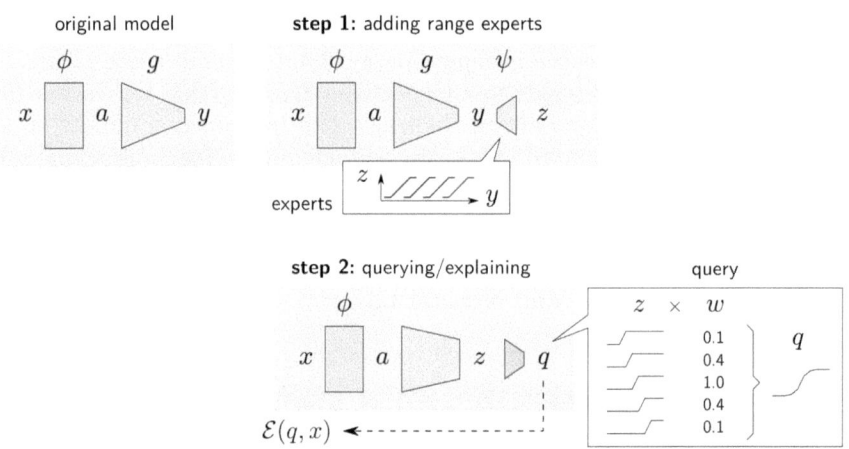

Fig. 2. Diagram of our two-step approach for obtaining fine-grained explanations from an existing regression model. The first step consists of adding a collection of range experts to the model. The second step synthesizes a query q from those range experts and produces a corresponding explanation (the exemplary query on the right is sigmoidal with the ML model's output but linear with the experts).

with multiple layers. We define the range experts as the following collection of functions building on the output of the ML model:

$$z = \begin{pmatrix} \rho_{0,\tau}(y) \\ \rho_{0,\tau}(y - \tau) \\ \rho_{0,\tau}(y - 2\tau) \\ \vdots \end{pmatrix} \tag{1}$$

where $\rho_{0,\tau}(y) = \min(\max(y, 0), \tau)$ clips the input to the interval $[0, \tau]$. A low τ corresponds to more specialized experts. The kind of transformation in Eq. (1) is also known as thermometer coding. The architecture that results from appending these experts is shown in Fig. 2. Assuming the values of y are always positive (which we can ensure through offsetting) we can reconstitute the output prediction by summing the experts' outputs:

$$y = \sum_m z_m \tag{2}$$

The mapping from y to z and back to y can be seen as a virtual layer which does not affect the input-output mapping, but that provides additional functionality. Unlike previous formulations of virtual layers [47], ours is placed at the output, enabling a disentanglement of the explanation in terms of output ranges.

Consider now the task of attribution. Classical explanation techniques would attribute y to the features of x (something we denote by $\mathcal{E}(y, x)$). The virtual layer allows us to compose two attribution steps:

$$R_m = \mathcal{E}(y, z)_m$$
$$R_{im} = \mathcal{E}(R_m, x)_i$$

where R_m denotes the contribution of expert m to the output y (in our case we simply have $R_m = z_m$), and R_{im} can be interpreted as the contribution of input feature i through expert m. The overall explanation can be seen as a matrix of size # features · # experts, from which it will be possible to formulate and answer precise user queries.

3.2 Querying/Explaining

Whereas the disentanglement performed above provides a more detailed view of the prediction behaviour than a simple explanation, the user is often interested in particular aspects of it. Our approach lets the user formulate a query (or 'explanandum') as a linear combination of the range experts:

$$q = \sum_m w_m z_m \tag{3}$$

An example of such a query is given in Fig. 2 (right). For example, if the user is interested in what makes a prediction $y = 60$ larger than a reference value of 50, the query q can be shaped in the form of a sigmoid centred at the reference value 50.

Once a query has been prepared (i.e. once the weights w_m have been defined), an explanation to that query $\mathcal{E}(q, x)$ can be generated by any state-of-the-art attribution method:

$$\mathcal{E}(q, x) = \mathcal{E}\left(\sum_m w_m z_m, x\right) \tag{4}$$

Note that for explanation techniques that fulfil the linearity axiom w.r.t. the last layer of representation, we can further develop the expression of the explanation as:

$$\mathcal{E}(q, x) = \sum_m w_m \mathcal{E}(z_m, x) \tag{5}$$

It shows that the explanation is a linear combination of the explanations of all basis elements z_m. This formulation can be advantageous when the explanation is associated with many different queries or when the query arrives in real-time, in which case the explanation basis can be pre-computed. We note that our approach satisfies some key desirable properties of an explanation:

Proposition 1 (Conservation). *If $\forall m : \sum_i \mathcal{E}(z_m, x)_i = z_m$, then $\sum_i \mathcal{E}(q, x)_i = q$, in other words, if each range expert z_m can be attributed to input features in a conservative manner, then explanations of any query q are also conservative.*

Proposition 2 (Irrelevance). *If $\forall m : \mathcal{E}(z_m, x)_i = 0$, then $\mathcal{E}(q, x)_i = 0$, in other words, if we verify that for a given data point, the feature is irrelevant for all range experts, then it is also irrelevant for any query built on those experts.*

These two results are easily retrievable by observing the specific structure of the explanation given in Eq. (5). Proofs can be found in Appendix A.

3.3 Structural Disentanglement

When the underlying explanation method relies not directly on the ML model's output but on its computational graph (e.g. LRP), the latter must be disentangled. Clearly, such a structural disentanglement is missing as the mapping from activations a to the expert's outputs z passes through a one-dimensional bottleneck y (the original real-valued output). We propose to replace the original mapping $a \mapsto (z_m)_m$ by a learned surrogate model (s_m):

$$a \stackrel{\theta}{\mapsto} (s_m)_m \mapsto (\widehat{z}_m)_m$$

where the second part of the mapping is given by $\widehat{z}_m = \rho_{0,\tau}(s_m)$, a hard-coded saturation forcing the surrogate and true experts to produce outputs in the same range. We then build for each expert the loss function:

$$\ell(s_m, z_m) = \begin{cases} \max(0, s_m) & z_m \leq 0 \\ |s_m - z_m| & 0 < z_m < \tau \\ \max(0, \tau - s_m) & z_m \geq \tau \end{cases}$$

which encourages that the surrogate's output is correct within-range and on the correct side outside-range. We then solve $\min_\theta \mathbb{E}[\sum_m \ell(s_m, z_m)]$ with $\mathbb{E}[\cdot]$ denoting the expectation over the training data. To preserve not only the prediction output of the original model but also its prediction strategy (i.e. the feature it uses) further steps are needed. One approach is to enforce the loss function not only on the data but also on perturbations of the data [44]. For example, activations can be randomly turned off (with a probability chosen between 0 and 1). This perturbation scheme ensures in particular that the Shapley value explanations of the original and disentangled models become similar (i.e. that they predict the same for the same reasons). Furthermore, we find that freezing the bias in the output layer is important to achieve the desired structural disentanglement.

3.4 XpertAI Evaluation

We evaluate our proposed approach qualitatively (Sect. 4) and quantitatively (Sect. 5). In both cases we rely on either a (constructed) problem that allows for validation against some sort of ground truth, or the observation of model behaviour under attribution-guided, meaningful input perturbations. [13] proposed a regression-specific metric called the area between the curves (ABC). The ABC is defined as the area between the model output when occluding a sample's features in the order of attribution magnitudes and a straight line connecting $f(x)$ and $f(x')$ (which corresponds to random sorting). Since sorting ascending and descending can result in asymmetrical curves, we sum over both areas [8]. For a balanced result, we normalize by the distance between the sample and the baseline when averaging. Higher values of ABC are better.

Furthermore, the challenge of including context in attribution methods (Sect. 2.2) naturally extends to occlusion-based evaluation (ergo, what to occlude with?). To ensure that we evaluate attributions within the relevant output range of function $f(x)$, where we account for context-specific (local) effects, we occlude with a domain-specific counterfactual [3,13]. Therefore, we sample conditional $x' = D(x|y = \tilde{y})$ from the available data set D with which we then occlude and average the respective ABCs over multiple draws.

4 XpertAI-Opinion: Insights Into Model Behaviour on Sub-manifolds

We now demonstrate how our *XpertAI* approach can help users disentangle local and global effects for meaningful insights in different case studies. First, we uncover output-scale-specific strategies for image regression problems (4.1). Then, we explain the quality of red wine (4.2) and the production losses of a wind turbine due to a technical malfunction (4.3). For each of the problems, we briefly introduce the dataset, model and *XpertAI* setting, before presenting the insights. We present results from using both, Integrated Gradients and Layer-wise Relevance Propagation (LRP). Details on all case studies can be found in Appendix C.

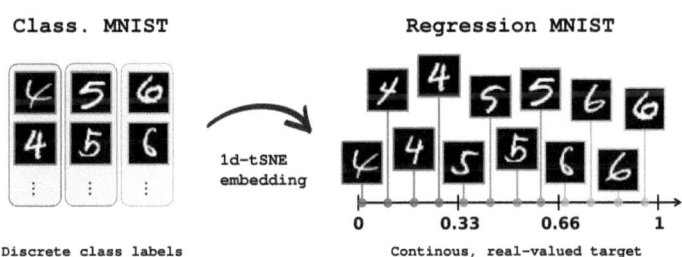

Fig. 3. Examples from three classes of the MNIST dataset for handwritten digit recognition (left) mapped to a real-valued scale with the help of a one-dimensional t-SNE embedding (right). Digits populate continuous ranges of the new target, and sorting within the digit ranges corresponds to digit rotations.

4.1 Uncovering Output-Scale-Specific Strategies

First, we adopt the well-known MNIST [11] dataset and transform it into a regression problem (*rMNIST*). For simplicity, we take the subset of only three digits (4,5, and 6) and calculate a one-dimensional t-SNE representation [30], which henceforth serves as a new label for each sample. Additionally, we ensure labels are distributed uniformly between values of zero and one. As a result, the individual digits populate continuous parts of the output dimension (in our case sorted by digit magnitude, which facilitates interpretation) while sorting within each digit bin is based on the respective digit's rotation (compare Fig. 3). We now train a vanilla CNN model architecture to learn this mapping from image to output scale. For contextualized insights, we train three range experts (one for each digit range). We first discuss qualitative results and present its quantitative evaluation in Sect. 5.

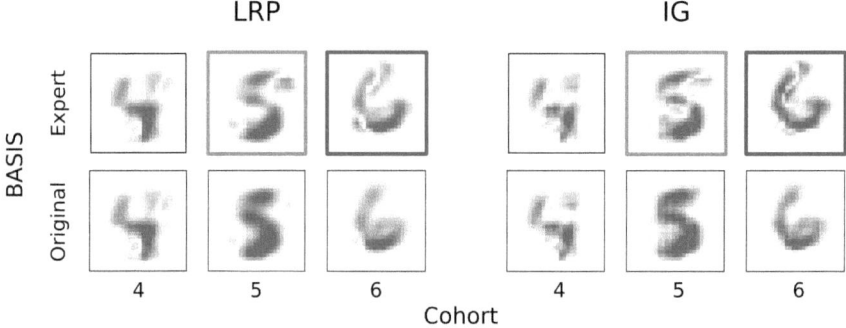

Fig. 4. Mean attributions over different cohorts of samples (columns) and basis functions (rows). The bottom row represents naive attributions. The top row corresponds to the respective range-specific expert *XpertAI* bases. Note, how only the latter exposes the digit rotation within the digit ranges (orange/blue). (Color figure online)

Figure 4 shows a comparison between the standard and the *XpertAI* explanations for both, LRP and IG. We contrast the average naive attributions over all samples *within* the respective output range (bottom row) with the explanations obtained with the respective range experts (top row). The explanations for the digit range *4* remain the same since both implicitly assume the same reference value (zero on the output scale). The expert attributions for the upper digit ranges (marked in orange and blue), enable more granular insights. It is visible how the range experts focus specifically on the rotation of the digit: a rotation to the right is associated with lower values (negative attribution, blue) and vice versa. See [Fig. 10] (Appendix C) for more basis functions. In Sect. 5, we will see that these qualitative differences in attributions also result in improved quantitative evaluation scores for attribution faithfulness.

Now, let's consider an illustrative regression task closer to real-world applications: biological age estimation from facial images [1,4,15] (see Fig. 13 Appendix C) for model and data set details. Intuitively, the explanation for a person with a high age should be structurally different when being contrasted with a much younger age or an only slightly younger one. We, therefore, focus on a high-age cohort (individuals predicted to be above 77 years) and train three range experts ($\tau = 38.5$ years). Figure 5, left, shows LRP attributions for the original model, averaged over the respective samples. Our proposed approach now allows us to disentangle these further using the respective age-specific basis functions. As expected, the explanation relative to the 'young' basis (centre) overall contains much more positive evidence than the one with respect to the closer reference value of 77 years (right). Additionally, we can see that the latter is more fine-grained with a remaining focus on the person's eyes and, surprisingly, we discovered a sign-flip for the oronasal region with a particular focus on lips and teeth. While the mouth has been reported to be an area particularly vulnerable to biases in age estimation from facial images [12], we put the faithfulness of these particular explanations to the test.

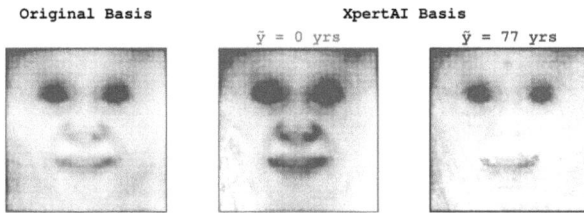

Fig. 5. Comparison of average attributions for standard LRP (left) and two different XpertAI basis functions. Red indicates positive, and blue negative evidence. We can see that the disentangled explanations allow for much more fine-grained conclusions. Interestingly, the sign flip of the mouth area was masked by the strong attributions with respect to the original basis. We test for its faithfulness in Fig. 6 (Color figure online).

In Fig. 6, we compare the effect of occluding the respective parts (eyes and mouth) of people's faces with a generic average over all images. One example of each is shown at the right of the figure. Recall that this means we mask the eyes and mouth section with a relatively 'younger' version. The chart shows the respective change in the model's output. In line with intuition, and the explanations, age is indeed consistently decreased when occluding the eyes. Masking the mouth area with relatively 'younger' mouths, however, indeed results in an *increase* of the model's average prediction in many cases. The *XpertAI*-basis therefore constitutes the more faithful explanation since the attributions correctly captured the sign flip in model behaviour.

In conclusion, the disentangled basis explanations enabled more detailed insights into the model's inner workings for both, the rMNIST and the age-prediction cases. They revealed effects that were not apparent from the naive explanations of the original model, since their highly aggregated nature did not allow for more fine-grained insights.

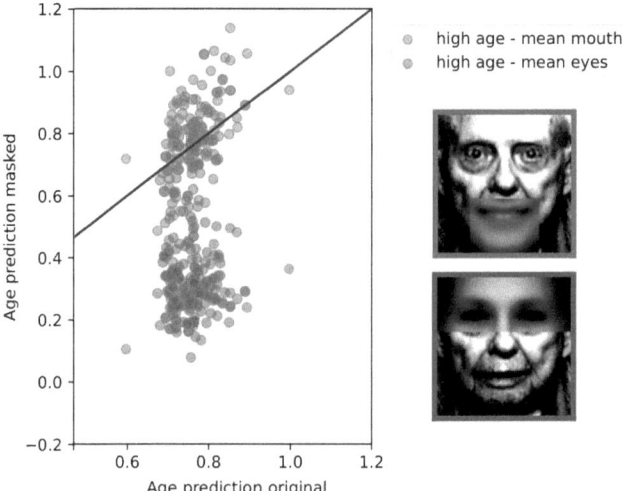

Fig. 6. Validation of findings from disentangling age prediction (compare Fig. 5). We occlude relevant parts of the image according to the disentangled explanations (eyes and mouth) with the dataset-wide average face (two examples on the right). We then observe the effect on the model output relative to the original model prediction. For the high-age cohort, the two areas have distinctly different effects. Occluding the eyes with a relatively younger pair results in a consistent decrease in the predicted age. Occluding the mouth region, however, results in an increase for many of the samples. This model behaviour is in line with our insights from the disentangled explanations.

4.2 What Sets Apart a Good Wine from an Excellent One?

As noted in the introduction, we now explore a more hedonistic and tangible example - red wine quality. We utilize Kaggle's *Spanish red wine dataset*[2] which contains several thousand wine samples. They are described by five numerical (year, price, as well as body, acidity, and quality scores) and four categorical (name of the winery and the wine, grape, region) features. The quality score, which is an 'average rating' given by thousands of testers (rating binned into 8 discrete quality levels), is our regression target. After data-pre-processing around 1700 samples are left. We have trained a small fully-connected ANN which achieved an R^2 of around 0.7.

We now want to learn what, according to the model, sets apart a good wine from an excellent one. We define wine as good when it belongs to the top 10% and excellent when it belongs to the top 1.5 % of the model output range. We train three range experts ($\tau = 0.33$) and compare the respective attributions obtained from standard IG with its application within the XpertAI framework. Figure 7 shows the decomposition of the excellent wine attributions into the

---

[2] https://www.kaggle.com/datasets/fedesoriano/spanish-wine-quality-dataset.

respective expert bases. Aside from the natural change in attribution scales, the most prominent difference in the explanations is the contribution of the price to the model outcome. For the naive IG attributions, the price is the by far most important feature (meaning high prices alone are the main indicator for excellent wines). The contextualized *XpertAI* attributions, on the other hand, give a much more balanced picture. Here, the outcome suggests that the price is the most important feature only for the low-quality range expert (meaning what distinguishes an average from a poor wine, blue). The relative importance of the price, however, is significantly reduced when compared to average wines (orange) and almost vanishes when compared to good wines (green). There, the sum of all other quality criteria is much more important than the price of the wine itself. This directly translates to some actionable (and intuitive) insight: if you next time buy a wine in the supermarket, don't go cheap to ensure you buy a decent wine. When looking for an excellent one though, you might be better off with the expert judgement of your local wine seller.

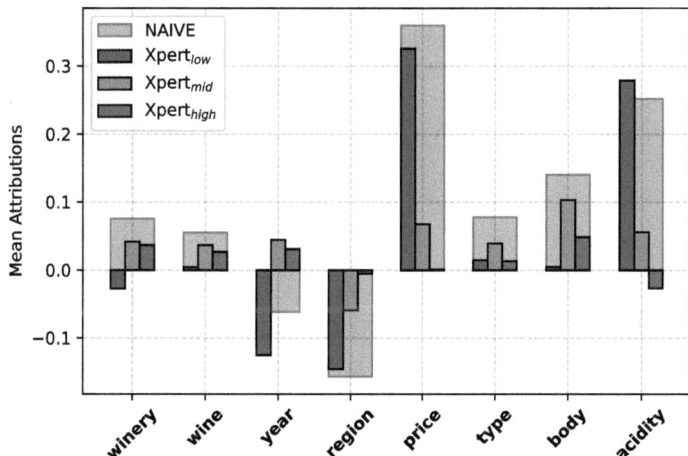

Fig. 7. Decomposition of naive explanations (grey) for samples from the high output range ('excellent' wines) with respect to low, medium and high-quality reference values (colourful). The XpertAI explanations allow for nuanced insights into what makes an excellent wine better than the worst (blue), a decent (orange) or a good (green) alternative. (Color figure online)

To make sure, our insights are not based on intuitive but unfaithful attributions, we also compare quantitative faithfulness for the and observe an average increase in the ABC metric by more than 10 % (see Sect. 5).

4.3 Why Does the Wind Turbine Produce Less Than Expected?

Wind power is one of the pillars of decarbonizing energy systems around the world. Wind turbines are often placed in remote locations and need to be operated and monitored from a distance, using data from their Supervisory Control and Data Acquisition (SCADA) system. Effectively leveraging this data is an active area of research [18], with the primary focus on detecting and diagnosing underperformance as the central challenge [33]. However, the detection of *under*performance is always context-specific since the implicit question is: 'underperformance relative to what operational state?' In the wind turbine case, it is the condition without the presence of a malfunction, given the context of prevailing ambient conditions.

We utilize data from a 2 MW wind turbine and a meteorological met-mast from an onshore wind farm on the Iberian peninsula[3]. SCADA data is available for two years and includes ambient conditions as well as technical turbine parameters as 10-minute averaged values (50,000 data points after pre-processing). We have trained a small fully-connected MLP to predict the turbine output from wind speed, air density, and turbulence intensity. The model achieves a competitive RMSE of less than 36 kW. Additionally, we have augmented the data with so-called yaw-misalignment losses. They occur when a turbine does not perfectly face the incoming wind direction, which reduces the effective area of the rotor. Detecting yaw-misalignment is an ongoing field of research [34,37] and attributing it by XAI methods has recently been proposed as an effective solution [25]. For such an approach to work, we need our XAI methods to faithfully attribute the losses induced by yaw-misalignment to the respective feature (difference of nacelle and wind direction). In our setup, we can directly compare attributions with the respective ground-truth-losses.

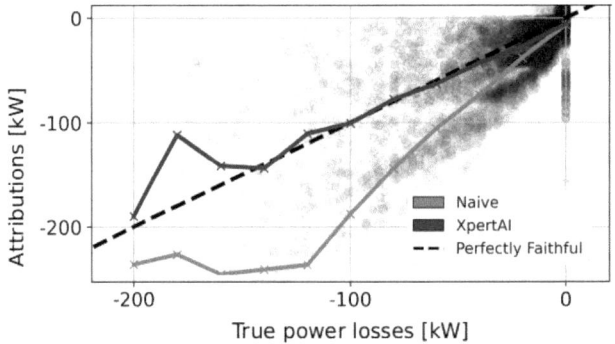

Fig. 8. Quantitative faithfulness when attributing yaw-misalignment losses to the respective feature with standard LRP (grey) and *XpertAI*-LRP (red) against the true losses (dashed line). (Color figure online)

We trained three range experts across the different operational regions of the turbine (see Fig. 13, Appendix C). Figure 8 shows the comparison of attributing the yaw-misalignment induced losses to the respective yaw-feature with standard

---
[3] https://opendata.edp.com.

LRP and our XpertAI-LRP variant. We can observe that the naive LRP application attributes exhibit a systematic overestimation (larger negative values) of losses caused by incorporating phenomena from outside the respective operational regime. Our proposed novel attributions obtained from the range-experts, on the other hand, are on average much closer to the ground truth. For turbine operators, this directly translates to better operation and maintenance decisions and therefore highlights the benefit of using sub-manifold-specific explanations in industrial or engineering applications.

5 Quantitative Evaluation and Sanity Checks of XpertAI-Faithfulness

After having presented some intriguing insights enabled through our *XpertAI* approach in the previous chapter, we now conduct a systematic evaluation of explanation faithfulness. Details on the respective experiments and additional insights for obtaining faithful range experts can be found in Appendix B and C.

5.1 Are XpertAI Attributions Faithful?

To answer this question quantitatively, we utilize the ABC score as introduced in Sect. 3.4. Table 1 reports the ABC scores of our *XpertAI* approach relative to a naive application of LRP and IG on the previously introduced data sets as well as several popular regression benchmarks [36]. For each of them, we trained three range experts and evaluated samples from the top range (see Appendix C). Overall, we see consistent improvements in ABC scores across all settings which means that our approach indeed can generate more faithful attributions with respect to a user-specific query. Note, that the advantage is significantly larger for LRP where our approach corresponds to a data-driven root-search strategy whereas naively, there is no such option. For IG we have already leveraged its inherent contextualization capability to some extent by utilizing the mean over all input samples as a starting point for the integration path. Our approach is still able to further refine the attributions towards a better contextualization.

Table 1. Comparison of faithfulness for different attribution methods applied naively and within the *XpertAI* framework. Relative improvement of ABC over naive application. Standard deviation over 5 different retraining runs for LRP.

dataset	LRP	IG
rMNIST	+50.7 % $^{\pm 3.5}$	+7.2 %
WINE	+19.8 % $^{\pm 1.2}$	+10.6 %
FRIEDMAN	+12.6 % $^{\pm 0.4}$	+1.9 %
CALIFORNIA	+2.5 % $^{\pm 0.9}$	+9.7 %
DIABETES	+3.8 % $^{\pm 1.6}$	+4.4 %

5.2 How Many Range Experts?

One practically relevant question is, how many range experts to train, which includes the choice of their respective ranges (τ). Conceptually, the method works best if every distinct sub-region of the output is covered by at least one *range expert*. In practice, these can either be domain-informed and therefore known apriori, or inferred by analyzing activation patterns (from an activation vs. $f(x)$ scatter plot, for example). In the context of our rMNIST case, selecting one range expert for each digit range, therefore three range experts in total appears to be the most intuitive choice. Since in practice, we might not know where exactly these boundaries lay, we compare settings for three, five, six, and nine equally spread range experts.

Table 2. Results for pixel flipping experiments for regression MNIST. Results within ranges: sample-flipping baseline pairs are within one expert range. ABC values are normalized by flipping distance. Values for naive methods differ because of the normalization. High values are better.

# experts	LRP Naive	LRP XpertAI	IG Naive	IG XpertAI
3	0.40	**0.56 ± 0.02**	0.93	**1.00 ± 0.05**
5	0.47	**0.70 ± 0.01**	1.16	**1.20 ± 0.01**
6	0.46	**0.75 ± 0.01**	1.22	**1.23 ± 0.01**
9	0.49	**0.78 ± 0.01**	1.32	**1.36 ± 0.01**

In Table 2 we see that our approach improved the ABC score across all settings. Also, we can see that LRP benefits in particular from adding extra range experts while IG results are more consistent across the number of experts. Note, that this also holds if the expert ranges are not aligned with known sub-concept ranges (as is the case for 5 equally distributed experts). In practice this means that the limit for the number of experts depends on the specific problem, computational considerations as well as the resolution of the available data.

5.3 (Diss-)aggregate XpertAI-Attributions

From Proposition 1, we can in principle derive an alternative way to obtain disentangled and contextualized attributions with respect to $\tilde{y}$. Instead of adding up the respective expert attributions, we subtract them from the original explanation in reverse order. Intuitively, only information relevant to higher-range bins should remain. We test this hypothesis empirically on the *rMNIST* dataset. We flip pixels to zero according to the order of the difference of attributions $\mathcal{E}(y,x) - \sum_m \mathcal{E}(z_m, x)$. Intuitively, the more evidence associated with lower-range concepts we subtract, the more evidence for higher values should remain, and therefore the flipping curve should decrease more slowly. In the ideal case, the only information with positive attributions is the one relevant for values larger than $\widetilde{y}_i$ and the flipping curve should therefore remain around that value for as long as possible. When testing this empirically, we indeed see such a behaviour (Fig. 9). Note also, that the plateaus of the different range experts do not cluster around the digit-transitions (0.33 and 0.66). This means, that despite the strong global concept shifts present in the data, the range experts were able to capture more subtle, local effects that guide $f(x)$ in the context of the respective reference values.

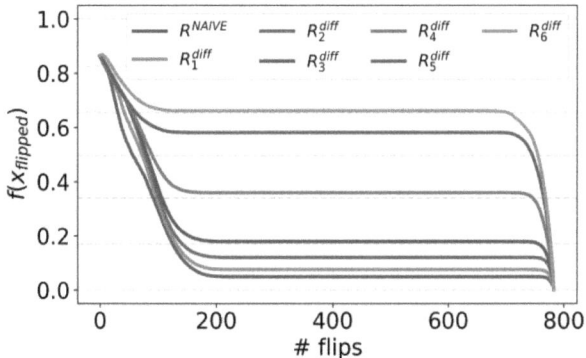

Fig. 9. Mean occlusion curves over all samples from the top bin of a six-expert-basis. When successively subtracting range-expert attributions from the original explanation and flipping pixels according to the remaining explanations, the flipping curves saturate in the proximity of the respective reference values.

6 Discussion and Conclusions

In this paper, we have proposed the *XpertAI* framework to achieve contextualized and disentangled attributions when explaining regression models. Inspired by the MoE approach, the framework divides the data into sub-manifolds, each of which corresponds to a certain predicted output range. Such a division is achieved by building a collection of *range experts*, which we equip with explainability. It enables for the first time a disentanglement along the output of the prediction strategy and the resolution of specific user-defined queries.

Empirically, we find that our XpertAI framework can distill locally relevant explanations from highly aggregated global standard attributions, as demonstrated by several quantitative experiments based on occlusion tests. Explanations associated with each expert range can be precomputed, so that exact user queries can be answered very quickly as a linear combination of the precomputed explanations.

Our approach can be interpreted within the framework of virtual layers, which has been instrumental in achieving various forms of explanation disentanglement. Furthermore, our approach provides an alternative to the more common approach of extracting reference points or counterfactuals and bypasses some of the challenges , such as their multiplicity and the need to search for them. Also, our approach differs from self-interpretable generalized additive models, by remaining applicable to a broad range of ML models, including deep neural networks.

We have demonstrated that our method can work alongside various explanation techniques, in particular, gradient-based techniques such as Integrated Gradients, or propagation-based techniques such as LRP. While this enables a seamless integration into existing explanation pipelines our approach naturally inherits potential shortcomings of these methods. Furthermore, it is necessary for propagation-based techniques to structurally disentangle the range experts. While we have proposed a surrogate modeling approach for this step, these surrogates need to be carefully trained and regularized to maintain the original model's prediction output as well as its prediction strategy. Also, retraining implies additional computational cost. Hybrid approaches, with the top layers handled by perturbation-based techniques and the lower layers with propagation, may eliminate the need for structural disentanglement while at the same time retaining high accuracy and computational efficiency. Enhanced approaches, inspired by model distillation or formally equivalent neural networks, could also be considered.

Overall, our work has highlighted the need to precisely formulate "what to explain" (the explanandum) and proposed a practical and flexible solution in the context of regression. The MoE idea our method builds upon, however, is more general, and our framework could be extended in the future to other decomposition of the predicted output, e.g. for structured output tasks such as time series prediction. Additional future work could furthermore focus on automating the optimal number of experts in a data-driven way. While we have shown that for sufficiently populated ranges of the output adding more experts improves contextualization, there certainly are limitations arising from data availability and computational constraints. Lastly, the application and evaluation to more complex models, such as regression foundation models [16], should be considered in the future.

Acknowledgments. This work was partly funded by the German Ministry for Education and Research [01IS14013A-E, 01GQ1115, 01GQ0850, 01IS18056A, 01IS18025A, 01IS18037A, and 01IS24087C], the German Research Foundation as Math+: Berlin Mathematics Research Center [EXC2046/1, project-ID: 390685689], the Investitionsbank Berlin [10174498 ProFIT program], and the European Union's Horizon 2020 Research and Innovation program under grant [965221]. Furthermore, Klaus-Robert Müller was partly supported by the Institute of Information and Communications Technology Planning and Evaluation grants funded by the Korean Government [2019-0-00079]. Our gratitude extends to Jonas Lederer, Pattarawat Chormai and Stefan Blücher for their invaluable comments and feedback that have contributed to enhancing the quality of the manuscript. Finally, we thank the XAI World Conference 2025 jury for the Best Paper Award.

A Proof of Propositions 1 and 2

Proposition 1 stating the conservation property of the proposed query explanation can be demonstrated through the chain of equations:

$$\sum_i \mathcal{E}(q,x)_i = \sum_i \sum_m w_m \mathcal{E}(z_m, x)_i \quad (6)$$
$$= \sum_m w_m \sum_i \mathcal{E}(z_m, x)_i \quad (7)$$
$$= \sum_m w_m z_m \quad (8)$$
$$= q \quad (9)$$

where in (6), we have injected the expression of the explanation in (5). From (6) to (7) we have permuted the sums. From (7) to (8), we have used the conservation property of the explanation of z_m. From (8) to (9) we have identified the weighted sum as being the query. Likewise, for Proposition 2, if some feature i satisfies $\forall m : \mathcal{E}(z_m, x)_i = 0$, then

$$\mathcal{E}(q,x)_i = \sum_m w_m \mathcal{E}(z_m, x)_i \quad (10)$$
$$= \sum_m w_m \cdot 0 \quad (11)$$
$$= 0 \quad (12)$$

B How to Train and Select Good Range Experts?

In practice, we need to select appropriate *range experts* for the XpertAI approach to enhance contextualization. This process may vary based on the respective XAI attribution method being employed. For occlusion- and gradient-integration-based methods, which do not require additional structural disentanglement (see Sect. 3.3), a simple shift-and-clip strategy is sufficient. For propagation-based methods, however, we need to learn the surrogate $a \mapsto (z_m)_m$ (see Sect. 3). Here, we want to highlight the need for appropriate regularization to avoid overfitting, which in the case of range experts would result in unfaithful model attributions. Analogously to regular model selection, we aim to choose the least complex range expert, that can sufficiently learn the respective mapping.

In case the latent representation a is already adequately disentangled, it is sufficient to fit a linear range expert (without bias term). We have observed this to work well for some of our low-dimensional benchmark datasets. Otherwise, we need to gradually increase range-expert complexity (adding neurons and reducing L2-regularization) until the mapping is learned sufficiently. Moreover, we have observed that instead of additional layers, (copying and) fine-tuning the top layer(s) on the range-expert targets z_m with small learning rates is a good strategy since it ensures the solution lays in relative proximity to the original model. If a new layer is added, initializing the weights with a projection to the latent principal components conditioned on the respective output range ($PCA(X|z_m)$) was found to speed up training and ensure good results. Furthermore, the Shapley-style data augmentation (cf. Sect. 3) is another crucial ingredient to prevent our experts from adhering to spurious correlations (that our original models did not use). This can be conveniently implemented with the help of a dropout layer on the surrogate input $\boldsymbol{a}$. Lastly, we can enforce the saturation of range experts outside their area of expertise by adding an explicit combination of ReLU functions that clip s_m to the desired range. These measures together ensure faithful and computationally efficient *range experts*.

C Details on Evaluation (Sect. 4 and 5)

C.1 Details Face-Age Regression Example

For this analysis, we have made use of a dataset containing $\sim$ 20k facial images associated with biological age[4] (biased toward younger ages). Each image is pre-processed so that all of them have the same size (200×200) and the faces are aligned and centred. We used a VGG-16 [42] model pre-trained on ImageNet [10,39] as a feature extractor followed by one ReLU layer with 256 neurons, a dropout-layer, and a final linear layer mapping the 256 neurons to a real-valued age prediction. In all cases we used LRP-$\alpha_1\beta_0$ rule [6,32] in the convolutional layers and LRP-ϵ rule [6] (where biases are ignored) for the fully connected layers.

C.2 Details Quantitative Evaluation

Here, we describe the details of our quanitative experiments. For the rMNIST experiments, we utilized a vanilla CNNs with two convolutional, ReLU and pooling layers, followed by three fully connected layers. The convolutional blocks were kept frozen, and only the fully connected layers were re-trained as experts, starting from their original model weights. The other problems (Wind, Wine, California and Diabetes) are based on tabular data. Here, we utilize a 4 layer-MLP with 20 neurons in each hidden layer. The last two were re-trained for each expert. Moreover, we utilized the PCA initialization trick, described above (Appendix B). w_m was selected to be 1 for all expert ranges between reference value and sample output, and 0 otherwise. More specific information on the implementation can be found in the published code repository[5]. Details, such as target distributions, model performance, and range-expert-performance across experimental setting can be found in Figs. 10, 11, 12 and 13.

C.3 Augmenting Wind Turbine SCADA Data with Yaw-Misalignment

We randomly add yaw misalignment of up to 15° to our data SCADA set, and adjust the respective targets (turbine output) with a yaw misalignment factor

---

[4] https://www.kaggle.com/frabbisw/facial-age.
[5] https://github.com/sltzgs/XpertAI.

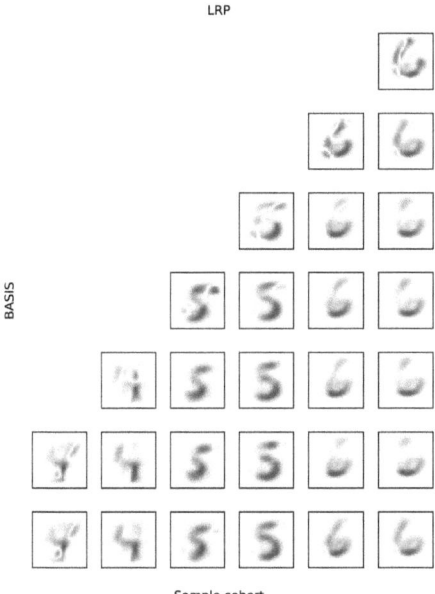

Fig. 10. Mean attributions over different cohorts of samples (columns) and basis functions (rows). Equivalent plot to Fig. 4 but for six range expert basis functions.

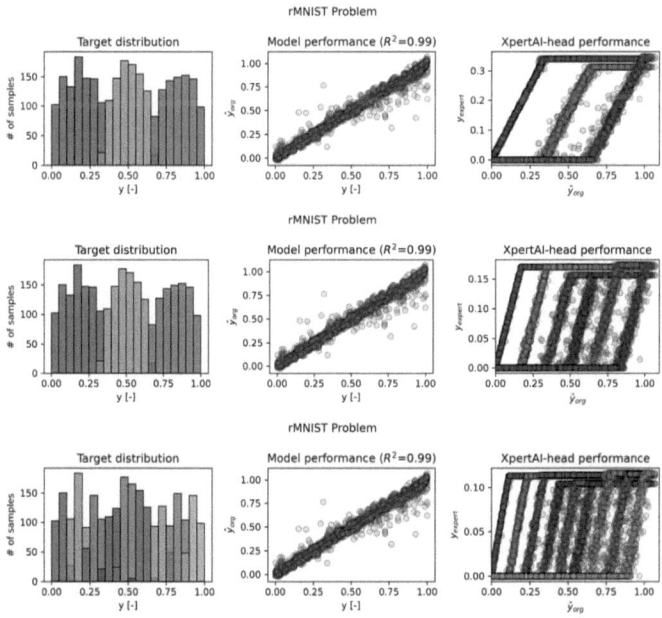

Fig. 11. Overview of model performance on the rMNIST problem for 3, 6 and 9 range experts (top to bottom).

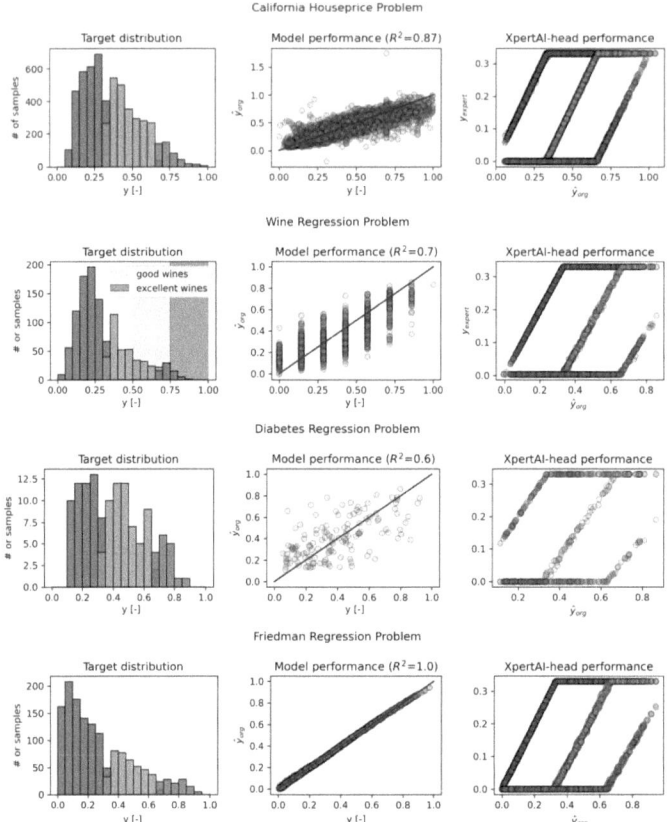

Fig. 12. Overview model performance for the regression benchmarks (Sect. 5).

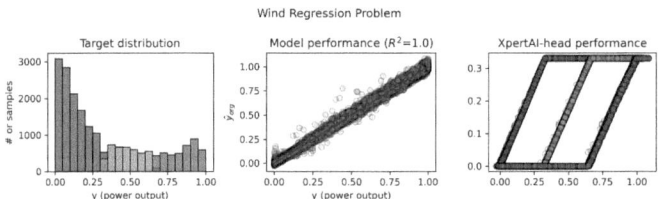

Fig. 13. Overview model performance wind turbine example (Sect. 4.3).

$c_{ymis,i} = cos^3(\Delta_{yaw})$, if $v_{w,i} < v_{w,rated}$. This approximation can be easily derived from static flow equations and geometric considerations, for more details on how yaw misalignment affects turbine output see [17]. After training and evaluation of the model on the augmented data, we can compare the magnitude of attributions to the ground truth.

References

1. Abdolrashidi, A., Minaei, M., Azimi, E., Minaee, S.: Age and gender prediction from face images using attentional convolutional network. arXiv preprint arXiv:2010.03791 (2020)
2. Achtibat, R., et al.: From attribution maps to human-understandable explanations through concept relevance propagation. Nat. Mach. Intell. **5**(9), 1006–1019 (2023)
3. Albini, E., Long, J., Dervovic, D., Magazzeni, D.: Counterfactual shapley additive explanations. In: ACM Conference on Fairness, Accountability, and Transparency, pp. 1054–1070 (2022)
4. Angulu, R., Tapamo, J.R., Adewumi, A.O.: Age estimation via face images: a survey. EURASIP J. Image Video Process. **2018**(1), 1–35 (2018). https://doi.org/10.1186/s13640-018-0278-6
5. Arrieta, A.B., et al.: Explainable artificial intelligence (XAI): concepts, taxonomies, opportunities and challenges toward responsible AI. Inf. Fusion **58**, 82–115 (2020)
6. Bach, S., Binder, A., Montavon, G., Klauschen, F., Müller, K.R., Samek, W.: On pixel-wise explanations for non-linear classifier decisions by layer-wise relevance propagation. PLoS ONE **10**(7), Art. no. e0130140 (2015)
7. Baehrens, D., Schroeter, T., Harmeling, S., Kawanabe, M., Hansen, K., Müller, K.R.: How to explain individual classification decisions. J. Mach. Learn. Res. **11**, 1803–1831 (2010)
8. Blücher, S., Vielhaben, J., Strodthoff, N.: Decoupling pixel flipping and occlusion strategy for consistent xai benchmarks. arXiv preprint arXiv:2401.06654 (2024)
9. Chormai, P., Herrmann, J., Müller, K.R., Montavon, G.: Disentangled explanations of neural network predictions by finding relevant subspaces. IEEE Trans. Pattern Anal. Mach. Intell. **46**(11), 7283–7299 (2024)
10. Deng, J., Dong, W., Socher, R., Li, L., Li, K., Li, F.: Imagenet: a large-scale hierarchical image database. In: CVPR, pp. 248–255. IEEE Computer Society (2009)
11. Deng, L.: The mnist database of handwritten digit images for machine learning research. IEEE Signal Process. Mag. **29**(6), 141–142 (2012)
12. Ganel, T., Sofer, C., Goodale, M.A.: Biases in human perception of facial age are present and more exaggerated in current ai technology. Sci. Rep. **12**(1), 22519 (2022)
13. Hama, N., Mase, M., Owen, A.B.: Deletion and insertion tests in regression models. J. Mach. Learn. Res. **24**(290), 1–38 (2023)
14. Hampshire, J., Waibel, A.: The meta-pi network: building distributed knowledge representations for robust multisource pattern recognition. IEEE Trans. Pattern Anal. Mach. Intell. **14**(7), 751–769 (1992)
15. Han, H., Otto, C., Jain, A.K.: Age estimation from face images: human vs. machine performance. In: 2013 International Conference on Biometrics (ICB), pp. 1–8. IEEE (2013)
16. Hollmann, N., et al.: Accurate predictions on small data with a tabular foundation model. Nature **637**(8045), 319–326 (2025)
17. Howland, M.F., et al.: Influence of atmospheric conditions on the power production of utility-scale wind turbines in yaw misalignment. J. Renew. Sustain. Energy **12**(6), Art. no. 063307 (2020)
18. Innes Murdo Black, M.R., Kolios, A.: Condition monitoring systems: a systematic literature review on machine-learning methods improving offshore-wind turbine operational management. Int. J. Sustain. Energy **40**(10), 923–946 (2021)

19. Ismail, A.A., Arik, S.O., Yoon, J., Taly, A., Feizi, S., Pfister, T.: Interpretable mixture of experts. Trans. Mach. Learn. Res. (2023)
20. Jacobs, R.A., Jordan, M.I., Nowlan, S.J., Hinton, G.E.: Adaptive mixtures of local experts. Neural Comput. **3**(1), 79–87 (1991)
21. Jacovi, A., Swayamdipta, S., Ravfogel, S., Elazar, Y., Choi, Y., Goldberg, Y.: Contrastive explanations for model interpretability, pp. 1597–1611 (2021)
22. Kim, B., Wattenberg, M., Gilmer, J., Cai, C., Wexler, J., Viegas, F., et al.: Interpretability beyond feature attribution: quantitative testing with concept activation vectors (tcav). In: International Conference on Machine Learning, pp. 2668–2677 (2018)
23. Klauschen, F., et al.: Toward explainable artificial intelligence for precision pathology. Annu. Rev. Pathol. **19**, 541–570 (2024)
24. Krenn, M., et al.: On scientific understanding with artificial intelligence. Nat. Rev. Phys. **4**(12), 761–769 (2022)
25. Letzgus, S., Müller, K.R.: An explainable ai framework for robust and transparent data-driven wind turbine power curve models. Energy AI **15**, 100328 (2024)
26. Letzgus, S., Wagner, P., Lederer, J., Samek, W., Müller, K.R., Montavon, G.: Toward explainable artificial intelligence for regression models: A methodological perspective. IEEE Signal Process. Mag. **39**(4), 40–58 (2022)
27. Linhardt, L., Müller, K.R., Montavon, G.: Preemptively pruning clever-hans strategies in deep neural networks. Inf. Fusion **103**, Art. no. 102094 (2024)
28. Lucic, A., Haned, H., de Rijke, M.: Why does my model fail? contrastive local explanations for retail forecasting. In: Proceedings of the 2020 Conference on Fairness, Accountability, and Transparency, pp. 90–98 (2020)
29. Lundberg, S.M., Lee, S.I.: A unified approach to interpreting model predictions. Adv. Neural. Inf. Process. Syst. **30**, 4765–4774 (2017)
30. van der Maaten, L., Hinton, G.: Visualizing data using t-sne. J. Mach. Learn. Res. **9**(86), 2579–2605 (2008)
31. Montavon, G., Lapuschkin, S., Binder, A., Samek, W., Müller, K.R.: Explaining nonlinear classification decisions with deep taylor decomposition. Pattern Recogn. **65**, 211–222 (2017)
32. Montavon, G., Samek, W., Müller, K.R.: Methods for interpreting and understanding deep neural networks. Digit. Sig. Process. **73**, 1–15 (2018)
33. Pandit, R., Astolfi, D., Hong, J., Infield, D., Santos, M.: Scada data for wind turbine data-driven condition/performance monitoring: a review on state-of-art, challenges and future trends. Wind Eng. **47**(2), 422–441 (2023)
34. Pandit, R., Infield, D., Dodwell, T.: Operational variables for improving industrial wind turbine yaw misalignment early fault detection capabilities using data-driven techniques. IEEE Trans. Instrum. Meas. **70**, 1–8 (2021)
35. Pawelzik, K., Kohlmorgen, J., Müller, K.R.: Annealed competition of experts for a segmentation and classification of switching dynamics. Neural Comput. **8**(2), 340–356 (1996)
36. Pedregosa, F., et al.: Scikit-learn: Machine learning in Python. J. Mach. Learn. Res. **12**, 2825–2830 (2011)
37. Qu, C., Lin, Z., Chen, P., Liu, J., Chen, Z., Xie, Z.: An improved data-driven methodology and field-test verification of yaw misalignment calibration on wind turbines. Energy Convers. Manage. **266**, 115786 (2022)
38. Ribeiro, M.T., Singh, S., Guestrin, C.: Why should i trust you?: Explaining the predictions of any classifier. In: International Conference on Knowledge Discovery and Data Mining, pp. 1135–1144 (2016)

39. Russakovsky, O., et al.: Imagenet large scale visual recognition challenge. Int. J. Comput. Vis. **115**(3), 211–252 (2015)
40. Samek, W., Montavon, G., Lapuschkin, S., Anders, C.J., Müller, K.R.: Explaining deep neural networks and beyond: a review of methods and applications. Proc. IEEE **109**(3), 247–278 (2021)
41. Shrikumar, A., Greenside, P., Kundaje, A.: Learning important features through propagating activation differences. In: International Conference on Machine Learning, vol. 70, pp. 3145–3153 (2017)
42. Simonyan, K., Zisserman, A.: Very deep convolutional networks for large-scale image recognition. In: ICLR (2015)
43. Stepin, I., Alonso, J.M., Catala, A., Pereira-Fariña, M.: A survey of contrastive and counterfactual explanation generation methods for explainable artificial intelligence. IEEE Access **9**, 11974–12001 (2021)
44. Stutz, D., Hein, M., Schiele, B.: Disentangling adversarial robustness and generalization. In: IEEE Conference on Computer Vision and Pattern Recognition, pp. 6969–6980, June 2019
45. Sundararajan, M., Taly, A., Yan, Q.: Axiomatic attribution for deep networks. In: International Conference on Machine Learning, vol. 70, pp. 3319–3328 (2017)
46. vielhaben, J., bluecher, S., strodthoff, N.: Multi-dimensional concept discovery (mcd): a unifying framework with completeness guarantees. Trans. Mach. Learn. Res. (2023)
47. Vielhaben, J., Lapuschkin, S., Montavon, G., Samek, W.: Explainable ai for time series via virtual inspection layers. Pattern Recogn. 110309 (2024)
48. Wang, X., Chen, H., Wu, Z., Zhu, W., et al.: Disentangled representation learning. IEEE Trans. Pattern Anal. Mach. Intell. (2024)
49. Zeiler, M.D., Fergus, R.: Visualizing and understanding convolutional networks. In: European Conference on Computer Vision, pp. 818–833 (2014)
50. Zhao, X., Broelemann, K., Kasneci, G.: Counterfactual explanation for regression via disentanglement in latent space, pp. 976–984 (2023)
51. Zhou, B., Khosla, A., Lapedriza, À., Oliva, A., Torralba, A.: Learning deep features for discriminative localization. In: IEEE Conference on Computer Vision and Pattern Recognition, pp. 2921–2929 (2016)

Open Access This chapter is licensed under the terms of the Creative Commons Attribution 4.0 International License (http://creativecommons.org/licenses/by/4.0/), which permits use, sharing, adaptation, distribution and reproduction in any medium or format, as long as you give appropriate credit to the original author(s) and the source, provide a link to the Creative Commons license and indicate if changes were made.

The images or other third party material in this chapter are included in the chapter's Creative Commons license, unless indicated otherwise in a credit line to the material. If material is not included in the chapter's Creative Commons license and your intended use is not permitted by statutory regulation or exceeds the permitted use, you will need to obtain permission directly from the copyright holder.

An XAI-Based Analysis of Shortcut Learning in Neural Networks

Phuong Quynh Le[1(✉)], Jörg Schlötterer[1,2], and Christin Seifert[1]

[1] University of Marburg, Marburg, Germany
{phuong.le,joerg.schloetterer,christin.seifert}@uni-marburg.de
[2] University of Mannheim, Mannheim, Germany

Abstract. Machine learning models tend to learn spurious features – features that strongly correlate with target labels but are not causal. Existing approaches to mitigate models' dependence on spurious features work in some cases, but fail in others. In this paper, we systematically analyze how and where neural networks encode spurious correlations. We introduce the neuron spurious score, an XAI-based diagnostic measure to quantify a neuron's dependence on spurious features. We analyze both convolutional neural networks (CNNs) and vision transformers (ViTs) using architecture-specific methods. Our results show that spurious features are partially disentangled, but the degree of disentanglement varies across model architectures. Furthermore, we find that the assumptions behind existing mitigation methods are incomplete. Our results lay the groundwork for the development of novel methods to mitigate spurious correlations and make AI models safer to use in practice.

Keywords: vision models · spurious correlations · disentangled feature learning · debugging models

1 Introduction

Machine learning models in classification tasks tend to learn spurious features that have strong relationships with the target labels are not causal. Models that rely on spurious correlations for their predictions would, for example, classify a bird as landbird based on the background feature, fail to recognize a cow on the beach, or predict the presence of pneumonia based on background features (see Fig. 1 for some examples). Especially in high-risk domains, such models could have serious consequences: a CNN predicting skin cancer using the presence of a color calibration patch (see Fig. 1, rightmost image) as a spurious feature fails to detect 68% of malignant cases when the color patch is absent [19].

During training, models heavily influenced by spurious correlations tend to learn these relationships and memorize samples from so-called *minority* groups where the spurious correlation is not present or which have inverse relationships [26]. This mechanism helps the models to achieve high average performance during training but leads to poor generalization on the minority group.

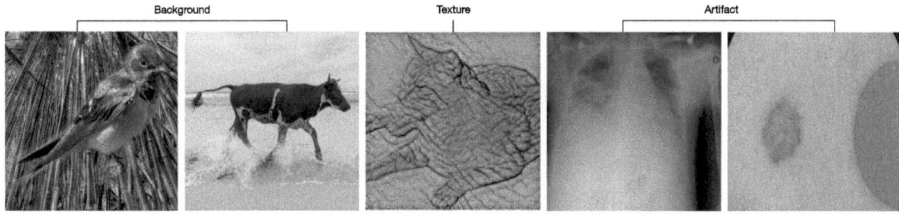

Fig. 1. Examples of variety shortcut types including backgrounds, texture and artifacts. The leftmost image is from the WATERBIRDS dataset, the three center images are from [7], and the rightmost image is from the ISIC dataset.

Therefore, the key objective of methods that mitigate spurious correlations is to improve the performance of minority groups.

Methods such as deep feature re-weighting (DFR) [11] and others [9,21] have successfully improved the performance of minority groups without extensive training to minimize group loss, even when models are trained in the presence of spurious correlations. These approaches assume that machine learning models are able to learn sufficient information about all features. Thus, by adjusting only the weights of the classification layer while leaving the learned representation unchanged, the performance of the minority group can be improved. On the other hand, other work [12] shows that DFR [11] works similarly to a last-layer pruning method, removing a large fraction of neurons that encode spurious features. However, even after re-weighting the classifier weights through DFR, the model still retains spurious information. The analysis in [12] provides some initial evidence that spurious features are not completely disentangled in the last layer, but a systematic analysis of how and where spurious features are encoded within models is still lacking.

In this work, we complete the investigation of the learning of spurious features in vision models by analyzing the phenomenon in both CNNs and ViTs models. We re-confirm the influence of spurious correlations and imbalanced data distribution. Further, we investigate the influence of spurious features within the networks, starting from the learned representation space and going deeper into the neurons and components of the models. We show the limitations of the underlying assumptions of existing spurious mitigation work and explain why they work and how they might fail. Specifically, our contributions are:

1. We show that both ViTs and CNNs learn spurious features and that this behavior can be explained by the representations in latent space (Sect. 4).
2. We introduce the neuron spurious score (s-score), an XAI-based metric to measure a neuron's reliance on spurious features (Sect. 3).
3. We show that the level of spurious feature disentanglement in neurons within the latent space differs between CNNs and ViTs. In CNNs, some neurons exclusively encode spurious features, while others encode both spurious and core features (Sect. 5). In contrast, in ViTs it is more difficult to find a clear set of neurons only encoding spurious features (Sect. 6).

4. We show that spurious features are encoded in different parts of the network, and that these neurons are not only located in the last layer but also in components of the neural network comprising multiple layers (Sect. 5 for CNNs and Sect. 6 for ViTs).

Our results provide evidence that unlearning spurious correlations is a complex task. While identifying and pruning spurious encoding components can be effective, it may not be sufficient due to the entangled nature of learned representations. Furthermore, pruning methods need to account for architecture-specific aspects, as spurious features are encoded differently in CNNs and ViTs.

The structure of this paper is as follows. First, we introduce the notion of spurious features (Sect. 2). We then describe the general setup of our experiments to analyze spurious correlations and introduce the **s**-score as an XAI-based inspection criterion (Sect. 3). Section 4 empirically shows that CNNs and ViTs are prone to learning spurious features and provides evidence that this is due to data manifold in representation space. Section 5 and Sect. 6 extend the analysis of representation space to all layers of neural networks using inspection techniques specific to CNNs and ViT, respectively. We discuss the main results in Sect. 7, review related work in Sect. 8 and conclude in Sect. 9.

2 Background

Spurious features $\mathcal{S}$ refer to statistically informative features that do not have a causal relationship with the target labels $\mathcal{Y}$ [7,25]. Models that learn spurious features often achieve impressive accuracy on the training dataset by exploiting spurious correlations present in the training data. In a dataset containing target labels $\mathcal{Y}$ and spurious features $\mathcal{S}$, we partition the data into groups based on the combination of labels and spurious features, denoted as $\mathcal{G} = \mathcal{Y} \times \mathcal{S}$. In general, within $\mathcal{G}$ of the training set, there exists at least one group that significantly has smaller size than others and does not contain the corresponding spurious features to the label, referred to as the *minority group*. Models that learn spurious correlations usually fail to predict this particular group during test time. For example, in the task of classifying bird types, where bird types are highly correlated with the background scene in the images, models tend to learn easier background features rather than bird characteristics (cf. Figure 1, leftmost image). A model that predicts based on background features performs well on the training (and i.i.d. test) data since most labels align with the background, and the model only needs to ignore or memorize a few remaining samples from *minority group* [26]. However, such models fail to generalize to birds on other backgrounds during test time.

Some types of spurious features can be easy to detect for humans, such as background and color [25], or artifacts in domain-specific settings [19]. However, some spurious features, such as texture or frequency patterns, may be imperceptible to the human eye [8,14]. Figure 1 shows examples of shortcuts[1].

---

[1] Following related work, we use the terms 'spurious features' and 'shortcuts' interchangably.

Table 1. Overview of the WATERBIRDS and ISIC datasets. Percentages in # **Train** presents the proportion of that group within the class $\mathcal{Y}$.

WATERBIRDS	$\mathcal{G}_0$	$\mathcal{G}_1$	$\mathcal{G}_2$	$\mathcal{G}_3$
$\mathcal{Y}$	landbird	landbird	waterbird	waterbird
$\mathcal{S}$	land	water	land	water
# **Train**	3,518 (95%)	185 (5%)	55 (5%)	1,037 (95%)
# **Test**	2,255	2,255	642	642
ISIC	BwoP	BwP	MwoP	MwP
$\mathcal{Y}$	benign	benign	malignant	malignant
$\mathcal{S}$	no patch	patch	no patch	*inserted* patch
# **Train**	6,314 (53%)	5,526 (47%)	1,571 (100%)	0 (0%)
# **Test**	3,158	2,763	821	821

3 Experimental Setup

In this study, we analyze the robustness of various models to spurious correlations. In this section, we provide details on the datasets, the vision models, and the evaluation metrics.

3.1 Datasets

We consider two datasets: WATERBIRDS [25] and ISIC [3]. Examples and data distribution for both datasets are presented in Table 1.

WATERBIRDS is a benchmark dataset for studying spurious correlations in learning. The task is to classify birds as either *water birds* or *land birds*. It is an artificially constructed dataset where bird images from the CUB dataset [29] are placed onto backgrounds from the PLACES-365 dataset [32]. To introduce spurious correlations, in the original training set, 95% of water birds are placed on water backgrounds, and 95% of land birds are placed on land backgrounds. However, in the test set, this ratio is balanced to evaluate model generalization. The four groups of the dataset are denoted as $\mathcal{G}_0, \mathcal{G}_1, \mathcal{G}_2$ and $\mathcal{G}_3$ with two minority groups $\mathcal{G}_1$ and $\mathcal{G}_2$ as in Table 1.

ISIC is a real-world data set for skin cancer detection. The data are obtained from the official website[2] and labeled as either *benign* or *malignant*. Prior studies [22] suggest that the dataset may contain several spurious correlations, such as color patches, rulers or surgical marks, black borders, etc. In this work, we focus on the color patch feature, which appears exclusively in the benign class in nearly 50% of cases. For evaluation, we construct an artificial test set where color patches are inserted to balance the spurious correlation. The four groups of the dataset are denoted as BwoP (benign without patch), BwP (benign with patch), MwoP (malignant without patch) and MwP (malignant with patch), with MwP representing the minority group.

3.2 Models and Hyperparameters

We evaluate both convolutional neural networks (CNN) and Vision Transformer (ViT) models. As representatives for CNNs, we use differently sized Resnet models, namely ResNet-18, ResNet-50 [10], and ResNeXt [30]. We evaluate two different ViT, namely ViT-B/16 [6], and DeiT [28]. All models use pre-trained weights from ImageNet-1K [24]. We do not adjust the hyper-parameters to optimize the worst-group accuracy. We follow the finetuning method of previous work [11,25] and use the following hyperparameter settings: each model is trained for 100 epochs with learning rate 0.001, weight decay 10^{-4} and SGD optimizer [23]. We adapt the batch size to the image input size to accommodate memory size and use 32 for WATERBIRDS and 64 for ISIC.

3.3 Evaluation Metrics

In our experiments, we use the standard metrics for evaluating reliance on spurious correlation: average accuracy and worst-group accuracy. To quantify the reliance of single neurons on a spurious input feature, we introduce the **s**-score.

Worst-group and Average Accuracy. In general, a model's robustness is measured by average accuracy—the proportion of correct classifications out of all predictions. Models that exploit spurious correlations often achieve high average accuracy (AVG) but perform significantly worse for a particular group within $\mathcal{G}$. The accuracy of this group is called worst group accuracy (WGA). Additionally, we denote the difference between AVG and WGA as GAP. A smaller GAP indicates greater robustness to spurious correlations.

---

[2] https://www.isic-archive.com.

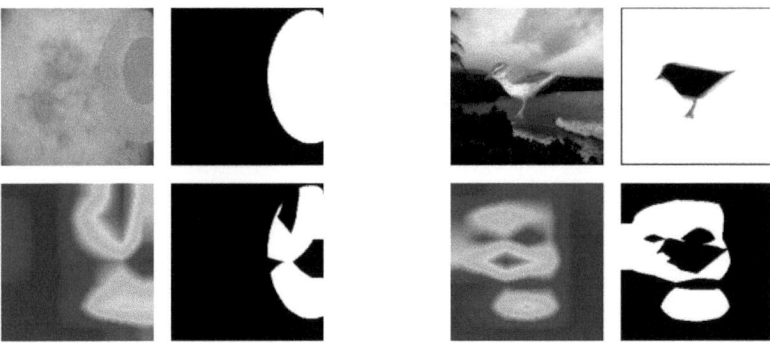

Fig. 2. Visualization of the s-score derivation by examples on ISIC dataset (left) and WATERBIRDS (right). A binary mask of the spurious feature (color patch or background) is obtained from the annotations in the training data set (top row). We use GradCam to obtain a feature attribution heatmap from a neuron and intersect its binarized version with the segmentation map (bottom row).

Neuron Spurious Score. In Sect. 5 and Sect. 6, we investigate whether there exist neurons in the penultimate layer that purely encode the spurious features. To measure the extent to which a neuron focuses on the spurious region in the input, we introduce the s-score. We consider a model f constructed by a feature extractor $f_{\text{enc}} : \mathcal{X} \to \mathbb{R}^d$ and a linear classification layer $h : \mathbb{R}^d \to \mathcal{Y}$. Given the input x_j, its corresponding penultimate representation $f_{\text{enc}}(x_j) = z_j \in \mathbb{R}^d$ and the spurious segmentation m_j given by a binary matrix (e.g., patch segmentation in ISIC), we use GradCAM [27] to compute the heatmap attribution over input, denoted as a_j^i, from neuron i of z_j. To emphasize the highly focused region identified by neuron i, we set a threshold α and binarize the heatmap a_j^i into b_j^i. The neuron spurious score, s-score, measures the proportion of the neuron's focusing region that corresponds to the region of the spurious feature. The s-score of neuron i is calculated by averaging over N samples

$$s^i = \frac{1}{N} \sum_{j=1}^{N} \frac{\sum b_j^i \odot m_j}{\sum b_j^i}$$

The neuron s-score s^i ranges between $[0, 1]$, where $s^i = 0$ indicates that either the neuron does not activate any input region or none of the focus regions overlap with the spurious segmentation. We consider a neuron with a high s-score a spurious feature-encoding neuron in the representation space. Examples of the input image, the segmented mask, the heatmap of a neuron and the s-score attribution of a single neuron are shown in Fig. 2.

4 Learning Spurious Features

In this section, we investigate the extent to which convolutional neural networks (CNNs) and vision transformers (ViTs) are susceptible to learning spurious correlations. First, we analyze the performance of the models for different groups in the data and with varying ratios of spurious correlations (Sect. 4.1). Second, we investigate whether this behavior can be explained by the representations in latent space (Sect. 4.2).

4.1 Performance on Groups

We fine-tune pre-trained CNNs and ViTs models on two datasets: WATERBIRDS and ISIC. The effect of spurious features is shown by the difference between the worst-group accuracy and the average accuracy during test time. Table 2 shows the testing performances across different models. Overall, all vision models tend to learn spurious correlations as shown by the significant gap (GAP) between the average accuracy (AVG) and the worst-group accuracy (WGA).

Table 2. Average (AVG) and worst-group accuracy (WGA) across 5 different runs on the test set for both CNN and ViT models trained on WATERBIRDS and ISIC. Showing mean and standard deviation.

	WATERBIRDS			ISIC		
	AVG	WGA↑	GAP↓	AVG	WGA↑	GAP↓
ResNet18	0.83 ± 0.01	0.46 ± 0.02	0.37	0.84 ± 0.01	0.37 ± 0.01	0.47
ResNet50	0.88 ± 0.00	0.63 ± 0.02	0.25	0.83 ± 0.01	0.22 ± 0.01	0.61
ResNeXt	0.89 ± 0.00	0.70 ± 0.02	0.19	0.86 ± 0.01	0.42 ± 0.01	0.44
ViT-B/16	0.87 ± 0.01	0.65 ± 0.01	0.22	0.83 ± 0.01	0.16 ± 0.01	0.67
DEiT	0.88 ± 0.00	0.66 ± 0.01	0.22	0.83 ± 0.01	0.12 ± 0.01	0.71

To analyze the extent to which models react to the presence of spurious correlations, we train a ResNet18 by varying the proportion of minority groups in the WATERBIRDS dataset during training (cf. Table 3). A minority ratio of 50% means that there is no spurious correlation in this modified dataset, and a ratio of 0% means that there is no minority sample in the training set. In the test set, we take the same number of samples from each group (i.e., a balanced subset). The two groups with an identical class label share the same foreground images, while the background is either water or land. Table 3 shows that the performance of the minority group gets worse as its proportion in the training data decreases (cf. $\mathcal{G}_1$ and $\mathcal{G}_2$), while the majority group performance remains nearly unchanged and consistently high—above 90% and even higher than when training without spurious correlations. However, even in the worst-case scenario (0% minority groups in the training set), the models can still correctly predict

Table 3. Influence of the correlation ratio of the spurious feature. ResNet18 on WATER-BIRDS. We keep the number of samples in the training set fixed (same as in the original dataset) and vary the percentage of the minority groups $\mathcal{G}_1$ and $\mathcal{G}_2$ within its corresponding class (originally 5%). In the test set, the two groups in each pair $(\mathcal{G}_0, \mathcal{G}_1)$ and $(\mathcal{G}_2, \mathcal{G}_3)$ share the same foreground images (the birds) while adapting to different backgrounds (water or land).

Minority Ratio	$\mathcal{G}_0$	$\mathcal{G}_1$	$\mathcal{G}_2$	$\mathcal{G}_3$	AVG	GAP↓
50%	0.98	0.98	0.84	0.83	0.91	0.08
25%	0.99	0.95	0.74	0.90	0.94	0.20
5%	0.99	0.78	0.46	0.91	0.84	0.38
0%	0.99	0.34	0.22	0.94	0.65	0.43

out-of-distribution (O.O.D.) samples in the test set, though with less than 50% accuracy. This shows that models not only learn spurious features but also capture core features.

Takeaways. Vision models are susceptible to spurious correlations but still retain generalization ability.

4.2 Analyzing Latent Space

We analyze the feature representations from the penultimate layer of the training data set of both CNN (ResNet18) and ViT (ViT-B/16). To visualize all data points, we show a t-SNE [16] projection of the output from the feature extractor f_{enc} of each model. In the ViT visualizations (Fig. 3, right column), both, ISIC and WATERBIRDS show a clear trend that samples with the same spurious features across classes blend in the representation manifold (BwoP and MwoP in ISIC; waterbird on water and landbird on water in WATERBIRDS). In the ResNet18 representation, we observe that even the boundaries between classes are separated in both cases, within each class, the data clusters according to spurious features. Note that in all cases, the models achieve close to 99% training accuracy. We hypothesize that depending on the model architecture, the spurious features are learned differently, however, in all cases, those features are well recognized and have a high impact on the classification result.

Takeaways. In both ResNet18 and ViT-B/16, we observe an identical phenomenon that samples with the same spurious features tend to lie closer to each other in the representation space, even with high training accuracy.

5 Encoding of Spurious Features in CNNs

In Sect. 4 we showed that the latent representations in the last layer of ViT and CNNs are governed by spurious features, i.e., clusters in latent space are defined

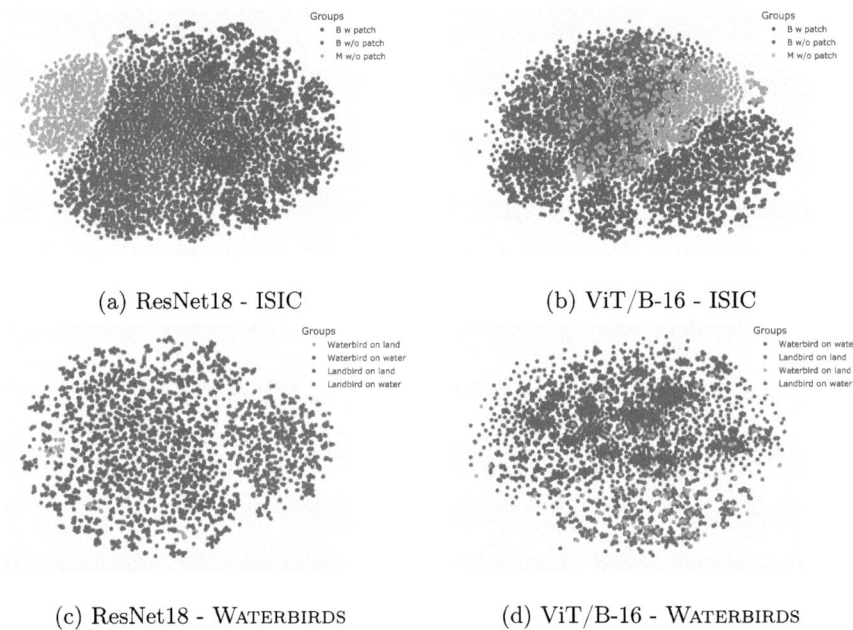

Fig. 3. Visualization of representation of last layers. Clusters are mainly defined by the spurious attribute (patch for ISIC, land/water for birds) and not by the classes (malignant/benign for ISIC and landbird/waterbird for birds).

more by the spurious features than by the target labels. In this section, focusing on CNNs, we analyze the extent to which this behavior can be attributed to individual neurons in different neural network layers. We begin by examining the disentanglement and entanglement of neurons in the penultimate layer (Sect. 5.1 and Sect. 5.2). For CNN-based models, we we investigate whether models learn disentangled information for different data groups (Sect. 5.3) using techniques for subnetwork extraction (so called network modulars) [5].

5.1 Neuron Disentanglement

We analyze single neurons in the last layer to test whether any of them are highly related to the spurious region. In each dataset, we compute the neuron spurious score **s**-score (cf. Section 3) over 50 random training samples.

On ISIC, the **s**-score of neurons ranges from 0.0 to 0.8. Visualization of three neurons from different score ranges is shown in Fig. 4. We determine the **s**-score ranges based on the proportion of the heatmap that overlaps with the mask segmentation of spurious features. A neuron receives a low **s**-score if on average less than 20% of the heatmap overlaps with the spurious mask (**s**-score < 0.2), and a high **s**-score if more than 70% of the heatmap focuses on the spurious region (**s**-score > 0.7). Otherwise, the neuron receives a mid-range

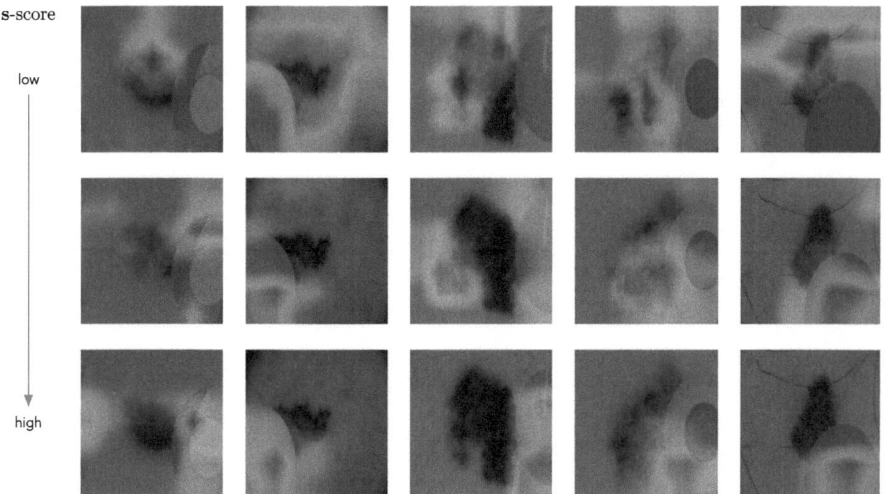

Fig. 4. Neuron heatmaps overlaid with original images, illustrating the activation of three different neurons (rows) across five sample images (columns).

s-score. For neurons with high or low **s**-score, the main focus region (more red areas) consistently highlights either the patch (spurious feature) or the lesion (core feature). Meanwhile, the neurons in mid-range **s**-score shift their focus between spurious and core features depending on the sample.

Table 4. Group accuracy of ISIC after pruning some sets of neurons in the last layer based on the neuron spurious score (**s**-score).

	BwoP	BwP	MwoP	MwP	AVG
ResNet18	0.92	0.99	0.57	0.37	0.84
Pruning (s-score > 0.7)	0.90	1.00	0.59	0.40	0.85
Fine-tune last-layer weights with group balanced set					
ResNet18	0.81	0.99	0.75	0.51	0.84
Pruning (s-score > 0.7)	0.81	0.99	0.77	0.56	0.85

Influence of Spurious-Encoding Neurons. By setting the weights connecting spurious-encoding neurons to the classes to zero, we observe a slight improvement in the WGA (Table 4, rows 1–2).[3] To reduce the influence of a highly imbalanced data distribution on the classifier, we additionally fine-tune the linear classifier using a group-balanced dataset in two cases: baseline ResNet18 and ResNet18 with spurious-encoding neurons deactivated (Table 4, rows 3–4).

---

[3] Here, we set the weights to zero without any retraining.

Table 5. Performance of applying DFR on ResNet18 for two datasets ISIC and WATERBIRDS. Prune$_h$ denotes the pruning ratio of the classification layer weights.

	Model	WGA	AVG	Prune$_h$	Avg. s-score
ISIC	Baseline	0.37	0.85	–	0.40
	DFR	0.71	0.79	80%	0.39
WATERBIRDS	Baseline	0.46	0.83	–	0.45
	DFR	0.82	0.87	52%	0.42

Fine-tuning after pruning some spurious-encoding neurons results in a slightly higher improvement in WGA compared to fine-tuning the baseline, indicating that the pruned representation better captures invariant features. From these experiments, we conclude that even though we can find some critical neurons (using labels and annotations of the spurious feature), we do not know how neurons interact with each other and, therefore, can not find a complete set of neurons that encode spurious features.

Takeaways. Our analyses in this section show that spurious features are represented and to some extend disentangled in the representation space and simply turning off those neurons improves robustness to spurious correlations.

5.2 Neuron Entanglement

Also in the direction of not retraining feature extractor f_{enc}, deep feature reweighting (DFR) method [11] and the subsequent analysis [12] suggest that using a group-balanced dataset to select essential neurons in the representation space and disabling all other neurons might make models more robust to spurious correlations.

DFR Method. DFR keeps the learned representation of trained models unchanged, retraining only the classification layer with a group-balanced validation set using logistic regression. The logistic regression hyperparameters are optimized for group performance with another group-balanced dataset. Under the assumption that trained models learn sufficient information despite the existence of spurious correlations, this approach uses a group-balanced set to seek the optimal neuron combination that is not influenced by spurious correlations.

Table 5 shows the effectiveness of the DFR method on CNN models trained with ISIC. DFR significantly improves the WGA while zeroing a large number of weights in the classification layer. This means that there is only information encoded in a small number of neurons of the embedding layer that is necessary for classification, and removing them makes models more robust. However, contrary to the naive approach of eliminating neurons that are strongly focused on spurious regions (cf. Table 4), our analysis shows that DFR removes a large number of unnecessary neurons while maintaining the same s-score distribution

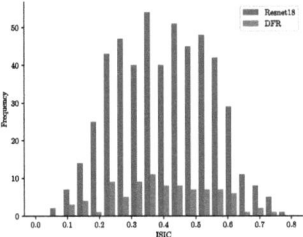 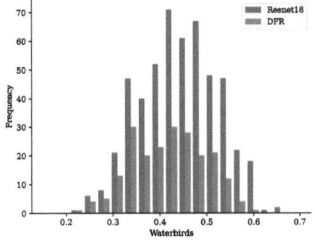

Fig. 5. Average s-score of ResNet18 and DFR trained on ISIC (left) and WATERBIRDS (right).

(cf. Table 5 and Fig. 5). This indicates that DFR does not change the *diversity* of the learned features, whether they are spurious or not. With a similar underlying hypothesis, the method of [9] also uses both learned core and spurious features in the latent space. This approach succeeds in improving the WGA by searching for a single weight of the classification layer that most activates for the minority group and editing only that weight.

We hypothesize that instead of genuinely selecting core features encoded in the representation space, the effectiveness of these classifier adaptation methods comes from learning new classifier weights to fit the new non-spurious data (group-balanced). This suggests that interactions between neurons strongly influence classification and that optimizing a subset of neurons and connection weights can improve group-specific performance. However, in alignment with the findings in [12], we conclude that these approaches do not truly eliminate the learned spurious correlations.

Takeaways. Without adapting the learned information, but the interaction between the representation neurons, we can significantly improve the performance of a particular group. However, there is no guarantee that the spurious correlations learned by the models will be completely eliminated.

5.3 Disentangled Components

As we showed in Sect. 5.2, retaining neurons with medium or high s-score while adjusting their influence on the classifier can reduce the impact of spurious feature learning. Therefore, we hypothesize that there are additional conditions or signals earlier in the network that allow the model to use these neurons more effectively in certain cases. In the following, we apply pruning and subnetwork learning to analyze their effect on spurious correlations.

Task-Oriented Pruning. We investigate whether pruning neurons in deeper network layers can help reduce reliance on spurious features. PruSC [13] and DCWP [20] are two pruning methods designed to mitigate spurious correlations. Notably, both methods prune neurons based on frozen trained weights by learning a mask on the weights, i.e., they refine the learned features instead of re-learning from scratch. Applying PruSC to ResNet18 with the ISIC dataset results in pruning 65% of the neurons in the last layer and 48% of the neurons across the entire model. Comparing the average s-score before and after pruning (cf. Figure 6), we observe that pruning effectively reduces the connections to spurious features. While improving performance for the worst-case group, PruSC yields a significantly lower average s-score, indicating a shift toward using less spurious features.

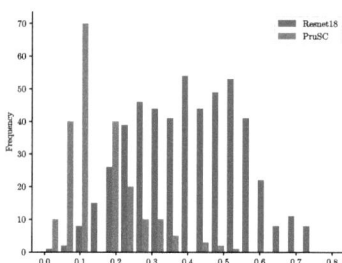

	ResNet18	PruSC
WGA	0.37	0.73
Avg. s-score	0.40	0.18
Prune$_h$	-	65%
Prune$_f$	-	48%

Fig. 6. s-score distribution. Prune$_h$ denotes the pruning ratio of the classification layer weights, Prune$_f$ denotes the pruning ratio of the entire model.

Group-Specific Components Learning. We further investigate how the relation between core and spurious features is encoded and whether those spurious features are learned and disentangled within the network. The ISIC dataset with training set $\mathcal{D}$ contains three groups: BwoP, BwP, and MwoP. We train model f fully on $\mathcal{D}$.

Applying a similar technique as [5], we freeze all the weights of f, and train a binary mask on each weight of f with a subpopulation of the training data. To avoid trivial results in a binary classification task, we can not remove an entire class as in the original paper. However, we hypothesize to obtain a subnetwork that removes all the relevant components that are purely responsible for a specific group. We conduct the study on two sub-dataset: $\mathcal{D}\setminus\{\text{BwP}\}$ and $\mathcal{D}\setminus\{\text{BwoP}\}$ by removing the group data BwP and BwoP from the training respectively. After pruning the model to 80% of the total number of weights[4], we evaluate the resulting model with the official test set. The results are shown in Fig. 7.

Case 1: Removing purely benign cases. By removing the entire group BwoP, the accuracy of this group drops significantly from 92% to 18%, while the performances of other groups are unchanged or increased. It proves that the group BwoP or the features belonging to the benign class are encoded and disentangled within the network, forming a benign-encoding component. Thus, deleting this component can lead to a significant drop in the performance of a particular group.

---

[4] We ensure that no layer is entirely pruned.

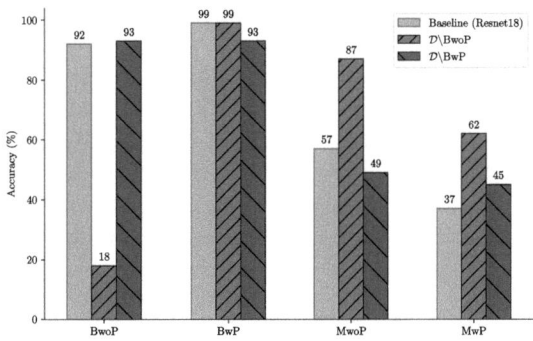

Fig. 7. Group accuracy of a subnetwork trained with $\mathcal{D} \setminus \{\text{BwP}\}$ and $\mathcal{D} \setminus \{\text{BwoP}\}$.

Case 2: Removing patches-containing cases. By removing the group BwP, we systematically test whether we can eliminate all the patch-encoding components within the trained network. The resulting performance after pruning is nearly identical between the two groups within a class (both groups of the benign class obtain 99% accuracy, and both groups of the malignant class obtain approximately 49% accuracy). This suggests that the removed connections are indeed responsible for encoding the existence of feature patches. However, we observe that when these connections encoding patches are removed, the performance of group MwoP drops. This means that the removed patch-encoding component not only contains information about the patches feature but also important information for predicting the malignant class.

Notably, the group BwP can be predicted by using either the patch-encoding or the benign-encoding component, and therefore, the group accuracy remains high in both cases.

Takeaways. We conclude that i) task-oriented pruning is a promising approach for mitigating spurious correlations by turning off connections that contribute to the spurious features, and ii) pruning methods are most effective when models learn features in disentangled subnetworks.

6 Encoding of Spurious Features in ViTs

In this section, we focus on analyzing the entanglement learning of spurious features in ViT models. Following a similar approach to CNNs, we begin by examining neurons in the penultimate layer (Sect. 6.1). Next, due to the unique multi-heads self-attention learning mechanism in ViTs, we focus on analyzing spurious features learned in attention heads (Sect. 6.2).

6.1 Last-Layer Representation in ViTs

In this section, we present the results of the analysis of whether there are spurious-encoding neurons in the representation space of ViTs. Figure 8 shows some examples of neuron heatmaps visualized with GradCam [27] (left) and the distribution of s-score averaged over 50 training inputs (right). We observe that even though there are some cases where the neuron focuses more on the core or spurious feature (more red region), the focus region of neurons in ViTs tends to be more distributed when projecting to the input. This leads to low overall s-score, i.e., 0.23 for ISIC and 0.14 for WATERBIRDS (cf. Table 6) - which are both in low-range s-score. We hypothesize that this phenomenon is due to the ability of global learning from the multi-heads self-attention of ViTs. This mechanism allows the model to simultaneously attend to both core and spurious features across the entire input, distributing the learned representations. In Sect. 6.2, we present an example in ISIC that under the influence of highly spurious correlations, ViTs show a clear entangled relationship between core and spurious objects in some particular attention head.

On the other hand, in alignment with the conclusion for mitigation methods that leave the latent space unchanged in CNNs (cf. Section 5.2), DFR [11] works well with ViT-B/16 (cf. Table 6). While significantly improving WGA in both ISIC and WATERBIRDS, the average s-score of models before and after applying DFR are nearly identical. This again confirms that DFR indeed changes the way neurons interact with each other to improve the performance of a particular group rather than truly eliminating the learned spurious features.

Table 6. Application DFR on ViT-B/16

	Model	WGA	Prune$_h$	Avg. s-score
ISIC	Baseline	0.16	–	0.23
	DFR	0.76	89%	0.26
WATERBIRDS	Baseline	0.66	–	0.14
	DFR	0.86	37%	0.14

Takeaways. With ViTs, we can not find a similar phenomenon of clear spurious-encoding neurons in the last layer as in CNNs. However, adapting neuron interactions works, suggesting the group-beneficial patterns when re-combining neurons in its representation.

6.2 Spurious Features in Attention Heads

The multi-head attention mechanisms in ViTs are designed to capture global information more effectively. We, therefore, investigate whether spurious and core features are disentangled in ViTs' attention heads.

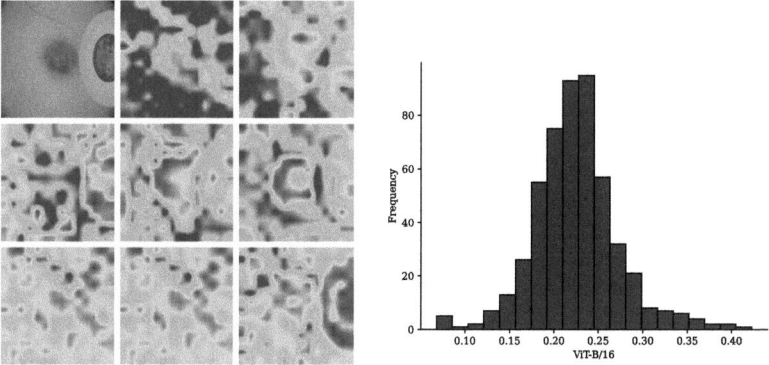

Fig. 8. Examples heatmap of neurons in the penultimate layer of ViT-B/16 (left) and s-score distribution (right).

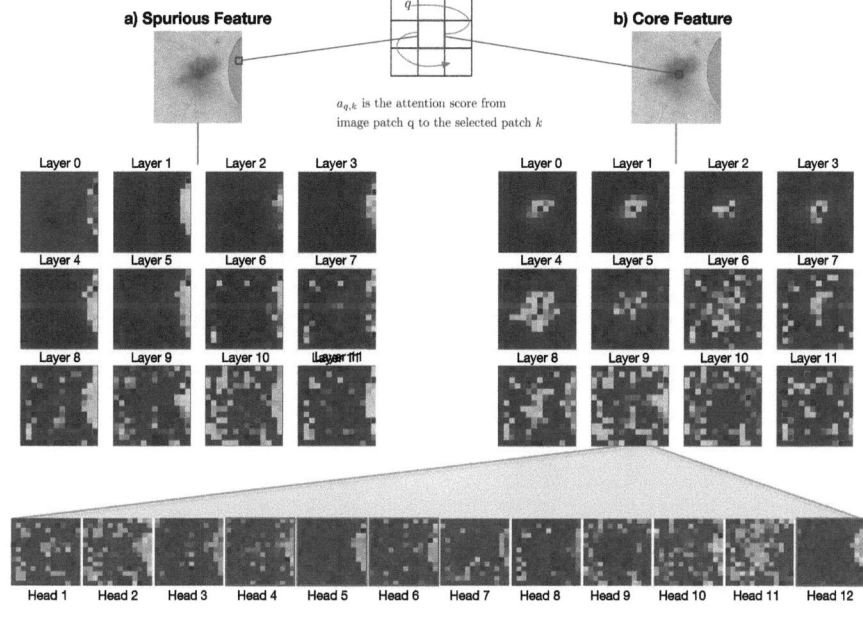

Fig. 9. Attention scores in ViT-B/16 of image patches corresponding to a) a spurious input feature and b) a core input feature. The feature maps in the middle show the scores per layer averaged over all attention heads. For the spurious patch (b), the highest average attention scores are from other spurious patches, making the outline of the spurious input part visible in the attention map. For an image patch from a lesion (a), the highest average attention scores are from image patches representing skin or lesions. However, there are layers that encode both core and spurious features because some attention heads are focused on the spurious feature (e.g., attention heads 4,5,6, and 12 in layer 9, highlighted with a red border). (Color figure online)

We analyze how much influence each image patch has on the encoding of one specific image patch, which either encodes a spurious (Fig. 9a) or a core feature (Fig. 9b). To visualize the attention map for a specific patch, we compute the attention weights in the transformer layers (averaged over multi-attention heads) when forwarding the input image through the model. From the attention weight matrix, we take the target row (indicating the target input patch) and visualize it as a heatmap. Figure 9 shows the visualizations across all transformer layers and single heads for a core feature in layer 9. We observe that even though the target patch is a core feature (see Fig. 9 a), some specific layers of ViT-B/16 show high attention to the spurious region (e.g. layer 8, layer 9) and that some neurons focus on the spurious region (e.g., attention heads 4, 5, 6, 12).

Takeaways. Under the influence of spurious correlations, we observe that ViT jointly encodes information of core and spurious features.

7 Discussion

This section summarizes and discusses our findings from the experiments in Sects. 4 to 6; a concise overview is given in Table 7.

Vision Models Exploit Spurious Correlations. We find that both CNNs and ViTs are susceptible to learning spurious features, and the ratio of minority and majority groups also affects the worst group accuracy. We also found that the spurious features can strongly define the representation space.

To Some Extent, There Are Disentangled Spurious-Encoding Components. In the representation layer, **s**-score can be used to determine whether neurons in the penultimate layer of the models can be separated into highly spurious-encoding neurons. Considering the deeper layer of the models, previous work [5] proves that within a trained model there are sets of neurons that are solely responsible for a specific class of data. Using a similar technique, our result shows that it is possible to extract components (in CNNs) that are responsible for specific groups or features. Therefore, with a careful experimental design, we can find a component that, when removed, mainly eliminates the effect of spurious features. In ViTs, due to the lack of an equivalent technique, we cannot further analyze whether there really exist spurious-encoding components. The existence of disentangled spurious-encoding components leads to a simple pruning approach to eliminate the learned spurious correlations.

Without Removing Spurious-Encoding Neurons, Adjusting The Interaction between Neurons Can Effectively Improve Performance. We found that the effectiveness of last-layer re-weighting methods does not come from really eliminating the learned spurious features, but from reconstructing the interaction between neurons. These methods may remove unnecessary neurons, but not necessarily spurious-encoding neurons. This leads to the assumption that the way neurons are combined during learning and predicting is important for generalization

Table 7. Overview of shortcut learning in CNNs and ViT.

	CNNs	ViTs
Prevalence of shortcuts	Learn spurious correlations, shown by a large gap between worst-group and average accuracy.	
Shortcut features in latent space	Classes separate clearly, but minority groups are clustered.	Latent space is more defined by spurious features than classes.
Last-layer spurious-encoding neurons	Neurons show a wide range of s-score, making disentanglement easier.	Spurious-encoding neurons are harder to detect, with average low s-score.
Spurious neuron combinations in last layer	Adapt neurons interaction, not necessarily remove spurious-encoding neurons, can form a more robust combination against spurious correlation.	
Disentanglement in earlier components	Exist components encoding both spurious feature and uncorrelated class.	Exist attention heads show high attention score between core and spurious patch regions.

ability. However, we do not yet fully understand the patterns when combining neurons.

There are also Components that Encode Multiple Features and Cause Models to Mis-learn. In the representation space, there is a large proportion of neurons with mid-range s-score. While this may be due to the limitations of the XAI-based technique (cf. Appendix A), previous work [12] has presented a qualitative example. In deeper components within CNNs, we find that removing spurious-encoding components also decreases the performance of the uncorrelated class. In multi-headed self-attention mechanisms, we find explicit cases where models fail to distinguish between core and spurious features. This suggests that in addition to a disentangled set of neurons encoding only core or spurious features, there are still neurons that activate both patterns.

Limitations of Existing Methods for Mitigating Spurious Feature Learning. Considering existing post-hoc spurious reduction methods, we hypothesize that: (i) last-layer re-weighting methods could prune a large fraction of neurons, but in fact still need information from all types of encoded features, such as core and spurious. Therefore, these methods would fail in the severe case that models under-learn information, which is hard to detect when the overall performance is still high based on learning spurious features. Furthermore, unmodified representation learning is ultimately not optimal because these methods cannot *correct* the earlier disentanglement of the model. (ii) For post-hoc pruning methods, we might prune some components or connections that are important for both core and spurious features. This could lead to the trade-off of improving WGA by reducing sensitivity to spurious features, but degrading performance for other groups by removing neurons that contribute to invariant features.

8 Related Work

A large body of work is based on the hypothesis that machine learning models tend to learn spurious features while under-learning invariant features. Therefore, a straightforward direction to mitigate the spurious correlations in learning is to focus on training group-robust models. Multiple approaches rely on human-annotated group labels and train models to minimize group loss [1,2,25]. To reduce the cost of collecting human-annotated group labels, many studies propose estimating pseudo-group information using predictions from early-stopped ERM models, followed by training a second robust model with pseudo-group labels [4,15,17,18,31]. Those methods assume that samples mis-classified by early-stopped ERM models are not holding spurious features. While these methods effectively improve the group-specific accuracy, they require expensive retraining, particularly when the existence of spurious information is unknown beforehand.

Recent studies have shown that despite the strong correlation between spurious features and target labels, machine learning models can successfully learn high-quality spurious and core features [11]. Therefore, post-hoc spurious mitigation or eliminating spurious correlations of trained models without extensive feature learning can be sufficient. Leaving the learned representation unchanged, existing work re-weights the classifier weights based on a group-balanced held-out dataset [11] or searches for and only adjusts a single weight that affects the minority group most [9]. Alternatively, it is possible to extract a subnetwork from a trained model that is more robust to spurious correlations [13,20]. These works empirically demonstrate the potential of models to learn both core and spurious features. However, it remains unclear whether these features are truly disentangled and to what extent the underlying assumptions hold.

9 Conclusion

In this paper, we showed that both CNNs and ViTs are susceptible to spurious correlations. We provide evidence that models can learn to disentangle spurious features, allowing us to extract neurons or subnetworks within a trained network that are specifically responsible for these features. However, models may also encode a mixture of core and spurious features or fail to learn perfect disentanglement. Based on the results, this paper shows how and why methods mitigating spurious features that either leave the representation unchanged or extract only subnetworks from frozen trained weights may fail.

A Limitation of s-score

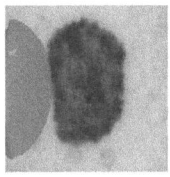 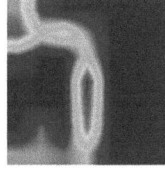

Fig. 10. Neuron with low score but potentially high spuriousness.

In this section, we discuss the limitations of using post-hoc explainable AI methods to calculate s-score. Explanation methods sometimes fail to capture fully what models are truly encoding. While heatmap attributions can visualize where the model is focusing within the input, they do not reveal what features the model is learning. For example, in Fig. 10, the s-score is low because the neuron's focus region has little overlap with the patch itself. However, to a human observer, it seems that the neuron is actually focusing on the *edge of the patch*.

References

1. Arjovsky, M., Bottou, L., Gulrajani, I., Lopez-Paz, D.: Invariant risk minimization. arXiv preprint arXiv:1907.02893 (2019)
2. Bao, Y., Chang, S., Barzilay, R.: Predict then interpolate: a simple algorithm to learn stable classifiers. In: International Conference on Machine Learning, pp. 640–650. PMLR (2021)
3. Codella, N., et al.: Skin lesion analysis toward melanoma detection 2018: a challenge hosted by the international skin imaging collaboration (ISIC) (2019)
4. Creager, E., Jacobsen, J.H., Zemel, R.: Environment inference for invariant learning. In: International Conference on Machine Learning, pp. 2189–2200. PMLR (2021)
5. Csordás, R., van Steenkiste, S., Schmidhuber, J.: Are neural nets modular? Inspecting functional modularity through differentiable weight masks. In: International Conference on Learning Representations (2020)
6. Dosovitskiy, A., et al.: An image is worth 16x16 words: transformers for image recognition at scale, June 2021, arXiv:2010.11929 [cs]
7. Geirhos, R., et al.: Shortcut learning in deep neural networks. Nat. Mach. Intell. **2**(11), 665–673 (2020)
8. Geirhos, R., Rubisch, P., Michaelis, C., Bethge, M., Wichmann, F.A., Brendel, W.: Imagenet-trained cnns are biased towards texture; increasing shape bias improves accuracy and robustness. In: International Conference on Learning Representations (2018)
9. Hakemi, S., Akhtar, N., Hassan, G.M., Mian, A.: Post-hoc spurious correlation neutralization with single-weight fictitious class unlearning, January 2025
10. He, K., Zhang, X., Ren, S., Sun, J.: Deep residual learning for image recognition. In: Proceedings of the IEEE Conference on Computer Vision and Pattern Recognition, pp. 770–778 (2016)
11. Kirichenko, P., Izmailov, P., Wilson, A.G.: last layer re-training is sufficient for robustness to spurious correlations. In: The Eleventh International Conference on Learning Representations (2023)

12. Le, P.Q., Schlötterer, J., Seifert, C.: Is last layer re-training truly sufficient for robustness to spurious correlations? arXiv preprint arXiv:2308.00473 (2023)
13. Le, P.Q., Schlötterer, J., Seifert, C.: Out of spuriousity: improving robustness to spurious correlations without group annotations. arXiv preprint arXiv:2407.14974 (2024)
14. Lin, Z., Gao, Y., Yang, Y., Sang, J.: Revisiting visual model robustness: a frequency long-tailed distribution view. Adv. Neural. Inf. Process. Syst. **36**, 59239–59251 (2023)
15. Liu, E.Z., et al.: Just train twice: improving group robustness without training group information. In: Meila, M., Zhang, T. (eds.) Proceedings of the 38th International Conference on Machine Learning. Proceedings of Machine Learning Research, vol. 139, pp. 6781–6792. PMLR, July 2021, https://proceedings.mlr.press/v139/liu21f.html
16. Van der Maaten, L., Hinton, G.: Visualizing data using t-sne. J. Mach. Learn. Res. **9**(11) (2008)
17. Nam, J., Cha, H., Ahn, S., Lee, J., Shin, J.: Learning from failure: de-biasing classifier from biased classifier. Adv. Neural Inf. Process. Syst. **33**, 20673–20684 (2020), https://proceedings.neurips.cc/paper/2020/file/eddc3427c5d77843c2253f1e799fe933-Paper.pdf
18. Nam, J., Kim, J., Lee, J., Shin, J.: Spread spurious attribute: improving worst-group accuracy with spurious attribute estimation. In: 10th International Conference on Learning Representations, ICLR 2022 (2022)
19. Nauta, M., Walsh, R., Dubowski, A., Seifert, C.: Uncovering and correcting shortcut learning in machine learning models for skin cancer diagnosis. Diagnostics **12**(1), 40 (2021). https://doi.org/10.3390/diagnostics12010040
20. Park, G.Y., Lee, S., Lee, S.W., Ye, J.C.: Training debiased subnetworks with contrastive weight pruning. In: Proceedings of the IEEE/CVF Conference on Computer Vision and Pattern Recognition, pp. 7929–7938 (2023), https://openaccess.thecvf.com/content/CVPR2023/papers/Park_Training_Debiased_Subnetworks_With_Contrastive_Weight_Pruning_CVPR_2023_paper.pdf
21. Qiu, S., Potapczynski, A., Izmailov, P., Wilson, A.G.: Simple and fast group robustness by automatic feature reweighting. In: International Conference on Machine Learning, pp. 28448–28467. PMLR (2023)
22. Rieger, L., Singh, C., Murdoch, W.J., Yu, B.: Interpretations are useful: penalizing explanations to align neural networks with prior knowledge. In: Proceedings of the 37th International Conference on Machine Learning, p. 11. JMLR.org (2020), http://proceedings.mlr.press/v119/rieger20a/rieger20a.pdf
23. Robbins, H., Monro, S.: A stochastic approximation method. In: The Annals of Mathematical Statistics, pp. 400–407 (1951)
24. Russakovsky, O., et al.: Imagenet large scale visual recognition challenge. Int. J. Comput. Vision **115**, 211–252 (2015)
25. Sagawa, S., Koh, P.W., Hashimoto, T.B., Liang, P.: Distributionally robust neural networks. In: International Conference on Learning Representations (2020)
26. Sagawa, S., Raghunathan, A., Koh, P.W., Liang, P.: An investigation of why over-parameterization exacerbates spurious correlations. In: III, H.D., Singh, A. (eds.) Proceedings of the 37th International Conference on Machine Learning. Proceedings of Machine Learning Research, vol. 119, pp. 8346–8356. PMLR, July 2020, https://proceedings.mlr.press/v119/sagawa20a.html

27. Selvaraju, R.R., Cogswell, M., Das, A., Vedantam, R., Parikh, D., Batra, D.: Grad-CAM: visual explanations from deep networks via gradient-based localization. Int. J. Comput. Vision **128**(2), 336–359 (2019). https://doi.org/10.1007/s11263-019-01228-7
28. Touvron, H., Cord, M., Douze, M., Massa, F., Sablayrolles, A., Jégou, H.: Training data-efficient image transformers & distillation through attention. In: International Conference on Machine Learning, pp. 10347–10357. PMLR (2021)
29. Wah, C., Branson, S., Welinder, P., Perona, P., Belongie, S.: Caltech-UCSD Birds 200. Technical Report, California Institute of Technology (2011)
30. Xie, S., Girshick, R., Dollár, P., Tu, Z., He, K.: Aggregated residual transformations for deep neural networks. In: Proceedings of the IEEE Conference on Computer Vision and Pattern Recognition, pp. 1492–1500 (2017)
31. Zhang, M., Sohoni, N.S., Zhang, H.R., Finn, C., Re, C.: Correct-N-contrast: a contrastive approach for improving robustness to spurious correlations. In: International Conference on Machine Learning, pp. 26484–26516. PMLR (2022), https://proceedings.mlr.press/v162/zhang22z/zhang22z.pdf
32. Zhou, B., Lapedriza, A., Khosla, A., Oliva, A., Torralba, A.: Places: a 10 million image database for scene recognition. IEEE Trans. Pattern Anal. Mach. Intell. **40**(6), 1452–1464 (2018). https://doi.org/10.1109/TPAMI.2017.2723009

Open Access This chapter is licensed under the terms of the Creative Commons Attribution 4.0 International License (http://creativecommons.org/licenses/by/4.0/), which permits use, sharing, adaptation, distribution and reproduction in any medium or format, as long as you give appropriate credit to the original author(s) and the source, provide a link to the Creative Commons license and indicate if changes were made.

The images or other third party material in this chapter are included in the chapter's Creative Commons license, unless indicated otherwise in a credit line to the material. If material is not included in the chapter's Creative Commons license and your intended use is not permitted by statutory regulation or exceeds the permitted use, you will need to obtain permission directly from the copyright holder.

Author Index

A
Abbaspour Onari, Mohsen 202
Ahmed, Taufique 327
Alves, Rodrigo 3
Amjad, Haadia 250

B
Biecek, Przemysław 264
Biecek, Przemyslaw 327
Biemans, Bram 44
Bogaert, Jeremie 310
Bonaita, Alessandro 225
Bortolussi, Luca 225

C
Cahlik, Vojtech 3
Cascione, Alessio 162
Cedro, Mateusz 91

D
Delač, Goran 68
Descampe, Antonin 310
Doumanoglou, Alexandros 376

G
Gneri, Jacopo 180
Göller, Kilian 250
Gozdera, Michał 264
Grau, Isel 44, 202
Guidotti, Riccardo 162, 180

H
Hanselle, Jonas 117
Heid, Stefan 117
Hüllermeier, Eyke 117

J
Jullum, Martin 19

K
Kaltampanidis, Yannis 376
Kapar, Jan 19
Knoll, Carsten 250
Koenen, Niklas 19
Kordik, Pavel 3
Kornowicz, Jaroslaw 117

L
Le, Phuong Quynh 424
Letzgus, Simon 400
Longo, Luca 327
Luque-Cerpa, Alejandro 351

M
Maeß, Johannes 289
Manjooran, Thomas 250
Martens, David 91
Montavon, Grégoire 289, 400
Müller, Klaus-Robert 289, 400

N
Nakajima, Shinichi 289
Nobile, Marco S. 202
Nuijten, Wim P. M. 44

P
Polgreen, Elizabeth 351
Pollacci, Laura 162, 180

R
Rajan, Ajitha 351
Rodriguez, Alex 225

S
Schlötterer, Jörg 424
Schnake, Thomas 289
Schwammberger, Maike 140
Seifert, Christin 424
Seitz, Steffen 250
Sienkiewicz, Elżbieta 264
Šilić, Marin 68
Standaert, François-Xavier 310

T
Tetzlaff, Ronald 250
Thommes, Kirsten 117
Tomaszewska, Paulina 264
Torfah, Hazem 351
Troubil, Pavel 44

U
Ullrich, Julian 250

V
Vascotto, Ilaria 225
Vukadin, Davor 68

W
Wenninghoff, Nils 140

Z
Zarpalas, Dimitrios 376
Zhang, Chao 202
Zhang, Yingqian 202

If you have any concerns about our products,
you can contact us on
ProductSafety@springernature.com

In case Publisher is established outside the EU,
the EU authorized representative is:
**Springer Nature Customer Service Center GmbH
Europaplatz 3, 69115 Heidelberg, Germany**

Printed by Libri Plureos GmbH
in Hamburg, Germany